Robert F. Huber

The Empire of the Seas

Consul General Robert Wilson Shufeldt, Havana, ca. 1861. Private collection.

The Empire of the Seas

A BIOGRAPHY OF REAR ADMIRAL
ROBERT WILSON SHUFELDT, USN

by
FREDERICK C. DRAKE

University of Hawaii Press
Honolulu

This book has been published with the help of a grant from the Canadian Federation for the Humanities using funds provided by the Social Sciences and Humanities Research Council of Canada.

©1984 University of Hawaii Press
All Rights Reserved
Manufactured in the United States of America

Library of Congress Cataloging in Publication Data
Drake, Frederick C., 1937–
   The empire of the seas.

  Bibliography: p.
  Includes index.
  1. Shufeldt, Robert Wilson, 1822–1895. 2. United States—History, Naval—To 1900. 3. United States—Territorial expansion. 4. Admirals—United States—Biography. 5. United States. Navy—Biography. 6. Diplomats—United States—Biography. I. Title.
E182.S564D7   1984   973.8'092'4 [B]   84-66
ISBN 0-8248-0846-0

For Val

Contents

Maps	ix
Preface	xi
1 Background of an Expansionist	1
2 An Education in Expansion	14
3 Consul General to Cuba, 1861–1862	28
4 Consul General to Cuba, 1862–1863	52
5 The Blockade of the Southern Coast	73
6 The Asiatic Station, 1865–1867	88
7 The China–Cuba–Mexico Axis, 1868–1870	114
8 The Tehuantepec Dream, 1870–1874	135
9 The Naval Theorist, 1875–1878	153
10 The Cruise of the *Ticonderoga:* Cape Henry to Cape Town	176
11 The Cruise of the *Ticonderoga:* South Africa to Japan	208
12 The Cruise of the *Ticonderoga:* The Mission to Open Korea	233
13 The Opening of Korea, 1881	257
14 The Opening of Korea, 1882	276
15 The Legacy of an Expansionist	305
Conclusion	334
Appendix 1: **The Sargent Letter**	355
Appendix 2: **Treaty of Amity and Commerce Between the United States of America and Korea, May 22, 1882**	363
Note on Sources	369
Abbreviations	373
Notes	377
Bibliographical Essay	431
Index	451

Illustrations follow pages 128 and 256

Maps

Map of the scene of naval operations against St. Mark's, Florida, March, 1865 — 84

Army map of the action at the Natural Bridge, St. Mark's, Florida, March, 1865 — 85

The Asiatic Station, 1866 — 93

Korea — 99

The Northwest Coast Rivers of Korea — 104

Tehuantepec as a Transit Route — 127

The Isthmus of Tehuantepec — 137

The Liberian Boundary Dispute of 1879 — 187

The Oil Rivers of West Africa — 203

Preface

Just over a century ago, the United States government dispatched a naval and commercial expedition under the command of Commodore Robert Wilson Shufeldt (1822–1895) to open new markets for American commerce in Africa and Asia. The culmination of that expedition, two years after the flagship *Ticonderoga* returned in 1880, was the opening of Korea to the trade of Western nations by the Shufeldt treaty of May 1882. The expedition, and the treaty, were examples of a movement into the Pacific toward Asia that had roots deep in American history. The commercial lure and the strategic drive attracted merchant capitalists, ships' captains, naval officers, and politicians. Among those who shared visions of maritime power during the Republic's first century were Benjamin Franklin, Philip Freneau, Hugh Brackenridge, John Adams, James Madison, David Porter, Langdon Cheves, Henry Clay, James Monroe, George Croghan, Timothy Dwight, John Jacob Astor, Asa Whitney, and William H. Seward; men who reflected deeply on the benefits and problems inherent in commercial expansion overseas. A variation of such a theme, the doctrine of the empire of the seas, which can be traced back through colonial American and English history to Roman, Grecian, and biblical times, found its greatest advocates in pre-Civil War America in William Henry Seward and Matthew Calbraith Perry. It was at the end of the nineteenth century that Alfred Thayer Mahan explored the historical influences of sea power and provided a rationale for the acquisition of the Philippines, Hawaii, Guam, the Panama Canal, and a battleship navy to defend the American thrust into the Pacific and the Caribbean.

To this select group of pre-Mahanian naval officers, politicians, commercial expansionists, visionaries, and thinkers, Shufeldt should be added as the key diplomatic and naval link between Perry and Mahan. Shufeldt gradually evolved a comprehensive theory of the empire of the seas based on commercial power and, between 1860 and 1885, devoted himself as theorist and administrator, consular diplomat, explorer, and naval attaché to implementing the schemes he designed for the United States. The subject of several articles and reminiscences during the period from 1890 to 1911 in relation to the opening of Korea, Shufeldt was virtually ignored by historians for the next sixty years. This neglect began to end in the 1970s. The Korean treaty has received citation in some diplomatic histories, and articles and books have been written on the opening of Korea as a diplomatic event, though none of them has placed that opening within the context of Shufeldt's writings and thoughts on the role of the United States in the world. Articles on Shufeldt's naval career began to appear in the 1970s, and a good comparative study by Kenneth Hagan has related Shufeldt's work to that of other naval officers in the 1870s and 1880s. In contrast to the numerous biographies of naval officers such as John Paul Jones, David Dixon Porter, Stephen Bleeker Luce, Matthew Calbraith Perry, and Alfred Thayer Mahan, there has been no full-length study of Shufeldt as either a diplomat or a naval officer.

Shufeldt's career is at least as important as Perry's or Mahan's for understanding the connections between American diplomatic, economic, and naval policies in the period from 1850 to 1890. His life is a case study in American expansion. With the exception of Secretary of State William H. Seward, there is scarcely another figure who links as effectively as does Shufeldt the territorial and continental expansion of the antebellum period and the postwar drive for commercial expansion overseas. Shufeldt is important precisely because, in his dual role of diplomat and naval officer, his career exemplified the interconnections between the growing problems in United States society, the pre- and post-Civil War expansionist trends in that society, and the characteristic use of the navy as a diplomatic instrument, particularly in Asia, in the latter half of the nineteenth century. Moreover, his life and career provide fascinating insights into United States diplomacy in Cuba, Mexico, Africa, Asia, and the Pacific in the years from 1850 to 1885. He reflected on the tensions apparent in reconstruction America and held strong views on the role of the United States as a regenerating force in the world. He sought to solve domestic problems—Negro slavery, the Negro presence, postwar depression, overproduction, and a declining navy—through a vigorous policy of commercial expansion.

The obscurity that enveloped Shufeldt came partially as the result of the actions of the Chester Arthur administration, which refused to acknowledge the role that Shufeldt, as an appointee of James G. Blaine, had played in Oriental and American diplomacy. The culminating event of Shufeldt's diplomatic career, the negotiation of the Korean treaty, was ignored. Such treatment naturally embittered him. In addition, he was sharply criticized by sections of the American press for a headline-making outburst against the Chinese and the Chinese empress in 1882, at the height of his negotiations for the treaty. Baffled, Shufeldt saw the glory that he hoped to reap, such as Perry had received for opening Japan, begin to elude his grasp. He became convinced he had been mistreated by his country, even after fellow officers in the navy rallied to his support and he was appointed president of the Naval Advisory Board that superintended the building of the White Squadron in the 1880s.

To weigh the life of such an individual requires a delicate balance that is difficult to achieve in any biography that is the first exposition of a man's life. The questions of how and why a society accepts the consequences of any individual's actions have to be balanced against the presentation of personal information. In this light, this book seeks to offer evidence to the debate among historians of American foreign policy on the nature and course of American expansion in the decades following the Civil War. By concentrating on the life of one man, it also provides evidence of the interactions between diplomatic, consular, naval, and governmental officers in the area of post-Civil War foreign policy. Several prominent works, notably by writers Kenneth J. Hagan, Peter Karsten, Clayton R. Barrow, Jr., Ronald Specter, and Robert Seager II, have been published in the field of naval history that reanalyze these interactions intelligently and add serious contributions to the pioneering works in post-Civil War foreign policy of Walter LaFeber and Fred Harvey Harrington. It is my hope that this biography of Shufeldt will add to such contributions in the fields of naval, diplomatic, and Korean history.

As in most biographies, the subject could have been approached by theme, chronological development, or by some combination of the two. At varying times of his life, Shufeldt was interested in the Caribbean and Central America. After the Civil War he focused on Asia and the navy. In the 1870s he analyzed the role of the navy in American life and directed his attention toward Africa and East Asia. During the 1880s he was dominated by thoughts of a treaty with Korea. In the last years of his life he worked on the redevelopment of the navy. To approach the recurring subjects in Shufeldt's life thematically would have meant not tracing the maturation of his thought patterns and actions through time on each theme as he related them to other areas of his thinking. The resulting fragmentation would have been too high a price to pay, particularly in a first full biography, and for this reason I have retained a more chronological approach as the most adequate method of showing the development of Shufeldt's thinking in juxtaposition with the problems he faced and the solutions he advocated. A concluding chapter pulls together the main threads and influences of his life. In addition, to illustrate Shufeldt's conceptions and thoughts on many subjects, full use has been made of direct quotations from his writings and reminiscences.

A work such as this leads the writer to incur many intellectual debts. The ideas that have helped in the development of my thinking on this book since its inception have been sharpened and honed by contact with many fine historians and teachers. To Walter LaFeber, teacher and friend, who focused my interests in United States foreign policy and naval policy with tolerance and skill, and who read the manuscript at a critical stage, I owe a special debt of gratitude. From David Brion Davis, Michael Kammen, Paul Wallace Gates, Frederick Marcham, the late Clinton Rossiter at Cornell University, and both Marcus Cunliffe and Maldwyn Jones at the University of Manchester, I gained lasting insights into American and British history. None of the above is responsible in any way for particular opinions or any errors, which are mine alone, in this work, though it has benefited from my contact with all of them.

I wish to acknowledge my grateful thanks for generous financial assistance offered in the research stages of this work by the Cornell Graduate School scholarship fund, by Tom Lloyd, administrator of the Cornell Faculty Research Fund, and by Deans Colin A. Plint, John McEwen, and Maurice Yacowar of Brock University, for funds to sustain research, purchase microfilm, and complete preparation of the manuscript. Moreover, I would like to record my gratitude to the Canadian Federation for the Humanities. This book has been published with the help of a grant from the Canadian Federation for the Humanities using funds provided by the Social Sciences and Humanities Research Council of Canada.

Librarians and libraries on both sides of the Atlantic have been especially helpful. Expert assistance came from the following: the staff of the Manuscripts Division and of the Thomas Jefferson Reading Room, Library of Congress; the archivists of the State and Navy departments records in the National Archives; Olin Graduate Library and the Regional History Room, Cornell; the Houghton Library, Harvard; the Sterling Memorial Library, Yale; Indiana University Library; Michigan Historical Collections Division, University of Michigan; Rush-Rhees Library, University of Rochester; Henry E. Huntington Library, San Marino, California; New York Public Library; Connecticut Historical Society; Tulane University Library; the General Services Administration, National Archives and Records Center, Washington, D.C.; the Federal Records Center, Suitland, Maryland; and the Probate Court, Washington, D.C. Collections used from these archives, libraries, and record centers are indicated in notes and bibliographical essay, and I

Preface

acknowledge with gratitude permission to quote from such materials granted by the respective institutions. British librarians who gave considerable help through interlibrary loan offices were those at the University of Wales, Aberystwyth; the Harold Cohen Library, Liverpool University; the National Central Lending Library; Newcastle University; Sussex University; the War Office Library; and the Public Record Office. In Ontario, the Brock University Library staff has likewise been of considerable assistance in locating and borrowing rare books and articles relating to Asia and American diplomacy. Helpful communications were received from Mrs. Lois Bayles, New Canaan Historical Society; Janet Penner, registrar of Middlebury College, Vermont; and Charlotte Thomson, librarian of the Red Hook Public Library. My thanks are also extended to Mrs. Mary Warner, who typed various copies of the manuscript with great skill.

My deepest gratitude is to my wife, Valerie, whose patience and good humor hauled me off many a lee shore during the writing of this biography.

1

Background of an Expansionist

Cuba, 1855

On a spring day in April 1855, a tall and rugged ex-officer of the United States Navy, Robert Wilson Shufeldt, visited the Spanish-held island of Cuba. Less than a year previously, Shufeldt had resigned from the navy following three years of inactivity and had joined the New York and Alabama Steamship Company as a captain on the Havana run. Shufeldt was familiar with the Spanish colony and its rulers, and his prominent features—high broad forehead, dark brown hair, and blue eyes over a full nose—were well known on the Havana wharves and to the Spanish authorities. Now, after his visit, he wrote from New Orleans to a group of newspaper owners that he had just returned from Havana by the same steamer that had brought to the press "items of news which are naturally of importance to us."[1]

Shufeldt's news concerned three incidents that had occurred in Cuba during his visit and that were to add fuel to the fires of expansionist sentiment throughout the United States during the summer of 1855. An American businessman, John Thompson, had been arrested at Sagua la Grande for hanging an American coat of arms in his counting room and refusing to take it down. A merchant vessel, the *El Dorado,* had been stopped by a shot across the bows from a Spanish war vessel. Third, a Cuban nationalist and leader of a group of gunrunners who had worked actively in the eastern provinces to overthrow the Spanish government of the island, Francisco Estrampez, had been executed by the authorities.

These incidents were merely the latest in a continuing series of diplomatic and emotional exchanges that had inflamed sentiment, especially in the southern United States, for the immediate annexation of Cuba. Scarcely had the Polk administration, which had deftly manipulated expansionist sentiment to increase the landed and seaboard boundaries of the United States, gone out of office than the covetous eyes of pro-slavery New Orleans opportunists and New York merchant steamboat owners were turned toward Cuba in daily expectation that the island was about to obey John Quincy Adams' Law of Political Gravitation. As southern polemics merged with serious debate in the United States administration and Congress between 1850 and 1855, resentments whipped up in the New Orleans press, fears of an "africanized" Cuban republic, and calls for annexation led to three attempted invasions of Cuba under Narciso López from 1849 to 1851 and two preparations to follow suit between 1853 and 1855 by General John A. Quitman, governor of Mississippi. In addition, the *Black Warrior** affair nearly brought the United States into war with Spain, a state of affairs the Spanish themselves almost adopted following the Ostend Manifesto, the most blatant attempt to pressure the shrinking Spanish empire in the western hemisphere since the events preceding the Adams–Onís Treaty of 1819. By 1855, Cuba was one of the flash points of Spanish–Anglo-American diplomacy.

Within this context of inflamed relations, which culminated during the first two years of the Pierce administration, Shufeldt's views showed that he was reluctant to associate himself with what he described as "the New York–New Orleans steamboat crowd" on the necessity of the immediate annexation of the island by the United States. Shufeldt had seen John Thompson in Havana and discussed the incidents of the arrest with him. Thompson had been brought to the capitol, interviewed by the captain general, instantly released and apologized to, and told that he might return to his business. Shufeldt acknowledged that the whole proceedings were arbitrary and an indignity but he added, "for if our papers constantly teem with abuse of the Spanish officials, it is but natural that they should resort to the 'lex talionis,' & seize so glorious an opportunity (within the law), of wounding our national pride by a public 'take down' of the 'American Eagle.' " Thompson, in Shufeldt's opinion, was only "an American gentleman residing at Sagua" and "had no claim to Consular protection."

In the case of the *El Dorado,* Shufeldt explained that a war vessel could stop a merchantman anywhere. Furthermore, he knew that the new captain general, José de la Concha, had issued a proclamation declaring the island of Cuba to be in a state of seige and subjecting all vessels coming into her waters to a visit from the men-of-war blockading the island. Thus he believed that the Spanish government "has the right, not only

---

*The *Black Warrior,* an American steamer usually employed in the New York to Mobile trade, was seized by Spanish authorities on February 28, 1854, in Havana for not having a proper manifest for her cargo. The incident provoked a considerable outcry mainly in the southern states, and especially in New Orleans, after the failure of the López filibustering expeditions to Cuba. Owing to the heated efforts of Pierre Soulé, then minister to Madrid, the seizure threatened to develop into a serious diplomatic imbroglio, but it was calmed by a Spanish apology and the cool work of Secretary of State William L. Marcy.

Background of an Expansionist

to board but to use force in keeping vessels from too near an approach to its coasts or from entering its harbors." Given this point of view, he explained, "I can not look upon the *El Dorado* affair in the light of an 'outrage.'"

Shufeldt deplored the distortions of these news items by the "usual correspondents" who assumed "an exciting character, injurious to a proper appreciation of events passing on the island of Cuba, and having a tendency rather to retard, than further the end they have in view." He did not doubt the sincerity of the news reporters, "shocked with the sight of the terrible garroté, and the sound of the rolling drum," and breathing an atmosphere "tainted with the 'vapor of a dungeon.'" However, he did question their fitness for the task of preparing the public mind in the United States to act intelligently "at a period not distant, upon the question whether Cuba is to remain 'always faithful' to her present government, or whether like another star she is to rise from her ocean bed, to add the brilliancy to that cluster which you and I, and every son of America, worships [*sic*] as devoutly as did those Wise Men of the East, the heralding star of the 'Advent'."

In adding his own celestial touch to John Quincy Adams' Law of Political Gravitation, Shufeldt did not favor any wild schemes for the conquest of Cuba. Like the famous Massachusetts statesman, he saw clearly the dangers inherent in grasping for new territory immediately to satisfy expansionist slavery desires. Moreover, in the execution of Estrampez, Shufeldt read lessons for American disunion. Somewhat romantically, he delineated the young Cuban revolutionary, who had been twice pardoned by the Spanish authorities and had still attempted their overthrow, as "young, ardent, heroic; actuated by the noblest impulses of humanity, which were artfully worked upon by designing men." He admired the Cuban's devotion to a cause that was hopeless from the first and he pitied his death. But neither could he condemn the Spanish authorities who had finally executed Estrampez and he declared: "If every enthusiast is to pursue his cause unchecked then the stability of all human institutions is at an end; (and not only the government of Cuba must feel the influence of every passing wind, but wiser and better governments might totter beneath the blows of *northern* fanaticism or *southern* disunion)."

In specifying the problem that John Brown and Preston Brooks were to dramatize within a few years, Shufeldt did not wish to appear as an apologist for the Cuban authorities. To his correspondents he wrote:

> I wish the readers of your paper to remember that there are two sides to every question; And I believe that the day is not far distant when this one will have to be met and answered by the American people viz. whether Cuba is for all time, to be the toy of her cruel mistress, or the pawn in the game of

English diplomacy, or whether America is to rise above the petty intrigues of [Pierre] Soulé or the insignificant protests of [Consul William H.] Robertson, & proclaim herself the mistress of the destinies of this western continent.

The United States had, in fact, already done this with the Monroe Doctrine and the statement only reveals the complete sense of Shufeldt's expansionist sentiments if the clause that he erased before he mailed his letter is added: ". . . whose influence must extend from Cape Horn to the Aurora Borealis."

This concern over the destiny of Cuba is the earliest recorded example of Shufeldt's views on the expansion of American influence in the world, and it is characteristic that, initially, it concerned an area closely adjacent to the continental United States. Expansionism was to become the great theme of his life after the Civil War, taking him from the Caribbean to the continents of Africa and Asia and leading directly to the opening of Korea to the trade of the western world. But in 1855 Shufeldt began writing on the topic at a time of tension and national debate over Cuba's relationship to Spain and the Union. One further clue to his attitude in this period emerged in 1873, at the time of more troubles with Spain over the *Virginius* affair,* when an old shipmate, John Fox, recalled discussing the problem of annexing Cuba in 1856. He reminded Shufeldt that "you and I had some talk about it . . . *you knew then* how to *take* Havana."[2] As a former naval officer Shufeldt had worked out the military details necessary for the conquest of the Cuban capital should war come, but they obviously did not include the type of filibustering activities that appealed to many of the "steamboat crowd" in the 1850s.

The Naval Apprenticeship: 1839–1854

There was little in Shufeldt's ancestral background that suggested a naval and diplomatic career, though according to family tradition at least one member was impressed by the British either during the American Revolution or the War of 1812. But the Shufeldts were mainly a farming family whose founding father came to New York with the large German Palatine migration of 1710 to make hemp, tar, and resin for the Royal Navy. The first record of a Zufeld (a Germanic rather than a

---

*The *Virginius* affair occurred late in 1873 when Spanish authorities in Santiago seized an American-registered gunrunning vessel, hunted for two years by the Spanish as a pirate, and executed captured rebel leaders and most of the crew. Although the crew executions were clearly illegal, the *Virginius* was illegally flying the American flag, her real owner was the Cuban junta, and the vessel did not conform to American law in registration. Nevertheless, the incident heightened tension for war without producing it between the United States and Spain.

Dutch name) is in the registers of the Palatine minister at the German settlement of West Camp, the Reverend Joshua Kocherthal, August 27, 1711. When the Palatines became restive under the restraints imposed on them and began moving out toward the Mohawk and Schoharie river valleys, at least one Shufeldt, "Jurie Toevelt," moved toward Rhinebeck on the east bank of the Hudson and settled with other High Dutchers. In 1714 the census for Dutchess County listed 445 people of whom 29 were slaves, and no Shufeldt or Toevelt was listed as a head of a family. But in 1718 Jurie Toevelt was on the tax roll assessed at £6 5s 7½d, well under the average of the 129 people whose total assessed valuation was £1,300. By 1723 Toevelt's tax figure was £17 0s 17d, and the family was on its way to becoming successful farmers, increasingly prosperous, who knew their interests and served them faithfully. By the 1740s both Jurie Toevelt and Jurie Adam Toevelt were listed as freemen among 240 so listed in Dutchess County. During the 1750s, when the county underwent a population explosion making it second only to Albany in New York state, with 13,289 whites and 859 slaves in 1756, they each owned a slave. As the revolutionary war developed, one branch of the family became numerically prominent in and around Claverack, Columbia County. In 1775 four Shewfelts—Jury Adam, Lawrence, Petrus, and Adam—were listed among 964 who refused to sign the revolutionary pledge against the British (compared with 1,820 who did), nor did a Shewfelt from Dutchess County serve in any of the seven county regiments or in Ezekiel Cooper's rangers during the war. However, by 1795 two Shufelts, Henry and George, along with many other farmers on Livingston Manor, presented the petition demanding an investigation into the Livingston's title. When the town of Red Hook was incorporated in 1812, the Shufeldts (the Rhinebeck Shufeldts retained the *d* in their names, unlike those from Columbia) were listed as being among the earliest families, conservative and relatively prosperous. It was in Red Hook, Dutchess County, that Robert Wilson Shufeldt was born, February 21, 1822, the second son of Mary Howey Wilson Shufeldt and George Adam Shufeldt.

Virtually nothing is recorded of Robert's early life in the 1820s on what is now known as the Homer Coons farm in Red Hook. Eight children—Alexander, Robert, Mary, Ellen, George A., Jr., Henry Howey, William, and Frances—were born to his parents. George Adam Shufeldt was a successful lawyer who wanted his sons educated for "good positions." Robert probably attended the local school in Red Hook during the 1820s and early 1830s and later, at sixteen, he entered Middlebury College, Vermont, as a freshman in 1837. No record of his academic work survives at Middlebury, but he left in 1839 without graduating during a period when the college suffered a drastic decline in enrollments. It is possible that young Shufeldt, who was increasingly attracted to a naval career, took the opportunity to enter the navy as a midshipman from New York when a vacancy arose in 1839. Certainly there was not much to appeal to a young man in Dutchess County in the late 1830s when the local agricultural economy began to decline.

Immediate family connections helped Robert considerably. His maternal uncle, Steven Bayard Wilson, was a commander in the navy and most likely smoothed the way for him. His father also gave his assistance. George Adam Shufeldt was a keen Van Buren Democrat who mourned the defeat of 1840. His early law training had been in the same law office, Abram Van Vechten's, where Martin Van Buren received his training. George Shufeldt was a political friend of Silas Wright, Daniel Dickinson, Elisha and Emmett Williams and John Nelles; a lawyer among lawyers. During Van Buren's presidency Shufeldt was appointed district attorney in New York City, leaving a similar post in Dutchess County. He wanted his son to read law, but Robert rejected his advice and chose the navy. The elder Shufeldt, who displayed a strong, possessive nature with his children, reluctantly acquiesced in the decision and used his influence with Van Buren to secure the midshipman's place for his son. Later George Shufeldt wrote to Robert, "I cannot determine whether you have done wisely in rejecting my advice to become a lawyer. I think that depends whether you feel an interest in your present profession or not."[3]

As the second son in a family of eight children, Robert Wilson was an individualist, at times a lone wolf. This characteristic was to surface repeatedly during his career in the navy and during diplomatic negotiations. He was impatient under restraint, independent, sometimes a dreamer and a romantic, given in middle age to writing poetry and musing about life, the sea, humankind—especially women—and power. He was also headstrong. The first memory that his younger brother Henry Howey recalled of him was of Robert, dressed in his midshipman's uniform, being chastised by a neighbor for picking apples in his orchard. Robert stood stiffly until the neighbor returned to the house and then, red-faced, denounced the farmer before striding away.[4]

The young man received orders on November 4, 1839, to leave his home near the Hudson and report to Commodore Charles G. Ridgely, USS *United States,* at New York.[5] After five months training in the Home Squadron, Shufeldt was ordered to join the USS *Potomac* on March 31, 1840. On May 12 his new ship left Norfolk and anchored in Rio de Janeiro harbor on July 3. Not until February 17, 1841, did a letter arrive from Shufeldt for his parents. In Rio the tall, blue-eyed and handsome midshipman had met his first love who, he recalled after twenty-five years, "won my heart there—with a bunch of flowers handed thro' the iron grating of their convent-like houses." The memory of the port and the town was so vivid that even after the Civil War he remembered, "it seemed but yesterday" since he had entered the magnificent harbor and wandered through the streets of the old city. Then he wondered what had become of his "dark beauty" and sadly reflected, "my first love I am sure died in [my] boyhood—tho' I remember well a resolve to return to Rio in Mature years to claim 'my nut brown maid'!"[6]

The absence of any mail disturbed Shufeldt's father, who found no tidings from his son "very strange & unaccountable!" George Shufeldt may have shrewdly guessed the cause of his son's preoccupation. "We thought that you would watch every opportunity to let us know all about you," he admonished his son, "but suppose that you are so much engaged & so much occupied in the new sights which daily come to your view that you had forgotten or had not leisure to think of those left at home." There followed a fifteen-page discourse, "this little relick" sent "as a means of keeping you in the path of virtue and of duty," about the perils that awaited a young man away from home. Commander Steven B. Wilson was held up as a shining example of sobriety and deportment for the guidance of his nephew.[7]

In August 1841, while still on the Brazil station, Shufeldt was transferred to the barque *Marion,* commanded by William J. Belt. At the beginning of February 1842, several of the Brazil squadron sailed for Buenos Aires. In that port the government was exacting a heavy toll on its political opponents. According to Louis M. Goldsborough, captain of the schooner *Enterprize* and soon to take command of the *Marion,* "Rosas, the head of that government, is shooting people almost every day." One hundred had been killed in three weeks, and over half of them, said Goldsborough, "were young men of the very best families of the country." The irate captain assumed that "if it were not for the actual presence of our men-of-war, the same scoundrel would shoot American citizens in the same barbarous manner."[8] Life for the young New York midshipman in the Brazil squadron, with love, fleet tactics, his father's recriminations, and a local rebellion to contend with was anything but dull.

For the two years between 1842 and 1844, Shufeldt served on a number of ships, and in August 1844, when stationed at Pensacola, he was instructed to attend the Naval School in Philadelphia.[9] This period of active service and rapid transfers led to Shufeldt's winning several accolades from his commanders. As he left the *Marion* Commander William J. Belt wrote to him that "it affords me much pleasure to assure you of my esteem & to state that your moral habits—gentlemanly and officer-like deportment—since we have sailed together in this ship have met my entire approbation." Similar testimonies to his prompt attention to duty came from the captains of the *Potomac, Ohio,* and *Bainbridge.*[10]

Shufeldt attended the Philadelphia Naval School, the predecessor of the United States Naval Academy, under its governor, Charles W. Morgan, until June 1845. In May of that year he was ill and had to be excused duties, but his illness did not prevent his passing examinations in seamanship, navigation, and mathematics by June 2. In July he reported for duty on the Coast Survey, placed there by a department that wished its younger, and surplus, officers to gain experience in hydrographic surveying. Almost immediately he was warranted as a passed midshipman. His eight months service on the Coast Survey was mostly on board the brig *Washington* under Lieutenant Charles Stacey Davis. By April 1846, he was ordered to report for duty on the frigate *United States* attached to the West African squadron, established to patrol the West African coast under the terms of the Webster–Ashburton Treaty of 1842.[11]

In September 1846, Commodore George C. Read, commanding the West African squadron, appointed Shufeldt acting master of the barque *Marion,* which he commanded for two years off the Congo coast and the Cape Verde Islands. Here he saw at first hand the practices and results of the slave trade. He was ordered to sail home via Gibraltar in August 1848. On September 1, in latitude 42°40′north, longitude 42°00′west, about twelve hundred miles southeast of Cape Race, Newfoundland, the barque was struck by a tremendous gale that ripped apart the fore storm staysail and battered the vessel for most of the evening and next day. The fury of the wind and sea might have led the barque to broach to, but Shufeldt had anticipated the direction from which the wind would hit as the vessel lay becalmed, and he arranged his canvas accordingly. Upon arriving at Boston he wrote a long account of his experiences to Messrs. E. and G. W. Blunt, whose published maps of storm routes he had read, praising the theory of storms developed by William C. Redfield, a meteorologist, for giving him the information that enabled him to escape the worst effects of the hurricane. Redfield requested, and received, permission to publish Shufeldt's letter in the *London Nautical Magazine* for 1849.[12]

Within a month of the *Marion*'s arrival in Boston in September 1848, Shufeldt was married to Sarah Hutchins Abercrombie, the daughter of the Reverend James Abercrombie of Philadelphia.* Henry B. Shufelt in *Our Folks: A History of the Shufelt Family,* claimed Shufeldt was married on October 16, 1847, but the year cited is an error. No record of any

---

*The Reverend James Abercrombie, D.D., was born in Philadelphia, January 26, 1758, son of James and Margaret Abercrombie, originally from Dundee, Scotland. Abercrombie's second wife, Mary Jane Mason (born November 28, 1783), was Sarah's mother. The Mason family was from Barbados.

return from the West African squadron by Shufeldt between 1846 and 1848 has been found. On October 22, 1847, he was issued a consulate pass to Seville, Spain, and one to Cadiz, by Alexander Barlow, American consul in Cadiz. The most conclusive proof that he was married in the fall of 1848 lies in a letter from Charles Stacey Davis, who wrote to Shufeldt from Cambridge, Massachusetts, on November 11, 1848, "I have received your note of the 8th . . . I congratulate you on your marriage & the Prospects of happiness it opens in life."[13]

Shortly after his marriage, Shufeldt applied for the Coast Survey again and his old commanding officer, Charles Davis, welcomed him back. There was little danger of the newly married applicant being sent overseas, and he was left without orders for five months. Only on February 27, 1849, was he told to report for duty with the survey, and he was assigned to the revenue cutter *Morris* for service in a hydrographic party under command of Lieutenant John N. Maffitt. However, the Coast Survey held only a limited appeal for Shufeldt. Within three months he applied to the secretary of the navy, William Ballou Preston, for service on the SS *Atlantic,* owned by the Collins Steamship Company.[14]

The Collins company, under the leadership of Edward Knight Collins, was preparing to compete with the British Cunard Company for control of the passenger and mail trade on the Atlantic. An act of Congress of March 3, 1847, had authorized the secretary of the navy to inspect Collins' vessels for the carrying of mail. After a successful survey, Collins was awarded the mail contract from the government, which specified that five new steamships, each of 2,000 tons gross with 1,000 horsepower, would be built. Collins seriously underestimated the costs of construction and his vessels were delayed, requiring machinery of then unprecedented power. By subsidizing the Collins Line with a mail award of $385,000 per annum, later increased to $853,000, Congress showed its willingness to engage with the British government, which subsidized the Cunard Line, in a bid to control the Atlantic passenger and mail trade. The terms of the contract required the Navy Department to place young officers on board for training, and Navy Board inspectors were to certify that the vessels had been built to government specifications. On October 25, 1849, Shufeldt was placed on "waiting orders" and the following April he was authorized to join the SS *Atlantic* as watch officer. In addition to Shufeldt, the Navy Department placed three younger midshipmen on board as junior officers.[15]

The race for supremacy on the Atlantic began in earnest in 1850. The *Atlantic* sailed on her maiden voyage from New York to Liverpool on April 27, 1850, under the command of Captain James West. When her sister ship, *Pacific,* joined her in early summer, followed by the *Arctic* and the *Baltic,* in November and December, they began to eat into the

Cunard monopoly, crossing at least a day faster than the Cunard vessels. For a short time a bitter struggle ensued between the two lines and Collins' share of passengers and mail revenues mounted steadily.

On January 5, 1851, however, the *Atlantic* broke down when her main shaft cracked through in a diagonal direction. For two days the ship hove to under storm canvas while the paddle wheels were lashed and the engine secured. After four days of trying to make headway against the winds, Captain West abandoned the hope of reaching Halifax or Bermuda and determined to run before the westerly winds of Cape Clear, 1,400 miles distant. With small spars, light canvas, 650 tons of freight, and useless machinery, the *Atlantic* averaged 150 miles a day and limped into Cork harbor on January 22.[16]

Before the vessel had left Liverpool, Shufeldt had suffered a bad fall that forced him to bed with a back injury. When the shaft broke the ship's surgeon, Samuel Boyd, was treating him. In the dramatic language of the *New York Evening Post,* Shufeldt "sprang from his berth, clothed himself without a moment's hesitation, and went on deck, where he remained in the midst of the terrible gale and snow storm . . . until the vessel was got under canvas, nor did he go off duty again until the vessel arrived at Cork." The *Evening Post*'s characterization was not based on an editorial policy of befriending young naval officers. The newspaper opposed the government's "regulation of commerce" and was trying to show that Shufeldt was needed in a crisis, since only three very young midshipmen were on board as officers. The editor could thus attack the government's "meddling with commerce" in placing the inexperienced three on the *Atlantic*. But he did not catch the logic of his praise of Shufeldt, himself only a midshipman, (though as first officer he was listed as lieutenant), who had also been placed there by the Navy Department. Not until fifty days after the *Atlantic* sailed did news of her safety reach the United States. Shufeldt's escape was celebrated by the people in his village.[17] By February, Shufeldt was in New York where he received many letters of thanks for his part in bringing the *Atlantic* into port.

Shufeldt's first child, christened Robert Wilson, Jr., was born on December 1, 1850, in a house on John Street, New York City. Shufeldt took his wife and small son with him on some of the crossings made by the SS *Atlantic*. In recollecting incidents of his youth when writing an autobiographical memoir in the 1920s, Robert Jr. recalled that he had often heard his mother say that when he was a small baby he had been taken across the Atlantic with her "aboard a merchant steamer which my father commanded." On one occasion a nurse engaged to look after the boy left him on top of one of the cargo bales near the ship's side. A sudden roll of the vessel sent the infant over the side, when he was caught at the last second by the panic-stricken nurse who desperately snatched hold of his long clothes and hauled him back on board. It was some time before the nurse, and Sarah Shufeldt, could bring themselves to reveal what had almost happened.[18]

Once his back injury healed, Shufeldt was detached from the *Atlantic* and assigned to the steamship *Georgia,* commanded by Lieutenant David Dixon Porter, and belonging to the United States Steamship Company controlled by the New York capitalists George Law, Marshall O. Roberts, and Bowes McIlvaine. Their intent was to institute a coastal service between New York and New Orleans, touching at Charleston, Savannah, and Havana. Thus began a fruitful acquaintance and friendship with Porter (that only soured in the 1870s when Porter apparently disapproved of Shufeldt's seeming friendliness with George M. Robeson, Grant's secretary of the navy), and Shufeldt's first contacts with the Caribbean trading area. Four months after joining Porter, Shufeldt contracted fever and left the *Georgia*. She was to be the last vessel that he served in for the Navy Department before the Civil War. From September 1851 to September 1853, he was furloughed at six monthly intervals and then granted an indefinite extension of leave by secretary of the navy James C. Dobbin of North Carolina. In March 1853, he was warranted as master, retroactive to February 21, and in May 1854, he was commissioned a lieutenant to date from October 1853. One month later he requested permission to resign and although he was then under orders to proceed to the USS *Massachusetts,* attached to the Pacific squadron, his request was granted.[19] At age thirty-two his first naval career was over.

A Highly Spiritualized Condition

For five years after leaving the navy, Shufeldt was constantly employed as a merchant sea captain. His first two years, until 1856, were spent on the New York–Havana–Mobile–New Orleans run for the New York and Alabama Steamship Company. There seems little doubt that the company had outbid the navy for Shufeldt's services, and he superintended the building of the *Black Warrior* and *Cahawba* for it. The lure of an increased salary, the absence of postings, and the necessity to settle his growing family (his second son, Mason, was born November 4, 1852, and his third son, George Adam, on May 3, 1854) proved sufficient grounds for resigning, especially as the opportunities for employment in the golden age of subsidized steam transport were increasing rapidly. In 1851 he bought a small cottage in Stamford, Connecticut. Three years later he set up residences in Mobile and New Orleans and at times took his family to the Crescent City.[20]

The only other occasion upon which Shufeldt's movements are revealed in the period from 1854 to 1856 was a highly personal one. On one of his voyages from New York to Pensacola he met the young and beautiful daughter of an army colonel stationed at Pensacola. Shufeldt did not give the exact date of meeting her, merely stating "In the spring of 185-." He recalled her name only as Kate and wrote that

> there were few passengers and we became intimate—There are times and there are persons in which & with whom life becomes intensified as it were and we live in a few days through years of feelings and passions—It was so in this case and when the hour came for parting—we both felt as if the bond had become too strong *ever* to be broken and that without a continuance of this friendship or rather love in its holiest sense—the world could henceforth afford no pleasure—nor heaven hold out a hope—As I took her hand in farewell she said with an angelic sweetness which foreboded sorrow—"fear not my friend, we will meet again."
>
> The month which followed passed with my mind & body in a highly spiritualized condition—the things of earth lost their significance and a future life of eternal harmony amid the music of the spheres pictured itself in brightest colors to an excited imagination . . . Love that divinest of passions lost its materialism & in its God-like company I walked the earth as one who treads alone its dusty paths—waiting only here below until "we should meet again."

A few weeks later Shufeldt was on his homeward voyage. Lying in his bunk one night he imagined that he heard her parting words again. At that moment he knew she had died, and a few weeks later he was not surprised to receive a letter from her sister saying that she had succumbed to yellow fever and that her last words were the ones Shufeldt had heard, and in the same hour. Many years later, in New York, Shufeldt went to see a medium, "Simon the Magician," at the corner of Bond and Broadway. As he entered he believed he saw Kate again. He recalled that "a terrible change came over my whole being—my mind & body became infused with the spirit of that departed friend," and he heard her repeat her parting words.

This episode with Kate, while giving one indication of the great attraction that women held for him throughout his life, also reveals the emotional drive that mysticism and spiritualism accentuated within him. Shufeldt used the incident to substantiate his belief that there was reality in a future life and "more consolation for sorrow and more hope for happiness—than can be found in any of the cold, clammy dogmas, preached for nineteen centuries—either by Jew or Gentile." This spiritualistic approach was typical of his views on religion, for he confessed that as the years passed even a "ressurection [*sic*] from the dead would

Background of an Expansionist

fail to convince me of the truth of any particular religious theory." But he did avow that mankind needed religion, and when his emotional drives were separated from the purely personal plane of an individual relationship or reflections on a future life, Shufeldt was to harness them to his ideas on the role of the United States in world affairs. He expressed a conscious desire to spread the gospel of the superiority of the United States to the "barbarians" who inhabited most of the rest of the globe. In 1855, in his early thirties, he was just beginning to formulate his opinions on such subjects. Because his constant visits as a ship's captain took him so often to Cuba, his attention was naturally fixed upon that troubled Spanish island which, he considered, would "rise from the ocean beds, to add the brilliancy to that cluster" which every son of America worshipped as devoutly "as did those Wise Men of the East, the heralding star of the 'Advent'." The prospects of embracing the Cuba of Estrampez and the *El Dorado* in the 1850s, as well as female companions on lonely voyages, could provide "the music of the spheres" for Shufeldt's "excited imagination."[21]

2
An Education in Expansion

In 1856, Shufeldt arrived in New Orleans and began to associate with prominent business and political leaders of the Crescent City at the height of their most visionary expansionist dreams. From this connection he developed a lifelong interest in the destinies of the transit route across the Isthmus of Tehuantepec, the southern Mexican isthmus between Ventosa on the Pacific and Minatitlan on the Coatzacoalcos River where the mountains dip to allow for passage of a railroad. While he was to grow increasingly suspicious of the motives of powerful Southerners such as John Slidell and Judah P. Benjamin in seeking to dominate the isthmus, he eventually wished to see it controlled by the United States government for both strategic and commercial reasons. For the next twenty years Shufeldt sought to extend American influence in the region.

The Louisiana–Tehuantepec Company

Throughout the middle decades of the nineteenth century American government officers, speculating companies, and private individuals displayed a keen interest in the Isthmus of Tehuantepec. As most of these interests centered in the port of New Orleans but attracted investment from New York, there emerged in that city after 1856 a combination of southern and northern speculators who eventually floated a company to control the right-of-way across the isthmus. Shufeldt's employment by this company, the Louisiana–Tehuantepec Company, threw him into contact with New Orleans and New York commercial expansionists. His involvement came just in time for him to witness the culmination of a five-year struggle among New Orleans companies for the control of the transit rights, as well as to color his views on southern efforts in Mexico. He once recalled that he had been hired in 1856 to command a steamer and to superintend the building of steamboats for the navigation of the Coatzacoalcos River. Later, when writing to William H. Seward, Lincoln's secretary of state, about his activities with the company, Shufeldt was sometimes confused in recalling its name, mentioning that "I was associated for two years with the New Orleans Tehuantepec Co." and elsewhere declaring "about a year subsequent to my connection with the Louisiana-Tehuantepec Company. . . ."[1]

While waiting for the directors of the company to negotiate a charter, Shufeldt became discouraged with his position. His future employment depended on an agreement being negotiated, and that did not seem likely over the winter of 1857. Thus in February he sought the position of consul to Trinidad de Cuba. He solicited the aid of General John A. Quitman, governor of Mississippi, whose filibustering preparations had alarmed the Spanish authorities in Cuba in 1854. Shufeldt, whose father had been tutored by Quitman's father at Kingston Academy, played on the family acquaintance: "You are aware of the interest I have always felt in the destinies of the island of Cuba," he reminded the general, then added, "I do not know whether your ambition still points that way, but I have long been anxious to connect myself with its future." What had previously prevented him from following this inclination had been the necessity of earning a living for his family. Now he feared that the vessel he commanded was about to be sold, and he began to look for employment elsewhere. The alternatives, as he saw them, were either in other seas or to settle permanently in Cuba. The first alternative would take him away from what he considered to be the great object of his life: "I am convinced that the inevitable progress of events will bring Cuba into our Confederacy or connect her prominently with a section of it—perhaps more consistent with her and its institutions—and I have the ambition, General to take a position in the course of these events."

Shufeldt believed that the post of consul at Trinidad de Cuba would be sufficient for his family purposes, but he dangled another incentive before the general's eyes. While in Trinidad, he believed, he would gain opportunities "of judging the genius of the people and the capabilities of the soil—These would be my study—and when the time comes—as come it must, when you or any other Statesman should need information upon these subjects—I would not only be ready to give it; but to join heart and hand in the advancement of a cause which as philanthropists we must regard as sacred and as Anglo-Saxons inevitable." In addition, he mentioned fifteen years in the navy and five years in the merchant marine "most of which has been in constant intercourse with the people and authorities of this island [Cuba] among whom I am well known."[2]

Shufeldt extolled Quitman as the exponent of southern expansionism, and expressed hopes that linking his destiny with the general's would give him "at least the chance of acting a subordinate part in the drama." He saw no inconsistencies in carrying out these ideas with the duties of an American consul. Furthermore, he claimed that he had the support of the "prominent citizens of this Consulate [Trinidad de Cuba]" and the backing of friends in Mobile to add to his qualification of speaking Spanish. There was no doubt that Shufeldt had caught the mystique of expansionism. Cuba was to remain in the forefront of his thoughts in the antebellum period. However, he did not receive the consular appointment, partly because he overestimated the amount of help that Quitman, then a discredited filibusterer, would be able to offer; he was left to take his chances with the Louisiana–Tehuantepec Company in New Orleans.

Following receipt of its charter from the Louisiana government, the company authorized its leaders, Judah P. Benjamin, Emile La Sère, José de Garay, William D. Lee, and Antoine J. Marigny, to negotiate with the Mexican government for a new transit concession. Despite the opposition of Pierre Soulé, a member of a rival canal faction who journeyed to Mexico to speak against the Louisiana–Tehuantepec Company, the group succeeded, probably by bribery (as was strongly hinted at in the New Orleans press), in gaining a new grant from the Mexican government.[3]

The company began operations almost immediately, under the presidency of Emile La Sère at 45 Carondelet Street. Shufeldt took over the command of the company's new steamer, the *Quaker City*, of 1,428 tons. She began to cruise between New Orleans and New York, via Mobile and Havana, in September 1857. During the same month the Mexican government promulgated the new grant, legalizing the company's operations. The *New Orleans Daily Picayune* declared that "The free passage of the isthmus is to us as much a necessity and a natural right as the free navigation of the Mississippi, the Gulf or the ocean." The editor believed that the company's leaders had a "future of brilliant promises before them" and contemplated that "no one can tell, indeed, the important part which this great transit route is destined to play in the development of that rich and fertile country."[4]

The future looked promising at first. Regular passenger trips over the isthmus by a light plank road began to link New Orleans and San Francisco. The company soon switched the *Quaker City* to the New Orleans–Coatzacoalcos route and added a smaller steamer, the *Suchil*, to take passengers to the town of the same name at the head of navigation on the Coatzacoalcos. Shufeldt's vessel began calling regularly at Minatitlan, at the mouth of the river. Shufeldt moved his residence from

Mobile to New Orleans and engaged rooms for Sarah and his son Robert in the Old St. Charles Hotel. He arranged for a tutor to give his son lessons in French twice a week and settled down for over a year to pursue his profession. Success appeared to be guaranteed by a government mail contract for carrying the California mails. Later, the chief New York financial backer of the company, Peter A. Hargous, decided to return the *Quaker City* to the New Orleans–New York run, which suited Shufeldt who had many warm friends in Cuba. Hargous knew from the newspaper in Havana that the *Quaker City* was "a favorite, & that Capt. S receives many flattering paragraphs."[5]

After April of 1859, the Tehuantepec bubble burst. Judah P. Benjamin's New Orleans friends first raised the specter that haunted all isthmian railroad or transit schemes—that a railroad network within the continental boundaries of the United States would bypass them when it linked both coasts. Such fears affected the directors of the Louisiana-Tehuantepec Company. It began to suffer from internal dissension and Hargous grew nervous. After R. D. Hatch, purser of the *Quaker City*, visited Hargous at the end of January, he informed Shufeldt, "I think he wished to see you in N[ew] Y[ork] to get among other things your opinion on *various* the persons connected with the enterprize in N[ew] O[rleans], Mr. [Lewis] Heyliger [secretary of the company] & those on the Isthmus." Hatch recalled that Hargous had mentioned many times Shufeldt's frank expressions of opinion concerning some new steamers and their fitness for the trade. "I feel sure of Capt. S.," Hargous had informed Hatch, "it is just what I need & want in these matters some one who is uncompromising in the expression of their true opinion when called upon." Internally, the company was dividing into two groups, with neither knowing what the other was doing and suspicious of each other.[6]

The crash came when Hargous found the returns on the transit route did not live up to expectations. The *New Orleans Daily True Delta*, editorially opposed to Benjamin and Slidell, sadly observed that the Hargous House had for a long time been considered "one of the staunchest within the limits of our erratic Republican neighbor [Mexico]," but that "it mixed itself up in the political intrigues, here and in Mexico, of the most equivocal character, for advantages in Tehuantepec, and this is the result." The newspaper revealed that the immediate cause of the suspension of the Hargous business was alleged to be the advances made to the company. It also estimated that Hargous was out of pocket by $600,000 to $1 million. Hargous later claimed that he lost $500,000.[7] Although he was able to remain in operation on the New York–Havana run, Hargous had to withdraw financially from the Tehuantepec venture. As an enterprise involving New York–New Orleans cooperation to control isthmian travel routes before the Civil War, the Louisiana–Tehuantepec Company was a dismal failure.

In October 1859, the struggling company suffered another heavy blow. An hour after midnight on Friday, October 7, Shufeldt's vessel the *Quaker City* smashed her engines completely, thirty-five miles southeast of Cape Hatteras. The vessel rode out a forty-eight hour gale with other ships standing by, but not until the steamer *State of Georgia* appeared and took over towing from the schooner *Kingfisher* did the *Quaker City* finally reach Hampton Roads on the thirteenth. In New York the unrest over the fate of the *Quaker City* continued for four days. The *New York Express* sent a reporter to interview Hargous, who claimed "no particular apprehension" for the safety of the vessel. One of the *New York Herald*'s correspondents explained why when he recalled that "Shufeldt is one of the ablest steam sailors afloat—clear headed, cool and resolute." The writer remembered Shufeldt as first officer of the *Atlantic* when she smashed her machinery and declared, "with a disabled engine he is qualified to meet any emergency of the sea." The vessel itself was staunch, with canvas and masts sufficient to stabilize her in a heavy sea.[8]

Shufeldt came out of the incident with a heightened reputation. One newspaper account noted that "the conduct of Captain Shufeldt is highly eulogized by every passenger." The passengers who remained with the *Quaker City* and who landed at Norfolk hoped that he would be given "some token of their appreciation of so gallant and worthy a man." All that Shufeldt received, however, was the grateful thanks of the New York Board of Underwriters, which had been saved the insurance costs of the vessel. The *Quaker City* was soon back in commission on the Havana run. Shufeldt remained in command until the opening shots of the Civil War. Although he was left with his ideas and dreams of controlling the Tehuantepec route, which were to occupy his thoughts for another fifteen years, in the more prosaic world of earning his living, the captain was now far from immediate contact with the Mexican scene.[9]

National Vessels for National Purposes

In May 1858, in a letter to the *New York Herald,* Shufeldt took a sharp look at the state of the nation's navy.[10] Royal Navy vessels had begun searching American merchant ships suspected of running slaves into Cuba or the southern states in 1858, and Shufeldt considered such actions "insulting and aggressive in a high degree" and that American resentment was "earnest and sincere." However, he also reflected upon the consequences of any American desire to resent such "insults" and "future aggressions" on commerce should a squadron be dispatched to the area. Should a British warship attempt to "visit" an American merchant vessel while an American warship was present, a collision would be inevitable. This could well be the beginning of a war, he wrote, that "few of us might live to see the end." He urged the readers of the *Herald* to understand that he was neither one of those men "born insensible to fear" nor one who accepted the attitude that every Englishman who landed on the shores of the United States "with hostile intent" would become "a prisoner or a bloody corpse." Even with a faith in the justice of an American cause and a determination to defend it, Shufeldt declared, "Our navy to-day is only equal to the task of getting us into a fight, and utterly powerless as a means of defence or aggression after we are well into it. . . ." In addition, he asserted that the only proper vessel of war was a steamer "and if possible, a screw steamer."

Having advocated the use of modern propulsion techniques, Shufeldt concluded his analysis by seeking to explode two popular myths. First, he assumed the days of reliance on the conversion of sailing craft, as in the War of 1812, were over. Furthermore, he asked the warmongers in his audience where the United States could find one steamer capable of conversion to a man-of-war. No such steamers existed and none could be built in less than nine months. Then came the rhetorical question: "what is to prevent England from lining our coasts in the meanwhile with her magnificent fleet of screw steamers?" The answer was self-evident. The second myth he identified was "a sort of mysterious faith abroad" in the powers of a "big gun" placed upon small vessels at short notice, which would "burn, sink and destroy" all who dared "to venture within its terrible range."

The former naval officer shared no such faith. Tactically, he still believed in close fighting using broadside batteries. The problem of naval combat between steam vessels had still to be solved, but Shufeldt could not imagine the captains of two American or English war vessels contenting themselves with the uncertain aim of long guns. Future combats for the purpose of capture, he considered, would be fought broadside to broadside and the victor would be, "other things being equal . . . the one with the strongest powers of offence and defence." What Shufeldt wanted for ships of war were "national vessels built for national purposes," and he urged: "let us seriously ask our legislators that if they really anticipate such an event, or contemplate sending a fleet to the Straits of Florida, why, in God's name, they don't do something at once towards placing the navy in a position which at least will not render disgrace inevitable? . . . The fight for 'free trade and sailor's rights,' if fought at all, must be between national vessels." Although he was clinging to one of the myths of the War of 1812 himself, when he anticipated that future action would be close-range broadsides, and he underestimated the conversion rate for steamers that took place during the Civil War, his readiness to accept steam as a means of propulsion, his preference for screw steamers over side- or paddle-wheel, and the skepticism he displayed over the dominant faith in the power of big guns on small ships, revealed a mind that had begun to grapple with some of the problems of naval tactics, technology, ordnance, and support for a national navy that were to be continually debated in naval circles from the Civil War through the 1890s.

The Cuban Slave Trade

At some time in the late 1850s, Shufeldt purchased a large frame house with an acre of land in Stamford, Connecticut. The house was surrounded by fine elms and a great number of different kinds of fruit trees. Shufeldt's son, Robert Jr. later remembered it as "a lovely old place on South Atlantic Street, which ran to the bridge that crossed the Mill River. . . . There was a large barn and a kitchen garden." On another occasion, he reminisced that it was "an old-fashioned New England home of the early sixties—with all of its cherished associations; with only four or five immediate neighbors, and the salt waters of the sound but a few steps from the front gate." Apparently, Shufeldt also purchased an eighteen-acre farm about two miles north of the Stamford home, which was farmed and cared for by "a fine type of Irish farmer," Jim Heffnen. The sons, Robert and Mason, attended the public school and on Sundays the family went to St. John's Church (Episcopal) where Drs. Todd and Mitchell were the pastors.[11]

As the Civil War approached, Shufeldt became acquainted with the former United States Whig senator, Truman Smith of Connecticut, who also lived in Stamford and was, most likely, one of Shufeldt's neighbors. Their first meeting probably occurred soon after Shufeldt purchased his Stamford home. As the war drew closer, Shufeldt discussed the Cuban slave trade with the powerful lawyer and former politician. Smith had once enjoyed considerable influence in Washington with Zachary Taylor; he had steered the Connecticut delegation toward Taylor in the presidential nomination for the Whig party in 1848. Taylor offered him the post of secretary of the Home Department, predecessor to the Department of the Interior. The Connecticut lawyer declined, however, preferring to enter the Senate and organize the Congressional Whigs. He served from 1849 to 1854, when he left to resume his law practice.[12] Shufeldt's friendship with Smith proved fortunate. The lawyer combined neighborly regard and political influence that benefited him considerably. In the days of Shufeldt's developing political thoughts, leading from Whiggish to Republican ideas, Smith proved to be highly influential, especially as he was moving to the Republican party himself. Through this contact, Shufeldt's career as a diplomatic agent, as well as a rising naval officer after the Civil War, began to flourish.

Late in 1860, Smith began to make a conscientious effort to understand the details of the slave trade and asked Shufeldt to write down what he knew about the "secret history of the 'Slave Trade' as it is carried on between the coast of Africa & the island of Cuba, in American ships." Smith's interest in the slave trade eventually secured for him the position of judge of the Court of Arbitration established in New York by President Lincoln, under the terms of the antislave trade treaty signed between William H. Seward and Lord Lyons, the British minister to Washington, on April 7, 1862. Smith was to serve on this court until 1870. In January 1861, Shufeldt briefed him on the traffic with an account that recalled his observations from his days with the West African squadron and his visits to Cuba.[13]

He informed the former senator that an organized company existed in Havana, with a capital of $1 million, whose sole purpose was to import Negro slaves into Cuba. Shufeldt noted the effect of American vessels and crews operating out of New York:

> those acquainted with the Government Officials in Havana—their sympathy with slavery and their natural affinity to bribery & corruption, need not be told how easily such a clearance can be obtained. (A Captain recently informed me that his cost him Six ounces $102)!—But this decision of Mr. Black & this action of our Consul—while it may be consistent with their own sympathies—& may also relieve them of direct responsibility—has not at least as yet, had the effect of diminishing the traffic under the national flag. On the contrary it has increased and is increasing every day. Mr. [Charles] Helm our Consul told me himself—that within the last twenty days he had passed thro' his office the registers of eight Am. vessels which he knew were going after Negroes.

Shufeldt outlined the shipping of the crew, the landings at the warehouses on the banks of the Congo, the evasions of the men-of-war, which called at the same depots for their coal supplies, and the life on board the crowded vessels. But it was Shufeldt's description of the economics of the voyage that especially interested Truman Smith. The slaving ship would anchor at Key St. Philip or one of the small islands abounding off the coast of Cuba and rendezvous with the launches waiting for its return. There with the aid of a corrupt customs official the Negroes were washed, exercised, and fattened for the market. The company's agent paid off the crew, the ship's anchor was raised, her plugs taken out, and sail made until the old craft "foul with crime—& full of all uncleanliness is started forth upon the sea—to sink inevitably & thus obliterate from the records all evidence of the cruise in which she has been an innocent participator." The ship's captain would then proceed to Havana with his register and a false bill of sale, which he forwarded to the New York customs house, according to the law, and "in the meanwhile present himself to his Principal with the following balance sheet:

	Dr.		Cr.
To fit cost of ship	$ 7,000	500 Negroes @ $800	$400,000
Advance wages	$ 1,500	Deduct bribes	$100,000
Cost of Negroes @ $50	$37,500		$300,000
Captain's wages	$ 5,000	Deduct first cost	$ 63,500
Super cargo & Boatswain	$ 5,000	Nett Profits	$237,500
Crew 10 men @ $750	$ 7,500		
	$63,500		

And so ends the voyage!"[14]

Shufeldt told Smith that the enormous profit that accrued to the trader (nine-tenths of whom, he claimed, were American) from such a voyage insured a constant supply, unless some means were found to stop the slave trade. He considered that the use of additional men-of-war around the island of Cuba had only the effect of increasing the number of vessels engaged in the trade. "It is a notorious fact," he added, "that more negroes had been landed since Jany. 1860, than the aggregate of the previous five years—a modest estimate places the numbers at 50,000 since the above date."[15]

The reason behind the trade lay in sugar. With a crop estimated at 600,000 tons and valued at $60 million, every Negro imported was an equivalent of one additional ton of sugar. At late 1860 prices a planter could buy slaves at a thousand dollars each and make 60 percent net profit on his gross outlay of capital. As it was the policy of the Spanish government to extract as much revenue from its colonies as possible, nothing but these large profits would enable the planters to meet the demands of Spain. Shufeldt noted that the income of the Spanish government from Cuba was $20 million per annum "or one-third of the total value of the several products." It was evident to him that before Spain stopped the slave trade she had first to reduce her taxes, and she was not likely to do that "unless actuated by some pressing emergency, not at present foreseen."

Shufeldt wished to see the United States modify its foreign policy and consent to joint action with other naval powers to permit rights of visit and search of all vessels in waters of Cuba.* He also recommended that the United States consuls in Cuba should be men "whose proclivities are rather against than for slavery." Hitherto, he did not consider that this had been the case. Consul General Charles J. Helm, the incumbent in Havana, was prosouthern in outlook. Although Shufeldt was prepared to give consuls credit for the intention of doing their duty, he had no doubt that their sympathies with slavery caused them to be lenient with "the criminal" who perpetrated the crime.

Furthermore, he drew conclusions about the fate of the Negroes seized by government vessels. He considered that the methods of disposing of them, adopted by the British and American governments, were open to serious objections. The governments did not improve the condition of the recaptured blacks, who were used for public and governmental work. He thought that the United States government, by landing the blacks on what was considered to be their native soil in Africa, especially Liberia, acted "with more humanity but perhaps less wisdom" than other governments. Those acquainted with Africa and the "utter difference in language, customs & religion of the various tribes—increased frequently by hereditary hostility," would know the poor prospects facing such Negroes of ever seeing their homes again. Shufeldt suggested some system of apprenticeship to southern planters for a term of years, under strict accountability, both for a humane exercise of their authority over the Negroes and the payment of their wages. But he did not stop to think what this would do to the existing slave population on the antebellum plantations, even though he considered it more humane and economical than the established practice. The effect of recaptured Negroes serving an apprenticeship and receiving payment would have led southern planters into complications with their own slaves that they would not have been able to solve and would have led toward gradual emancipation. The real tragedy, Shufeldt thought, was that a Negro taken from Africa "*never* can get back again to the point from whence he came!"

This long analysis of the Cuban slave trade brought Shufeldt face to face with the problem of Cuba. If the rate of Negro increase into the island continued, he believed that "by the Eternal Law of compensation" the island would become africanized; the master and tyrant of that day would surely become the slave and victim of tomorrow. In spite

---

*It is obvious that Shufeldt had modified his attitude toward Royal Navy vessels searching American ships, expressed in May 1858 (see page 119). Most likely, his growing repugnance for the slave trade accounted for this shift in attitude. Yet, even in May 1858 he had taken the pragmatic view of the searches by reflecting on the consequences rather than upon manipulating the tension, which hardly qualified him as an outraged critic.

of his earlier citations of sugar and taxation figures he declared that Spain had no interest in the future of Cuba and he informed Truman Smith that:

> she knows that someday it will pass from beneath her sceptre—She legislates therefore for that Colony only for the present—revenue from it is what she wants—& she exacts that & would draw blood if it could be turned into gold! The real future of Cuba is bound up with the destiny of our own country—but more especially with the Northern portion of the country. Between it & the South there is an antagonism arising from the similarity of institutions & similarity of products. But the North wants her crops & she wants Northern manufacturers & northern products & she looks in that direction & clings to that support more & more every day.
>
> It is therefore the right & the duty of the government today—whether this Africanization of the island of Cuba shall go on until it ends in the blood & carnage, rapine & devastation, & finally in the barbarism of another San Domingo—or whether by checking the future importation of negroes—she may yet shine forth from the warm bosom of her tropical sea as another bright Star in our Country's diadem—with all the radiance of a Queen of the Antilles!

Shufeldt's association of the island with the future of the North, and his awareness of the growing antagonism with the South in the immediate pre-Civil War days, clearly placed his sympathies among the swelling ranks of the Republican party. Through Truman Smith he met William H. Seward, soon to be Lincoln's secretary of state. As the leading exponent of American expansionism in central America and Asia and a firm antislavery advocate during the 1850s and 1860s, Seward was to influence the development of Shufeldt's thinking on imperialism, manifest destiny, and expansionism. In the early 1860s, however, it was not merely the consideration of the slave trade that led Shufeldt toward Seward, Smith, and other Republican leaders. His personal leanings were in that direction as he remembered the actions of the prosouthern leaders in the Louisiana-Tehuantepec Company.

The Completion of an Education

In 1861 Shufeldt recalled that during 1857 or 1858 he began to have suspicions about the aims of the Louisiana-Tehuantepec Company in controlling the isthmian canal route. Writing to Seward from Havana in November 1861, he informed the new secretary of state that in joining the company he had entered, at first, "with more than usual zeal into a project, which if it had been consummated then, would have done so much to enhance the grandeur of our western Empire."[16] It was in

1861 that Shufeldt was just beginning to develop a conception of the destiny of the United States that intertwined commercial and landed expansion. Thus he advocated that any transit route should be nationally owned. Consequently, he warned Seward that the right-of-way across Tehuantepec, "which altho' always deemed worthy of the attention of our government, at one time to the extent of an offer of $15,000,000 for the privilege," had been bandied about from one company to another, "each time losing something of its character & prestige." The reason for these losses lay in the "want of money & honesty" in the corporation that held the grant, until it finally fell into the hands of the Louisiana-Tehuantepec Company "of which the Hon. J. P. Benjamin of Louisiana was the soul—& P. A. Hargous Esq.—of New York the sufferer." Shufeldt asserted that because of a chronic lack of capital and honesty the company failed to fulfill its obligations, in spite of being sustained by the Buchanan administration, principally through the influence of John Slidell, with mail contracts amounting to $250,000 per annum. This led to "the utter ruin financially of Mr. Hargous & to the last tattered shred of honesty of Mr. Benjamin."

This picture of private corruption would have held little of value for Secretary Seward unless Shufeldt could have produced an argument of stronger force to inspire him to action. This he did with the revelation of a conspiracy that would confirm Seward's worst fears. A year subsequent to his connection with the company, he recalled, "circumstances occurred which led me to believe that the acquisition of that Grant by the above Company controlled by J. P. Benjamin & Jno. Slidell of Louisiana, was only part of the present scheme of 'Secession.' " According to Shufeldt, both Benjamin and Slidell used the Buchanan government for treasonable purposes. A glance at the map, he told the secretary, would show the "immense advantage which would have accrued to this ideal Southern Republic by the acquisition of Tehuantepec with the Gulf of Mexico in its control." The secession of southern California could be confidently anticipated and the United States' longer and more exposed Panama route would be "completely outflanked."

Shufeldt enlarged upon the threat posed to Cuba and Mexico in the 1850s by the expansionist southern secret society, the Knights of the Golden Circle: "You know better than I do Sir, that this idea of an immense Southern Republic, based upon the institution of slavery, has for years been the dream of many of the prominent men of the South—divulged to me some time ago by the late Genl. J. A. Quitman. To the compete fruition of this dream Cuba & Mexico were necessary—in the conquest of the former Genl. Quitman failed—Tehuantepec yet remains to become the prize of some race capable of developing its resources."

A full decade later Shufeldt was to reiterate many of these accusations. Then he even believed that Benjamin was the president of the company, and recalled:

> the object of the company was political rather than commercial. James Buchanan then Prest. of the U.S. loaned his Executive power in the organization of a route, which was intended by these Southern men [Benjamin and Slidell] to bring California within the limits of the foreshadowed Southern Confederacy—as early as the year before mentioned [1856] the seeds of secession had been sown. You may depend upon it—for I speak of my own personal knowledge—that it was intended by these leaders of the South, in the event of the election of a republican Prest., in 1860—to subvert the govt. of the U.S. if need were to appeal from the ballot to the bullet.[17]

Shufeldt's letter to Seward revealed that wartime rancor had been added to his opinion of the southern leaders of the company that had employed him as skipper of the *Quaker City*. The second recollection in the 1870s showed that he still held those opinions a decade later.

Behind Shufeldt's concern was his growing awareness of the problems of territorial expansion. As early as 1855, in his comments on the rebel Estrampez, he demonstrated that he welcomed the acquisition of Cuba as the wise men of the East welcomed the "heralding Star of the Advent." In February 1857, he could gladden the heart of the filibustering General Quitman by asserting his belief that the "inevitable progress of events" would bring Cuba into "our Confederacy or connect her prominently with a section of it—perhaps more consistent with her and its institutions." When he wrote those words he edged as close as he ever did to sanctioning southern policies, but they were partly designed to secure the position he sought and partly to express the superiority and inevitability of the spread of Anglo-Saxon institutions in Cuba. By 1861 he still held the view that expansionism was desirable, even into Mexico. Where he diverged from the leading spirits of the Louisiana–Tehuantepec Company was over the question of who would control such expansion and whether it would be slave or free territory. Shufeldt came to realize that unbridled expansion was acceptable only when conducted under the political aegis of the North.

In 1855, with the execution of Estrampez, he had been aware of the possibility that the factionalism and strife that had affected Cuba could spread to "wiser and better governments," and he hoped that America would rise above the petty intrigues of individuals to proclaim herself the mistress of the destiny of the western continent. In the Quitman letter of 1857, the "Confederacy" that he mentioned was deliberately ambiguous, but for his own purposes he was referring to a national and not a sectional one, even though the recipient of the letter probably inferred the latter. Continentalism, even if it embraced noncontiguous territory like Cuba, was to be directed by the North. By 1860, however, Shufeldt was recoiling from the prospects of an "Africanized" Cuba because it might bring "the barbarism of another San Domingo." If Cuba were to shine forth "as another bright Star" in the American diadem as "a Queen of the Antilles," it would only be by checking the future importation of Negroes. He had begun to see that as the United States were being bound together with improved transportation and communication facilities, the political fabric was disintegrating. By the time he had examined the Cuban slave trade and written to Seward in November 1861, the tragedy of this dilemma had revealed itself at Bull Run.

3
Consul General to Cuba, 1861–1862

Peacetime commercial pursuits aimed at controlling the Isthmus of Tehuantepec soon ended for the thirty-nine-year-old captain. For the first two years of the Civil War Shufeldt served a diplomatic apprenticeship as a consul general in the Spanish island colony that had excited his expansionist dreams. As the American Union shattered and the imperial dreams of Napoleon III centered on Mexico, Shufeldt used his consulate as a diplomatic listening post tuned into the affairs of the Confederacy, France, Spain, and Great Britain, especially when they concerned the future of Mexico. He also transmitted information about blockade-running to the captains of the northern blockading vessels. From his Cuban experiences, Shufeldt eventually gained a reputation for diplomacy, which, though not fully warranted at the time, was later to attract the attention of successive presidents and secretaries of state after the war.

A Bout with the British

The inordinate speed with which Shufeldt changed professions in April 1861 was remarkable. Two weeks after the firing on Fort Sumter, he was refitting the *Quaker City* in the New York navy yard for wartime operations within the Capes of Virginia. On April 25, Samuel L. Breese, commandant of the New York navy yard, informed Secretary of the Navy Gideon Welles that the *Quaker City* had been armed with two 32-pounders and that Shufeldt had assumed wartime command on behalf of General John Wool's Union Defence Committee. Just two days later, Shufeldt was on board the first available steamer, the *Karnak,* on his way to take over the United States Havana consulate and purchase all of the American coal in the city for the government with fifteen hundred Spanish doubloons furnished by the New York shipping firm of Howland and Aspinwall. He went with the backing of Truman Smith, Governor William Buckingham of Connecticut, and Secretary of State Seward. Most probably at Smith's request, Seward had recommended Shufeldt to Lincoln for the Havana post, and the president agreed.[1] While Shufeldt's appointment can be partly explained by the opportunities created by the Civil War, with pro-Southerners vacating government posts, it had also been offered because Shufeldt's own political interests and personal background commended him to the leaders of the Republican party in two states and because his views on Cuba corresponded closely with Seward's.

As consul general, Shufeldt initially boarded with an American family, the Fairchilds, who lived in an old-style house two or three blocks from the Tacon Theatre on the Paseo. Not long after taking over the position, Shufeldt wrote to his eldest son Robert, just before his eleventh birthday, one of the few private family letters from him that have survived. It reveals his attitudes to home, sexual stereotypes, and manners.

> I had much pleasure in receiving your letter by the Steamer *Bienville*. You are improving very nicely in your writing and spelling and you can tell Mr. Glendenning so with my kind regards. When you come out to Havana you must make up your mind to learn Spanish and assist me in the office.
>
> I hope that as you are now getting old enough, you do not give your dear mother more trouble than you can help, and that you set a good example to your brothers—remember that in my absence you are the head of the family and as such you must behave like a man and a gentleman. I hope that our friend the Major [a big mastiff] is a well behaved dog and not saucy because he thinks he is getting to be a big dog! Teach him manners!
>
> Tell Jimmy [Heffnen, the Irish hired hand] to keep the place in nice order for you know that I am very proud of my home and I would not like to have anybody go by it and say "Whose *slouchy* looking home is that?" I had much rather that they should say—"What a neat place that is of Capt. Shufeldt's," wouldn't you? So you help Jimmy to keep it clean.
>
> My boy Aweng [his Chinese servant] is very anxious to look like other boys, so he went and cut off his long "pig tail," which all Chinamen wear, much to my disappointment, for I wanted to bring him home *pig tail and all!*
>
> Give my kind regards to all friends who ask you about me, and with much love to your dear mammy and your noisy brothers, I am Affectionately, Your Father. Remember me to Catherine very kindly.[2]

Within a few months Shufeldt brought the family to Havana and established them in an ancient adobe house, four miles out on the Paseo, on a side street, the Calle Tulipan. The house had an acre of land attached with a wide variety of tropical fruit trees, splendid plants, a passion vine, roses, and garden flowers. Shufeldt sent his three sons, Robert, Mason, and the young George, to a private school run by a

Danish woman who taught eight or ten other boys and girls from families in the immediate vicinity. Later, Robert went to a Spanish-speaking school run by a Cuban. At family meals Shufeldt would allow his son only as much food as he could ask for in Spanish and, as Robert recalled, "thus it came about that I, in a few months, could speak Spanish almost as well as English, especially as I constantly associated with the Spanish-speaking boys and girls of the neighborhood."

The house on the Calle Tulipan echoed with the noise of receptions, which many officials and well-known Havana families attended. Robert Jr. remembered that the parlor was typical of an old-fashioned Spanish house. The walls were "exceedingly thick, the two tall windows and the front door had great recesses, and the former had heavy iron bars set vertically in the masonry, as we see it in prisons, while the shutters were of massive wood." In this rather elegant Havana house, flanked by an English family, the Tolmeys, on one side, and with the McGregors and the Laborde family close by, Shufeldt settled down to the task of raising his family and dealing with the Spanish authorities and the consular representatives of other nations.[3]

The British consul general in Havana, Joseph Tucker Crawford, had held his post on the island since 1842. A generation older than Shufeldt, he was zealous, with a keen sense of the need to uphold British dignity, maritime rights, and commerce. From Havana at the beginning of the Civil War, Crawford notified Lord John Russell, British secretary of state for foreign affairs, of the arrival of Confederate envoys William L. Yancey and Pierre A. Rost from New Orleans on April 3. The two Confederates had requested that Crawford present them to the Spanish captain general of Cuba, Don Francisco Serrano, which Crawford had done. By April 17, the British consul general had heard of the firing on Fort Sumter. Fearing a blockade of the southern ports and "foreboding a cruel, fratricidal and exterminating Civil War in that Republic," Crawford worried about the protection of British trade and commerce. He warned Rear Admiral Sir Alexander Milne, commander-in-chief of British naval forces on the North American and West Indies station, of "the great Interests which Great Britain will have exposed during the coming struggle, which it is to be feared may interrupt the supply of Cotton to our Manufacturers as well as interfere with the consumption of British Goods which, it is known, are on their way to the Southern Ports of the American Union to an unusually large amount."[4] Despite his concern about protecting British trade and commerce early in the war, Crawford's task was somewhat easier than Shufeldt's. Soon his worries were to fade as increasing numbers of American ships' masters and owners began to abandon the American flag and register under British colors.

The presence in Havana of these two proud and sensitive representatives of rival commercial nations soon led to friction. On May 6 the steam tug *W. H. Webb* arrived under the American flag, and her captain, James B. McConnell, applied to Shufeldt for clearance. He refused to give it, for the port of New Orleans, from which the *W. H. Webb* had cleared, was officially in a state of blockade, even though there were then no United States cruisers off the mouth of the Mississippi. The *Webb*'s papers and ship's register had endorsements by Confederate officials, and her crew list and clearance from New Orleans had not been forwarded to Shufeldt. He refused to clear the vessel for any port unless the voyage was to one not covered by the blockade, that is, a northern port where the civil authorities could decide the legal position. The consul general thus applied to the Spanish port authorities to prevent the ship from leaving harbor until they received a regular clearance from his office, and they complied with his request.[5]

On May 10 the British consul general wrote to Shufeldt that the *W. H. Webb* had been purchased by William Smithett of London, and he asked for information to fill out the register. This letter did not reach Shufeldt until late on May 11. In it, noting that the vessel was British property, Crawford asked that Shufeldt "at once" withdraw his interdict at the office of the port captain, as he was "not aware of any right which the Consulate of the United States had to interfere for the detention of a British vessel." This cool request angered Shufeldt. He immediately wrote to Crawford expressing surprise at "so palpable a violation of international courtesy, as the hauling down of an American flag on an American vessel and substituting in its stead the English colors, without the slightest notification either formal or informal to the U.S. Consulate-General." Furthermore, he declared the *Webb*'s owners had not conformed to the laws of the United States regarding the sale of vessels in foreign ports. No crew list or ship's register had been deposited with him. Shufeldt thus suspected the *Webb* of treasonable purposes, and he declared that the matter of detention was between him and the port authorities. Consequently, he questioned the validity of the sale and the vessel's right to carry any other than the American flag. In the middle of this heated correspondence, the port captain, Don Blas Garcia de Quesada, inquired whether the vessel was British or American. Shufeldt considered that in the absence of proof she was still American. This, however, was not sufficient for the port captain, and on May 12 the *Webb* left under British colors. In informing Seward on the fourteenth, Shufeldt concluded that "if through the liberality of the British Navigation Laws, English Consuls in foreign ports are empowered to issue provisional registers to foreign vessels such power in unfriendly hands could be made a source of incalculable mischief in the present condition of our national affairs." In addition, at noon on the twelfth, he had received a letter from Crawford stating that he had nothing to do with any infringements and irregularities while the vessel was under the American flag. As Shufeldt had indicated that he was going to refer the matter to his government, Crawford added that "all further correspondence respecting the *W. H. Webb* between us will be unnecessary."[6]

With the vessel's departure all Shufeldt could do was to appeal to the captain general of the island. In a lengthy letter he requested cooperation from Don Francisco Serrano and urged upon him that "Your Excellency can not fail to see that if the laws of the United States in reference to the sale of American vessels in foreign ports are to be so entirely ignored, and that before references can be made to the Supreme Authority of the Island such vessels are permitted to leave, there can be no security for the Commerce of the United States in this port, and no power to prevent such vessels from covering the neighboring seas as pirates and privateers." The captain general proved to be of little assistance, for he observed that whatever irregularities had existed in the *Webb* case could not be removed after the vessel had sailed. He thus refused to intervene. Shufeldt was left to express the hope to Seward that his prompt action in this case would prevent the recurrence of similar ones.[7]

In this, too, he was disappointed. The *Webb* affair was really a test case. The promptness of Shufeldt's actions counted for little against the final result. Soon wholesale transfers of southern vessels were being made to the British flag. The result of such actions was clearly reflected in the quarterly returns for shipping at the consulate. For the quarter beginning April 1 to June 30, 1861, 140,860 tons cleared at Havana. From October to December 1861, the total fell to 40,564 tons. In June Shufeldt wearily informed Seward that "it would be agreeable to me to receive instructions from the State Department—as to what ought to constitute a legal sale of American vessels in this Port." His embittered attitude toward his British counterpart filtered through his request for instructions when he declared, "as the British Consul Genl. seems to feel himself bound to issue temporary registers upon the mere application of parties claiming to have the power to sell & without reference to the American register for the purpose of seeing whether such power has been granted by the true owners of the Vessel or not, I have found it impossible to . . . collect the fees due the Consulate arising from such transfer of flags, and the consequent discharge of the crews."

Thus in June, Shufeldt suggested to the government the great importance of having an American man-of-war in harbor as frequently as possible for the aid and assistance of his consulate. By the end of that month, Gideon Welles had commended Shufeldt's suggestion to the consideration of Flag Officer William Mervine, commanding the Gulf squadron at Key West. The blockading forces were stretched so thinly, however, that it was not until November that Shufeldt's suggestion could be followed.[8]

The *Trent* Affair

The one incident that proved the increasing efficiency of American naval forces was the removal of Confederate commissioners James M. Mason and John Slidell, with their secretaries MacFarland and Eustis, from the British mail packet *Trent*. This action by Captain Charles Wilkes of the USS *San Jacinto* is usually studied for its diplomatic significance as the first serious Anglo-American confrontation of the Civil War. Its impact was of obvious importance. The crisis between the United States and Great Britain threatened the continued survival of the United States. For this reason it has been amply covered by historians. But in focusing on the diplomatic interchanges of Seward, Lyons, Russell, and Adams, one loses the essence of the key events that developed in Havana preceding the capture. These events reveal that the claims that Captain Wilkes alone conceived of the capture of Mason and Slidell are erroneous. They also illustrate that the *Trent* affair was only one episode, though the most important, that grew out of the increasing friction that developed very early in the wartime period between the British and American consular representatives in Cuba.

In one sense it is hardly surprising that Wilkes should be accorded sole responsibility for conceiving of the capture. In his report of November 15, 1861, to Gideon Welles, Wilkes declared that the *San Jacinto* had been cruising off Cienfuegos, Cuba, after returning from the African squadron, when he learned that the Confederate commissioners, their families, and secretaries had set off from Charleston en route to Havana. The commissioners had left Charleston in the *Theodora* on October 12, 1861, arrived at Nassau on the fourteenth, departed for Cuba on the sixteenth, reached Cardenas on that date, and continued after a few days rest to Havana, which they reached on the twenty-second. After taking in sixty tons of coal the *San Jacinto* left Havana on October 26 to intercept the *Theodora,* but Wilkes missed his attempted interception and arrived at Havana on October 31. He coaled his vessel and then left, intending to cruise on the route that the British mail packet boats to St. Thomas would take. He first sailed to Key West, Florida, hoping to find the *Powhatan* or some other steamer to accompany him to the Bahama Channel "to make it impossible for the steamer in which Messrs. Slidell and Mason were to embark to escape either in the night or day." Unfortunately, the *Powhatan* had left the previous day, and the next morning the disappointed captain took his vessel to the north side of Cuba in order to communicate with the United States consul at Sagua la Grande on November 4. Here Wilkes hoped to receive a telegram from the United States consul general in Havana giving him the time of the *Trent*'s departure. Wilkes reported that "in this also I was disappointed," and so he took the *San Jacinto* ninety miles eastward, to where, in sight of Paredon del Grande Light House, the Old Bahama Channel contracted to a width of fifteen miles and to her famous rendezvous with the *Trent*.[9] What stands out in Wilkes' report, other than the ship's movements, are his three "disappointments"— missing the *Theodora*, the *Powhatan*, and the time of the *Trent*'s departure —all of which were unable to thwart him from his single-minded, self-conceived goal of capturing the *Trent*.

Shufeldt's initial reaction to the news that Mason and Slidell had already landed in Cuba on October 16 and were to meet Don Francisco Serrano in Havana was one of pessimism. He notified Seward that he found "a growing feeling here in favor of the South and a buoyant belief that this Confederate oligarchy will receive formal recognition from the maritime powers of the world before the 1st Jany. next." The arrival of Mason and Slidell at Cardenas and the subsequent movement of the steamer *Theodora* to Havana had, to the consul general, "perhaps somewhat enhanced this feeling of sympathy which however has always been ready to exhibit itself as well among our own countrymen as among foreigners." He concluded that the only means he possessed in Havana to offset the influence of Mason and Slidell was a dignified maintenance of the justice of the northern cause, both in public and in private. Somewhat significantly, however, he declared that "A *vigorous blockade* would keep such a pernicious influence from getting abroad—and it is a matter to me of the most profound regret that this steamer particularly should have escaped to a place of safety with these men, one of whom [Slidell] I had hoped would have remained at home to meet a juster fate." Already Shufeldt was thinking of blockade and internment as an answer to the problems posed by the southern commissioners. Secretary of State Seward was also impatient for the capture of the commissioners. A month before they were eventually detained, he had pressed Gideon Welles to use his blockading vessels to capture them, although Seward would have preferred to capture the envoys on board a Confederate vessel.[10]

The presence of the Confederate commissioners in Havana also sparked off another bout of diplomatic infighting between the British and American consular representatives. Apart from his official position as consul general, Crawford was also the agent for the West Indies Mail Line, which owned the *Trent*, and he booked the passages for Mason and

Slidell. In addition, when a request from a private citizen of Havana to present Mason and Slidell to the captain general was refused, Crawford introduced them to Don Francisco Serrano as "private gentlemen from the Confederate States of America." The captain general told Shufeldt later that he had declined to receive the commissioners officially but had seen them merely as private persons. After the furor over the *Trent* affair had broken, Crawford became incensed at newspaper reports in the United States that declared he had presented the commissioners officially. On December 2 he recalled his relationship with them for the sake of the British minister in Washington, Lord Lyons:

> I think it necessary to State to Your Lordship, that, I neither presented nor accompanied those Gentlemen to the Captain General in uniform or other ways.
>
> Mr. Slidell is an acquaintance of mine since 1825 and Mr. Mason's brother was my very intimate friend, when he was Secretary of the U. States Legation in Mexico under Mr. Poinsett, long ago—I certainly did myself the pleasure of calling on those Gentlemen as Strangers and shewed them such civilities as were in my power, but I never thought of rendering them any official Services. I presume they were fully aware that, had they needed any such assistance, I could not have given it, and none was ever applied for.

Despite his denial of "other ways," Crawford certainly allowed the commissioners to accompany him to the captain general's palace. Shufeldt later claimed that the British consul general had treated them with "marked civility" in introducing them to Don Francisco Serrano.[11]

Not to be outdone by the movements of the British consul general, Shufeldt accompanied Captain Wilkes and his officers in full dress to the palace.* He considered that the officerlike bearing "and the fluency with which Capt. Wilkes conversed with the Capt.-Genl. in French" had a marked effect on Don Francisco. The party was later invited to the Spaniard's house, and Shufeldt mentioned the incident to the secretary of state because he considered it was important "to meet whatever social influences Messrs. Slidell & Mason may exert upon this Government by every means in our power." According to Shufeldt's report of the meeting, the captain general expressed little respect for the commissioners and "of Mr. Slidell particularly he spoke in terms of derision."[12]

Back in the consulate Shufeldt and Wilkes mulled over the international repercussions that would follow if Wilkes successfully seized Mason and Slidell. Shufeldt consulted the authorities on international law in the consulate but found none that mentioned a case similar in its

---

*Shufeldt's son, Robert, recalled in later life that when he was eleven (1861) Commodore Wilkes and later Admiral David G. Farragut visited the family home on the Calle Tulipan.

character to the one he proposed to raise with Wilkes. He later admitted to Seward, "at first, such a measure [as the intended seizure] would seem to be a violation of the rights of neutrals upon the ocean, yet upon reflection it is one which admits perhaps of a more favorable consideration and Captain Wilkes after much thought upon the subject & in view of the great importance of the capture of these persons with their dispatches came to the decision of intercepting this steamer as before stated, & taking them from her by force if necessary." Thus on November 4, Shufeldt informed Seward that the *San Jacinto* had sailed on the second "with an object in view—which if carried out will probably be reported by Capt. Wilkes." He sent this obvious hint of the seizure in a secret dispatch by sailing vessel, for he did not wish to reveal the nature of the news, mainly from fear that the means of communication were "so uncertain."[13]

Later, on November 9, the day after the capture but two weeks before the news of it reached him in Havana, Shufeldt justified Wilkes' actions to the secretary of state. They had decided to go ahead with the planned capture, he reported, in language very similar to that used by Wilkes in his undated document "Grounds for Capture," because Mason and Slidell were not "innocent travellers upon the ocean" but were "avowed enemies of the Govt. of the U.S.," going aboard the *Trent* "as the accredited Ministers of the Confederate Government"! Shufeldt stressed that the steamer was a private vessel under contract to convey the Royal West India mails "and in no sense can be considered a [British] national ship." He considered that whether Wilkes' intended action was to meet with the approbation of the government or not, the captain had "been actuated by the highest patriotism & the sincerest desire to serve his country." Furthermore, he readily admitted, "I gave him all the information in my power."[14]

Shufeldt's description of the meeting with Serrano, his subsequent consultation with Wilkes of the authorities on international law, and the final decision reached "after much thought" by the captain, to intercept the *Trent*, does not support historical assertions that Wilkes alone thought of the plan or that he had no doubts about removing the envoys. Neither can the claim be sustained that Wilkes only began to "rationalize" the seizure of Mason and Slidell after the capture, as the *San Jacinto* was steaming toward Charleston. Furthermore, the suggestion that Wilkes' undated, handwritten document "Grounds for Capture" was written *after* the capture is, at least, highly doubtful.[15] The consultation of Shufeldt's consular law books took place in the consulate between October 31 and November 1, for the *San Jacinto* sailed for Key West on November 2. It appears likely that Wilkes jotted down the various reasons justifying the seizure of Mason and Slidell in Shufeldt's office before the *San Jacinto* left Havana.

A few days before the *Trent* sailed, Joseph Crawford's wife called upon Shufeldt's wife, Sarah, when Shufeldt was present. During the conversation she turned to him and remarked that "a rumor had got afloat that the *San Jacinto* had gone out for the purpose of seizing these gentlemen etc. Did you ever hear anything more ridiculous Mr. Shufeldt?" He gleefully reported his reply to Captain Wilkes: "No Madam never heard anything so ridiculous in my life—making her a very low bow, as ridiculous as it seemed to the Madam it nevertheless made her *sick* I am told for a week." He assured the captain of the *San Jacinto* that not a soul knew of the intended seizure, "and it came upon them like a clap of thunder!" To Seward, Shufeldt proclaimed, "The *Trent* sailed on the morning of the 7th inst., having the whole party on board—unsuspicious of any untoward interruption of their voyage."[16]

In this belief Shufeldt was only partially correct. James M. Mason knew of the activity created by the appearance of his party. He later recalled: "our presence in Havana and our mission to Europe as well as our purpose to embark in the mail steamer which was to leave Havana on the 7th of November was well known in the city. We knew it had been spoken of and commented on by the Consul of the United States at Havana and thus would, of course, reach the ear of Captain Wilkes."[17] That the commissioners' intentions had already reached Wilkes' ear via the consulate is evident from Shufeldt's dispatches to the secretary of state and Wilkes' reports to the secretary of the navy. Both the Union and Confederate factions in Havana, however, were in doubt on other matters. The southern commissioners did not know precisely what course of action would be taken after Wilkes heard of their intended purposes. Neither Wilkes nor Shufeldt knew the exact time that the *Trent* would sail on the eighth, but Shufeldt arranged to telegraph this information to Wilkes via the consul at Sagua la Grande as soon as he learned of it.[18] Wilkes thus left for Key West looking for the *Powhatan* to help him intercept the *Trent* in the Bahama Channel. The *San Jacinto* then returned to lie off Sagua la Grande, where Wilkes expected to receive Shufeldt's telegram. At this point the chain of communication broke.

By the morning of November 6, Shufeldt had discovered the *Trent*'s time of departure. Consequently, at 2:00 P.M. on that day James H. Horner, United States consul at Sagua, received the following telegram from Shufeldt: "I will see it in the afternoon of day six. Forward it as directed in my letter of the 29th."* Shufeldt's "day six" was after Wilkes was due to sail on the second, that is, November 8. As Horner had received no letter before or with the telegram, he did not understand the message and telegraphed for information or orders. Horner

---

*"Lo veré en la tarde del diá seis manden como dirigido en mi carta del veinte y nueve."

had the impression that Shufeldt was on board the *San Jacinto,* which would touch at Sagua, and that he wanted to see him. Thereupon Horner decided to go to the port. Then a letter came from Lieutenant Breese of the *San Jacinto* informing him that he should see Shufeldt immediately. Horner telegraphed that he would come to the port by train, there being no other means of transportation available. The train was delayed, however, and when Horner arrived he found the boats of the *San Jacinto* had left about ten minutes earlier. The officer in charge indicated they would return for the consul at 6:00 A.M. the following morning, and Horner waited. He left on the seventh at 1:00 P.M. only after the officer and boats had not appeared.

Not until November 8 did Shufeldt's explanatory letter, sent on October 29, reach Horner informing him that the *San Jacinto* would probably call at the port between the fifth and seventh and that, in the event of his receiving a cable from the consul general's office, to consider that it belonged to Captain Wilkes and to deliver it to him. Horner later explained to Wilkes that had he received this letter before the telegram he would "have had everything in readiness and would have delivered it at any trouble or inconvenience, for I knew what it *meant* as soon as I knew it was for you, but having no clue to its meaning till two days after its receipt I would not suppose that a message addressed to me was for another person." Neither could Horner tell why or where Shufeldt's letter had been delayed. When he received the telegram, he went to the post office and asked if a letter addressed to him had been overlooked. He was assured no letter for him was there. Horner wrote his explanation to Wilkes because he understood "from Boston that an impression had been received that I had failed to do my duty in not communicating with you when the *San Jacinto* was off this port," and he was concerned to rectify this impression "in order that you may see that it was from no want of sympathy with the object of the cruise of the *San Jacinto* that I failed to communicate with you, but solely from the fact that I was not properly informed of what I ought to do." Later, Shufeldt explained to Wilkes, "I telegraphed you at Sagua—of the sailing of the *Trent*—as we had agreed—but your boat left the wharf about 15 mins. too early." Wilkes thus sailed to his rendezvous in the Bahama Channel "disappointed" in his hopes to learn the *Trent*'s time of departure.[19]

After the interception, Wilkes was lionized in the North for his part in the capture. He was received by the mayor and city government of Boston at Faneuil Hall and given a dinner by the merchants at Revere House. New York City entertained him and his family as guests of the city. "The Navy is rapidly becoming popular," wrote G. J. Abbot, a senior clerk in the State Department, to Shufeldt, "and a large addition & appropriations will be made." Abbot praised Shufeldt's own services to the government and maintained that Seward frequently called Gideon Welles' attention to the "wisdom of your suggestions, emanating, as he stated in his letters, from one practically acquainted with the sea." Wilkes himself wrote to Shufeldt that "long ere this you have heard that I bagged our friends as I told you I would," and informed him, "I have many a time had a good laugh over the whole affair which I assure you came off just as I had arranged it should." Confident in his newly won popularity, Wilkes added that his notions of the international code "have been fully endorsed by those learned in the law and they are satisfied that sea officers could read and study as well as interpret international law."[20]

Shufeldt praised Wilkes for the capture. He considered "the affair was managed admirably & you deserve the credit which you are receiving." The consul general had received the news of the capture when the *Trent* had returned from St. Thomas and testified that "it then created a furious excitement not confined to English subjects, but more particularly developed of course by Mr. Crawford & his clique." War was predicted as inevitable, and Shufeldt reported that Crawford had declared the captain of the *Trent* ought to have shot Wilkes' officers on his own deck.[21]

Crawford certainly responded dramatically to the news of the seizure. On November 23, having just received the first dispatch from the *Trent*'s officers upon the vessel's return from St. Thomas, he wrote to Lord Lyons about the "outrage of the British Flag" committed by Wilkes. Crawford also pointed out that the USS *Santiago de Cuba* was cruising within sight of the Morro castle guarding Havana harbor, "avowedly to intercept and Capture four or five British vessels which have been trading *uninterruptedly* between this and Savannah and Charleston." The British consul general considered such "hostile intention" to have been openly expressed by the captain of the *Santiago de Cuba,* and he advised British ships' masters not to put to sea. "If this State of things is authorised by the U. States Government," he asserted grimly, "there is only wanting the formal declaration of War." Unfortunately for Crawford, as he confessed to Lord John Russell, there was no British ship-of-war available to escort British merchant vessels.[22]

Crawford's belligerence was soon modified. Shortly after copies of American newspapers reached Havana with news of the *Trent* affair, he found himself charged with interfering by taking Mason and Slidell to meet the captain general. He felt constrained to defend his conduct against "these malicious statements of the American press, which I have no doubt were furnished by the U. States Consulate of this place." He informed Lord Lyons that he would have passed over such statements had he not believed that their reproduction "might be intended to be applied in justifying the Act committed by the U. S. Frigate on the *Trent*." Crawford thus notified the British minister in Washington of his official movements in relation to the Confederate commissioners in order that Lord Lyons could contradict "such infamous fabrications" in the United States capital.[23]

Without a British gunboat on hand and feeling compelled to defend his personal honor from press comment, Crawford responded with whatever weapons were available. When Shufeldt sent the official American mail bags to the British consulate for shipment on board a British steamer to Veracruz, they were refused by the vice-consul acting on Crawford's instructions. However, the public mail bags were taken for passage. This action not only raised Shufeldt's ire but later brought Crawford a reprimand from Lord John Russell. This latter proved no consolation to the infuriated Shufeldt, whose anti-British feelings had been heightened by the refusal. When the angry consul general discovered that a suspected Confederate agent, J. W. Zachary of New Orleans, was allowed to sit in Joseph Crawford's office reading the official report of the Royal Mail agent on the *Trent* interception, he regarded this as a "palpable violation of official privacy and manifestation of active partisanship between a British officer and a rebel agent." He termed the British consulate a rendezvous for southern agents and charged Crawford with aspiring to be the first British minister to the Confederate states in the event of recognition. If it were found that the *Trent* affair was a violation of neutrality, then he considered that the "constant aggressions and active hostility" shown by Crawford would demand ample apology and "as complete reparation as that of the former" incident.[24]

What concerned Shufeldt more than anything else, however, was the rumor that Crawford had requested the British admiral on the station for a man-of-war to convoy the blockade-runners beyond the reach of American steamers. Such an action could produce future tension and possible involvement with the Royal Navy. Before a vessel appeared, Shufeldt followed the *Trent* blueprint and had Commodore T. Ridgely "take old Zachary of N. O. out of an English Schr. & land him safely at Fort Taylor." At that time Shufeldt was also wrestling with a claim by the skipper of a French brig, the *Jules et Marie,* which had been hit by the *San Jacinto* before the *Trent* incident, who charged that Wilkes had abandoned him to sink on the high seas. Despite a request by the French consul to refer the matter to Washington, Shufeldt hoped the incident would be settled without causing any unfriendly feeling with the French government, "as I wish to keep on good terms with them at least until we have whipped Jno. Bull."[25]

But even at the height of his anger over Crawford's manner, when

Shufeldt reflected that Crawford's excitement "would have been more natural to a younger diplomat," he did admit that the British consul general had not exhibited such open emotion, however flagrant the insult, on any other occasion. Crawford had responded so vehemently because of his deep personal interest in the *Trent*'s sailing and the affairs of the commissioners. The United States consul general was willing to acknowledge the special interest of his British counterpart, the first sign that the tension between them since the *Webb* case might ease somewhat. With a British squadron then arriving in Cuban waters this was a necessary and heartening manifestation.[26]

The final effect of the *Trent* affair in Cuba was to strengthen Shufeldt's relations for a short time with the Spanish authorities. As Shufeldt's relationship with Crawford became strained, the Confederate agents in Havana hoped to capitalize on the situation by pressuring the Spanish government in Cuba for recognition. Shufeldt's adversary in this respect proved to be his predecessor, Charles J. Helm. Early in November, Shufeldt heard from Wilkes that Helm was at St. Thomas, where he had also served as consul, hoping to use his influence with the governor of St. Thomas to gain "an informal recognition of the Confederate flag in that port." In this he was unsuccessful, and he immediately transferred his attention to Cuba. Shufeldt had warned Assistant Secretary of State Frederick W. Seward in October that Helm "might do us some hurt in Cuba," and he urged that steps be taken to prevent Helm's departure from the United States. Helm, nevertheless, escaped to the Spanish island where he proved to be a thorn in Shufeldt's side on several occasions.[27]

Robert Shufeldt, Jr., remembered one incident that revealed the passions running between Union and Confederate factions in Havana and that had dangerous overtones for his father:

> I was present upon one occasion when a man made an attempt to assassinate him. One morning I was in the rear office, which had no windows and so was quite dark—a room one had to pass through to reach the main office—there came a knock at the door leading into the hall. Mr. Walcott, my father's clerk, opened it, and I stood near him as he did so. A young man dressed in black appeared in the hallway, wearing a keen, not to say fierce expression, and seeming to be somewhat nervous. He wanted to see the consul, but the clerk declined to let him enter. He made a move as though he intended to force his way in, but Mr. Walcott succeeded in preventing him. At this time he produced a big and most vicious-looking knife, and gave the clerk to understand that had he succeeded in reaching the Yankee consul, *that* was what he had for him, shaking the weapon in Mr. Walcott's face. There was, in those days, a reward of $12,000 offered for my father's head, printed on big posters displayed in public places in Mobile, New Orleans, and else-

where in the South; he paid not the slightest attention to it, but it worried my poor mother a great deal.[28]

Overall, however, Shufeldt considered that the seizure of Mason and Slidell had produced a marked effect on Spanish opinion in Cuba. He informed the secretary of state that "the Spanish Authorities and the people of the island native and foreign have been once more awakened to the fact that we are still a nation, which will not forget even in the midst of civil war, to maintain its rights & its dignity. Spanish officials in their proneness to sympathize with the cause of rebellion tremblingly expect that their turn will come next & entertain the cowardly hope that England will resent the 'outrage' and thus screen them from their old dread—revived of our strength & promptness to avenge our wrongs."[29] Therein lay the problem. English officials did resent Wilkes' action, but as the *Trent* affair passed off the Cuban stage, cooler heads than Shufeldt's, Wilkes', and Crawford's were to deal with the problem of reaching a solution short of war.

The Spanish Ogre

Although his attention was occupied by the altercation with Joseph Crawford and the activities of blockade-runners, commerce destroyers, and Confederate agents, Shufeldt became increasingly concerned over events in Mexico. Three years of civil war had been brought to an end when the Liberal forces of Benito Juárez entered Mexico City on January 11, 1861. The Mexican treasury was exhausted during the struggles, and creditor nations such as Britain, France, and Spain were concerned over the value of their Mexican bond holdings, issued by the Conservative government of General Felix Zuloaga, and the safety of their nationals. The rival groups claiming to be the government of Mexico were caught up in diplomatic pressures to honor the debts. In April 1859, the United States minister to Mexico, Robert M. McLane, had forwarded recognition of the Juárez government. The Buchanan administration had been interested in completing a loan by treaty, which, had Mexico not been able to pay, would have meant foreclosure on the territory used to guarantee the loan. Such lands included Lower California, Sonora, Chihuahua, and the transit rights across Tehuantepec. Buchanan's Mexican policy encountered severe opposition in Congress, ending with the defeat of the McLane–Ocampo Treaty negotiated on December 14, 1859, and rejected by the Republican opposition on May 31, 1860. The territory was thus saved from absorption or virtual protectorate status by internal difficulties in the United States.

On July 17, 1861, the Mexican government suspended the payment of interest on the foreign debt. As Spain, France, and Britain began to mount a joint expedition to force repayment, Shufeldt watched the proceedings from Havana. While his suspicions over the allies' intentions mounted, the number of his dispatches on the subject increased. In August 1861, while convalescing from yellow fever, he visited Washington and discussed the Mexican problem with Seward. In the 1870s Shufeldt recalled: "In the year 1861 . . . I found myself in Washington in official connection with Mr. Seward. . . . I brought to his notice the important fact that having failed in the effort to embrace California within the limits of the Southern Confederacy—Messrs. Benjamin & Slidell had ceded the right of transit across the Isthmus of Tehuantepec to the French Government, & that—this was really the secret of French intervention in Mexico.[30] This recollection, however, should be treated with caution, for it ignores several distinct phases of Shufeldt's thought and telescopes together others on the subject of the Confederate, French, and allied attitudes toward Mexico, and particularly Tehuantepec, during the developments of November 1861 and June 1862.

In November, Shufeldt indicted the expansionist designs of the Confederacy's officials toward Mexico and warned Seward that the Tehuantepec grant "expires with all of its privileges in *April* of the coming year." Shufeldt still had a consuming interest in the transit route through the southern part of Mexico. While he bracketed past attempts to gain the isthmus with Cuban filibustering movements, he was now concerned to jolt Seward into action on behalf of the federal government. He politely reminded the secretary of state that to the statesman controlling the destinies of a nation "& even marking out the future work of unborn millions—it becomes a grave duty to contemplate all possible eventualities." Among these was the possible realization of a southern confederacy. Should that event occur, then the acquisition of the right-of-way and colonization of the isthmus was a matter of the highest consideration:

> We can not permit—educated as we are to believe that free institutions and free labor are the inalienable rights of every human being,—We can not permit, I say, a Republic based upon principles utterly repugnant to these rights, to extend itself over this virgin soil—serpent like to wind its poisonous way along the streams and over the hills of that beautiful country, and worse still to demoralize an innocent people as its great prototype did in former times in the garden of Eden. The acquisition of Tehuantepec would effectually circumscribe the limits of this Confederacy and prevent it from spreading its obnoxious influence to the shores of the Pacific.

It is doubtful whether the Mexican people would have been able to distinguish with the same finesse as did Shufeldt the biblical differences between two colonizing powers. But out of Shufeldt's Adamite fears that the Confederacy could accomplish on the isthmus what he had hoped a national government might undertake, until prevented by civil war, developed the bitterness that he directed at Benjamin, Slidell, and other members of the Louisiana–Tehuantepec Company. Such hindsight, however, would have remained only as an interesting example of one Northerner's frustrated views of an expansionistic southern company but for the appearance of other serpents in the Garden of Eden.

Despite his anti-French recollections in the 1870s, Shufeldt was not unduly worried in November 1861 by French designs on his envisaged paradise. He warned Seward that the French minister to Mexico, Monsieur Alphonse Dubois de Saligny, was an intimate friend of Judah P. Benjamin who, before leaving France, had gained the backing of the emperor and the capitalists of Paris in an attempt to secure Tehuantepec as an international highway. Shufeldt had met Saligny, who informed him that he anticipated the rebellion of the southern states, with Tehuantepec naturally falling into the hands of the Confederacy. From his short acquaintance with Saligny, Shufeldt believed him to be fully in sympathy with the rebellion, and ready to assist any southern agents to perpetuate the rights of the Louisiana–Tehuantepec Company. But there was nothing in his analysis in 1861 that suggested that Benjamin and Slidell had ceded the right of way to the French government or that the French intended to move against Mexico independently of the other powers. Instead, Shufeldt remained optimistic, "But full in the Faith and Hope that the unity of our country will be restored—still Tehuantepec presents to the eye of the modern statesman as it did to Cortes in the time of its conquest the best natural highway between the Atlantic & Pacific Oceans—and the shortest for us between our Eastern & Western possessions by over 1000 miles of sea travel—and presenting no obstacles which American ingenuity can not overcome or American labor accomplish."[31]

Seward and Thomas Corwin, United States minister to Mexico, were concerned with the efforts of Confederate leaders to acquire part of northern Mexico, rather than Tehuantepec. The secretary of state had already contemplated authorizing Corwin to negotiate a treaty with Mexico whereby the United States would agree to a loan to cover the interest at 3 percent on the Mexican debt of $62 million for five years from the date of suspension, provided that the European powers forebore from hostilities. Against a pledge to reimburse the money at 6 percent Mexico would offer as collateral a lien on the mineral rights and public lands in the states of Lower California, Chihuahua, Sonora, and Sinaloa, an interest scheme similar to the one proposed by the Buchanan administration. As Corwin began to negotiate he considered that Seward's proposed pledge of the public lands in four Mexican states would probably end in the cession of sovereignty to the United States, from which two consequences would follow—the end of all hope of extending a separate southern republic and the cessation of any further attempts to establish European power on the continent. Corwin neglected to add the third consequence, obvious though it was—the expansion of the American leviathan state at the expense of Mexico. On July 29 he admitted that "this would probably end in the cession of sovereignty to us. It would be certain to end thus if the money were not promptly paid as agreed on."[32]

Within this diplomatic context, Shufeldt's concern for Tehuantepec was initially channelled into observing the flow of allied troops toward Mexico. From his Cuban vantage point he considered that the main threat to that country in November and December 1861 came not from France but from Spain. This misapprehension first arose because of Shufeldt's close proximity to Spanish government circles in Havana. As early as October 25 he had spelled out the details of the naval and military expedition that the Spaniards were preparing. Don Joaquin Gutièrrez de Rubalcava, the Spanish admiral, would command a force of six powerful screw frigates, six side-wheel steamers, and two sailing sloops of war, totaling about 340 guns. Accompanying this squadron would be six battalions of troops, 140 horses, two hundred sappers, and two companies of artillery. Shufeldt anticipated a total of ten thousand to twelve thousand troops with seven thousand already in Havana.

Before warning Seward of the aims of the Confederacy, Shufeldt had heard that Don Francisco Serrano had "positively prohibited the shipment of any arms or munitions of war from the island of Cuba to any ports of Mexico." At first he was delighted and regarded the Spanish action as fortunate for the United States, for it prevented Confederate agents from shipping arms to Matamoras for smuggling into Texas. But soon Shufeldt saw the full implications of the Spanish order. He informed Seward that the Spanish naval and military expedition against Mexico was now ready. It only delayed while waiting the arrival of the steam frigates *Concepcion* and *Sealtad.* Spanish artillery was already on board the troop vessels. While the expedition was thus preparing to sail, he met the Mexican consul, Ramon Diaz, and learned that England and France would probably cooperate with Spain.

As the three-power expedition was readied, Shufeldt still concentrated on the Spanish. By December 5, the day after Seward officially declined to accept an allied invitation to cooperate with the allies in the Mexican intervention, Shufeldt forwarded detailed information that the Spanish naval and military expedition had finally sailed from Havana between November 29 and December 2. Twelve war transports and merchant troopships with six thousand seamen and marines and seven thousand troops fully equipped for the campaign were escorted by six screw- and seven side-wheel steamers. The military forces were under the command of the second officer of Cuba, Major General Don Manuel Gasset, and the second military officer of Puerto Rico, Brigadier General Carlos de Nargas y Muchucas. This expedition eventually seized the port of Veracruz on December 17.[33]

Shufeldt reported that this force had been fitted out at Cuba's expense at a cost of $2 million drawn from the treasury and $1.5 million in drafts from Madrid on the intendente. This official had been obliged to borrow $1.3 million from the Spanish Bank of Havana. As the parallel Spanish expedition to reconquer San Domingo had also been made at the expense of Cuba, Shufeldt considered it evident that if Spain were to depend on Cuba entirely for the means to carry out her new colonizing policy, "she must not only soon exhaust its treasury but render the taxpayers of the island much dissatisfied & disaffected—A result which I think is already manifesting itself."

To the former naval officer's practiced eye, the expedition was creditable in every respect: the ships and troops left in splendid naval and military condition. The new diplomat, however, was dismayed. He had no doubt that the expedition was intended to restore Spanish rule in Mexico, and he sadly observed,

> Whether England & France have been deceived by Spanish diplomacy into the belief that its real object is the ostensible one of settling the claims of Spanish citizens against Mexico—or whether they are willing at this propitious moment, to add their weight in crushing out free institutions upon this Continent—must be a question—the answer to which will materially interest us as a republican people—It is a matter to me of profound regret that we are not in condition at the present time to hoist again the "flag of freedom" over the walls of "San Juan d'Ulloa."[34]

Shufeldt proposed his solution to the problem of Spain in Mexico to the assistant secretary of state. Writing privately to Frederick W. Seward, he pointed out that as the expedition had drained Cuba of both men and money, he believed *"this island could be starved out & taken in 30 days—by a blockading fleet."* Obviously this was an incitement to action as well as being overly optimistic. Second, he wished to see five thousand men and $1 million sent into Mexico to form the nucleus around which the Mexicans could rally "in strength sufficient to drive these fellows back into the sea." As a reward for this assistance, he considered that the United States would be able to obtain from a grateful Mexico "valuable concessions & objects . . . on the isthmus of Tehuantepec."[35]

Sooner or later Shufeldt deemed a collision with Spain certain, unless the United States renounced the Monroe Doctrine. He was convinced that Spain meant to reconquer Mexico and reintroduce slavery. As he believed that country looked to the United States for assistance, and as the country was "stronger in a military sense than we ever were," he desired the government to assist the central American republic in her hour of need. Accordingly, he volunteered his services to the government to guarantee to raise men and go to save Mexico. "I know Mr. [Benito] Juárez & many of his friends," he told F. W. Seward, "& I will either succeed or die in the effort to vindicate the cause of republican freedom upon this Continent." Alternatively he argued, "I consider Cuba to be almost in a defenseless position." What Secretary of State Seward thought of these obvious hints, repeated and enlarged upon in a confidential letter to his son, cannot be precisely determined. Seward was still waiting to hear whether his plan to aid Mexico with a loan had been acceptable to the Mexicans. But Shufeldt's suggestion probably planted in his mind the idea of sending his consul general to Mexico, though not in the role that Shufeldt had so dramatically cast for himself. It was apparent that Shufeldt still greatly desired Cuba and thought that it could be taken by the United States. His own personal dreams prompted his suggestions on a course of official action over Mexico.[36]

The new year brought fresh hope to the despairing consul. On December 28, he had watched a French squadron of one line-of-battle ship, three frigates, and two sloops disembark a force of twenty-six hundred in Havana under the command of Rear Admiral Jean Jurien de la Gravière. Three days later he was pleased to reveal to Seward that the newly arrived French admiral had expressed great dissatisfaction that contrary to the tripartite convention, and much to his surprise, the Spanish expedition had sailed before his arrival. Gravière also heard from Veracruz that the Spanish flag had been hoisted over the harbor's fortifications and over Government House in the city, without reference to the French or English powers and without consultations with the commanding officers of these forces. Most important of all, the French admiral declared he would by no means consent to the assumption by General Don Juan Prim, Marqués de los Castillejos, of overall command of the combined forces in Mexico. Shufeldt was convinced that these facts would interest Seward, "as tending to show a want of harmony in the actions of the allied powers—& the possibility that Spain will soon be left alone to prosecute her war upon that weak nation."[37]

In view of these developments, Shufeldt increased his proddings of the assistant secretary of state. He volunteered for any service the government might intend toward Mexico. Never one to disguise his opinions of other people or nations, Shufeldt reaffirmed his belief that Spain intended to restore her rule over a slowly regenerating Mexico and that the three powers maintained their show of force in the gulf "not more to threaten republicanism in Mexico than in our own territories." Repeating his old theme that the Mexican cause was identical with that of the United States, Shufeldt added a new suggestion. As it was possible that the allied powers would occupy Matamoras, why not anticipate them, he asked? "It is needless, of course, to point out to you," he nevertheless indicated to Frederick Seward, "the great importance of this point as the key to Western Texas, &, in fact, at this moment the only port thro' which commerce passes unrestricted into the Southern Confederacy." Blithely assuming full insight into Mexican policy, Seward's man in Havana had no doubt that the government of Mexico would cheerfully consent to such occupation, and he was satisfied that two hundred or three hundred men could hold the Rio Grande without difficulty. In order to avoid complications with foreign powers, he urged that any movement into Mexico be done secretly, the alternative being to make Brasos de Santiago a base of operations. Reaffirming his intense desire to see the invaders driven from Mexican soil, he expressed his willingness in this cause "to sacrifice my life or create my fame."[38]

The day after Shufeldt swore this undying allegiance to the cause of Mexican independence, he wrote privately to Charles Sumner, the powerful senator from Massachusetts. Shufeldt reflected that the civil and political difficulties in Mexico were "in many respects as identical with our own." He began to pull together the great themes of his life for the senator's benefit. Carefully, he pointed out:

> Intimate all my life with the negro—in his various conditions of existence—from the shores of Africa—to the mildest form of slavery in our own country [*sic*]—I have long since made up my mind—that he is capable of a self sustaining position.
>
> Prest. Lincoln suggests the purchase of some territory—for the trial of this experiment—with the negroes at present & those which may come in possession of the Govt. I beg leave to ask your consideration of the advantages which the isthmus of Tehuantepec present to that purpose.[39]

For the other objects and purposes that rendered the isthmus worthy of immediate consideration, Shufeldt directed Sumner to consider his letter to Seward of the previous November warning against the expiration of the Tehuantepec grant. Shufeldt, like Lincoln, was groping toward a solution to the joint problems of what to do with the Negroes captured as "contraband of war" during the first two years of the Civil War, and what to do about the threat of Spain, Britain, and France in Mexico. While Lincoln contemplated colonization in Haiti, Chiriqui, or Liberia, Shufeldt proposed a settlement in Tehuantepec, thereby relieving the government's embarrassment over contrabands and using the freed slaves in the construction of an American-dominated transit route. By appealing to Sumner's antislavery views and using the blacks as a means, he hoped to solve the problem of his transportation scheme. Given his earlier views on Tehuantepec there is little in the approach to Sumner to suggest that his primary aim was to help the freed slaves.

Early in January of 1862 Shufeldt heard that the allies had occupied Veracruz and had determined to go to Mexico City "by diplomacy if possible, by force if necessary." For the first time he was forced to confront the possibility that the allies planned to establish a constitutional monarchy by appeal to the people. Once established, he believed, the powers would combine into a quadruple alliance with Mexico in a movement against the United States, by raising the blockade and placing a force on the banks of the Rio Grande. Thus at the end of that month, Spain was still the country Shufeldt feared most. He enclosed the address that the allied powers had issued to the Mexicans, and the ultimatum of the Spanish commissioners to the Mexican government, in his dispatches to the State Department. Furthermore, he revealed that Mexican general Miguel Miramón, leader of the Conservatives opposed to Juárez, had arrived in January with ten thousand muskets and five thousand uniforms purchased at Spanish government arsenals in Cadiz and Barcelona. When Miramón left Havana on January 23, under a passport made out to M. Fernandez, with a suite of sixteen persons on board the English steamer *Avon* bound for Veracruz or Tampico, Shufeldt informed Seward:

> I adhere to the opinion which I before have expressed to you—that it is intended on the part of Spain to use Miramón—as the means of restoring her power in Mexico—as Sant Ana [*sic*] was used in San Domingo.
>
> I have no idea that England will permit her forces to go into the interior—France will retire after her claims are settled—and Spain will be left to follow up her intentions in that country in her own way.

He disgustedly added that it would be easy to say that the European powers would not permit this, as it was said in reference to San Domingo six months earlier, but which was later acquiesced in universally. His only hope lay in the news that Colonel Llorencez and other officers of the Spanish army had returned to Havana "disenchanted" with the spirit of independence in Mexico. More importantly, he reported much sickness prevailed among the troops in Veracruz, and gleefully noted that "500 or one-twelfth of the Spanish troops being in hospital," progress into the interior was "greatly hampered."[40]

While Shufeldt reported these setbacks to Spanish hopes, other pressures were being exerted on Seward. A month after landing, the allies issued a proclamation to Mexico that they had come neither to conquer nor to revolutionize the country but to settle their financial claims. But complications were to arise not only out of the huge sum of $205 million demanded by all creditors from Mexico, but also from the production by Dubois de Saligny of the Jecker debt claim. This debt, contracted in February 1859 by decrees of General Miramón in order to defeat Juárez, had never yielded more than one-third of the value to Mexico of the original sum of $75 million. As the French produced this demand for repayment, the United States secretary of state could only remain watchful of events taking place in Mexico.[41]

Early in February, Shufeldt's hopes were still buoyed as the allied powers ran into difficulties. The commander of the English forces, Commodore Hugh Dunlop, had taken General Miramón on board and detained him for being implicated in the seizure of £660,000 stolen from the British legation in Mexico by Conservative forces on November 17, 1860. To both the Spanish authorities in Cuba and to Shufeldt the move was unexpected, but whereas it dismayed the former it delighted the latter. Shufeldt had considered Miramón's departure for Veracruz part of the program of Spanish invasion. The press news and correspondence from Veracruz confirmed his opinion. The general tenor of conversations and speculations in Havana exhibited "an ill concealed chagrin and disappointment." On the one hand, it convinced him that "England at least will not lend herself to the foul designs of Spain"—about the only time he complimented the English.[42]

The consul general had occasion for further celebration. The Spanish expedition had been orginally under the command of General Manuel Gasset and had been raised in Cuba by Don Francisco Serrano. Both were discontented by General Juan Prim's arrival directly from Spain as commander-in-chief. Gasset resigned his position and returned to Havana when Prim reached Veracruz. Admiral Rubalcava "and most of the prominent officers of the Army" followed him. To Seward, Shufeldt joyously commented, "you can easily imagine that General Serrano is not in the most amiable mood in regard to the whole affair." To add to Serrano's disgust, Prim, who found few resources of any kind from customs dues in Veracruz, was obliged to draw on the Havana treasury for an additional $400,000. "Thus far, therefore," observed the happier consul general, "the revolt in Mexico has had a gloomy effect here."[43]

In ebullient spirits Shufeldt allowed his imagination free rein. He proclaimed to Seward: "the result of this interference—which must be disastrous—or at least fruitless—will I hope teach the European powers the folly of meddling with the domestic concerns of American Republics

—and *now* is the time, as it occurs to me—for the Nations of the Continent whose Governments are based upon the rights of man—to form an alliance offensive & defensive—for the maintenance of these rights—against the combined despotism of the world." To Seward the prospect of an alliance with the United States' weak neighbor, at the time of the allied invasion, would hardly hold the attractions that Shufeldt imagined. But the consul's optimism bore him along without the careful analysis that the situation required. To Shufeldt, the "petty revolutions" that disturbed the good government of the smaller American republics were "but the struggles of entailed ignorance & superstition—in the grip of the undying principles of human progress." Shufeldt read this lesson in the struggle that the Civil War "on a grander scale is so magnificently exemplifying." He remained confident, however, once Spanish weakness had been demonstrated, that "in the midst of these revolutions we still possess the strength—which God has given to Man—to defy that power—which in blasphemy—claims to rule over fellow men by 'divine right'."[44]

The strength Shufeldt drew from his own divine benefactor enabled him to feel more at ease over Mexican affairs. But his reflections had revealed one great flaw in his assumptions up to February 1862. His single-minded concern with Spain as the archetype of evil in the Mexican Garden of Eden had caused him to ignore other dangers. As late as February 6, he confided to Seward, "I leave England & France out, in writing of Mexican affairs because I believe that arrangements will be made with these powers by the Commissioners at present in Vera Cruz."[45] But, as the French began to move independently in Mexico, it soon became apparent that Shufeldt had concentrated too heavily upon the Spanish ogre. The overanxious consul general suddenly discovered that it was Napoleon III who really wore the seven-league boots.

4

Consul General to Cuba, 1862–1863

The Mexican Problem

From February to May 1862, Shufeldt's interest in Mexican affairs increased dramatically as he devoted considerable time to reporting officially to Secretary of State Seward and unofficially to Frederick W. Seward, Charles Sumner, Truman Smith, and Edward Lee Plumb, the attaché of the United States legation in Mexico City. In return he was kept informed by these five of developments in current government policy. His office was also in close contact with the consulates at Tampico and Veracruz, and with Thomas Corwin in Mexico City. As the allied expedition gathered, Havana City became a source of news and rumors to which Shufeldt paid close attention. Though his relations with Plumb and Corwin were complicated by their dislike of one another, Shufeldt used both to good effect for information. In addition he kept a watchful eye on the allied fleet and personnel movements in Cuba. The Havana consulate thus became a clearinghouse for information on Mexican events. As a result of Shufeldt's intelligence activity, Seward wrote to him in March that he was greatly interested in the correspondence on Mexican affairs and hoped that he would continue it.[1]

In February 1862, the prospect of United States action in Mexican affairs increased following the Union's western victories at Forts Henry and Donelson and the nomination of General Winfield Scott as minister extraordinary to Mexico. Edward Plumb, who had passed through Havana on his way to Washington with two treaties on extradition and postal conventions, negotiated by Thomas Corwin with the Mexican government, was elated over "the glorious victories," which, he informed Shufeldt, "have at last settled the rebellion." Shufeldt had recommended Plumb to Frederick Seward as a man "more conversant & with a better appreciation of Mexican affairs than any American I have recently met." When Plumb arrived in Washington with the treaties he found more interest in Mexican affairs than he had expected. Writing to Shufeldt that "the want of action seems to be caused in Mexico, not here," a thinly veiled attack on Corwin, Plumb reported that several members of the Foreign Relations Committee were favorably inclined toward the payment of interest on the Mexican foreign debt, but not to a mere loan of money, which had been Corwin's original plan.[2]

Indeed, on February 18, the committee unanimously authorized its chairman, Charles Sumner, to report resolutions to the Senate empowering the Executive to enter into treaty negotiations with Mexico, by which the United States would assume the payment of interest on the Mexican foreign debt and accept her drafts in favor of the allies for the amount of their immediate reclamations. This would take effect only if the allies withdrew their forces and released their mortgages on the Mexican customs houses. Sumner, who conferred with Plumb at Seward's request, had asserted that the presence of the great naval expedition in the Gulf of Mexico was directly hostile to the United States and that the situation was grave. Plumb observed that the committee's resolutions were expected to be reported and acted upon within a week. Meanwhile, the Senate ratified the postal convention with Mexico and it was anticipated that the extradition treaty would soon follow.[3]

On February 19, however, the ministers of Spain, France, and Great Britain met at Soledad with the foreign minister of the Juárez government and signed a preliminary convention recognizing that government and agreeing to negotiate a settlement of their claims at Orizaba. The Soledad Convention stipulated that the allied powers disclaimed all designs against the sovereignty and territorial integrity of the republic of Mexico. Exactly one week later the United States Senate declined to approve any policy that would lead to the assumption of any part of the Mexican debt. The discussion on the Senate resolution, reported from the Foreign Relations Committee, was so unfavorable that a decision could not be reached on the day allotted to foreign relations and the resolution was later defeated by a vote of twenty-eight to eight. With the news, Plumb disgustedly informed Shufeldt that the senators "have been influenced first by their state of profound ignorance" and secondly, by a feeling "which has grown with extraordinary rapidity since our late victories, that it may be as well to leave open some field of employment for our enormous army."[4]

As Seward was left to formulate a new policy, following the Senate's refusal to ratify Corwin's debt treaties, Shufeldt grew elated in Havana. He cheerfully reported that allied affairs had gone badly, the troops were still suffering from sickness, and their leaders could not agree among themselves. Spain had used up her available men and supplies.

Conditions in Havana were bad. The treasury doors were now closed. Dissatisfaction was apparent among the island's people, with a "desire to free themselves from Spanish rule being inherent." Shufeldt hinted that Mexico needed arms and spoke with Admiral David Glasgow Farragut about occupying Matamoras. Farragut thought the idea a capital one, and Shufeldt believed the occupation would give material assistance to Mexico and check trade with the Confederacy. He was greatly pleased by the Union army's march southward toward Corinth and informed his superiors that "the echo of its tramp reverberated from the shores of Cuba." He also reported that Don Francisco Serrano thought that Spain and France were "in a snarl" in Mexico, that England would retire from the contest, and that if the Civil War ended quickly, the North would have an army of a million disciplined men in the field.[5]

At this time Shufeldt was rethinking his attitude toward intervention in Mexico. He heard through Mark Hill Dunnell, consul at Veracruz, of the meeting between General Prim and the Mexican foreign minister, Manuel Doblado, at Soledad. Completely erroneously, Shufeldt suspected that its purpose was to make Prim dictator. Prim, however, had learned of the French movement to make Maximilian of Austria the absolute ruler of Mexico. Shufeldt thus had something new to add to his stories of Spanish financial exhaustion. The French movement disgusted the Spanish authorities in Cuba. Whereas Shufeldt had been previously almost wholly anti-Spanish, his elation over Spanish misfortune was chilled by French intentions. He now noticed for the first time that General Juan Nepomucene Almonte, the soul of the monarchical movement in Mexico whose arrival in Havana he had recorded earlier, had left for Veracruz "impatient to regulate the affairs of Mexico" for France. "Your disgust at the cool impudence of the Monarchs of the old world," he confessed to Seward, "must be equal to my own—in thus endeavoring to tread upon a soil consecrated to a higher order of government."[6]

When Shufeldt found out about the Soledad Convention he considered that the recognition of the Juárez government was a singular acknowledgment to make after the allies had proclaimed it their mission to restore peace and order to Mexico. However, he still clung to his original assumptions about Spain. He told Seward that Prim would try to subvert the Juárez government and by pronunciamento secure a replacement to favor Spanish interests. But he was forced to admit that Spanish officers in Cuba and Mexico had not succeeded in what he assumed to be their objectives. On March 3, however, Shufeldt was badly shaken by the news from Dunnell, who usually proved accurate, that twenty-five thousand French troops were expected. The consul general passed the news in a private letter to Seward that revealed a plea for pan-American union as well as Shufeldt's own headstrong and emotional streak:

> I have no desire to become a martyr—but if there is any one principle—for which I would be willing to lay down my life—it is this—that *America* must be ruled by *Americans,* and it gives me great pleasure—to see this feeling developing itself throughout the western hemisphere—because altho' the lesser republics may individually be weak—Yet united they will be able to resist any combination which Europe can bring against them—Any such movement must be under the lead of our own government—and I trust that when our own war shall have ended—it will become the policy of the government to assume this leadership—the first field for which will of course be found in the present condition of Mexico.[7]

Shufeldt's "martyrdom," however, was dependent on how Washington's officials reacted to the changes in Mexican affairs.

In both Washington and Havana, Seward and Shufeldt undertook reassessments of the Mexican dilemma. Seward notified the various American legations abroad that "a monarchical government established in Mexico, in the presence of foreign fleets and armies, occupying the waters and the soil of Mexico, has no promise of security or permanence." Shufeldt's own changed point of view was also demonstrated when he asserted that "the policy of France underwent a sudden change —& so inexplicable that Mons. de Saligny found himself under very different instructions from those of Admiral La Gravière." The French minister had protested against the Soledad conference as contrary to his instructions, though Gravière had signed the convention as being in accordance with his. The result was not only a serious disagreement among the French but also between themselves and the Spanish commissioners, who became incensed. Prim urged the Mexican foreign minister that the time was "*now* or *never* for Mexico to receive a govt. consistent with her antecedents & her sympathies." Otherwise, he warned, a French force would thrust upon Mexico an alien and obnoxious prince. The reply was unfavorable, and Prim began reembarking the Spanish troops and army stores as the French pushed farther inland. Shufeldt's information on these occurrences came from an inside source, an officer of the government and "an intimate friend of Genl. Prim." The consul general forwarded it to Seward with the comment that the whole of it "is not inconsistent with what I have hitherto written."[8] To a certain extent he was right, but only if he admitted that he had magnified the Spanish threat previously and was still magnifying it until March and April when Prim was a spent force in Mexican affairs.

As the French danger increased in March, to a level that Shufeldt estimated equalled the Spanish threat of December 1861, he suggested a similar solution: the use of a confidential agent in Mexico. Such an agent, he pleaded, while being neither a minister nor an official representative of the country, might be able to act as circumstances required for the benefit of the United States and, at the same time, identify with the interests of Mexico. Shufeldt proposed a plan whereby the president could restore him to the naval service with a commission to act in an entirely confidential capacity for the government. This move would give weight and importance to his position with the Mexican leaders and people. He indicated to Frederick Seward that he would "go to Mexico for the purpose of instilling American ideas—of fostering the republican sentiment—of infusing courage to resist European encroachments—and finally to place in its true light the present contest going on in our own country—& its intimate relations with the immediate future of Mexico." He proposed to visit the capital and principal towns of the republic and contact their leading men to whom, he claimed, he was not unknown as a supporter of the Juárez government. He also asserted that he knew the genius of the Mexican people and their institutions, that he had been a good deal in the country and, above all, that he possessed "that faith in the living principle of republican democratic institutions—upon this continent." Should he be unsuccessful, he informed Seward, "then it will be because I am not an anointed apostle in the eternal faith—which teaches the right of every man to *himself*—his own government & his own religion."[9]

Shufeldt expanded on the theme for the benefit of the assistant secretary of state. The message was remarkably similar to the one he gave to Quitman in 1857, with Mexico now substituted for Cuba: "Mexico is the field towards which I have long looked—& upon which I am anxious to consecrate the rest of my life in the defense of free governments—& the amelioration of the human race." He returned to the problem that he had last raised with Charles Sumner, the question of what to do with the emancipated blacks in the United States: "yet to me, it seems sure —that the time must come—& that not far distant—when the future home of the *emancipated* negro must be found—in the genial climates of the more southern latitudes. . . . The limits of this letter prevent me from bringing to your notice—the advantages which the Isthmus of Tehuantepec offers for the colonization of the negro—& the higher interest it offers in view of Americanizing that point as a transit to our pacific shores." Shufeldt then volunteered to spend his annual leave of absence in Mexico. As he explained to the younger Seward, "In the war at home the field is already occupied—the harvest of fame has been gathered—Mexico—identical in her cause—is yet untrodden—I wish to go there—under the full belief—that God controls the destinies of men —and that I may become an instrument however humble—in the maintenance of the rights which he has bequeathed to every man—whatever may be his station or his complexion." To further this end Shufeldt agreed to supply the United States government with information. The responsibility, he added, with scarcely a thought toward the controller of his destiny, would be his alone. For that reason he informed the assistant secretary of state, he would dislike to have on the records any evidence that might "be construed into more enthusiasm than is 'compatible' with the position I have the honor to fill."[10]

The process of Shufeldt's self-hypnosis with Mexico was nearly complete. Two days after he suggested using a confidential agent, he accused the French minister of being fully committed to the interests of the South. He leveled the charge that "there was a complete understanding with Southern men—and perhaps the approbation of the Emperor—as to the course he should pursue in Mexico—in connection with the fore-shadowed policy of the Southern States." This was the first solid link between the French and Confederates that Shufeldt forged. In 1870, when recalling the incident, he ignored the fact that he made the link in late March 1862 and not in November 1861, when he had been much more fearful of the Spanish.[11]

Secretary of State Seward soon responded to Shufeldt's urgings. He notified William Lewis Dayton, United States minister in France, that "reports from the United States Consul General at Havana . . . indicated that France aimed at the subversion of republican institutions (the American system) in Mexico." Seward also instructed Dayton that "we have more than once . . . informed all the parties to the alliance that we cannot look with indifference upon any armed European intervention for political ends in a country situated so near and connected with us so closely as Mexico." The secretary of state then authorized Shufeldt to be absent from his Havana post for two months in order to proceed to Mexico. But Seward was careful to warn his consul that,

> At the present moment, divided and distracted by attempted revolution, we can do little more than watch with care the operations of intrigue in the neighboring republic.
>
> It is to be hoped, however, that the Mexicans may find sufficient encouragement to protect themselves, in the manifest improvement of our own political condition, and in the divisions which have occurred among the European states which have entered their territory under invitations as disloyal in their character as the appeals which our insurgents are making to foreign nations for intervention in the affairs of this country.[12]

Shufeldt's confidence shot up at the news. "Matters in Mexico have at last taken a tangible shape," he wrote to Seward. From Veracruz, however, news arrived of the meeting on April 9 between the allied plenipotentiaries at Orizaba, which led to the British and Spanish withdrawal from Mexico and the decision of the French to push on alone. Under the protection of the French flag, General Almonte had issued a pronunciamento declaring himself the supreme chief of the Mexican republic and calling all soldiers and citizens to annul their allegiance to the Juárez government. Shufeldt correctly considered Almonte merely a front for Maximilian of Austria. As the French under General de Lorencez advanced, the consul general regarded the war as finally commenced, and he was apprehensive about its conclusion. He expected the French troops to reach the capital and the Juárez government to flee into the interior. Mexico would be plunged once again into civil war just when it appeared to be emerging from such complications.[13]

In his overanxiety for the fate of the weak Mexican government, Shufeldt betrayed his headstrong nature. France, he claimed, had left out of her calculations the chances of Juárez's receiving foreign aid "and consequently the *rear* of her forces will be unprotected." Veracruz was in a position to be taken easily by a few thousand men. What, he asked, if Juárez were to authorize some person to create a force abroad and come to his assistance via Veracruz? Could this be done without compromising such a foreign government, or would it be considered a cause of war between France and the government "indirectly" permitting such aid to leave its ports? Clearly, the newly appointed agent envisaged a military role of greater magnitude for himself in the destinies of Mexican resistance. But he was prepared to await the outcome of his journey to Mexico before elaborating on this theme.[14]

The Mission to Save Mexico

Shufeldt landed in Veracruz in time to observe the French troops begin their advance toward Mexico City, accompanied by a straggling band of General Almonte's followers. On April 19 the French retired from Orizaba but returned the next day on the pretext that their wounded had been threatened. To Shufeldt "this flimsy veil was made to cover one of the greatest violations of national honor on record." As an observer he was acutely aware of the general breakdown of law and order in the wake of the French forces, with bands of guerrillas organizing both for and against the Juárez government. With the Spanish return to Havana on board English vessels, the French military officers and civilian officials treated the retiring Spanish with profound contempt. Seward's courier joyously reported that "the rupture in the Holy Alliance has become intensified into an undisguised hatred." As he imagined the English were also mortified by the French action, he was now aware that the main danger to Mexico came from the French.

However, even at this late date, he did not entirely discount General Prim, whom he characterized as "still intriguing or negotiating secretly with General Doblado," and he added a warning:

> It is needless to say to you that the Govt. of Mexico at the moment of entering upon a war against One-fourth of its citizens in rebellion, aided by a powerful Nation with men and money—is wretchedly poor—its soldiers & even its officers in the field literally famishing with hunger. Without aid of some kind—sooner or later Mexico *must* yield to her enemies—and in her submission our own institutions must receive a terrible shock. . . . At the present moment *action* on our part in the affairs of Mexico—immediate urgent—is of vital necessity as well to her as to us—As in the case of our own rebellion the hour of argument has passed—We must either aid her—directly or indirectly or she must *perish*. Without us she had no hope.

Once France possessed Mexico, he informed the State Department, "does it not occur to you that the Emperor of the French may make the non recognition of the Southern Confederacy dependent upon our recognition of the Almonte Govt. in Mexico?"[15]

In May Shufeldt proposed to see President Juárez and advocate a plan for a force of three to five thousand men, recruited in the United States, to hold the Isthmus of Tehuantepec. Shufeldt visualized himself as commander-in-chief under a Mexican commission but financed and sustained with money loaned by the United States under the proposed terms of Minister Corwin's treaty, signed April 6. This money, he told Seward, "ought to be expended in a way to advance *our interests* in that country." Furthermore, he declared his intention to suggest to the Mexican government that the isthmus should be thrown open to colonization, drawing emigrants from California as well as the Atlantic seaboard, and affording "admirable advantages for the colonization of our contraband negroes." Strategically, apart from the Pacific seaports, the isthmus represented the only position where forces could come from abroad to assist the Mexicans without directly attacking the French. Setting a price on the venture, the ambitious envoy estimated that $1 million would effectively secure the isthmus "for Mexico—& eventually for ourselves if Mexico is to be divided up—Poland like—by this modern Holy Alliance." Shufeldt was not averse to joining in the partition of the Mexican state if the United States received its share. He recommended active aid and money to establish a United States protectorate in Mexico, even though he was well aware that the money granted under Corwin's intended treaty would dwindle by bribery and corruption by the time it reached any point to be of use in the struggle. As Edward Plumb joined him in Veracruz, with dispatches for Thomas Corwin, Shufeldt urged, in this point of view therefore it becomes *US* to look out for a slice of this unhappy country in order that we may not only in this portion maintain alive the principles of republics—but also from it be able to operate & co-operate against these Allies or perhaps in the turn of events assist in the reintegration of the Republic under a liberal & constitutional Govt.

By the way—I believe that Mexico needs absolutely a foreign element— and that *our* safety as a nation requires that this foreign element should be American. . . . I therefore propose to infuse this American Element by the military occupation of the isthmus of Tehuantepec.[16]

In Shufeldt's eyes the expansion of American influence into Mexico would allow the United States to control the rich states of Oajaca, Tabasco, and Eastern Veracruz, effectively forestalling the attempted French takeover of Tehuantepec and the establishment of a French route to the Pacific. Shufeldt informed his superiors that he would speak to Doblado and request a commission as general with the power to confer military rank. The crusading consul optimistically anticipated an eager acceptance by the Mexican foreign minister, but he urged the State Department to approve his plan. To Shufeldt the policy of lending money to Mexico under Corwin's proposed treaty of April 6 was only wise in proportion to the hold it gave the United States on that country. Expecting much of the loan to disappear, he argued that "We ought to take possession of Tehuantepec! . . . It therefore becomes us—to use this money or a part of it—in such a way as will not only benefit Mexico —but *Ourselves*—we must act as if we were Co-heirs—in this country. Once in Tehuantepec—I will guarantee that no foreign flag shall fly there—it will be Mexican until *We* want it."[17]

Shufeldt's earthbound progress into Mexico was more difficult. The stagecoaches by way of Orizaba were not allowed through the French lines, and those by way of Jalapa went once a week. Most of the available horses had been seized by the Mexicans or hired by the allies. Eventually, Shufeldt and Plumb, travelling together, had to purchase mounts on which they reached Jalapa on May 6. At this time the French forces were about four leagues from Pueblo, having brushed aside the forces of General Zaragosa at the Cumbres of Aculcingo, ten leagues above Orizaba. Edward Plumb complained, "I do not at all like the present appearance of my journey. The reactionary guerrillas are hovering on both sides of the French lines most of the way from Perota up." Shufeldt, who wanted the United States "not only to take the matter out of the hands of the French—but the Mexicans also," found himself the focal point of Mexican curiosity. He concluded that the appearance of United States troops would be hailed with great enthusiasm, for "I am asked every day when they may expect to see them."[18]

On May 9, the day after the French and Mexican forces were locked in battle at Puebla, the two Americans set out from Jalapa and arrived at Mexico City only on the fourteenth. Here Shufeldt had an interview with Thomas Corwin about his colonization plans. He was obviously persuasive, for Corwin responded enthusiastically to the project and later informed Seward that "Lincoln's proposition to colonize free Negroes" had been received everywhere with cordial approval. Describing the Isthmus of Tehuantepec as "almost vacant from sea to sea," Corwin wrote to the State Department that "the power to avail ourselves of this great advantage with the least expense to ourselves and the happiest results to the black man, whether looked upon in either the light of economy or philanthropy presented a motive of great weight with me for adopting at once the treaty in question, before the opportunity should be lost."[19]

Shufeldt next submitted a long dispatch to Foreign Minister Doblado dealing with the possible settlement of the emancipated Negroes from the United States on the relatively uninhabited isthmus. He posed five questions to Doblado, aimed at establishing whether the Mexican government would view with favor the colonization project under the auspices of the United States and approve of the purchase by that country, in the name of private individuals, public or private lands for the settlement of the former slaves. If the Mexican government agreed to such a scheme, Shufeldt desired to know if it would exempt the supplies and effects of such immigrants from duties, their lands and property from taxation, and themselves from military service for five years. In all other respects the immigrants would conform to the laws of Mexico. Furthermore, he inquired if the government would agree to a fully armed United States force on the isthmus, "for the proper protection of said immigrants; said force to be withdrawn on the termination of said [European-Mexican] war." Finally, he stipulated that the affairs of the immigrants "and their charge and control" would be in the hands of agents "duly appointed for that purpose and for as long a period as may be necessary by the United States."[20]

In spite of Shufeldt's plea that the purchase of public and private lands by the United States would not compromise nor interfere with Mexican sovereignty, his ebullient statements on military adventures and colonization to Seward clearly show that was his aim. With American troops, colonists, and financial power extended into the region, and a corresponding absence of Mexican financial power in the form of taxation and duty exemptions for five years, together with exemptions from military service for the citizens, there would be little that Mexico could do to exert her own laws if they clashed with United States aims in the area. Under these circumstances Mexican sovereignty would have been alienated even more rapidly than was accomplished by the Stephen Austin party in Texas during the 1820s. Both Shufeldt and Doblado obviously knew this.

Doblado's reply was extremely guarded, and he linked any acceptance of even part of the scheme with the ratification by the United States Senate of Corwin's loan treaty of April 6. From the Mexican National Palace he replied to Shufeldt on May 19: "If the treaty recently concluded . . . is ratified by the Senate of the United States the scheme of colonization of the negroes liberated in that Republic will be practicable, and the Mexican Government . . . will accept the conditions detailed in your communication (that I am answering) excepting those which are incompatible with the independence and Sovereignty of the Constitutional Government." If the treaty were not ratified, he continued, then his government regretted that it would not be able to enter into the colonization project. A duplicate treaty with the British had already been prepared in the event of nonratification by the United States Senate. Then, Doblado observed, "nothing could be done without the consent of England."[21] He had not only cleverly tied in acceptance of the scheme to future acceptance of the Corwin treaty, and raised the prospect of British rivalry, but has also provided an escape route for his government by way of the undefined "exceptions" that would appear incompatible with the government's independence and sovereignty.

As Corwin exchanged ratification of the postal and extradition treaties that had been brought to Mexico by Plumb, his loan treaty had already failed to pass the United States Senate. Consequently, Shufeldt's scheme, tied as it was by Doblado to the fate of that treaty, was already a dead letter. Ignorant of this fate, Corwin urged Shufeldt to go directly to Washington with Plumb, who was returning with the Mexican ratification of the treaties he had brought, and offer Seward the results of his personal observations in Mexico. That Shufeldt had impressed the diplomat was obvious, for Corwin notified Seward that, "he seems to me to be a very cool sound man & certainly his patriotic & personal feelings are all on the right side. His long acquaintance with the Spanish American race give to his opinions well deserved weight . . . I trust our Consul at Havana will not be censored for his trip to Washington, I am sure it is necessary."[22]

Shufeldt's journey to Washington never materialized. He started back from Veracruz on May 22, just after the news reached Mexico of the capture of New Orleans by Flag Officer Farragut's forces, and he arrived in Havana the morning of June 5. Once there he found orders from Seward, dated May 23, directing him to return immediately to the duties of the consulate general.

A Debate on National Policy—and the Reckoning

Shufeldt had sent five dispatches from Veracruz and Jalapa, dated May 1, 3, and 8, all of which were received at the State Department on May 23. Their combined effect created deep concern. Seward wrote immediately to his agent informing him that his suggestions would be taken into consideration, which they merited "when offered by an intelligent observer not unfamiliar with the scene." But then came the measure of Seward's concern:

> it is, however, noticed, not without some regret, that you seem to suppose yourself clothed with diplomatic powers. This was not the purpose of the government when it sanctioned your visit to Mexico. You will consequently abstain from official correspondence with any person in authority, and as it is presumed that by the time this reaches you, you will have noted and reported upon everything in that quarter which it may be desirable to know here, you will return to Havana and resume your duties there.[23]

This letter caught Shufeldt by surprise. Nothing that he had received from the secretary of state, he claimed, would have warranted such a suggested assumption of diplomatic powers on his part. As his instructions had reached him too late to prevent his address to Doblado on the colonization project, Shufeldt sent Seward a copy of the correspondence with the explanation that "it was expressly understood that this correspondence was in my individual character—and arose from my knowledge of the part of Mexico alluded to." The consul general admitted that the letter was written from the American legation in Mexico City and had met with Corwin's "endorsement and approbation." He hoped this would be sufficient apology for the act, particularly as the question was "harmless" in its nature and only "intended to create an interest on a subject which at some future time must be of great importance to ourselves, and might be of vast advantage to Mexico."[24]

Shufeldt believed this official explanation was not sufficient to reveal his motives, for he wrote privately to Seward to restate his case. "I simply threw them out as hints and in undisguised candor," he told the secretary of state, "and in entire accordance with the tone of my previous *private* correspondence." He repeated his readiness to lay down his life to help a divided, impoverished, and demoralized Mexico throw off the invaders. With the state governors of Guerrero, Yucatan, and Zucatecas refusing to send troops to defend the capital, and with the French already controlling the states of Veracruz, Puebla, and Mexico, he envisaged complete disruption under the current French policy. Shufeldt's remedy was still to lend Mexico money. Though he believed it would be misapplied he anticipated that it might help to maintain the central government. In return, however, the United States government could secure the rights of property in the republic. This was essentially the basis of the proposed Seward loan plan and was ultimately incorporated in the Corwin treaty. But Shufeldt developed it one step further: "the administration of this property would necessitate *intervention*—both civil & military—to encourage emigration and secure tranquility to the emigrants—and without *intervention* in my opinion—Mexico can never rise in the scale of Nations to that dignity—which her territory or resources would justify. . . . It is *European* intervention which I deprecate. . . . Its reconstruction however must be upon the basis of a democratic government."[25]

On July 24 Seward thanked Shufeldt sincerely for the "valuable information and very suggestive hints" contained in his letter. To Seward the danger was not that the Confederate insurgents might succeed in overthrowing the Union government, for he considered it strong enough to defend itself, but that "some foreign nation or nations invited by our division" might "enter the breach and subvert the Republic." To prevent such action was his duty and, he warned his consul general, "it must be performed with the utmost caution and energy." Seward then clarified the reasons why Shufeldt had been recalled on May 23.

> You went to Mexico to learn facts and communicate them to this Government. You were expected to practise the utmost reserve. Your letters showed a degree of enthusiasm which led me to apprehend that you might forget that reserve, while I know that in whatever you might say you would be supposed to speak for the Government of the United States. No Government could conduct its foreign relations successfully if it suffered itself to be, or seem to be, committed by Agents not invested with diplomatic functions and amenable to diplomatic restrictions. You were therefore recalled.

Seward thus related the possible consequences of Shufeldt's mission to potential excuses to justify foreign intervention in the Civil War. Nevertheless, he offered a crumb of comfort to the smarting consul general when he indicated that the "seeming necessity" for the recall had not in the least diminished "the respect and high appreciation" of his ability and discretion entertained by both Lincoln and himself.[26]

Shufeldt responded to this rebuff with a high degree of sarcasm combined with a spirited defense of his conduct. He assumed that a proper disposition of the rapidly increasing number of emancipated Negroes in the United States was a subject in which every citizen had a right to, "and ought to feel," a deep interest. With a nice touch of irony the consul general remarked that he trusted he "did not transgress the limits of official duty" in expressing this interest to the State Department. Admitting that he had initiated the colonization project with the Mexican government while understanding that he had no authority to do so from his government, he declared his purpose had been to present the scheme for Seward's consideration upon his return to Washington. Trapped in the web of his own enthusiasm, Shufeldt claimed that Doblado's reply was "as favorable as could be expected under the circumstances." He maintained "no doubt" that such an arrangement could be made with the Mexican government. The result would be to the great political and commercial benefit of the United States, arising from an international transit route between the eastern and western coasts of America. The occupation of the isthmus, he noted, "by colonists under the guarantee and good faith of the U.S. would give our Govt. an indirect control in Mexico—which our own interest and safety seem absolutely to demand." This was the key to his scheme, not any genuine concern for the emancipated slaves. They were pawns for the success of flanking movements leading to his commercial scheme. He considered it pertinent to add that by the establishment of such a colony, with inhabitants speaking the American language, imbued with American religious and social customs, and based upon the principles of free labor, a check would be offered to any slave-holding nation that might desire to extend itself in that direction. If the Confederacy could not be defeated, it might be outflanked.

Shufeldt then proposed to Seward a convention between the governments of Mexico and the United States. Five of the eight points he advanced for this meeting merely repeated the provisions of his plan forwarded to Manuel Doblado. But he added three further points for discussion. Under the fifth, sixth, and eighth points the United States would pay Mexico an annual sum of money for a fixed term of years in return for free use of two seaports, one on the Gulf of Mexico and one on the Pacific coast, for the importation of articles needed by the colonists for the construction of railroads, for improvements of river navigation, and for exemption from taxation. The colonists would have free navigation of the rivers and all rights and privileges granted to various corporations for the right-of-way over the Isthmus of Tehuantepec. If that right-of-way had expired, the Mexican government would "bind itself—to grant a *new* charter to an *American* Company—under such guarantees as were heretofore held by the former corporations—but free from all the liabilities of the same—except such as may have been incurred in the surveys and other legitimate purposes for the development of the project."[27] The ghost of the old Louisiana–Tehuantepec Company still lingered in Shufeldt's mind.

To answer the point raised by Seward of the danger to the United States occasioned by the Mexican imbroglio, the consul general took a different stand. It was true, he admitted, that the United States was in a struggle "so terrific—that if the principles involved were not immortal we might fear our own destruction." But even that struggle, he pleaded, "ought to render us the more alive to the duty of aiding that people among whom the same issue—is likely to meet with disaster and temporary defeat . . . the Mexican people have not the elements of resistance to any foreign Power." It was this basic difference in assumptions over the source of greatest danger that distinguished Shufeldt's arguments from those of the secretary of state.

This difference became more apparent when Shufeldt tried to influence Seward through his son, Frederick. Shufeldt wanted possession of the Mexican isthmus and pointed out that Mexico was prostrate. He directed the attention of the State Department to the bustle of Spanish activity in Central America, the outfitting of a Spanish fleet under Admiral Puizon for the Pacific, and the "next movement" by Spain, the restoration of Spanish influence on the American continent. "In the midst of all this effort," he asked the younger Seward, "are we to remain powerless to resist?" At the same time Shufeldt indicated his awareness of the extreme difficulty that would attend any action by the United States as the tide of battle ebbed and flowed at home: "I feel how strong we are when successful—and alas! how weak we seem to be when we meet with a check—how tremendous is yet the work we have to perform in the rejuvenation & reconstruction of our own land and government—but would the project I submit to you—necessarily involve us with foreign powers? If not I am convinced that the advantages we would gain in obtaining indirect control of the Isthmus would at a day not distant be of immense importance.[28]

Shufeldt had really thrown away his case with the easy assumption tacked on to his plea for intervention. On March 3, he had been prepared to wait for any lead by the United States government "when our own war shall have ended." Once in Mexico, however, he began to argue for immediate action. Then in his letter to Frederick Seward, he urged action but conceded only an "if not" about the possiblities of foreign intervention. It looked remarkably like formulating his question to fit the desired result. Equally as sure was the secretary of state's reply on June 24 that the project was fraught with danger. Seward could well have asked what would have been the result if Shufeldt's project did bring involvement with another power?

The consul general was in reality asking Seward to provide the right solution to contradictory questions. Shufeldt was gambling that militant action to take control of the isthmian route might not invite retaliation by the French or bring danger of possible disruption to the political center of the empire from which such control would come. Seward wanted above all else to safeguard and consolidate the United States, to crush the internal rebellion even at the expense of temporarily losing control over communications routes and adjacent areas. He maintained this position consistently throughout the course of the Civil War. Probably the most famous example of his attitude came in a dispatch to John Bigelow, consul at Paris, sent on May 21, 1864, at the time of General Nathaniel P. Banks' ill-fated Red River expedition: "With our land and naval forces in Louisiana retreating before the rebels instead of marching toward Mexico, this is not the most suitable time we could choose for offering idle menaces to the Emperor of France. We have compromised nothing, surrendered nothing and I do not propose to surrender anything. But why should we gasconade about Mexico when we are in a struggle for our own life?" Control over adjacent areas could always be gained once the political center was strong, the armies triumphant, and the economy sound; hence the secretary's policy of watchfulness and sending fact-gathering reporters to Mexico.[29]

Shufeldt should have picked this message out of the June 24 letter in which Seward pointed out the possibility of a foreign nation entering the breach and subverting the Republic. That he failed to do so was obvious from his enthusiastic proposals to run the French gauntlet to Tehuantepec. Given the two alternatives, Seward's policy, based on the assumption that if the United States went under so would Mexico, was more soundly based than Shufeldt's view that if Mexico went under then republican principles in the United States would suffer a fatal blow. In 1862 no one could answer Shufeldt's implicit question about the consequences of possible involvement, and Seward could not afford the risk of inviting success for the rebellion by foreign intervention following a rash Mexican aid program. Not that Seward's expansionist dreams were any less forceful than Shufeldt's; they were only tempered by his being at the center of diplomatic operations and not in a consulate daily conditioned by resentment of Spanish, French, and British intrigue, real or imagined. Seward's assumptions kept the course of diplomatic alternatives within his grasp: Shufeldt's would have given the choice to his diplomatic opponents and possible future adversaries.

If Seward merely lectured his man in Havana at the end of June, he gave him a sharp rap on the knuckles in July. He had submitted Shufeldt's dispatch of July 4 proposing a convention between the governments of Mexico and the United States to Lincoln. He also bluntly observed that a law of the United States forbade any citizen unauthorized by the president to enter into any diplomatic correspondence with any foreign power. Shufeldt had acted in derogation of that law "and incurred the President's very decided disapprobation" for opening a correspondence, without the necessary authority, with General Doblado, "the very able and enlightened Minister of Mexico." While Shufeldt's eight-point proposal had been forwarded to Lincoln, Seward doubted if any such scheme for the treatment of contraband slaves would pass the Senate or House. Furthermore, with the Senate's "recently manifested . . . conviction that it is inexpedient to loan or advance monies to Mexico in the present conjuncture," Seward doubted the wisdom of any actions toward Mexico that could lead to complications with the allies: "While the national heart is strong and confident, and may be relied upon for the boldest and most determined defense of the Country against any foreign encroachment upon its rights or honor, there is by no means any such unanimity of popular sympathies with Mexico as could weaken the hold of the traditional policy of avoiding foreign entanglements upon the public favor at the hazard of complicating our relations with foreign nations."

For these reasons Seward advised that Lincoln could not authorize any diplomatic agent to make overtures to Mexico of the nature that Shufeldt had made to Doblado. "You need not be told," he adroitly informed the errant consul general, "that it is unfortunate that you have excited expectations on the part of Mexico which your Government cannot fulfill." Again came balm for wounded pride. Seward praised Shufeldt's "distinguished fidelity and ability in the exercise of the proper functions of the important consulate," which had won the president's "highest respect and consideration." Lincoln was induced by these circumstances to overlook Shufeldt's error. Nevertheless, it remained an error, and Shufeldt's only consolation lay in Seward's confidential handling of the matter in order to save his agent any practical embarrassment "or any pain beyond the necessary vindication of the authority and dignity of the Government."[30]

For all practical purposes Shufeldt's mission to save Mexico foundered on Seward's logic. Yet it did have some impact on diplomatic negotiations outside the United States. John Slidell, Confederate commissioner to Louis Napoleon, wrote to Confederate secretary of state Judah P. Benjamin on July 25, 1862, enclosing a memorandum of his interview with the emperor. Slidell had raised the subject of Corwin's treaty, which, he argued, was "a subsidy of $11,000,000 to enable Juárez to carry on the war against France." Napoleon correctly predicted that the Senate would not ratify it. Slidell then declared: "I said that I heard from what seemed to be good authority, although I did not pretend to vouch for the truth of the report, that Shufeldt, U.S. Consul-General at Havana, had gone to Mexico and placed at the disposition of Juárez $2,000,000, being the cash installment stipulated by the treaty;

and if this were so, the Mexican Army was now waging war against France with means furnished by the Federal Treasury."³¹ Had Shufeldt known of Slidell's imaginative assessment of his journey, he might have gained solace from it. Had Slidell guessed anywhere near the truth of Shufeldt's eight-point proposal to place colonists and troops in Tehuantepec, and realized the compromising effects this would have on northern diplomacy, he might have had a stronger argument to offer to Louis Napoleon.

Shortly after his return, Shufeldt wrote a confidential letter to Seward about Mexican affairs that mentioned his "deep sense of mortification" upon receiving the president's disapprobation. He added that "in times like these mere personal feelings ought and do sink into utter insignificance before the Great events which are hurrying us along." He also wrote in the same vein to F. W. Seward. Many years later he glossed over the whole Mexican incident and inaccurately recalled his role in it.

> Mr. Seward sent me to Mexico—by authority of the President to ascertain from that Government the practicability of settling our Southern negroes on the isthmus of Tehuantepec. Lincoln's plan was to purchase them at an appraised value & to force them to emigrate. The scheme was quixotic, if you please—but it was humane—Lincoln dreaded the shedding of fractricidal blood—At all events it came too late—the country was already enveloped in the murk & gloom of war—blood began to flow—& those who believed in the integrity of the Union—had to be baptized.³²

There was little doubt at the time, and later, that Shufeldt considered himself one of the baptized martyrs.

Like a Lion in a Cage

After his return from Mexico, Shufeldt remained consul general in Havana for ten more months, but the important diplomatic events in his term of office were over. He enjoyed a quiet spell of routine work, free from the cares of Mexico, between June and August 1862. His exequatur finally arrived from Madrid in August, and he concentrated on reporting the increasing number of blockade-runners, merchant ships, and foreign war vessels that called at Cuba. Until the end of the year, Shufeldt's duties lay mainly in solving two incidents involving foreign vessels and United States warships. One was the *Jules et Marie* case, which had dragged on since November 1861. The other involved a British vessel, the *Blanche,* burned by the crew of the USS *Montgomery* while beached under the protection of the Spanish flag hoisted by the Alcalde de Mar. Shufeldt negotiated the former case with the French consul general in Havana, Bernard des Essard, and eventually damages of $9,500 were accepted by the French owners. The *Blanche* affair took much longer, and at the end of December 1862 the negotiations were still at the stage Shufeldt considered would "take some time." His greatest difficulty lay with the Spanish indignation that had welled up after the *Blanche* had been left a gutted wreck. Several Spanish warships had left Havana harbor on receipt of the news, but they returned without a clash with any Federal cruiser. On January 24, 1863, Shufeldt wrote to Seward:

> the Spanish authorities were very indignant at the violation of territory, and it will be difficult to prove in the face of the captain's protest that [Commander] Hunter's men did not set fire to her. I tried very hard to get the evidence of the crew of the *Blanche,* but they were kept out of my way. I regret the affair so far as the Spanish authorities are concerned, but insomuch as John Bull may bluster and threaten I confess that it gives me pleasure. We have a reckoning with him, which I hope, under Providence, to live to see settled.[33]

In the difficult period following the Union defeat at Fredericksburg, in December 1862, Shufeldt was placed on the defensive with regard to Spanish pressure and actions. Don Francisco Serrano was recalled to Madrid and a new captain general, Lieutenant General Domingo Dulce, took office on December 10. The new ruler of Cuba was more hostile to northern interests than his predecessor. The *Blanche* affair was only settled when an apology was delivered to the Spanish authorities. Shufeldt wanted to resist doing so because he thought an apology would lead to Spanish arrogance. That the arrogance was not altogether one-sided was evident when he complained that he felt humiliated; a condition that a few years earlier he would not have deemed possible "for an American to submit to." He expected the new Spanish administration in Cuba would be unfriendly and Spanish sympathy would rapidly disappear "before the inexorable logic of events."

Shufeldt felt particularly angry as a result of his inability to influence events. Somewhat bitterly he asserted that "our weakness to these people is as apparent as the noon day sun," and with overtones of superiority still glimmering asked, "are we indeed so near destruction that even Spain can begin the process of bullying us?" According to the disconsolate consul, the Spanish captain general had replied haughtily when Shufeldt asked for the release of the crew, mainly American, of the brig *Estelle,* destroyed by the CSS *Florida.* Shufeldt's surge of anger at Dulce's reply, which made his cheeks "tingle," was one that he found it difficult to subdue.[34]

As difficulties mounted for United States vessels chasing Confederate commerce destroyers such as the *Florida,* Shufeldt's relish for his position decreased. The crest of the wave on which he had ridden during the *Trent* affair had left him floundering in the shoals of Seward's displeasure and Spanish resentment. His request for leave of absence was turned down in August. Then came the loss of his relations with Don Francisco Serrano and the arrival of the unsympathetic Dulce. The position no longer held any excitement. With Spanish administrators reacting unfavorably toward the United States and helpfully toward Confederate agents in January 1863, Shufeldt was further discomfited diplomatically by the news of the Union defeat at Fredericksburg. On January 24, exasperated by the Spanish, he wrote to Seward, urging that "unless some degree of resistance is shown—it will lead them to a manifestation of feeling against us—which to your agents abroad will become almost unendurable. . . . I trust I may be forgiven for giving vent to feelings which are pent up here within my own breast—until I feel almost like a lion in a cage—disposed to roar even in fruitless rage."[35]

By the end of 1862, therefore, Shufeldt was giving serious consideration to reentering the navy. He had toyed intermittently with this idea since November 1861, but now acted on it and asked Truman Smith to intercede with the administration in Washington. Smith soon felt his lack of political bargaining power in his efforts to aid Shufeldt's cause. If only he still held his old Senate seat, he complained, he could act much more effectively than he was able to at the moment. However, Smith's persistence paid off over the winter. He spoke with fifteen or sixteen senators during visits to Washington. "The result I have come to," he informed Shufeldt, "is that you are pretty certain to be invited home in the course of the Winter to take your place in the Navy." The only opponents of the move were expected to be Senators John Parker Hale of New Hampshire and James Wilson Grimes of Iowa, both on the Senate Committee on Naval Affairs, and Smith caustically termed them "narrow prejudiced men and not very well liked in the Senate." On March 14, Gustavus Vasa Fox, acting secretary of the navy, informed Seward that Shufeldt had been confirmed by the Senate as a commander in the navy.[36]

When Shufeldt received the news he contacted Seward. On April 15 the secretary of state commended him for his conduct in Havana as consul general, and two days later Shufeldt was ordered to report to Rear Admiral Hiram Paulding in New York for the command of the steamer USS *Fort Jackson.* He did so on April 20, 1863, and sent in his resignation to the State Department. Frederick Seward notified him of its acceptance and assured him of the "high appreciation" with which his "laborious and faithful services amidst the embarrassments and responsibilities" of his late position was regarded by the government. The younger Seward indulged in "the confidential expectation that a brilliant career" lay before Shufeldt, honorable both to himself and useful to the country.[37] Shufeldt had the same dream, but did not intend it to be applied only to the naval service during a period of Civil War. Unfortunately for him, the attempt to apply it to the Isthmus of Tehuantepec had failed not once but twice already.

5

The Blockade of the Southern Coast

The Charleston Blockade

Shufeldt's Civil War naval career was primarily involved with duty in the South Atlantic and East Gulf blockading squadrons. It began on May 8, 1863, when Shufeldt was detached from the *Fort Jackson* and ordered to report to Commodore Cornelius K. Stribling in Philadelphia, for passage in the USS *Bermuda* to Port Royal. He was then attached to Rear Admiral Samuel F. DuPont's South Atlantic blockading squadron, and took command of the gunboat *Conemaugh,* a sidewheel steamer of 955 tons with a powerful eight-gun armament.* Shufeldt joined DuPont's squadron on May 25 and found his officers and crew in good condition, but the *Conemaugh* needed caulking, for her long exposure to the sun had opened her seams. He requested a relief vessel in order to return to Port Royal for the necessary repairs. Dupont, however, needed the *Conemaugh* in Winyah Bay, South Carolina, and was unable to grant the request.[1]

Shufeldt was soon in action against Confederate forces. Opposite his usual anchorage in the bay was an artificial causeway through a marsh that connected South Island to the mainland. Where the road crossed over a stream a bridge had recently been destroyed. On June 8, a landing party dispatched to reconnoiter in the direction of the bridge was chased back by the picket guard. Acting Ensign G. F. Morse reported that the bridge was being rebuilt. At 1:00 P.M. Shufeldt ordered the *Conemaugh*'s first cutter to be manned with twenty seamen and marines under Masters J. W. Stapleford and Morse, and sent them to destroy the bridge across the creek. Twenty minutes later, the *Conemaugh* moved up the river to cover the landing party and command the causeway and a larger party in the distance. The Cat Island battery was hit by two

---

*One 11-inch and four 9-inch guns, one 100-pound rifle, and two 24-pound howitzers.

100-pounder rifle shells. Stapleford reported finding the bridge rebuilt with great care, evidently for the purpose of transporting artillery to South Island to play upon the *Conemaugh*'s anchorage. The bridge was burned and Shufeldt ordered another cutter into Mosquito Creek and the canal near Cat Island for a mile-and-a-half, to check if more bridges had been built. Another party reconnoitered North Island, marching twenty miles in a complete circuit. Shufeldt reported that "it would be difficult if not impossible" for any artillery to be brought there, and the expedition returned without loss. While he knew it was only a small affair, he felt assured that if another occasion of more importance occurred, his officers and men would respond with similar "alacrity and cheerfulness." DuPont thought the results were very satisfactory and expressed pleasure at the spirit and readiness developed. But he recommended caution in any future reconnaissances, "as the rebels are on their own ground and . . . might entrap a small party."[2]

A completely different kind of incident took place in Winyah Bay. During the blockade, an old, gray-haired slave, who had lived for ten months in the swamps building a canoe, came down the river with a ragged shirt flying as a flag of truce. Shufeldt sent him down below to have breakfast and created a commotion among the crew, who "thought they were better than a d--n nigger anyhow." He did not blame the men for being "exponents of an idea which prevailed throughout the land" or for their reaction to the contraband who, "never wavering, never faltering until he reached the protection of that flag—which he had heard was making *all* men free," had starved and hunted in the swamps in order to escape.[3]

The episode led Shufeldt to discourse upon the plight of the black in the Civil War. The ironies built into the "contraband status" and the effects of the war in the trenches moved him to reflect at length on the slavery problem:

> Strange inconsistency—wonderful paradox! Our tears have flown in continuous streams for the poor African slave—but not a word of pity is heard for the hundreds who perish in the trenches—or worse still for the women and children who die daily from starvation & neglect.
>
> Contraband indeed! Unfortunate Ethiopian—unless you can change your skin—you will find no practical sympathy from the white man—Either in the North or in the South—in the one you are doomed to slavery—in the other to social ostracism . . . I know that the Negro is at once the fountain & origin of our evils (fons et origo malorum)—that he stands in the way of an inexorable destiny *but he* is innocent in all this; He neither made himself a slave—nor has he made the effort to become free. He is simply the victim to a law of progress—which neither he nor we can control. . . . I protest that I have no prejudice of color—I have enjoyed the intellectual society of many great and

good negroes—in Liberia—& St. Domingo—and yet with that detestable weakness which makes man cower to men—I have shrunk from contact with colored men in America.

I am no advocate for miscegenation—I believe that social distinctions ought to exist & that a mixture of these races would be an unmixed evil—but in the name of God—treat the Negro as if he were human—possessed by the same hopes—actuated by the same fears—and if your religion is true an inheritor in common with yourself of all that Heaven can offer!

Shufeldt later sermonized on the incident: "let us pray my friends—let us kneel down in our cushioned pews—lay our heads upon our scented handkerchiefs and thank God with smiling self complacency—that 'we were not like other men,' more especially that we are not like this 'd--n nigger' this modern pariah—this poor unfortunate weak old contraband—who for fifty years has sweated & groaned for others profit—but who is—thank God—free at last—for my dear Sir—he is dead!!" Though he wrote more eloquently at other times on the problem of the black in American society and later developed some racist expressions himself, on this occasion Shufeldt revealed both a compassion for the plight of the individual swamp slave and a heavy irony directed at self-righteous northern attitudes midway through a war that was ultimately to free all the slaves.

After the small success at Winyah Bay, DuPont ordered Shufeldt to blockade Georgetown, South Carolina, and then to lie off Charleston harbor. Joint army and navy preparations for an assault on Battery Wagner were being made, and the admiral wished no news to leak out. By July 8, the *Conemaugh*'s boats were landed on Folly Island, the sandspit home of Battery Wagner. The fleet steamed along the shores of Morris Island, weaving a curtain of shells above the fort. But Shufeldt did not participate in the abortive Union attack on the battery on July 18-19. After towing the *Weehawken* to Nassau, the *Conemaugh* went to Port Royal to have a rifled gun and carriage fitted. Her return was delayed by bad weather, a broken cylinder head, and rudder and valve repairs. Shufeldt reported to Rear Admiral John A. Dahlgren, who had replaced DuPont as commander of the squadron, on July 27.[4]

Early in September 1863, Shufeldt was detached from the *Conemaugh* and ordered to the *Kaatskill*, an ironclad with two guns and a crew of seventy-four. He was extremely unwilling to serve in the smaller, hot, and unmanageable ironclad, though he reported for duty. The discontented captain felt, moreover, that he had to get to Washington in order to settle his consular accounts from Havana, which the Treasury Department wanted cleared, and also to apply for a commission on the West Indies station. His disgust at the appointment to the *Kaatskill* was apparent in a letter to Gideon Welles in which he noted, "I am unsuited physically for service on an Iron-Clad—being too large & too full blooded for such a confined space." Dahlgren gave in to Shufeldt's wishes and revoked his orders. Given Shufeldt's indication that he would appeal to the Navy Department if he did not, there was little that he thought he could do.[5]

Secretary Welles, however, regretted Shufeldt's wishes. He did not see how he could change his orders. He would neither dicuss the circumstances that made Shufeldt's case peculiar nor argue the necessity of retaining the "able officers of the South Atlantic Squadron" on duty "while their strength will admit." In justice to the other commanders, he felt disinclined to make the changes that Shufeldt desired. Welles, who knew that the "dry blockade" was tedious and irksome, and service in the monitors was "debilitating and exhausting," argued that it could not be permitted to officers to select the service where they were to be employed. He believed that withdrawing Shufeldt from the South Atlantic squadron, in order to give him an independent cruising command, would cause dissatisfaction among the other officers and impair confidence in the department, neither of which results he thought Shufeldt would desire to bring about. In short, Welles told Shufeldt to go back to the squadron and forget his request for the present.[6]

Welles was obviously disturbed by the request, for he entered in his diary for September 15 a full comment upon it:

> Commander Shufeldt, an officer of [more than ordinary] ability, gives me trouble by a restless but natural desire for change and more active employment. Wishes an independent command, is dissatisfied [to be] in the South Atlantic Squadron. Inadmissible. It is only recently he has been reinstated in the service, on my [special] recommendation and by my efforts, against the remonstrance of many officers and [others] [their friends in and out of Congress]. Now to give him choice of position over others who never left the service would be unjust. I cannot do it. Duty on his present station is arduous, irksome, exhausting; someone must perform it were he to leave.[7]

Welles did, however, appreciate Shufeldt's opinions about the difficulties facing the force off Charleston. A strong indication of his views emerged from an interview he had with Welles immediately after the latter's letter of September 17 had reached him. Shufeldt made the journey to Washington and Welles later revealed that:

> Commander Shufeldt called on me. Thinks the capture of Charleston impracticable by the force now there. Says Dahlgren had been a good deal ill, and there has been much to discourage him. The Army, he says, fails to do justice to the Navy, without which they would be speedily driven away. There have been some mistakes, errors which seem to have caused irritation

between the two branches of the service. Dahlgren has not spared himself, and his long and arduous labors have been such as would wear down a more robust man. More than exhausting physical labors have been the mental anxieties he has endured—The loss of his two fleet captains, jealousies as to his professional advancement without corresponding sea service or naval achievement in battle, the morbid hostility of such of the DuPont clique as remain in the squadron, army antagonism, and ignorance and prejudice fostered by it.[8]

It was obviously not a very reassuring picture of the blockade that Shufeldt drew for Welles, but the latter held firm in his belief that the numbers of the fleet were to remain at least as high as before Shufeldt came to see him. In his written reply to his restless commander, Welles gave his opinion of the value of capturing Charleston. He conceded that many difficulties were to be surmounted before such a capture and acknowledged that other places existed where the rebels might fortify themselves. Nor was he able to say whether Charleston was superior from a strategic point of view over many other places. But he did declare that the moral effect of its capture, to the Union forces, to the South, and to the world, was of great importance, and he thus desired its capture.[9] For members of the South Atlantic squadron, the "dry blockade" was to continue.

The Cruise of the *Proteus*

In spite of the long explanation urging Shufeldt back to Charleston, Welles soon gave him a change of command, transferring him, in October, to the USS *Proteus,* originally built to carry cattle for troop supplies but now converted to a gunboat; a third-rate of 1,244 tons, listed as carrying eleven guns. She was a sturdy steamer, schooner-rigged, and fully seaworthy, with a first-class crew of 210 and a battery of eight 32-pound smooth bores on the berth deck, a 200-pound Parrot rifle amidships on the spar deck, together with two 12-pound brass howitzers. In addition, on the forecastle and on the poop deck, over the captain's cabin, was a 32-pound Parrot rifle. When Shufeldt reported for command to the New York navy yard on October 9, 1863, he found the vessel would not be ready until the following March. During the intervening five months he went home to spend the winter in Stamford; his wife Sarah was ill after the loss of their son, Charles, who died at eighteen months. This loss, combined with the lonely life, the strain of bringing up their three boys, Robert, George, and Mason single-handed, and the infrequent intervals of Shufeldt's visits, took their toll emotionally. Sarah Shufeldt was ill for much of the time of Shufeldt's furlough, only recovering slowly in February. Shufeldt drew a reprimand from his mother for not sending news of the family, and she invited them to visit. But her son was anxious to be at sea again after the trying winter, and when he heard that the *Proteus* was nearly completed he headed for New York in mid-February to supervise the shipping of the crew. He decided to take his eldest son, Robert Jr., with him and had him fitted out in the uniform of a warrant officer in the navy. Robert was to serve as captain's clerk and undertook the duties of a signal officer. By mid-March the *Proteus* was ready for sea.[10]

On April 5, Shufeldt received sailing orders to cruise between Bermuda and Nassau for the protection of commerce, to intercept blockade-runners until his coal was nearly exhausted, and then to report to Acting Rear Admiral Theodorus Bailey at Key West for duty in the East Gulf squadron. From Bailey he received orders to cruise at his discretion in an area to the northward of 28° latitude and eastward of 79° longitude, to intercept and capture blockade-runners. Shufeldt thus had a roving commission to investigate and destroy, if necessary, behind a wall of blockading vessels that lay off the harbors of the eastern Gulf of Mexico and the Atlantic coast of Florida. The gunboat *Tioga* was to undertake a similar task to the southward. Permission was granted to touch at Havana or Matanzas for information, and prizes were to be sent to Boston for adjudication. Before sailing, Shufeldt's orders were modified to allow him to cruise anywhere on the Bahama Banks, or north and east of them as far as Crooked Island passage, the limits of Theodorus Bailey's command.[11]

At the end of May, Bailey ordered the *Proteus* to cruise off Cardenas, through the Nicholas Channel on the north side of Cuba to Cap Haitien, to act as a liaison with vessels of Admiral James L. Lardner's squadron and to correlate information on the movements of CSS *Florida,* known to have sailed for St. Pierre, Martinique, on May 9. From there the *Proteus* was to proceed to the northwest of Mantanilla Reef, or to the best position available to capture the *Florida,* if possible, and to intercept the commerce of the blockade-runners between Confederate ports and the Bahama Islands. Under orders such as these, the *Proteus* cruised four thousand miles and Shufeldt's crew boarded or hailed twenty-four vessels in the search for blockade-runners. But Shufeldt captured few prizes in the Civil War. He had thin luck generally, gained only $550 in prize money, and the vessels boarded usually got rid of their cargoes when the *Proteus* hove in view. Shufeldt picked off small schooners, but the big, fast steamers eluded the slower Federal vessel.[12]

At the end of June the *Proteus* took the steamer *Jupiter,* heading for Wilmington, but lost the *Let Her Be,* making for the same port, when the *Proteus* was outsteamed. This lost chance rankled with Shufeldt and he told Bailey: "from information I have obtained & from my knowledge of the ground, that if I could have a good sea going steamer, capable of 11 to 12 knots speed, and of remaining at sea fifteen days in each month, I could do much toward breaking up the illegal traffic between Nassau and Wilmington. The *Proteus* wants speed."[13] Shufeldt had similar luck in August and September. In August his crew boarded the American steamer *Santa Martha* and the British schooner *Guiding Star*, but had no evidence to detain either. At the end of the month, after taking the *Proteus* northward to lie across the Galveston-Havana line, he captured the British schooner *Ann Louisa*, from Havana, with an assorted cargo, and sent her into Key West. But two days later, in the same position, a Confederate steamer showed her heels to the *Proteus* and outran her. Robert Jr. recalled that the suspicious steamer was very nearly the same size as the *Proteus:* "We gave chase, but soon found that she was a very fast boat. We fired some fifty-six shells at her, but she kept pretty well out of our range. At one time she swung round broadside to us and hoisted a big Confederate flag—the white one that was used during the latter part of the war. We ran her into Galveston, where she loaded up with 500 bales of cotton! And with this magnificent cargo she steamed out one dark night, cautiously making her way to Havana." She was the *Francis,* a New York steamer on her first trip, and Shufeldt complained to Captain T. P. Greene, officer in charge at Key West, "this is the fourth Str. we have chased within sixty days & failed to catch for want of speed." In pursuing the steamer into Galveston, Shufeldt had abandoned chase of a schooner that he could not find on his return. "It at any rate seems a matter of regret," he added to his report, "that so many opportunities for destruction of rebel commerce should be lost for the want of an additional ½ knot per hour [*sic*]."[14]

Toward the close of 1864, Shufeldt continued cruising near the Bahama Banks and Nassau. The news of the presidential election of 1864 pleased him, and he wrote to Truman Smith that the continuation of Lincoln's administration was likely to be much better for the country than anything else. But he had not always thought that way. In August 1864, with a mixture of cliché and self-revelation, he had confided to his diary:

> I approach politics with extreme caution. I criticize our Politicians with great diffidence—I only know that the gallant old ship "Constitution" is among the breakers—I hear the roar of the torrent—I feel the force of the gale. I see the whirl & dash of the waves—and I cry—oh for the man at the helm—who can ride the storm—who can defy the elements—who can *create* destiny—*control* fate! . . . I do believe in that attribute of the human mind which links the created with the creator—which asserts its will on every thing that God has made. I pin my faith to the individual—What is history but the life of the Individual? The mere mass of humanity is the sand of the desert—blown

hither and thither by every wind of doctrine—It is the Individual who vindicates our Immortality—Whose voice is the voice of God! I believe in General Butler!

There was also more time for relaxation and thinking about others. Shufeldt swam with his son, rode horses around Key West with him, and, on one occasion, saved the boy's life when he was caught in quicksand on one of the west coast Florida beaches. The boy also found that his father did not spare him in the kind of tasks he gave to him, expecting him to bring the mail aboard ship from visiting vessels in dangerous seas. Robert Jr. remembered that "My time aboard the *Proteus* never hung heavy on my hands. I read some of the books in the captain's library; transcribed every day the ship's log into a big black book, which was to serve the captain for future reference; painted a bit, answered the letters from my mother and brothers, and enjoyed myself generally." However, Shufeldt realized the boy was not going to make a naval officer, being more interested in becoming a naturalist, and so he sent him north in the steamer *Union,* with a captured Confederate crew stowed as prisoners on board.[15]

Shufeldt began to write to his family after a long neglect. More importantly, from the perspective of his own developing ideas, he began to set down his thoughts on paper, composing poems and short essays, some crudely thought out, spliced with sea phraseology and exclamations on such topics as "Oh Woman," "At Sea," "Contraband," and "Spiritualism" but with increasing awareness of the problems of the slave in the United States and relations with other countries. He was beginning to focus on the twin problems of race and empire arising out of the Civil War.[16]

In turning to poetry to celebrate his forty-third birthday, Shufeldt reflected both poignancy and ambition:

> Thro' the thick mists of departed time,
> I trace life's pathway of hope & fear—
> As here, & now in full manhood's prime
> I stand on the brink of another year—
> I stand on the brink of "Forty-Three",
> And I look at life as it seems to me—
>   it seems to me
> Like a ship, upon a far-off sea.

The poem, which Shufeldt headed "Quarante Trois," continued in this reflective vein to recall his childhood home, "Youth's verdant shore," and the ghosts of dead friendships. The fifth verse was perhaps the most revealing of the younger man's ambitions, after which the poem groaned along to this melodramatic ending:

> But saddest of all is Ambition's wreck,
> As it floateth by, with patriot aim—
> And glorious hope on its ghostly deck
> Lost in the dirge of the Main—
> > Wailing as it sinks & for ever more
> > Deep in the Sea, which hath no shore
> > > Which hath no shore!
> Lost! Lost! for ever and ever more.
>
> Is there no port for this ship that sails
> Laden with sorrow, burthened with grief,
> Where borne along with fav'ring gales—
> She may reach—a haven of pure relief!
> > There is I'm told in an *Unknown Sea*
> > An Island as lovely as one can be,
> > > As one can be—
> Ah! there I would rest at "Forty Three"![17]

Obviously time weighed heavily on Shufeldt's hands in the last months of 1864. As the operations of the war entered their final phase and the northern armies of Grant and Sherman pincered their way toward a junction outside Petersburg, the navy was left to maintain the pressure around the beleaguered coasts. General Winfield Scott's anaconda plan had succeeded in much of its tactical application and, to many, the end was clearly in sight. Shufeldt's brother George urged him to leave the navy and come to Chicago where he would find him employment. Shufeldt declined the offer as he wished to remain in the navy for the rest of his career.[18]

In January 1865 he was ordered to cruise to Tortugas, Cape Antonio, and the Campeche Banks, with no particular limits to his cruising, within the overall area of Rear Admiral Cornelius K. Stribling's station. It was on this cruise that Shufeldt chased his last prize of the war. On February 27, in latitude 20°10' north, longitude 83°30' west, the *Proteus* fell in with the steamer *Ruby,* supposedly bound for Belize, Honduras, but suspected of aiming for St. Mark's, Florida. Among the cargo not thrown overboard was a quantity of lead. The *Ruby* was run on shore by her crew and her skeleton left for the waves to wash.[19]

The Expedition against St. Mark's, Florida

With the loss of Wilmington and the fall of Fort Fisher, the last major ports of the Confederacy were closed, and the blockade-runners had to make for smaller inlets, insecure harbors, and even sandy beaches. St. Mark's, Florida, was the last available location still in southern hands that could be used by blockade-runners of oceangoing size. Rear Admiral Stribling and Brigadier General John Newton, in command of the military district of Key West and Tortugas, determined to attack St. Mark's after a plan to land troops at Tampa or Cedar Keys, to cut off a Confederate force thought to be in the Lower Florida Peninsula, proved to be impracticable. Newton embarked the Ninety-ninth United States Colored Infantry, the Second United States Colored Infantry, and three companies of the Second Florida (United States) Cavalry (dismounted), on board the USS *Magnolia* and USS *Honduras* and moved off to Ochlockonee Buoy, near St. Mark's bar, thirteen miles from land, to meet the assembled naval force. By March 2, the steamers *Mahaska, Honduras, Magnolia, Stars and Stripes, Hibiscus, Spirea, Fort Henry,* and *Britannia,* with the schooners *O. H. Lee, Matthew Vassar,* and *Two Sisters,* had assembled, the whole force commanded by Lieutenant Commander William Gibson but soon to be turned over to Shufeldt's command. Shufeldt noted, "I have no doubt that preparation had been made by staking the channel, removing obstructions and garrisoning the fort, to make St. Mark's in some sort a compensation for the loss of Wilmington," words repeated in Stribling's report to Welles.[20]

On March 2, Stribling ordered Shufeldt to take command of the naval force and "render all the aid and assistance possible to the expedition." Shufeldt took the steamers *Proteus, Iuka, Isonomia,* and *Hendrick Hudson* to join the fleet already off the bar and on March 5 assumed control. He found that Newton and Gibson had already worked out plans to land troops to attack Newport, destroy the public establishments there, cross the St. Mark's River, take the town in the rear or, alternatively, strike the railroad between St. Mark's and Tallahassee, and disperse any isolated bodies of the enemy in order to prevent concentration against the raiding party. Smaller bodies were to land and destroy the railroad bridges over the Ochlockonee and Aucilla rivers and break the Tallahassee–St. Mark's railroad. Meanwhile, a naval force was to engage and silence the batteries at St. Mark's, land a force of five hundred to six hundred seamen at Port Leon to cover the land expedition, prevent any movement in its rear between St. Mark's and Newport, and threaten St. Mark's itself.[21]

Delays hit the expedition from the start. The naval vessels had to ride out a gale until the morning of March 4. When the fleet got underway, the pilot ran the leading vessels, *Spirea* and *Honduras,* containing troops, hard against the bar. The army forces were delayed until the fifth before they advanced toward their first objective, the East River bridge. The timing of the enterprise was out of alignment as Shufeldt arrived to command the naval force.[22]

Shufeldt found the *Honduras, Fort Henry, Hibiscus, Stars and Stripes, Britannia,* and *Mahaska* in St. Mark's Channel attempting to ascend the river but "owing to the tortuous channel and shoal water all of them more or less aground." During the day the vessels succeeded at high tide in advancing one-half mile farther. They left the *Spirea* aground by the lighthouse where she remained until lightened and towed off by the *Isonomia* on March 7. On the sixth the squadron progressed another half-mile during high tide, mainly by kedging,* the difficulties not diminishing as the vessels ascended. By Shufeldt's order, Gibson, now second in command, sent a party of men on shore to hold the bridge that connected Light House Island with the mainland and provide assistance to the land forces in any way.[23]

The naval forces pulled slowly up the river. A reconnaissance by Lieutenant Martine convinced Shufeldt that there were no artificial obstructions in the river up to the point where the *Fort Henry*'s guns would be in range. He intended to take the vessel up to Port Leon if the army were not compelled to fall back. On the morning of March 7, Shufeldt was within a mile-and-a-half of Port Leon and could see from the deck of the *Honduras* that the town was occupied with troops, probably those engaged the day before in an action with Newton's forces. The fort at St. Mark's carried four guns of heavy caliber pointing directly down river. Shufeldt later heard from Newton that a number of guns had been brought down by railroad from Tallahassee for the defense of the town. The Confederate steamer *Spray,* believed to mount four guns, could be seen in the river "actively employed during the tedious ascent either in obstructing the river near the city or in planting torpedoes." She was not expected to form more than a slight obstacle to the advance of the *Fort Henry.* Altogether, Shufeldt considered that "the town was in a better state of defence and there were many more troops in the country than I fancy Genl. Newton expected to encounter otherwise I presume he would have waited until our gun boats could have been got within supporting distance—then he could (by landing at Port Leon) have carried the works by assault."[24]

As the navy struggled up the river, the army was engaged in a bloody little engagement at the Natural Bridge. Newton had been compelled to make for the Natural Bridge when he discovered the Newport bridge had been fired by the Confederate defenders, who drove off any attempts to quell the flames. On the sixth he made two attacks on the Confederate forces at Natural Bridge and was beaten back both times. The army forces withdrew to Light House Island, reaching it at 4:00 A.M. on the seventh.[25]

---

* Winding in a hawser attached to an anchor laid some distance ahead of the vessel by the crew of one of the ship's boats.

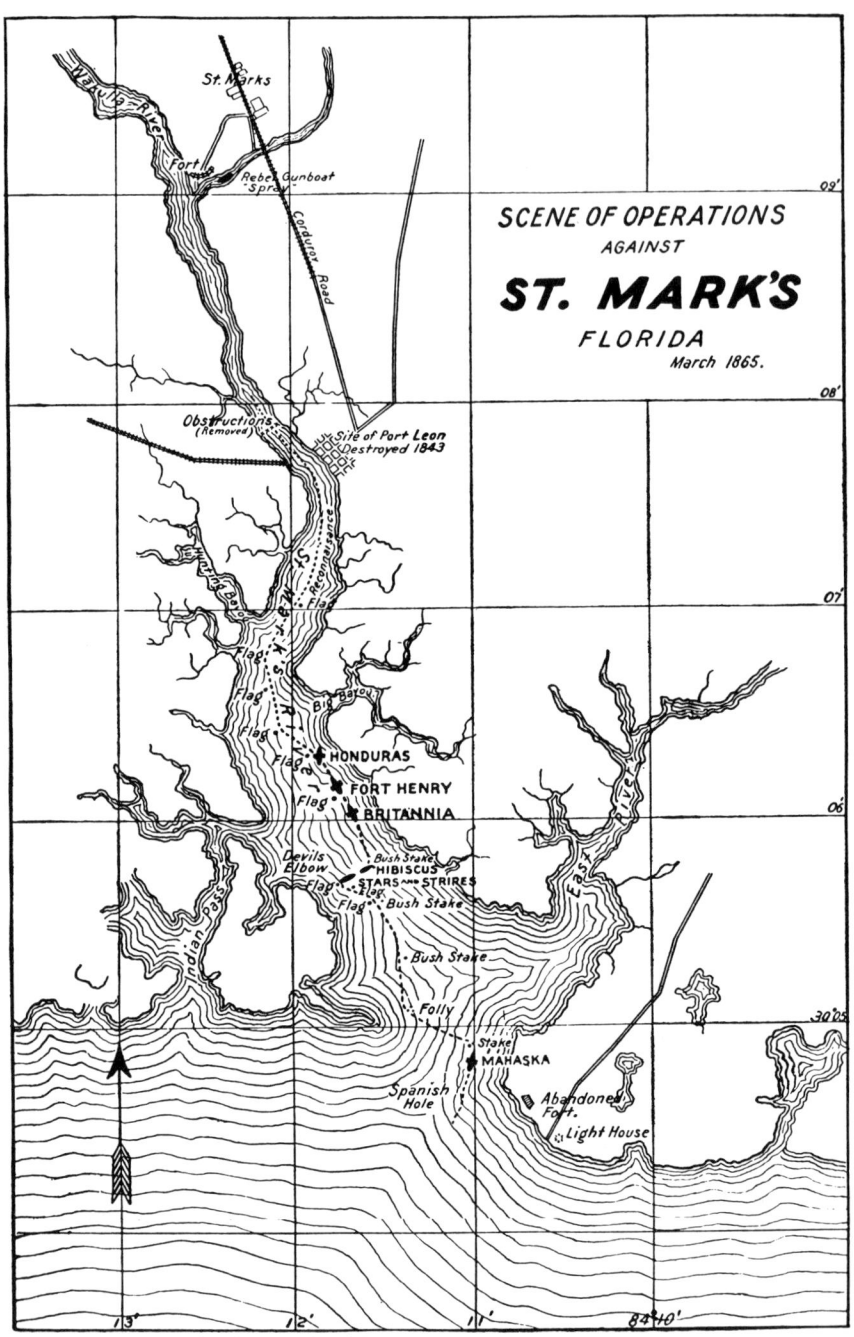

Map of the scene of naval operations against St. Mark's, Florida, March 1865. From *Official Records of the Union and Confederate Navies in the War of the Rebellion* (Washington, 1894–1914), ser. 1, 17:813.

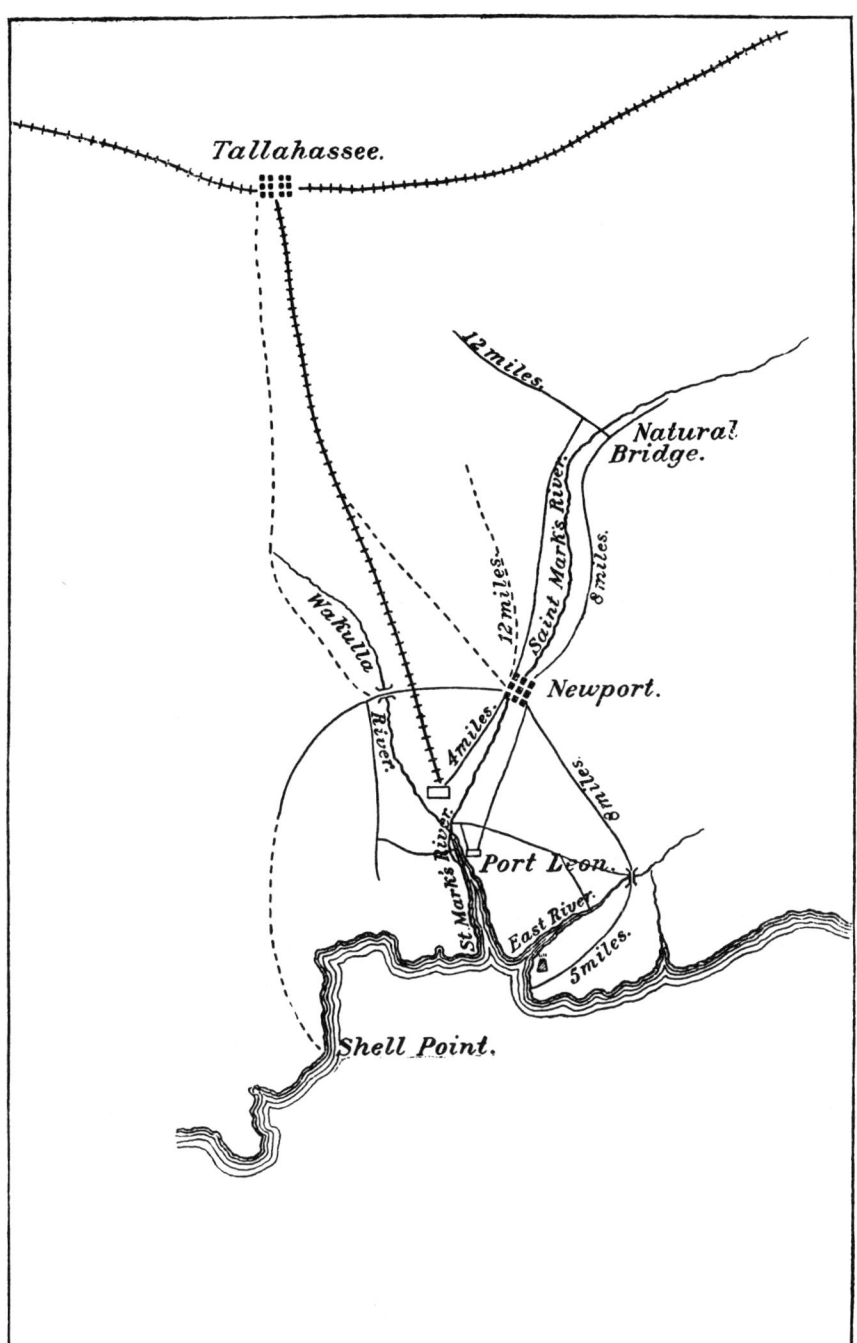

Army map of the action at the Natural Bridge, St. Mark's, Florida, March 1865. From *Official Records of the War of the Rebellion* (Washington, 1880–1901), ser. 1, 49 (1): 68.

Faced with more troops than anticipated, and with the retreat of the Union land forces, Shufeldt decided that "no successful attack could be made" with his resources. There was no reserve of ammunition or coal, and only the *Fort Henry* of all the fleet could have ascended the river with a battery of sufficient weight to bombard the fort. After an interview with Newton on the morning of March 7, during which the general stated that he had accomplished all that he contemplated for the present, Shufeldt ordered the squadron to drop down river and anchor off the lighthouse at Spanish Hole. All that the navy required, and all that it could use, had been gained by blockading the mouth of the river, for the channel above was "too shoal and crooked to make St. Mark's of any practicable Naval use." With the exercise of ordinary vigilance, Shufeldt considered that it would be impossible for the Confederates to drive the gunboats away, and equally impossible for blockade-runners to pass.[26]

The expedition failed to accomplish all of its planned objectives, despite the satisfaction that Newton had expressed on the morning of March 7. Complaints came later from Newton, who had a defeat to excuse. That the navy generally, and Shufeldt in particular, was not fully satisfied with the results is certain. Stribling reported that although the expedition "has not been attended with the success expected," it had been the means of showing the temper of the officers and men of the East Gulf blockading squadron who, "from the nature of the blockade service, have not been so situated as to render any brilliant service" but who were ready and anxious for an opportunity to show they were made "of the same stuff that gained such glorious victories at New Orleans, Fort Morgan, and Fort Fisher." Shufeldt reported that his officers and crew had shown "untiring zeal and activity" and whose disappointment at not geting under fire "had been general and sincere." Stribling wrote to Shufeldt that "the result has not been such as we expected, but there appears to have been no want of zeal on the part of the Navy." He praised Gibson's arrangements before Shufeldt's arrival and commented that "the zeal, intelligence, and industry of Commander Shufeldt, ably supported as he was by the officers and crews of the vessels, in ascending the rivers, is worthy of commendation." As the navy preened itself, all the dissatisfaction was thus expressed by General Newton.[27]

Few of the overall tactical objectives of the expedition were accomplished. Several public establishments at Newport were destroyed by the defenders in their panic, but the attacking forces did not cross the St. Mark's River, take St. Mark's in the rear, strike the railroad between there and Tallahassee, or prevent an enemy troop concentration. Neither were the railroad or river bridges over the Ochlockonee and

Aucilla destroyed. The naval force did not get to St. Mark's to silence the batteries, land a force of five hundred to six hundred seamen at Port Leon to cover the land expedition, or threaten St. Mark's. The Confederate forces did not cross the river between St. Mark's and Newport to threaten Newton's rear, but the Union naval forces could not have prevented it if they had chosen to do so. In short, the Federal forces had met with a decided repulse. But they had caused the destruction of one iron foundry, one grist mill, one saw mill, and a salt works, burned by Confederate forces, the loss of which were disasters to the people of Wakulla County. Despite these seemingly small tactical gains, the greatest strategical accomplishment belonged to the navy. Vessels of the squadron were across the bar off the mouth of the river. As Shufeldt aptly stated: "as the Navy now has possession of the mouth of the river, the only point which is of any Naval importance whatever—I consider that the object so far as we are concerned to be fully gained." The navy, however, had been across the bar on the morning of the fourth, its object gained before the troops departed.[28]

The expedition against St. Mark's virtually ended the war for Shufeldt. After returning to Key West, he patrolled to the south of Cuba, visited the principal ports of the island, and then returned to protect commerce and maintain the blockade, but he scarcely saw any blockade-runners. In Havana he was "uniformly received with courtesy by the Military and Naval Authorities of Cuba," which must have caused a wry smile to cross the face of the former consul general. At the end of April, he was ordered to take his vessel north. News of the ending of hostilities was celebrated before the *Proteus* could leave. On April 24, he was ordered to report to the commandant of the New York navy yard. Shufeldt arrived on the twenty-ninth and one week later was detached from the *Proteus* and told to await orders.[29] The long night's watch on the blockade was over.

6

The Asiatic Station, 1865–1867

Some Problems for the Postwar World

After Shufeldt left the *Proteus* and shook the sound of the Civil War out of his ears in Stamford, he soon heard from Commodore Henry Haywood Bell, newly appointed commander of the Asiatic squadron, who offered him the flag captaincy of the squadron in the USS *Brooklyn*. Shufeldt was flattered by the offer: "I trust that an association which promises to be both lengthy & intimate," he answered the new commander, "will never be otherwise than agreeable to you." Bell also imagined the "friendly regard" that he had always entertained for Shufeldt would be "closely cemented" by their future association. Both estimates proved to be overly optimistic, as relations with Bell were not to live up to Shufeldt's expectations. But his two years on the Asiatic station were crucial to his development. He learned at first hand some of the problems of American involvement in Asia. It was also the beginning of a twelve-year period during which he sought answers to questions that he raised on the role of the United States in world affairs. After 1877 he attempted to put into practice the solutions he reached during more than a decade of investigation.[1]

Soon after Shufeldt heard from Bell, the flagship was changed from the *Brooklyn* to the *Hartford,* symbol of northern pride after her prestigious Civil War success under Admiral Farragut at New Orleans and Mobile. Both Bell and Shufeldt were pleased to receive the newly overhauled *Hartford,* and the commodore urged Shufeldt to select a good sailing crew and executive officer, as he intended to run the ship under canvas. She left on August 11, 1865, making for Rio de Janeiro as her first port of call.[2]

As the flagship slipped southward, Shufeldt began to keep a diary "a sort of daily journal of the incidents and events which may transpire during the coming cruise."[3] This resolution came after Shufeldt listened to the ship's chaplain preach a "plain, sensible sermon" on the third Sunday out from New York. He considered the truth of the sermon to be found "in the deep sea beneath us and the calm blue sky above us than in words which at best must fall far short of the magnificent eloquence & musical swell of grand old ocean." After that Shufeldt checked himself. He would refrain that day from writing of his emotions. But his very next sentence mentioned the wind sighing through the rigging "with soft and melancholy cadence," reminding him of home. He confessed that the striking of the ship's bells on the hour sounded as the "knell of increasing distance from those I love." He asked himself if it was necessary to test the strength of human affection. Why did love from home, he wondered, increase in proportion to distance from it? With the sweeping generalizations that he loved to produce, he dismissed all humanity as "inconsistent" for being "only happy when we are miserable." Shufeldt's moods on such occasions were sometimes put in verses, such as a piece called "A Dream":

As over these Southern seas, I steer—
Out of the deep, doth a form appear.
E'en now this dreamy form comes to me
As night spreads her pall, upon the sea—
And stars shine bright & tropic breezes blow
Towards the North, where colder than its snow
Are my dead friendships—Come to me again
Like distant music from o'er the Main,
Comes, with that strange & mystic power
Which regilds the past, recalls the hour,
    When first I felt a bright illusion end
    Knew I had *lost* myself, nor gained a friend!

By the beginning of September he felt that he had gone so far it was "difficult to *look back*"; already he had begun to look "*ahead* thro two years of time." Surely, he asked, man must be immortal, for how could he contemplate spending two years, "so much of life's brief span . . . in the simple anticipation of returning home?" Those who went down to the sea in ships did so with a brief period of pain and a long, lingering look behind them. Then it was face forward to "the bright star—Hope" beckoning one onward until the earth was circumnavigated and home was reached "only by going away from it." On September 2, in the evening moonlight, he confessed to his diary, "I believe that God made heaven and earth—but I am sure that He made *the sea.*" Later he wrote: "I love the sea because it brings into play that part of my being nearest akin to *Power.* In the storm I glory in the consciousness of strength—In strength not to defy but to control the elements. In the calm—I rest upon the swell—like the sea bird seeming to hear music in the eternal harmony of the waters . . . the beautiful, the vital, the joyous power of *Motion!*" He considered that the sea was "Godlike" in its indestructibility and revealed, "I had almost said—Godlike it is Eternal." Shufeldt's restless moodiness after three months at his Stamford farm showed a romanticism, mysticism, and power consciousness within a mind easily triggered by contemplating sun and sky in an open vessel. By mid-October his diary writings were reinspired by the memories of his visit to Rio twenty-five years previously. He toured, and remembered, the part of the city in which he had met his first love; a moment that seemed to be "but yesterday." A quarter of a century of experience had had its effects, however. Shufeldt attended a ball on HMS *Narcissus,* met several of his countrywomen there "& flirted with them all," which he considered was "an irresistible tendency on my part to that delightful occupation—altho I am just getting into that category, which lays me liable to the approbation of 'an old fool' when thus engaged."

While in Brazil, Shufeldt renewed his acquaintance with James Watson Webb, United States minister to Brazil and the focal point of American interests there. With Webb he had a long talk about the United States' "true policy with reference to the American Republics—Empire etc." The minister agreed with his visitor that the United States government should inaugurate "a more decided American diplomacy" and let Europe "go to the d---l." This feeling was reinforced when Shufeldt was on board HMS *Narcissus.* He confessed it was difficult to forget "that before our war ended we were the subjects of their sneers & insults—I am very anti-English in my tendencies—but I think that our true policy *at present* is *peace.*" When Shufeldt ruminated on Brazil he ventured the opinion that it was destined to "become a 'black' empire and will present to the world the best field for the solution of the problem—whether he [the Negro] is capable of self government & progressive civilization."[4]

Such thoughts remained with Shufeldt after the *Hartford* moved on to South Africa by mid-November. Cape Town impressed him with its agricultural and physical attractions, but when he saw the huge earthworks being dug to improve the harbor by over six hundred convicts principally native black Africans, he devoted a long analysis to the advance of "Civilization":

> Bowing & smiling with all the amenities of cultivated life beaming upon her countenance—She [civilization] tramples upon & crushes unoffending barbarism—What law of their own—made by themselves in their own Country—have these people violated—that they should be compelled to do this thing? . . . There is *nothing* more inhuman—than the humanizing process of

civilization! No wonder that wild beasts flee before the march of progress—even the instinct of the animal—teaches it that cultivated humanity never permits mercy or justice to check its onward & fearful stride! Talk of the softening & humanizing influences of Civilization & christianity upon barbarians—they civilize & christianize—as the unmuzzled ox treadeth out the corn—by trampling & flattening upon it! Did the Creator of Man establish any arbitrary standard of human happiness? If not then has not the Kaffre and the Hottentot a right to be happy in his own way & in his own country? Show me the Divine Law for the punishment of these ignorant people by compelling them to work in chains upon an undertaking intended to increase the power of their conquerors—simply because they at some time or other have broken laws which they neither knew of or understood—I am weary of this eternal quackery in the practice of humanity—the unmeaning clatter in the preaching of Christianity. It is the argument of the Southern Slaveholder—that he christianize the Negro! Yes—as Christ was christianized upon Calvary—in blood & sweat & upon the Cross!

Shufeldt discovered that the colony had been pro-Confederate during the Civil War and had only changed its attitude when northern forces had proved victorious. Consequently, his own inclinations after studying the plight of the American Negro slave, allied with his experience in South Africa, led him to the strongest denunciation that he ever made of slavery as the "foulest blot upon the escutcheon of any nation."[5]

Cape Town, however, represented something more than an example for Shufeldt's skepticism about the advantages of civilization; he also sensed that it was the last link that bound him to the Western ways of life that he had known for over forty years:

Henceforth we are to pass two years—among a people entirely different from ourselves—a people not even seeming to have a common humanity—a people whose thoughts & feelings & sentiments flow in other channels—As people who worship other Gods—a people who claim another civilization—Like the sun—everything that is bright has risen in the *East*—Let us go & see if this brightness & glory hath forever departed from the land of its birth: Let us try & discover which of these types of Civilization & religion is the best (if any)—for *all* the sons & daughters of Man![6]

For two years Shufeldt's tour of duty thus covered a personal quest as well as his professional responsibilities as flag captain of the squadron.

Asia and the Asiatic Squadron

After running the gauntlet of tremendous seas, gales, and intense cold south of Cape Town, the Asiatic squadron soon patrolled the warmer South China Sea. Three American vessels, *Hartford, Wachusett,* and

Wyoming, began shuttling between Macao and Hong Kong. Their arrival coincided with a long plea from Isaac J. Allen, United States consul in Hong Kong, to Secretary of State Seward on the need for the protection of American commerce from Chinese pirates. In three weeks, between January 20 and February 10, 1866, six cases of successful, and a number of attempted, piracies had been reported to the consul. The pirates operated fleets of ten to twenty junks, often in sight of the harbor and in open defiance of Chinese government vessels. These junks could not be recognized once they had slipped among the others in the harbors. The only foreign patrol vessels were some old Crimean War gunboats maintained by the British, who pointed out that other nations should also provide protection for commerce.

Consul Allen desired a cooperative national effort to stamp out piracy. The alternative that appealed to him would have been disarming all junks and subjecting them to search with "the possession of arms *prima facie* evidence of piratical character." He lightly dismissed the extent to which such procedure might impinge upon the sovereign prerogatives of China. Instead, he concluded in his appeal, "if in demand thereunto, the Chinese Government should fail, or confess its inability, to restrain its own subjects from these piratical depredations upon the public commerce of other nations, those other nations might well apply such measure and mode of coercion as would best establish the security of their commerce." Allen thus hoped that the United States would cooperate actively with other powers in any measures for suppressing the crime in the Hong Kong area.[7]

Such demands on Bell's squadron kept the vessels moving over the China seas, bolaslike in their controlled orbiting near the main ports. The commodore's main instructions were to cruise for the protection of American commerce and lives. Shufeldt, under Bell's personal direction, cruised extensively in the *Hartford* between February and September 1866, touching at eight different ports in China and Japan—Macao, Hong Kong, Whampoa, Amoy, Shanghai, Nagasaki, Yokohama, and Yeddo (Tokyo)—on at least twelve separate occasions. In addition, other vessels visited Canton, Swatow, Foochow, Ningpo, Chefoo, Newchwang, Tangchow, and Taskee in China and Osaka in Japan. Shufeldt finally escaped the routine of disciplinary activity on board the *Hartford* following the untimely death of Robert Townsend, captain of the *Wachusett,* in August 1866. He was appointed to command the vessel on September 5 and immediately inherited two primary duties from his predecessor. One was to use the *Wachusett* as a flying vessel between different ports to protect American commerce against piratical depredations. The second was by way of counterpoint to this theme. Bell had instructed his commanding officers to "co-oper-

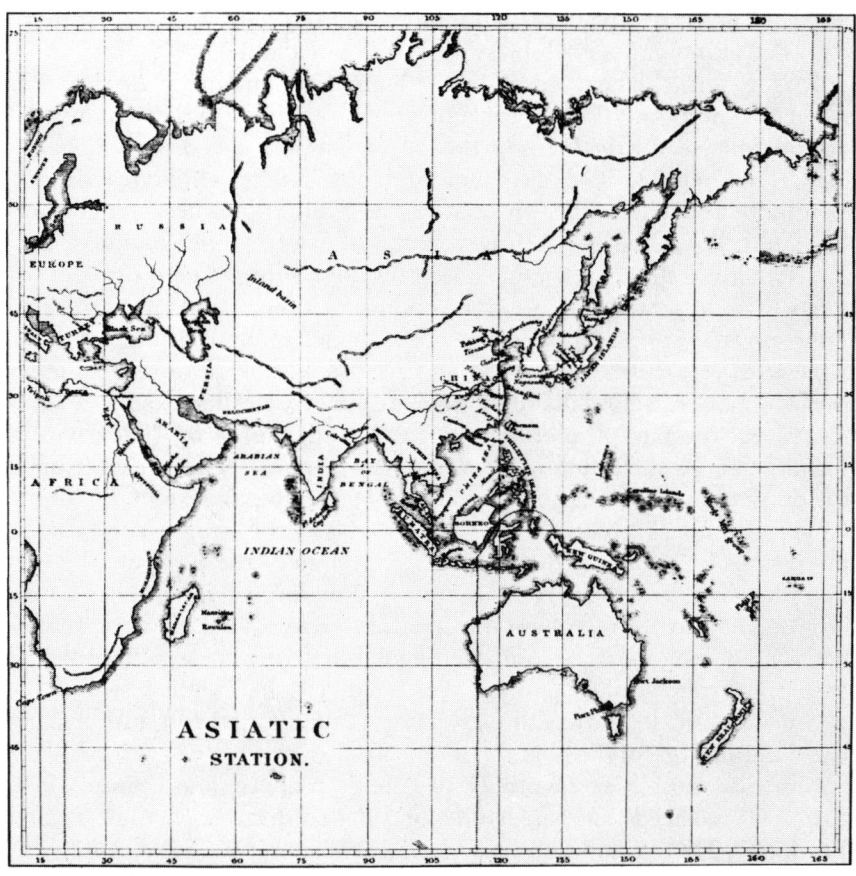

The Asiatic Station, 1866. From *Report of the Secretary of the Navy being part of the Message and Documents communicated to the two Houses of Congress at the beginning of the Third Session of the Forty-Sixth Congress* (Washington, 1880), p. 444.

ate with the British Naval Commanders, should they desire it, for these objects," and "with any Chinese authorities available."[8]

Just as Shufeldt arrived at Hong Kong on September 29, Isaac J. Allen was notifying the secretary of state of an act of piracy committed on the American brig *Lubra* of Boston, which had sailed for Yokohama on September 22. Two days out of Hong Kong, off Pedro Branco headland, the brig had been boarded by Chinese pirates, her master, Benjamin P. Holmes, and three seamen murdered, one wounded, and the remaining three crewmen chased up the rigging. The pirate group, thirty strong, looted the vessel searching for opium and treasure. The *Lubra* pirates were later caught and the leader sentenced to death after American residents in Hong Kong raised a $1,000 reward to spur on the local police. Before that denouement, however, Allen expressed anxiety about the fate of another American ship, the *Parsee,* laden with a valuable cargo including large amounts of opium. The consul judged the opium to be "a commodity peculiarly tempting to the cupidity of the Chinese pirates." He knew that the loading of the drug was known to the pirates by means of their espionage system at the port, and he was apprehensive. For these reasons, "as well as to give general assurance of protection to our merchant marine in these seas," he asked the *Wachusett* to escort the *Parsee* beyond the headlands of the coast, within which area the pirate junks operated. Such an act, he claimed, would be appreciated by the parties directly interested and by the "entire American community" of the port.[9]

Shufeldt responded favorably to Allen's request, and opium worth $100,000 received safe passage beyond Pedro Branco, en route to San Francisco. He notified Bell, now acting rear admiral, that despite various remedies made for suppressing piracy, "so long as Hong Kong is made a huge smuggling mart for the whole coast of China it must attract the rascals and desperadoes of a superabundant and not over scrupulous population." To Shufeldt piracy was "the natural companion to smuggling," which would continue as long as smuggling was made "the permanent interest of the British Govt. and the British Merchant." He counted five hundred junks at Swatow alone. In view of this numerical evidence, he asserted that piracy could not be suppressed without a very large naval force "or untill the whole character of European trade is changed." Commerce, however, could be protected. All that was required, so far as the American flag was concerned, was a comparatively limited force escorting small vessels or those containing valuable cargoes of opium or ammunition "calculated to tempt the Pirates to follow them out of Port." No inward bound vessel that Shufeldt knew of had ever been attacked, and escorting outgoing ships proved to be satisfactory to the American consul and residents of the port.[10]

Bell approved of the convoy by the *Wachusett*. He hoped Shufeldt's arrival in Hong Kong would enable him to take successful action against the perpetrators of the *Lubra* piracy but warned that as junks and fishing vessels could cruise a long way off the coast "this plan of protection will be very local in its action." With the United States warships *Shenandoah, Ashuelot,* and *Monocacy* expected in Hong Kong by the New Year, Bell was optimistic that there would always be at least two vessels in those waters. The admiral also expected to take the *Hartford* to Hong Kong in mid-December, but when he did Shufeldt was to miss this rendezvous.[11]

While cruising off the China coast, Shufeldt had a chance to study the activities of illegal traders and American missionaries. During October, as the *Wachusett* cruised among the islands between Macao and Hong Kong, Shufeldt observed the desolation and famine along the coast to the north and south of Macao, caused by the great activity in the coolie trade. Prisoners taken in local wars, as well as the young men of the villages, were sent as prisoners to Macao for the illegal trade, part of which was supported by the American steamer *Spark*. Though participation in the coolie trade was not permitted under the American flag, the *Spark* was openly active. Shufeldt regarded the trade "as a great scandal to that civilization which we profess to bring to China" and hoped that Bell would inform the American minister in China of the *Spark*'s activities.[12]

In mid-November, when the *Wachusett* visited Amoy, the United States consul, William Patterson Jones, requested a delay in Shufeldt's plans to sail again quickly. A party of Hunan soldiers who had arrived at "Chang Chow" in his consular district had "illegally taken possession of a chapel at that place belonging to certain American missionaries," headed by the Reverend John Van Nest Talmadge. The soldiers had expelled the native helpers and quartered themselves in the building. When they left, before Shufeldt arrived on November 17, they either destroyed or appropriated for their own use everything movable about the premises. Jones desired an extension of the *Wachusett*'s visit until the matter could be settled with the local taotai (intendant of circuit). Together with Jones and the British consul, Shufeldt interviewed the taotai at Amoy, who promised verbally to guarantee payment for any damages and to issue a proclamation of prohibition to avoid such troubles in the future. Had the taotai not made this promise, Shufeldt would have sent the *Wachusett* seven miles up the river and taken Jones twenty miles farther in the ship's boats, in order to gain satisfaction from the taotai at Chang Chow who, he assumed, "will immediately attend to the matter."[13]

Though Shufeldt believed that the case of the Hunan soldiers was an infringement on the rights "plainly guaranteed to Am. missionaries, in our treaties with China," and while he was prepared to use force to safeguard these rights, he was personally unhappy over missionary activity in the Orient. He considered it was a matter of regret "that these missionaries, preachers of a gospel of peace, should seem so often to need the interpretaion of a Gunboat in order to make the heathen understand them." A year later, while cruising among the Chusan Islands, Shufeldt debated the issue with an American missionary named Knowlton, based at Ningpo. Shufeldt remarked that if he had his way he would clear the lot out of China. Knowlton was stung sufficiently to write a long letter justifying Christianity and the work of the Ningpo mission as the greatest boon available to the Chinese. Shufeldt's response to Knowlton was seemingly not preserved, but he later published a damning indictment of the work of the missionaries and Christianity in China.[14]

Nevertheless, Shufeldt helped to satisfy the missionary demands at Amoy. When Jones had not received a direct reply from the Chang Chow taotai, he sought a personal interview with the acting taotai at Amoy in an effort to obtain that official's written guarantee of the payment of damages. The latter would not provide a document, merely admitting the principle of reclamation, and promised to write to the official at Chang Chow "recommending payment of just damages." Jones, however, remained both optimistic yet cynical. Granting these declarations as "the basis of only a moderate measure of good faith," he informed Shufeldt, it would be possible to settle the affair satisfactorily without further reliance upon "the tacit but potent support of your immediate presence at this port." Later Jones informed Shufeldt that everything had been settled, for the day after the *Wachusett* left Chang Chow a rumor swept it, creating great alarm, that the foreigners were going to destroy it. The taotai and the local prefect visited the chapel and damage was estimated at $40. "The authorities here are profuse in their civilities; for all of which we feel that we are much indebted to you," the grateful consul informed Shufeldt. Before that, however, Jones had informed the captain that his request need no longer influence the *Wachusett*'s movements, and Shufeldt thus took her to Whampoa for a thorough refit.[15]

Investigating the Fate of the *General Sherman*

On August 9, 1866, the *General Sherman,* a centerboard trading schooner of eighty tons (with two 12-pounder guns mounted in broadside), owned by an American named Preston and chartered by the British shipping house of Meadows and Company, based at Tientsin, set sail from Chefoo, bound for Korea. She never returned, and after the *Wachusett* had been refitted in December, Bell delegated Shufeldt to investigate the news of her loss on the west coast of Korea.[16] It was rumored that after the vessel entered the "Tai Tong" (Taedong) River her crew had been murdered and the boat burned. Other rumors mentioned survivors. From the inquiry that followed, Shufeldt began to develop an interest in Korea that eventually supplanted his Mexican-Tehuantepec dream and provided him with an idée fixe for the remainder of his life. In 1866, therefore, the investigation was important as a stage in his thinking on strange new worlds and as an excellent example of the work of the United States Asiatic Squadron after the Civil War.

Little was known in official United States government circles about Korea, a condition of ignorance common to most Western nations in the midnineteenth century.[17] The first recorded visit of any European to the country was that by a Spanish Jesuit, Father Gregario de Cespedes, in 1593. Other contacts included Dutch shipwrecked sailors in 1627 and 1653 and visits by French and British men-of-war in 1787, 1797, 1816, 1832, and 1845–1847. French Catholic missionaries gained access to the country at the end of the eighteenth century and managed to remain despite a lack of sympathy displayed by Korea's monarchical government and proexclusionist forces. In 1855, the first Americans ever to set foot in Korea, four shipwrecked sailors, were sent overland to China, but gave only brief depositions of their experiences when they met the American consul at Shanghai. In 1854 and 1866 Russian warships also visited Korea. The Russian gunboat that arrived in 1866 dropped anchor in Wonsan harbor and a letter was sent to the capital, Seoul, asking for freedom of trade with Korea. The Korean court answered that Korea was a vassal of China and the matter must be negotiated at Peking. Only a semiannual mission from China for trade and tribute was allowed across the Yalu River. But the pressures on Korea were beginning to grow and 1866 marks the beginning of the last decade during which the Koreans successfully maintained their exclusiveness.

On February 6, 1866, the regent of Korea during the minority of King Kojong, the Taewon'gun, head of the antiforeign party in Korea, ordered the expulsion of the French Roman Catholic missionaries in the country. The Chinese refused to intercede when approached, and the French government thus prepared an expedition that landed at "Île Boisée" (Kanghwa Island) in the summer of 1866, captured and burned the town of Kanghwa, but was so roughly handled by the Koreans that in the eyes of the Koreans and the Americans on the scene it suffered a severe repulse. Against this background of French demands on China and a military expedition to Korea, the attitudes of Koreans, who were normally tolerant to outsiders, native converts, and shipwreck cases, naturally hardened. In June of the same year, the American schooner *Surprise,* commanded by Captain McCaslin, had been wrecked on the west coast of the peninsula and the crew members, supplied by the local officials, sent overland to the northern "Korean gate" and passed on to the Chinese. But a different fate awaited the *General Sherman*'s crew in the Taedong River in August.

The first news of the destruction of the schooner was brought to Chefoo by Admiral Pierre Gustav Rose, commander-in-chief of the French fleet returning from Korea. At Chefoo the United States consul, E. T. Sanford, began inquires into the incident and wrote to Rose asking him to furnish all the information that he possessed. The admiral informed him that the *General Sherman* had been burned and the crew executed by order of the regent, after a request for instructions by the governor of the district in which the vessel had been wrecked. At this stage Rose was probably hoping to implicate the United States Asiatic Squadron with Korea following the French repulse. Apparently Rose had gathered most of his information from a French Catholic missionary, Father Felix Rydell, one of three French priests who escaped from Korea after being hidden by converts.[18]

Sanford, whose newsgathering activities proved to be excellent, immediately notified the American minister to China, Anson Burlingame, of the fate of the schooner. Like the French earlier, Burlingame first approached Prince Kung, head of the Tsungli Yamen (the "Office for General Management"), and apprised him of the affair. Kung disavowed all responsibility for the Korean action "and stated that the only connection between the two countries was one of ceremonial." The reply was similar to that given to the French when they sought redress for the antimissionary activity in Korea. To Burlingame, as it had done to the French, the answer implied that China was not responsible for the activities of the Koreans and that Korea was responsible for her own domestic and foreign policy. As the French had attempted to take reprisals against the Koreans, Burlingame likewise desired independent action against them. He thus wrote to Admiral Bell suggesting that action should be taken, for he supposed that following the French defeat there would be a large French fleet off Korea in the spring. The issue, he astutely observed, "will be the opening of the country," and he wished for an American presence "to rather restrain than promote aggression, and to serve to limit action to such satisfaction only as great and civilized nations should under the circumstances have from the ignorant and weak."[19]

Similarly, when Bell first heard of the *General Sherman* affair from Meadows and Company, he sought to interest the Navy Department in an expedition the following spring. He notified Gideon Welles that the squadron could be reinforced from the Pacific coast with light draft vessels and two thousand troops landed at Hamilton harbor on the largest

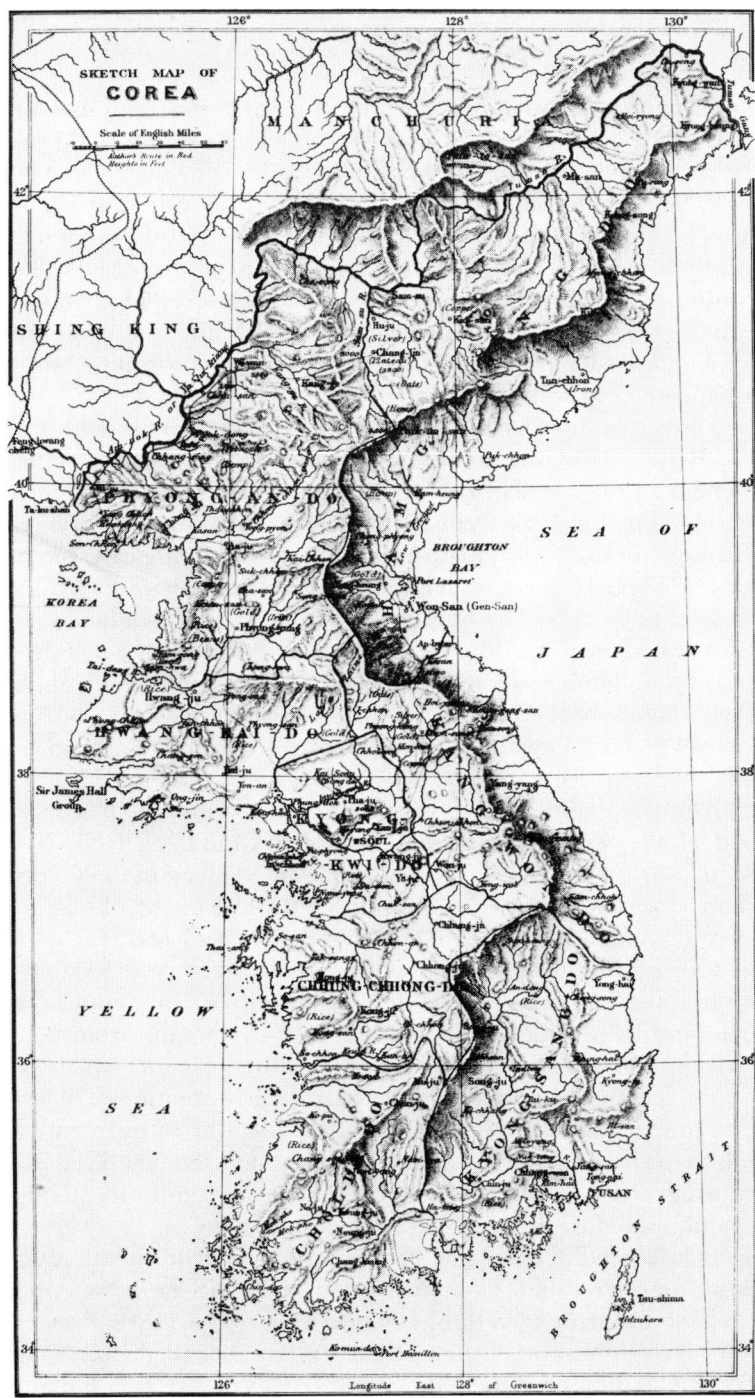

Korea in the 1880s. From William Richard Carles, *Life in Corea* (London and New York, 1888), frontispiece. Reprinted with permission of the publishers, Macmillan Press Ltd.

of a small group of islands (Nan Hoo) about forty-five miles off the southern coast of Korea. Bell believed such an expedition could capture Seoul and humble the Korean king. The benefits of such a move were obvious, he pointed out: "A blow so struck, promptly and efficiently, followed by a quiet withdrawal of our forces to California as soon as our demands are satisfied would awe not only Japan and the court of Peking into profound respect for American views and interests but would disclose to the world who are the masters of the Pacific, and make American diplomacy easy in the East as well as on our northern boundary from Vancouver to Newfoundland."[20]

Thus at the end of December 1866, Bell dispatched Shufeldt to Chefoo and Korea to investigate the circumstances of the murder of the *General Sherman*'s crew, which, besides her owner W. B. Preston, included two Americans, Page and Wilson, as master and mate, two Malays and five Chinese for crew, two British subjects, George Hogarth, the supercargo, and Robert Jermain Thomas, a Scottish missionary, together with a Chinese shroff. The only additional news that Bell could offer to Shufeldt was that a Mr. Mackie of the branch house of Meadows and Company at Chefoo had interviewed the Chinese junk pilot from Shantung who had apparently seen the *General Sherman* in Korea during the summer. The junk captain, knowing Robert Thomas, the British missionary, had agreed to pilot the *General Sherman* up the "Ping Yang" River. After four tides he discerned that the local inhabitants were hostile and left the vessel, returning in his junk to China.

As this was the only authentic information received of the schooner's fate and place of misfortune, Bell ordered Shufeldt to obtain all the information in his power at Chefoo and then proceed to the "Ping Yang," north of latitude 38°, east of longitude 125°, on the northwest coast of Korea and ascertain its defenses, approaches, depth of water, and rise and fall of tides. Moreover, he was to demand from the chief authorities "the delivery . . . on the deck of the *Wachusett*" of any survivors of the schooner, and make "such further investigation of the case as may be practicable." From there the *Wachusett* was to proceed to Port Hamilton, a sheltered anchorage on the largest of the Nan Hoo islands, off the south coast of Korea, and Shufeldt was to examine its advantages or capabilities before reporting to Bell in Shanghai.[21]

Shufeldt arrived at Shanghai early in the new year and conducted a series of interviews with Captain Bochet of HIMS *Prinoquet,* who had been on the French expedition, Captain Haswell of HMS *Pelonis*, who had met the Chinese junk pilot at Chefoo and believed from him that the *Sherman* had entered the Yalu Kiang (river), Francis P. Knight, the United States vice-consul at Newchwang, then visiting Shanghai, who informed him that Meadows and Company had revealed to him their desire to explore the Yalu Kiang, Ernest Oppert who had been in the British steamer *Emperor,* up the Kiau Kiang, and Captain McCaslin of the schooner *Surprise.* Shufeldt also obtained a chart of the Kiau Kiang in latitude 37°30′ north, longitude 125°53′ east, from Jardine, Matheson and Company.

From these conversations, in which the evidence given was sometimes contradictory, Shufeldt inferred that owing to the lateness of the season, the crew of the *General Sherman* might be en route to China and not yet heard of at the Korean gate. The only reason to suppose their treatment would be different from that received by the crew of the *Surprise,* he informed Bell, would be "the course of subsequent events with reference to the French," which "may have involved all foreigners at that time in the Country." This proved to be an accurate assessment of the conditions involving the *Sherman*'s crew.

Shufeldt's witnesses also united in declaring the coast too much unknown and of too dangerous a character to approach in midwinter, especially as the rivers, the principal means of communication with the interior, would be frozen. Given all due allowance for hastily formed opinions and imperfect knowledge, Shufeldt considered that if he took the *Wachusett* to Kanghwa, scene of the French landing, in order to communicate with the Korean government, he would identify the United States with the French and be received in a hostile manner. If he did not go to Kanghwa, where could the *Wachusett* go? There were five rivers, each of which had its advocates among the interviewees and each dangerous to approach. Shufeldt's own inclination on January 8 was to go to "the harbor of Choson [Inch'on]," about seventy leagues from Seoul. There he hoped to communicate with the authorities, first of all thanking them for their kindness to the crew of the *Surprise,* and then enquiring about the crew of the *General Sherman.* Shufeldt supposed the crew might be alive until he learned the opposite. His subsequent proceedings would not be prejudiced by such a course of action and it would, in the meanwhile, "avoid a serious difficulty." But he regretted that Bell was not in possession of more definite information before giving him his orders, and he hoped that if he diverged from his instructions the admiral would consider "the mist in which this whole thing has been involved and the absolute necessity for the exercise of individual judgement when removed so far from superior authority."[22]

In this frame of mind Shufeldt met Father Rydell. From the French priest he learned that the crew had definitely been murdered and the boat burned in the Taedong River. This river emptied into the Yellow Sea about 120 miles northwest of Seoul in the province of P'yongan. Rydell doubted if Shufeldt could obtain a Korean pilot to take the *Wachusett* to Kanghwa Island even if the rivers were not frozen. He explained that the natives would either all run away or, if questioned by Shufeldt's party, would be beheaded with all their families by officials after Shufeldt's departure. Shufeldt thus deemed it would be inadvisable to attempt to reach the mouth of the Taedong River in winter and doubted if any communication could be held with the Korean government at any point other than near to Choson (Inch'on).[23]

From Shanghai, Shufeldt moved to Chefoo, where he arrived on January 14. There he interviewed the Chinese pilot, who confirmed the evidence that Bell had passed to Shufeldt. The *Sherman* had cleared for Posyeta, a Russian port on the northeast boundary of Korean and Russian possessions. After touching at Chefoo she had entered the Taedong. But a serious discrepancy developed in the testimony of the Chinese pilot and Father Rydell. The priest asserted that there were about nineteen or twenty people on board, who were captured or beheaded by order of the regent, the Taewon'gun, a natural enough inference from one who had been smuggled out of Korea to avoid persecution. The pilot maintained there were twenty-seven people on board, who were murdered by the mob of a native village. The mob was convinced that the schooner was a pirate vessel and became incensed the higher she ascended the river. When the *Sherman* was carried by unusually high tides over Crow rapids, normally an impediment to vessels of her size, and then anchored just above Yang Jak Island, the crowd set fire to the vessel with fire rafts and murdered the crew on shore. Eventually, Shufeldt reached the conclusion that the murder was committed by the mob, that the Chinese pilot was correct, and the affair was not officially ordered by the Korean government.[24]

The pilot's account naturally cleared the Korean government of any direct implication in the massacres. The event was, therefore, not to be confused with Korean policy toward French priests and their converts. But Shufeldt reminded Bell that if the Chinese government disclaimed all control over Korea, then the voyage of the *General Sherman* was not illegal, for the vessel had violated none of the treaty obligations with China by endeavoring to enter the ports of an independent country. Thus in 1867 Shufeldt had already stumbled across the vexing question of Korea's legal and diplomatic status that was to hamper his efforts to negotiate with that country fifteen years later (see chap. 12). For his immediate purposes, however, he concluded that while the fact of China's declamation may have been unknown to the captain and charterers of the *Sherman*, it did remove the "appearance of illegality" from the voyage and give it "a more lawful claim" on the protection of his government. Such a claim could be negotiated with the Korean government directly, without the intercession of the Chinese.[25]

The First Visit to Korea

On Monday, January 21, 1867, the *Wachusett* finally set sail for Korea. Shufeldt secured the services of the Chinese pilot who had provided him with so much information on the fate of the schooner and the assistance of the Reverend Hunter Corbett, an American missionary based at Chefoo, as interpreter. Two days later the *Wachusett* anchored off the coast of Korea in latitude 38°4' north, longitude 124°50' west. Shufeldt mistakenly believed this was the mouth of the Taedong River, but he had anchored his vessel just to the north of the Sir James Hall group of islands. While there Shufeldt confirmed that the schooner had gone up what he thought was the "Ping Yang" River, fifty miles to the north of his anchorage. As the mouth of the river was frozen, and his pilot showed a marked reluctance to go near the mouth of the "Ping Yang" (the Taedong River), Shufeldt ordered the *Wachusett* to remain in "Wachusett Bay" near the Neu-to (Sir James Hall) Islands, in what is now the TaeDong Man (bay). Shufeldt was proud of the fact that his vessel was supposedly the first of foreign description to anchor on that part of the Korean coast. But Shufeldt's charts had led him to confuse the geography of the west coast of Korea. He was at a different river from that entered by the *General Sherman*.[26] Shufeldt's correspondence was thus with officials of Hwanghae Province when he should have been communicating with those from P'yongan Province.

At Wachusett Bay Shufeldt discovered that the town of "Ping Yang-so" (P'yongyang, the present capital of North Korea), the only town of any importance on the Ping Yang (Taedong) River, could not be reached by the *Wachusett* even if the vessel had moved up the coast. She could not have ascended the northerly river more than half way because only five fathoms of water were to be found thirty miles upstream. There were no official cities on the coast, although a number of fishing villages lay close by. At his anchorage, Shufeldt heard from the local people and the headmen of the two nearby villages that the crew of the *Sherman* were all murdered by villagers and not by order of the mandarin.[27]

On January 24 Shufeldt addressed a letter to His Majesty, the King of Korea, thanking him in the name of "the whole American people" for the kindness offered to the crew of the *Surprise* in June 1866 and asking what evil the people of the *General Sherman* had done "that they should have been made to suffer such cruel treatment." He requested any survivors to be delivered to him on the *Wachusett* or at any more convenient port that the monarch wished to choose. This action was especially desirable, he noted, "that the peace and friendship which has

The Northwest Coast Rivers of Korea.

hitherto been uninterrupted for many years may still continue between America and Corea." He desired a "speedy answer" in order that he "may depart in peace." Shufeldt also sent greetings to the presiding officer of the district of "Chang Yuen Heen," requesting him to forward the letter to the king.[28]

While waiting for a reply to these letters, sent through the agency of one of the local headmen and his son, Shufeldt made inquiries among the local fishermen and learned that ten of the *Sherman*'s crew were Cantonese, a people hated for their habit of coming to the Korean coast to rob and plunder. The Chinese pilot confirmed these raids "to the great dread of the whole seaboard." Furthermore, Shufeldt discovered that Hogarth, the English subject on the *Sherman*, was known for his reckless character, and "his acquaintances suppose that if a riot occurred, he would be very likely to have been one of the means of causing it." At this time Shufeldt considered that the Korean people were primarily responsible for the *Sherman* affair, but that they had an excuse from the fact that the whole of the west coast "is annually the scene of depredations and robbery on the part of the Chinese. . . . Our Pilot says that failing to purchase two Corean ponies the Capt. of the *Sherman* had determined Chinese fashion to steal them on his return down the river." Nevertheless, he believed that the government of Korea would, sooner or later, learn the lesson "taught to other Eastern nations, that it can no longer maintain that contemptuous exclusiveness which disdains all explanation or responsibility for its own acts or those of its people."[29]

About fifty miles east of the *Wachusett*'s anchorage was "HaeChow Poo" (Haeju), the capital city of the province of Hwanghae. On the morning of January 29, an official named Le Ke Yung came from this city and was brought on board the *Wachusett*. In answer to Shufeldt's questions about the letter to the king, the wreck, and the fate of the *Sherman*'s crew, Le Ke Yung replied that he knew nothing about any of these matters and he urged frequently and monotonously, that the *Wachusett* should depart immediately and return to the United States. As an official spokesman for Hwanghae Province, Le Ke Yung was correct in denying that he knew of the incident that had taken place in P'yongan Province, even though he probably would have heard of it unofficially. Shufeldt, however soon tired of his repetitions and asked what objections could there be to the *Wachusett*'s waiting for a reply. He informed the Korean that if he were obliged to leave without an answer to his dispatches "many more armed vessels" would return. Le Ke Yung declared this would be "exceedingly unjust," while to return to the United States would be "praiseworthy." At this point Shufeldt lost patience and the interview ended abruptly:

SHUFELDT: To allow your country to murder our men without cause of provocation cannot be passed over.
LE KE YUNG: I do not know anything about this business.
SHUFELDT: If you know nothing, I have nothing more to say to you.[30]

For Shufeldt the interview was unsatisfactory. He has no doubt that Le had "lied systematically from the beginning to the end," and that he was either the governor of Haeju or some high officer in his confidence. He did not imagine his letter to the king of Korea would go further than Le, the official superior of the mandarin at "Chang Yuen." He also noticed the great dread of the local population in Le's presence and did not expect further intercourse with the Korean population at that point. Shufeldt considered Le was "utterly beyond the reach of reason or agreement." He feared that the old chief and his son, both of whom had acted as his messengers, would have paid for their friendship to the Americans with their heads (which proved to be correct, for the Reverend Hunter Corbett revealed that the next year a Dr. C. W. Mateer, acting as interpreter for Commander John C. Febiger in the visit to Korea of the USS *Shenandoah,* had discovered this melancholy detail). Le's "haughty and imperious" manner had rankled with Shufeldt, who considered the Korean to be "the most perfect type of a vindictive savage." He revealed the extent of his anger to Bell when he wrote, "I determined to leave him abruptly with the impression on his mind that the result of the conference was not at all satisfactory and that it would not be the end of the investigation."[31]

Baffled by Le Ke Yung's intransigence, aware that the ship was gradually being frozen in, and fearing that he might not be able to leave until the spring, by which time the provisions would have been exhausted, Shufeldt ordered the *Wachusett* southward. He sailed toward Port Hamilton to make the survey requested by Bell. But he intended to return to his anchorage in the spring after reprovisioning. Thus when the *Wachusett* returned from Korea to Shanghai on February 5, Shufeldt forwarded charts of his anchorage and urged Bell that in view of the dangerous and uncharted waters along the coast of Korea it was advisable for a visiting ship always to have a consort with her to render proper assistance. He retained the Chinese pilot at $30 a month as the only one acquainted with the true Taedong River and the west coast of Korea, especially "as the English Naval officers already knowing him would in all probability obtain his services in the Spring."[32] Cooperation with the British had its limits.

Shufeldt was mistaken in assuming that his dispatches to the king of Korea probably went no further than the governor of Haeju. In the spring of 1868, following a report that four of the *Sherman*'s crew were still alive, Commander Febiger of the USS *Shenandoah* went up the Taedong River to investigate. He communicated with the local authorities and received a dispatch from an inspector of the Imperial Board of Directors, addressed to Shufeldt, informing him that the destruction of the *General Sherman* had arisen from the aggressive actions of the crew. Furthermore, on July 18, 1868, the *China Overland Trade Report* published a reply from the intendant of circuit in the Hwanghae district. The dispatch indicated what were the existing Korean rules for the provisioning of shipwrecked sailors and their transport overland to China. It claimed the *Sherman* affair arose from the provocation of the schooner's captain, intent on pushing up river to the provincial city. It mentioned a Frenchman, "Isuy," not described in any of Shufeldt's evidence, who seized the adjutant general of the provincial city as a hostage and who had also fired on Korean trading vessels. Eventually the crowd on shore attacked in an attempt to rescue the official. The report mentioned "tens of people" killed by cannonballs before the crowd rushed in a mass that proved irresistible. Finally, the powder store of the vessel exploded, burned the ship, and killed all on board. With considerable irony the report blamed American attempts to open the country for causing the affair: "It appeared from your honourable communication that the vessel of our guest [Shufeldt] is of a different nationality from that obtained by this Isuy. The beginning and end of this affair amount simply to this—That your honored countrys customs greatly tend to produce propriety in intercourse with others, is well known to all the province, as well as to our illustrious neighbor—China."[33]

Many years later, in the 1880s, Shufeldt indicated that after returning from Korea to Shanghai after his first visit he conceived the idea "and considered it possible to make a treaty with this Hermit Nation without the exhibition of force." But this recollection was mellowed by twenty years reorientation in his thinking about Korean affairs. In 1867 Shufeldt recommended a solution based on force. After leaving the Korean coast, en route to Port Hamilton, he notified Bell that:

If the disaster to that vessel is regarded as an act of the people of Corea, and without sufficient provocation, then it only remains to go up the "Ping yang" river at the proper season and inflict proportionate punishment at the scene of the outrage, but if viewed as an act of the Corean Govt. which may and ought to influence our policy in the East, it occurs to me that we would punish that Govt. quite as much by assailing them in the South, at Chosan for instance, a point which might eventually be of use to us to retain, rather than by going up the W. coast where the French are already operating, and which if occupied could be of no national or commercial importance.[34]

Either of these solutions would have meant the use of force and Shufeldt was quite ready to inflict it on the Koreans as a matter of national or commercial policy.

By the time he had surveyed Port Hamilton, on the largest of a group of islands which he called the "Nan Hoo" islands, off the southern Korean coast, Shufeldt expanded on his earlier views of American policy. The "Nan Hoos" were "two Gibralters [sic] on a small scale, facing each other and guarding the harbor between them." They would make an excellent base in the Far East as well as a suitable sanatorium for curing fever among the fleet's crews. Thus, though he noted privately to Bell that it had been evident that the crew of the *General Sherman* had brought its fate upon itself by imprudence and marauding intentions, he believed the Korean government ought to be taught "they could no longer maintain that contemptuous indifference to foreign power." He declared that he had withdrawn "for fear of compromising" Bell's future course of action, and he counselled the admiral: "it will not require any larger force than you have—to take possession of the whole *coast*. I believe it to be entirely defenseless, but going into the interior is of course another thing. Why not occupy Port Hamilton? We want just such a place & you have a very good pretext—& from there operate upon the *Southern* coast of Corea until that Govt. is *forced* to acknowledge at least its responsibility to foreigners?" Shufeldt's annexationist venture would have brought the United States directly into the Asian theater of war, immediately with Korea and possibly with China. The later failure of the Low-Rodgers expedition to Korea in 1871 revealed Shufeldt's mistaken assumptions about the numbers required to hold "the whole coast." But that expedition also demonstrated that Shufeldt's missionary drive and imperialism in 1867 were duplicated in official circles less than five years later.

Bell thanked Shufeldt for his activities in Korea and noted the "zeal and intelligence" that Shufeldt had shown in executing his duties. He indicated that he could lay before the Navy Department "information of a nature definite enough for the Government to act upon." Bell, in fact, recommended what Shufeldt had suggested—a punitive force to occupy Port Hamilton—to the department.[35] For the captain, however, the Korean mission was over and the *Wachusett* moved to Shanghai to resume the patrol of the Chinese coast.

Opening the Yangtze Door

Soon after his arrival at Shanghai, Shufeldt informed Bell that he intended to visit Ningpo and then proceed up the Yangtze River as far as Hankow. Consequently, when Colton Salter, the first United States consul at Hankow, wrote to him that the *Wachusett* was needed there because "we are not respected as we should be by the native authorities," Shufeldt seized the opportunity to move up the river. Salter, who had left Hankow when he deemed the local taotai had insulted the American flag, wished to return from Shanghai with the backing of a warship. Willie P. Mangum, the United States consul general at Shanghai, approved Salter's request and considered the steamer's visit would have a "happy effect in strengthening the influences of our consuls at the river ports, with the natives." Shufeldt desired to take the *Wachusett* upstream because no American man-of-war had visited Hankow since 1861, and the effect just then, he considered, would be "highly beneficial." He was concerned with more than just Salter's prestige.[36]

At that time the Shanghai Steam Navigation Company, operating under the presidency of George Tyson and the American flag, had exclusive control of the Yangtze River navigation. The *Wachusett*'s visit, Shufeldt believed, would "undoubtedly have a beneficial effect upon the Chinese Authorities . . . added to the fact that the steam navigation of the Yangtze is now exclusively an American interest." To the enthusiastic captain, the port of Hankow, in the center of the Chinese river trade, was of the "greatest importance" to the United States trade, and he could think of no other place in China where a visit from a warship was more essential.[37]

Bell approved Shufeldt's excursion. Although other United States naval vessels had entered the Yangtze River, on March 6 Consul Salter returned in triumph to Hankow, on the deck of the largest United States warship ever to visit that port to that time. The *Wachusett* remained for nine days, and Shufeldt exchanged the usual courtesy visits. On March 13, as the *Wachusett* sailed for Kiukiang, Shufeldt observed on his way down river that the north bank of the Yangtze, from twelve miles above Kiukiang to within forty miles of Hankow, was in the possession of West Nien fei banditti. The south banks were covered with destitute refugees. In the evening Shufeldt had counted seventeen towns and villages on fire. The local taotai informed Shufeldt that this band of rebels was the remnant of a force lately defeated by General Pao Ch'ao. Several of the Nien fei had been caught in Kiukiang, and the alarmed Chinese authorities had ordered a levée en masse to oppose them. With refugee country folk pouring into the city, the local taotai asked Shufeldt's support and subsequently sent an official letter declaring that while protecting foreign property, the *Wachusett* was indirectly protecting the Chinese. Shufeldt offered what aid he could, consistent with his duty, and determined to stay in the river wherever it was necessary, "until this condition of things" ceased. The Chinese naval authorities in the river, under Chin-tai-ting and the admiral of the inner river, with the gunboats of Sun, secured Kiukiang and forced the rebels back.[38]

Shufeldt claimed that the Nien fei on the bank opposite Kiukiang had been restrained by an English gunboat and the *Wachusett*. He gave no information to Bell of the activities of the Chinese gunboats, which had kept private vessels out of the Nien fei's hands. In doing this Shufeldt was probably not seeking to denigrate the Chinese performance, which had been impressive in preventing the rebels from crossing the river, so much as to justify the retention of the *Wachusett* at Kiukiang for another reason. He wished to use the vessel to promote American business interests. Shufeldt pointed out the benefits to Bell: "The immense freighting business on the Yangtze, now almost exclusively an American trade, deserves to be fostered and protected by our Government, and if in the coming revision of foreign treaties the American Minister were to succeed in opening the river to I'chan 400 miles of navigable water above Hankow—he would confer a great benefit upon the Steamboat interest which in China must always be more or less of advantage to American enterprise and Capital." This proclivity for the American freighting business was apparent in Shufeldt's connections with the Shanghai Steam Navigation Company. He had borrowed a company pilot named Gould during his cruise up river, and, in thanking President George Tyson for the services, Shufeldt hoped the voyage of the *Wachusett* had "advanced to some extent" the company's interests in China. In any case, he continued, "I know now that it is a trade which deserves all the protection which our Government can give it, and it will be a part of my duty and pleasure in connection with our voyage to report it." He reaffirmed his desire to see the river opened to the company's steamers.[39]

The effect of the *Wachusett*'s visit to Kiukiang was less decisive than Shufeldt had anticipated. Only after reaching Shanghai on March 30 did Shufeldt realize the widespread devastation and the large-scale proportions of the rebellion of the Nien fei; an uprising of much greater scope, and more successful, than the usual rebellious unrest in China. The Nien fei uprising came shortly after the Taiping Rebellion and absorbed many of the Taiping refugees. By April 9 the rebels had returned to Hankow and were threatening the city again. Colton Salter reported that the Chinese community was in "a very excited state," with hundreds of refugees flocking into the city. Nien fei spies were again reported among them, and Salter feared they were being supplied with arms and powder by foreigners in the town. He appealed to Shufeldt to serve the interests of commerce in the vicinity by revisiting Hankow and remaining for a month or two. Shufeldt attempted to return but the *Wachusett* only got to Shanghai from Foochow. He was prevented from steaming up the Yangtze again because large cracks had recently been discovered in the after part of the ship's main crankshaft, and she could not make sufficient headway against the Yangtze current under sail power alone.[40]

If Shufeldt's impact at Kiukiang was not as great as he imagined, the effect of the cruise up the Yangtze on his thoughts was deep and profound. He realized the commercial and strategic importance of the river for China and America. After discussing the opening of "the Child of the Ocean to Ichang" with Colton Salter, he prepared a scheme for Commodore Thornton A. Jenkins, chief of the Bureau of Navigation, that would have effectively lent government support to American attempts to open the river—"the best channel for American enterprise in the East"—to American trade. The "peculiar construction of Am. river steamboats" and the "aptitude which Americans possess" were the two factors that he believed gave American business a head start against other nations. He quoted the Shanghai commissioner of foreign customs to show that Americans were "in the ascendant as regards shipping" at Shanghai and "every where else." On the Yangtze, at the particular time that Shufeldt wrote, seven steamers out of nine were American-built.[41]

These steamers were owned by the Shanghai Steam Navigation Company, whose stock was held by Chinese but whose management was under the control of the American house of Russell and Company. By 1872 the company increased its fleet to nineteen vessels. In 1867, six of the vessels sailed under the American flag and two under the English, though all were American-built. Over the six hundred miles between Shanghai and Hankow the amount of foreign and domestic products carried in these vessels, from the open river ports of Kiukiang and Chinkiang, was 170,000 tons, valued at $50 million in 1866. The Chinese government received $799,351 in tonnage and export dues. Shufeldt asserted that the interests of the American and Chinese were identical in this trade; to each it was a matter of "national importance."[42]

Shufeldt was not satisfied with this harmonious state of affairs, however. He wished to push the American trade frontier four hundred miles upriver to I-ch'ang, the port from where the junks shipped nearly all of the products that went farther upstream. To reach I-ch'ang by steam, which Shufeldt considered feasible, would have meant bypassing the junks and the middlemen and opening the rich province of Szechuan, "the Garden of China." In the center of the rich tea and silk districts east of that province lay Tung-t'ing Lake, which also opened into the Yangtze a hundred and fifty miles above Hankow. Shufeldt proposed a survey to examine these waters and, following the revision of the United States treaties with China in 1868, to open the Yangtze, which would "tend very much to enhance American interests in that Country." The survey would only be a preliminary "and an entering wedge for the other which sooner or later would follow." Naturally, Shufeldt volunteered for such a survey.

Having defined the Yangtze River and I-ch'ang within the American trading orbit, Shufeldt proposed a survey of the coast of China between Yangtze and Shantung and from Tengchow (now P'eng-lai) to the Priho (Peh River near Tientsin) including part of the Yellow River, the Hwang Ho, which he declared was "at present a geographical mystery." From there he proposed to survey and report on the west coast of Korea and the islands adjacent to its southern coast. He dangled the prospects of finding gold in Korea, and if mines existed there, he speculated, "California would inundate the peninsula—as soon as it became known —& American interests would be rapidly developed." Finally, Shufeldt claimed that: "China and Japan—are both looking towards America— with most friendly gaze—not only for the trade & intercourse which they expect from the Pacific—but with a sort of feeling that the American Element is an element antagonistic to that European power whose encroachments they dread." It was, in short, an expression of the classical American assumption about China.

Shufeldt's ambitions to lead in the surveying and opening of the Yangtze and Hwang rivers, Korea, and the adjacent islands were soon thwarted. He remained at Shanghai throughout May and June, coordinating the movements between Rear Admiral Bell and the various patrolling vessels of the Asiatic squadron. Then, after Bell returned from a punitive expedition in southern Formosa (Taiwan), he ordered the *Wachusett* to cruise under sail alone among the Chusan Islands, off Chekiang Province, against pirates and "other interruptions." Bell wanted the *Wachusett* to return to Shanghai by September 1, reenter the Yangtze, and proceed as far as Nanking.[43]

After this cruise Bell decided to send the *Wachusett* back to the United Staetes with the crew members whose terms of service had expired in the other vessels of the squadron. Shufeldt mournfully confessed to Fannie V. Mangum, wife of the United States consul general Willie P. Mangum, both of whom he had become very friendly with in Shanghai, that he would leave China with regret. His family had apparently slipped into the back of his mind, and he glumly noted that "fate and the Admiral have decreed that I *must* test the question [of returning]."[44]

As the reinforced squadron assembled in Hong Kong harbor, Shufeldt believed the seven vessels were "quite magnificent," causing both pride and anxiety to the admiral. In an obvious reference to the Reconstruction measures in the United States, Shufeldt wished that before he left "we might have a dash before I go—at some foe worthy of our steel.

A war would be a blessing to the Nationality of America—make heroes *common* to the whole country—Ex Parte heroes must one day come to a discount—They deserve well of their government—but if we are to be one People—they must expect *oblivion*." He also revealed that his relationship with Bell had deteriorated. Consul Mangum considered Bell a statesman, but Shufeldt declared that "Mangum's statesman is fond of showing his power & perhaps a little of his spite—because I did not rejoin his ship—but I'd rather go home on a raft than join the *Hartford* again." Shortly after Shufeldt left China, Bell was drowned in a boating mishap. In March 1868, Shufeldt received the news and noted: "We had telegraphic news of the death of Admiral Bell. I left him at Hong Kong with a decided feeling of displeasure, but his sad fate & memories of his many virtues & many kindnesses too, have changed that feeling into one of remorse. Oh if we only knew, if we could peer into the future how much & how often would be taught the lesson of charity—How much we would forgive, if we knew that our offender would never meet us on Earth again."[45]

Shufeldt took the *Wachusett* out of Hong Kong harbor at sundown on September 18, 1867, bound for New York. He found the four-month passage via Singapore, Cape Town, and St. Helena "terribly tedious" and confessed to looking back rather than ahead for a long time—a similar trait displayed on the journey to the Orient. By the time the vessel docked at New York January 29, 1868, he had completed his reports for the heads of the Bureaus of Ordnance, Construction and Repair, and Navigation.[46] His initial exposure to Far Eastern civilization, Chinese pirates, American missionaries, consuls and diplomats, the opium trade, Koreans, and the American shipping interests in the Yangtze River valley was to be over for a decade. But it was soon clear that his thought patterns, previously concerned with Caribbean and Central American problems before the journey to the east, had now expanded to dwell upon Asiatic dilemmas for Americans, including himself, to solve.

7

The China–Cuba–Mexico Axis, 1868–1870

Dreamland Takes the Shape of Shanghai

Shufeldt's return to Reconstruction America produced emotional problems of readjustment for him. His wife was ill and "bordered closely on death" from an overdose of aconite administered by a bungling doctor. His children had outgrown his recollections. The sense of family estrangement was paralleled on the political level when he tried to acclimatize to the realities of postwar America. The state of the country disgusted him. He was aghast at the amount of money required to support his family because of inflation and considered that one could not live without a fortune. Between June and November 1868, however, he moved his family to a farm in New Canaan, six miles north of Stamford, which he acquired in exchange for the Stamford house. The farm was an estate of 213 acres; the house was about two miles from the post office and the telegraph station. He also found the domestic political scene depressing, and when writing to the Mangums in Japan, he observed that "partisan feeling in the North is intensely bitter & in the South—the sentiments which caused the war are gathering fresh strength . . .—I lose my faith, at times in the capacity of my people for self government." Glumly, he informed his friends to remain in Japan for their own political and economic well being.[1]

Depressed and despondent, Shufeldt sought solutions to the problems of financial inflation, partisan bitterness, and the reemergence of sectional antipathies in expansion, but this time he was to include Asiatic areas for consideration as well as Caribbean and Mexican. In sum, between 1868 and 1870 he tried to interest officials in the Navy Department and Congress to send surveying expeditions to China, Cuba, and Mexico. When he finally received powerful backing for survey of Tehuantepec in 1870–1871, he also reached the conclusion in the same year that the panacea for the ills of the United States was imperialism.

At first, in 1868, Shufeldt dispelled some of the ennui that haunted him by lecturing on "Western Civilization in the East" and talking on some of his "Outward Bound" experiences to the people of Stamford and New Canaan.[2] The former lecture, printed for local circulation, provided a close insight into the forty-four-year-old commander's thinking on the Orient after two years of exposure to its influences. His disgust with missionary activity, already evident in his years on the Asiatic station, surfaced early in his talk. He considered that the "introduction of protestant Christianity implies a complete subversion of society as at present constituted in China." Moreover, he had found that the missionaries he had encountered were generally living in luxurious surroundings. He presented damning testimony to his Connecticut audience, based on firsthand experience, of the imagined "hardships" that missionaries were supposed to undergo "in pursuit of their high calling in China." His cryptic comments revealed both his dislike of the pressures placed on the Chinese for religious reasons by American missionaries, and their reliance upon the power of the United States Asiatic Squadron to back them in their efforts to spread a gospel of peace.

Similarly, Shufeldt offered an exposé of the influence of opium when he discussed commerce in the Orient, pointing out the demoralization that the drug caused to large sections of Chinese society. He spoke also of the evil effect of the Chinese coolie trade, with its annual export of fifty thousand to eighty thousand coolies to Demerrara, Cuba, and the guano islands of Peru. He blamed "Western Civilization" for fostering the crime of piracy, even though he was reluctant to assert that such civilization's development of the opium trade had been the means of creating it. Although the *Wachusett* had escorted the *Parsee* and the *Lubra* out of Hong Kong when they were carrying opium, and the American vessel *Spark* had been one of the chief culprits in the coolie trade when Shufeldt was cruising off Canton, he neglected to mention these episodes to his Stamford listeners.

Instead, Shufeldt aroused the anti-British sentiments of his audience. In his conclusion he reminded his listeners that "in the foregoing remarks—it must [be] remembered—that the 'western civilization' alluded to—is purely of the European or more strictly speaking of the English type—America lies *East* from China—and now the tide which had been 'backing up,' from the West to the East—forcing English capital & power from the Indus to the Yangtsze [*sic*], is about to resume its natural flow." Such a tidal wave, he anticipated, would swamp any rival power in the Pacific for, he proposed, a new era was dawning for those distant lands:

> as everything that is bright comes from the East—even as the sun rises in the East & as still the Star of Empire westward takes its way—so China must

look to the shores of America for a new Civilization & a more vigorous regeneration. This is the natural course of events, the true march of human progress, the irresistible flow of the human tide.

A civilization will come from California, more rough & uncouth, but with kindly sympathies, it may kick & cuff & curse & swear, but it will shake the hand & if need be lend a hand to their [*sic*] pig-tailed friends, it will not hold itself aloof with haughty indifference to the joys & sorrows of Chinese life, as if it was a being of another sphere as English civilization has hitherto done. In a word China is bound to come into the family of nations—thro' the rough & tumble process of Californian energy—unpremeditated—against her will—in fact before she knows it there will be a total topsy turvey change at least on the sea borders of that inimitable Empire.

The pacific is the ocean bride of America—China & Japan & Corea—with their innumerable islands, hanging like necklaces about them, are the bridesmaids, California is the nuptial couch, the bridal chamber, where all the wealth of the Orient will be brought to celebrate the wedding. Let us as Americans—see to it that the "bridegroom cometh" . . . let us determine while yet in our power, that no commercial rival or hostile flag can float with impunity over the long swell of the Pacific sea . . . It is on this ocean that the East & the West have thus come together, reaching the point where search for Empire ceases & human power attains its climax.

Shufeldt expected that America would "have her own" when Americans would no longer be known as "No. 2 Englishmen" in the East and when farsighted statesmanship had interlocked Russia with America, "making their interests mutual & their power irresistible." With an obvious side-glance at the purchase of Alaska, the captain had reached the same conclusions about America's westward march that Alexis de Tocqueville and Seward had, even if he viewed the interests of the two powers in a more optimistic light than they did.

This message proved enormously popular with his listeners, and the proud lecturer was pleased with his "universal success." Inspired by his reception he eagerly made plans to address the Navy Department on the prospects for his survey of the Yangtze River and to volunteer to return to China and carry out this project. He also believed that the election of 1868 would help his plans for the future. He began to look forward to a change of administrations after spending two days listening to the impeachment proceedings for President Johnson and seeing the finale or, as he succinctly put it, "la commencement du fin." As the election approached he considered Grant's victory "*almost* a sure thing," and he believed it was "essential to preserve tranquility and future progress." Over the summer he toyed with the idea of applying for consular service again, even asking Truman Smith and William P. Jones, the latter now a neighbor in New Canaan, to write to Seward for him. But he eventually changed his mind, although offered the Havana post, because, as he told the Mangums, "the political horizon is too unsettled to leave a certainty in the Navy for your branch of the public service."³

Apart from a brief spell of court martial duty in Philadelphia in October and November, however, Shufeldt remained at home in New Canaan for most of the summer, clearing the farm with his sons by day and conjuring up ancient and more contemporary spirits from the navy and China, by means of the planchette board, in the evenings with his family. He regarded the navy as "absolutely stagnant." At the end of October the assistant secretary of the navy expained to him that in all probability he would remain unemployed for a long time. Shufeldt thus feared he would be placed on waiting orders unless he struck out "on some new path." But if Grant were elected, he anticipated that Admiral David Dixon Porter would become secretary of the navy and would inject new life into the service. In the meantime, he confessed to the Mangums in Nagasaki, he would like to return to the Far East, especially to those haunts connected with his last few months at Shanghai. Even "dreamland," he admitted, "always takes the shape of Shanghai, Pootoo, etc." As fall came to New Canaan his nostalgia for the not-too-distant Chinese past was rekindled, and he instructed Fannie Mangum to tell her husband that "I long for China—I even wish for Nagasaki."⁴

The Cuban Revolution of 1868—and *The Imperialist*

Although Porter was not appointed secretary of the navy, the election of Ulysses S. Grant in 1868 opened new channels of opportunity for Shufeldt in a service essentially restricted by postwar financial retrenchment. On November 13 Shufeldt was ordered to proceed to the New York navy yard and report to the commandant, Rear Admiral Sylvanus W. Godon, on December 11 for the command of the Naval Rendezvous situated at 22 Market Street. The position was an administrative one superintending the enlistment and discharge of men. Shufeldt also found that it placed him in close contact with the activities of the Cuban junta in New York between November 1868 and January 1869. The city was in a state of excitement with daily parades in support of the Cuban revolution that had broken out when Don Manuel de Céspedes, a lawyer-planter, had raised the flag of rebellion against the Spanish government in eastern Cuba on October 10, 1868. Shufeldt's own emotional attachment to Cuba resurfaced when he produced a series of articles, on the influence of the Spaniard and the Negro and the role of the Creole on the future of Cuba, for the *Philadelphia Press*.⁵

Shufeldt's articles criticized the Spanish slaveholders, the "repressive Government," and "insidious Jesuitism" for degrading the Cuban Creoles. Cuba's only salvation was due to its proximity to the United

States, and the erstwhile commander considered that its political "regeneration" must come from the same source. Thus he proclaimed that the "distinctive Americanism" found in the natives of the island could be relied upon for "the final regeneration of Spanish America." Such was his scorn for the Cuban, however, that he believed not even a "century of progress" could bring the Creole up to a position enjoyed by the citizens of the United States.

At the end of January 1869, Shufeldt was instructed to relinquish command of the New York Naval Rendezvous. As the revolutionary storm progressed in Cuba, he reset his emotional barometer and once again contemplated applying for the postion of consul general in Havana. He wrote for help to Porter, still the senior admiral in the navy, and sent along copies of testimonials received from the State Department in 1861 and 1862. Shufeldt reminded the powerful admiral, incorrectly as it happened, that he had been recalled on account of his "loyalty to Americanism" in 1862-1863. Now, he declared, he hoped to represent the same idea on the island with advantage to the Grant administration. If Porter agreed, Shufeldt wished him to intercede with the president on his behalf. Should the position of consul general be offered, he would now accept it.[6]

In mid-April 1869 Shufeldt also got the ever-faithful Truman Smith to write twice to Charles Sumner, chairman of the Senate Foreign Relations Committee, and to Secretary of State Hamilton Fish, stressing Shufeldt's familiarity with the affairs of the island, his reliability as "a man of honor," and his high intelligence. Shufeldt, however, informed Admiral Porter that he was "unwilling" to join in "the throng of office seekers for that or any other positions." This was more calculation than modesty on Shufeldt's part. He informed Porter that his resignation from the navy would benefit others "more deserving" than himself in that service. Despite such altruism, he then referred Porter to two of his backers, senators Orris S. Ferris and William Buckingham of Connecticut, for further information and suggested that if Porter did not approve of the scheme he should return the letters and the testimonials. The admiral's views are not recorded, but the documents nestle safely in the Shufeldt papers. Instead Shufeldt soon received orders to take command of the ironclad *Miantonomoh*.[7]

At the height of his desire to find his cause among the Cuban revolutionaries, Shufeldt's pen ran riot. He produced manuscripts on the "Independence of Cuba," "The Future of Cuba," "The Annexation of Cuba," and prepared at least one general lecture on these interrelated themes.[8] Shufeldt's response was interesting, especially in view of his beliefs of the 1850s and his Civil War experiences. As a representative of northern thought on annexation in the antebellum period, he had backed away from the possibility because of its potential effect on southern expansionism and power. Even in early 1869, he still rejected the notion of annexation because it would be "the extension of the area of disaffection in our own country," which would prove to be "the most desirable to the most disloyal" and also "revive the hope of a future Southern Confederacy."

The Cuban slave also caused Shufeldt to discountenance annexation. Such a slave, he opined, would have to remain in a state of vassalage for years because "no construction of the laws of humanity" could place him "within the limits of citizenship—He is an absolute barbarian—totally unfit for the duties & responsibility of civilization." Consequently, Shufeldt asserted that the problem of the future status of the Cuban slave was one that could be solved by Cuba alone. To bring the Cuban to the United States would be to add to "the complications both here & there." The annexation of Cuba would serve as a source of weakness and distraction to the United States. To reconcile this view with his earlier expressions of 1855, Shufeldt was forced to play down the usefulness of Cuba as a naval base. The advent of steam and ironclads, he now argued, had robbed her of the title "Key of the Gulf." Cuba could offer no advantage that the United States did not already possess in Key West or Tortugas and, from the naval point of view, Shufeldt argued she was not as desirable as Bermuda, Nassau, or even St. Thomas.

On this antiannexationist point Shufeldt remained constant until May 1869. For example, in "The Independence of Cuba," written between April 13 and 25, 1869, he stated that

> the question of annexation to the United States is more difficult [than Cuban independence]. Few Cubans really desire it now—formerly yes as a perpetuation of slavery—but the Native Cuban cannot & does not care to identify himself with Anglo-Saxon progress . . . annexation to the United States means for the Cuban annihilation & or at best subordination to the Yankee . . . the question of annexation is for us still more complicated. What will we do with 600,000 Negroes—as savage as on their native coast—or the 200,000 Chinese—the lowest dregs of Canton—Will the rule of Universal suffrage work here? Extension of our domain in that direction is encouragement to another rebellion—is a reward for past treason. Let Cuba work out her own salvation.

Despite this racialistic reluctance over annexation, Shufeldt considered American influence over the future course of Cuban history was inevitable. In "The Future of Cuba," he asserted, "Our Country, by virtue of her position ought to be & by her pledges is forced to be, the mistress of Cuba's destiny, the arbiter of her fate," a type of pre-Spanish–American War sentiment akin to the later Platt Amendment. In mid-April, as he prepared to join the *Miantonomoh,* he believed that Cuban independence had already been achieved, arising out of emancipation in the United States and aided further by the revolution in Spain. Holding aloof from annexation, Shufeldt nevertheless eulogized the United States as "the exponent of liberal ideas—as the Mistress of the Western Continent" who would have a direct interest in Cuba "to see that she meets with [no?] undue interference or comes under undue influence."

To Shufeldt, the problem of Cuba also meant a chance for Americans to free themselves from European diplomacy. Thus, he passionately advocated that over the Cuban question, "heralded by the inauguration of a higher America—in the person of General Grant . . . let us take a new stand—assert our prerogatives as the mistress of this Continent & the circumadjacent islands." However, given his reluctance to see Cuban slaves gain immediate freedom, Shufeldt suggested a gradual emancipation. This would, he affirmed, need the "restraining force of military power executed by friendly hands." Loath as he was to accept annexation, Shufeldt nevertheless wished to prevent "anarchy" by sending in a regiment or two and the West Indies squadron to superintend this emancipation. Believing that the matter could be settled by merely stating his solution, Shufeldt imperiously declared in "The Independence of Cuba": "We sail under the flag of that diplomacy which asserts its pure & distinctive Americanism—which is personified in General Grant & J. Lothrop Motley—Let this Spirit pervade our Government & direct its course & Cuba under its genial influence will form the nucleus of another American Republic—developing another race towards human perfection."[9] The overall context of Shufeldt's arguments was something more than the familiar nineteenth-century theme that man was steadily moving toward an attainable perfection. He implied that this perfectionism could only be obtained within the limits of the American system, however slowly it might proceed because of the Cuban slave's innate "barbarism." Regeneration required involvement with the United States.[10]

By mid-May, however, Shufeldt had become pessimistic about the activities of the Cuban junta in New York.[11] As far as he could ascertain, the junta had $100,000 in New York banks. This money was being spent on the purchase of arms and the charter of vessels, "and getting up *spontaneous* 'mass meetings.' " The junta bought a steam tug, the *Henry Burden* from Fernandina, Florida, the schooner *Grapeshot,* which at the time Shufeldt wrote had sailed from New York and lay at Beaufort, North Carolina, and the steamer *Perritt* carrying General Thomas Jordan, late of the Confederate army, which had not been heard from since she sailed on May 4. Jordan later landed in Cuba as one of the military leaders for the junta. Altogether, Shufeldt estimated these vessels carried ten thousand arms with ammunition, "a few field pieces," and about three hundred men, of whom one hundred had returned. He was also aware that the *Quaker City* had been purchased for $86,000 for gunrunning, though she was not owned by the junta but by an unknown Englishman. Shufeldt conjectured that maybe she had been purchased by Spanish merchants in Havana, to be fitted out as a man-of-war and chartered to the Spanish government. This was unrealistic thinking on his part, for the *Quaker City* was arrested late in May 1869 in New York harbor, suspected of filibustering activity, and the Spanish had their own war vessels to deal with those belonging to the junta.

In New York City, Shufeldt observed the mass meetings and remarked laconically that "if the army of Cespedes—is as large and well clothed—as the army of Cubans who daily march up & down Broadway—The independence of the island is a fixed fact." But he openly scorned their efforts in a characteristic outburst: "of all the rising generations of men on the face of the Earth, there is none less fit to grasp the occasion, to cope with impending events than the young Cuban, degraded by a long course of moral and political servitude—contaminated in blood by miscegenation—it will take centuries to raise him to the dignity of real manhood." Shufeldt thought that the Cuban women in the city possessed much more energy than the men in the cause. He denigrated the premature outburst of the revolution and claimed it had been betrayed by a Cuban Creole, whose "treachery & deceit" as a representative of his race were "the sad results of his past education—& prophecies of his future conduct."

To Shufeldt there appeared to be a fatal want of unity of purpose, secrecy, reliability, and above all of money, as well as a "sad lack of patriotism" for the Cuban cause. Though he believed no Cuban bonds had been sold, Shufeldt knew the junta hoped to acquire two monitors being built in Peru. He wanted the Cuban group to purchase the *Hornet*, a Clyde-built paddle steamer of 870 tons. Yet when he was later offered the command of the junta's naval forces or the captaincy of the *Hornet*, he turned both offers down with the excuse that he could not jeopardize his professional career for a private enterprise. Eventually, the disappointed Shufeldt confessed to having no faith that the island would ultimately become independent. He deemed as mere pretense any efforts "to ask for forbearance in Cuba—on account of the *popular* revolution in Spain." In that country Shufeldt was convinced that the Prince of Asturias would become monarch in place of the recently abdicated Isabella II. But whatever resulted, there would be "*no* hope for Cuba," for the "terrible colonial rule" was "as fixed & inelastic as the laws of the Medes & Persians." He estimated that the best that could be maintained in Cuba in 1869 would be a desultory warfare in the mountains.

With Spain holding the seaports and "both parties equally relentless & blood-thirsty" carrying destruction and ruin wherever they could not rule, Shufeldt prophesied that "the fairest isle of the sea will become a jungle & a desert."

By the end of May 1869, Shufeldt's mental gymnastics on how to break the deadlock led him to advocate a solution he had previously rejected—annexation, "however repugnant to most of the creoles, & unacceptable to our own people." Shufeldt asserted that Cuba was a "purely *American* problem," humane, politic, and "in the end inevitable." Succinctly defining the problem in a diplomatic context, he hoped the day was not far distant "when we can let go the skirts of *European* diplomacy—to which we have been hanging ever since we were a nation." He imagined that day had dawned until jolted back to reality by the *Alabama* claims* and the Cuban dilemma. Helplessly, he watched the course of Spanish pressure on the rebels. Recalling the two and a half years of his own consular position in Havana, Shufeldt considered that he had been "crucified daily." Grimly he asked, "wouldn't the silent eloquence of the *Miantonomoh* convince the authorities of Cuba—that the American flag is sufficient protection for American citizens?" He answered himself when he added, "I should like to try it." Charles Adams, an old Civil War shipmate on the *Proteus,* thought that Shufeldt would be pleased to have Cuban troubles result in a "direct blow out with old Spain." He added, "I know you have much of the milk of human kindness and are neither revengeful or vindictive, but if I were your prisoner I should hail from anywhere except old Spain." Later still, Shufeldt commented to Willie P. Mangum that "the process of despotism had rendered them [the Cubans] unfit to be free & yet annexation only widens the sphere of our own disorders . . . we are hurrying on to our destiny with accelerated pace."[12]

As the Spanish pressure on Cuba continued, Shufeldt was detached from the New York scene. For a while he wove Chinese and Cuban desires together. He returned to his old plan to survey the Yangtze as a means of employment and began to seek information on the work of the transcontinental railroads binding California to the East and bringing commerce from the Pacific to New York. To Shufeldt, Shanghai was the

---

*The *Alabama* claims were the American demands for compensation from Great Britain arising out of the alleged unneutral acts of the latter during the Civil War, particularly the failure to stop the CSS *Alabama* from sailing from Liverpool to a career of commerce destruction of Union merchant vessels. The claims were complicated by the political opportunism of Senator Charles Sumner of Massachusetts, who raised them initially; traditional dislike of Britain, Fenianism, and Fenian raids on Canada; and the American urge to take Canada in compensation for settling the claims. Part of the claims were settled in the Treaty of Washington, May 8, 1871, and the remaining "indirect" claims were arbitrated at Geneva in September 1872.

natural terminus of the Pacific railroad. Bringing an Asia that he had recently experienced and enjoyed into the American orbit seemed then to be more promising than wrestling with solutions for a Cuba that both fascinated and yet exasperated him after more that a decade of reflection on her destiny. He therefore petitioned Porter for the command of either the USS *Ashuelot* or the USS *Monocacy* for three years. He considered that the growing importance of American interests in China and Japan would merit a survey of the upper waters of the Yangtze, and he carefully outlined the same project to Porter that he had suggested to Commodore Jenkins in 1867.

To his earlier plan, stressing the commerce of the Yangtze, Shufeldt also added a survey of Japanese waters with their "10,000 islands still comparatively unknown, tho' each successive year increasing in interest & importance." He considered it a matter of national mortification for the United States to derive constant benefits from English surveys of the China seas and yield none in return. Moreover, he confidently asserted, there would be no objection from the peoples whose borders were surveyed, "as we are known to be free from territorial aggrandisement in that direction—& are invariably regarded as protectors from European encroachments." Shufeldt's conception of Chinese views of American intentions assumed a purity about political motives strangely unrelated to economic behavior; a Reconstruction version of using the eagle's wings to shield the Chinese dragon from St. George. Porter thought the scheme worth considering on merit but was forced to reject it. In the winding down of the postwar navy, he despaired of any action. "If we live long enough to get any vessels together your ideas should be carried out," he advised the eager commander, "but at present we are so deficient that we can get but two vessels to send to Cuba, and these only for three months and with rotten rudders." Mournfully, he added, "the Navy is all gone!"[13]

Unable to procure a vessel to visit China until Cuban matters had been resolved and not yet decided on whether Cubans were fit to be admitted into common citizenship with Americans, even when he began to argue annexation, Shufeldt sat out the summer of 1869 waiting for orders and examining the state of the country. He analyzed just what was wrong with the United States for the benefit of Willie P. Mangum in Japan.[14] The president appeared to have yielded to congressional influence. The rule in government seemed to be that holding office under ex-President Andrew Johnson was *prima facie* evidence of disloyalty. Shufeldt thus counselled caution for Mangum, especially vulnerable as a Southerner, for the rush for appointments had been "absolutely *startling.*" Somewhat disillusioned, Shufeldt reflected that this state of affairs furnished to all thinking men "a sad commentary upon our system—& preparing them for a revolution which seems sooner or later to be inevitable." He also revealed to Mangum that he had been in Washington during and immediately after Grant's inauguration and had "never felt more profound disgust—at the unscrupulous intrigue—the reckless political immorality which seems to pervade every branch of the Government." Patriotism and honesty, both cardinal virtues for Shufeldt, seemed to have been submerged in a vast sea of corruption, and he told Mangum that "there is but little here that does not sadden the true lover of his country—weigh him down with a sense of impending calamity."

Understandably, he watched the course of events. One straw in the wind that he noted was the founding of a newpaper in New York, *The Imperialist*, with a crown on its masthead and the motto "Let us have peace." Four years earlier, he observed, it would not have had a single reader. Now it professed to be the organ of a "wide spread but secret order" whose object was "empire for the security of property & the preservation of liberty." He told Mangum that the United States was hurrying to its destiny with accelerated pace. Above the whirl and the rush, in words later recalled in the views of Brooks Adams at the turn of the century, Shufeldt imagined that he saw "the man on horseback." Unlike Adams, who found his apocalyptic figure in Theodore Roosevelt, Shufeldt discovered the image "does not resemble 'the hero of Appotomax' [*sic*]." But Shufeldt's sense of impending gloom was similar to Adams' fears. Despondently, he reached his conclusions for the future, and he implied that he accepted the *Imperialist*'s arguments on race:

> Every age says the Philosopher has its infallible remedies for humanities ill & every succeeding age discovers their fallacy—Negro emancipation was the panacea—which was to cure all of our political evils—The Negroes free & equal & lo! our troubles have only commenced. The Chinaman is also coming upon the scene—What the darkey is to the South, the Irishman to the East—Johnny Chinaman is to be to the West—& again the question is bound to come up—of the inferiority of races—Universal suffrage (male & female) in this mixed condition of races & colors, is simply impossible—the result therefore appears to be inevitable viz. Imperialism.

As Shufeldt cut the Gordian Knot, his personal problems were not so easily solved. "As for me," he told the Mangums, "I am not what I am —I am a creature of illusions—phantasms. . . . The shadow is the thing I grasp—the reality is gone forever." He asked the Mangums if they had read Grant's message on Cuba: "He deliberately kills Cuba—slaughters the infant Republic in cold blood—A lesson he learned in the war . . . America crushes out the germ of liberty on the beautiful isle . . . I abjure America—shall I come to China and find true liberty!" In mourning Grant's solution for Cuba, and prevented from returning to the Far East for the present, Shufeldt's restlessness welled up once again. As a solution he directed his thoughts to yet another project that would fall under this imperial mantle and also fulfill his personal ambitions. Almost inevitably, his eyes once more turned toward the Isthmus of Tehuantepec. Whether or not he was about to chase another illusion, he was succumbing to the lure of dominating the isthmus again.

Negotiations for an Isthmian Survey

At the end of April 1870, Shufeldt was detached from the command of the *Miantonomoh* and offered a choice of two shore commands, as either inspector of ordnance at Portsmouth navy yard, New Hampshire, or officer in charge of the New York Naval Rendezvous. His wife Sarah, ill with heart problems, depressed and lonely, wished him to take the former. But he had other ideas. He had been commissioned a captain, to date from December 31, 1869, and he did not intend to be tied to a desk job in a shore establishment that offered no prospects for expansion. Thus, though he took the Portsmouth position during the summer of 1870, Shufeldt used it as a stopgap until he could bring pressure to bear on the government for a survey to determine the practicability of an isthmian canal at Tehuantepec.[15]

Initially, Shufeldt was concerned about the problems of American commerce, but he also had other things in mind. He carefully jotted down the reasons why such a survey of the isthmus would be justified in terms of access to Asia:

> An experience of 12 years in the Commercial service on this Atlantic seaboard—has convinced me—that the supremacy of the Atlantic ocean—has gone from America. The great Powers in Europe, viz England, Prussia & France, are so to speak "too many guns" for us. . . . The Pacific Ocean, with its long swell & gentle breezes lies waiting for the American flag. Alaska & the Aleutian isles form the arm which America is stretching out to embrace the Nations & the commerce of the East. A recent cruise of three years in China & Japan—has imparted to me the full conviction—that we in accord with the laws of progress—are destined to civilize & control those nations. A Canal somewhere between the Atlantic & the Pacific is for this purpose—an absolute & an inevitable necessity.
>
> Wilfully to ignore this law of progress is a barbarism. No nation can be truly great without external Commerce—witness China.[16]

Shufeldt quickly gained powerful support. On March 18, 1870, Reuben E. Fenton of New York brought before the Senate a joint resolution that, after two readings, was referred to the Committee on Foreign Relations. It stated that it was important for the commerce of the world "and more especially that of the western hemisphere" that a ship canal should be constructed across "the American isthmus." The president was authorized to obtain the permission of the Mexican government to send a corps of engineers to survey the summit of the Isthmus of Tehuantepec to ascertain if there was sufficient water for a canal.[17]

Not until the final removal of the French from Mexico in the spring of 1867 did the United States government move toward a realization of the dream of controlling the transit route across the isthmus. On October 6, 1867, the Mexican government had granted to a company formed by Emile La Sère the privilege of opening interoceanic communications across the isthmus "by railway, carriage road, and telegraph line." This concession included large grants of land and exempted company vessels from tonnage duty at Gulf and Pacific ports on the route. The capital of the company was exempted from any import duties or taxation except the payment of 8 percent of the net profits of the company "whenever dividends shall be paid to the stockholders," and 12 cents for each through passenger carried. This grant was confirmed by the Mexican Congress, December 29, 1868, approved by President Juárez, January 2, 1869, and published in the official *Gazette* January 4. The concession fixed a time limit at May 22, 1872, subsequently extended to January 2, 1874, and re-extended until December 14, 1874, and January 2, 1876. In order to pursue the concession, La Sère formed the Tehuantepec Railway Company, incorporated in Vermont with a capital of $18 million. Nothing in the grant mentioned a ship canal and Shufeldt may have been suspicious of La Sère as one of the southerners interested in the old Louisiana–Tehuantepec Company of the 1850s. La Sère's grant was similar to others offered to private companies, whereas Fenton's resolution of March 1870 brought the United States government directly into contact with the problems involved in surveying and constructing a canal across Tehuantepec and the benefits to be reaped for American commerce if such a canal were to be American-owned or -dominated. Spurred on by the opening of the Suez Canal, President Grant and American capital investors, backed by government surveys, turned to Darien (Panama), Nicaragua, and Tehuantepec to find a shortcut to the riches of the eastern world. Thus Shufeldt refocused his thoughts on an isthmian link in a line that stretched from the Caribbean to Asia and rode the crest of a rising wave of public interest as Tehuantepec came into prominence as an alternative route for a ship canal.[18]

The navy's newest captain wrote to Senator Buckingham of Connect-

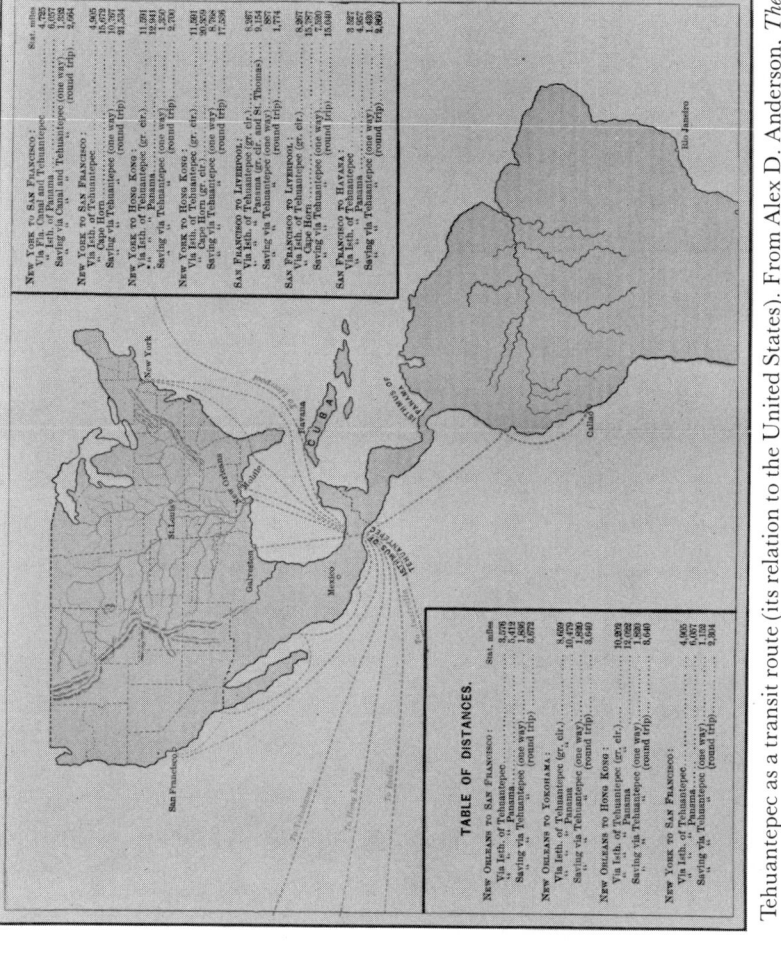

Tehuantepec as a transit route (its relation to the United States). From Alex D. Anderson, *The Tehuantepec Inter-Ocean Railroad* (New York and Chicago, 1880), following p. 58.

icut and sent a box of cigars to his mentor, Admiral Porter, informing them both of his desire to lead a surveying party to Tehuantepec. Porter assured him that he would do all that he could "to forward your views about the Tehuantepec business and when the time comes will provide you with the means of locomotion." Shufeldt had finally interested the Navy Department in one of his schemes. Between 1870 and 1873 the secretary of the navy ordered at least four different surveys for an isthmian canal route and each survey was to examine at least three possible routes at Darien and Nicaragua, as well as the one at Tehuantepec.[19]

Shufeldt was concerned not only with the technical problems of surveying a canal route but the reasons for its being cut. He discussed with close friends the serious decline of American commerce during the decade commencing with the Civil War. Whereas some of his acquaintances supported a bill introduced into Congress by Benjamin F. Butler to give differential duties (up to 20 percent in wooden ships and 25 percent in iron ships) in favor of American tonnage, Shufeldt was fully committed to making American shipping favorably competitive by shortening commercial routes in America's favor. He wished to capture the Pacific trade by means of an isthmian canal.[20]

Shufeldt's old acquaintance from the Louisiana–Tehuantepec Company, John McLeod Murphy, tried to dampen Shufeldt's ardor for the route.[21] Murphy declared that even if a route existed, which he doubted, "the attempt to construct one, would cost more than the suppression of the southern rebellion, and take longer than it did to build the Chinese walls or the pyramids of Eygpt." But Shufeldt was not dismayed by Murphy's coolness. Before June he received the blessings of the Navy Department when the secretary promised him the necessary ships and men. Shufeldt asked Murphy's help in acquiring books and maps of the area and received from his friend a copy of a map drawn in the 1850s for the Tehuantepec Railway Company, to which Murphy added some notes from his own experience on the isthmus. Murphy also suggested a possible canal route based on his own survey of the Coachapa River in 1866, and he opposed Shufeldt's choice of the Coatzacoalcos River, which was protected by a bar at the mouth that had from thirteen to seventeen feet of water, depending on the tide. Like Senator Fenton, Murphy stressed the central problem of such a survey: "the question of the *possibility* of a ship canal across the Isthmus turns wholly upon the existence of a sufficient supply of water at the summit." Using his findings from 1851, Murphy strongly doubted the possibility of such a canal. But he admitted that he had not then been looking for a ship canal, and his judgment could thus be in error. One thing was certain, he told Shufeldt, "here is 'the heart of the mystery,' and it is in your hands old fellow to 'pluck it out.' "

The USS *Potomac*. U.S. Naval Photographic Center.

Captain Charles Wilkes *(right)*, USN, Havana, November 1, 1861. This photograph, shown for the first time, is from a private collection. Sarah Abercrombie Shufeldt *(below)*, wife of Robert Wilson Shufeldt, with their infant son, Robert Jr. Daguerreotype taken in January 1851 near the time when the boy was almost lost overboard on a voyage across the Atlantic. Published by Robert Jr. in his "Life History of an American Naturalist," *Medical Life* 31, no. 3 (March 1924): 104. Reprinted with permission. Sarah Abercrombie Shufeldt *(bottom right)*, Havana, November 1861. Private collection.

"Collaborators against the *Trent*." Consul General Robert Wilson Shufeldt and Captain Charles Wilkes, Havana, November 1, 1861. Private collection.

Shufeldt's sons *(above)*, George, Robert Jr., and Mason, with Bruno, the family dog, Stamford, Connecticut, winter 1863. Robert Jr. (seated) is in the uniform of a warrant officer. The photograph was taken about the time he served with his father in the USS *Proteus*. Private collection; also published in "Life History of an American Naturalist," *Medical Life* 31, no. 3 (March 1924): 112. The crew of the USS *Proteus* boarding a brig *(right)*, drawn by Robert W. Shufeldt, Jr., and published in "Life History of an American Naturalist," *Medical Life* 31, no. 5 (May 1924): 196. Reprinted with permission.

erdeck turret, USS *Kaatskill*, Charleston Harbor. U.S. Naval Photographic Center.

The USS *Hartford (above)*, flagship of the first post-Civil War Asiatic Squadron. U.S. Naval Photographic Center. Rear Admiral Henry Haywood Bell *(right)*, commanding the Asiatic Squadron, 1866–1868. U.S. Naval Photographic Center.

USS *Wachusett,* shown here drying sails in 1874, was Shufeldt's command after the *Hartford* on the atic station. U.S. Naval Photographic Center.

Captain Robert Wilson Shufeldt, USS *Wachusett,* ca. 1867. U.S. Naval Photographic Center.

Shufeldt's proposals for solving such a mystery rejected many of the experiences of previous surveying expeditions. He suggested to Murphy that he would go down before October, during the rainy season, and remain over the winter. Murphy fully concurred in this decision, for it was the only time when the river courses and watersheds of the country could be properly observed. Through Murphy Shufeldt became acquainted with several of the engineering problems, and the best means of solving them, before he had even begun to enumerate the requirements of the expedition or plan its composition.

During June, Shufeldt pushed hard for the survey. He wrote to Henry Howard Starkweather, representative from Connecticut in the Forty-first Congress, asking for his aid. Although he personally favored Shufeldt's plan, Starkweather was not too optimistic and informed the captain that "there is a positive lack just at present among the leading men in Congress of appreciation in this direction." However, he promised to urge Shufeldt's survey upon others. Starkweather personally hoped for its success in one of the sessions of Congress and intimated the great pleasure it would give him if Shufeldt led the expedition. Shufeldt found Admiral Porter equally as helpful. In reply to Shufeldt's letter soliciting aid, Porter told him to come to Washington and "look out for the canal business." In an added postscript Porter promised, "I will do all I can to help the cause."[22]

Prospects for the Tehuantepec survey received new impetus following the failure of Commander Thomas O. Selfridge's survey to locate a route across Darien. Shufeldt hoped to obtain money and a new resolution from Congress. He asked Truman Smith to intercede with Senator Buckingham in favor of Tehuantepec. Smith did as requested and used all the contacts that he had among his old associates in the Senate, including Congressman Dawes on the House Appropriations Committee. Shufeldt also went to see Charles Sumner, who listened with interest to his plans. Sumner promised help and proved as good as his word. On July 1, 1870, he reported a joint resolution to the Senate authorizing an expedition and survey of Tehuantepec and Nicaragua and on July 4 proposed an amendment to a House bill making appropriations for sundry civil expenses of the government for the year ending June 30, 1870. Sumner's amendment authorized the president "to appoint a commission for the purpose of making an exploration and survey of the routes of Tehuantepec and Nicaragua, in order to ascertain the practicability of a ship-canal at these places between the Atlantic and Pacific Oceans." On July 11, the Senate accepted a House appropriation of $30,000 for the commission to explore and survey the two routes. From there it went to the House for final approval.[23]

Meanwhile, having failed to obtain any canal concession in the grant of 1867, the Tehuantepec Railway Company attempted to remedy the deficiency by actively pressuring Congress for aid. In April 1870, the company dispatched its engineers to the isthmus, under Colonel John J. Williams, to make the necessary surveys for a railroad and carriage road and prepare the maps and plans for submission to the Mexican government. The estimated cost of the railway and rolling stock was $7.5 million for 162.5 miles. The Mexicans approved the expedition in July 1870. Simon Stevens, president of the New York-based Tehuantepec Railway Company, and a Nicaraguan commissioner named Hollenbeck, with steamship interests on Lake Managua, were working together in Washington for the proposed survey. A powerful Nicaraguan lobby built up in Washington. Shufeldt was well aware of Stevens' interest in the outcome of his visits to Charles Sumner and William Buckingham. He used John Q. A. Ziegler, chief engineer from the *Miantonomoh,* to procure the company's pamphlets, books, and maps under the pretext of displaying an interest in the surveys.[24]

Rival canal factions appeared in Washington during June and July. The Tehuantepec Railway Company claimed it would commence work on a railroad in September. Shufeldt's chief engineer from the *Miantonomoh* did not believe it was possible, and on July 18 Ziegler notified Shufeldt that, as far as he could learn, the company had no new charter from the Mexican government. In this Ziegler was mistaken. Stevens received help from Hamilton Fish. On October 22, 1870, Fish authorized Thomas H. Nelson, United States minister in Mexico City, to negotiate the changes for the company.

> In an instruction . . . of the 10th of June, 1869, you were authorized to propose to the Mexican Government a Convention with the United States for the purpose of revising certain stipulations contained in the 8th article of the Gadsden treaty so called on behalf of the Tehuantepec Railway Company. It appears from the letter of Mr. Simon Stevens, the President of that Company . . . that it contemplates obtaining from the Mexican government a grant for the construction of a Ship canal also across the Isthmus. Mr. Stevens consequently wishes that the stipulations, desired with reference to the railway may also be made applicable to the Ship Canal.

The Tehuantepec Railway Company, however, did not approach Shufeldt too closely during the summer. He had not been officially appointed for the survey. The company directors could afford to wait and see the direction that events took. The Nicaraguan pressure group around Hollenbeck, which was having an iron steamer built at Chester, Pennsylvania, for use on Lake Nicaragua, also wished the United States government to survey its route and supported Shufeldt's survey for Nicaragua as well as for Tehuantepec. But it was threatened by a rival group, headed by Marshall O. Roberts, which was just then publicizing its own projected survey of the isthmus in New York City.[25]

In July Shufeldt went to see Congressman Butler to ask his support in the House of Representatives. Butler, like Sumner, promised help and delivered it. Truman Smith added his weight by writing to members of the House Appropriations Committee and prominent generals. On July 28, 1870, Shufeldt finally heard that the bill appropriating the $30,000 for his survey had passed the House. Later he publicly eulogized both Sumner and Butler for their efforts on his behalf. Without their help it would have been virtually impossible for him to have succeeded in obtaining the survey. With a cry of "Eureka," Captain William Temple, head of the navy's Bureau of Ordnance, passed on to Shufeldt the news of the appropriation in Bill 183, together with a message from Admiral Porter informing him to see the president. Because the Franco-Prussian War was creating a mild flurry of activity in the Navy Department, whose officials were finding out that for the first time since the end of the Civil War there was now a serious dearth of vessels, Porter could only initially offer a tug of 350 tons and a good steam launch for Shufeldt's survey.[26]

Shufeldt had not yet been appointed. The final decision lay with President Grant as to which service would use the appropriation to carry out the Tehuantepec survey. Porter promised to speak to Grant about the question when both were at Narragansett Bay late in August. He later wrote to the waiting captain that he had not had a chance to mention the subject to Grant. Porter warned that he would not be back in Washington until the beginning of October, and he gave Shufeldt a letter of introduction to the president in case he wished to see Grant at Long Beach. The letter described Shufeldt as a candidate for the Nicaragua-Coatzacoalcos survey and mentioned that "in case you conclude to give the work to the Navy I recommend him for the duty."[27]

Some time at the end of August or the beginning of September, Shufeldt saw Grant, who favored an isthmian canal controlled by the United States. The president decided to give the survey to the navy. Shufeldt later recalled: "If General Grant is anything—he is an American. He believes fully in the expansiveness & in the ultimate expansion of our institutions over the whole Continent—limiting the United States within the natural boundaries of Cape Horn & the Aurora Borealis! On the occasion he evinced exact knowledge of the country which I asked his authority to visit & predicted that by means of American Canals & railroads Mexico would sooner or later become an integral part of our own dominions." Shufeldt prepared a draft of a letter to Grant in which he noted that Tehuantepec "will remain as a monument to your fame & your patriotism." On September 3, he was formally detached from the

Portsmouth navy yard and told to report for the command of USS *Kansas* and USS *Mayflower,* both fourth-rates, to spearhead the surveying expedition for both routes. On the eleventh he finally took charge of the project that he had been assiduously working for during the previous six months.[28]

Immediately the appointment was announced, the president of the Tehuantepec Railway Company tried to influence Shufeldt's choice of staff for the survey. Simon Stevens offered all maps, plans, books, and charts of the Barnard and Sidell surveys of the 1850s, and the recent reports and maps of John J. Williams that were published in July 1870. Stevens suggested "that you do not name a principal assistant until you see him & hear his views—As a consulting Engineer Col. W[illiams] has few equals & no superiors in matters pertaining to Railways & Canals . . . His return from the Isthmus in July—having crossed over the whole line, gave him *fresh* information." Shufeldt, however, declined the offer. Murphy, who knew Williams from 1851, had informed Shufeldt that he had no faith in any report that Williams might make. Instead, Shufeldt tendered the post to the experienced engineer Silvanus Thayer Abert, who had surveyed the isthmus and in 1870 published an account of isthmian transit problems entitled *Is a Ship Canal Practicable?* Abert could not accept the post and Shufeldt next offered it to Estevan A. Fuertes, a Spanish-born engineer, a graduate of New York Polytechnic at Troy, employed by the Ministry of Public Works in Madrid from 1860–1864 and later in Puerto Rico, then in charge of one of the bureaus of the Croton Aqueduct Department of New York City Engineering Office for six years. The choice was a fortunate one. Fuertes accepted and was to prove an excellent engineer. Shufeldt struck up a friendship with him that lasted long after the expedition returned from Mexico. Shufeldt also approved the choice of Fuertes' principal assistant, R. H. Buel, and welcomed John C. Spear to the party as surgeon. One other person he attempted to appoint to the surveying expedition was Lieutenant Commander Alfred Thayer Mahan. Mahan, however, told Shufeldt, as he had told Commodore James Alden previously, that he had strong personal reasons for wishing to remain ashore near his home. Shufeldt invited George Collier Remey to be attached instead, and Remey accepted.[29]

While all of the bustle of preparation was being displayed by his engineers and assistants, Shufeldt collected his thoughts on the end purpose for which a canal, if practicable, would be needed. He carefully drafted a letter to Secretary of the Navy George M. Robeson[30] in which he stated his basic assumptions about a canal: "If it is conceded, that an interoceanic Canal through any of the Isthmus passes of the Western Hemisphere, is a necessity for the present or prospective commerce of the world; then it becomes a matter of interest to the American Govt. to select that route, which while satisfying interoceanic demands, will at the same time, conduce the most to the development of our own foreign and domestic trade." Shufeldt firmly believed that Tehuantepec assumed a primary importance over all other isthmian routes. He estimated that the canal would start from some point in the Gulf of Mexico, probably the mouth of the Coatzacoalcos River. The reason was clear in his mind: "A glance at the map will show that this Gulf could be held against any European Naval power. The channels between Cuba and Florida on the north and between Cuba and Yucatan on the West, being in the aggregate only (140) one hundred & forty miles, with Key West as a base, could always be closed effectually by our own Navy." No other isthmian route, Shufeldt pointed out, held this military advantage, and he declared that over no other would it be probable that the United States could maintain supremacy in time of war. This theme was to remain at the center of all his writings on the advantages of a canal.

The second advantage offered by Tehuantepec was that it was the shortest route between the eastern and western possessions of the United States. Shufeldt estimated the gain over Panama, between New Orleans and San Francisco, would be 1,350 miles, with proportionate advantages over other routes. Thus a steam canal boat could load at any point on the Mississippi and deliver her cargo at San Francisco in eleven or twelve days from New Orleans. It was obvious, Shufeldt noted, that a canal at this point "becomes a part of our internal water communication, as well as affording a channel for the external commerce of ourselves and of the world." In his rough drafts of these messages, Shufeldt linked these ideas about Tehuantepec, in particular, to the more sweeping ideas of capturing the commerce of the Pacific.

Both from a military and a commercial point of view, Shufeldt deemed Tehuantepec to be a point of first importance. He wished the expedition to go there first and then on to Nicaragua. The cutting of a canal would involve only the question of expense, once it was determined if there was enough water to fill it. To this problem the attentions of the expedition would be directed. Should it be solved, Shufeldt proposed to explore the lagoons on the Pacific coast in search of a natural terminus and harbor and also examine the sand bar at the mouth of the Coatzacoalcos to ascertain the possibility of dredging it to deepen the channel. Then the expedition would survey the points between the two coasts to determine the character of the soil, the natural obstacles, and the liability to inundation during the rainy season.

Shufeldt did not propose to define the character of the work to be constructed or to estimate the cost. An undertaking of such magnitude, he claimed, should not be commenced until every foot of the way had been thoroughly examined and every possible contingency calculated. His small party did not desire to be considered anything more than pioneers and explorers in the van of those who would follow in broader paths with more minute investigation and with more scientific knowledge. With these limitations defined, Shufeldt reported to Rear Admiral Melancton Smith at Washington navy yard on October 4, and, two days later, he was ordered by Robeson to proceed to Mexico and seek the permission of the Mexican government to survey the isthmus. As the expedition made ready to sail, Shufeldt brought his wife Sarah and his niece Mary "Molly" Miller on board with him. Shufeldt hoped that the expedition would give them a chance to learn something of the isthmus that had captivated his imagination for so many years. He may also have hoped that the sea cruise would revive his wife's spirits and health, but he did not know that she had less than six months to live.[31]

8

The Tehuantepec Dream, 1870–1874

The Isthmian Survey, 1870–1871

As Shufeldt prepared to take a United States surveying expedition to the isthmus that he had pressured Seward to occupy with troops and colonists during the Civil War, he did so with the belief that the construction of a canal across the isthmus would help to solve the problem of America's declining commerce. Such a canal would allow the United States to compete on favorable terms for the trade of the Pacific and Asia. Even when he served on distant naval stations after his survey of Tehuantepec was completed, Shufeldt's thoughts continued to be dominated by the isthmus. Not until the route was rejected in 1874 by a presidential commission to investigate canal routes did Shufeldt give up his Tehuantepec dream and bring to an end twenty years of personal endeavor to control the area.

In anticipation of the surveying expedition's arrival in October 1870, Thomas H. Nelson had effectively smoothed the way for Shufeldt. On October 19 Nelson invited him to Mexico City and notified him that the canal concession had passed the Mexican Congress the previous day and only needed the president's signature to become law. Delayed by a hurricane that damaged both vessels and delicate surveying instruments, the expedition did not arrive at Minatitlan, near the mouth of the Coatzacoalcos, until November 11. Once there, Shufeldt found that the Mexican government had already issued the necessary authority and permission to execute the survey. Although he visited Veracruz on November 17, Shufeldt declined Nelson's invitation to visit the capital. He had hoped to find Mexican commissioners to accompany the party but, unable to do so, he informed Nelson that it would be better for such officials to join the expedition at Chivela near the headwaters of the Coatzacoalcos.[1]

At Minatitlan, Shufeldt organized his work force into subgroups, ready to start for the interior on the twenty-eighth. One party, under the command of Lieutenant Commander Norman H. Farquhar, was detailed to take the *Kansas* to the bar at the mouth of the Coatzacoalcos River and make a line survey of the river, from the Uspanapa tributary to the sea. Together with soundings and tide surveys along the coast rivers and tributaries, this work went on under Farquhar's competent guidance over the winter, finishing in March 1871. In addition, the expedition's surgeon, John C. Spear, was given the major task of compiling a report covering the geological structure and materials, timber, agricultural products, inhabitants, and climate of the proposed route. Subjects of botanical, zoological, and archaeological interest, together with details of Indian tribes, petroleum springs, and asphalt lakes were to be studied and portable collections, where possible, made of the botanical and zoological specimens for the Smithsonian Institution museum.[2]

Shufeldt determined to lead the major surveying parties himself. On November 28, four canoes with eighteen members of the expedition on board left Minatitlan at 6:30 A.M., towed upstream by the *Mayflower*'s steam launch. When the launch broke down next day, Shufeldt returned with it to the base camp, but the canoes continued upstream powered by Indian muscles. Shufeldt soon rejoined them and for eight-and-a-half days the canoes moved into the interior until they reached La Puerta at noon on December 6. Once there the party took to mules, slowly winding up to the Chivela plains for another four-and-a-half days, hampered by runaway animals and stubborn muleteers. At Chivela the expedition established its headquarters in a house owned by an American. Shufeldt organized his inland groups while the scientific instruments were checked, notified John N. Wolf, United States vice-consul at Tehuantepec, of the expedition's arrival, and requested that he pass on the news to the military authorities of the state of Oaxaca. A band of Juchiticos Indians, in rebellion against the state authorities, passed through the camp, but Shufeldt considered them "most friendly." He was unperturbed by them and by December 14 had organized parties headed by Lieutenant Commander John R. Bartlett, George C. Remey, John C. Spear, and Estevan Fuertes.[3]

For two months, as the various groups went out in the field, Shufeldt acted as a public relations officer with the Mexican government and the members of the expedition. On December 20, he conversed with Feliciana Garcia, colonel-in-chief of the Oaxaca militia, because "the surrounding country has seemed to be in full possession of the revolutionary party in arms against the State Government." But Shufeldt did not ask for any protection, for an armed escort might "perhaps provoke an attack." At the end of December he left maps and instructions at

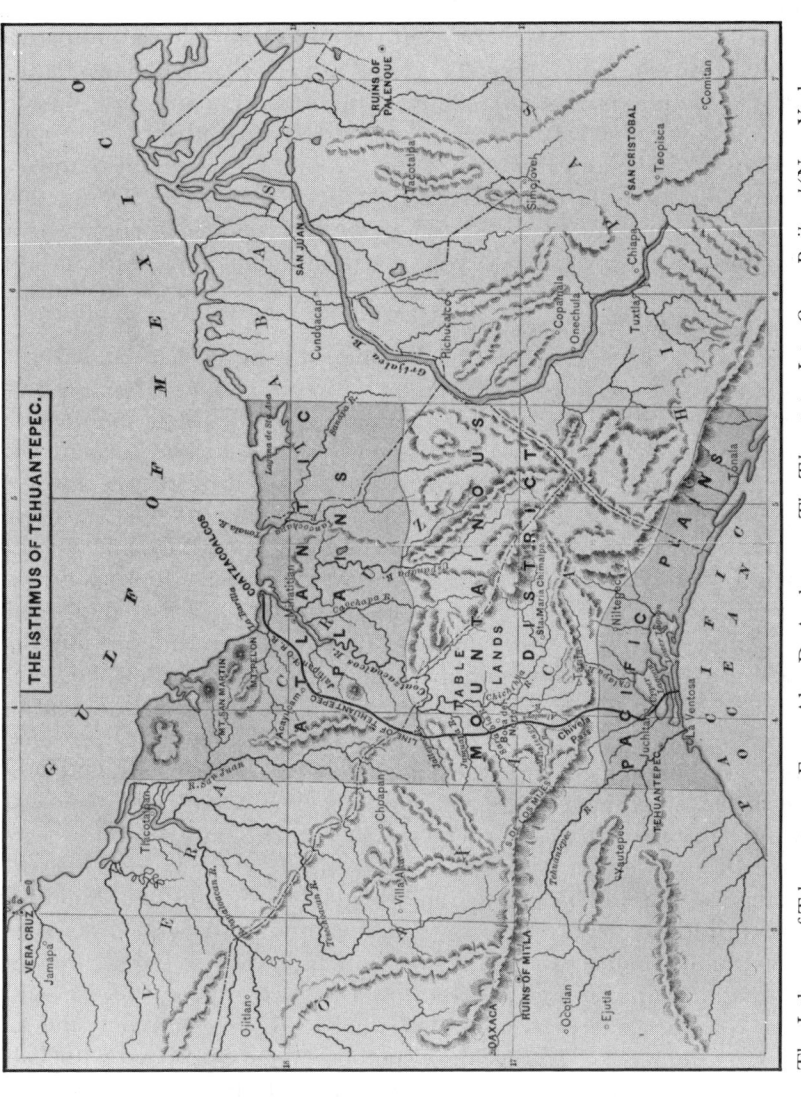

The Isthmus of Tehuantepec. From Alex D. Anderson, *The Tehuantepec Inter-Ocean Railroad* (New York and Chicago, 1880), following p. 18.

Tehuantepec for the officer from the Pacific fleet, Lieutenant Commander Alfred Hopkins, assigned to survey the proposed routes through the Pacific lagoons at Boer Bara and Ventosa. Shufeldt estimated that he would next visit the Pacific coast again about January 20, 1871, where he hoped to meet Hopkins. He was still unable to send definite news to Secretary Robeson, but he directed a reunion of working parties on his return to Chivela on January 20. There he found these parties "scattered over the plains & mountains in small numbers earnestly engaged in the work for which we were sent out." At Minatitlan, the work was as far advanced as he anticipated, though delayed by attacks of intermittent fever among the men. Farquhar's team had proceeded up the Coachapa River to survey the branch of the Coatzacoalcos, commenced operations at the bar, and had begun a preliminary reconnaissance of the Tierra Nueva River. Even at this stage, Farquhar had ruled out the Coachapa as a possible starting point.[4]

Shufeldt also found a party of Tehuantepec Railway Company engineers under Colonel John Williams at Minatitlan. The company had prepared to send the party to the isthmus at the end of November. Simon Stevens had informed the secretary of the navy that Williams would leave with "a sufficient Corps of Engineers to commence and prosecute the construction of the Tehuantepec Railway." The "breaking ground" ceremony had been set for Christmas week, and Stevens wanted the secretary to send instructions to Shufeldt's party to permit it to participate in the celebrations. Robeson left Shufeldt to exercise his own pleasure in the matter, however, and he was elsewhere on the isthmus at the time of the ceremony.[5]

Stevens' company had realized the danger that a canal, national or private, could pose for its rail interests. Pressure on the Mexican government finally gained an extension of the original concession to include the establishment on the isthmus of a canal navigable for vessels drawing not more than six meters. But the railroad activities were focused on the west bank of the Coatzacoalcos, while it soon became apparent from Shufeldt's survey that the most reasonable line should be placed on the east bank. The company eventually suspended work on the west bank pending the results of Shufeldt's survey. Later Shufeldt disclaimed all connection with "any inter-oceanic railway communication, or with any enterprise upon this isthmus, represented by individuals or by companies." In revealing this disclaimer to M. Z. Chazaro, president of the junta Popular de Sotavento, Shufeldt noted, "should we find the Isthmus of Tehuantepec capable of canalization, we can such congratulate our fellow citizens upon a discovery as grand in its future results, as any that has hitherto marked the onward march of men or contributed to the wealth & power of nations."[6]

The Tehuantepec Dream

Throughout January, Shufeldt travelled between Minatitlan, Chivela, Tehuantepec, and the headwaters of the Coatzacoalcos. But on February 8, he was urgently recalled by Norman Farquhar, who informed him that his wife, Sarah, had "a succession of her attacks with which I believe you are familiar, and also know how serious and dangerous they are." Sarah Shufeldt had experienced heart and liver problems for a long time. Farquhar urged Shufeldt to return to Minatitlan as soon as possible. He thus departed from Chivela with Dr. John Spear but on the way received news of his wife's improvement. Consequently, while Spear continued to the coast to examine Sarah, Shufeldt returned to the interior camp at Chivela and then on to Tehuantepec once more.[7]

The key to possible success of the survey lay with Estevan Fuertes' party in the mountains near Santa Maria Chimalpa. Shufeldt knew how crucial Fuertes' findings were. At the time of his wife's illness, he wrote to the engineer:

> Aside from the cause, I regret the necessity of being absent at this, perhaps the most critical moment of our visit to the Isthmus, but I know that everything will be done by you and the Corps of Officers to make the result of your work at least final, if not satisfactory. . . . I shall return at the earliest possible moment. . . . Lt. Comdr. Bartlett writes me very favorably, & if you can find the water he thinks he can find the pass & I do trust that the hopes which we have formed will be realized & that your travels through the mountains of Mexico will not have been in vain.

Fuertes, accompanied by Mexican commissioner Manuel Fernandez, had experienced trouble with the Indians, who had proved "insulting & unwilling to furnish food or assistance for the expedition." Indirectly, this proved to be a boon for the party. It drove Fuertes' men deep into the mountains for their explorations and threw them back on their own resources. They often went where the Indians would not have taken them, even if they had been more cooperative. Fernandez, however, insulted by the local alcalde, set off to bring troops, and on February 15 a company of eighty men arrived at Chivela.[8]

Two days later Fuertes wrote to Shufeldt, "I can hardly suppress my 'good spirits' and would like to scream Hurrah!!! loud enough to reach Minatitlan. *The Canal is an accomplished fact!*" Fuertes' assistant, R. H. Buel, had found a tributary of the Corte River, the Rio Blanco, about two hundred feet above the level of Chivela, that had "enough water apparently for two canals; enough power to supply turbines to pump an immense amount of water; enough height not to resort to pumping and in plain sight above this point there are two heavy falls." Fuertes modified his optimism somewhat later when he noted: "I find I say the '*Canal* is an accomplished fact.' It means in as far as the main difficulty of water and elevation is concerned. It may be possible that the route for the feeder might prove impracticable, but I have sufficient reasons to believe that such is not the case. The final success depends now, *mainly* upon the skill and energy displayed in hunting out a rout [*sic*], and not as before this last discovery, upon the eventuality of nature's shape."[9]

Highly pleased, Shufeldt notified Robeson that while there had been nothing much to report on the exploration and examination of other routes proposed by previous engineers (which he found proved to be either impracticable or too expensive for the purposes contemplated), now he was "encouraged with the hope that both the water from natural sources has been found, of sufficient elevation, & a pass through the Sierra of sufficient depression to fill & conduct a surface canal over the summit level of the Isthmus of Tehuantepec." Should this hope be realized, he wrote, the main obstacle would then consist of conducting the water from the point discovered to the pass. The next undertaking would thus be a survey of the probable line of this feeder. Shufeldt was optimistic about the results, especially as Bartlett had reported, "we have found the place for a canal, if Mr. Fuertes can find the water." To the secretary of the navy, Shufeldt pointed out: "a reference to the map of the Isthmus will show that if the reports above referred to are verified, it will only be necessary to bring the water from the Corte at the mouth of the Rio Blanco to San Miguel or its vicinity by means of natural & artificial reservoirs & aqueducts in order to fulfill the object of our exploration."[10]

In March, Remey reported that Fuertes had already traced a feeder route to the Tarifa plains to bring water for a canal. Shufeldt then drew up a memorandum asking his chief engineer to establish the exact elevation of the point selected on the Corte for the feeder, to determine the amount of water in the river at that point, to report whether a feeder could be brought from that point, to visit the Corte as near to Tarifa as possible where by means of pumps water could be raised in sufficient quantities, and to ascertain if from that point the water could be conducted to Tarifa. While Fuertes' and Bartlett's parties worked on these problems, Shufeldt carefully bottled his optimism. He informed Robeson that the Rio Corte contained sufficient water at a proper elevation for the supply of a canal but at such a distance from Tarifa pass, roughly sixty miles, that "it becomes a question whether a Canal can be considered 'practicable' when the requisite Aqueduct will involve an expense almost equal to the main work." Shufeldt believed such a canal would have to be a surface canal. He counselled that this route "above all other routes, presents the greatest advantages to our Country." Hence he was reluctant to report it was "impracticable" until every point had been given the most serious thought "and every resource has been exhausted."[11]

Finally, on April 4, Fuertes reported officially to Shufeldt that a ship canal across the Isthmus of Tehuantepec was not only practicable but that the topography presented "no extraordinary obstacles to its construction." The summit level would be reached by a feeder of about thirty miles, with water taken from the Corte near the confluence with the Blanco. Nothing else remained for Fuertes' party to do except to establish by use of the level, the true height of the summit at Tarifa. Shufeldt relayed this news to the Navy Department on April 18 and proclaimed that "it is a source of great gratification to be able to say that an interoceanic Surface Canal of any necessary dimensions may be constructed across this Isthmus." Shufeldt notified Robeson that he had arrived at this conclusion while guarding against considering "the interests of individuals or companies" and avoiding the "partial opinions of previous Explorers." The survey, he declared, had demonstrated "the practicability of this important work."[12]

In making his report, Shufeldt devoted four pages to the political condition of Oaxaca: "This state has been for years in a condition of revolution & internecine strife—resulting at the present in irreconcilable geographic divisions—In political 'partidos' whose governing motives are revenge—in insecurity for life & property & lastly as most significant for ourselves in distrust & dislike for every foreign element however apparent it may be that the introduction of that element alone can bring peace & develop the resources of the country." Shufeldt estimated that treaties would be necessary before any public works could be undertaken and deemed that if an interoceanic canal were built, "the first stipulation should be, the right of protecting American interests & the lives of American citizens." This is an excellent example of the naval officer's perennial concern to focus on the primacy of American business and commercial interests by preserving "stability" and "order" in the region.[13]

A Death and a Dream

Having accomplished his intended purpose, Shufeldt's only remaining official duties on the isthmus were involved with clearing the survey work on the Pacific coast and, at Minatitlan, packing the expedition's equipment for the return to the United States. Lieutenant Commander Alfred Hopkins reported that the survey of the Pacific lagoons was finished. His initial impressions were that "it would require a vast amount of money and constant dredging, to make a harbor in the Lagoon," but a much smaller outlay would provide for "a very good and safe harbor" at Salina Cruz. By the time Shufeldt left on April 27 Fuertes had also made his preliminary report, which reflected the optimism first expressed in his letter to Shufeldt of February 17. Fuertes estimated that the construction presented fewer difficulties than the geographical condition of the isthmus would have led one to anticipate.[14]

On April 18 the *Kansas* sailed for the United States. Some of the party went to Veracruz to return home on the mail packet boats bound for New York. Shufeldt and his family left aboard the *Mayflower*, which, after touching at Sisal, Yucatan, called at Havana. Five days later the *Mayflower* put to sea in midafternoon. Not long afterward Sarah Shufeldt, long-suffering and the victim of an apparent heart attack at Minatitlan, died on board. There is no direct evidence of how Shufeldt took the loss of his wife, though he ordered the *Mayflower* into Tybee Roads, Savannah, on the evening of May 15 and requested permission to leave the vessel to return home overland. He left the ship the next day and went directly to New Canaan. Over the summer he was morose and depressed, but there is little correspondence that reveals his thoughts during this time. Later, Shufeldt's sons, Robert and Mason, charged their father with neglect in their mother's death. There was no substance in the accusation, founded more out of jealousy at their father's growing preference for the company of his niece, Mary (whom he was soon to refer to permanently as Molly), than for his sons' company. The death of his wife was the first stage in a developing estrangement between Shufeldt and his sons that led eventually to his spurning them and adopting Molly Miller as his daughter. Robert Jr. indicated that Mary (whom he called Minnie) was some twelve years older than himself (therefore born in 1838) and in 1924 recollected that "She became a prominent factor in our family life and a disturber of the peace." The estrangement held throughout their lives. In 1924 Robert wrote that Mary, then eighty-six, lived in Washington and declared, "Personally I never come in contact with her and only see her from time to time on the streets, the last occasion being on the 9th of August, 1923, when she stood close to my wife and myself upon a street-car platform on 'F Street'."[15]

In the midst of his private grief, Shufeldt's major task over the summer of 1871 was to complete the survey results and present them to the Navy Department. He performed this task with a remarkable report that included his initial memorandum to Robeson of September 26, 1870. Shufeldt stated the assumed dimensions of a canal to be: breadth at top, 162 feet; bottom, 60 feet; depth, 22 feet. These dimensions had been taken as the basis for a canal because they would be sufficient to accommodate "at least nine-tenths of the commerce of the world, and certainly wide and deep enough for our own domestic trade." To feed the canal an aqueduct of about 27 miles would be required in addition to tunnelling for three miles and making some heavy cuts. He judged the total length of the canal would be 144 miles and it would have 140 locks. Shufeldt firmly believed that a canal could be constructed over his surveyed route. He considered that "throughout this route I am warranted in the opinion, concurred in by the joint commission, that there is no natural obstacle to the construction of a canal which engineering, science, and liberal capital cannot overcome." Yet he was reserved in his recommendations, knowing that a decision lay with Congress. He contented himself with the observation that, "taking into account these circumstances, a canal supplied with water by such a length of aqueduct, through mountainous and tropical country, can only be deemed practicable to the extent of its political and commercial necessity, measured by the progress of the age."[16]

Shufeldt's own views on the necessity of a canal, however, plainly showed that he considered the effort worth making. He judged that such a canal would be more advantageous to American, rather than world, commerce. Before the opening of the Suez Canal, it was his belief that an American canal would be regarded as "a work of great *international* necessity." However, he now estimated that Suez was the "short connecting-link between the capital, political influences, and the trade of all Europe, and the teeming population of the East." Consequently, he saw canal communication in the western hemisphere as "*American,* and local in its main object, incidental only to the rest of the world." That he meant "American" to be synonymous with "United States" was revealed when he argued that one need only glance at a map to demonstrate the necessity for a canal and its location: "each isthmus rises into prominence as it lies nearer to the center of American political and commercial influence, and the intrinsic value of this eminently national work ought to be based upon the inverse ratio of the distance from that center."

With this assumption of the United States as a hub of political and commercial influence, Shufeldt's thoughts took wing. He saw the canal in relation to the national development of American commerce. A canal through the Isthmus of Tehuantepec, he argued,

> is an extension of the Mississippi River to the Pacific Ocean. It converts the Gulf of Mexico into an American lake. In time of war it closes the Gulf to all enemies. It is the only route which our Government can control. So to speak, it renders our own territory circumnavigable. It brings New Orleans 1,400 nautical miles nearer to San Francisco than a canal via Darien, and such is the character of the intervening waters, that it permits a canal-boat to load in Saint Louis and discharge her freight in California with but little more than the risk of inland navigation. As a matter of political economy, therefore, as

well as of commercial necessity, a canal here assumes the gravest proportions. It may be that the future of our country lies hidden in this problem—whether, in the demonstration of which, our principles of government, and our commerce under the flag which represents them, are to go hand in hand to further development, until are reached and taught the remotest corners of the East and the rudest barbarians of the Pacific Isles, or whether resisting the struggles and checking the aspirations of the American heart for space and freedom, we are to live in disregard of natural law, and leave to another nation a glorious mission unfulfilled.[17]

Shufeldt was calling for exclusive American control of an isthmian canal. Though he was using phrases similar to those that Truman Smith had used with him before he went to the isthmus, about the Gulf of Mexico being an American lake, Shufeldt obviously meant them to be understood in the context of westward expansion and American mission. He was much closer to President Grant's position, also in favor of exclusive control, than to that of Secretary of State Hamilton Fish, who still preferred some type of international arrangement. The change in opinion among leading members of the administration away from international toward United States regulation began when Seward inaugurated a policy of American control of the isthmus, six weeks before Grant was sworn in in March 1868 and Fish moved into the State Department. Grant wanted a monopoly over an isthmian canal and was prepared to follow Seward's policy. Fish, however, had to contend with the Clayton–Bulwer Treaty, which coupled the United States with Great Britain in any moves to cut a canal. Both the president and the secretary of state wished to retain the anticolonization features of that treaty, thus keeping the British out of Central America, but Grant wanted, somehow, to overlook the treaty's canal provisions. The dilemma was too great for Grant to solve during his term of office, but he gave prominent support to the "relatively new concept" of exclusive control for the United States, which he linked to his desire to acquire San Domingo. After Grant, most American chief executives stressed this policy in regard to any isthmian canal.[18] It was obvious that Shufeldt supported such policies.

Shufeldt picked up the notion of exclusive control very quickly. He was not concerned as much with the implications of the Clayton–Bulwer Treaty as with the opportunities American control over an isthmian canal would give to the United States in the expansion of commerce and propagation of ideals. The first stage in exploiting such control, he conjectured, should be a collaboration between government and business to furnish the means whereby American expansion in the Pacific was to be continued. The American mission would then be to extend to all areas, civilizing barbarians, and then on into the East, until the "heart for space and freedom" was achieved. Shufeldt thus cleverly linked the isthmian canal with his earlier proposals for surveys in China, Japan, and Korea. Falling into place in his mind were the sections of a great circle of civilization that stretched from Cuba through the isthmus, over the Pacific, and into Asia. Control of the Pacific and the building of a canal were interrelated links in that chain. Later he wrote:

> it is here . . . upon this [Pacific] sea . . . the ocean bride of America, that the East & West will join hands & the great circle of civilization will be complete— . . . This canal is within the compass of modern science—within easy reach of our resources—it is demanded by the times & is worthy of the Nation. The Pacific Ocean is to be hereafter the field of our commercial triumphs—we have been driven from the Atlantic by superior weight of metal. Let us see to it that no rival flag floats upon its Pacific bosom. It is upon these shores that our ambition must cease—for it is here that our Empire terminates. The Pacific Ocean *is* & *must* be essentially *American*. Through it & by us—China & Japan must acquire a new civilization & adopt a new creed—for it is in this sense that "Westward still, the Star of Empire takes its way."[19]

In this declaration, Shufeldt not only coupled the canal to the Pacific ocean but introduced the competitive reason why that ocean was so important. As continental, territorial empire ceased, commercial opportunities inherent in continentalism, denied on the Atlantic, together with propagation of a gospel of Americanism, were substitutes that still allowed Americans to find a new frontier on the Pacific.

To realize this dream, the development of an isthmian canal was essential. Shufeldt had watched the failure of the Louisiana–Tehuantepec Company at first hand in the 1850s. The problem was to find efficiency of operation in the building of a canal. For Shufeldt there was only one possible way to do this: bring in the national government. His own experiences and his urgings from Cuba in the Civil War dictated this solution:

> for twenty years the Isthmus of Tehuantepec has been the butt of speculation, the sport of railway financiers. People, both native and foreign, have lived and died there, in the vain hope of the coming of the "company" which was to build railroads and develop the river navigation. They have lost confidence in American enterprise, and have left but little faith in American projects. This work, of so much importance to ourselves and to the world, ought to be placed beyond the pale of speculation—out of the region of doubt. It needs national resources and national guarantees. It should be based upon a treaty between the two governments. A simple canal concession, subject to revocation by the same power which granted it, is valueless. It neither interests our Government nor inspires confidence among capitalists. . . . I would

make the Tehuantepec Canal bear the same relation to the trade of the United States that the Erie Canal does to the State of New York. In a few years it will have tended as much to the aggrandizement of the whole country as that canal has to the "Empire State."

With these remarks, which refect the disillusionment of his Louisiana-Tehuantepec days, Shufeldt concluded his surveying activities. He was to have gone to Nicaragua after the Tehuantepec survey was finished, but, while coordinating the survey reports over the summer, he became too ill to attend to the plans.* On August 11, he asked to be relieved of the command of the Nicaraguan expedition. Five days later he completed the final report of the Tehuantepec survey.[20] His direct connection with surveying was finished, and he was assigned to other duties. Only his dreams for his route continued as strongly and persistently to affect his future thoughts.

Dreams in Abeyance: The European Station, 1871–1873

With the completion of his reports, Shufeldt was ordered to the European squadron for two years. Just as his vessel, the *Wabash,* was due to be commissioned as flagship of the squadron, under the command of Rear Admiral James Alden, he made a request to be detached from the vessel. He still yearned to make the trip to Central America to conduct the Nicaraguan part of the survey. He informed Admiral Porter, who had helped him to secure the command of the *Wabash,* that he wished to be detached for health reasons. Porter promised to see what he could do but wanted an outline of the new Nicaraguan project to show to the president. Before Porter could promote Shufeldt's scheme, the unpredictable captain had given up the project and rejoined the *Wabash.* Much later, he recalled for his friends the Mangums that his health and spirits had been affected by the happenings on the isthmus and that he had accepted the *Wabash* command to escape from the scenes and memories of Connecticut. Porter was pleased, for he feared that if Shufeldt returned to the isthmus his health would break down completely. "You looked badly when here," he wrote, "and I am satisfied that a return to that region would either finish you entirely or you would wind up with the same suffering that I have gone through."[21] Moreover, Porter had already received Shufeldt's charts of the Tehuantepec survey and had estimated that a two-year wait was necessary to see if the dredged sections of the Coatzacoalcos River would refill.

For many naval officers the European cruise meant a continuous

---

*His replacement, Commander Crossman, was drowned in a boating mishap.

The Tehuantepec Dream 147

round of social invitations on board different vessels in many ports of call. This proved to be the case with Shufeldt, although the Franco-Prussian War and the outbreak of the Spanish Carlist Revolution of 1872 were interesting diversions that kept him moving through Europe with the squadron. He took his youngest son, George, and adopted daughter, Molly, with him to enjoy the continent, where he hoped to regain his health and spirits. His eldest son, Robert, went to Cornell and the other son, Mason, joined the Naval Academy.

While in Marseilles, Shufeldt switched commands from the *Wabash* to the *Congress* and had time to mull over the events that had brought him to the European station. Even after six months the Tehuantepec project was still on his mind. He confided to the Mangums, safely on the other side of the world, that he was only "waiting for the calming down of the political cauldron—to go at Congress again for more money." By this time he was bored and restless on the station and told the Mangums that retrospective pleasure was like still champagne; life had departed from what gave sparkle and zest. He speculated that he might never see them again. In 1890 Shufeldt recalled the memory of that European cruise:

> The European Squadron . . . consisted of the best ships in the Navy, & its principal occupation was to exhibit itself before the fashionable society at Nice or, during the yachting season, at the Isle of Wight in England. Although notified by the Naval Authorities of France that its constant occupation of the harbor of Ville France [Nice] was an embarrassment to them; it remained there for months apparently because it had the fashionable society of Nice, consisting largely of Americans on the one hand; & the celebrated gambling establishment of Monte Carlo on the other. The truth of the matter is, that outside of these considerations, there is not a single reason, national or commercial, for the presence of an American squadron on the European Station.[22]

Shufeldt's depression at this time also arose from money problems. In August of 1871 he had borrowed $1,000 from Rebecca Watson, a friend of the family, in order to prepare his New Canaan farm before selling it. In September 1872, faced with the loss of her position as a governess, she wished him to repay the money and thus caught him in financial difficulty. He wrote for help to Molly and asked her to authorize her mother to repay the money, saying that he would reimburse her when the farm was sold the following year. The financial problem was heightened by a series of headaches for which he could find no efficient remedy. When, in addition, he had to turn over the command of the *Congress*, which he wished to retain, to Alexander C. Rhind, and take command of the *Plymouth* in October 1872, he wrote to Molly that he was "not very happy today—these two affairs coming together have rather struck in." However, the unhappy captain considered that an hour or two of his daughter's loving care could cure him.[23]

In January 1873 Shufeldt was finally given orders to return to the United States via the west coast of Africa, which gave him the chance to renew his contact with the waters he had patrolled in the 1840s with the antislave trade squadron. Thus, as Shufeldt's drive to establish Tehuantepec as the only canal route for Americans to develop was about to reach its climax, the ambitious captain was re-exposed to yet another area of the world into which he could plan to extend American influence if his hopes for Central America were blunted.[24] While the question of Tehuantepec was awaiting resolution, he awoke to the commercial opportunities offered by Elmina, Cape Coast Castle, Fernando Po, the Gabon River, and St. Paul de Loanda. Like Henry Morton Stanley, the Anglo-American journalist and adventurer commissioned by James Gordon Bennett of the *New York Herald* to find David Livingstone in 1870, Shufeldt was to become one of the first to point out the vast commercial possibilities of Africa to his fellow Americans. Before that, however, his desires for the isthmian canal were finally resolved.

The Death of the Tehuantepec Dream

By June 1873 Shufeldt was back in the United States and restoring old Connecticut friendships disrupted by the European cruise. The *Virginius* crisis filled his thoughts for a while, but the old urge of annexation of Cuba was tempered by his fears of the impact of the island's racial mixtures on the United States. Instead, Shufeldt prepared to act as executive officer of the New York navy yard, and for just over a year he carried out the routine of administering one of the navy's largest yards.[25]

During this fourteen months at the New York navy yard, Shufeldt's future in the navy was affected by the rejection of the Tehuantepec canal route by the Inter-Oceanic Canal Commission, established on March 15, 1872, by President Grant to study all previous surveys and make recommendations for the most suitable route. Initially, the commission consisted of Brigadier General Andrew A. Humphreys, United States Army chief of engineers, Professor Benjamin Peirce, mathematician and superintendent of the United States Coast Survey, and Rear Admiral Daniel Ammen, head of the navy's Bureau of Navigation. Later Captain C. P. Patterson of the Coast Survey joined. In February 1874, Shufeldt received orders to appear in Washington before the commission to discuss his ideas on the practicability of the route he had surveyed. Rear Admiral Ammen wrote to alert him to points of reference for all the surveys in which the commission was interested: the fitness of

The Tehuantepec Dream

existing harbors at either end of the canal, the estimated cost of constructing and improving harbors, the length of line proposed, elevation of the total amount of excavation proposed, the estimated cost of obtaining full water supply, and the gross estimate for putting the canal in working order at its proposed depth.[26]

Shufeldt turned for answers to his old engineer, Estevan Fuertes, by this time professor of civil engineering at Cornell University. Fuertes' reply went thoroughly into canal costs and provided as well a grand total figure and two separate estimates for every different section of the canal—the tunnels, feeders, dams, trenches, and locks.[27] The professor was convinced that the joint habilitation of the Tehuantepec harbors would cost "less than the improvements on the cheapest single harbor of the Nicaraguan route." His total estimates for the construction of a canal across Tehuantepec, which he had calculated in 1872 for a talk given to the American Society of Civil Engineers, ranged from just over $69 million to $109 million, depending on the number of locks used or required and the types of cuts made to supply the canal with water. But Fuertes also put his finger on the great disadvantage of the Tehuantepec route—the height of its summit level. At the time of writing to Shufeldt in 1874 he felt unable to determine how much should be allowed toward offsetting this Tehuantepec drawback against the known advantages and disadvantages of other routes.

Fuertes revealed in his letter to Shufeldt how much contact with him had influenced his thinking on isthmian routes. He articulated his "clear and deliberate conviction":

> For the purposes of this canal, Cuba is as much a territory of the U.S. as the District of Columbia; and Cuba will be an American state before the canal will be finished. Cuba, Key West, Yucatan & Tehuantepec, are Gibraltars to the "American Mediterranean," but far more important. The American harbors of the Gulf will act as magnets to the immense trade of the East. The Tehuantepec route is shorter more direct. It passes through the territory of that republic called by common consent, the Sister republic. . . . The difficulties of this passage, and of fostering our National interests, will increase with its removal Southward. In case of a foreign war, our commerce with the East & C[hina?] will be constrained to pass before the guns of the numberless European colonies in the West Indies.
>
> The ascendency of Europe over the West Coast of South America makes it impossible for us to determine who shall control the Southern Isthmian routes; and unless we occupy the Isthmus by force, the means of defending our pacific coast & commerce will be at the mercy of the amorphous governments of Central America.

Shufeldt forwarded Fuertes' estimates, together with his own 1871 report, as the basis of his evidence for the commission.

The press during this time was pessimistic about Tehuantepec, and Robert Jr., studying at Cornell, considered it "looks hard for Old Tehuantepec but there is no telling yet what may turn up." Then on February 10, Shufeldt read that Tehuantepec had been laid aside by the commission and that an expedition was due to go to Darien and Nicaragua to examine the relative merits of these canal routes. Angrily, he declared that if such press reports were true then the commission had either decided the Tehuantepec route was "manifestly impracticable, or that the survey is incomplete & does not possess the necessary data, in order to make a comparison with its rival."[28]

Shufeldt objected on both counts. He had never characterized Tehuantepec as impracticable, and he wanted the question of geographical position to enter into the commission's decision. "I take for granted," he exclaimed, "that if it is the policy of the Government to build a canal it will be built primarily for the advancement of American interests & incidentally only for the benefit of the world at large." On the survey itself, he rightly pointed out that it had not been intended as anything more than a reconnaissance to establish the fact of water supply at the summit and the feasibility of deepening and improving the terminal harbors. The line of the canal was not particularly defined, although all possible emergency difficulties were noted. Thus, Shufeldt argued, the Tehuantepec survey might compare unfavorably with those of "more elaborate" detail—the Darien and Nicaragua surveys—because less time had been spent on it. In the case of Nicaragua, much valuable data had been accumulated by previous surveys.

Shufeldt was also perturbed because the officers who had conducted the other surveys, Thomas O. Selfridge and Edward Lull, had been called before the commission "fresh from the field of their labors," while he had been abroad "engaged in a widely different branch" of his profession. He had submitted his report for "the most rigid scrutiny" and wrote that justice to himself and those serving under him demanded that it should not be laid aside. Daniel Ammen's reply to his appeal merely indicated that the commission had not issued any proclamations about its proceedings and did "not purpose entering into a newspaper discussion as to the relative advantages of the different routes." It would confine itself to its instructions in the discussion of the subject.[29]

Shufeldt was not mollified. He published an article in the *New York Herald* stressing the advantages of the Tehuantepec route over its rivals and attacking the estimates for a canal along those routes as being too low by comparing them with Fuertes' for Tehuantepec. Urged by Norman Farquhar, Shufeldt next complied with his orders and went to Washington and appeared before the commission to argue his case. Nothing short of the commission's stated preference for the Tehuantepec route would have satisfied him, however, and he came away disappointed. Brigadier General Humphreys wrote to console him, saying that his appearance was not a mere matter of form, though Humphreys did not see how it was possible to make "a merely personal examination of the two routes" before the return of the parties sent to Nicaragua and Darien to resurvey the routes. Shufeldt was irked by press comments on Tehuantepec and suspected that they emanated from the commission. Humphreys denied this:

> I knew nothing about it, neither did the Commission, and no one was directed, authorized, or permitted to make such publication; . . . I have not seen what you refer to in connection with your name; but it is very certain that it is impossible for the Commission to have said, done, or tolerated anything that might seem to convey a reproach to you, or to express any other sentiment than one of cordial esteem for you both officially and personally, and the very great satisfaction they had in listening to your lucid exposition of the characteristics of the Tehuantepec route.[30]

Shufeldt did not give in easily. He appealed to Fuertes for help, and the Cornell professor agreed to cooperate "against the Triumvirate" in furthering Shufeldt's "pet scheme." However, he would have to see the reports from the other surveys. Fuertes was prepared to be cross-examined on Tehuantepec, but both he and Shufeldt, he warned, would need to be aggressive and find the weak points of the other routes. He believed his own report was "honest & scrupulously faithful," in which "there cannot be a single flaw (excepting its horrible mis-prints)," but he cautioned that its invulnerability as to accuracy would not settle the matter of the relative merits of the routes. Fuertes' weak point was that he did not know the full capacity of the water at Tehuantepec. Making rough calculations, he estimated that twenty-five feet of water could be supplied, but he unwittingly supported the relative merits of the Nicaraguan route when he declared, "in so far as the water supply for ship canal purposes is concerned, no other route can oppose Tehuantepec on this point. Though Nicaragua has a larger supply, that of Tehuantepec is ample. . . ." Despite such testimony the Inter-Oceanic Canal Commission eventually accepted the Nicaraguan route. Daniel Ammen was known to favor it over the others, and the amount of water available in Lake Nicaragua influenced the decision. The Nicaraguan government maintained a lobby to press the demands of its route and, compared with this pressure, Shufeldt's efforts were futile. He was left with little solace except from the faithful Norman Farquhar at Annapolis.[31]

The dream of "Old Tehuantepec" died hard with Shufeldt. He had gone on the European station knowing that the commission would discuss the relative merits of the various routes, but had been advised that it would not meet until after his return. Now all was lost for the isthmus. As a last resort, he wrote to the *Nautical Gazette,* analyzing the various routes. He dismissed Darien, because Selfridge had failed to find a through-cut, and he dealt harshly with Nicaragua, which, while possessing a magnificent lake nearly at the summit, ensuring a boundless supply of water, had no harbors at either end nor the material to construct them. If these difficulties could be overcome, Shufeldt speculated, then Nicaragua would be the chosen route. But he did not dismiss Tehuantepec:

> I take for granted that the United States will not permit any Power to build a canal through any part of the Isthmus of the Americas—which will militate against our own interest—We already hold the right of way across the Continent by means of our railways—& it is not the policy of our Govt. to create a transit route—which would conflict with this & almost certainly throw the commerce of the Pacific into the hands of England . . . the French Govt. committed this grave mistake at Suez—England now virtually controls the Canal at that point. The location of a Canal therefore resting with our Govt. by virtue of its Controlling influence upon this hemisphere—it remains for the people of the U.S. to decide the point of transit.[32]

By this time Shufeldt was not writing about the tactics of any one canal being constructed, but about the strategy of having a canal at all. Commerce could now be channelled over the transcontinental railroads. The obvious question was why build a canal at all? Like Suez, there was the possibility that it would fall under English technical and economic control. The Pacific could well slip into English commercial hands as the Atlantic had done. Though Shufeldt was not to pose such a question in the context of rejecting any canal for another decade, it was obvious that in the post-Tehuantepec rejection of 1874 these thoughts were taking shape in his mind. It might mean the abandonment of twenty years of endeavor to control Tehuantepec (and an admission of failure), but it was a step that Shufeldt would be prepared to (and did) take. Already his energies were turning to other tasks and projects.

9

The Naval Theorist, 1875–1878

The Coming Man

As the prospects for Tehuantepec faded, Shufeldt turned increasingly toward naval administration as a secure platform for his career. From 1875 to 1878 he served as chief of the navy's Bureau of Equipment and Recruiting. At first he was concerned with the navy's personnel and took steps through his bureau to attack conditions in the service. Then he called for a complete overhaul of the recruitment and punishment systems within the navy. Next, as the country was hit by the savage economic depression of 1873–1877, adding to the political crisis that Shufeldt had observed on his return from the East, he began to conduct a series of inquiries into the navy's needs and purposes. He eventually looked to the continents of Africa and Asia, especially Liberia and Korea as entry points, for a trade expansion program to solve America's commercial problems. Moreover, he personally proposed to find the solutions himself, rather than leave the quest to others.

Shufeldt came to the Bureau of Equipment and Recruiting post against keen competition from other naval officers, including Captain George Ransom of the *Colorado* and Stephen B. Luce, later the founder of the War College. Shufeldt's support for the position was considerable. In February Stewart L. Woodford, lieutenant governor of New York and later minister to Spain at the outbreak of the Spanish–American War, recommended Shufeldt to Secretary of the Navy Robeson for the position. By March Truman Smith had lined up several of the Connecticut delegation to Congress. Smith modestly confessed to doing nothing but waiting on "Gov. Buckingham" to make a brief statement about Shufeldt's career, to which Buckingham responded with "great enthusiasm . . . promptly and effectively." With this, Shufeldt's chances had increased dramatically. Norman Farquhar, then commandant of the Naval Academy, did not believe anyone below Shufeldt in rank would receive the appointment "unless it may be Luce who has a very strong hold on [Admiral John] Rodgers." Farquhar added that "The Admiral [Porter?] told me one day without my saying a word that he favored you for it, and Preble says that Luce told him that you were the 'coming man.' " Rear Admiral Foxhall Parker also considered that Shufeldt would get the bureau as "[Isaiah] Hanscom [the naval constructor] says he considers your calling and election *sure*."[1]

By July, as the Navy Department was reaching a decision on the bureau, Shufeldt received an invitation from Rufus Hatch to join the Pacific Mail Ship Company. He toyed with the idea of asking for a year's leave in order to join the firm, especially when its president, Russell Sage, wrote to Robeson stating that the company's board of directors had decided to appoint Shufeldt commodore of the line. When Foxhall Parker heard that Shufeldt might go he felt pleased that the captain was about to enter a life "more congenial to your restless, aspiring spirit," yet regretted he would not be able to consult with Shufeldt in Washington. Robert H. Wyman in the hydrographic office was more blunt: "Let no promises induce you to leave the service again, work what you can out of it, but hold on." The department refused to let him go, however, and Shufeldt sorrowfully informed Hatch that he hoped he would find better men to aid in the restoration of the company "to the pre-eminent position it deserves—as the standard bearer of our commercial supremacy in the East." Nevertheless, he did survey the company's steamships—*City of Peking* and *City of Tokio*—for the Navy Department under the company's mail contract with the Post Office. He also tried to interest Hatch in a Tehuantepec railway route to San Francisco—to no avail.[2]

The "coming man" was aiming to be chief of one of the Navy Department's eight administrative bureaus at a time when the navy was declining. David Dixon Porter's anguished cry to Shufeldt in 1869, that the navy was no more, was to re-echo through the 1870s with increasing relevance. The United States Navy, which had been a world leader in applying such aspects of naval science as steam propulsion, armor for war vessels, and revolving turret monitors, all battle-tested during the blockade of the southern coasts, had become bogged down with congressionally inspired restrictive economizing. While there may well have been good reason for this relative austerity, some naval officers, including Shufeldt, began to react to the stagnation that they deemed a threat to their careers.

Against this background and long before he entered the bureau, Shufeldt was well aware of the unrest over the state of the navy. His correspondence from 1872 onward is filled with letters from fellow officers complaining of the navy's condition. For example, James Mullany at the Philadelphia navy yard informed him that "the Navy is just now suffering from the effects of mutual admiration as it did when the Board of 1855 met in Washington & retired many officers who were quite their [*sic*] Peers in every Prospect." Norman Farquhar bluntly told Shufeldt that the navy was not popular with the people at large and that "our existence depends on one keeping up a high standard of usefulness."[3]

Among the navy's rank and file the conditions were often terrible. One of the reasons Mullany wanted to see Shufeldt in the Bureau of Equipment and Recruiting was because he considered "the entire Navy will have to be changed as far as the manner of dealing with sailors is concerned." For a long time, he explained, he had believed that the old system of keeping men on board ships in the harbors and denying them shore leave would have to be abandoned. He cited the example of the USS *Worcester*, flagship at Key West: "here is the crew of this ship a well disciplined orderly crew who do all their work as well as could be expected of them. Well—they had liberty last March—and if we are kept down here during the sickly season it will be from six to eight months before they will be permitted to put a foot on shore in a decent place." Yet when Mullany had spoken to William Reynolds, Shufeldt's predecessor at the bureau, about going north to give the men liberty, Reynolds had replied that if the ship went "the men would *run away.*" Of course they would, argued Mullany, "until a radical change takes place men will run away." Mullany expected that Shufeldt, in control of receiving-ship policy, would energetically improve the life of the ordinary recruits in the naval service and reverse the hoary policies that stipulated the men had to be held down by iron discipline and harsh punishment.[4] Ultimately, however, despite Mullany's optimism, the final arbiters of any policy changes would be the individual captains of the navy's vessels, and convincing them might be a harder task than convincing the bureau chief.

With obsolete and rotten ships, poor charts, too many officers for too few positions, an overly optimistic Naval Academy with an outdated teaching program (as testified to by Shufeldt's own son, Mason, then at the academy), and very little money for new vessels, the United States Navy in the early and mid-1870s had a host of abuses in administration that any enterprising officer could attack. It also had an entrenched conservative corps, as Mullany had indicated, against which such an officer might waste his leverage. Nevertheless, the early 1870s did produce a group of reformers outside of the main corridors of power in the navy eager to champion their own kind to work for reform. Good officers like Mullany and Farquhar were ready to lend their voices and help Shufeldt initiate change through the bureau he controlled. Rear Admiral Foxhall Parker summed up the desires of this group when he told Shufeldt that he looked forward to seeing him in Washington for occasional consultations "for the good of this poor Navy, which is now in a state of paralysis that seems to foreshadow certain dissolution if a remedy for its diseased condition be not soon discovered."[5]

The "restless, aspiring spirit" thus held on through the remainder of 1874. After serving on Courts of Inquiry, as secretary of the Board of Examiners at the Naval Academy, and working on a manuscript history of the New York navy yard for the remainder of 1874, Shufeldt was detached from duty in New York on January 18, 1875, and ordered to report to Washington as chief of the Bureau of Equipment and Recruiting.[6]

The Bureau of Equipment and Recruiting

Administratively, the Navy Department was divided into the office of the secretary of the navy and eight bureaus: Equipment and Recruiting, Construction and Repair, Ordnance, Steam Engineering, Yards and Docks, Medicine and Surgery, Provisions and Clothing, and Navigation. The last two employed the greatest number of officers and staff but Shufeldt's bureau was the only one jointly concerned with ship maintenance and personnel. Under his control were nine officers and employees. He took over at the beginning of February, and found that much of his work was concerned with the sheer routine of dealing with discharged, deserted, and pensioned sailors, inspecting equipment in the various navy yards, ordering supplies, preparing annual estimates for Congress, authorizing the disposal of condemned stores and articles on board ship, and directing the recruitment of new seamen in the various receiving ships.* He soon began to keep a daily log, neatly bound in four leather volumes, which he maintained for four years, directed solely to jotting down notes on the business of bureau administration. It shows the regularity and patience with which Shufeldt kept the daily record and the careful attention he paid to administrative duties and details.[7]

For months Shufeldt was busy adjusting to bureau routine. He checked huge deficiencies in the inventories of the Boston and New York navy yards and, over the summer of 1875, his work took him to New York, Philadelphia, Norfolk, and Baltimore. In May the weary bureau head wrote to Molly that he had started out "on a spree" the previous evening but had turned at the front door and gone to bed. Later, he explained, "the Secretary has kept me nearly all the morning in his

---

*Vessels employed at ports and harbors to receive and provide for naval recruits. Sometimes they were used for men already in the service waiting to transfer to a new assignment.

office & so I must write up my morning's work after hours." Shufeldt was even prevented from going to the theater by pressure of work, and told his daughter that his only relaxation had been in flirting with a woman staying at his hotel during a convention. When she left, Shufeldt resigned himself to work again. "I have been very busy—& feel tired tonight," he wrote to Molly, "Secy. goes away for a week & so crowds all anticipated work of the week into one day." On September 21, however, he was promoted to the rank of commodore. His future progress in the navy now depended on seniority and attrition rate among older colleagues.[8]

One major excursion that Shufeldt made for the department came in November 1876, when he travelled to New Orleans to take command of the naval forces there following the riots over the summer in the Crescent City. Louisiana politics since the election of 1868 had been conducted in an atmosphere of violence, intimidation, graft, and corruption, especially at election time in 1872, 1874, and 1876. The Knights of the White Camelia in 1868, the White League of New Orleans in 1874, the disputed elections of 1872 and 1874, culminating in the pitched battles at Colfax, Grant Parish in April 1873, and New Orleans in September 1874 all served to stamp Reconstruction Louisiana as a violent community. In 1876 the militant wing of the conservatives, which had successfully demonstrated its strength in 1874 against Governor William P. Kellogg, restricted its activities in the hope of depriving the returning board for the Rutherford B. Hayes–Samuel J. Tilden election of any pretext for rejecting Democratic votes. Riots still broke out during the summer of 1876. On November 8, following the disputed count in the presidential election, when Louisiana was one of three southern states with a majority of popular votes for Tilden converted into a majority for Hayes by the actions of the returning board, President Grant ordered army and navy units to New Orleans. Two days later he requested a number of prominent northern Republicans to "witness the count" in the city.

Shufeldt was accompanied to New Orleans by Senators John Sherman of Ohio, William D. Kelley of Pennsylvania, and Eugene Hale of Maine and Congressmen Edwin W. Stoughton of New York and John A. Kasson of Iowa. On November 16, Shufeldt met General Philip Sheridan, commander of the army forces in the city, who informed him that he anticipated no serious trouble "at least for the present." Laconically, Shufeldt noted that "the presence of the troops & ships has a very *soothing* effect—no doubt however as to the disposition to make a row—provided the election goes against the Democratic party." Despite his strong Republican sympathies, Shufeldt intended to keep away from the politicians of both parties who were crowding the hotels. He stayed with Paymaster Stephen Rand of the USS *Canonicus,* and his wife "in the quiet friendly part of the City," determined to remain in New Orleans only as long as he considered it necessary. After two days he told Molly that the crisis, as for as New Orleans was concerned, had passed.[9]

Shufeldt watched the returning boards in session with witnesses from both parties. Displaying his characteristic Republicanism, he remarked that "if the fraudulent votes are thrown out the State will go for Hayes —otherwise not." But he acutely observed that "the people seem less interested in the Genl. than the State election—& I believe if the Dem. State ticket is counted in Tilden might go to the d---l for all they care." On the general situation in New Orleans, he reflected that the people "though externally quiet—are at heart turbulent & threatening they hate us—with a force worthy of the 'old-boy.' I am however getting indifferent to their frowns." What helped his coolness, however, was the "wonderfully restraining influence" that the presence of the ships had on the population. Shufeldt believed the people would accept "the inevitable" with a philosophy based on wholesale respect for the army and navy. So convinced was he of the effectiveness of the precautions taken, that by the beginning of December he returned to his bureau in Washington. New Orleans was pacified and the electoral votes announced in the city on December 6, leaving a majority in the presidential election for the Hayes electors of 3,437. Shufeldt had participated in a peacetime naval exercise in social control during one of the most important election campaigns in American political history.[10]

Just prior to his journey to New Orleans, Shufeldt's business proximity to George Robeson pulled him into an argument between the secretary and Shufeldt's old friend David Dixon Porter over pay for officers on the retired list. This dispute had sweeping repercussions. Robeson eventually faced a congressional investigation into malpractices in the Navy Department. Porter nursed a grievance that led him to send the correspondence to Shufeldt, presumably with a request for his opinion on the matter. Shufeldt was caught between Robeson and Porter, both of whom had helped his career to that point. It is highly likely that Shufeldt failed to give Porter the complete satisfaction that the aggrieved admiral felt was his due. The episode of Porter's pay seemingly soured relations between Shufeldt and the admiral. This estrangement may have developed from Porter's disillusionment with the navy and the bureau chiefs in 1876 and possibly, from a feeling of inadequate support from Shufeldt. However, it also indicated that Shufeldt no longer needed help from Porter to gain a position of power in the navy's bureaucracy. After 1877 there was not much communication between the two men.[11]

During his four-year term, Shufeldt strove to convince Congress, usually unsuccessfully, of the need to improve the equipment for which his bureau was responsible—steel hawsers, anchors, contents of ships' galleys, chains, and wire. Shufeldt was concerned that items of American manufacture were inferior to English equivalents. His greatest success in this area came in 1878, when he had the satisfaction of reporting that an iron-rolling mill had been installed at the Washington navy yard, efficient enough to furnish all of the round, bar, and flat iron required for use at the several navy yards.

Part of Shufeldt's work was estimating the worth of new inventions for improving the navy's equipment. In April 1865, he recommended a royalty of $50 be paid for each boat-detaching apparatus invented by Master Maxwell Wood and already fitted, or to be fitted in the future, to naval vessels, but he did not recommend that the patent be purchased. Such apparatuses proved to be popular inventions in the mid-1870s. In April 1877, junior officer (and later rear admiral) Bradley A. Fiske recalled that his own boat-detaching apparatus had been successfully examined at sea and a favorable report given by his captain. Armed with this report Fiske had seen Shufeldt in Washington. The latter told Fiske that he would be ordered to the New York navy yard in order to take up the manufacture of his invention with a private firm, as he proposed to test Fiske's apparatus alongside Wood's in several ships. From his experience Shufeldt found that work of that kind could be done better and in quicker time privately. "Besides," he added, "it gives the inventor a little royalty, and that acts as a stimulus to invent things."[12]

Shufeldt found greater scope for his reforming zeal in the condition of the navy's personnel. In October 1875, he devoted most of his annual report to the problems of recruitment and punishment. He painted a grim picture of the navy's receiving ships "crowded . . . without sufficient facilities for their [recruits'] comfort and cleanliness . . . without shelter, disease of nearly every form appeared among them." The recruits, sick and discontented, either deserted or were drafted unfit to serve. The commodore thus elaborated a program for improving conditions and spent the next three years pressing for its introduction.

The key to Shufeldt's plan was the redevelopment of the naval apprenticeship scheme, which had been allowed to lapse, in order to provide for an adequate number of trained seamen. This proved to be his most effective contribution to the recruitment program. Working closely with Stephen B. Luce, who is usually cited as being the first to introduce an apprenticeship scheme in the navy, Shufeldt strove through the summer of 1875 to provide training ships, such as the *Sabine, Supply,* and *Minnesota,* and adequate clothing for the boys. It was Shufeldt who introduced Luce to Isaac Bell, New York commissioner of charities on April 29, 1872, and recommended Luce, then returning from the European squadron, "with the very laudable intention of interesting the Government & the people of the country in the establishment of a training school for seamen." He told Luce that his ideas for using old sailing ships were excellent and "will not be allowed to lie fallow." Later still, he told him that after the plan was put into operation, "I should think it would suit you to become the Genl. Superintendent of training schools."[13]

Though only an experiment in 1875, Shufeldt's naval apprenticeship scheme grew in importance between 1876 and 1878. As Congress cut the number of seamen in the naval establishment from 8,500 to 7,500 in 1876, Shufeldt enlisted 260 young trainee seamen and suggested an increase of the apprentice boys to 750. In 1877 he recruited 569 and proposed an addition to the training program that would allow apprentice seamen to be eligible for good conduct badges at age twenty-one, with courses of instruction leading to petty and warrant officer rank for those "peculiarly deserving through proficiency and good conduct." He hoped his program would be made permanent when "in a short time the Navy will be manned by intelligent and native-born seamen, and many boys rescued from idle and vicious lives." Perhaps as much as Luce, Shufeldt deserves credit for taking steps to counter the decline of the navy's personnel (and, possibly, to reduce the number of foreign-born sailors). For most of 1877, Shufeldt worked closely with Luce over superintending the training ships for naval apprentices. The boys recruited in the mid-1870s were to be the able seamen who manned the White Squadron of the 1880s. The revival of the apprentice seamen's training scheme was one of the major reforms in a decade normally typed as stagnant in naval affairs.[14]

As bureau chief, Shufeldt moved to improve conditions for recruits and attempted to modify the use of harsh punishments. The commodore desired to educate the men for the service, giving them inducement to remain in it by consulting their wants, both mental and physical. He wanted them to have adequate clothes, a clothing allowance of $50, credited after three months service to offset the amount charged to a recruit's account for clothing received upon entry into the navy, and the payment of interest at 4 percent on amounts due to enlisted men, to bring seamen's savings into line with soldiers' savings. This was revolutionary dogma for the navy in the 1870s. Shufeldt had obviously taken notice of James Mullany's complaints about depriving men of their liberty leave. Referring to records of the department, he did not hesitate to attack the flagrant abuses in the punishment system. Fear of punishment did not deter men from deserting. "Take away the provocation for desertion," he argued, "and this demoralizing crime will diminish." If it still continued, then Shufeldt would punish it with all the rigor of the law. As far as he could discover, only one or two laws of a negative nature, such as the abolition of flogging (1851) and the banishment of the grog tub (1862), had been the sum total of the legislation concerned with improving the navy's rank and file. The commodore warned Congress of the dangers when he asserted, "the apex of the pyramid has been adorned, but the foundation-stones lie in an inchoate condition, threatening at any time to bring the whole structure to ruin." What particularly distressed Shufeldt was that nothing more than spasmodic attempts had been made to "elevate and enlighten our men." Even these efforts, he considered, had been rendered futile "either through prejudice or inattention."[15]

Under Shufeldt's leadership the receiving ships were improved to constitute a reserve class of warships with steam power and formidable batteries, rather than left as mere hulks in which to cram newcomers with little opportunity for drill. He also protested against the "constantly increasing tendency" for officers' accommodations on board navy vessels to encroach upon the space allotted to the crew. He initiated a series of surveys of war vessels to show how much cubic capacity was allocated to officers and men. The surveys revealed, for example, that for every 58 cubic feet per man on the *Swatara,* the officers had 324 cubic feet. Shufeldt wanted staterooms built in accord with actual need "and not left to the discretion of the constructors, who often build or alter them to suit the natural, but selfish, desires of officers who expect to occupy them."[16]

To the reforming commodore, the health of the crew was of primary importance as a matter of naval efficiency. "A ship [of war] may be ever so perfect in its construction and armament," he warned Congress in 1877, but "she loses her significance as a man-of-war unless manned by a vigorous crew." This theme was to permeate all of his writing on the navy. Shufeldt urged a study of the ventilation of ships' quarters by a group of medical officers, and he condemned the practice of placing the ship's sick bay deep in the bows, where it was "eminently well calculated not only to make a man sick, but to keep him so, from its position, the absence of light and air, and the usual want of the convenience which a patient requires." The practice of situating the ship's hospital in the forward part of the bows had been abandoned by every navy but the American. In 1878 a board of officers met to carry out ventilation experiments on the USS *Richmond.* Shufeldt passed on its recommendation for exhaust fans and enlarged air ports to Congress—to no avail.[17]

Allied with these problems was that of excessive punishment inflicted by overzealous officers. Shufeldt conscientiously examined the quarterly conduct reports forwarded to the bureau from all ships in commission. He felt that he had not only become cognizant of the character and qualifications "of every enlisted man in the Navy," but had been able to check "hasty and often needless punishment of the men." As a general rule, Shufeldt found that "the less the punishment on board, the more efficient the ships." He thus demanded "an intelligent revision of the naval code" in order to "harmonize it with the spirit of the age." It was one of the Navy Department's "most pressing duties."[18]

When he was leaving the bureau, Shufeldt laid stress in a final report on the gradual but marked improvement in the moral and professional character of the enlisted men in the service. Punishments, which in 1877 had stood at 22 percent of the men afloat (6,106 men to 1,366 punishments), were down to 14 percent the following year (6,135 to 864). Desertions, which totalled 1,203 in 1876, fell to 818 in 1877 and to 669 in 1878. Shufeldt attributed this reduction to a growing belief among seamen "that a more liberal system of discipline is about to prevail in the service; one based upon encouraging men with rewards for doing their duty rather than by punishing them for its neglect." In his "Fragment on Naval Affairs," written in either 1876 or 1877, he declared, "I now make the somewhat novel assertion that both ships & guns are *subordinate* in importance to the proper education of officers & men—in other words that the personnel constitutes a *Navy* rather than the material." At the same time, he suggested to Richard Wigginton Thompson of Indiana, who had succeeded Robeson as secretary of the navy, that a rigid examination and inspection be carried out into the methods of admission into the service at the different rendezvous and recruiting stations in the country. He wanted a medical inspector to tour these points at least once in every six months and to file a report on each visit. "It will occur to the Hon. Secretary of the Navy," he prompted Thompson, "that the efficiency of the Navy depends in a very great degree upon the physical condition of its personnel"; such an inspectorate would have helped to remedy the defects in the crude system then operating.[19]

Shufeldt, advocating efficiency, became known through the fleets as a friend of the ordinary seamen. Even after his term in the bureau had finished, the commodore continued to enjoy a reputation of having their basic interests at heart. With this record, Shufeldt commended any officer who was willing to step outside of the conservatism of his rank and take an interest in the common sailor. "Say what you will," he again drove home the lesson for the benefit of Congress, "the efficiency of the Navy depends upon its officers and men and not upon its ships and guns." The latter, Shufeldt argued, changed with "every fashion or whim of the day," but the former would remain the same "as long as human nature endures." This message won increasing support for the commodore in the press as well as in the ordinary ranks of the navy.

The program of reform for navy personnel and naval efficiency, however, had mixed success. Although Shufeldt failed, as did David Dixon Porter throughout the 1870s, to obtain legislation of clothing allowances and banking facilities for the seamen, he was successful in reintroducing the naval apprentice scheme. He was also able to get better facilities for recruits and to mitigate severe punishments. The navy's rank and file appreciated his concern for them, even if his goal was efficiency rather than humanity, and the fall in desertion rates can be attributed to his influence and policy (although the general economic decline in the 1870s may have had an effect). But in each instance of success it was apparent that the innovation had come directly through the bureau, in matters over which he had direct control. Wherever changes involved congressional legislation or dependence on other sections of the Navy Department, Shufeldt was unsuccessful in producing results. Outside of the bureau his power leverage was nullified by a Congress that had different priorities and, for the first two years that Shufeldt held the post, by a secretary, George Robeson, who was content with the navy as it was.[20]

The Role of the Navy

While investigating the internal requirements of the navy, Shufeldt allowed his imagination free rein on the position of the navy in the political and economic life of the country. The picture before him was a gloomy one. Added to the personal tensions that he had experienced in 1868-1869 and 1872-1874 over Cuba and Tehuantepec were his observations of the political and social unrest in New Orleans. Furthermore, he was forced to reflect on what was the worst year of the severest depression yet encountered in the United States. Militant labor and agrarian radicals in both the eastern and western parts of the country had begun to make it clear to the Republican party that the South did not have a monopoly on discontent. The props of Republican wealth and moneyed society—the protective tariffs, banks, and congressional support for railroad expansion—were openly threatened. Socialist groups had developed in the years after the panic of 1873, and the wounds of the 1877 general strike had left poorly healed scars on the American body politic. Many joined with capitalist Jay Gould in expressing fear of a "great social revolution." Shufeldt had feared just that from the political corruption he had found after his return from the Far East in 1868. In 1877 it appeared more imminent. As he had turned to Tehuantepec to provide an answer in 1870, he now accepted the solution proposed by President Hayes and his secretary of state, William Maxwell Evarts, in 1877, that American trade had to expand and provide outlets to siphon off surplus manufactures. Shufeldt developed this idea as he reexamined the role of the navy during 1878.

On January 14, 1878, Secretary Thompson posed a series of questions to Shufeldt, Daniel Ammen, William N. Jeffers, and William H. Shock, the heads of the Bureaus of Equipment and Recruiting, Navigation, Ordnance, and Steam Engineering, respectively. Thompson's letter virtually marks the beginning of the movement from within the Navy Department hierarchy to create a new navy after its decline in the years following the Civil War.

The new secretary wished to know, some ten months after taking office,

> what annual expenditure appropriated for a score of years would be necessary for building vessels to supply the waste from losses and decay?
>
> If $3,000,000 were thus appropriated for this purpose how could it be most effectively applied and upon what kind of vessels?
>
> What is the efficiency of the present naval vessels and what repairs would be judicious in their maintenance, that is to say, what are the general and what are the special conditions that should control the question of repairs to those vessels; or of selling them, or of using them simply for subsidiary purposes?

Thompson established a committee of four—made up of the bureau heads whom he had queried—under the chairmanship of Daniel Ammen to consider these problems. He also counselled: "On a subject of such vital importance involving so many elements, many untried and unsolved, an actual agreement in detail would hardly be possible, but such general agreement may be found to exist, as will point out in a clear manner, what the initiatory steps should be, in the building up and maintenance of an effective Naval force under the changing circumstances which might involve that subject."[21]

This survey of and concern over the "initiatory steps" and the expenditure for "a score of years" to be taken to build up the navy sheds a somewhat different light on Secretary Thompson's efforts, and those of the Navy Department, from what most naval historians are willing to acknowledge. Harold and Margaret Sprout, for example, unfairly dismissed Thompson as a secretary "so densely ignorant of naval affairs as to have expressed surprise, so it was reported, on learning that ships were hollow.... Ignoring the inadequate condition of the regular Navy, Thompson talked largely about the advantage of a strong merchant marine, from which we [sic] could easily 'improvise a navy in ... an unexpected emergency.'" Apart from the fact that one of the best ways to ensure the increase of the navy was to talk about the strengthening the mercantile marine, the Sprouts were incorrect in their assumption that Thompson ignored the condition of the navy, as his letter to the bureau chiefs reveals. Of much greater significance was the fact that Thompson asked his bureau chiefs for their investigations within a few months after he first began to preach to Congress of the vast importance of the navy for the development of American commerce. He was not only seeking (and thereby learning) answers to questions on the size of the navy deemed most feasible to his experienced advisers, but he was gathering ammunition that he proceeded to fire at Congress every year in his annual reports on the crucial importance of expanding American commerce. Shufeldt and Thompson were to agree later on the primary areas where the expansion should occur.[22]

Two days after receiving Thompson's request, Shufeldt replied with the basic assumptions underlying his views of the navy's role.[23] To the first question, the commodore said that if an effective force afloat was considered to be fifty cruising ships (and he was taking into account the naval policy of the United States as indicated by existing congressional legislation and annual appropriations), then it would be fair to estimate that if 10 percent of the aggregate tonnage was renewed annually, the cruising force of the navy could be kept up to a proper standard of efficiency. The aggregate tonnage, he thought, should be distributed as follows:

8 of the *Trenton* class	2,500 tons and upwards	20,000 tons
8 of the *Alaska* class	1,500 tons	12,000 tons
8 of the *Marion* class	1,000 tons	8,000 tons
12 of the *Adams* class	500 tons and upwards	6,000 tons
16 gun boats	300 tons and upwards	5,000 tons
	Aggregate tonnage	51,000 tons

Consequently, Shufeldt imagined that 5,000 tons annually would be required and, as the navy was most in need of flagships, this total represented two vessels of the *Trenton* class at a cost of $1.5 million each. The *Trenton* was a 3,900-ton vessel with thirteen 8-inch converted rifles, two Gatling guns, and a compound steam engine that gave fourteen knots.

This $3 million expenditure also answered Thompson's second question, but the commodore had reservations about purchasing two flagships immediately. He explained that "as the *defensive* force of the country is perhaps of equal if not greater importance than the active cruising force," the $3 million might be applied to the completion of five double-turreted monitors then under construction. These ships, added to the fleet of monitors, would afford to the most important seaports "an appreciable defensive force." Shufeldt believed they should be the limit of United States construction in that direction "until time and genius develop more clearly than at present the character of ships required for purely defensive purposes." As a third alternative, he considered allotting half the appropriation for the monitors and half for a flagship. Thus, in two years he could have two flagships and the completed monitors.

On the issue of current naval policy, Shufeldt remained pessimistic. He clearly stated his opinion that "the sea going foreign-cruising Iron-Clads neither come within the limits of our probable means, nor is [*sic*] demanded by the foreign policy of this country. We neither wish to carry on an aggressive war, nor have we Colonies to defend." Neither did Shufeldt see any urgent need to build torpedo boats. There were plenty of tugs in the principal harbors that could be modified for such purposes and if destroyed would represent only a small replacement cost. To Shufeldt, the torpedo boat was "the forlorn hope of an attacking force." With little faith in them, he desired that their possible destruction should represent the least possible amount of money. Instead, he considered the steam-powered ram the most formidable instrument of destruction known to naval warfare. One or two such vessels should be built, he argued, but he thought a special appropriation should be requested so that the $3 million Thompson had originally specified could be applied to purposes beyond the reaches of experimentation.

To Thompson's third question, Shufeldt replied that it would be injudicious to spend more than 50 percent of the prime cost of any one vessel on its repair in the event of need. The navy had a cruising force in January 1878 of about fifty vessels totaling fifty thousand tons. Eleven of these vessels were single-turreted monitors of the *Ajax* class, in a good state of repair and commissioned in reserve. Shufeldt urged that the cruising ships should be kept in commission for a period of six years, though not necessarily on the same station or with the same officers and crew. Ordinary repairs could be done on board by the crew and expenses kept at a minimum. Shufeldt's estimates assumed a naval force of eight thousand enlisted men and 750 boys as apprentices. In droll fashion, he remarked that the Navy Register should be corrected in accordance with his suggestions, by dividing the list into "efficient, reserved and the condemned" classes, "in order that the Congress and the Country may know the actual condition of the Navy."

Most of these suggestions by Shufeldt were incorporated in the report the Ammen committee made to Thompson. Shufeldt was in basic agreement with his fellow bureau chiefs, with the possible exception of William Jeffers who urged an expenditure of $5 million per annum. More importantly, the majority of the committee members had made their suggestions within a framework of existing naval policy, congressional legislation, and annual appropriations. Naval officers and lobbyists were operating within the limits of the financially possible, not the context of the readily desirable. Shufeldt's recommendations in January 1878, therefore, conformed to what was attainable. Even so, he had concentrated heavily on securing the "defensive" naval force, avoiding any demands for a strong overseas cruising navy.[24]

Later in 1878, Shufeldt moved to a much more outspoken position. Partly because of the cry to export more of America's industrial surpluses, partly because of bureau frustrations created when Congress refused to implement all of his plans for naval personnel, but mostly because of the sickening impact of the depression, he began to think in terms of an active navy in overseas waters. The keystone of his naval theories was added when he published *The Relation of the Navy to the Commerce of the United States,* a letter written by request in 1878 to Leopold Morse, a member of the House Committee on Naval Affairs.[25] This small work was more concerned with the role of the navy as Shufeldt hoped to see it established, rather than the navy that was deemed within reach in 1878.

In his opening sentence Shufeldt voiced the opinion that "no nation can be really great without an external commerce." He cited the example of China as a grouping of four hundred million people with no status in the world as a nation, "an aggregation of people without external force." The commodore blamed this state of affairs on China's exclusiveness or, as he defined it, "the absence of interchange of ideas through the absence of interchange of commodities in her own ships and under her own flag." He warned that the United States seemed to be pursuing a policy that would make her as weak beyond her limits as China.

Concerned over the depression and the labor strikes, Shufeldt explained that the United States was losing the fruits of its own vast internal trade because it was not controlling its external commerce with the world under its own flag. The nation was courting contempt from its commercial rivals and cultivating its own insignificance by surrendering its commercial power on its own coasts to these same rivals. Thus, he added,

> in addition to this fact, which is true as a matter of political economy, we are urged imperatively to the re-creation of our commerce through the absolute necessity of procuring a market for our surplus products.
>
> At least one-third of our mechanical and agricultural products are now in excess of our own wants, and we must *export* these products or *deport* the people who are creating them. *It is a question of starving millions.*[26]

With a grossly overinflated economic surplus, and the fear of losing control over the nation's commercial power, Shufeldt saw only one solution: government intervention that would pledge security against total loss to capital investors who would otherwise be loath to invest in steam navigation. Such capital investment was slow to develop, he believed, because of the risks involved in seeking trade and the larger investment required to inaugurate it. Let an enterprise gain a footing, he continued, and then it could compete on its own merits or fail for want of them. He was particularly concerned with emphasizing this problem. "*In no other* way," he claimed, "can our commerce be re-established or our prestige restored upon the ocean. In no other way can the country be relieved of its surplus products, or an additional impetus be given to its industries." This analysis paralleled the thinking of Secretary of State Evarts in 1878.[27]

The commodore proposed granting subsidies to specific routes in proportion to the normal amount of trade and maritime risks, using the cost of marine insurance on the capital invested, which then stood at about 8 percent per annum, as a just estimate for a government subsidy. No subsidy should last ten years, he counselled. Subsidized steamship lines were "essential to the commercial prosperity of the country and our real greatness as a nation." At this point in the argument the navalist took over. It followed, Shufeldt asserted, that the steamships should be so constructed "that while they are *commerce savers* in time of peace, they may become *commerce destroyers* in time of war. In other words they become part of a navy, utilized in commercial pursuits in time of peace." The work that Shufeldt envisaged for them was clearly defined. They were to be very fast mail packet boats, "faster than the fighting ship, pure and simple, can be made," combining other qualities essential for a man-of-war. Because of their great speed, these mail steamers would become "the skirmishers of the ocean in time of war, as useful to the friend and as fatal to the foe, owing to their great speed, as the more ponderous regular war ships." Shufeldt also anticipated their usefulness as troop and stores transports. He did not at this time develop his views on "the ponderous regular war ships," but he probably meant the defensive wall of monitors and the flagships of the *Trenton* class. At this stage he was more concerned with demonstrating to Congress the adaptability of steam vessels for possible use in time of war, a series of potential *Alabama*s, with additional use to the mail packet service and the navy.

Shufeldt had given a clue to his thinking on this point in May of 1875, when he revealed to Stephen Luce that,

> I am not quite conformable when you "groan" over the disappearance of our sailing ships. They seem to me things of the past—& if we can't build

steamers to suit the want of the Navy—then in a short time we will have no Navy at all. But I do not despair yet. The Naval Powers of the World are all at loss as to what kind of ships they want—& the only difference between ourselves & them seems to be that while they without a policy are spending money at random—We without a policy are at least saving millions—until the problem is solved. Whether when we know what we want—we shall build a Navy—is to be sure a matter of great doubt—but hope also. In the meanwhile we are getting a small number of cruisers—full powered steamers which we can employ at advantage—& thus keep this service from complete dissolution. To be able to *man* this Navy of the future—is the work before *us* now. It needs but little legislation—but it requires our hearty good will & determination—& any aid—co-operation—assistance or advice to the Chief of the Bureau under whose cognizance it comes will be gratefully received.[28]

In his letter to Congressman Morse, Shufeldt also considered one of his favorite topics—what the merchant marine had contributed to the navy. Using the Civil War as an example, he listed the forty-five hundred officers and the sixty-five thousand men who by joining the navy had "jumped as it were into fighting gear at a moment's warning from the peaceful pursuits of commerce to the intricate duties of the man-of-war." Should another war come upon the nation, he asked (and, if so, he hoped it would be a foreign war), where were the ships, officers, and men to come from unless from a rejuvenated mercantile marine? With mounting rhetoric he demanded to know: "Are we to hire some belligerent to fight our battles? Is the boundless empire of the oceans, is the sceptre of the sea, to pass entirely from our hands under a policy which fears to risk a dollar for the chance of gaining a thousand? Are the United States and China to be joint apostles of inertness and consequent insignificance upon the world's great battlefield—the mighty deep?" From the stirring climax, begging its own answers and emphasizing the essential qualities of the merchant marine for the navy, Shufeldt passed to an examination of those qualities that made the navy no less indispensable to commerce. "The Navy is, indeed, the pioneer of commerce," he affirmed, affording to the trader seeking "the unfrequented ports of the world . . . the constant protection of the flag and the gun." The trader, he continued, combining Napoleonic dictums with racial overtones and motives, "deals with barbarous tribes—with men who appreciate only the argument of physical force. The old paths of commerce are well known, but as manufacturers increase, new markets must be found and new roads opened. The man-of-war precedes the merchantman and impresses rude people with the sense of the power of the flag which covers the one and the other." The mission of the navy, as Shufeldt defined it, lay in the aid and aggrandizement of American commerce, and this task would never end "unless Congress cripples this arm of the national defense." The navy was the guardian of

American commercial exports and imports, which amounted in 1877, he claimed, to $1,132,000,000.[29]

Equally so, the navy was the guardian of the six hundred boys, saved from idleness, vice, and crime to enter at age twenty-one into the merchant service. In time of war a corps would be ready to rally to the flag. "Do not these facts compensate in a great degree for the expense of maintaining a navy?" he asked the naval committee members of the House. He obliged them with his own answer: "If they do not, then this nation is a mere myth, and natural progress an utter absurdity. I, for one, however, still believe in the inherent greatness of our people. I believe that our merchant marine and our Navy are joint apostles, destined to carry all over the world the creed upon which its institutions are founded, and under which its marvellous growth in a century of existence has been assured."

Inspired by his apostolic vision, Shufeldt enumerated the steps by which it could be achieved: a subsidy to steamship lines for carrying mail, ships of iron, three thousand tons and upward, manned by American seamen and compelled to take as apprentices five boys for every thousand tons burden and thirteen knots speed. These ships were to be inspected regularly by a board of naval officers reporting to the secretary of the navy and the postmaster general. Secondly, Shufeldt desired a complete reorganization of the executive departments of the government, to place all governmental maritime interests under one marine department, headed by a secretary of marine. From this reorganization he hoped for harmony and economy of men and materials. "The time is now opportune," he noted, "for a simplification of a complex system without violating the obligations which the Government has incurred toward any body of men." Foremost in his mind was the congressional reduction of one thousand men in 1876. He wanted all marine services, some of which were superintended by the treasury and war departments, simplified without injuring the interests of the ordinary seaman. Thirdly, he wanted the training system to be made permanent, similar to the public school system, and operated by the Navy Department. He did not wish it to remain subject to the judgment or discretion of any individual secretary. Lastly, he suggested that the rank and file of the Navy, "hitherto . . . neglected as if education was not important to the seaman as the officer" should be fostered as a class "who contribute in a large degree to [the nation's] prosperity in time of peace and to its protection in time of war."

Shufeldt's considerations of a navy limited by annually small appropriations and congressional legislation, culminating in his farsighted view of the kind of navy needed for the commercial growth of the country, perfectly exemplify what Robert Seager has characterized as the dual nature of the Navy Department's advice to congressional leaders, who were at the department's mercy for informational purposes.[30] By advocating commercial expansion, naval leaders sought naval growth as well. Shufeldt's writings of 1877 and 1878 show that he was in the vanguard of those naval thinkers, such as Stephen Luce, Francis Ramsay, Richard W. Meade III, George Ransom, Daniel Ammen, and Francis Roe, who were supplying Congress with information fifteen years before Alfred Thayer Mahan published his famous works on sea power and history.

The Navy's Open Door: The American Colonization Society and Liberia

A perfect example of Shufeldt's speculations on the role of the navy in developing the nation's natural commercial outlets for its surplus agrarian and industrial goods was provided by his views on Liberia and Africa. Following the official death sentence on Tehuantepec rendered only by the Inter-Oceanic Canal Commission in 1876, Shufeldt had written to his daughter that the isthmus was exhausted as an outlet for southern commerce. He gloomily added, "we have given up politics." But this assertion was only half correct, for he merely changed the direction of his ambitions. As Tehuantepec faded into the background as the target for his commercial and evangelizing efforts, the small African republic of Liberia, born of America's desire to solve its internal racial problems by exporting them, became the focal point for those energies in Shufeldt that combined, like poles in a magnetic force-field, his desires to foster American commercial expansion and to find a solution to the problems of the Negro in American life.[31]

After 1876, Shufeldt had become active in the American Colonization Society, which had flourished before the Civil War by encouraging Negro emigration from the United States to Liberia. When the war was over, the society went into decline; it had no message that American blacks wished to hear. Colonization had been rejected as a means of solving the country's racial problems. The executive committee of the society, however, was still appealing for funds to send "worthy colored people" to Liberia, which was to be "the great agency for planting enlightened and civil institutions and Christianity upon that vast and populous Continent." Late in 1875, William Coppinger, the treasurer and later secretary of the executive body of the society, wrote to Shufeldt about the outbreak of war at Cape Palmas, Liberia, between Liberian troops and local tribes. Coppinger hoped that an American war vessel could be dispatched to Liberian waters "to protect them [citizens] and commerce." Shufeldt responded by scheduling a lecture for the annual general meeting of the society in the New York Avenue Presbyterian Church in Washington on January 18, 1876. Unfortunately, he had to withdraw at the last moment because he was travelling on bureau business, but his address, entitled "Exodus of a Race," was read for him on the nineteenth by Reverend Dr. Edward W. Appleton of Philadelphia and was warmly received. Members of the society from New York, New Jersey, and Connecticut wished him to address meetings in their cities and states, and John Orcutt, general secretary of the New York branch of the society, urged him to accept, for "the cause would thereby receive an impulse which it very much needs."[32]

The message in Shufeldt's lecture was clear from the title.[33] Commencing with the point that "political liberty is indispensable for personal liberty," as well as to "the protection of property," Shufeldt declared that a crisis had come upon the Negroes in the South, for they were "no longer considered as a portion of the People of America." In the face of southern white complacency, the only remedy, he urged, was emigration en masse from the region. He compared the Negro plight to the various migrations of peoples, from the Israelites to the Pilgrims, and counselled Negro leaders to found a new nation in a new world. "The finger of destiny points to Africa as the home of the black man of America," he persuasively argued to an audience that was unaware of the extent of his previous involvement with Central America as the object of the divine phalanx. In such a new home the blacks would be "the pioneers of a new nation, the conquerors of a new world." Why not emigrate to Liberia, he proposed, for it had government, laws, and was established. Above all, he contended, "it is essentially an *American* state." Though it was obvious that any emigrants would face hardship in leaving, the commodore stressed the advantages of doing so. "Remember," he advocated to the blacks present, "that you are instruments in the hands of God for the redemption of your race from a bondage worse than slavery."

Shufeldt was not only concerned with redeeming Africa through regenerative agents that he simultaneously wished to see removed from the United States, but he was also conforming to preconceived notions of geographical social Darwinism. "The Continent of Africa presents itself to you as the natural home of the black men," he advised at the end of his lecture, "the yellow race flourishes in Asia; the white race develops its full vigor in Europe. . . . each race has its allotted portion of that part of the earth's surface." The implications were obvious; the Negro would only flourish in his "allotted" sphere. An exodus to Africa would solve the problem of white and black Americans and for the Negro "plant the seed of a vigorous race upon the soil and within the latitudes for which he was destined from the beginning, and to lay the foundation of a civilization, which, if not equal at first to that of the boasted Anglo-Saxon, will at least be bounded only by his own will and powers, and not by the arbitrary dictum of a senseless race prejudice."

Shufeldt made up for the disappointment of not being able to deliver his address in person in January 1876 by giving one the next year entitled, "The United States Navy in connection with the Foundation, Growth and Prosperity of the Republic of Liberia."[34] Here he concentrated more fully on Liberia itself, especially the role that United States naval officers had played in helping the foundation of the republic. Those naval officers, as well as the natives, were well aware that "the power of gunpowder is the power of civilization; in the mind of the untutored heathen it is divinity personified, and on the borders of barbarism, the American gun, under the American flag, is a most powerful ally to the American missionary." Shufeldt's view of power in this context combined Christian, racist, and commercial attitudes with the concept that force prevails. For Shufeldt, whether it was the navy impressing "rude people" with the sense of the power of the flag or gunpowder and the American gun allied against the barbarians, God was on the side of the big battalions.

The commodore had learned this lesson, and observed the alliance between flag, gun, and missionary, when he had been a young midshipman in George Read's African squadron, and while returning home from the Mediterranean in 1873 aboard the USS *Plymouth,* when he had called at various ports on the west coast of Africa. For his audience he recalled his thoughts when he walked through the streets of Monrovia, Liberia's capital: "I thought to myself . . . Liberia is a *fixed fact.* No reflux tide can wash her into the sea. . . . Liberia is there to *stay.* An island in the ocean of barbarism: a little cloud out of the sea, like a man's hand, yet full of portent to Africa; a herald of the coming of that army of civilization which, by an inexorable law, exterminates where it cannot convert."

To his audience of clergymen, philanthropists, and Negroes, Shufeldt preached a sermon like a Sunday divine raising the bogey of "Mohammedanism" to stir his listeners:

> If you believe that Christianity is the religion of the future of Africa, essential not only to her salvation, but to her temporal welfare, then I beg you to consider Liberia as an important bulwark against the encroachment of the followers of the Prophet, and as a point whence to start Christian propagandism into the heart of Africa. Most of the foreign settlements on the coast are simply trading posts, and the duty of christianizing the country is lost sight of in the pursuit of gain. Liberia, on the contrary, is a Christian community, founded as such. Upon it, and upon its friends, devolves this positive mission

of preaching the Gospel to the heathen. It is our duty to assist her in this mission by every possible means—Liberia is the initial point for American effort in the Christianization of Africa. . . . One by one the dark superstitions will disappear in the ever-increasing light, till in the brightness of mid-day the Son of Righteousness will cast His beneficent rays over the whole area of that broad and now benighted land.

Dazzling his audience with his vision of African regeneration, Shufeldt reopened their eyes to the obstacles in the way. He had harsh words to say about the British trader on the coast, who substituted a trade in rum, tobacco, and gunpowder for the old slave trade. He believed the pressure of such traders on the British government had led the British to take under their control fifteen hundred miles of African coastline. What was required, therefore, to offset the equally offensive obstacles represented by the followers of the Prophet and British traders was the moral influence of the American-African on "the surrounding mass of barbarism." American Negroes would be the cutting edge of Christian propagandism into the heart of Africa. Liberia's light would radiate over the whole continent, recharged by the batteries of an American warship stationed in Monrovia harbor, for Shufeldt meant Liberia to be closely tied to the United States. The commodore also wanted the establishment of a line of mail steamers to run directly from the United States to Liberia. With the American Navy present and the American merchant marine in close attendance, the two "joint apostles" were ready to carry the American creed to Africa and secure the trade of Liberia for the United States. By 1878, in which year he was appointed to a position of vice-president of the American Colonization Society for his efforts in 1876 and 1877, Shufeldt was urging the government to countenance these steps and send him to Liberia.[35]

A Further Role

Shufeldt's term at the Bureau of Equipment and Recruiting was a transitional one in his thinking on naval and commercial affairs. He accepted the government's rejection of a Tehuantepec canal and henceforward regarded the isthmus as an area for his private relaxation only, an Adamic Eden to which he might retire at the end of his career. In its place he substituted first Liberia and later Korea as the natural foci for commercial ventures backed by the United States government. As Central America faded, Africa and the Far East began to fill his thoughts.

The period at the bureau also produced changes in Shufeldt's attitude toward the condition and role of the navy. Previously restless under authority, as his career in Cuba as consul general, his naval service in the Civil War, and his postwar career in the Asiatic and European squadrons had demonstrated, he now buckled down to routine work and administration. Between August and October 1878 he served as acting secretary of the navy when Thompson was away from Washington. In the same years at the bureau, he began to develop his special naval service interests and undertook his personal inquiry, later used by Congressmen William H. Kimmel and Leopold Morse, into the role of the navy in Liberia and in the commercial life of the United States. The drive and energy that Shufeldt displayed in his work and thoughts eventually convinced Secretaries Thompson and Evarts that Shufeldt was the logical choice to lead an official commercial and naval expedition to Africa and Asia.

Accordingly, on November 1, 1878, Shufeldt notified Thompson that "as the Department has indicated the intention of assigning me, at an early day, to special duty at sea, I . . . tender my resignation as Chief of the Bureau of Equipment and Recruiting, to take effect when orders for sea service are issued, or at any time . . . most convenient for the public service." To Stephen Luce, he revealed his satisfaction that the secretary had a clear sense of the necessity of continuing the training system but confessed he was tired of "the wear & tear of Bureau life." Thompson was genuinely sorry to lose Shufeldt's high administrative qualities as bureau chief and adviser. He also regretted Shufeldt's separation from the department on personal grounds. They had been friends as well as colleagues, and Shufeldt had often rendered considerable assistance to Thompson in the discharge of his duties. Thompson extended his earnest wishes for Shufeldt's welfare on the forthcoming cruise and said that he looked forward to "most beneficial results," especially ones that would "greatly benefit our commerce" and also add to Shufeldt's personal and official reputation.[36] With these sentiments ringing in his ears, Shufeldt left the bureau and prepared to spearhead the American drive for commercial expansion in Africa and the Far East.

10

The Cruise of the *Ticonderoga:*
Cape Henry to Cape Town

Opening the Doors of Africa and Asia

Africa was far better known by the American public and government officials in the nineteenth century than most historians of United States foreign policy have been willing to concede. Apart from the detailed knowledge of coasts and peoples gleaned from the slave trade connections, American interest had been honed throughout the century by reports of naval officers, merchant captains, whalemen, Salem traders, missionaries, explorers, and adventurers. The west coast was often the focus of special consideration, particularly after the establishment of Liberia as a colony of freed American Negroes in 1821, but the east coast of the continent also received its due share of attention. New England trading connections with it went back to the late seventeenth century. By 1832 the Navy Department had dispatched Commodore David Geisinger with two warships and an envoy, Edmund Roberts, to open trade relations with the sultan of Muscat, whose territory then stretched from the Persian Gulf to the south of Zanzibar. The treaty was ratified and exchanged in 1835. Similarly, American commerce with the north coast of Africa commenced well before the wars with the Barbary powers at the beginning of the nineteenth century. The United States government opened its first North African consulate at Morocco in 1791, its first southern African consulate at Île de France (Mauritius) in 1794, and its first southern, mainland consulate, under John Elmslie of Pennsylvania, at South Africa during 1799. As of 1862 the United States government had twenty-five consular and commercial agencies, together with the offshore West African squadron (from 1843 onward), protecting American interests on the continent.

These interests—private, commercial, and governmental—sharpened considerably by the 1870s. American explorers such as Paul Belloni Du Chaillu, Charles Chaillé-Long, Arthur Donaldson Smith, and

Alan S. Southworth, together with the American Geographical Society, helped disseminate information about the "Dark Continent." After James Gordon Bennett, Jr., commissioned Henry Morton Stanley's spectacular adventure in search of David Livingstone in 1870, the readers of his *New York Herald* were soon informed of the vast commercial possibilities of central Africa and the Congo. Stanley himself was perfectly clear, as were others, about the commercial prospects of the Congo River and Africa. After a long review of the founding of Liberia and the work of the American Colonization Society, Methodist Episcopal bishop Gilbert Haven forecast in the *North American Review* of July 1877: "Look at the colony after the lapse of this half-century . . . see if America in Africa has any value to America in America. We shall leave out of consideration its religious and educational conditions, since the scope of our purpose will not allow of that examination. The commercial and political condition and relations of Liberia will occupy our attention."[1] This was not long in coming. By 1878, after issuing a clarion call for foreign markets to take up the slack of the United States industrial and agricultural output, Secretary of the Navy Thompson was ready to work closely with Secretary of State Evarts on a joint policy to include African markets among those that should be opened and reopened to American produce. Shufeldt's coming mission was the first indication by the Hayes administration that it stood poised to join with European powers in the economic scramble for Africa and Asia. For Shufeldt, it was the culmination of a lifetime of expansionist projects. Appropriately, this one was designed to girdle the globe.

The instructions for Shufeldt's world cruise were drafted jointly by the Navy and State departments.[2] The commodore's initial task was defined by Thompson on October 29, 1878. Praising Shufeldt's "capacity, discretion and peculiar fitness" for the duty, the secretary directed the vessel offered to Shufeldt, the USS *Ticonderoga,* to visit the "unfrequented ports of Africa, Asia, the islands of the Persian Ocean, and the adjacent seas, particularly where there are at present no American Commercial representatives with a view to the encouragement and extension of American Commerce." While much was left to Shufeldt's discretion with regard to the ports visited and relations with the inhabitants, Thompson was certain that his agent would have no difficulty "in ascertaining the main and important objects of the Department" in outfitting the expedition. Evarts believed that it would "redound much to the public's advantage."

The commodore was expected to report on the articles of export and import and the commercial facilities afforded by the laws of the respective countries, especially the ports of entry, and encourage American influence by visiting countries such as Liberia, where the United States had treaty relations, or Muscat and Zanzibar, where treaties possibly needed revising. Evarts requested that Shufeldt clarify the changes at Muscat, which had affected the United States treaty of September 21, 1833. As the sultan of Muscat was thought to reside at Zanzibar, Evarts desired to know what political events had led to the change of residence and when they had taken place. Because the State Department had been informed that American vessels were not allowed to take in cargo at ports under the control of the sultan of Zanzibar, but that all the products of the sultan's domains on the mainland were carried to Zanzibar for export abroad, Evarts wanted this restriction removed, especially as it increased the cost to the foreign consumer. Failing such a removal, Evarts wished to discover if such restrictions were general in application. If not, he intended to claim the same privileges under Article IV of the 1833 treaty.

Thompson informed Shufeldt that he was expected to contact tribes on the coast of Africa not already under the control of European powers "for the purpose of familiarizing them with advantages of trade with the United States." He was also instructed to visit Madagascar and Burma, where American citizens had been maltreated, "circumnavigate the island of Borneo," and interview its sultan. Only two trading posts existed on Borneo (Brunei), and Thompson pointed out that previous attempts by the British and Americans to establish trading stations with the sultan's consent had failed.

Evarts clarified these directions.[3] He told Shufeldt that the treaty of 1867 between the United States and the queen of Madagascar needed improvements. Shufeldt was also ordered to confer with A. G. Strider, United States consul at Singapore, on whether the sultan of Borneo (Brunei) had "ceded or leased to individuals or companies parts at least of the main Island and smaller islands adjacent thereto." Evarts challenged the sultan's competency to do this "in disparagement of his treaty with the United States," even though Joseph W. Torrey, United States vice-consul at Bangkok in Siam, managed one of the companies, the "American Trading Company." The company's lease had been declared void by failure to comply with conditions, especially the annual payment required by the sultan. Evarts explained that because "the extent of that Island and its resources, mineral and otherwise, are so great . . . it is important that the whole object should be carefully inquired into."

Shufeldt was also ordered to visit "some port of the Corea with the endeavor to re-open by peaceful measures negotiations with that Government." This decision was inspired by Senator Aaron A. Sargent of California, chairman of the Senate Committee on Naval Affairs, who introduced a resolution into the Senate on April 8 calling for a commission to negotiate a treaty with Korea through the friendly offices of Japan. Sargent described the Koreans as waiting patiently to be "opened" as Perry had opened Japan; a "new people . . . in need of our manufactures." Thompson hoped that the American attack on the Korean forts in 1871 could be satisfactorily explained, for a "moderate and conciliatory course towards the Government would result in opening the ports of that country to American Commerce." Shufeldt was urged to give "special consideration to this subject." The invasion of 1871 by United States marines, arising out of the determination of Frederick F. Low, United States minister to China, to engage in commercial relations with Korea, had led logically to the Korean government's assumption that war existed between the two countries. Nothing had been done since 1871 to heal the breach. Evarts speculated that the Korean monarch "during whose reign our overtures for diplomatic intercourse were rejected" had been dethroned. He did not know if the old dynasty still continued, and he advised Shufeldt that if it did then he "might cautiously sound it as to its inclination to enter into a treaty of Amity and Commerce with the United States similar in spirit and purpose to those already in existence with other Oriental Countries." The succeeding dynasty might be more favorably disposed. Shufeldt was asked to report on this possibility as soon as he could, mainly because information about the Korean-Japanese treaty of 1876 (especially those provisions relating to the return of shipwrecked mariners, not only of the two nations but of other nations) had been received by the department. To Evarts, this represented "proof of intimacy" between the two governments that could work to the advantage of his agent.

In addition to commercial and treaty-making tasks, Evarts and Thompson had other duties for Shufeldt.[4] The State Department requested that he make reports "in reference to the condition of all Consulates in the ports of the world visited," and pass on any other information that the department may desire. Evarts wanted the commodore to comment on the expediency of establishing more consulates. Furthermore, any information "for the development of American trade" with the regions visited would prove "gratifying" to the department as well as "of public interest and importance." At Aden, Shufeldt was to check on the qualifications of Pieroslaw Burjorjee Sorabjee, an applicant for the consulate post that had been vacant since consular agent William H. Nichols had retired in 1869. Secretary Thompson wished Shufeldt to use the cruise to rectify errors in longitude and latitude, where found to exist, and to make sailing directions and take tracings of unexplored coasts to add to scientific knowledge and give additional security to navigation in the seas visited.

Evarts had a specific diplomatic task for Shufeldt in Africa. In April

1878, the British government asked the State Department to detail a naval officer to act as arbitrator in the dispute between the British colony of Sierra Leone and Liberia over the northwest boundary between the two countries. Commander Robert F. Bradford, commanding the USS *Marion,* had originally been assigned to this duty, but when the State Department heard that the commission to discuss the boundary question had been deferred until January 1879, Bradford was ordered home from Gibraltar and the duty passed to Shufeldt. He was instructed to communicate with the British authorities upon reaching the African coast and act in conjunction with the commission. Moreover, he was authorized to remain independent of commanding officers on special stations and report directly to the secretary of the navy on all matters connected with the expedition. He was permitted to ascend African rivers, stay ashore if need be, and employ native boatmen without checking with area commanders. Thompson impressed upon him that "the Department attaches great importance to this Expedition in view of its probable bearing upon the future of American Commerce. All increase in the exchange of the productions of Africa, Borneo and the islands of the Indian Ocean for those of the United States is imminently desirable, and there is no reason why our Merchants should continue behind those of other nations in this respect." Thompson also informed him that he had been selected "for this special and important duty in view of your experience, ability and enlarged commercial views."

Four days after Shufeldt received Evarts' instructions, the secretary sent him detailed directions on his role in the Liberian boundary dispute. He was to act as arbitrator of questions before the Mixed Commission, made up of Sierra Leonese and Liberian officials. The State Department had been alerted by John H. Smyth, United States minister in Liberia, that the British and Liberians had finally selected representatives. Smyth had described the disputed territory as a commercial locality that was extremely valuable to the Liberian republic. Evarts sent him the news that Shufeldt had superseded Bradford and instructed him to forward the information to the Liberian government. The secretary also informed the British of the change in arbitrators.

Once these diplomatic instructions were relayed to Shufeldt, his immediate task was to board the *Ticonderoga,* a 225-foot, 2,200-ton vessel, fully rigged but also propelled by 800-horsepower engines. She carried two 8-inch rifled muzzle-loading guns (originally 12-inch smooth bores with steel rifled tubes inserted), six 9-inch muzzle-loading smooth bores, a Gatling, and two or three small steel breech-loading howitzers. Her small arms were Remington rifles and pistols, with Springfields for the marines.[5] The flagship, however, did not appear until after November 27, and Shufeldt heard from her captain, Commander Bartlett J.

Cromwell, that she had stuck on the rocks in Gloucester harbor when setting out for Norfolk. The commodore told Molly "it blew like thunder" while he waited in Norfolk navy yard. It was probably "a foretaste of the cruise," he reflected, but added, "I stood like the old sea dog that I am!" His patience, however, was wearing thin. Finding Norfolk dull, uncongenial, and "so awfully stupid," he filled his time reading *Jane Eyre*, which he thought was "a wonderful book" and whose characters fascinated him. Not until Saturday, December 7, did Shufeldt take his last glimpse of the United States for two years, off the Virginia Coast at Cape Henry, when he wrote to Molly that he had prayed they would all meet "as if we had been parted but for a day." On that nostalgic note the flagship finally slipped out to sea.[6]

Cape Henry to Sierra Leone

The *Ticonderoga* passed quickly from Cape Henry via Madeira to Porto Grande, Cape Verde Islands, arriving on January 5, 1879. The commodore anticipated being off Monrovia about February 1 and decided to sail from Porto Grande about the eighth. He parcelled out the work "to set all hands to *thinking*—an unusual thing on board of a ship in the Navy." He took stock of his officers' capabilities and assigned them specific tasks observing and recording events in each port visited. He hoped after his return to the United States to "compile an interesting and valuable book." The officers' tasks included making complete surveys of every port touched, taking note of the trade, commerce, economics, military affairs, cities, towns, religions, transport, communications, customs, physical and political geography, climate, and vessels, crews, and cargoes that came into each harbor. These reports, which were designed to accumulate maximum information in the shortest time for the State and Navy departments, were eventually used as the basis for a two-volume history of the cruise of the *Ticonderoga* that still lies unpublished in Navy Department archives.[7]

Shufeldt's nephew and Molly's brother, Lieutenant Frederick Augustus Miller, who was serving on the *Ticonderoga*, kept a daily journal of the events and progress of the cruise, which eventually ran to three volumes. In its introductory pages Miller neatly captured the spirit and intent behind Shufeldt's career and the cruise when he noted,

> the Centennial taught the lesson, not alone to foreigners, but to many of her own people, that this country was the great producer of the world, not only of food, but of manufactures, and a very general movement took place, of seeking of outlets for the streams of supply started or augmented by that knowledge; Commodore Shufeldt had long time foreseen this, and in many ways

had identified himself much more prominently with the commercial interests of the country than any other naval officer; To him therefore was consigned the performance of the duty of seeking and developing new markets for our products, and to Africa he directed his first attention, for that country is certainly the greatest underdeveloped market of the world for the principal exports from the United States; cotton goods, food, and tobacco.

Similarly, Petty Officer G. Allen on board the *Ticonderoga* noted that the cruise was "for the advancement of American commerce," a phrase nearly duplicated by Shufeldt himself when he informed Thomas Brown, United States consul at Bathurst, Gambia, on December 29, 1878, that he was engaged on a special service "with a view to collecting information which may tend to the development of American Commerce."[8]

Shufeldt was impressed by Porto Grande as one of the most important ports on route to the west coast of Africa. He hoped that the United States would commence "a steam commerce with Africa" via the port, especially as it was visited by English, French, German, and Portuguese shipping lines and served as a link station on the Lisbon-Brazil telegraph cable. The commodore wanted the American consul stationed at Porto Praia, on São Tiago, to be transferred to Porto Grande. He urged that American cottons should be sent out to take advantage of the market offered by five hundred merchant ships and two American merchant houses, Messrs. Bateman and Allen of Boston and Portland. Shufeldt also promised his daughter that when the *Ticonderoga* reached the coast he would send her information to open a correspondence with the *New York Herald* "and get paid for it." James Gordon Bennett's *Herald*, which included on its masthead the slogan "Let the Congo be opened to the trade of the world," did not pick up many of the descriptions of the cruise. Eventually, it was the *New York Daily Graphic* that gave illustrated and prominent coverage of the *Ticonderoga*'s mission, although the *Herald* and other New York newspapers later followed suit.[9]

At noon on January 15, the *Ticonderoga* dropped anchor in the harbor at Freetown, the capital of Sierra Leone, and saluted the British flag. Shufeldt was proud of his promptitude in arriving exactly on the day he forecast, two months to the day from which the vessel was commissioned for the cruise. When the commodore went ashore with the ship's captain, Commander Bartlett J. Cromwell, and Lieutenant Daniel P. Mannix, commanding the ship's marines, he was met by a "gorgeous Policeman," who welcomed him in a loud tone, a battalion of troops, and a full band, which escorted his party to Government House. As Shufeldt sweated his way up the hill toward the official residence he was surrounded "by thousands of natives—men & women whose demonstrations were of the most exuberant kind." It was a scene, he informed his daughter, "where civilization & barbarism endeavored each in its way to outvie the other in the warmth of my reception."[10]

At Sierra Leone, Shufeldt found the Liberian commissioners already on hand to discuss the boundary question, but the British commissioners had not yet arrived. While waiting, he investigated the affairs of the United States acting consul, Dr. John A. Parm, in following Thompson's orders. He recommended that Parm be given full possession of the consulate, and Parm's grateful wife promptly organized a lunch for the commodore. This, together with dinners with the governor and chief justice of the colony, a breakfast with the senior British naval officer at Sierra Leone, and the entertainment of the Liberian commissioners on board the *Ticonderoga,* constituted a series of gastronomic events that were part of the standard features of naval visits to British colonies. Shufeldt wrote to Molly that they were "an intolerable bore."[11]

The commodore was also proud to disclose to his daughter that both the English and French were watching his movements carefully, a fact that, he admitted, "I rather like!" He made certain that the authorities of the two countries had adequate knowledge of the reasons for his visit, outside of the arbitration proceedings. He passed information to the *West African Reporter,* which glowingly headlined "The American Naval and Commercial Expedition to Africa" and referred to it as "one of the most important results of the workings of the practical American mind as well as one of the most potential of the schemes of modern commercial ingenuity and enterprise." The *Reporter* added that the expedition had been projected "by the sagacious and philanthropic mind of Commodore Shufeldt and most liberally seconded by his Government." Using quotations on the role of the American Navy that came straight out of Shufeldt's pamphlet *The Relation of the Navy to the Commerce of the United States,* the editorials trumpeted loudly that the *Ticonderoga* would add "fresh laurels to grace the achievements of that illustrious Navy" in a cause "of infinitely greater importance than South Sea discoveries or Arctic investigations." The editor felt certain that Shufeldt's expedition would leave "a distincter and wider impression upon this continent" than any since the days of the Portuguese adventurers. "American zeal and energy will tear the veil asunder and admit the world," the paper speculated and added, "it may be reserved for the youthful and energetic nation of the West to utilize more largely than any other the vast resources to which attention had been directed."[12] This reasoning is so close to Shufeldt's own as to indicate that the editor probably did little more than check over the text provided. The *Reporter* provided good publicity for the mission, and Shufeldt took advantage of it. But it was little wonder that he felt the British and French were watching his movements closely.

Shufeldt showed that he was ready to vie with the aims of the original Portuguese adventurers in his eagerness to exploit the commercial possibilities of the region. He discussed this with Dr. Edward Wilmot Blyden, who had helped bring about the discussion on the northwest boundary question while serving as Liberian minister plenipotentiary and extraordinary to the Court of St. James. An African of pure descent, born in St. Thomas, West Indies, in 1832, Blyden was the foremost literary figure in Liberia, a professor and author of several articles and books published in American and British academic circles. He had been brought to Shufeldt's attention by a mutual friend, Edward Morris of Philadelphia, a Quaker member of the American Colonization Society who owned eight hundred acres in Liberia. Blyden dreamed of an African state running into the hinterland from Boporo, and he wanted such a state to be tied to the coast by light railroads running from Monrovia along the St. Paul River into the Niger Valley and the heart of the Sudan.[13]

Such a vision dovetailed with Shufeldt's. He sought to use Blyden, who spoke Arabic fluently, as a roving consul for the interior of West Africa where Islam was established, and he was gratified when the professor enthusiastically took up the suggestion. Shufeldt explained to the Navy Department:

> The importance of employing such a man can not be overestimated. Africa with its immense commercial possibilities with a population greater than that of China, and with much greater external needs—has as yet scarcely been brought in contact with civilized nations.
>
> Europeans have skirted the Continent very much as a fly travels around an egg—always indeed finding the natives eager for barter and capable of supplying all the demands of trade, and yet making no perceptible effect upon their resources beyond the mere borders. . . . It is not perhaps my province to urge this appointment upon moral grounds, and yet the United States should not be laggard in the work of civilizing this Continent.

In the two-volume manuscript copy detailing his cruise experiences, which he later prepared for a publication that never took place, he added the words "we should claim our share in such honors and reap the reward of our zeal." He also told Blyden, "I take the liberty of expressing the opinion, that while the U.S. is in harmony with the Powers of Europe in the desire to advance Africa in the scale of civilization, and in that respect you might well represent the nations of the earth, but that in its commercial aspirations it is in a measure the rival of Europe, and if you accepted the service it would be your first duty to keep this fact in sight." Inspired by the possibilities for Blyden's intended role, Shufeldt later authorized Lieutenant Franklin J. Drake and Master Charles E. Vreeland to survey the St. Paul River and its banks in order to determine the feasibility of a Liberian light railroad route into the interior. Though Blyden was not appointed, both he and Shufeldt found it convenient to work together to promote the opening of the interior.[14]

In addition to his correspondence in regard to Blyden's talents as a potential consular officer, Shufeldt sent the first of his commercial dispatches from Sierra Leone. He considered Freetown's harbor one of the best in the world. A line of steamers connected the British colony to England. But despite the large amount of traffic at Sierra Leone and adjacent points occupied by Europeans, Shufeldt believed that "Africa proper has scarcely been touched by foreign trade." His remedy was to push aside the obstacles caused by lack of internal communications and build light railroads into the interior for a hundred or two hundred miles, in order to "open up a commerce of world wide importance." This trade would be of "peculiar value" to the United States, he later proclaimed, putting his finger directly on the problem facing depression-ridden America: "The great and increasing surplus of agriculture and mechanical products in America will force our citizens to look abroad for markets. . . . Africa with its teeming population presents a tempting field for the sale of these articles, which, so to speak, are the peculiar products of our own soil viz. cotton and tobacco."[15] Shufeldt added rum and kerosene for the secretary of the navy, omitting them in a copy to Blyden. With Blyden as a roving consul, linking the United States with the interior tribes, with the New York firm of Yates and Porterfield already trading at Freetown in hides, ivory, rubber, groundnuts, palm oil, cotton, tobacco, rum, and kerosene, and with light railroads opening up the interior of Liberia from the coast, one of Shufeldt's main purposes—the relief of American surpluses by entrance into the anticipated, vast, interior African market—would have been virtually accomplished.

The Liberian Boundary Question of 1879

The Liberian boundary question that Shufeldt had been selected to arbitrate had a history spanning a quarter of a century. The British government recognized the sovereignty of Liberia from Cape Palmas in the south to Sugaree in the northwest. Liberians claimed beyond that to the Gallinas country and the land to the north to the Shebar River, basing their claims on treaties made with the Gallinas chiefs in 1851. The Liberians declared their treaties were treaties of cession by purchase, but the local chiefs asserted that the treaties of 1851 were treaties of friendship only. The territory in dispute, claimed by the Liberians, thus lay between the Sugaree (Sugury) and Shebar rivers, and included the districts known as Mannoh (Mano), Mannoh Rock, Solyman (Sulima), Gallinas, Cassa (Kasa), and Gumbo. The British Foreign Office had neither accepted nor renounced Liberian claims in its treaties with local chiefs, which meant, naturally, that it did not recognize Liberian claims. A commission established in 1863 to resolve the discrepancies had failed to reach an agreement. Since then the Liberians had engaged in abortive attempts to establish their claims over the Gallinas tribes.

At Freetown, Shufeldt found that the Liberian commissioners— Joseph W. Hilton and James S. Smith, both government officials, together with H. W. Johnson and John Wallace Worrell, a senator from Grand Bassa County, as counsel—had been waiting since January 1 for their British counterparts to arrive. He informed the secretary of the navy that he anticipated "a long and somewhat tedious discussion and examination of this boundary question," including detailed examinations of chiefs of tribes and witnesses of both parties. "I apprehend a longer stay in the vicinity than I originally contemplated," he added for Thompson's benefit. To his daughter, however, he indicated that a longer delay on that part of the coast was likely to prove agreeable; "the question at issue is of great importance to Liberia & to satisfy that country will necessitate a partial investigation." Yet the nonappearance of the British, he implied, showed that the British government thought the boundary question of but little importance or, at least, that the Liberians "can await H. B. M.'s convenience." The commodore pessimistically forecast that Liberia would have "a poor show in the coming Commission." He revealed his own prejudices by stoutly declaring, "I wish I was here as an *advocate* rather than an arbitrator—for the Liberians."[16]

The Liberian commissioners held little hope that the commission would ever meet. Only one British commissioner, David Hopkins, British consul for the Bights of Benin and Biafra, the Niger River, and Fernando Po, had arrived by the end of January. Even after the major British commissioner, William Warren Streeton, acting chief justice and queen's advocate for Sierra Leone, appeared the delay was extended because no instructions had been received from England. When these finally came on February 10, the Liberian commissioners were in a waspish mood, and the commission was scheduled to meet the next day. Shufeldt soon found he would be kept at least a month longer than he had anticipated. "The blessed Commission is not yet organized & one cause of delay follows another," he moaned on February 10 in a letter to Molly, going on to say, "I believe the truth to be that the English dont [*sic*] want *me* to act as their judge & arbitrator." "I may be mistaken," he added as an afterthought, "but the delay is quite unaccountable."[17]

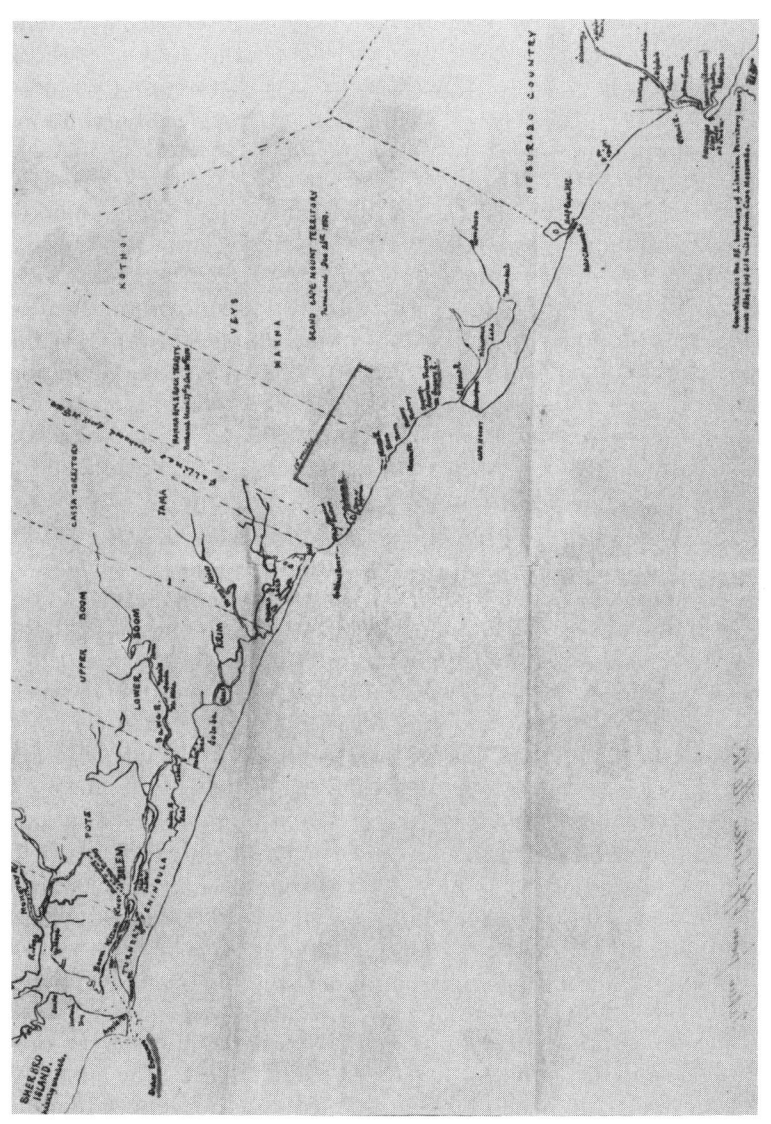

The Liberian Boundary Dispute of 1879. From the Robert Wilson Shufeldt Papers, Manuscripts Division, Library of Congress.

Shufeldt was too egocentric in assessing British procrastinations. The British case rested so much on the status quo that government officials were wary of bringing it to arbitration by anyone. Shufeldt's position as arbitrator thus proved to be the first source of disagreement between the two bodies of commissioners. One of the Liberian commissioners, Joseph W. Hilton, proposed that Shufeldt should be invited to preside over the commission, but Streeton objected that there would then be three commissioners against two. He suggested that the commodore be invited to attend meetings at pleasure. Despite a lengthy discourse from Hilton, the British position was eventually agreed upon, signed, and a copy sent to the commodore. He would be used only to settle referred points in dispute and not attend as president of the commission with a casting vote.

The commission next dwelt on the finality of the award. The British commissioners stated that the British foreign secretary, the Marquis of Salisbury, had requested that they ask the Liberians to give an assurance that the Liberian Senate would abide by the award that might be agreed by the commission. The Liberians countered by making the same request of the House of Lords. No such assurances could be given by the British, but they did inform the Liberians that their government would abide by the award if agreement and a decision were reached. The Liberian commissioners retorted that the commission's decision was to be considered final and absolute. In the event of a disagreement between them, the points in dispute would be arbitrated. Similarly, they added that their government would be bound by the draft proposals of 1870, which had been drawn up for discussion in another commission on the same problem. The considerations of these 1870 proposals had yet another bearing upon Shufeldt's role as arbitrator.

Streeton and Hopkins were bound by their instructions from the British Secretary of State for Foreign Affairs. In drafting these instructions, Lord Salisbury had referred to his predecessor Earl Grenville's instructions for the guidance of the proposed 1870 commission. In 1870 the British and Liberian governments had agreed on what was to be the basis for discussion. That basis, identified in the 1870 instructions, was also to guide the 1879 commissioners, and they were not permitted to go beyond it. When this was made clear to the Liberian commissioners, and after a short adjournment to consider the instructions, they agreed that their government would be bound by the award, as specified in 1870. In turn, the British agreed to accept this Liberian assurance, with the important proviso that,

> subject to the recognition by the latter [Liberian commissioners] of the fact that in the statement in the [1870] proposals referred to that Her Majesty's

Government recognize the limits of Liberia "as comprising the coast line between Cape Palmas to the South and the South Bank of the River Solyman to the North West," "Solyman" is written in mistake for "Sugaree," and that such statement should read as if the word "Sugaree" had been contained therein instead of the word "Solyman."

The Liberian commissioners wanted this question settled by the arbitrator, hoping that the British clerical error of writing Solyman instead of Sugaree would work to their advantage by giving them fifteen miles of coastline northward. But Streeton and Hopkins replied that according to the Grenville instructions of 1870, they could not recognize Solyman when Sugaree had been intended nor settle the boundary question without further inquiry into the claims of Liberia to the line of coast north of Sugaree territory. They considered there was no question at all to submit to Shufeldt until such an inquiry had been pursued "on the spot."[18] Over this question the commission became deadlocked for a second time.

On this vital issue Shufeldt agreed with the British. Privately, he accepted the interpretation that the arbitrator should only decide in the case of disagreement after an on-the-spot investigation. He was unofficially upholding Grenville's instructions of 1870 as the proper basis for negotiation and accepting the British insistence on beginning the inquiry at Sugaree. His acceptance of the British argument kept the *Ticonderoga* at Freetown until the investigation could occur. Shufeldt sardonically informed his daughter of the squabble, which both times caused an adjournment *"sine die"* and then resulted in another meeting the next morning as if no altercation had occurred. "In this way we presume to spend the cruise in Sierra Leone," he wrote, adding that he intended to tell both parties "to-morrow—being 30 days of tedious waiting . . . that we are getting tired and that any further shilly shallying will no longer be endured by your patient & long suffering daddy!"[19]

On Sugaree or Solyman the commission deadlocked. Not until February 14 did the Liberian commissioners Hilton and Smith agree to commence investigations of the northwest boundary from Sugaree territory to the river Shebar. If the British commissioners were not content with that proposition then the Liberians requested an adjournment to enable them to obtain powers from their government to make the admission—that Solyman was a clerical error for Sugaree and that the commission should meet "on the spot" at Sugaree—required by the British commissioners. Their point—and with it virtually the dispute—won, Streeton and Hopkins stated they still desired the admission to be made before proceeding with the inquiry. They thus consented to an adjournment until April 1 at the latest. By so doing they were removing the chance of a later repudiation by the Liberian government, in the event of dissatisfaction with the final verdict, at the risk of a refusal at that point to begin at Sugaree. News of this six-week adjournment caught Shufeldt completely by surprise. He had been expecting a dissolution and had not been present on the final morning. When the Liberian commissioners failed to notify him of the adjournment and did not answer an inquiry from him on the subject, he showed his acute displeasure by writing to the Liberian secretary of state, Garretson Wilmot Gibson. The latter was left with no alternative but to apologize for "this reprehensible omission on their part."[20]

Despite his anger over the discourtesy of the Liberian commissioners, Shufeldt was not blinded to the plight of the country. Grimly, he issued a stern warning to the American Navy and State departments:

> The retrocession of this territory to the natives, to be eventually absorbed by the Colony of Sierra Leone will be a serious blow to Liberia; it virtually dismembers the Republic and entirely destroys its prestige upon the Coast. *But I do not see any remedy unless the United States Government should directly intercede with Great Britain for a less stringent and exacting basis of agreement for the settlement of the Question.*

Native chiefs, backed by traders, would always deny the deeds of cession, he counselled, striving hard for State Department support. "Liberia is the *objective* point of American trade on this coast, and is really the garden of Africa," he preached to Washington officials; "the time cannot be far distant when it will become of the greatest commercial importance to the United States." He was apprehensive that the Liberians, technically, had no case on the boundary issue and that the colonial officials of Sierra Leone, who controlled the British commission, would exact "the pound of flesh." The outcome, he prophesied, would be the absorption of the republic into the colony of Sierra Leone or its diminution into an insignificant missionary station. The British government, Shufeldt acknowledged, had always been generous with the Liberians (for him a major concession), but the "pressure of trade" and the "national ambition of colonial officials" would serve to exercise a "constant and perceptible influence" on the home authorities until such a result as he gloomily predicted occurred. Consequently, on February 16, 1879, he notified Thompson that

> the United States, aside from the mere question of philanthropy, is interested in the permanence of this republic. It is the objective point of American trade on the vast west coast of Africa . . . no American can be blind to the fate of this only American colony. National indifference is but the forging of another link, in that chain of commercial inactivity, to keep bound prisoner his flag

and ship from off the ocean world. . . . What future is there for the Republic if neglected and unsupported by the Mother Country?

Shufeldt carefully marked on the margin of page 26 of a copy of the twenty-ninth report of the American Colonization Society (1846), sent to him by William Coppinger in November 1878, a statement by Secretary of the Navy Abel P. Upshur in 1843: "This Government will be, at all times, prepared to interpose its good offices to prevent any encroachment by the Colony upon any just right of any nation, *and it would be very unwilling to see it despoiled of its territory, rightfully acquired,* or improperly restrained in the exercise of its necessary rights and powers as an independent settlement."[21] Thus the commodore resolved to stay and help to see the commission through to a finish, even though there was a danger to his crew in the unhealthy rainy season and the cruise had already been delayed for thirty days.

The Tabou District and the End of the Commission

With six weeks to wait and a shortening temper to contain, Shufeldt could well reflect that his decision to remain ultimately resulted from his acceptance of the British case with regard to the "on the spot" visit to Solyman. Yet he also agreed to remain at the request of the Liberian government, even though he wrote to Molly that the commission had "fizzled out altogether." Moving to Monrovia from Freetown, he spent his birthday visiting Mrs. Jane Roberts, wife of the former president and an old acquaintance from his visit of 1873. "The relief in getting away from the English influence at Sierra Leone is great," he confided to his daughter. His sense of frustration, however, was just as keen in the cooler climate of Monrovia. "I am trying to do something for the good of Liberia & my own country, to wind up my public service," he mentioned in yet another letter to Molly, "after this cruise I shall live for *you.*"[22]

The commodore soon found that he was being dragged into Liberia's domestic troubles. In Liberian eyes, the cause of the northwestern boundary troubles lay with the activities of British traders who were encouraging the native chiefs to resist Liberian claims. Similarly, Liberia was experiencing troubles with traders in other areas of the country. Secretary of State Gibson informed the United States minister in Liberia that an American named Julio, together with a German named Lehman, were violating the navigation, commerce and revenue laws of Liberia by trading with Liberian territory at Tabou and other places south of Cape Palmas without complying with the trade laws on that part of the coast.

After the *Ticonderoga* arrived at Monrovia, Shufeldt visited Minister

Smyth and discussed the full details of the Julio affair. On February 25 the minister forwarded Gibson's dispatch to the commodore. He told him that under the treaty of commerce and navigation between the United States and Liberia, concluded at London on October 21, 1862, and ratified February 11, 1863, the right of interference in such matters seemed to be given to the United States, conditional upon a precedent request by the Liberian government. Smyth thus reinforced a request from Gibson that Shufeldt should intervene. Later, when informing Evarts of the affair, Smyth related that Shufeldt had expressed the opinion "that under the treaty, authority was given for interference by the United States government, the request being duly made by the Liberian Govern't." Evarts and the State Department's law officer later rejected this interpretation of the treaty clause. On February 26, however, Shufeldt declared himself willing to take "such action in the premises as the treaty . . . might seem to require."[23] Accordingly, he prepared to lend the weight of the *Ticonderoga*'s guns to the authority of the Liberian government in its dispute with Julio. Secretary Gibson acknowledged that Shufeldt had agreed to "call at such point or points: assemble the chiefs and endeavor to impress upon them the several considerations," which included Liberia being regarded as joint owner of the boundary. This question would be settled as soon as circumstances would allow.

Shufeldt left Monrovia on March 5, confident that the ship's visit had been "a most triumphant one for the *Ticonderoga*." The nation's president had given an official breakfast to the ship's officers, and the city of Monrovia had entertained the ship's company to luncheon "in grand style." All this, Shufeldt cynically observed, was "in gratitude for anticipated favors—for the Commission has not yet settled the 'vexed question.' " He warmed the hearts of the assembled company by speaking on the important role that the United States Navy had borne "in planting a colony here, and its relations to the Republic of Liberia." After that he left to put his words into practice by placing the flagship at the material service of the republic.[24]

Secretary of State Gibson appointed James T. Gibson, superintendent of Cape Palmas, to accompany Shufeldt. Gibson's task was to name to Shufeldt any of the local tribes who were "inclined to repudiate" Liberian jurisdiction. Traders were expected to "respect Liberian laws, and vessels plying between Cape Palmas and the San Pedro river were to hoist the Liberian flag with which they would be furnished." The Liberian secretary of state wanted to appoint a local, reliable chief as head police officer of the district at $100 per year, to keep order, fly the Liberian flag, and hoist it on the approach of any vessel.[25]

Anchoring his vessel off the Tabou River on the eighth, Shufeldt sent word to Julio to account for his disregard of Liberian revenue laws.

Julio declared he was perfectly willing to pay the revenue duties to Liberia, but the native king, old King Nimleh, the blind ruler of the Grebos, would not allow him to pay anything. Shufeldt sent for the king, who excused himself from coming on board but sent various chiefs and head Grebos. The headmen were told that the frigate would return in sixty days for an answer. The same conditions were repeated to them that had been laid down for Julio. Shufeldt estimated that the insubordination along the whole line of the coast from Cape Palmas to the San Pedro River, aimed at the authority of the Liberian government, was based on the hope for a settlement unfavorable to Liberia from the northwest boundary commission. This would provide an opportunity to revolt and appeal to Great Britain for a settlement of the southwest problem. Most of the trading illegalities were caused by the fact that the traders could not do business without the consent of the native chiefs, and the Liberian government did not have the power to enforce its laws upon them.[26]

The commodore felt frustrated over the outcome of his talks with Julio, Nimleh, and the headmen, fearing for Liberia should a general uprising of the native tribes take place on the disputed borders of the republic. What was needed, he urged, was a war vessel "to impress insubordinate tribes with a sense of the power and interest of America," for a gunboat was the only restraint "upon a rude African." This was only half the problem. The absence of permanent Liberian power in the area was a reflection of the republic's military weakness. Shufeldt knew this when he expressed concern over the possible fate of the small Liberian garrison at Harper and worried that in the event of a massacre it would be "too late . . . to regret that the flag of her Great Mother Republic has not for years been seen in her harbor." Overall, however, the expedition to the Tabou coast had demonstrated that neither the United States naval representatives nor the Liberian government could influence local traders or chiefs in areas where the Liberians could not exert their own control.[27]

After returning to Monrovia, Shufeldt prepared another series of reports dealing with local surveys made by teams of the *Ticonderoga*'s officers. The country in the vicinity of Cape Palmas had been surveyed by a party headed by Franklin Drake and Charles Vreeland, who had also completed a survey of Stockton's Creek and the St. Paul River. Drake and Vreeland had penetrated a short distance beyond the headwaters of the river in the direction of Boporo, with a view to adding "in some degree to the knowledge of the interior of Liberia." Drake reconnoitered Stockton's Creek, the river, and the interior, eventually recommending the building of a narrow-gauge railroad. His report furnished the first reliable information on the St. Paul River and the adjacent countryside and brought to fruition the dream of Lieutenant Mayo C. Watkins, U.S.N., a Virginian who had first wanted to make the survey in 1851.[28] Later Drake completed surveys of the Sugury and Mahfah (Mafa) rivers and Fisherman's Creek.

Shufeldt posted Drake's reports to the secretary of the navy and added:

> Liberia is and must be the objective point for American trade upon the Coast of Africa. It fronts the richest and the most populous region which can be tapped by means of light railways from its shores, more readily and economically than from any other point on the West Coast.
>
> England and France are now actively engaged in dividing up the Continent of Africa, and are rivals for the possession of its immense commerce. Even Liberia the only quasi American colony is now undergoing a scrutiny as to her rights upon the coast.
>
> If the Government and People of the United States remain indifferent to these facts, then, when too late, they will have to mourn over the loss of one of the most valuable outlets to our trade, and leave out of our estimates, the commerce of a Continent which consumes more than any other country the natural products of our own soil and the fruits of our own industry.

To tie Liberia more effectively to the United States, Shufeldt pressed for a government line of steamers subsidized by the United States and exempted from paying port duties by the Liberian government. Such vessels, plying monthly between the two countries, would have established a Liberian-American customs union undermining the trade of rival nations. To this Shufeldt wanted to add links to Madeira, Fernando Po (modern Bioko), the key to the west coast palm oil trade, and the Mandingo tribe of the interior, "the great traders of Central Africa," as he justifiably termed them, who would bring the riches of the interior over the narrow-gauge railroad mapped out by Drake's survey to Monrovia.[29]

The reason Shufeldt wanted to see the whole area fall under the economic dominance of the United States is clear. To his supporters in the Navy Department, he explained: "Such schemes may seem visionary with prospects of profit too remote to be practicable, but we must bear in mind that with the old markets overstocked with goods, that Nation will be wise which taking time by the forelock, seizes upon at least its share of the only remaining unoccupied mart in the world, such as the virgin soil of Africa with its teeming population really is today." He attempted to stimulate interest among American manufacturers by sending cloth samples to the Navy Department, and firms such as Van Volkenburgh and Leavitt of North Street, New York, responded eagerly. Altogether, Shufeldt could have given no finer description of the rationale behind his expedition to Africa and the willingness with which he had gone down the coast to lecture traders and native chiefs on the responsibilities of the allegiance to Liberian authority.[30]

Shufeldt's grandiose schemes and his lack of success with the chiefs left him with fluctuating emotional responses. Once back in Monrovia, he penned a lonely letter to Molly, advising her, "don't plan plans for me—I am done with ambition." "Hereafter," he continued, "Paul may plant & Apollus water & whatever of good may come of it—let others *reap*. I have done my share—I want rest." But later he proudly confessed to his daughter that he was not content to leave others to harvest the glory. He revealed that the *Ticonderoga* "remains the Lion of the Coast & we get invitations individual & general from corporations & counties to accept hospitality unbounded." The Liberians regarded the flagship with special favor and Shufeldt boasted, "if I am or was a 'big injun' in Washington—you may comfort yourself by knowing that out here I am growing in altitude & circumference—until if vain I might fancy myself —the great Man of Liberia!" Patronizingly, he referred to the Liberians as "these poor helpless people" who "had so little sympathy."[31]

At the end of March, Shufeldt took the *Ticonderoga* to Solyman, where the reconvened boundary commission was due to meet on April 1 to hear testimony from the Gallinas chiefs. He was exasperated. For two and a half months, he wearily exclaimed, "we have been dancing attendance upon this Commission & today it is to commence for the first time in real earnest." He scathingly assessed the chances for both sides: "the British Commissioners determined men backed by a sense of the power of the British Crown are here to face the Liberians who flounder about in the meshes of the law as interpreted by the British Crown lawyer— confronted with witnesses all suborned by British traders—& sitting in a Negro town— the real King of which is an Englishman!" Under these circumstances the commodore considered the result would not be difficult to predict. To Molly he wrote, "Liberia will probably lose her case —Even the Arbitrator can not help them outside of the Evidence presented. But Liberia is not blameless & the people have never tried to cultivate the friendship of the natives while the English traders ply them with 'dashes' [bribes and gifts] on all occasions." Shufeldt had put his finger on the crux of the Liberian problem, the extreme dislike by the native tribesmen of the "imported brother." In his eyes the Liberian government did not possess "a friend on earth." The American people upon whom they relied, "if in their self conceit they rely upon anybody," were far too distant and "too indifferent to the impending fate of the Negro Republic."[32]

The second meeting of the boundary commission lasted from April 4 to 24 before breaking up without reaching a settlement. For this session the Liberian government changed its commissioners to William McCall Davis and John Wallace Worrell. At Solyman, the Liberians desired to know the names of the parties disputing Liberia's claim to the territory. The British assumed their Liberian counterparts would produce witnesses in support of the alleged deeds of cession to Liberia and thus declined to furnish any names. In reply, the Liberian commissioners implied "that the native Chiefs had not raised the objections of themselves but had been invited to do so by Her Majesty's Government." The British claimed that the object of the proposals was not whether any particular kings or chiefs were entitled to the districts in question but whether the Liberian commissioners could show a title to the districts "as would justify Her Majesty's Government in ignoring the repudiation by the native kings and Chiefs of the claims put forward by the Liberian Government to the North of the Territory extending between Cape Palmas to the South and the Sugaree Territory to the N.W. both inclusive." The onus of proof lay with the Liberians, and the British were prepared to wait until the native chiefs came forward themselves in support of their own denials of the cession.

Shufeldt was invited to be present at the opening, but he declined. He charged the British with one-sidedness, but Streeton turned aside the charge and invited him to come see the commissioners "working very industriously & in perfect harmony," which was, he stressed, "quite a contrast to Sierra Leone." Shufeldt asserted that his services were only required "under special circumstances," and he remained on board the *Ticonderoga*. On April 7 every commissioner at Solyman requested his presence, but he still refused. He indicated that he would leave next day for Sierra Leone to replenish the rapidly dwindling stores of his ship. He was piqued at the Liberians for failing to notify him of the end of the first session of the commission, a fact that still rankled him in April. But the blame for refusing to join the commission lay with him alone. The point is of some importance in view of his claim later that the British froze him out. For his daughter's sake he assessed the significance of the Liberian dispute. When its history came to be written, he ruminated,

> you will have no reason to be ashamed of the role I am playing—The fact is, that the British Commissioners have been terribly afraid of poor me! They have declined to give me the presidency of the Board—for fear that Liberia would have too strong a friend! They have . . . dallied for 90 days afraid to go on & yet not daring to stop. All in a diplomatic way of course. . . . They had hoped for an Umpire—a milder mannered man. The question grew in importance when the *Ticonderoga* came. Through the haze of an African atmosphere they saw American aggression & Yankee annexation![33]

Shufeldt was inaccurate in personalizing the British objections to him. The British commissioners were willing for him to join the commission, but they occupied the position of strength in the negotiations; to admit Shufeldt as president, as he and they well knew, would mean a pro-Liberian bias. By keeping him out of the presidency they prevented their numerical equality from being undermined. In this position they outwaited him and outmaneuvered the Liberians.

Having replenished the ship in Sierra Leone, Shufeldt returned to Solyman on April 21. Here he found the two delegations still deadlocked. The British denied that the Liberians had established their case through failing to substantiate their claims to the coast. Consequently, they declared there was nothing to lay before the arbitrator. Also, the British considered that the Liberians had not established any boundaries by treaty. They denied the existence of a "Manno" territory, which the Liberians claimed. When Shufeldt arrived, Alfred W. King, secretary of the Liberian group, complained to him of "some very arbitrary proceedings" in his absence and concluded that Shufeldt's services were indispensible to the commission.

On the twenty-first the Liberian commissioners issued an ultimatum. The British had offered to take Shufeldt's "opinion . . . on certain points" but would not regard it as binding on, or affecting, the British government, unless concurred in by each government. This meant each government would have the power of review over Shufeldt's opinion. The British would not accept the decision unless it proved favorable to them. The Liberians declined the British proposition, very properly in Shufeldt's eyes, as derogatory to the character of the arbitrator and his government. By this time Shufeldt had defined the British commissioners as both judge and jury. For the information of his secretary of the navy he enumerated the points of the proceedings that struck him as *ex parte:* Solyman, though nominally in the disputed territory, was actually a British trading post (a dangerous admission for him to make); the British trader, John Myers Harris, possessed all of the powers of a chief or king controlling the surrounding tribes entirely; the same natives were witnesses in the case against Liberia; over fifteen hundred tribesmen had come to the post, being called to it and fed by the British authorities; and the Liberian commissioners were surrounded "by these savages more or less hostile to them, . . . so to speak in a hostile camp." This militated against a fair trial. The commodore informed his superiors in the State Department that "if the British Home Government intended, as I have no doubt it did, that Liberia should be treated not only impartially but generously, in this, to her all important question, it would have been much better to have divested the British Commission of its *Colonial* [i.e., Sierra Leone] character; [as] the thirst for territory and the feeling of jealousy existing at Sierra Leone against Liberia is very intense, not to say unscrupulous."[34]

To Shufeldt's mind, the three months on the West African coast had passed without his once being invited to perform any official function, yet the correspondence between the English and American governments had envisaged an active part for him in the commission. The Liberians had a case to take before the great powers of the world. He hoped the United States government would not be "the last to enter her protest" if the smaller republic should "lose" a strip of territory. Likewise, the editor of the *Monrovia Observer* charged that the motive behind Sierra Leone's fight was the wish to expand into Liberia, assuming that for this purpose the Sierra Leonese "had got up a case" against their neighbor. Shufeldt's view took into account that the commission "had gone up" when the British commissioners had refused to refer the case to him as Arbitrator, and when the Liberians, "having more pluck" than he thought, insisted on referring it. As a result, "the whole thing exploded." Personally, he was glad for he felt it gave Liberia another chance later for land. Meanwhile, it called "the attention of the world to the greed of Great Britain—seized at this time with the thirst for Empire." Shufeldt was overly optimistic. Liberia did not get another opportunity to negotiate. In 1882, long after Shufeldt had passed from the coast, Great Britain annexed the disputed area following a display of force by the Royal Navy.[35]

Following the failure of the negotiations, the Liberian government gave Shufeldt a handsome letter of thanks, which he took to be more for what he did not do than for what he did. To his daughter he compared the state of Liberia with what she had seen in 1873:

> Liberia has not gathered any strength since we were here in the *Plymouth*—on the contrary she grows weaker. If not enough harrassed by foreign traders both within & without her borders the people have now begun the agitation of the *color* question—the pure blacks against the mixed bloods. There is no foretelling the result of this antagonism. It has been the real cause of all the revolutions in Hayti & will be the cause of revolution here. I confess that I am losing my confidence in the Republic—I see no help for it except the direct intervention of the U.S. . . . there will be enough & to spare of forthcoming trouble in our own country without borrowing the troubles of this insignificant nation.

Later, in the manuscript he prepared for publication, Shufeldt developed this criticism of Liberia's color problem:

> There are other disintegrating influences also constantly at work. For thirty years the Liberian has despised and ignored the African. There is no repugnance of race in America to compare with the feeling existing between the imported and the native races—an affectation of superiority on the one hand, met by contempt and hatred on the other. No effort has been made to

amalgamate these discordant elements. On the contrary the Liberian builds away at an oligarchy. Imported from the Southern States he has brought with him the imitated air of hauteur, the fancied tones of superiority which he seems to think the characteristics of mastership. . . . There is no unity of thought or action in the body corporate of Liberia. Strange as it may seem in a negro republic, the "color-line" is strongly marked. The black man, pure and simple, hates the mulatto.[36]

Shufeldt also warned the Navy and State departments of French moves to occupy the island of Matacong, and the fears in Liberia of a French move to assume a protectorate over the country. He recommended the detachment of a gunboat from the European squadron to assist Liberia. Secretary of State Evarts and Alvey A. Adee, the assistant secretary in the State Department, investigated and pointed out to American representatives in European capitals the "increased Politico-economic importance" that Liberia possessed. Repeating sentiments that had been issued in 1843 by Abel P. Upshur, Evarts warned American ministers in London and Paris that "the United States are not averse to having the great Powers know that they publicly recognize the peculiar relation between them and Liberia, and that they are prepared to take every proper step to maintain them." Thus the United States government kept careful watch on French and British moves that might tend to "assimilate or extinguish the governmental rights of the native peoples on the African coast in the neighborhood of Liberia."[37]

As Shufeldt left Liberia for the last time, he paused to reflect that his labors had not been entirely in vain. But on May 6, off the Bonny River (now in Nigeria), he struck an entirely different note in his estimates of the future of Liberia. For Secretary of the Navy Thompson he defined Liberia as "the real center of American interests on the West Coast of Africa north of the equator." All of Africa that he had visited, with the exception of Liberia, had been divided between England and France; there was "not a single American trading establishment at any point or at any native towns where by its presence American trade could be encouraged or the flag utilized." Believing that Liberia would be absorbed by Britain or France unless protected by some friendly power, he outlined the problem specifically for Thompson's benefit:

> Liberia presents a front of six hundred miles upon the sea, behind which lies the most fertile portion of the Continent: it is a tempting prize to any Nation in search of new markets, but she is only a rope of sand stretched along the beach and cannot be held together much longer without the cohesive power of a stronger Government. I make these remarks after thoughtful consideration and not so much in the interest of that Republic as in the extension of the foreign commerce of our own Country.

Although pressing for the self-interest of his own country before the official policy-making bodies in the United States, Shufeldt had a more doleful view to offer to Molly. "Poor Liberia," he wrote to her, "I often think of that forlorn yet complacent Republic—& could weep for her—if one could weep for a people in a collective sense." No doubt tears for Molly's sake would be as soothing as the balm of economic opportunity would be for Thompson and American commerce.[38]

On to Cape Town

On April 11, Shufeldt had received further instructions from the State Department. Early in February, Evarts notified the Navy Department that Colonel Henry Shelton Sanford, former American minister to Belgium and an American entrepreneur with a strong interest in Africa, had suggested that Shufeldt be instructed to observe American commercial interests on the Congo River. Sanford wished to prevent any sanctioning of the doctrine, preached by the Portuguese, of any right to exclusive control in that region by fact of first discovery. Evarts believed that the impracticability of such a rigid insistence on exclusive control could be easily demonstrated. Furthermore, he declared, "the general commercial world" would not accept a doctrine "offensive to the general and peaceful pursuit of that commerce," without the closest scrutiny as to its fundamental merits. The *New York Herald* also demanded commercial freedom for all nations in the Congo, identifying its interest in its masthead slogan. Evarts' letters were forwarded to Shufeldt for his future guidance. He thus determined to call at the Congo en route Cape Town.[39]

The *Ticonderoga* left Monrovia on April 29, bound for Fernando Po (Bioko, Equatorial Guinea), Gabon, and the Congo. Early on the morning of May 7, Clarence Peak, on the Spanish island of Fernando Po, jutted out of the morning mists as the *Ticonderoga* slid into her anchorage at Gravina Bay. The prospects of the Spanish-held island, used as a prison for political prisoners, excited the visiting American as "the key to the palm oil trade" of the eight principal palm oil rivers of West Africa, "the natural terminus of an American steam ship line employed in the African trade." Shufeldt urged the appointment of a consul for the Bights of Benin and Biafra. He desired the extension of the jurisdiction of the consulate at St. Paul de Loanda over the Congo. Returning to his old theme on the navy, he stressed the need for United States control over the island:

> The actual possession of the Island of Fernando Po by the United States would be of immense advantage to our Commerce but in the absence of any such desire on the part of the American Government or People—as mani-

fested in our foreign policy, it would be (in my opinion) very desireable to lease from the Spanish Government any one (say Gravina Bay) of the harbors for a coaling station. . . . It would seem to me that part of wisdom to have at least a coaling station scattered here and there among the islands of the Globe, and I venture the prediction that as uninteresting as Africa is to our merchants today, the time is not distant when a continent of 300,000,000, of non-manufacturing people will form no insignificant item in the manufacturing business of America.[40]

Despite his excitement over the potential of the Spanish colony for American commercial domination of the palm oil rivers, Shufeldt felt disillusioned over his impact on Africa generally. He wrote to Molly, "if I could feel any certainty as to the future & the future policy of our own country I might make much more of an impression here but the feeling constantly intrudes itself of its inability—we have no policy—it is a mere matter of haphazard." Dangling at the end of a 3,000-mile communication line and out of touch with departmental strategies, Shufeldt could only fulminate against the "pertinacious designs" of the English and French to divide up the continent. He lectured Molly that Fernando Po, which Spain "only nominally owns," could become "of the greatest commercial importance" to the United States because it was the key to the trade of the entire palm oil region, "yet who in America cares?" The commodore was not so far in front of official thinking in Washington as he assumed, though he made himself despondent at what he imagined to be the lost opportunities for commercial enterprise.[41]

After touching at the Gabon mission station, the *Ticonderoga* anchored in the Congo River on May 27. She proved too large to ascend the river for more than thirty or forty miles and then against a very strong current and the constant hazard of shifting sand and mud bars. Shufeldt sent Lieutenant Franklin Drake thirty miles upriver in the steam launch to negotiate with the chiefs of the Mussarango tribe. Shufeldt described them as "incorrigible rascals and robbers, and can only be restrained by the constant presence of a gun boat." The main chiefs with whom Drake conferred were kings Kala, Parker, Inpaca, Pala Bola, Natudy, and Asumba, while he was prevented from speaking with King Inballa when the steam launch broke down. The talks with Pala Bola, originating in the maltreatment of an American crew some years earlier, proved to be inconclusive.[42]

Shufeldt found the Dutch in complete possession of Banana, a collection of large trading factories run by about thirty Europeans and three hundred natives, at the mouth of the river. Thirty or more of these factories belonged to the Afrikaansche Handelsverenninging Company of Rotterdam, which controlled the river trade and a large strip of the adjacent seacoast with its fleet of schooners. Shufeldt believed the river trade was but one remove from the old slave trade, selling rum and gin to the natives. Disgusted by what he saw, he told Thompson: " 'The opening up of Africa' viewed from this stand point with reference to its Civilization is a mere deceit and delusion. The natives of the lower Congo who have been in contact with whites for nearly four hundred years have only had ingrafted upon their innate barbarism the lowest vices of civilization." The Dutch did not take kindly to the commodore's presence. When the ship's launch broke down, the company refused to charter a steam tug to the Americans. Consequently, Shufeldt left a week earlier than he had anticipated, partly because of the Dutch attitude and partly because his ship's sick list was growing astronomically in the sticky heat of the river.[43]

For this area, as at Fernando Po, Shufeldt advocated the appointment of an American consul or commercial agent with extended jurisdiction on the coast, though he expected the Dutch to claim sovereignty. He recommended to his government that it take this point into consideration, especially "in view of the importance of this river to the commerce of all nations." He had his paymaster, William J. Thompson, draft a commercial report on the area. From his point of view of the Dutch activities, Shufeldt advised that United States interest in the region should be "one calculated either to christianize or civilize the Africans." The true line of American commerce, he advised, lay north of the equator, "embracing the oil regions of the Bights and the fertile region which lies behind Liberia and extends to the valley of the Niger."[44]

Shufeldt also hoped to set the minds of the secretary of state and Colonel Sanford at rest on the problem of Portuguese intentions in the area. There was nothing to be apprehensive about from them. The province of Angola, he estimated, owed much of its prosperity to Antonio Francisco da Silva, who had served at some time as a United States consul at Loanda (Luanda) and whom Shufeldt mistakenly called an American. Da Silva, known as Silva Porto, was born in Portugal, served a merchant apprenticeship in Rio and Bahia, and dominated the interior of Angola for nearly fifty years. Shufeldt hoped to turn his expertise to American advantage. Portuguese trade, while increasing, was partly an intercolonial slave trade with other Portuguese colonies. Shufeldt did not recommend frequent visits by American men-of-war to the river because of its "little relative importance" to the United States, its unhealthy climate, and the difficulties of navigation after one hundred miles. Furthermore, he expected the Dutch to claim the Congo, an event that he stood ready to condemn: "It is another advent in the 'opening up of Africa.' It is another stretching out of the hands of Commerce; the fingers of one clasping and creeping over the rich domains of

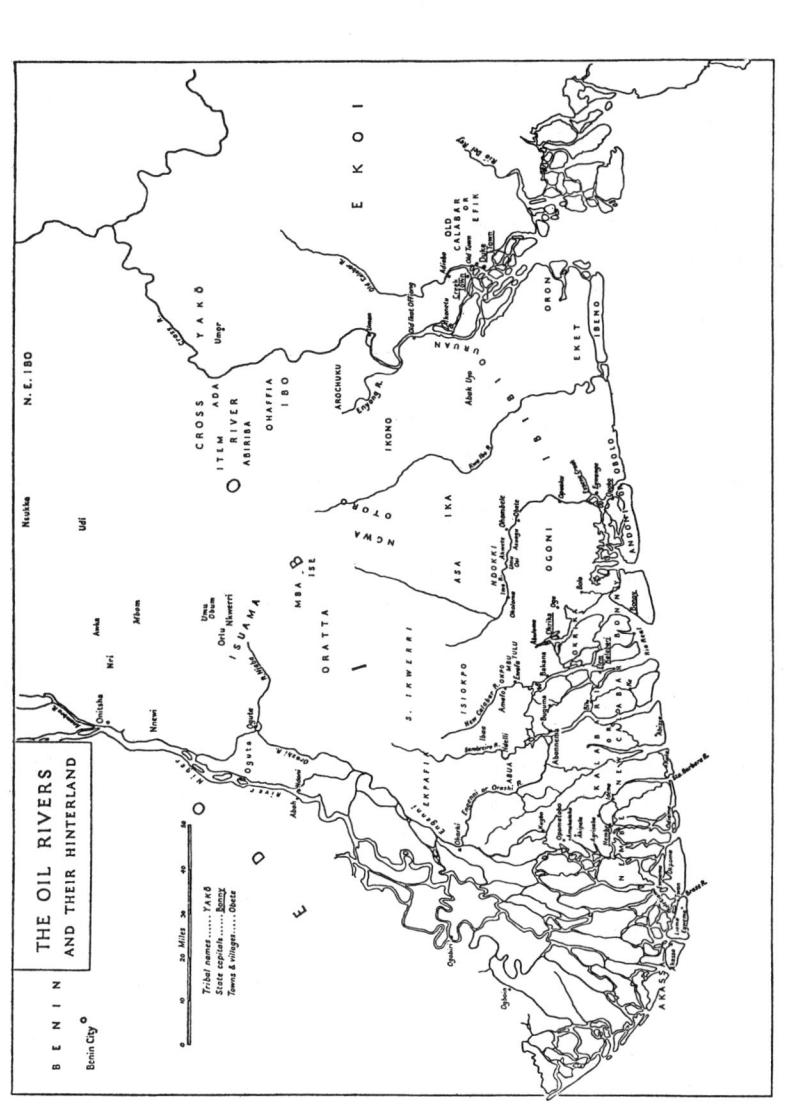

The Oil Rivers of West Africa. From G. I. Jones, *The Trading States of the Oil Rivers: A Study of Political Development in Eastern Nigeria*, published for the International African Institute by the Oxford University Press (Oxford University Press, 1963), p. 9. Reprinted with permission.

a barbarous and unknown continent; the other extending in the name of reward and of Civilization, the debasing influence of vile liquor, to degenerate and degrade natives, by nature 'already debased.' "[45] Although Shufeldt had continually urged the stretching out of the hands of American commerce, he assumed it would uplift and civilize the native inhabitants. Moreover, he was frowning on the use of alcohol by the Dutch, but he later advocated the sale of rum products to Africans if it eased the problem of the depression in the United States. In the long run, the only distinction between the two types of control, Dutch and American, lay in the commodore's assumption that American civilization would uplift and regenerate, as he had implied it would in Cuba, Tehuantepec, and the Pacific islands, whereas Dutch penetration would lead to degradation and degeneration.

A Consular System for the African Coast

En route to Cape Town, Shufeldt called at St. Helena to allow his crew to recuperate from fever and to distill his thoughts on the commercial importance of the west coast of Africa, relating that importance to the tasks confronting the United States if it wished to seize a share of the African market.[46] In the first instance he defined the problem:

> The Continent of Africa is today the great commercial prize of the world. England, France, Holland and Germany are aware of this fact, and are striving for its possession, and, whatever may be the impression at home, the cruise of the *Ticonderoga* on the West Coast, has been to these Powers a matter of jealous interest.
>
> But if we are to have the share in this rapidly increasing trade that our products entitle us to, it will need the active protection of our Government. Hitherto the foreign trade of the United States has been of spontaneous growth, arising in a great degree from the indifference and blindness of foreign nations to the genius of our people, and the immense resources of our Country; now however, those Nations are fully alive to these facts and when we enter the field it must be in the character of a rival—prepared to contest every inch of the ground.
>
> The enterprise of the individual American Merchant can not be expected to succeed against the combined influence of the capital and power of Europe, unless sustained by the active force of his own Government.

There were two ways that such a force could be applied to the situation, he argued, without "trespassing upon acquired rights" of European nations or upon the "natural rights" of Africans: one was to provide an efficient consular service and the other was to provide naval protection.

Such a consular service, Shufeldt envisaged, would extend jurisdiction along the whole west coast, "so that every mile of the beach shall by means of Agencies, so far as our people and trade are concerned, be under the protection of the American flag." He cited the British example as sufficient justification for his scheme. If any outrages took place on British merchant vessels, the British consul went to settle them in a gunboat. "So it should be in a degree with us," he demanded. At that time, he added, American merchant vessels were often dependent on British protection. He acknowledged Britain as a generous rival, surveying rivers, buoying harbors, patrolling rivers at a cost of money and lives, all of which resulted in protection for stray traders as well as her own. Shufeldt had a vision of American consular and naval protection on a similar scale to the British. The minister resident in Liberia should be appointed the consul general for the whole coast. Within his immediate district of Liberia, Shufeldt wished to allot him powers to appoint commercial agents at four or five points within the territory; Tabou, Cape Palmas, Sinou, or Cape Mount. Such a minister should also be a white man, he urged (and in his mind he may well have thought of himself), for it was no compliment to Liberia "to appoint a black man to that office." A Negro would be both subject and object of dislike to the Liberians and would fail "to inspire the respect among the natives which seems to be the inherent right of the white man in Africa."

Outside of Liberia, Shufeldt desired to see consuls at Sierra Leone (with jurisdiction over Senegambia and agencies at the Senegal and Gambia rivers), Fernando Po (with control over the coast of Guinea), the Bight of Biafra (including agencies at every one of the oil rivers of the west coast), at the Gabon River (with a commercial agent at the Congo), and at Loanda (with jurisdiction from the south bank of the Congo to the southern limit of Angola). Such a division of consular authority was flexible, he postulated, for it was not intended to be an arbitrary system, only suggestive, but such a pattern as this should be erected for it was "essential to our Commercial progress on the coast." Furthermore, it required full government support. Shrewdly using a western simile, Shufeldt declared, "our commerce like our mining interest, has ceased to be the mere haphazard hit of the wandering mariner or miner and now demands, as does mining, the steady support and guidance of capital and organization."

As a corollary to this system, Shufeldt required the presence of American gunboats with specific orders to assist the consuls. He poured scorn on the Navy Department's instructions to naval commanders who were permitted "to consider the coast as a fit place for 'black listers' from the Mediterranean," who were sent without definite orders or distinct ideas of the importance of the rivers. At least keep one ship of the European squadron on the coast, he pleaded, and provide a small vessel to survey the coast and rivers of Liberia, not only in the interest of that country and its identification with the United States but also for "the development for our mutual benefit of its dormant riches." Once again Shufeldt pressed for a mail subsidy for a Liberian–United States steamship line. Then, he had faith that American products would soon find "constant and abundant sale" on the coast, and "the American flag be restored to its former prestige."

Despite this intense drive to push and pull the Navy and State departments in the direction of his own thinking, Shufeldt was pessimistic about the final outcome of his efforts. When the *Ticonderoga* arrived at Cape Town on August 4, he revealed his surprise that he had not received "one line from the Dept.—either of encouragement or discouragement—we seem to be left to our own devices." To his daughter, he characterized the alleged indifference of the government as "sad evidence of its decay—& a forerunner of its downfall." The commodore's resentment at the "political bummers" who were being appointed to consulates that required first-class men to compete with the foreign consular corps and his dislike of foreign men-of-war protecting American citizens as well as foreign steamships carrying American mails were evident in his letters home. Privately, he overstated his sense of isolation. To Molly, for whom his messages were more emotional than thoughtful and in contrast to those for Thompson, he confided: "The possibilities for the future of America are so great—that I grit my teeth at the indifferences of our Govt. & the supineness of our citizens—but what avails this gnashing of teeth & why should you & I worry? I shall go on—filling quires of paper, with matter which is never read, until the end of the cruise & then I shall subside into my easy chair & in the curling of my cigar smoke—see all my labor vanishing into the thin air!"[47] With his vision of omnipotence wafting on a smoke cloud of despair, Shufeldt finally came to the end of his tour of the west coast of Africa. Before him stretched all of the lands bordering on the Indian Ocean and the Asiatic seas. He intended to observe the activities and the influences of the British work of colonization in South Africa. He had this aim in mind as he brought the *Ticonderoga* into Cape Town harbor during the first week in August.

The cruise of the *Ticonderoga* was not greeted with the indifference in government circles that Shufeldt conjured up for his daughter's benefit. Evarts twice notified Thompson that Shufeldt's dispatches on the American consulate at St. Helena and a consular system for the west coast of Africa were "of much interest and will have careful consideration" and were "important and valuable."[48] Shufeldt's interests in consular activity apparently bore fruit in October of the following year when the State Department issued the first volume of its *Reports from the Consuls of the United States on the Commercial Manufacture etc. of their Consular Districts.*

Shufeldt's advocacy of a comprehensive consular network to cover the entire West African coast was a rational scheme to win "the great commercial prize of the world." The commodore looked to African markets to end America's economic depression. He faithfully followed his instructions to seek the openings whereby the United States government could join the economic scramble for Africa. His promptings of the Navy and State departments followed logically from his investigations into the consular service. Prevented from solving the boundary question, Shufeldt had a far greater vision for Liberia than the extension of her territory a few miles northward. He wished to use her, and the palm oil rivers close to Fernando Po, as open doors to Africa. While some in the United States agreed with him in overall African strategy (for example, the African Trade Society, organized to promote steamship intercourse with Africa, which demanded in 1884 the establishment of a mail service between New Orleans and Liberia), most observers of Africa, however, looked to the Congo in future years rather than to Liberia.

Thus President Chester A. Arthur's annual message of 1883 suggested possible cooperation with other commercial powers to promote trade and residence rights in the Congo, and the following year the Senate Committee on Foreign Relations inquired into trading rights in the Congo Valley and was called upon to report on the necessary action to further American commerce. Senator John T. Morgan of Alabama offered a resolution to Congress, February 26, 1884, recommending that the president "secure freedom of access and traffic for American citizens in their legitimate enterprise in the Congo Basin by assuring protection to traders and missionaries and by denying the rights of any one nation to exclusive sovereignty." Senators John Sherman of Ohio and George F. Edmunds of Vermont called for an open door for all nations. Eventually, Secretary of State Frederick T. Frelinghuysen commissioned Willard P. Tisdel as a roving agent in 1884, to report on the political and commercial situation in the Congo. The Navy Department dispatched Lieutenant Emory H. Taunt, who seconded Tisdel's reports. This interest culminated in American participation in the Berlin Conference of 1884–1885, to discuss freedom of commerce and navigation, outlawing the slave trade, and establishing freedom of religion and rules for the occupation of the interior of the Congo. Shufeldt's activities, like Stanley's and Sanford's, intensified American interest in West Africa, and Shufeldt was one of the great commercial pathfinders into western and central Africa. But the trails he urged Americans to follow would have brought them to the Niger Valley through Liberia, while the ones that finally were followed by later Americans led into the Congo basin.

11

The Cruise of the *Ticonderoga:*
South Africa to Japan

As the *Ticonderoga* sailed along the coast lands bordering the Indian Ocean, Shufeldt's main task was to carry out Evarts' and Thompson's instructions as they applied to the various countries and ports en route. He also used his time and imagination to comment on the political and commercial control exercised by the British in these seas. As the cruise progressed, his examination into the nature of power intensified. Soon he found himself on the horns of an expansionist dilemma. He often deplored British political control yet envied the extent of that nation's commercial dominance. Constantly exhorting Americans to redouble their efforts to secure commercial supremacy, he was deliberately vague on the question of whether this implied political control for the United States. Secretary of the Navy Thompson also proved to be vague on this topic when he claimed, "It is confidently expected that material benefits to our commerce will result from this expedition, and that it will become the means of establishing new relations between this country and the continent of Africa and the adjacent islands." While not defining "new relations," Thompson clearly agreed that the cruise served as a practical effort to extend American commercial influences, as Shufeldt continued to seek solutions to the country's problems in a world still beset by the lurching booms and slumps of economic dislocation.[1]

Cape Town, South Africa

Shufeldt began his comparisons with Britain immediately upon reaching Cape Town. He compiled a detailed report concerning the political problems and industrial conditions of South Africa in which he compared the colony's development with America's own.[2] Defining the colony as "a central point for the exchange of the productions of that Continent for the manufactures of Europe and America," he believed it was crystallizing into a new nation "possessing all the characteristics and qualities of Anglo Saxon nationality" and with social, industrial, and political questions similar to those of the United States. He defined the first problem as one of consolidating the great expanse of the country, with its preponderate proportion of natives to colonists, under one government. Next, he predicted the annexation of the Orange Free State, asserting that the government must be essentially "a White man's Government." Eventually, he envisaged the whole of South Africa being brought into contact "with the civilizing influences of commerce and intercourse with superior races."

The key to this expansion and consolidation, in Shufeldt's estimation, was the rapidly developing railroad system of South Africa, with 450 miles completed and 400 under construction. He dwelt at length on the beneficent effects that railroad building was having on the country and drew the lesson for Americans:

> The French are perfecting railway schemes which are intended to penetrate North West Africa through Senegambia; the English will extend their power by the same means from the Cape of Good Hope to the Equator, and if Americans care to take their share in this mission, they have Liberia through which may be entered the heart of Africa, and thus the whole of the "Dark Continent" would be brought, so to speak, "into the market" and its people taught by their necessities to aspire to a higher plane of civilization.
>
> It may not be out of place for me to say here that the native of Africa is infinitely better off under the rule of the white man however despotic, than under his own Chief, who at the best is an unfeeling savage. The conquest of Africa therefore will be a benevolent act and I care not who undertakes it, for in the end it will redound to the good of its people and to the benefit of the whole world.

Shufeldt's views on the role of railroads were very similar to his analyses of the role of men-of-war. The railroads not only linked eastern and western seaports but, in the absence of navigable rivers, he calculated, a railroad system was vital to the imperial and commercial development of the country, for "the railway must precede the settler, and . . . as it opens up the interior, the country will become populated, traffic will increase, and the indirect benefits to the revenue will more than compensate for any remaining burden upon the Treasury." He also drew attention to the construction of telegraphic communications connecting Cape Town with the important towns of the eastern seaboard, Delagoa Bay and, ultimately, Zanzibar, Aden, and England.

Shufeldt also saw English policies coinciding with American over the problems of "the color line" and internal tribal warfare.[3] The commodore, who observed "an irreconcilable antagonism of races," was concerned over opinions that were openly declared in the colonial parliament by the attorney general "that the whites and blacks were natural enemies—that the blacks were only fit to be tillers of the soil—that whether friend or foe they should be disarmed and not permitted to carry any weapons, but [be] confined—strictly bondsmen in fact, if not in name—to their legitimate occupation as hewers of wood and drawers of water." Thus he feared that if the policy of repression (rather than concession) being urged by a majority of the colonial government were implemented, then a general rising of the black population or else an exodus of the population caused by profound discontent would take place.

Similarly, the encroachment of the pioneer on the tribal lands was bringing him into almost constant collision with tribes, in much the same way that the American pioneer had come into contact with Indian tribes. Shufeldt described the situation plainly:

> Injustice, and often cruelty on the one part is met by revenge on the other. Substitute "Sitting Bull" for "Ketchwhyo," and "Big Horn" for "Isandhlwana," and you have the history of our Indian war repeated in the Kafir war in Africa.
>
> To be sure the Kafir is a different creature from the Indian, the one being a cattle-raiser and the other a hunter, but both are migratory, and possess the qualities which cause them to struggle against the encroachments of the European Settler. To both, civilization means extermination. . . . The policy that has brought about this [Zulu] war—at the bottom of which lies the Craze of Imperialism—has also succeeded in creating another hostile element on the borders, consisting of a tribe not despicable in the art of war, with whom in their defeat, the other Kafir tribes must naturally sympathize.

As a result of his analysis, Shufeldt recommended that the preliminary step by the United States government should be to raise its consulate at Cape Town to a higher class. He desired an independent consulate at Port Elizabeth, Algoa Bay, which possessed a virtual monopoly of the export trade with the United States and a general commerce almost double that of Cape Town. Generally, Shufeldt found the consular service on the entire West African coast "beneath the dignity of the country it represents," but he blamed the inadequacy of salaries rather than methods of selection or the Cape Town incumbent, W. W. Edgecomb. Given his preconceptions of the paramount demands of American commerce, together with his drawing of parallels between the courses of United States and South African history, Shufeldt's conclusion was also self-evident: "Much has been done by the visit of the *Ticonderoga* to the Cape to bring these two Nations into fraternal relations, and I only hope that this communication may have the effect, in its limited way, of arousing a similar interest and feeling in the United States."

Treaty-making from Madagascar to Zanzibar

From Cape Town, the American vessel cruised for two weeks toward St. Augustine Bay on the west coast of Madagascar, one hundred and sixty miles north of the southernmost point of Cape Sainte Marie. On September 19, 1879, the *Ticonderoga* moved on to Tullear Bay, which Shufeldt regarded as "one of the finest harbors I have ever entered . . . perfectly secure and healthy." As British and French rivalry for colonial acquisitions embraced the eastern shores of Africa, he wanted to extend American opportunities by using the bay as a coaling depot for United States warships, with a consular agent also present at the place. To implement his desires within the context of Thompson's instructions, Shufeldt entered into two agreements, on September 17 and 20, with King Balambé and King Lamarese, chiefs of the Malagasy and Sakalava tribes, who controlled the tribal confederation around St. Augustine and Tullear bays. These agreements were made in order to provide protection and coal to American trading and whaling ships engaged in the Chinese, Indian Ocean, and East African trade, which frequently visited Tullear Bay and the surrounding coast.[4] According to Shufeldt and the tribal chiefs, the government at Antananarivo, capital of the island, exercised no rights of sovereignty over the western part of the island. The chiefs declared that the Antananarivo government had never controlled the coast from Cape St. Vincent southward, one-third of the coastal strip. Only one point—a military garrison—existed on a thousand miles of west coast where the government had any authority. As vessels of all nations, especially English and French, traded along the coast without regard to the Antananarivo government, paying dues to the local kings and receiving protection from them, Shufeldt considered some agreement with the chiefs was essential for the protection of American commerce and the acquisition of rights to deposit coal for naval vessels.

Shufeldt made his agreements with knowledge of the United States–Madagascar treaty of 1867, which he did not consider binding on the west coast, "for if it was construed to cover the whole island of Madagascar it would virtually exclude our flag from at least one half of the island leaving to other Nations the most profitable part of the trade." This was a remarkable reversal of Shufeldt's attitude as manifested during the *Ticonderoga*'s visit to the Tabou River at the request of the Liberian government. There the commodore had upheld the central government against the native chiefs and illicit traders; in Madagascar he was repudiating the authority of the central government, backed by a treaty with his own country, by making formal agreements with local kings for the benefit of American trade. The latter was the operative factor to

Shufeldt: in both countries he expected his actions would lead to an increase in trade with the United States.[5]

Shufeldt's original instructions had specified calling at Madagascar to investigate the possible maltreatment of an American citizen, a request that originated from the United States consul at Tamatave, W. W. Robinson. The consul had also suggested a revision of the treaty of 1867, mainly because cotton goods belonging to the Salem shipping house of John Bertram were being lost en route from Tamatave, the principal port, to the capital. Robinson, however, had established a close relationship with Queen Ranavalona II and the Hova government at Antananarivo on the east side of the island. Shufeldt's actions in negotiating with tribal chiefs of the west coast, who were resisting the Hova government and the Manjaka royal family, threatened to undermine the queen's authority on the west coast. The rumor spread to Tamatave that Shufeldt had raised the American flag. As a controversy brewed over the arrival, in August, of a French diplomatic agent, which was judged by some to be a preliminary step in the establishment of a French protectorate, Robinson was extremely concerned over the strength and survival of the island's government.[6]

Shufeldt was more concerned that the Hova government did not control more than one-third of the island; in the northwest there was not a semblance of obedience to Hova law where there was not also a Hova garrison. He saw the Hovas using British help to extend their power while fearing French influence. As American trade amounted to $300,000 annually and as French silver coin was used in the island, it occurred to Shufeldt "that if our merchants engaged in the Madagascar trade could introduce the 'trade dollar' into that country—it would afford no insignificant market for our silver, as these dollars being cut up would never return into circulation." He desired all of the advantages of the 1867 treaty but wished to confine it exclusively to the Hova government "and only to that part of the island over which it has exclusive jurisdiction," together with the advantages of his own agreements with the Malagasy and Sakalava tribes, even if it meant ignoring the Hova claim to sovereignty over the whole island. Such a revision of the 1867 treaty would have taken three months to accomplish, he informed Thompson, so he took the *Ticonderoga* from Tullear Bay, called twice at stopping places on the west coast, and finally left the island to sail northward on September 26.[7]

Consul Robinson managed to neutralize Shufeldt's work on the west coast. On January 21, 1881, Charles Payson, third assistant secretary in the State Department, informed Robinson that Shufeldt had decided that American commerce would be able to compete successfully on the west coast if aided by consular representatives providing protection.

The State Department was willing to consider the question of another consular post on the southern part of the west coast, but before acting the department's officials wanted to know certain information: what was the most favorable point for its establishment; what were the powers of the Hova government to protect American traders on that coast; what was the power of the Hovas over the Sakalava tribe; what was the advisability of trading directly with the west coast traders "until such time as the Hova or Madagascar government shall have established their authority over the whole of the island"; and how were the treaties with the Sakalava tribe regarded? The State Department was obviously sensitive to the points raised in Shufeldt's dispatches (which undermined his claims to Molly that he was being ignored), though Payson informed Robinson that no further action would be taken on Shufeldt's treaties other than an acknowledgment of their receipt. But Payson did warn Robinson that

> should the Hova or Madagascar government fail to establish their [*sic*] authority over the Sakalava tribe of the West Coast, and should their officers at the few ports in their possession continue their actions upon our Commerce reported by Mr. Stanwood [who had worked with Shufeldt on the treaties], or in a word, should the necessities of our commerce seem to demand it, the Department is prepared to avail itself of Commodore Shufeldt's agreement, and to hold relations with the natives of the West Coast, pending the settlement of the question of disputed sovereignty and authority in that section of the Island, at the same time, the government of the United States is quite willing to recognize the authority of the Hova or Madagascar government over the whole Island.

Shufeldt's visit placed the State Department in a position to put pressure on the Hova government through Robinson. It used the commodore's agreements as bargaining weapons to extract from that government the best terms possible for the protection and expansion of American commerce on the island. By May 13, 1881, Robinson had persuaded the foreign minister to sign a new commercial treaty.[8]

Leaving Madagascar the *Ticonderoga* passed to Johanna (Anjouan), the central island of the Comoro group situated in the Mozambique Channel about 275 miles from the northwest of Madagascar. The total population of just over ten thousand on the small island was governed by an independent sultan. The town of Johanna, on the north side of the island, had a population of nearly three thousand and served as a port of call for American whalers. Upon arrival Shufeldt noted for Molly's sake, "we are now in a different world—the Arab & Moor have taken the place of the Negro pure & simple. We are beginning to have a taste of the Orient." Unfortunately for the commodore, this taste included an unpalatable altercation between American citizens and the sultan of the island.[9]

The main American commercial interests on Johanna were in sugar, coffee, and hides. Dr. Benjamin F. Wilson, M.D., a former acting assistant surgeon in the United States Navy, was the island's second largest sugar producer. His estate, "Patsey," outstripped the sultan's own plantation. Another American, T. P. Robinson, of the firm of Hondlette and Company of Mauritius, had introduced coffee production into Johanna and was engaged in the hide trade. Both were involved in disputes with the sultan over the purchase of machinery, though Wilson did not let his sugar partnership with the monarch suffer as a consequence. Robinson, however, had a further grievance. He claimed that the sultan had allowed others to occupy land belonging to him. At the suggestion of W. H. Hathorne and Dr. John Kirk, United States and British consuls in Zanzibar, to whom Robinson had applied for redress, the case had gone to the arbitration of a British resident named Robert Sunley. Robinson refused to accept the decision and appealed to Shufeldt for aid when the *Ticonderoga* arrived.

Shufeldt, however, considered Sunley's decision "to be eminently just and reasonable." Robinson had revealed that he had attempted to take possession of certain lands in advance of any leave granted by the sultan and while the latter was absent from Johanna. On his return, the sultan had ordered the lands disposed to others. Shufeldt had a dim view of Robinson's action and told consul Hathorne, "it was an arbitrary and unjustifiable act on his part—arousing the hostility of the natives, and placing himself so decidely [sic] in the wrong, as would render it improper for any United States officer to interfere in the premises." He told Hathorne that he should advise Robinson "to cultivate more friendly feelings with the King, under whose protection he voluntarily placed himself, and who seems to be desirous of doing him justice." Thus he refused to aid Robinson, and the latter appealed to the State Department for redress.[10]

Shufeldt had good reason to denigrate Robinson's actions. On October 4, he signed a treaty with the ruler of Johanna in the latter's palace.[11] The treaty was designed to encourage commercial relations between the United States and Johanna. Peace and friendship were declared and liberty of trade accepted by both parties. Sultan Abdallah agreed to provide for the protection and security of property and the persons of resident Americans; trade was to be perfectly free, subject only to customs duties, and American goods were exempted from internal duties and "injurious regulations." The treaty included protection for shipwrecked sailors and property, with recovery provisions for the owners. Furthermore, Abdallah permitted the appointment of a consul or commercial agent or "any other officer duly appointed for that purpose," who was to be responsible for trying and adjudging crimes committed by Americans, even in disputes with Johannese, without any interference, molestation, or hindrance on the part of any Johanna authority before, during, and after litigation. The treaty would have made the consul the arbiter of the island's commercial and judicial activities as far as they involved an American in a dispute. On February 27, 1880, President Hayes submitted the treaty to the Senate, where it died.

Sultan Abdallah explained in a letter to the president that he had wished for such a treaty for a long time. Urged on by Shufeldt, he requested that Johanna be made a protectorate of the United States. The sultan was concerned over the extension of English and French authority around him and feared annexation by one of them. Mayotte, one of the Comoro Islands, had been ceded to the French in 1841. Abdallah believed that Zanzibar would soon fall into English hands. As his domain had been visited by American whalers, he declared, "we have a better feeling of friendship with them than any other nations." Shufeldt encouraged this feeling with a gift of a Springfield rifle, five hundred rounds of ammunition for the sultan, and fifty pounds of powder from the *Ticonderoga*'s magazine to fire the salute as the American flagship moved out of harbor.[12]

Zanzibar proved to be even more exciting than Johanna for the visiting Americans. They arrived on October 9, receiving an official reception from the sultan. While the reception at Johanna had been "unique," Shufeldt informed his daughter, and "gorgeous in its barbaric ways & his [Abdallah's] return visit filled the ship with the turbulent Turk . . . this was outdone by the Sultan of Zanzibar. To reach his palace—we marched thro' files of troops to the music of an excellent band, playing our own airs—to be met at the foot of the stairs by the Sultan himself accompanied by a Staff dressed in all the splendour of an Eastern court." He entertained the sultan and the American consul, W. H. Hathorne, who also represented the Salem firm of John Bertram and Company, on board the ship.[13]

Evarts' instructions required Shufeldt to discover if the United States treaty with the sultan of Muscat and Zanzibar, negotiated by Edmund Roberts and ratified September 21, 1833, was in need of revising. The terms of the treaty allowed American citizens to trade freely in any of the ports of Sultan Seyyid Said's dependencies. The 7.5 percent duty on imports in American ships was reduced to 5 percent, and no export or pilotage charges were made. A most-favored-nation clause and extraterritoriality were granted, and the president of the United States was allowed to appoint consuls to reside in any of the ports where trade was carried on. Such consuls appointed were to be exclusive judges of all disputes and suits in which American citizens were involved. Shufeldt hoped to sign a revised treaty with the sultan, especially as he found in Zanzibar, as everywhere on the east coast of Africa, "a most friendly feeling for Americans & great respect for the American flag," based on sound knowledge of the United States by the ruler of Zanzibar.

Shufeldt found difficulties with his treaty revisions, however. Zanzibar was no longer attached to the sultanate of Muscat, for when Seyyid Said had died in October 1856 his possessions had been divided between his sons. Despite family murders and threats by the eldest surviving son, Seyyid Thuwain of Muscat, to attack Zanzibar's ruler, Seyyid Majid, the two sections remained separate, and Muscat acknowledged Zanzibar as an independent state after 1866. On investigation, Shufeldt found that Sultan Barghash, who had succeeded Seyyid Majid in 1870, accepted the treaty between the United States and his father, the sultan of the two territories. "This treaty [of 1833] is an advantageous one for us," the commodore told the secretary of the navy, "in as much as it does not contain the following clause reserving to the Sultan a monopoly in Ivory and Gum Copal between Tangate [Tanga] and Quiloa [Kilwa]" on the African coast. Shufeldt gleefully reported that American vessels and merchants enjoyed "all the privileges possessed by the most favored Nation" in Zanzibar.[14]

The clause acknowledging the sultan's monopoly had been inserted in the British treaty with Zanzibar on May 31, 1839, the French emperor's treaty of November 17, 1844, and the treaty with the senates of the Hanseatic republics of Lübeck, Bremen, and Hamburg of June 13, 1859. On March 10, 1847, the sultan had written to President Polk asking that the treaty might be changed, but on October 7 Polk declined to make any change or to abandon any privilege secured by the treaty. Consul Hathorne informed Shufeldt that but for the absence of such a clause in the United States treaty, "a European company might recently have obtained from the Sultan a monopoly of the trade of the articles mentioned." Shufeldt thus felt it necessary to obtain the incumbent sultan's acknowledgment of the 1833 treaty, since it was in every way satisfactory to American merchants in Zanzibar. One disadvantage of the treaty was that restrictions existed that did not permit foreign vessels to take in cargoes at some places on the African coast, but as such restrictions were general in application to the traders of all nations, Shufeldt believed Americans had the best of the treaty privileges. Consequently, he did nothing to revise the treaty of 1833. But to his daughter he confided his opinion of American inactivity in those waters. "What a shame it is to keep a fleet at Nice," he ruminated, "& send three ships to Zanzibar in thirty years!" He regarded the island as "the key of the commerce of East Africa."[15]

Mare clausum Britannicus—Combatting the British in the Indian Ocean

Shufeldt despaired over Zanzibar's future. He believed that the island would be absorbed into the British empire. In a detailed study of the East African slave trade, Shufeldt bitterly indicted British activity. The English, he argued, had seized the commerce of a region under the guise of destroying the slave trade. English merchants had moved into the area when the Royal Navy confiscated the slave factories on shore and took control of the chief defensive areas to support its operations. The result was a "huge Leviathan which swims through the seas and gorges itself upon islands and their inhabitants and which is now so fondly called by its subjects—the 'British Empire.' " The naval searches of Arab dhows and American merchant vessels stirred Shufeldt's blood, and the appointment of a British resident, to serve as a power behind Zanzibar's throne, irked him. Yet he omitted his opinion of the British empire as a huge Leviathan in that chapter of his manuscript he believed would be published. Shufeldt's anti-British feelings were detected, and partially reciprocated, by John Kirk, the British representative in Zanzibar, who wrote, "Commodore Shufeldt although seemingly a man of considerable common-sense is devoid of the tact and address needed for the occasion."[16]

In Zanzibar the American shipping houses of Arnold Hines and Company of New York, George Ropes and Company of Boston, and Ropes, Emmerton and Company of Salem, dominated the shipping of cloves, hides, ivory, and gum copal to the United States at a value of $60,000 to $100,000 per annum and imported American cottons and oils. They had enjoyed a supremacy in trade rivalled only by the German house of O'swald and Company, which Shufeldt mistakenly believed was the oldest trading house in Zanzibar. By late 1879, though American firms remained important to Zanzibar trade, they were rapidly losing business to others. In 1883 there were forty-seven English, seventeen French, eleven German, and only four American citizens on the island. "The American Consulate was the Sultan's Foreign Office," Shufeldt wistfully asserted when recalling a previous state of affairs. That consulate, established in 1836-1837 by Richard P. Waters and later reestablished by Commander John Aulick and the USS *Susquehanna* in 1851, had been the first of any nation in Zanzibar. Then the British had moved against the slave trade. Whereas the island had been "stamped thereon [with] an American nationality," Shufeldt claimed, it was "just now in the process of obliteration by a more politic, if not a more powerful nation than our own." The American flag, he pointed out, was "growing smaller and smaller—before long it will appear in these seas 'no bigger than a man's hand.' " The result was a commerce controlled by the British and "the ousting of American supremacy at Zanzibar where for years she was the mistress of its trade, as she lost years ago the immense possibilities of the West African Commerce."[17]

The results of such British action against the slave trade, Shufeldt pointed out for the benefit of his superiors in Washington, always redounded to British commercial advantage: "both the government and people of Great Britain are often led into the acquisition of territory against their wishes by the irresistible pressure of the Trader—or the inordinate ambition of the Colonial officer."[18] Despite identifying this as a general principle of British colonization, he cynically added, "I do not believe that the English people really want Zanzibar, neither did they want Zululand or Afganistan." The specter of British expansion into adjacent areas of the East African, Persian, and Indian seas was to haunt him for the rest of the cruise. Everywhere the *Ticonderoga* touched, from Zanzibar to Hong Kong, the commodore found the supremacy of the British trader had ousted American influence and led to British dominance and control. Grimly he spelled out the lessons for the secretary of the navy when he declared that he could not avoid calling attention to

> the peculiar and almost parallel cases, in our commercial history, on these vast stretches of continent the East & West Coasts that are represented in Zanzibar and Liberia. To me—to the American merchant—to any future possibilities of trade revival, these two countries are the *only* two left wherein to enter the wedge of rivalry. They are the respective keys of a rich and almost boundless land. The future of Africa may be the question of another age, another century. But a future it has and if we are to be actors on the stage of progress and development abroad as well as at home, we must get out of our car cushioned with national conceit and rescue the flag now lost in the smoke of the thousand steamers of the "Mistress of the Seas."

Shufeldt illustrated the point forcibly. In the first six months of 1879, ten American vessels, all sailing ships, had called at Zanzibar; in the same period fifty-three English vessels—forty-three steamers and ten sailing ships—had called. In 1879 ships and tonnage for trading nations were as follows: Britain sixty-nine ships, 761,265 tons; Germany thirteen ships, 5,940 tons; United States ten ships, 5,283 tons; France four ships, 1,975 tons. The articles imported in that year in American vessels, mainly cloth and beads, were valued at well over $640,000, and exports to the United States—coconuts, vanilla, coffee, rubber, horses, gum copal, ivory, and cloves—amounted to over $680,000, which the commodore considered was "not a bad exhibit in these days of our commercial decadence abroad."

However, compared with the British portion, the American performance was slight. Between 1871 and 1879, British shipping increased sevenfold, following the opening of the Suez Canal in 1869. It was stimulated further by the Aden to Zanzibar telegraph in 1877 and the opening of a monthly subsidized mail steamship service to India in 1872. The United States position depressed Shufeldt. "When it is remembered that Zanzibar is the key to the vast commerce of the great West [East?] African Coast," he pointed out to the American public, "this showing is a melancholy one for the greatest of modern empires."

A further clue to the state of Shufeldt's concern over the future of Zanzibar emerged when the French representative on the island, Le-Doulx, notified his government that Shufeldt had told the sultan that he could count on the United States for aid if Zanzibar's independence were ever threatened. It is difficult to disagree with Norman Bennett's assessment that there was little justification for this assertion, for though Shufeldt might promise, "the United States, as the Sultan was soon to learn, might not necessarily deliver."[19] Nevertheless, Shufeldt was positively "rescuing" the flag in much the same way that he had attempted to do in Tehuantepec for Foreign Minister Doblado in 1862: by making unauthorized promises of aid in the face of foreign pressure.

When the *Ticonderoga* sailed into Aden harbor on November 3, thirteen days out from Zanzibar, she once again entered British-dominated territory. Shufeldt found Aden to be an entrepôt for the contiguous countries of Arabia and Africa, "a military position . . . of great strength," which controlled the Red Sea as "the Gibraltar of the East." It was ruled by a British political resident, the brigadier general who commanded the garrison. Shufeldt felt as if he were in a new country, with the Negro replaced by the Arab and the camel being the predominant moving figure. The commodore drove out to the Arab sector of the town and found "scriptual wells & picturesque men & women drawing water for camels to drink. . . . Jews, Hindus, Somalis and English soldiers mixed up & jabbering in all the languages of Babel."[20]

In the British colony of thirty thousand people, Shufeldt found a large agency of the American business houses of Arnold Hines and Company of New York and John Bertram and Company of Salem. He noted that the scope offered by the port could only support "a commercial agency from which the fees would be only a trifle," and he recommended James I. Williams, who had served in the Union Navy in the Civil War, as "a creditable and responsible man" for the position. Shufeldt thus rejected the merits of Pieroslaw Burjorjee Sorabjee, the previous applicant for the post, who ran a chandler's business. In Aden, Shufeldt found every nationality but American represented commercially by the respective governments. He deemed it essential for American interests to establish an agency at the earliest convenient time, especially as Aden was soon to be linked by submarine cable to Cape Town via Zanzibar, Port Mozambique and Delagoa Bay.[21]

Shufeldt moved the flagship on to Muscat, and for ten days the *Ticonderoga* lay in the calm waters in view of the shore. The trade of the sultanate had dwindled since its separation from Zanzibar. Its current ruler, Seyyid Turki, was maintained on his throne by the support of the British India government and a British gunboat anchored in the harbor. The effective political power lay with the political agent of the British India government, desirous of controlling all routes to India and the trade of adjacent countries. Shufeldt was irked by the title of political resident maintained by the British consuls, which gave them more local power, recognition of two guns more in ceremonial salutes, and which placed them ahead of United States consuls in order of ceremonial rank. Insult was added to injury when the commodore found out that two-thirds of Muscat's trade was American, mainly in cotton goods, and that the storehouses were filled with American goods. Consequently, he recommended a consular agency particularly as trade was increasing and needed protection "for its growth and extension into the Persian Gulf."[22] On November 19 Shufeldt entertained Sultan Turki on board. He found him "a melancholy man—uncertain in tenure of office" and also "poor." He sounded the ruler about the possibility of a consular agency and, after some hesitation (inspired by guessing what the British political resident would think, Shufeldt estimated), he agreed to the request. The commodore grew excited by the prospects. He gauged that American trade, especially in cottons, was "capable of almost indefinite expansion," and he envisaged that the Aden and Muscat consulates, under James I. Williams and Louis S. Maguire, both representatives of American commercial houses at their respective ports, would serve American interest well in this area of British political control. Both consulates could be subordinated to the United States Bombay consulate, which would have paralleled the organization of the British consular staff.[23]

Above all, Shufeldt urged the appearance of American men-of-war in the adjacent seas. It had been thirteen years since one had visited Muscat and yet, Shufeldt asserted dogmatically, merging commercial and racial comments, "there is no place in the world where the physical manifestation of power is so necessary for the diffusion of the knowledge of the moral power of a civilized Nation as among the semi-barbarous and barbarous peoples that dwell upon these shores." It was an axiom among merchants wherever the *Ticonderoga* had called, he recounted for Thompson's edification, "that in the mercantile [*sic*] world Africa is the only 'nut left to crack'—we can get our share of the kernel if we are only present at the 'cracking.' "[24]

The major obstacle was the dominance of the British in the area. Fifteen English war vessels patrolled the Indian Ocean, mostly gunboats of 500 tons but backed by two or three corvettes of larger size. Shufeldt wanted a small squadron of American war vessels in the Indian Ocean, patrolling from Ceylon to the Cape of Good Hope. For Thompson's sake, he declared that he knew of no part of the world where the navy would contribute more to "pay its own expenses" or furnish "a more tangible argument for its 'raison d'être.' " To his daughter he revealed his ambition: "The English are terribly jealous of our movements—& this going into the Persian Gulf—looks to them like a mission in the *Russian* interest—I don't mind exercising them a little—these rulers of the land & sea—these modern Romans who claim the world is their Empire—What a lot of filibustering I could do out here if our dear Uncle Sam wouldn't object."[25]

Early in December, Shufeldt took the flagship to Bushire and Basra on the Euphrates River and eagerly proclaimed to the American people "this is the first American Man of War & almost the first American ship that ever entered the Persian Gulf—but our fame precedes us & wherever we go we are welcomed." The ship had moved through the waters where Alexander the Great met his naval commander, Nearchus, in 320 B.C., near Hormuz and then steamed seventy miles up the Shatt-al-Arab, the section of the river between the junction of the Tigris and Euphrates and the sea, to Basra, the seaport of Mesopotamia. For his daughter, Shufeldt conjured up pictures of himself "in a maze over the thousand thoughts which flow in upon the brain—as he wanders & wonders in this old old land—older than history—than time itself." He gloated over the American presence and boasted to Molly that the *Ticonderoga* was not only the first American ship of any kind to enter the river but that she was the largest of any nation, "so we are *real* curiosities—our decks are thronged & you may imagine both English & Turkish are fearfully mutilated—but everybody is aimiable [*sic*] & we make friends by the score."[26]

Part of the time Shufeldt compiled long dispatches on the Persian Gulf for the Navy Department. The commodore still believed that they would not be read or, at most, would be glanced over. He asked Molly why he should write such reports at all, why he should not do as others did and "inform the Navy Dept. that after arrival the Turkish flag was saluted & the salute returned . . . Why not?" He wondered if he was being urged on by his "destiny," striving for different things and performing work that "meets often with a sneer & always with indifference." He concluded that he would not want to work any more after the cruise; he would be willing to go to some quiet spot "under a mango tree—by the banks of a river."[27]

Shufeldt was too pessimistic in assessing the use made of his dispatches. Evarts informed Thompson that "these reports [Nos. 55–59] have been read with the attention called for by the importance of the subjects of which they treat and the thoughtful care shown in their preparation. No. 56, in particular, in relation to the East African Slave Trade, has had considerable perusal. . . . Nos. 57 and 58, in relation to commercial openings between this country and Madagascar will have careful consideration." Thompson notified the directors of the Board of Trade in New York that Shufeldt's work in Africa enabled the department to provide samples of trade goods sold in Africa, Persia, and Arabia in order to encourage American manufacturers and exporters "to compete with the merchants of other nations in supplying their markets." Several American firms wrote to the Navy Department for the cotton and silk fabric samples, including Wilson and Bradbury of Philadelphia and New York; Aub and Hackenburg, machine and sewing silk manufacturers of Philadelphia, Baltimore, Chicago, and Cincinnati; Brainerd and Armstrong, silk manufacturers of Philadelphia and New London; Van Volkenburgh and Leavitt of New York; W. L. Strong, commission merchants of New York, Philadelphia, and Boston; and T. O. Hauge and Company of New York. Edward Atkinson, the special agent of the Customs Department at Boston, requested samples. Van Volkenburgh and Leavitt wanted samples used in the trade on the west coast of Africa and "such goods as the market requires." Aub and Hackenburg thanked Thompson for forwarding Shufeldt's samples and observed, "it is very apparent that all these goods can be manufactured in the U.S. at greatly reduced prices on quotations in the schedule."[28] Obviously, to the cotton and silk merchants of the eastern seaboard Shufeldt's cruise was opening new trade possibilities in Africa and the Persian Gulf.

Despite his gloom over what he imagined to be the fate of his dispatches, Shufeldt devoted more than twenty pages to the political and industrial questions of the Persian Gulf. The ports of Bushire, Lengeh, Bandar Abbas, Basra, Kuwait, Qatif, and the pearl fishing center of Bahrain all passed under his close scrutiny. The commodore revealed the extent of Turkish penetration around the gulf, with over four hundred miles of coast acquired. Certainly much of the coast had passed from Arab to Turkish rule; Shufeldt found the alleged "sick man of Europe" far from moribund in the Persian Gulf. But this Turkish vitality still did not interest him as much as the operations of the British in the area.

Shufeldt described the Persian Gulf as an English lake with English vessels patrolling the Persian shores. A British political resident was established in Persia, and the Arabian section of the coast was under the protection of the Bombay government. Through their agents, the British controlled the gulf and its commerce, estimated at approximately $5 million per annum. The commodore considered there were favorable opportunities for the introduction of American manufactured goods into Persia and Turkey in Asia, yet the area was remote from American steamship lines. Any increase in American trade would be conducted indirectly through London or Bombay or perhaps by American sailing vessels to Muscat. But the obstacles to this increase were formidable and Shufeldt counselled the secretary of the navy:

> practically we cannot expect to sell our goods to people who do not know of the existence of our Country—a high Persian Official could with difficulty be made to apprehend that the *Ticonderoga* and all that belonged to her was not of English workmanship; he thought the United States, if not England, must be Germany.
>
> The cruise of this ship has been useless—if it has not convinced our Government of the vital importance of a reorganization and extension of the Consular system—whereby the flag many be familiarized among the semi-civilized nations of the earth. . . . An American flag hoisted over a Legation at Teheran its capital, which we know would even now be most favorably received, would under such circumstances not only add to the dignity of our Country, but confer a real and lasting benefit to the world at large.

In 1883, following a House of Representatives resolution of February 1882, a United States legation was established in Persia. Though it is not possible to attribute its establishment directly to Shufeldt's mission, the pressure he put on the State Department undoubtedly contributed to that result.[29]

Shufeldt looked to Persia, especially the hinterland of the Shatt-al-Arab and the Karun River, for trade concessions. He anticipated that Persia would probably be a battlefield between Russia and England "for the supremacy of the East" and noted that in this struggle Persia leaned toward Russia and repelled English attempts to establish any more political residencies in the country. He drew attention to the Karun River ("An admirable waterway into the very heart of Persia," with rapids at one point but navigable for 135 miles), because he believed that what the shah had refused the English he might grant to the Americans. Shufeldt envisaged an American company, possibly the merchant house of A. and T. J. Malcolm, operating at Bushire, inaugurating a shoal water steamboat navigation business on the river, not only profitable in itself but the precursor of other profitable enterprises left almost exclusively to the English. Such a challenge had moral, religious, and sacred as well as commercial overtones:

> the spirit of civilization cradled in the valley of Mesopotamia has gone abroad throughout the world and in the process of time America has been

born, the instrument perhaps, though the youngest of the nations—to bring back to the Euphrates—the blessings of a liberal religion and a free Government. . . . In almost a moral and religious sense therefore the display of the American flag, in these sacred waters and over the cradle of civilization, is a duty we owe to mankind—as well as to ourselves.

The mercenary who would use the American flag abroad for the sole object of gain, and the ward politician who uses it at home, do not, it seems to me, quite understand its significance. The Government of the United States is the product of ages of experiment. Its flag represents the result up to the 19th century of the Christian era. It is the sign and symbol of modern civilization—It involves a responsibility and dictates a course of action.

Given this high moral purpose, and the introduction of American commercial interests into competition with the English, Shufeldt was uncertain over any future developments in the area, especially between Russia and England. He warned the secretary of the navy that being "allied" to England, gaining knowledge from the same sources and with ideas running in the same channels, Americans were apt to consider her as "all powerful in the East." Her strengths were known, but he pointed out that most Americans did not know her weaknesses, particularly the weakness "arising from a heterogeneous people, strung upon a thread, which reaches around the world, and is called an Empire." The main defense of this empire was obviously thrust upon the Royal Navy, for the "defenceless Condition of most of the Colonies" was a familiar fact to anyone who had travelled around the world. Shufeldt assessed that a navy would have to possess the qualities of Providence itself to defend all such colonies, and he questioned the loyalty of them all. Furthermore, he warned, "English rule in the East is dictatorial—such a government may be necessary but it does not create a grateful people. . . . If ever the British Lion loses his teeth, or his claws become blunted, figuratively speaking, there will be a knife at the throat of every Englishman in the East. . . . Be all this as it may, the one fact is patent, viz: that the Persian Gulf must be considered under the present Imperial policy—an 'English Lake.' "[30] The lessons that Shufeldt learned were important. The real teeth and claws of the British lion were the ships of the Royal Navy, which held together the various areas of noncontiguous territory. A strong empire needed a powerful navy. Furthermore, while such a navy might be able to repel attacks on the empire by another naval power, it would not be able to defend the colonies against internal rebellion. A strong empire needed a stable internal policy. The British empire had the former, but the observant American doubted whether it had the latter.

After three weeks analyzing British policy in the Persian Gulf, Shufeldt was glad to escape its trying climate. He caught a severe cold that irritated him almost as much as the evidence of English activity in the area. The American flagship sailed for Bombay on December 15, 1879, with the crew spending their second Christmas away from the United States at sea en route to India. Shufeldt was already thinking ahead to the Far Eastern part of his mission. To Molly, he revealed flashes of ambition amidst declamations of only doing his duty:

> While I inspired with a desire to do in these later years of my life some little thing more toward the interests of our country & the good of mankind—have travelled over 20,000 miles of sea & through every variety of climate—whether we deserve any reward—or deserving it whether we shall obtain it—is perhaps a question which we ought not to entertain, but to rest satisfied with the consciousness of having tried to do our duty. . . . It will be desirable if you can quietly find out from him [William Shock] whether or not the Secy. intends to give it [the temporary command of the Asiatic squadron] to me & write by return mail—I am almost indifferent to the decision—but at all events I would like the Dept. to define (by that time) the route by which we are to return to the U.S.[31]

To Shufeldt's mind, the culmination of the cruise would become apparent in his negotiation with the Koreans, and he hoped that the temporary command of the Asiatic squadron would give him far greater leverage to secure his treaty.

In Bombay by December 27, Shufeldt took the opportunity to relax on the shore for a few days. As in Persia, he ventured into the streets and bazaars, drove among "the motley inhabitants of this really wonderful town," visited the Parsee tower of silence, met American missionaries, and was introduced to the English admiral, Gore-Jones, whose pay and allowances, totaling $25,000 per annum, aroused his envy. In his contacts with British officialdom in India, Shufeldt experienced some hostility. He believed that the visit of former president Grant earlier that year had exhausted the hospitality of Bombay, and the arrival of the *Ticonderoga* "was not at first received in the warmest manner." He was virtually ignored by British officers at the opening of the new Prince's Dock and snubbed many in return. The crusty commodore ironically noted that "Bombay is a marvellous city—wonderful because 800,000 Natives permit themselves to be arbitrarily ruled by a few hundred troops & bullied by a domineering & cruel race—as the English undoubtedly is in India."[32]

Shufeldt developed this theme of British aggression for Secretary Thompson:[33]

> British rule in Asia and Africa is at present so aggressive in its character as to be more or less antagonistic to the interests of every civilized and semi-civi-

lized nation of the Earth. Under pretext of suppression of piracy, destruction of slavery, protection of Commercial routes and rectification of frontiers—it is really a mere grasping for universal Empire—a usurpation of authority—an ill-concealed intention to become the "Paramount Power" over the world at large, as it already styles itself in India.

But in this age another Roman Empire is impossible and I have faith that before it is too late—the sober second thought of England will rend this veil of imperial illusion and remand the Country back into the sisterhood of Nations, as the equal and not the Autocrat of other nationalities—otherwise some day not distant the British Empire will receive a shock from which it will not easily recover—for outside of England, and least of all in India, it has in itself no intrinsic strength. Its colonies and its commerce would be helpless before any Combination of Power. The British Navy—granted to be the most powerful in the world, after deducting the squadron necessary for home defence—could no more protect these Colonies or this commerce from an enemy than from a stroke of lightning or the shock of an Earthquake.

In this instance he was reflecting on the dangers from without, rather than from within, posed to a widely scattered empire based on long lines of sea communications and a strong navy. But his analysis was not as carefully thought out as his earlier discussion of the internal strength of the British empire. He underrated the power of the Royal Navy in 1880. Its task in the last quarter of the nineteenth century was not to scatter and defend all colonies but to concentrate in sufficient strength to be more powerful than any hostile naval combination that could be brought against it. British admiralty policy was designed to produce a navy that was stronger than the combined force of its two largest rivals. Squadrons for "home defence" would be part of the Royal Navy, and of other navies, too, but not the only part. Not until the British lost their ability to maintain a navy stronger than its two nearest rivals was the British empire threatened from without. That threat, increased by air power, was reserved for the twentieth century, long after the first indicators of internal trouble had appeared in the Indian Mutiny of 1857 and the Boer War of 1899–1902.

Perhaps with memories of the Indian Mutiny in mind, Shufeldt declared that the incorporation of India into the British empire was a mistake. It was illusory to think of making India Christian or loyal. He noted for Thompson:

> As Americans however, we are interested in the products of these events; as a nation which in the process of time must become the center of Commercial power, we have interests and rights in these seas and on these Continents—At present it is as if we had no existence—The struggle goes on between this great "Paramount Power" and these weak, discordant, effeminate races,

and America has no voice in the matter. Do we really mean to "extend *American* influence" or are we to continue to play the role long ago assigned to us in China—of No. 2 Englishmen?

Yet he concluded his survey with the prediction that "not many in Bombay realize that a nation is growing up in America destined in a very few years to overshadow the Indian Empire even in its own markets."

The commodore gave the lie to his earlier assessments of the weakness overseas of British sea power, when he gauged British naval power in the area. What impressed Shufeldt most as a manifestation of British power in the East was the enormous steam fleet that Britain possessed outside of its navy, especially the five troop ships of 4,000 to 5,000 tons such as the *Malabar*, which he visited in Bombay harbor, each built at a cost to the Indian government of £270,000 and capable of taking two thousand troops each between Bombay and England two or three times a year. Shufeldt was still convinced that fast cruisers, which could be converted into commerce destroyers in time of war, represented a more desirable naval force than a concentration of heavy ships. Hence the extension of American influence that he so desired would come by commercial and moral pressures as much as by naval.

Shufeldt omitted the Burmese part of his expedition. He wrote to the Navy Department to explain his reasons: the British were in control of the whole of the seacoast and for two hundred miles up the Irrawaddy River; the ship would have to anchor at Rangoon, where fever raged; and it would take six weeks to reach the capital, Mandalay, seven hundred miles upriver from Rangoon. In addition, he mentioned internal dissensions in the country. The local ruler was "a brutal tyrant usually maddened by liquor." The commodore considered these were sufficient reasons to discourage his visit, which might involve more responsibilities and cause more delay than the best interests of the cruise would justify.[34]

Shufeldt also rejected an invitation from David B. Sickels, United States consul at Bangkok, who wanted the *Ticonderoga* to call. Sickels promised an interview with the king of Siam and hoped that Shufeldt's visit would increase the trade between the two nations, but Shufeldt was tired. Rather wistfully, he asked Molly not to forget his birthday, for "it will remind you of an old man—who feels so old that he would like to be near to his dear Child . . . to draw the strength & comfort from her which he does not find anywhere else." He revealed that he was thinking of bringing the cruise to an end, especially if the secretary did not give him temporary orders to command the Asiatic squadron. "The work is rather telling upon me," he grumbled, "it has been a constant strain—& altho' you will not let me say so—yet I do feel myself growing too old for this constant activity." But he did draw some comfort from his past activities. "I fancy the London *Times* would like to get hold of some of my despatches on English affairs in the East," he confided to his daughter in faraway Washington, "they would be good documents for Gladstone."³⁵

These were not happy days for Shufeldt. Trouble on the *Ticonderoga* between Molly's brother, Frederick A. Miller, the acting executive officer, and Captain Cromwell led to Miller's leaving the ship at Singapore when Shufeldt backed the authority of the captain. Shufeldt also heard of three or four deaths in his family in quick succession. "The scythe is indeed cutting a swathe among my relatives, the only question is whose turn will come next," he observed on one occasion and added disconsolately, "the grain is ripe for the harvest." He was also dejected over the fact that he had written to the secretary personally, twice, and had but one reply. In addition, the upcoming elections in the United States made him gloomy over the possibilities of a Democratic victory. Characteristically, he was able to produce a solution for the country's problems, if not his own:

> The country will be convulsed again in the coming elections—the man on horseback is really coming—As old Toombs said in Georgia the other day— We are to have "Grant & his Empire by G-d." Rather Grant than the Democrats—but "is the Republic a failure"? Just now too, is America's opportunity—with Europe discontented & hungry—Monarchs threatened & the masses threatening—We could with peace in our own borders—rise to the dignity of the first Nation on Earth—I find all over the East—Our Country liked & our flag respected—I could "annex" the whole "Orient" under our starry banner.³⁶

Obviously, the British had influenced him more than he cared to admit.

Borneo and the Spanish Colonies in the East

Shufeldt's instructions from Evarts called for a close inquiry into whether the sultan of Borneo (Brunei) had ceded or leased parts of the main island or smaller islands to Joseph William Torrey and the American Trading Company, which had subsequently passed to the English trading firm of Dent, Overbeck and Company, in derogation of the United States treaty of June 1850. That treaty, negotiated by Captain Joseph Balestier of the United States Navy, together with another negotiated with Sarawak in May 1850, was designed to secure reciprocal trading rights, most-favored-nation status and protection for American shipping in the harbors of northern Borneo. In addition, it gave Americans the right to acquire property in areas under the sultan's control.

While in Singapore, Shufeldt had interviewed W. H. M. Read, the agent general of Dent, Overbeck and Company, and A. G. Strider, United States consul, and discovered that the sultan of Brunei had in fact ceded a large portion of his territory to the company, including some of the land covered by the Borneo–United States treaty of June 1850. Through the agent general, Shufeldt found the company was exercising sovereign rights, and he bluntly told Read that the United States government did not acknowledge the competency of the sultan to cede or lease to companies any portion of his dominions "in disparagement of the stipulation in his treaty with the United States."[37]

Shufeldt sailed for Borneo at the end of February 1880 to discover the sultan's reasons. On March 1 he sent Lieutenant Daniel P. Mannix in the steam launch up the Brunei River to interview the ruler. After stopping at the British consulate to pick up an interpreter, Mannix proceeded to the palace where he met the sultan and the Pengeran Těměnggong, Hassim, son of the late Sultan Omar Ali Saifeddin and heir to the throne. Mannix found that the concessions of territory to the company had been approved by the ninety-five-year-old sultan, Abdul Mŭmin, and Hassim, both of whom believed the Dent, Overbeck concessions were pleasing to the United States and England. Shufeldt had ordered Mannix to protest at the possibility that the privileges of American citizens, especially "the right of reclamations under the treaty," might be violated by the nature of the concessions. The commodore also informed the Navy Department that it would be up to the United States government to take further action if it deemed it necessary.[38]

Once more Shufeldt detected the perfidious influence of the British. The British-owned island of Labuan, the governor of which was also the consul general for Borneo, lay near the mouth of the Brunei River. Shufeldt considered it was the point "from which emanates the policy of the Sultan," and he chortled over the surprise that his visit would cause to the English government. The treaty had been lying dormant for so many years that he believed it was more probable that it had been overlooked by the partners in question and its existence forgotten by the sultan. Nevertheless, he warned the Navy Department, there was no question of the importance of revising and maintaining the treaty, "because if we wish to create a prestige in the East for the benefit of our Commerce these surrounding Powers [Dutch to the east, Spaniards to the north, British to the west, and the rajah of Sarawak to the south], as well as the Sultan of Borneo [Brunei] himself, must be made to understand that we are not unmindful of its privileges."[39]

The question of prestige in the East remained in Shufeldt's thoughts as he directed the *Ticonderoga* to Manila in the Philippines. Relaxing in the home of an American merchant, Shufeldt pondered his coming mission. "If the Corea does not open itself like an oyster," he told his daughter, "we shall have nothing left to do but come home." He expected no assistance from either naval or diplomatic officers in Asia. "Personal pleasure & official inertness are the principal obstructions to any work expected from the modern naval officer," he mused, adding as an afterthought, "I have often felt discouraged & have promised myself that no desire of my own will tempt me again into any enterprise which requires any Naval aid."[40] Like all such promises that he made to himself on the cruise, this one was destined to be broken.

Shufeldt took the opportunity in Manila to make a formal study of the Spanish colonies in the East. He informed Thompson that Spanish rule in the Philippine Islands had created "a contented and prosperous people . . . converting them from a low type of heathenism to a moderate standard of Christianity," and noted that the intervention of the two thousand priests in the islands had helped ease the despotic nature of the military rule. But Shufeldt's main interests were in the commercial opportunities "this great Colony the Philippines" offered to the United States,

> many of the products of which—principally sugar and hemp—go direct to the United States and many of the manufactures of our own country, under a more liberal tariff, and freed from the restrictions placed upon the importation of American goods in American ships might be exported to these islands in exchange for their products. Spain is a non-manufacturing country and it should be the policy of the United States, if possible, by modifications of existing treaties to obtain access to so large a number of people who, there as everywhere else, would give the preference to American Cotton goods as well as to other articles of American manufacture.

The commodore wanted proper consular representation at two of the most important ports, Manila and Iloilo, with a consul general to insist on settlements with the governor general. These requests were heartily echoed by Vice-Consul Edward A. Youngs, who reported that the *Ticonderoga* had arrived March 9 and that Shufeldt "created a very favorable impression with both the Authorities and American residents of this City." He regretted that Shufeldt could not stay longer, "as could he have visited the adjacent ports of Iloilo and Cebu, I think it would have been beneficial to the interests of Americans, especially at Iloilo where the leading export firm is American." Likewise, Shufeldt desired a consul general and consular agencies at Makassar and a port on Sumatra in the Dutch East Indies, with a minister resident at Bangkok.[41]

Siam attracted Shufeldt because it was independent. He declared that since the visit of General Grant to the East there existed "a manifestation on the part of Eastern people to place themselves in a more intimate relation with the people of the United States." Voicing a popular belief of the 1880s, he stressed that such peoples had obviously discerned "in the Great West a barrier against European domination." Siam alone was independent of foreign rule, and with the French at Saigon, Cambodia, and Annam, and with British Burma stretching to meet the British colonies of Penang, Malacca, and Singapore, Shufeldt believed either of these two powers would "wipe out this independent kingdom." Such a destruction of native sovereignty would be hostile to the interest of the United States for economic reasons:

> England, more particularly, wherever she goes fosters her own industries and thrusts upon her alien subjects her own manufactures. France contents herself with the propagation of "moral ideas" and protects "the Church" but in so doing she is exacting and arbitrary to the injury of the commerce of other nations.
>
> It seems to me to be the interest of our Government to protect as much as possible—under treaties such countries as Siam from these encroachments and to encourage commercial intercourse and more intimate relations without interfering either with their policies or their religion.[42]

How Shufeldt was going to achieve more intimate relations with countries such as Siam without interfering in policies or religion was a question he never satisfactorily answered. Possibly he hoped to do so by upgrading the consular service. But he also tied that in with an active naval policy based on deployment of naval units to foster and protect commerce in the "distant seas which wash the shores of Continents and Islands . . . where the wooden gunboat still remains an element of power." Whether consuls backed by men-of-war would abstain from interfering in the internal affairs of countries if the local administrations did not encourage American commerce to the extent deemed sufficient by the same consuls, was a point Shufeldt never reached in his analysis. Perhaps he did not need to, for his call for the deployment of wooden ships in distant seas, where such vessels could still represent power, points the way his thoughts were moving on this issue.[43]

Beneath Shufeldt's concern for American commercial advantages lay the assumption that political interference was quite distinct from the economic and commercial advantages to be wrested from a country. Despite a world cruise of 28,000 miles to that point, through many of the imperial holdings of the world's great empires, Shufeldt still clung to the belief that the United States could refrain from internal political interference in securing and maintaining commercial advantages. Yet, as he had frequently pointed out for the benefit of Thompson, Evarts, eastern seaboard merchants, and ultimately the American people, especially when analyzing the motives of the British in Africa and Asia, such a separation was impossible; the examples of British penetration had revealed to him over and over that the one led to the other. As the commodore took the *Ticonderoga* from Manila, bound for Hong Kong and Japan, he clung to the notion that what the United States wanted for countries such as "the independent kingdom of Siam" was a marriage ceremony in which the bridegroom took the dowry and the bride retained her virginity. Whether he was prepared to embrace Korea on these terms remained to be seen. But his one fear, as he intimated to Molly, was that he did not know if his activities in the East would be sustained by the government. "I am determined to assert—at least here & there our own nationality—I am tired with sailing under the shadow of the English flag," he noted for his daughter.[44] With that thought on his voyage around the rim of the Indian Ocean, he directed the flagship toward Yokohama via the Liu Ch'iu (Ryukyu) Islands, but adverse winds forced her into Nagasaki.

12

The Cruise of the *Ticonderoga*: The Mission to Open Korea

The Problem of Korean Independence

As the *Ticonderoga* ploughed her way through heavy seas into Nagasaki harbor, Shufeldt was preparing to navigate the far rougher waters of Far Eastern diplomacy. The major problems that he had to face in negotiating a treaty with Korea were the relationship of that country to China and Japan and the factional strife within the Korean court. When Shufeldt visited Korea in 1867, the Hermit Kingdom was generally regarded by foreign governments as being within the Chinese empire. During the late 1860s, however, that empire came under increasing pressure from France, Britain, Russia, Japan, and the United States. After 1866 China's imperial officials sought to guard its dependent provinces and tributary states, only to see the loss of southern Annam, lower Burma, Liu Ch'iu, and Formosa. France and Britain sliced off the former two dependencies; the Japanese successfully disputed China's claims to the latter two. In addition, the Russian threat along the northern Chinese border increased each year, culminating in the crushing Treaty of Livadia, September 3/15, 1879, when the tsar took another large segment of Chinese territory.

Like other nations, the United States created difficulties for the Chinese world order. Her naval and diplomatic pressure on China and her actions in Korea contributed to this end. In 1871, Frederick F. Low, United States minister to China, cooperated with Rear Admiral John Rodgers in an attempt to force the Koreans to open trading negotiations with the United States. Low pointed out to Hamilton Fish in July 1871 that the commerce with China, Japan, and Russian Manchuria required vessels to skirt the coast of Korea and thus "brought prominently into view the undesirability of allowing a country directly in the track of a great commerce bounded on two sides by the sea, to remain with its coasts, outlying islands and dangerous passages, totally unexplored." To the United States minister, who grounded his argument on natural law, "the sea is the great highway of the nations, which no country is at liberty to obstruct with impunity," and mariners and their property should be returned when shipwrecked. He informed Fish that Korea was an independent nation. It was obvious that he also regarded it as situated at the crossroads of empire in the northern Pacific. Accordingly, Low, Rodgers, five ships, and over twelve hundred seamen and marines sailed for Korea in an attempt to open trade with that country, using the *General Sherman* affair as a means to initiate contact. The results of the expedition have been chronicled in a number of works, generally chauvinistic, that have emphasized American military efforts. The Low-Rodgers expedition, however, was a diplomatic failure, did not open Korea to American trade, and added considerably to the many troubles that China had to experience over the Korean peninsula and its crumbling empire.[1]

The problem of the relationship of Korea to China was to bedevil the Far Eastern diplomacy of Western powers throughout the last quarter of the nineteenth century. The problem was whether Korea was "independent," and therefore fully responsible for its own actions in relations with other powers, or was a protected area in the Confucian family of nations under Chinese dominance. China's relations with surrounding areas, territories, and dependencies were colored, as John King Fairbank has observed, by "this concept of Sinocentrism and an assumption of Chinese superiority." Chinese officials thought of their country's "foreign relations" as manifesting the same principles "that were manifested internally within the Chinese state and society." One problem of such a Sinocentered world order, however, was that although "it was not coterminous with the Chinese culture area," Korea lay within the Sinic zone "umbilically tied to China by cultural bonds such as the Chinese written language and Confucianism."[2]

The nature of Chinese suzerainty was unknown to Western nations and legal systems, for it was based on the tenets of Confucian society, familistic and natural, not "legal" in the Western senses of legality. Western concepts of the "state," "sovereignty," "the legal equality of states," and "international law," were lacking in the Chinese system. Professor T'ung-chi Lin of Nankai University, Tientsin, believed the Chinese-Korean relationship was "alien then to the Western juridical concept." The closest analogy in modern times that Lin found was the relationship of the Dominions to the British Crown within the British Commonwealth. Professor Tingfu Tsiang of National Tsing-Hua University defined such a relationship:

> in law and ceremony, the subjection [of Korea to China] was even abject. Korean Kings received their investiture from Peking; every year tribute mis-

sions were sent. On the accession and death of a Chinese Emperor, Korea must send representatives to attend the ceremonies. When the Emperor sent an agent to Korea, the King himself kowtowed to him. In case of internal trouble or foreign invasion in the vassal state, the suzerain was obliged to send aid. Otherwise, Korea was left entirely to herself. . . . China with her tributary states formed a family as it were, with China as the big brother and the tributaries as the younger brothers.

The cement that bound this empire together was mixed from Confucian cultural and intellectual materials. Korea accepted the language, religion, laws, arts, education, manners, customs, trading missions, and calendar of China, and the ceremonial connection between the two countries was regarded by the courts of China and Korea as meaning an inferior status for Korea within the Confucian world order.[3]

In June 1871, after the Low-Rodgers expedition had withdrawn, the Korean monarch memorialized the Chinese Board of Rites, which dealt with the relations of China's tributary areas: "I humbly hope that the Board of Rites will lay before the Throne all the facts connected with this matter and that the Emperor will issue a special edict to exhort and instruct the envoy of the said country [United States] so as to overcome doubts and dispel his anxiety and thus each may be left to himself without trouble." The submissive tone and content of the entire dispatch led Low to believe that it amounted to a Korean acknowledgment of the supremacy of China. Lin has pointed out, however, that it was "a practical appeal, announcing that Korea would not in any way have intercourse with the foreigners . . . to accuse it [the Chinese government] of evading responsibility is to assign to it a responsibility which was non-existent." Yet the memorial concluded that "the contents of the letter of the American envoy do not indicate that a reply is expected; nor should I. The ruler of a colonial state, dare not commit such a breach as to trouble the honorable Board to forward a reply."[4]

In 1876, the Koreans were forced to sign a treaty with the Japanese that became the first overt step in Japan's moves to detach Korea from China's orbit. China accepted the Japanese right to negotiate a treaty only after a Japanese diplomatic, military, and naval expedition had anchored off Korea and a long debate over the nature of Korea's tributary status had taken place between Chinese officials and Mori Akinori, the special envoy Japan sent to China. The naval expedition to Korea, led by Kuroda Kiyotaka and Inouye Kaoru, negotiated the Treaty of Kanghwa, the first article of which stated that "Korea, being a self-governing nation, enjoys the right of equality with Japan." The Japanese had already signed a treaty in 1871 with China that stressed the equality of both countries. In Japanese eyes, the implication of the Kanghwa treaty was the Korea would thus hold a similar position in relation to

China as well as to Japan. Neither China nor Korea, however, took the first article of the Japanese–Korean treaty as a departure from the long-established position that defined Korea as China's vassal. Nevertheless, Japan began to use the treaty to provide a definition of Korea's independence of China; a denial of Chinese suzerainty over Korea.

Li Hung-chang, who came to dominate Chinese-Korean affairs after being made viceroy of Chihli (Hopei) and northern superintendent of trade in 1870, was alarmed sufficiently by the Japanese treaty to reiterate Korean dependency on China at every conceivable opportunity. Particularly after 1879, when Japan annexed the Liu Ch'iu Islands, Li intended to neutralize Japanese influence by countering it with that of the Western States, on the principle that one poison was often the effective antidote for another. He became even more concerned when Japan added a supplementary article to a commercial convention with Korea, which declared that if any foreigners were shipwrecked on the coast of Korea they would be delivered to the Japanese authorities, who would take responsibility for returning them to their homes. Li determined that while the recognition of Korea as a self-governing nation in the treaty with Japan did not necessarily contradict China's suzerainty, the omission of any reference in the treaty to China's suzerain position might in future "give rise toward misunderstandings." Consequently, he decided that it might be desirable for Korea to open trade relations with the outside world. He also assumed that within any treaties with Western powers there should be inserted a clause stressing Korea's dependency. This decision was to have profound implications for Shufeldt's treaty negotiations in two successive attempts to open Korea to American trade.[5]

One other development in the 1870s was to affect the context of Shufeldt's attempts. There emerged within Korea a deep division among the families and social groups that generally provided the leadership of the country over the correct approach to take to the threats, and the possibilities of opening trade that such threats aroused, from outside nations. During the 1860s, following the accession to the Korean throne of the twelve-year-old King Kojong (Ch'ol jong), the Taewon'gun, as prince regent and the boy's father, generally ruled Korea strongly with a policy of centralizing and revitalizing administration in royal hands. The regent aimed to undermine the power of the *yangban* and *ajon,* the Korean nobles, bureaucrats, and family gentry; attack the power of the pro-Chinese Confucian scholars such as Yi Man-son, Kim P'yong-muk, and Ch'oe In-hyon by abolishing Confucian shrines; and build public works such as the Kyongbok Palace in Seoul. Early in his rule he adopted a fierce anti-Christian and antimissionary stance that led to the expulsion of the French priests whom Shufeldt had met when investigating the *General Sherman* affair.

Such activity, which was to some extent anti-Chinese and anti-Japanese as well, produced many enemies and rivals for the Taewon'gun. Quite apart from the foreign, non-Korean people, who generally adopted a hostile antiregent stance because of his intention to drive out Christian missionaries, the regent was faced by powerful opposition within Korea. In 1873 the leaders of an antiregent group, organized around the queen, a member of the Min family, and composed of displaced *yangban,* Confucian scholars, and office-seekers, succeeded in ousting the Taewon'gun from office. He was retired, the Min family came into power, the strongest antiforeign and proexclusionist forces were removed from the Korean court, and the queen replaced the Taewon'gun as the center of effective policy and decision making.[6] After 1873 factions emerged within the court based on more "conservative," pro-Chinese Confucianists, antiforeign Taewon'gun supporters, and more "progressive," anti-Chinese, proforeign elements. These broad factional groups continued to dispute for effective power through most of the period from 1873 to 1894, when the defeat of China by Japan allowed the Japanese to use the Taewon'gun as a puppet to terminate the power, and the life, of the queen.

The 1876 treaty with Japan was attacked by orthodox Confucianist intellectuals who desired to retain the Chinese connection with all of its cultural values. One of the leaders, Kim P'yong-muk, published works on antiwesternism and was finally exiled in 1881, losing the debate because of extremism rather than because of the nature of his pro-Chinese arguments over the course of Korea's future. By the late 1870s the pro-Taewon'gun, anti-Min, and antiforeign movement had also lost the debate and the struggle for power, but still retained sufficient hopes and strength to attempt an *émeute* directed against the Min family in 1882. It was the increasingly powerful Min faction, which wished to control the reins of Korean court power through a slow rate of modernization designed to keep it in control during the 1870s (until 1882, when temporarily overthrown by a Taewon'gun coup), that came to dominate Korean political life. Early in the 1880s there also began to emerge a more progressive group, led by Kim Ok Kyun, Park Yong-hyo, Soh Kwang Pom, and Hong Yong-shik, that wished to see Korea modernize and adopt more rapidly Western and Japanese techniques. It began to compete with the Min faction. Thus, the control by the queen's group and the mounting opposition by differently motivated factions within the Korean court and government created the internal setting that eventually allowed Shufeldt to negotiate a treaty with Korea.[7] Shufeldt himself, in 1880, as the *Ticonderoga* approached the shores of Japan, had little inkling of these internal dynamic elements in the country he confidently expected to open like an oyster yielding a pearl.

The Initial Approach

When Shufeldt telegraphed to John A. Bingham from Singapore, the United States minister to Japan had no knowledge of Shufeldt's intended journey to Korea. Despite not being informed by the State Department, Bingham promptly initiated proceedings in Japan by requesting letters, on March 12, 1880, from the Japanese minister of foreign affairs, Inouye Kaoru, recommending Shufeldt to Japanese officials in Korea and to Korean officials. Secretary of State Evarts eventually approved Bingham's actions and ordered him to "extend all possible facilities to Commodore Shufeldt to enable him to successfully attain the desired result as regards the mission with which he is charged."[8]

Inouye Kaoru, who had been vice-minister plenipotentiary on the 1876 diplomatic-military expedition to Korea, initially informed Bingham that he could not recommend Shufeldt's mission to officials of the Korean government, for "a very few years have elapsed since the conclusion of the treaty of friendship between Japan & Corea and that the time has not as yet arrived for putting into full execution the stipulations of the said treaty; . . . I fear that it [an introduction for Shufeldt] might give rise to some complications whereby the execution of our treaty with that Country might be somewhat prevented." The Japanese foreign minister considered that he could not comply with Bingham's wishes for the present, but he was willing to advise the Japanese officers in Korea "to do the best in their power in facilitating the said mission." Consequently, Inouye notified Kondo Masuki, the Japanese consul at Fusan (Pusan), Korea, that upon Shufeldt's arrival at the port, "you will in no way interfere with his mission, but having the Treaty of friendship existing between Japan and the U.S. you will give him every possible assistance that he may require at your hands, during his stay at your port." In addition, the foreign minister provided nine copies of charts to help Shufeldt navigate Korean waters. In view of the claims by historians such as Charles O. Paullin and Tyler Dennett casting doubt on Japanese sincerity in this initial approach to Korea, it is worth noting that Evarts instructed Bingham on June 25, 1880, to tender the thanks of the Navy Department, through his office, to the Japanese government "for its friendly act of courtesy to Commodore Shufeldt."[9]

Bingham tacked on his own warning to Shufeldt by revealing that in an interview of April 19 with Inouye and the vice-minister for foreign affairs, Wooyeno Kagenori, the foreign minister had asserted, "the

Coreans are exceedingly jealous of foreigners and [Inouye] reminded me of the ill-treatment of Japanese vessels etc. by that people only a few years ago when they went to Corea on a friendly visit." As Bingham erroneously believed that only Fusan was open to the Japanese (the Korean-Japanese treaty of 1876 opened three ports as well as a legation) and no port to any other power, he suggested that Shufeldt should not attempt to enter Korea by any port other than Fusan. Furthermore, he wished the commodore success in his journey and regretted that the Japanese government did not feel at liberty to respond "more satisfactorily" to the request.[10]

While Bingham was working in Tokyo, Shufeldt arrived in Nagasaki. Not only was this port much closer to Korea than his original destination, Yokohama, but it was the one place in Japan where he could obtain the information that he needed about Korea. Kondo Masuki was on leave in Nagasaki, and on April 18 he readily gave Shufeldt "all the desirable points" of information, including a good Japanese map of Korea. Shufeldt also learned from the French vicar apostolic of Japan that the Korean government had adopted a more lenient policy toward the Christians in the country, ceasing to persecute them and releasing Christian captives. In addition, on April 20 the commodore conversed with the Chinese consul in Nagasaki, Ü Tsing, who informed him that the Chinese government had advised the Koreans "to make treaties with foreign powers—as a means of resisting the encroachments of Russia on its northern frontier." Under these circumstances, Shufeldt felt encouraged to start for Fusan at the beginning of May. He asked Willie P. Mangum, his old friend from the 1866-1868 China tour, now the United States consul in Nagasaki, to accompany him as a translator. Mangum telegraphed for and received permission from the State Department. The commodore also cabled Secretary of the Navy Thompson to ask for further instructions, but the secretary only repeated the orders to proceed to San Francisco via the Sandwich Islands "unless something should be developed on your visit to Corea which would warrant you remaining longer in Japan and asking advice by cable."[11]

Shufeldt had been angling for the Asiatic squadron in one last effort to secure command. To his daughter he sighed, "If I only had the squadron now for a few months—to add to the prestige of the flag—I would be almost sure of success—but I shall go *anyhow*—for here in the East—the opening of the Corea—is regarded as the one unaccomplished event—of final importance to Western Nations." The analogy with Perry's opening of Japan weighed heavily on his mind. He confessed that he often asked himself, "why work & worry over matters which after all are no good to you or yours—If there is no reward hereafter, there certainly is no reward here for disinterested labor." For

Molly he added that, in his view, "the men who idle their time at the dining table or in the salons of Washington are the ones who reap the harvest sown by humbler hands." Later he told her that he did not want the thanks of Congress nor would he join "the hordes who are seeking for personal advancement," and he was unconcerned whether or not the department gave him the squadron. At this stage, he declared, he was only going to Korea to open a correspondence and then return to await events.[12]

By May 4, the *Ticonderoga* lay off Fusan harbor. Shufeldt wrote a letter, translated by Ü Tsing, to the king of Korea "to bring about the amicable intercourse" between the two countries, which "owing to a misunderstanding" had been "unfortunately interrupted for several years past." This "misunderstanding" was the United States attack on the Korean forts of the Han River in 1871. He reminded the king that he had visited Korea while investigating the *General Sherman* affair in 1867. Moreover, he felt obliged to add, notwithstanding the attack on the forts, that "the Government of the United States entertains most friendly feelings toward the Government and people of Corea." Then came the crux of his argument. He hoped that in view of the progress of events in China and Japan, as well as in Korea, the monarch had concluded that "the present time is opportune for the commencement of a new era by offering to the United States, under treaty, such commercial privileges as are granted to it by the two nations just mentioned." The kingdom of Korea, he reminded the king, was "of all nations the only one remaining which excludes other nationalities from its territory." Furthermore, Shufeldt added, the United States "have never sought by aggression to extend their sovereignty in these waters, nor have they ever meddled or interfered with the religious or political institutions of independent nations." Consequently, the United States government asked only two things: "*first* for the protection of its citizens if stranded upon foreign shores, and *second,* for such commercial facilities as nations universally grant to each other in the present day."[13]

Kondo Masuki attempted to deliver this letter for Shufeldt to Yaku-Gaku-Liu-Ko-Shaku, a Korean officer residing at Fusan. The Japanese consul advised the Korean to meet Shufeldt personally, but he replied that he could not decide what he should do with the letter. Balked by this indecision, Kondo Masuki went to Torai-fu on May 5 and met the governor, Chin-To-shin, who not only refused to transmit the letter to his government without an order from that government, but told the consul that he could not receive or transmit any such letter sent by a foreigner with whom he had never had any intercourse. The governor asked Kondo Masuki if America was the same country known to the Koreans as "Melikan," and upon being told that it was, he angrily responded, "America is the enemy of Korea, and once threatened to bombard our cities in the bay of Kokwa. It is quite immaterial whether Japan concerns herself in this matter or not, we will never accept any propositions made to us for friendly intercourse with America." Those words signaled the end of Shufeldt's initial attempt to gain entrance to Korea through Fusan. The Japanese consul expressed his sorrow at the result of the endeavor. "I have done for you as much as I can," he told Shufeldt, who acknowledged his "kind efforts to render us service in this matter."[14]

Returning to Yokohama, Shufeldt confessed to his daughter, "we have been to Corea—& found the *gates closed* . . . If I can only get the gate ajar to the 'forbidden land' I think I can get in—it is worth trying for even if it takes all summer." At this point Shufeldt was grateful to the Japanese consul for his efforts. It is inaccurate to conclude, as Paullin and Dennett have done, that Shufeldt was suspicious of Japanese motives during this time. He asked Minister Bingham for interviews with the Japanese foreign minister and then hoped to return to Korea "if armed with additional powers." Failing that, he concluded, "we may go to China & try the Chinese authorities."[15]

The Second Attempt

On May 12 and 20 Shufeldt and Bingham met Inouye Kaoru for interviews on the Korean question, and Shufeldt asked the foreign minister to forward his letter to the king of Korea directly to the Korean government. In this request Shufeldt was actively supported by Bingham, who informed Inouye,

> I am instructed by my Government to ask the good offices of H. I. J. Majesty's Gov. by personal or official letters to the Gov. of Corea to aid Commodore Shufeldt in transmitting a friendly communication in writing to that Governor. Y. E. already knows that Commodore Shufeldt is possessed of a letter addressed to him some years ago by order of the King of Corea in which the Corean Prime Minister among other things expressly says that the written communication which Com. Shufeldt had at that time addressed to the King was improperly delayed by the local Corean Magistrate for which neglect of duty that official "rec'd a demerit mark" thereby showing it was the wish of H. M. the King of Corea, as it was H. M.'s duty to receive the friendly communication of Com. Shufeldt which was wrongfully delayed by the local magistrate until the Com. was constrained by the severity of the weather and the demands of duty elsewhere to quit Corea.

Bingham thus formally requested Inouye to forward Shufeldt's letter, stressing that the Japanese government would not incur any responsibility but would be giving another assurance of goodwill toward the United States. Bingham expected the Japanese government to comply, and he asked for a speedy reply to his letter, repeating again that he did not doubt "that Y. E. will be pleased to do this act of kindness for my Government." Inouye advised Shufeldt to take the *Ticonderoga* nearer to the Korean capital and make a display of force, but the commodore refused to entertain the suggestion. The Japanese foreign minister then informed Bingham and Shufeldt that the request to forward the letter would require the consent of the Japanese Council of State, which would meet next on May 24.[16]

While waiting for the result of the discussion, Shufeldt confessed to being worried by the desire "to complete this last undertaking creditably" and do all he could in Korea. "I pass uneasy days & sleepless nights," he told his far-distant daughter, adding, "I do not know of anything in the Dept. to work against my interest—I have never asked officially for the Squadron—& all of [*sic*] I have suggested has been complied with—but if I had rec'd the command for the summer—I am almost sure I would have accomplished more in the Corea than we probably shall now."[17]

On the afternoon of May 24, Bingham notified him that the Japanese foreign minister recommended to the Korean government that it "should comply with the request of the United States Government made through you in a friendly spirit." Inouye informed Bingham that he did not doubt that the Korean government would forward the desired answer. He sent Bingham a copy of his letter to the Korean minister of ceremony, in which he informed the Korean that he had prevailed upon Shufeldt not to visit Fusan again and that the American would wait sixty days at Nagasaki for a reply. Inouye claimed that Shufeldt intended "simply to repeat the former request" for a treaty of friendship. Stressing his own experience, Inouye offered his advice to the Koreans in dealing with this approach because "the general state of the world is now very different from that of olden times, and we know from our own experience the impossibility of rejecting foreign intercourse, and China also has the same experience." He stressed this would be the means of guarding against the "Contempts from abroad, and of securing the right of independency of your country." There is no evidence at all of any reluctance by Inouye or the Japanese to further Shufeldt's mission or that they requested Shufeldt to remain in Nagasaki in order to make the Americans appear as though they were dealing with Korea through Japanese channels. After the first rejection at Fusan, both Shufeldt and Bingham would have been the first to acknowledge they were dealing through Japan. The important point is not that Shufeldt was in Nagasaki waiting for a reply, but that the Japanese foreign minister was the agent through whom he and Bingham wanted to send the letter to Korea and was, of course, Shufeldt's deliberate choice. Evarts again asked Bingham to express appreciation for Japanese cooperation, noting that "From these numerous papers it is observed that the Japanese Government has been of material assistance, with the help you have been able to extend, to Commodore Shufeldt, and I will thank you, therefore, to suitably convey the thanks of the Government of the United States to that of Japan for the steps so courteously taken by it, to forward and promote the object with which Commodore Shufeldt has been charged."[18]

While waiting for Korean events to develop, Shufeldt informed Thompson,

> The Corean Question is of great interest here in the East and it would seem that the prestige which we acquired by the treaty with Japan should be maintained by being also the first to make a treaty with Corea.
>
> If therefore after the present overtures (which are of the most friendly character) are received, that Government should refuse to entertain any proposition—especially for the protection of shipwrecked mariners and property stranded upon the Corean Coast, it will be for the Government of the United States to decide upon the propriety of using other and perhaps more forcible means.

What these means would entail, he speculated, was "a display of our naval force in these seas" on the Korean coast that "would bring about intercourse at least, and perhaps a treaty." In that eventuality, he hinted broadly, "the squadron is strong enough to attack and hold any desirable point on the coast."[19]

Inspired by the possibilities arising out of the Japanese foreign minister's note to the Koreans, Shufeldt stayed up all night preparing a history of the stages of the negotiation for the government to give officials "a clear idea of the present status of the Corean negotiations" in case he should have to telegraph for instructions. He sought Navy Department approval of both the tone and the character of his letter to the king of Korea, especially as he found it extrememly difficult "without loss of dignity" to open negotiations with the country, "the last contact with which was on its part considered an act of unprovoked hostility." Despite being haunted by the Low-Rodgers expedition, Shufeldt was sanguine of success, especially after the intervention of the Japanese government, "which after much hesitation has now acted with vigor and judgement." If success did not come from these efforts, he informed the secretary, then it would remain for the American government either to abandon the idea of opening the country, or, to use force:

> A mere display of force upon different parts of the Coast, at unexpected moments would so intimidate the authorities as to bring them to terms. This,

of course, might in an unguarded moment bring about a collision, if so, our present naval force on this station would be found quite ample to meet the emergency. . . . We should take possession of these islands [Port Hamilton] and hold them until the Corean Government yielded to reasonable terms. This I am convinced it would soon do rather than have our Naval force so near their coast—but if it did not, then this port, so convenient to China, Japan and Corea, could be justifiably held as a means of protection against the risks of our commerce upon the Corean Coast.

The diplomat of 1880 still wore the armor of 1868. Futhermore, he told Thompson that if the department would place the Asiatic squadron under his command, in the event of no answer coming from Korea after sixty days he would endeavor to bring the affair "to a creditable and successful conclusion—a matter which although comparatively unimportant would nevertheless add very much to the power of the United States in the East, and . . . might be considered as giving eclat to the present administration." From Nagasaki he confessed to his daughter of a yearning to visit Korea "in more force than I now possess," but anticipated returning home in the *Ticonderoga*.[20]

Shufeldt was under a good deal of pressure at this time, mental and physical. His letters about his nephew, Molly's brother, Frederick Miller, leaving the ship at Singapore after a quarrel with Captain Cromwell, had reached his adopted daughter, and her replies were so gloomy they filled Shufeldt with despair. In addition, he had not heard from his sons for at least six months, and he grew savage in his condemnation of them. The break with his sons, which had grown after his wife's death, widened irreparably in these years: Mason had not written for six months, George sent only the briefest of notes, and Robert sent nothing at all. Shufeldt was "tired of this selfish, unfilial conduct & I see no remedy but to shut up the shop—& live the life of a wanderer." He felt no responsibility for their support. Furthermore, Shufeldt was physically tired by the cruise. On arrival at Nagasaki in April, he had spent a wretched three days shaking off the effects of fever. Then came the sixty-day wait for the Korean letter. Rear Admiral Thomas H. Patterson declined to turn over the command of the squadron to him and take home the *Ticonderoga*. In addition came Secretary Thompson's reply cabled immediately after receiving Shufeldt's dispatches of May 29 and 31, to "use only persuasive means with Coreans, Avoid hostilities." Thompson was keeping tight reins on the crusading commodore, who notified the secretary on July 1, "Cable orders received and will be carefully obeyed."[21]

At the beginning of July, Shufeldt disclosed to his daughter that his plans were more widespread than merely waiting for the reply to Inouye's covering letter. In order to have his letter to the king of Korea translated correctly, he had consulted Ü Tsing, the Chinese consul in

Nagasaki and a confidant of Li Hung-chang, the viceroy of Chihli, guardian of the emperor, commander-in-chief of eighteen provinces and, as Shufeldt correctly believed, the most powerful man in China. Ü Tsing gave Shufeldt the impression that his letter so pleased him that he wanted to send a copy to Li. This was somewhat naive on the commodore's part, for Ü Tsing wanted Li to see what events were transpiring in, and over, Korea. But Shufeldt was flattered sufficiently by Ü Tsing's praises to search out his only copy of the 1868 lecture on China he had delivered in Stamford after his return from the East and give it to the consul. He believed Ü Tsing was "so much delighted to find a single foreigner who would or could write in favor of his Country" that the lecture was translated and "circulated throughout the 'flowery kingdom.' " As the absorbing topic within Chinese councils was the probable war with Russia and the defenseless condition of the Chinese seaboard, Shufeldt guardedly informed his daughter, "at this moment China wants a Naval officer of reputation . . . to relieve herself from English influence which has been & will always be oppressive & expensive." "I would *not be surprised,*" he remarked confidentially, "if all this ended in my receiving an invitation to visit Peking—for the purpose of consulting with Li Hung Chang on the Corean question & perhaps to have the offer made of supreme naval command of the Chinese forces." What reinforced his belief, apart from the obvious hints of Ü Tsing, was the "impressive attention" given him by the Chinese embassy officials in Tokyo and "by the anxious wish of the Consul" for him to visit China. "At all events," he sardonically declared, "it is something to know that a prophet is not without honor save in his own country."[22]

With this prospect in mind, Shufeldt began to feel more optimistic about the fate of the Korean venture. Kondo Masuki indicated that the Korean government would reply within the stipulated time, and Inouye Kaoru refused to respond to foreign inquiries about whether the Japanese government had used its good offices in aiding the United States government in its negotiations. Although Shufeldt was in the dark about Thompson's intentions to reallocate the squadron, "the only persuasive power which Corea or any other Eastern nation recognizes," he soon heard from China. Li Hung-chang had written to Ü Tsing expressing his desire to secure Shufeldt's services but informing the consul that the matter would have to be referred to the Tsungli Yamen. Shufeldt reckoned that he would not hear anything more about the Chinese Navy until August, but he did enthuse over the opportunity this might afford him. "China has a Navy of about 60 vessels of modern type," he calculated, adding for his daughter, "To be made its Commander in Chief would in the present aspect of affairs be a distinction both in Europe & America which I can scarcely realize."[23]

On August 8 Ü Tsing formally delivered Li's letter of July 23 to Shufeldt. The viceroy had written that he had heard of Shufeldt for a long time* but had not the pleasure of meeting him. "I respect you very much for being a clever and just man and having a good feeling towards China," Li wrote, inviting him to Tientsin in order to have "a personal meeting with you and talk over matters." The commodore notified the consul that he would accept the offer immediately if his government would permit him to do so. He informed Li ("the Chinese Foreign Minister" as he termed him) that he would telegraph for permission.[24]

Within a week after receiving Ü Tsing's covering letter, Shufeldt's Korean plans had been resolved. The latest news from Korea had been Kondo Masuki's favorable letter to the Japanese Foreign Office. He had kept this letter until August 10, the last date for the reply from Korea to reach him within the sixty-day span, before sending it to his superiors in the Navy Department. But as it was the typhoon season, Shufeldt declared he would wait until the middle of September before sailing for San Francisco. This would give the Korean government ample opportunity to reply to his letter. He offered the department three probable lines of action: going to Fusan in the event of a favorable reply, returning home in the event of an unfavorable one, and waiting further, with the possibility of receiving no answer from Korea. Four days later he tacked on a fourth possibility, that of going to China, so that "the interests of the cruise would be extended thereby." He told Thompson of Li's offer and proclaimed that it would be discourteous to neglect the invitation. Moreover, he reassured the secretary, the visit "will have no other than a pleasant effect upon the relations between the two Countries, and will in no wise interfere or conflict with either the Diplomatic or Naval Authorities in this part of the world."[25]

Privately, Shufeldt sang a different tune, for he believed he would go to reorganize the Chinese Navy. His hopes of receiving the command of the United States Asiatic Squadron had foundered when rumors of the appointment of Rear Admiral John M. B. Clitz to succeed Patterson began to filter through from San Francisco. If these rumors were true, Shufeldt speculated, then it was obvious the department had determined not to give him the command. "I think it makes a mistake," he confessed to his daughter, "because I have reason to believe that my personal influence both in China & Japan is greater than that of any naval officer of whatever grade or nationality." Still, he hoped to wake up "the Rip Van Winkles in Washington" with the announcement of his promotion "to the grade of Admiral in Chief to H.C.M. the Emperor of China & the 'Son of Heaven'!" In an addendum to a letter of August 13, added at 8:00 A.M. on the fourteenth, he wrote, "I shall

---

*He had not heard of him well enough to avoid calling him "Sheffield."

accept it—It would be such a position as I ought not to decline being far above anything I could expect at home."[26]

It was at this point that Shufeldt's Korean hopes shattered. The letter forwarded by Kondo Masuki and the prefect of Torai-fu to Hanabusa Yosimoto, the Japanese minister to Korea, had been presented to In-jisho, the Korean minister of ceremony. In-jisho returned Shufeldt's letter to Inouye Kaoru, via the consul at Fusan, firmly and somewhat impolitely, making clear that Shufeldt's letter was unacceptable. In-jisho explained:

> It is well known to the world that our foreign relations are only with Japan neighboring to us, which has been maintained since three hundred years, and that other foreign nations are not only situated far from us, but there has never been any intercourse with them. The letter of the American Mission bears the address of "Great Corai"; this name of the country was used in the period of the late dynasty. Now the name has been altered. Even if the letter were addressed "Great Chosen," how can I receive and present to my August Sovereign the letter which has been addressed directly to His Majesty? If he should wish to send any communication, he might better address it to a local officer or to the Minister of Ceremony.
>
> Upon deliberation of the matter I cannot receive the America Mission's letter.[27]

It would be straining credulity and ignoring Korean resistance to regard this as evidence of Japanese duplicity. The Koreans regarded their relations with Japan as going back to the Hideyoshi invasions (1592 to 1598) during the Wan-li period of the Ming dynasty. Also, three Japanese trading missions had existed on the south coast of Korea from about 1440 to 1512. Fusan was the center of a Japanese-Korean trade down to the formal opening of the treaty ports in 1876. The conservative Korean minister of ceremony was being very specific; to the Koreans there had been no other foreign intercourse and, thus, no reason to disturb the status quo.[28]

In-jisho's suggestion, of sending another letter to a local officer, held only the faintest of chances for Shufeldt, who predicted that "without some exhibition of force upon the Corean Coast it will be difficult to convince that Government of the earnestness of our purpose secluded as it has been for so many Centuries from contact with the outside world." But he felt that he and the *Ticonderoga,* like Commodore Biddle in the *Columbus* before Perry's visit to Japan, had inaugurated a movement that would most likely continue until Korea was open to commerce and foreigners were permitted to visit its shores under treaty protection. It would be inaccurate to conclude, however, as Hag-w'on Sunoo has done in "A Study of the U.S.-Korean Treaty of 1882," that after Shufeldt received the news from Korea, "he was very much discouraged," —a comment that underestimated Shufeldt's tenacity and perseverance and neglected the possibilities of Chinese help.[29]

Bingham consoled Shufeldt over the "evasive reply to this Government." Shufeldt had good precedent in having addressed the king of Korea previously in 1867 and having had his letter received and answered. The minister promised to apprise the government of the transactions, considered that the Japanese officials in Korea should not have permitted the return of the unopened letter, and suggested that the Japanese government should return it "for a fitting answer thereto, and that as the Minister of Ceremony of the King of Korea has been pleased to ask H. E. Mr. Inouye 'to do his utmost to arrange it,' viz—the blunder of the Minister of Ceremony, this Gov. should repeat its request." Bingham wanted Shufeldt to bring the Korean minister of ceremony "to a right understanding of his duty" and offered his services in case Shufeldt wished to send further communications, though he warned that it was by no means clear that "this very unsatisfactory letter to Mr. Inouye gives any assurance that a letter addressed to the Minister of Ceremony would be received and be favorably considered by the Corean Government."[30]

The Chinese Gambit

Shufeldt left Nagasaki on August 19 and took the *Ticonderoga* to Tientsin for an interview with Li Hung-chang on the twenty-sixth. During the three-hour meeting, Shufeldt asked Li if China would use its influence to secure a Korean–United States treaty of amity. The reason he gave was that Korea lay in the line of ocean commerce and travel between America and the East; it was important to secure protection by treaty for American lives and property that might be stranded on Korean shores. After a prolonged discussion of the strategic position of the Korean peninsula with reference to Russia, China, and Japan, Li agreed to use his influence with the Korean government. In fact, he told Shufeldt that China had used her influence to effect the treaty between Japan and Korea. Li also informed his guest that he wanted the opinion of a naval officer, "in whom he had confidence," on the probable result of a war between China and Russia, so far as naval operations on the Chinese coast were concerned. He promised the answer would have full force and effect, not only with himself but "in the counsels of the Nation." Shufeldt replied that in view of the formidable naval force on the coast of China (in July 1880, twenty-one Russian warships had been sighted in the Sea of Japan), "the result could only be one of disaster to China." Li seemed "much impressed," he thought. The viceroy assured him no war would occur between the two nations if China could avert it. The two empresses, the "Prime Minister," Prince Kung, and Li himself were all in favor of peace.

During this interview Shufeldt was filled with admiration for Li's intelligence and judgment and with pleasure over the treatment he received in Chinese hands. To the secretary of the navy, he revealed that Li had expressed the hope, when peace was assured, that the United States government "would permit me to assist China in the organization of its Navy." This, he considered, "is a matter to some extent personal in its nature, but if consumated [sic] would add very much to American influence in China and probably end in the construction of ships for that Government in American Ship Yards."[31] Shufeldt judged that he would receive a distinct proposition from China by the time the *Ticonderoga* arrived in San Francisco.

While en route from Kobe to Honolulu Shufeldt carefully set down his thoughts on "Corea & American Interests in the East" for Secretary Thompson. This fourteen-page dispatch was not only the culmination of his thinking on the mission to open Korea, but was typical of his beliefs, sharpened through two years of contact with Africa and Asia, on the aims and role of the United States in relation to other Far Eastern countries. As an exponent of commercial expansionism, he noted: "The acquisition of Alaska and the Aleutian Islands—the treaties with Japan, Sandwich Islands and Samoa are only corollaries to the proposition that the Pacific Ocean is to become at no distant day—the commercial domain of America." Shufeldt considered that the Atlantic Ocean was dominated by the "immense weight of European Capital." "Under natural law," however, the flow of commerce as of migration was from the East toward the West. The geographical position of the United States "in conformity with this law" pointed to the Pacific Ocean as the main channel of trade and to the United States "as the source from which these Oriental people must obtain whatever they need in the way of Commercial exchange." In all probability, he estimated, "within the next half century the United States will find its largest market in Asia rather than in Europe." Thompson's report of 1881 echoed Shufeldt's sentiments very closely, especially when the secretary informed Congress, "our acquisition of Alaska and the Aleutian Islands, and our treaty relations with Japan, the Sandwich Islands and Samoa, together with our present commercial intercourse with China and the East Indies, place us upon such equal terms upon the Pacific with other powers that it will be our own fault if the advantages now promised to our commerce shall be lost."[32]

To Shufeldt, within this context a treaty with Korea became "but another link in the chain which binds the East to the West and would give to our Country that moral precedence in Corea which is so universally conceded to it in Japan." Shufeldt dwelt at length on Korean aversions to any foreign intercourse, covering the past French, American, and Russian pressures on the country. He steadfastly urged, "if any means can now be found to get beyond the 'barred gates' and to reach the central goverment—I am convinced that Corea could be made to understand not only the policy of a treaty with the United States—but its absolute necessity as a matter of protection against the aggression of surrounding Powers." He reflected that the country would become the battleground of any future war between China, Russia, or Japan, but he did not consider that would have been sufficient reason to keep clear of the area.

To accomplish the desired treaty, Shufeldt estimated there should be evident the same earnestness of purpose that characterized Perry's course in Japan. That meant "some outward and visible sign of the power of his Government" should be given to the commissioner chosen to negotiate the treaty. He was satisfied that moral suasion with Orientals, especially Koreans, "who have seen so little of the world, though clothed in the most powerful language, would fail to convince even those most willing to believe unless they saw evidence of the power of the nation which sought their friendship." At this point in the argument, he offered additional justification for the use of this power, culled from his own experiences that summer:

> Besides in the intervention between the United States and Corea, I am not satisfied that Japan has been acting in perfect faith—it is her policy indeed to monopolize the commerce of Corea. She possesses in that Country extraterritorial rights, and rules the Coreans with an iron rod. Striving to free herself from the obnoxious array of foreigners upon her soil—she is unwilling to have these foreigners see how she has imposed these same laws in an aggravated form—upon her defenceless neighbor.

This was the first occasion upon which Shufeldt charged the Japanese with not acting in good faith during the negotiations of the summer. Only in October 1880, after transferring his hopes of achieving anything from Japan to China, did Shufeldt begin to blame the Japanese. Despite being given prominence by Paullin and Dennett, Shufeldt's opinion is not proof of Japanese duplicity in May and June. Moreover, such a notion implies that success or failure could only have come through the Japanese Foreign Office, an opinion that ignores the power of the conservative and antiforeign forces then dominant in the Korean court, who were the prime movers in rejecting the initial approach to Korea.

It is possible that Shufeldt had reflected seriously and deeply on

Inouye's role by October, but this was not very likely at a time when he confessed to feeling weary and in need of mental rest. Much more likely as the reason for the outburst was Shufeldt's conversation with Li Hung-chang. Three pieces of internal evidence point to this interpretation. Shufeldt was describing how the Japanese were treating the Koreans in Korea, yet he had not been in the interior, only touching briefly at Fusan, where, he later recalled, the ship had been placed in quarantine.[33] The imagery of the "iron rod" was more of the type used by Chinese observers reporting to the Chinese viceroy and describing the efforts of the rival Japanese to dominate a country that China considered lay within her orbit. Secondly, Shufeldt had mentioned Korea as a battleground between three contending powers, and he told the secretary of the navy that he had discussed the strategic position of the Korean peninsula at some length in the early part of his interview with Li Hung-chang. Thirdly, in Shufeldt's letterpress copies of his official correspondence to people other than the secretary of the navy, there is a letter to Bingham dated September 10, 1880, in which Shufeldt revealed that "Li Hung Chang expressed *confidentially* a want of faith in the good offices of the Japanese. I hope that he is mistaken in this conception."[34] Shufeldt obviously did not accept Li's judgment as late as September 10, but by the time he wrote to Thompson a month later he had seemingly accepted the viceroy's conception. It appears most likely, therefore, that Shufeldt's changed notions about the Japanese, especially considering his letter of thanks to Kondo Masuki and Inouye Kaoru, only developed in the post-August depression when In-jisho's letter reached him and after he had been exposed to the astute diplomatic pressures of the viceroy of Chihli. To place undue emphasis on Shufeldt's frustrated outburst of October as evidence of Japanese motives in May would also mask the fact that his change of mind could have been encouraged by the prospects of a place in the Chinese Navy should the peace be maintained between China and Russia.

After his outburst, Shufeldt drew the lessons for the United States. The *Ticonderoga*, like Commodore Biddle's *Columbus*, had inaugurated a movement. If the country desired to extend its influence in the East and follow up Perry's movement in Japan, it should place a squadron "under the command of a discreet officer"; otherwise, he warned, "we shall bestow upon some other nation the *prestige* and *power* which *of right* belongs to ourselves."* There was a further reason for the United States to act:

> it is a duty which we owe to these people to become the pioneers of a more enlightened policy in the East. European power is not employed to "civilize"

---
*My italics

orientals—but to subordinate them and to keep them subordinate for the purposes of trade or proselytism. . . . The United States should take higher grounds and while demanding protection for its citizens, should ask for nothing more than she is willing to concede. . . . The object of the *Ticonderoga* was to do away—in the first place with this unfavorable reminiscence [the Low-Rodgers expedition of 1871]—and in the second to endeavor to pave the way to such a treaty as would at least give to the United States the right to protect its citizens and their property if wrecked upon the Corean Coast, at present we submit to the humiliation of such protection from the Japanese Government, the only one, which thus far, has such right under treaty.[35]

In contrasting the United States in the East, as the dispenser of a "more enlightened policy," to the "non-civilizing" European powers, Shufeldt was postulating opinions similar to those expressed on his round-the-world cruise. The higher moral character of American policy was juxtaposed with the lower tone of European policies designed to subordinate the dominated areas for commercial reasons. Yet when he discussed Korea as a peninsula that jutted out into the ocean highways of the world, Shufeldt showed the same keen awareness of trade rights, even countenancing the use of force, if negotiation failed, to achieve this end. Submitting to Japanese protection would be a humiliation. Arguing softly yet carrying a big stick would bring about the opening of Korea. To Thompson he noted:

While acceding to the desire and even the right of Corea to remain secluded from the family of nations—no one I presume will deny to other countries the prerogative as well as the duty of protecting their Citizens whenever they may be found. . . . Commerce insists upon the right to travel upon this track [the ocean highways of the world] and the mercantile world is justified in demanding its protection.

I do not wish to see the United States use coercive measures in Corea or anywhere in the East—yet as I have said before, America is the pioneer of the Pacific—a position which she should not only recognize but claim. For this reason—if for no other, I hope she will not resign her place in Corea to other Powers both willing and anxious to retard her progress or cripple her prestige in the East.[36]

The commodore did not enlighten the secretary of the navy as to which should be sacrificed, the moral suasion, the commercial privileges, or the use of force, if ever any of these began to run counter to the others in the bid to dominate the Pacific. He merely brought the *Ticonderoga* home to San Francisco by way of Honolulu. On November 8 the flagship dropped anchor two years, more than fifty ports of call, and 36,000 miles after she had cleared Cape Henry.[37]

The Empire of the Seas

The cruise of the *Ticonderoga* had mixed results. Considering the various diplomatic tasks he had been given, Shufeldt could hardly claim success with many of them. He had failed to achieve a settlement of the Liberian boundary question, though given the assumptions of both British and Liberian commissioners and the attitudes of the tribal chiefs disputing Liberian authority, it was doubtful if any arbitrator could have achieved a solution. The treaties with kings Balambé and Lamarese in Madagascar and with Sultan Abdallah in Johanna were rejected by the Senate. At Borneo, the impact of Shufeldt's notification that the sultan and Dent, Overbeck and Company had overlooked the United States treaty of 1850 was negligible. In Korea, though there was a promise of dividends from the Chinese, the move to approach the Hermit Kingdom through Japan yielded no profits for American trade in 1880.

Yet there were also some successes. In Korea, Shufeldt's approach helped to remove the unpleasant memories of the Low-Rodgers expedition and gave ammunition to the groups at court who wished to establish contact with the outside world. In Zanzibar and Persia considerable progress had been made. Shufeldt had decided that the United States–Zanzibar treaty of 1833 was more beneficial for American trade than a revised one would be; a positive reaffirmation of the commercial status quo. In Persia, where a legation was established in 1883, Shufeldt had, in the words of the secretary of the navy, "brought our form of modern civilization in immediate contact with that prevailing among those who represent the oldest civilization known to history."

In a commercial context the cruise was much more of a success. It is important to realize that the cruise of the *Ticonderoga* was an official expedition of the United States government, no less important through being made at sea instead of on land. It placed Shufeldt not only in the naval context of explorers like Charles Wilkes and Commodore Perry but in the national context of explorers who had opened the American West since the time of Lewis and Clark. The commodore thus served as a standard-bearer for the United States goverment in extending that West into the Pacific. Though the specific treaty-making agreements bore little fruit, the instructions of Evarts and Thompson in Hayes' cabinet proved to be an indication of American interest in siphoning off the commercial riches of both Africa and Asia. Shufeldt himself was a powerful exponent of the idea, defined in his instructions, that "all increase in the exchange of the productions of Africa, Borneo and the islands of the Indian Ocean for those of the United States is imminently desirable." For that purpose he welded together a strong reporting team, headed by Franklin J. Drake, Kossuth Niles, Charles E. Vreeland, Frederick A. Miller, and Paymaster William J. Thompson, to keep the government informed of the ports and countries of call. Both Navy and State departments attached great importance to the expedition in view of its probable bearing on the anticipated future of American commerce. In 1880, the secretary of the navy described the benefits to be derived from the cruise that "had special reference to the increase of our commerce." Thompson constantly reminded Congress that Shufeldt was sent to other countries and natives in Africa to "enable them to appreciate the advantages of trade with the United States." He judged the results to have "not only been eminently satisfactory" but the information communicated during the voyage would "contribute materially to our knowledge of the commercial wants of the peoples who have been visited." Large quantities of manufactured goods used in different markets had been forwarded to the department and distributed among American manufacturers to enable them to determine whether they could compete in these markets with European manufacturers. The cruise, in this sense, was a fact-finding research mission of undoubted success. Thompson drew the attention of Congress to the result:

> An exchange of our products for those of the East is fast becoming a necessity to all the oriental people, and their interests, as well as ours, suggest the adoption of the most efficient measures on our part to increase our trade with them. Even in Corea our manufactured goods are preferred to those of England, but they find their way there through the Japanese, with whom the Coreans have a treaty of amity and commerce. The benefits derived in this way, however, are indirect, and would be greatly increased if the ports of that country were opened to our merchant vessels.[38]

The cruise also had great personal importance for Shufeldt. It placed him squarely in the van of commercial expansionists. On the west coast of Africa his notable commercial-diplomatic contribution was in proposing a consular service for the whole of the coast. He identified the efficiencies and deficiencies of the existing service and pointed to the efficacy of providing new consulates in ports then without them. Furthermore, he relayed a tremendous amount of firsthand information on the commercial possibilities and the actual state of American trade with the west coast of Africa, Cape Town, Madagascar, Muscat, Zanzibar, the Persian Gulf, and the Orient.

Shufeldt was one of America's earliest and most prominent commercial pathfinders in Africa. His dream of dominating the palm oil rivers from Fernando Po, his desires to establish steamship routes from the United States to Sierra Leone and Liberia, and his mission to extend American influence eastward through Liberia into the heart of Africa, or westward from Zanzibar, demonstrated that Africa, in his mind, could be a market for American produce. In 1887 former Senator Roscoe Conkling of New York took up the idea, first pressed in America by Shufeldt, of a commission to discuss with other governments the possibility of a trans-African railroad. Africa became the subject of a considerable debate in the country, but the fruit of Shufeldt's enterprises were not gathered until after the 1890s.

In discussing the consequences of such forceful commercial expansion, however, Shufeldt exhibited uncertainty, doubt, and vacillating attitudes. En route he had touched at the imperial holdings of the world's great empires. He had observed the British in Sierra Leone, Cape Colony, Aden, the Persian Gulf, Muscat, India, and Borneo; the Spanish in Fernando Po, Borneo, and the Philippines; the Dutch in the Congo and East Indies; the French in Gabon, Madagascar, and the Comoro Islands; and the Portuguese in Angola. He attacked the Dutch for their "degrading" of Congolese natives, sneered at the Portuguese, and feared the French and British. More and more, as the cruise progressed, he was drawn to an examination of British power, imperial strength, and weaknesses. He pointed out that the success of British imperial ventures was based on the protection provided for British traders by men-of-war and consuls bringing the trader under the aegis of the consular flag. He deplored the extent of British political control, yet envied that country's commercial dominance. He recognized that the activities of the Royal Navy in suppressing the slave trade and the supremacy of the British trader had ousted American influence and led to British hegemony and control. Furthermore, he had put his finger on the weaknesses of the British empire in the event of internal violence and revolt and on the force of British naval power in threading together widely scattered colonial holdings.

Yet when Shufeldt's solutions to America's problems are compared with his analyses of British imperialism, they reveal a marked similarity. For example, Shufeldt wanted to relieve American production surpluses by entrance into the anticipated, vast, African market. Liberia and Zanzibar would be the wedges into Africa to offset any British and French division of the continent. The Liberian trade outlet would be tied to the United States by subsidized steamers and mail services. No port duties would mean favorable conditions for the influx of cheap American goods. Beyond lay the Niger Valley, to be linked by Blyden's proposed railroad from Monrovia. Zanzibar would play a similar role on the eastern side of the continent. In Asia, Korea would be the same kind of wedge into the Asian market. Here Shufeldt was ready to use a display of force to achieve his objectives. He was prepared to seize Port Hamilton until the Korean government acceded to his demands for a commercial treaty. That was one reason why he wanted the command of the Asiatic squadron. His desire for increased commercial entanglements had led to his readiness to use gunboats to back up his demands. Yet this was the basis of the British "Paramountcy," that he analyzed on his cruise. All Shufeldt had left to fall back on, therefore, to distinguish his own brand of political persuasion from British, Spanish, Dutch, French, or Portuguese was his belief in the regenerative effects of a "higher civilization" and the assumption that such entanglements might not lead to political control. To the commodore, the American flag represented "the result up to the nineteenth century of the Christian era." In a moral and religious sense the American empire would be one distinctly superior to others. But in two years of close reflection on the subject, Shufeldt failed to resolve the dilemma posed by his observations, that increased commercial expansion led toward increasing military and political intervention.

Captain Robert Wilson Shufeldt when he served as the U.S. Navy's representative in charge of naval preparations for the funeral of George Peabody, Portland, Maine, February 8, 1870. Private collection.

The USS *Miantonomoh,* double-turreted monitor and mainstay of the harbor defense navy. U.S. Naval Photographic Center.

James Robert Madison Mullany. U.S. Naval Photographic Center.

Rear Admiral Stephen Bleeker Luce. U.S. Naval Photographic Center.

George Maxwell Robeson *(left)*, Secretary of the Navy, 1869–1877. U.S. Naval Photographic Center. Admiral David Dixon Porter *(above right)*. U.S. Naval Photographic Center. Richard Wigginton Thompson *(above left)*, Secretary of the Navy, 1877–1881. U.S. Naval Photographic Center.

Secretary Richard W. Thompson and the chiefs of the navy's bureaus, 1878. Top left clockwise: Robert W. Shufeldt (Equipment and Recruiting); William H. Shock (Steam Engineering); John C. S. Howell (Yards and Docks); John W. Easby (Construction and Repair); George F. Cutter (Provisions and Clothing); William D. Whiting (Navigation); William Grier (Medicine and Surgery); and William N. Jeffers (Ordnance Brady photograph; private collection.

The USS *Ticonderoga* flying the pendant of Commodore Robert Wilson Shufeldt, Table Bay, South Africa, 1879. Shufeldt Papers, Manuscript Division, Library of Congress.

Rear Admiral Robert Wilson Shufeldt, ca. 1884. Library of Congress.

Commodore Robert Wilson Shufeldt (third from left) with Viceroy Li Hung-chang (center) and mandarins of Li's yamen, who were most likely Ma Chien-chung, Cheow Fuh, the Hai Kwan taotai, Cheng Tsao-ju, Lo-fông-loh, and an interpreter. Private collection.

William Eaton Chandler *(above left)*, Secretary of the Navy, 1882–1885. U.S. Naval Photographic Center. *(above right)* "For the Children" from their grandfather, Robert Wilson Shufeldt, Thanksgiving, 1884. Private collection. Robert Wilson Shufeldt's gravestone *(right)*, Arlington National Cemetery. Photograph by the author.

13

The Opening of Korea, 1881

Forging New Links

After the failure of his attempt to complete the *Ticonderoga*'s cruise by negotiating a treaty, Shufeldt was determined to open Korea. By now he regarded a successful entrance into Asia through the Hermit Kingdom as the culmination of his life's work. But first he had to rebuild his political support in the United States. The Hayes' team of Evarts and Thompson had left office when he returned at election time. Sick and weary, feeling the first symptoms of "some organic derangement" with his heart, he feared he might "sink into a chronic invalidism." Psychologically, he prepared himself for retirement under a Democratic administration. To Molly he explained, "there is nothing left for me to do —& but little 'vim' to do anything." But he expected the Democrats, if elected, to pursue a vigorous foreign policy and, he guessed, that would probably be of service to him in China. He learned that the threatened war between China and Russia had receded and believed there should be no reason why the government should refuse him permission to enter the Chinese naval service. "I quite expect a prominent & lucrative position," he confessed to his daughter, "& if my health will permit shall accept a proper offer—if not I shall go on the retired list."[1] Shufeldt did not extend his analysis of the Russian-Chinese rapprochement far enough. If the threat of war had passed there would be little reason for Li Hung-chang to offer him a lucrative naval post. This conclusion became all too obvious in late 1881, but it escaped Shufeldt in San Francisco in November 1880.

The election of James Abram Garfield in 1880 meant that the retired list was not to be Shufeldt's haven for another four years. The commodore had arrived in the United States at the end of a bitter campaign in which the issue of Chinese immigration had played a significant part on the West Coast. He had strong views on the desirability of reducing

Chinese immigration and became acquainted with California senator Aaron A. Sargent, a "warm friend of Garfield," and a leader of the anti-Chinese movement in California, who had introduced the resolution into the Senate in 1878 on the need to open Korea. In 1879, just before President Hayes' veto of the Chinese exclusion act, when racial prejudice was running high in California, Shufeldt had written to Molly from Sierra Leone that "Sargent is not *all* wrong on the Chinese question whatever may have been his motives—We don't want another race of inferior people in our Country—You may depend upon it—the Chinese are *slaves* really when sent here." Shufeldt was to retain the connection with Sargent (and his prejudices) and display them prominently at a crucial time in the Korean treaty negotiations of 1881-1882.[2]

Over the winter of 1880-1881, Shufeldt turned his mind to the solution of many problems concerning commercial expansion. He wished to see a Bureau of Commerce established under the secretary of the navy and staffed by naval officers on the active or retired lists. This bureau would have brought the commercial activity of the nation directly under central regulatory control as far as such activity affected the crews, condition of the vessels, and the quality of ships' masters. Shufeldt was still concerned over the paucity of the American merchant marine and cited the appalling treatment of sailors at sea as working against adequate commercial expansion. At the conclusion of his proposals he told Americans, "you may ask, 'where are our ships.' and I ask, 'where are our men to man them?' "[3] He also worked over his 1877 pamphlet on the navy, with a view to publishing it. Reflecting on the course the country might take, and the implications for the navy, he lectured,

> But if the maritime spirit of the country is really dead and we accept without humiliation the fact that we are no longer to contest for the empire of the sea —that not only our means of travel over the ocean, but our lives and our property abroad are to be under the protection of foreign flags—that we are to possess this continent in selfish and solitary grandeur, without a mission to our fellow men or participation in the world's affairs, and I had almost said without any responsibility to an over ruling Power as an exponent of free institutions, while there remains yet so much of despotism and 'divine rights' —if, in a word, we are to maintain a position of defiant isolation, it must at least be conceded that we need a navy for the purpose of defense. To be without the means of national defense is simply to invite attack.

He also inserted some comments inspired by the voyage of the *Ticonderoga*. During the cruise he had not encountered another warship of the United States, but had met the men-of-war of most other maritime nations. Such vessels conveyed "to the barbarians a sense of the power of their governments to protect and punish," but he had missed "the flag which proclaims to the world a nation founded by the people and for the people." All over the world, he recalled sadly, oppressed peoples looked in vain for the starry banner. As far as these people were concerned the American flag was a mere abstraction, "something the oppressed long for as for the coming of Messiah," but in vain. He revealed that at times he had felt ashamed of the United States because he deprecated "the parsimony and false economy which prevent her from taking her proper stand as first and foremost among the nations of the globe."[4]

The requirements of commerce and the navy also led Shufeldt to consider again the advantages and disadvantages for the United States of a transisthmian canal. As the secretary of state in Garfield's administration, James G. Blaine, attempted to negotiate changes in the Clayton-Bulwer Treaty with England, Shufeldt wrote to the *Washington Post* to add his view to the proposed modifications.[5] He took the "unique ground" that a canal or ship railroad anywhere upon the American isthmus "would be rather detrimental than conducive to the commercial interests of the United States from the fact, that already possessing the right of way by means of our transcontinental railway system, any such trans-Isthmian route would give to the world a means of transit which we now monopolize." He regarded the arguments of the supporters of a Nicaraguan route as fallacious and did not consider it the duty of the American government "to authorize, under any National charter, the construction of a canal for the mere sentimental purpose of benefitting the world at large." He pointed to the Suez Canal as an example of one canal route that had fallen into the hands of England after being built by the French; he presumed the same result would follow the opening of any means of transit for ships across an American isthmus.

Shufeldt knew the mood of the incoming administration favored the construction of a canal. Consequently, he asserted that if the government and people wished a means of transit to be built, it should be at Tehuantepec. The reasons were the same as he had given in 1871; it was the shortest line between the eastern and western seaboards and would be the only route that could be controlled by the United States in time of war. Commerce and strategy dictated Shufeldt's views on this point. The Gulf of Mexico was an American lake, he reminded his readers, drawing their attention to the fact that the American railroad frontier was pushing toward, and inside of, Mexico. In the "logic of events" the railroad system would not only connect with the Mexican capital but push on to link up with the interoceanic railroad then being built. Shufeldt thus considered that in the event of war with any maritime power, "it would be easy for us to throw into Mexico a body of troops within thirty days, sufficient to hold not only the entrances to the canal or other means of transit, but every mile of it over the Isthmus." Despite this high-handedness with Mexican sovereignty, Shufeldt believed that Mexico should be a partner with the United States against the aggressions of any European power. Mexico, he asserted, "should be a country with its own autonomy, fostered and encouraged by the United States, but never absorbed or otherwise than morally protected." Presumably this moral defense included the ability to "throw" the body of troops into Mexico to defend the canal—a partnership of senior and junior, scarcely of equals.

As Shufeldt wrestled with such commercial, naval, and isthmian problems, he never lost sight of Korea. He was delighted to receive news from Li Hung-chang, shortly after the *Ticonderoga* arrived in San Francisco, mentioning the possibility of reorganizing the Chinese Navy. In later years he claimed that in August 1880, he had declined this naval project because the United States had friendly relations with both China and Russia, and he did not want to side with one more than the other. There is no evidence that supports any offer of the naval post by Li. However, Shufeldt had recommended that Li employ Daniel Mannix as an instructor at the torpedo school. The viceroy promptly wrote to the Navy Department for Mannix's services. In addition, Li praised Shufeldt as "a man of superior intelligence" and declared, "Although I should be very proud of getting your Excellency's assistance in organizing the Chinese Navy, but as you said in your letter the pending difficulty between China and Russia, it may not be advisable for the present to entertain the idea. But I trust in some future time I may still indulge the hope of availing myself of your services and experience. In the meantime indulge me the pleasure of hearing from you often, as if I am talking to you face to face."[6]

Better news soon followed for Shufeldt. On March 3, 1881, Charles L. Fisher, United States consul at Tientsin, notified him that during a two-hour interview on March 1, Li made many kind inquiries and wondered why he had not heard from the commodore. Li told Fisher to write at once and inform Shufeldt that Li had written to the Korean minister stating his wishes and that a favorable answer had been received "that they were willing to negotiate with you." The Korean minister had asked Li what Shufeldt might demand, and Li had made up "a sort of Memo. for their guidance" about what would be just to ask and to give. Fisher concluded by saying: "The Viceroy says be sure and tell the Commodore to come out in the spring and accomplish the work so well inaugurated and after that is accomplished—he wants you to come here and see and have long talks upon the many questions that are surrounding China—and he says he feels sure that when he sees you again you can come to some final arrangement about staying with him —as he wants your advice continually."[7]

When this letter reached Shufeldt, he acted with vigor prompted by the concern that he might be forestalled, in what he now regarded as his own personal dream, by other officers in the navy. From Fisher he had the assurance that nobody else had been informed of the matter mentioned by the viceroy. He immediately went to see James G. Blaine, gaining from the secretary of state a full assurance of support. On March 15 Blaine wrote to the new secretary of the navy, William H. Hunt of Louisiana, who had taken office ten days earlier, that it was desirable that a naval officer of rank and reputation should be attached to the United States legation at Peking. Thus within less than a week of receiving Fisher's letter, Shufeldt was notified by Hunt of the State Department's request and that he had been suggested for the duty. Later he recalled, "I proceeded at once to Washington and through the earnest assistance of Mr. Blaine—then Secretary of State—I was sent to China as Naval Attaché to the American Legation, with a secret authority, to make a Treaty with Korea." The press caught wind of Shufeldt's task and began to speculate on the possibility of his reorganizing the Chinese Navy.[8]

On May 9 Blaine issued Shufeldt specific orders to report as attaché to the United States legation at Peking, headed by James B. Angell. He could stop at Tientsin to relay any information he might receive "as to the readiness of the Corean Government to resume the negotiations for a treaty of amity and commerce." Blaine told Shufeldt to forward duplicate dispatches to Angell and then wait for further instructions either at Peking or Tientsin "or such other point as may be selected upon consultation between yourself and the United States Minister to China." He also wished to be kept informed of the naval and military organization of the Chinese empire and the "present condition and probable extension of our commerce there." The commodore was to leave San Francisco on May 19, if possible, taking with him the newly ratified immigration and commercial treaties with China.[9]

High Hopes and Long Delays

Determined to take his daughter with him to China, Shufeldt engaged her as his secretary and official hostess for necessary social functions. Together they left San Francisco and landed at Shanghai via Kobe and Yokohama. To Molly the port of Shanghai, with its handsome waterfront buildings, including the United States consulate close to the steamship landing, its shops and well-paved and -lighted European section, seemed exciting and safe after the cold and rainy voyage across the

Yellow Sea from Japan. To Shufeldt, however, the city was neither so strangely new nor exciting. Visitors began to crowd into the consulate to see him a few days after his arrival on June 21, but he was anxious to commence his mission, and so told his daughter they would be leaving on the morning of the twenty-third for Tientsin. Though delayed, they arrived there on June 29 and informed the minister of their presence. Angell was surprised by Shufeldt's intended purpose. Although not piqued with Shufeldt personally, "is it not a little singular," he asked him, "that the govt. has not notified me of your coming much less of your having the Treaties and of your Corean Mission?" The notification had been locked at the last minute in the dispatch box he was to deliver to Angell.[10]

On July 1 Shufeldt was received by Li Hung-chang. Much later, in a more hostile mood, when his relationship with Li was at its lowest ebb, Shufeldt characterized him:

> He is fifty-nine years of age; six feet two inches in height, has a clear, cold cruel eye, & an imperious manner. He is a thorough Oriental, & an intense Chinaman. These imply contempt for Western nations, & hatred for all foreigners. Li Hung Chang is the Bismarck of the East; he keeps together an incongrous Empire & an effête dynasty by the repressive force of an indomitable will. He suppresses rebellion by decapitation, & quiets the turbulent with the bamboo—yet he is great—not because he is so much in advance of his countrymen, but because he is not so far behind as they are in an appreciation of the arts political & physical which govern the modern world. He at least recognizes the value of these forces; he buys ships of war; constructs forts, experiments in torpedoes, & drills troops with modern arms. . . . Li Hung Chang, as the Viceroy of the Imperial Province, guards & garrisons with his own provincial army the capital city of Peking. He has a partially trained force of about 35,000 men, armed with breech-loaders, & a complement of field pieces. He has also in store 200,000 or 300,000 stand of arms & several hundred pieces of artillery. His forts on the seaboard of the gulf of Pechihli, are of modern construction, & are armed with heavy modern ordnance. But, although his troops have been more or less drilled & organized by foreign officers, they are at all times liable to be dispersed for labor upon the public works, thus continually destroying what their instructors are endeavoring to create in them; namely, the *elan*, & spirit of a military corps.

James Angell gave a much softer and more favorable picture of Li in his diary recollections, and, in July 1881, Molly considered Li "a decidedly fine looking man, & carries himself well." This powerful figure promised Shufeldt that he would use his "friendly efforts" to bring about a treaty between Korea and the United States. Li had engaged in a long conversation with a Korean officer (Pak Won-Kuei) visiting China who, "although not a Minister, or officially authorized to represent the Corean Government, was yet a man of influence." The Korean was favorably impressed with the advantages of trade with the United States. Li had subsequently written to the Korean government about a treaty but to that date there had been no reply. Shufeldt considered that the Korean government had previously been afraid that Russia, in the event of a war with China, would seize some Korean ports. To offset this it was willing to enter into treaty relations with Western powers. With the treaty of peace signed between Russia and China, this apprehension diminished and, in Shufeldt's eyes, Korea reverted to "its desire for isolation."[11]

The commodore estimated that two parties had seemingly developed in Korea resulting directly from the visit of the *Ticonderoga,* "one for, and the other against, opening the country to foreign commerce." Li Hung-chang had stated that the king and court officials belonged to the first of these parties, while many *yangban* and lesser officials in the minor offices of government were opposed to any foreign intercourse whatever. For his secretary of state, Shufeldt explained Li's reasoning behind the approach to Korea:

> The Viceroy also says that while he is satisfied that the influence of China would have great weight with the Government of Corea, in effecting the treaty contemplated, which he himself is anxious to secure, yet he apprehends that if any direct action is taken on the part of his Government in favor of the United States, the Representative of every Western nation would demand the same in behalf of their respective Governments. While therefore, he does not see at present exactly what course to recommend in the matter, leading me to have patience as he has the conviction that a treaty can eventually be made.

In Shufeldt's eyes, Li seemed to be annoyed over an effort that he understood had been made by John Bingham in Japan, through the Chinese embassy in Tokyo, to persuade the Korean government to send an envoy to Japan to confer with him about a treaty. Shufeldt told the viceroy that he knew nothing of the matter and that Bingham had not mentioned it to him during his brief visit to Japan en route to China.[12]

During the interview Li also asked Shufeldt about the importance of the Korean treaty to China. However, he sidestepped this crucial issue and later told Blaine, as he told Li, that he would rather confer with Minister Angell on the subject, as he had "no authority at present other than to ascertain the present condition of things." Shufeldt had learned that lesson from Seward nineteen years earlier over Mexico. But he was also aware that the Russian threat, which spurred Li's actions in 1880, had been removed. The effect was obvious, he told Blaine, for "it will be readily understood that neither the Viceroy [n]or the Chinese Government feels so earnestly the necessity of securing the integrity of Corea by means of treaties with Western Powers." Even so, Shufeldt was optimistic in assessing the eventual result. He predicted that in the course of the next few months the friendly offices of China might be obtained and a commissioner might succeed in making a treaty on Korean soil. Such an eventuality would require the presence of a ship of war. The "few months" eventually stretched to ten before the treaty was accomplished.[13]

Next day, July 2, Shufeldt met Li again. During these interviews the viceroy neglected to mention the possibility of organizing the Chinese Navy, the carrot that he had dangled before Shufeldt's eyes from September 1880 to March 1881. The appointment was very much in Shufeldt's mind. He told Angell that it was one of the reasons for his visit to China and, in consequence, informed him that "neither of these interviews were quite as favorable as I had been led to expect." As a result, he decided that he was not quite prepared to write to the Department of State. His hopes for personal advancement had suffered a serious blow. By July 3 the somewhat dispirited commodore found that "nothing seems likely to be developed here at present." He thus decided to start for Peking the next morning to deliver the two treaties to Angell. Before he set out (by houseboat and ox-cart), however, he observed a drill with Li Hung-chang, given in English by Chinese officers, on board a Chinese war vessel.[14]

After presenting his credentials as attaché to Angell, Shufeldt hoped to escape with only a three-day visit to Peking, but he also wished to pay an official visit to the Tsungli Yamen. Angell asked for an interview for him on Friday, July 8, but Prince Kung, head of the Tsungli Yamen, wrote that it was not possible to see him before Tuesday, July 12. Shufeldt was disgusted, for it meant he would not be back in Tientsin until the fifteenth. Angell, however, used Shufeldt's visit to arrange a reception at which "the whole foreign element" was present. Shufeldt met Robert Hart, the British inspector of Chinese customs, and liked him. He also sardonically noted that "dinners of course commence when a new subject joins the charmed circle which diplomatically bulldozes China."[15]

The latest recruit declined most of these official dinner invitations in Peking with a plea of being very tired, though he reluctantly agreed to attend one given by the British minister, Sir Thomas Wade, on the twelfth. However, the news of the attempt on the life of President Garfield led Angell and the American community to decline all such invitations. Issuing a "Laus Deo" for missing the dinner, though not for the cause of its cancellation, Shufeldt left Peking after his interview with Prince Kung. He borrowed a horse from Mrs. Angell for the ride back to Tientsin, vowing he would have walked the entire distance rather than endure a cart journey again.[16]

In Tientsin once more, Shufeldt immediately requested an interview with Li. He wished to talk about Korea, sourly commenting to Angell that Li would have to "take the initiative if he desires to talk of the Chinese Navy." At this interview, however, Li told Shufeldt that he did not wish him to discuss Korean matters with the Tsungli Yamen nor communicate on the subject with Prince Kung. Li was dealing with the negotiations in person; he did not wish the Tsungli Yamen to handle them. Shufeldt reported to Angell that Li "has inaugurated a movement which he believes will have a successful termination, and wished to reserve to himself the proper time for consulting with the Chinese Government should it become necessary." Operating from his Chihli base, the viceroy was virtually a semi-independent authority mediating between the Koreans and Shufeldt. For the next five months Shufeldt was to accept this situation; he stayed away from the Tsungli Yamen and played the game according to Li's rules.[17]

Li was a master of leaking just enough information to keep Shufeldt curious. He informed the commodore that he had sent a letter to the Korean government "as will at least elicit a reply, if not be the means of sending over a Corean Official of rank to consult with him in reference to a treaty with the United States . . . within the next ninety days." He wished Shufeldt to remain and meet this expected official or to ascertain the contents of any communications sent from Korea. Moreover, the viceroy wished for some person, preferably Shufeldt himself, to meet the Korean official formally, to discuss the points involved in the treaty. Shufeldt noted the position correctly when he informed Angell that "the Corean naturally being ignorant of the mode of making treaties would be governed by the advice of H[is] E[xcellency]." No matter how Shufeldt later tried to wriggle away from admitting Korean dependency on China, his own definition of Li's role, and his initial acceptance of Li's rules, were to stand in his way.[18]

Before the interview ended, Li proposed that after "a proper discussion and arrangement," Shufeldt should go to Korea with a Chinese official and the Korean negotiator "in order that the Treaty may be made in that country itself." The viceroy wanted him to be empowered by the United States government to discuss the treaty in order to avoid delay. In March Li had ordered two of his staff members, Chêng Tsao-ju and Ma Chien-chung, to prepare a treaty draft to help the Korean government. Significantly, he also suggested to Shufeldt that the Japanese-Korean treaty of 1876 might be made the basis of negotiations, subject to any emendation that the United States government might desire. To James Angell in Peking, Shufeldt noted:

> While I do not propose myself as Commissioner for this purpose, should our Government determine to enter upon the negotiation, I feel it my duty to state that owing to my connection with this matter and to the confidence reposed in me by H. E., the Viceroy, as well as to my experience gained during two visits to the Corea, this authority conferred upon me would perhaps lead to a more successful result than if given to a stranger. At all events if our Government concludes to make this treaty, prompt and immediate action seems to be imperative.

Next day, the letters crossing in the mail, Angell notified Shufeldt that he had urged the State Department to confer full honors on some person to make a treaty with Korea and that he trusted "the work will fall into your hands."[19]

During the summer of 1881, Shufeldt found that events moved slowly. He waited impatiently for the Korean envoy or some communication about the treaty. The latter could only arrive at Li's Chihli yamen (office or headquarters) when the struggle between the opposing factions within the Korean court had been resolved in favor of the king's backing Li's proposals for a treaty. In addition, in the United States, the uncertainty over the fate of President Garfield resulted in a similar state of delay and confusion in government circles. Blaine's attention was directed more toward observing the political actions of Roscoe Conkling, his great political rival and leader of the New York Stalwarts, and to the health of the dying president, than to the mission of his special attaché in China. For Shufeldt this meant he was still bound by Blaine's original instructions of May 9, which had authorized him to wait for further instructions at Peking or Tientsin.[20]

On August 3 Shufeldt visited Li's yamen for further discussions. The viceroy wished to know if any State Department action had taken place about the Korean question. The commodore informed him that Angell had advised the American government to appoint a commissioner to open Korea. Li asked if it were possible that Shufeldt would receive the appointment. When he replied that he did not know, Li revealed to Shufeldt that "he had interested himself in the matter solely on my account & that unless I was selected to conduct the negotiation he would have nothing to do with it . . . he was anxious however for my sake & for the sake of our govt. to bring about a treaty with Corea—it would complete in a creditable way the duty assigned to me—when in China last year." Somewhat regretfully, Shufeldt told Angell that he knew the government would not be governed by such consideration and he was only mentioning it "in a personal way." Earlier, on July thirtieth, he had informed Angell that he had only disclosed this because he thought the viceroy would take more active steps over the treaty if he negotiated it: "*Personally* I feel quite indifferent—for to tell you the truth I am growing old & weary of any active duty—A trip to Corea—particularly in the winter would not be a pleasure excursion." However, he reaffirmed he would go as commissioner or associate, if the government desired it.[21] He was also well aware that Angell's recommendation could influence the State Department.

The End of the Naval Dream

Shufeldt also began to worry over the question of his services in the Chinese Navy. After observing Li's coquetry on the subject on July 14, he noted that the viceroy "likes very much to have me near him—but he seems to be satisfied with a friendly neutrality." At the end of July, Shufeldt asked Angell if he could see any way in Peking to bring about his appointment to the Chinese Navy, as he was "not quite content to 'hang on by the eyelids.'" At the interview on August 3, he learned that Li intended to offer him "an important position in the Chinese Navy" after the Korean matter had been concluded. Already the intended position had diminished from the one that Shufeldt expected in 1880, and it would now follow and not precede the Korean negotiations. Li, however, invited Shufeldt to Taku and Port Arthur to see Daniel Mannix at the Chinese torpedo school and inspect the Chinese forts.[22]

Angell was dismayed with the news of Li's order of priorities. On August 1 he had warned Shufeldt that he thought it wisest to find out whether Li really desired his services. On the twelfth he bluntly told Shufeldt, "to be frank, I do not like the results of your interview with Li. While I earnestly desire you to adjust the Corean matter, I confess my study of Chinese character leads me to suspect that Li has abandoned the idea of employing you, unless new clouds of war appear, but still wants to keep you within reach for an emergency." Angell advised him to be extremely guarded in deciding what fraction, if any, to believe of what any Chinese official told him, except in a written contract. Remember, he warned, "they count documentary testimony alone as of any value," and urged Shufeldt to "get things in black & white." Meanwhile, although Shufeldt still found that Li treated him with marked civility, he confessed to Angell, "whether he refrains from making me an offer on account of embarrassment or whether he really does not intend to do so at all—as you seem to feel—I do not know & do not really care."[23]

Within three days Shufeldt was called to Li's Tientsin yamen for a discussion on Chinese naval matters. For the basis of this discussion he prepared a paper on the Chinese Navy that accurately forecast the impending conflict between China and Japan and argued for a policy of coast defense with regard to Western nations but a policy of offense with regard to Japan. Shufeldt considered the fleet "by no means a despicable one—every ship at least is of the most modern type—& only needs a crew to make it formidable." He recommended a navy of ten ironclads, ten steel corvettes, thirty mosquito (river) boats, and thirty torpedo launches; a roster of five admirals, sixty captains, four hundred lieutenants, and nine thousand seamen, with an additional fifteen hundred in the torpedo corps. While at the yamen Li told him that when the two new corvettes arrived from England in September or October, he would make him a substantial proposition. Shufeldt replied that until then he would still be subject to orders from his own government. Molly Shufeldt caught the glitter but not the reality—"Father continues to be great friends with the Viceroy"—and noted that "H. E. asked him to go over to Port Li [Arthur] to inspect its qualifications, sent his own yacht to take him as far as Taku at the mouth of the river." Shufeldt, however, informed Angell that he would be very careful to avoid giving offense to others and confine his advice to naval affairs.[24]

Shufeldt's hopes for the naval appointment were built on sand. In the viceroy's employment were two French naval officers, each with a salary of £8,000 per annum. Their services had never been utilized by the viceroy, and Li would have been hard pressed to appoint Shufeldt over them. The commodore recognized this, for he told Angell that if he were employed the French officers and French minister would "probably be very much annoyed." Even so, official Tientsin was alive with rumors about Shufeldt's relationship with Li Hung-chang. The considerations Shufeldt was receiving from Li caused Angell to change his mind about Li's intentions. He explained his disgust at the lying he had found in China, which had triggered his pessimism. As Angell prepared to leave China, he expressed his hopes, for Shufeldt's sake, that his suspicions had been erroneous. Shufeldt merely told him that the viceroy's final offer of the command of the Chinese Navy was being deferred from day to day, "like the Millerites prophecy of the resurrection—It *may* come."[25]

Two events beyond Shufeldt's control helped to disrupt his plans. News came of President Garfield's death and the turnover in personnel within the divided Republican party. Blaine's Half-Breeds were replaced when Roscoe Conkling's Stalwarts, though not Conkling himself, came into power with the new president, Chester Arthur. Li Hung-chang called on Shufeldt on September 30 to ask if Garfield's death would effect any change in the policy of the government. Shufeldt believed not, but declared it was impossible for him to say what changes might take place in the cabinet. Meanwhile, Li had decided to move to Peking from Tientsin for the ceremonial funeral of the more senior but politically impotent Chinese empress, Tzu An, co-regent with Tsu Hsi, about October 10. He planned to remain until November 10 and then go to his winter residence at Pao-ting-fu. Shufeldt was left with the alternative of staying in Tientsin or going south. He planned to finish surveying the naval and military affairs of China and then return home in the spring. Feeling his mission had failed, he blamed foreigners for besieging Li with advice. Angell was surprised by Shufeldt's mood, for he felt the chances of Shufeldt's receiving the appointment were better than a month earlier. But the vacillating Angell had second thoughts and advised Shufeldt to leave Tientsin for either Shanghai, Foochow, or Canton, unless Li moved quickly. As Angell had already turned over the legation to Chester Holcombe, the new chargé d'affaires, he tendered his advice privately.[26]

The low point of Shufeldt's diplomatic and personal ambition in China thus came in October 1881. No news had come from Korea or from the United States about the appointment of a commissioner to negotiate the treaty. The prospect of a new administration was not appealing. Li had cooled off toward the naval appointment. All that remained to fill the vacuum was Tientsin's rather routine social life, to which Shufeldt had already been introduced by Li, and an occasional visit to a naval establishment. Shufeldt attended several tiffins, dined with Li, and enjoyed excellent social contacts with him before his departure for Peking. Once the viceroy had left for the empress's funeral and Pao-ting-fu, however, and with Angell also gone, Shufeldt turned to Chester Holcombe for advice on what to do. He explained to the sympathetic Holcombe, who had spent twelve years in China, that he had decided to remain in Tientsin, contrary to Angell's advice, partly because he had been asked by Li, "by his own particular request," and partly because he thought it his duty, "although not at all sanguine of any satisfactory result." He was at a loss to know why the viceroy should wish to be discourteous, especially after his return from Peking. Shufeldt had grown openly impatient. He believed that he had seen a change in the viceroy's attitude since Angell had passed through Tientsin on his way to Shanghai. He did not know whether Li disliked Angell or if he had given the viceroy the impression of paying too much attention to the view of his own minister, but he claimed to have "received this impression at that time." The new chargé thought Li's actions "surprising and . . . discourteous," agreeing with Shufeldt that it was probably the result of intrigue against him by the representatives of the other powers. Holcombe urged Shufeldt to reconsider his decision to spend the winter in Tientsin, for "it would be better to pass the coming months almost anywhere else than there." Shufeldt, however, explained to Holcombe, "I have a very remote reason to believe something may yet be done in the Corean matter, and therefore I did not wish to get too far away from Peking at Present. Again I do not quite like to be driven away now."[27]

Shufeldt desired to put an end to some of the speculation and intrigue among the foreign representatives. Accordingly, he wrote to Lo-fông-loh, Li Hung-chang's naval secretary:

> Since my residence in Tientsin reports have been circulated both in the native and foreign press that I was about to take service in the Chinese Navy.
>
> These reports have no doubt disquieted the minds of the foreign officers already in that service and have caused discussions among the Chinese Officials, and while they remain uncontradicted render my stay here subject to the unpleasant suspicion of being an applicant for such position. Will you therefore do me the favor to say to all parties interested that I have never been offered a post under the Chinese Government by any one authorized to confer it.
>
> My residence in China is subject entirely to the orders of my own Government—as an Attaché of the U.S. Legation at Peking.

The note was in many ways a calculated insult to Li, especially the reference to conferment by "authorized" persons. Shufeldt considered it would "account for my remaining in Tientsin, should it be advisable either for professional or personal reasons to do so." Given the situation, his assessment was realistic, if personally disagreeable, for it freed him from the viceroy's pretenses and the machinations of the foreign representatives designing to stop his naval advancement.

Writing the note must have caused him deep regret over the blunting of his personal hopes, for he bitterly complained to Holcombe about the final outcome of his quest. He could only guess it was caused by the viceroy's own conceit, "his ill concealed contempt for foreigners," the "general faithlessness of the oriental character," or, worse still, the "intrigues of foreigners who would thus stoop to means as base as the 'heathen Chinese' himself." Shufeldt's disillusionment surfaced when he told Holcombe, "For four months I have waited here—careful to do or say nothing offensive—rather reluctant than desirous to assume the responsibilities of the Chinese Navy, but hoping that I might be directed to try and secure a treaty with Corea, through the Viceroy's assistance. Came here by the Viceroy's invitation—all to reach at last this lame and impotent conclusion." Furthermore, he told Holcombe that although what had passed in the naval matter was of a purely personal nature, by no means reflecting on the dignity of the United States, yet it could not be considered other than an unfriendly act toward one of its officers and therefore "worthy eventually of official consideration." Finally, after Lo-fông-loh asked if Shufeldt's letter could be published, he informed

Holcombe that he would leave if the chargé thought he should, provided he could get away "after the next American mail arrives." Soured by his treatment and blaming either English, German, or Russian intrigue for preventing his appointment, Shufeldt commented that if it were not for the fact that American officers would tend to create an influence in China of importance to the United States, he would say that in any intervention on his part with those intrigues "the game was not worth the candle." In other words, it was nationally but not personally.[28]

As Shufeldt wavered in his resolve to remain in Tientsin, Chester Holcombe changed his advice. Assuming that the viceroy was to pass the winter in Tientsin, Holcombe had told Shufeldt that should he also remain, it would have appeared "in spite of his cavalier treatment of you, you were still waiting in hopes of some favor at his hands, and he might be led to do something even more offensive than his course in the Taku matter." But when Holcombe heard Li was to go to Pao-ting-fu for the winter, he estimated that the situation was relieved and advised Shufeldt he could see "no serious reasons why you should not remain if you prefer." On the Korean treaty matter, Holcombe was more pessimistic. He had "little or no hope" of any developments, telling Shufeldt that the only reasons why the Chinese would desire foreign powers to enter into treaty relations with the Koreans would be if Russia had any serious intentions of occupying that country. As the Tsungli Yamen had been officially assured by the Russians that the tsar had no designs on Korea, Holcombe did not think China would aid the United States or any other power "to make a treaty with her tributary." He thus admitted Korean dependency on China.[29]

Shufeldt agreed with Holcombe on the state of Korean affairs. He believed the Russian consul had dissuaded Li from any intention of assisting him in obtaining the Korean treaty. He also thought that even when Li had stated he would help, he meant "we should insert in our Treaty, as the price of his assistance, a clause asserting the sovereignty of China over Corea." Shufeldt thus put his finger directly on the great problem of Chinese attitudes toward Korea's relations with other powers. If such a clause were submitted to the United States government, he expected a doubtful result, "particularly as China has permitted Japan to make a treaty [in 1876] with Corea upon the basis of its *own* independence." He obviously anticipated the question of Korean sovereignty would be the major problem of the negotiations.[30]

The arrival of the American mail revived Shufeldt. He notified Holcombe that he had received an unofficial notification that Blaine would forward instructions in regard to his appointment as commissioner to Korea in the following mail, "provided that he remained long enough in Washington to have them properly drafted." If not, then instructions "of the same nature" might be sent to the new minister in Peking by the incoming secretary of state, Frederick T. Frelinghuysen. Consequently, Shufeldt intended to remain in Tientsin for the next official mails. His accreditation as United States commissioner would relieve him of the pressure of seeming to be a suppliant for a naval appointment no longer regarded as feasible. Though the position as commissioner was highly dependent on political affairs in the United States, the information did produce a subtle change in Shufeldt's mood. To Holcombe he confided, "I do not feel sanguine of success, nor do I overrate the importance of such a treaty, nevertheless, in connection with our interests in the East, it is a question whether it would not be worth while to undertake it." The game was worth the candle after all, and Shufeldt resolved to play it, though he now knew that there was little that could be accomplished in Korea until the following spring.[31]

Lame Duck Instructions: Blaine's Korean Policy

On November 14, shortly before he left office, Secretary Blaine sent new instructions and credentials.[32] Blaine based his detailed instructions on Shufeldt's considered opinion, given in July 1881 after the early meeting with Li Hung-chang, "that a successful effort can now be made to open commercial relations with the Kingdon of Chosen." The latter name was adopted by the State Department because of the slight offered by the Korean minister of ceremony when Shufeldt's original letter addressed to "Great Corai" and sent through Inouye Kaoru had been returned in 1880. Blaine warned his envoy that the propriety of his renewed effort must be determined by his own discretion, "governed by the condition of things, existing at the time of this despatch." The irony was that Shufeldt had found conditions continually changing at Tientsin. But Blaine was specific in his aims and warned Shufeldt, "I should impress upon you, that the government of the United States is not willing to subject itself to another refusal at the hands of His Majesty the King of Chosen." Consequently, it was only on the assumption that Shufeldt was in possession of evidence "to furnish reasonable grounds for very confident hope" that he was authorized to execute his instructions. The government would be seriously dissatisfied with the commodore, Blaine warned him, if his anxiety to accomplish the work (in which Blaine recognized he felt "a natural and honorable interest") should so far mislead him "as to subject the friendly advances of the United States to another repulse."

Blaine wished a letter to be delivered from the president of the United States to the king of Korea, but, he noted, if access to the capital of

Korea was not allowed, then negotiations should take place at Fusan with some representative of the Korean government. Shufeldt had to take care that such negotiations would not be with local or provincial officials but with a negotiator appointed to meet him who "has full and direct authority from His Majesty to discuss and sign a Treaty." He was also required to "transmit properly and honorably" the president's letter to the king "with a guarantee that it will be received and answered."

Blaine notified the commodore that he considered "*it may perhaps be judicious*—to put forward as the prominent purpose of your visit, a Treaty for the relief and protection of American vessels and crew who may be shipwrecked on the Corean coast." For such a purpose Shufeldt was to take his instructions from the United States–Japanese treaty of May 17, 1880. But Blaine was concerned with gaining much more than a mere shipwreck convention. He counselled his envoy carefully that "Should the temper and disposition of the Corean government be such as you anticipate you will secure the right of trade at such port or ports as may be open. . . . Such a privilege would scarcely be satisfactory if it was anything less than the privilege of trade secured by Treaty to the citizens of the United States in the open ports of Japan and China." Blaine believed that a tariff regulated by treaty was not advisable. He urged Shufeldt to seek "an equality of duties, the rates being the same as those imposed upon native merchants or the most favored nation." Moreover, Shufeldt had to take special care to make certain that import and export duties were to be paid only once at the ports of entry and shipment; no further dues or internal taxes were to be levied on merchandise *in transitu*. Blaine also wanted to obtain "the right of free travel into the interior for the purpose of trade" given the maintenance "of a proper respect to the native laws and authorities and a sufficient and liberal protection of our own citizens." The commodore was to insist on extraterritorial jurisdiction for consuls and other officers, exactly as granted by the Japanese and Chinese governments. Consuls were to be given the right to communicate directly with the authorities at the capital "until Diplomatic representation is the necessary consequence of such a Treaty."

With these clear instructions, specifying American desire for more than shipwreck relief, Blaine discussed his hopes for such a treaty. With a phrase that has caught the eye of many historians, Blaine commented that "while no political or commercial interest renders such a Treaty urgent, it is desirable that ports of a country so near to Japan and China should be opened to our trade and to the convenience of such vessels of our Navy as may be in those waters, and it is hoped that the advantages resulting from the growing and friendly relations between those great Empires and the United States will have attracted the attention and awakened the interest of the Corean government." He looked forward "with confident expectation" to the success anticipated by Shufeldt, but did not wish to see a complicated treaty. "If the government of Corea (or Chosen) is willing to open its ports to our commerce as China or Japan have done," he confidently told Shufeldt, then he would be willing to establish friendly relations with pleasure, but he did not propose "to force or to entreat such action."

The section of Blaine's instructions contained in the above paragraph is usually the only part to elicit comment from historians. It is obvious, however, that Blaine's directions were much wider than the point about "no political or commercial interest" rendering such a treaty urgent. Moreover, he used the word "urgent," not the word "necessary." His opening remarks were concerned with securing a right of trade in Korean ports at least equal to that gained in the open ports of Japan and China. Anything less would "scarcely be satisfactory." That would have been a parallel situation to the opening of the Chinese and Japanese ports, to which Blaine made a direct reference. In view of this, one can take issue with such comments as Alice Felt Tyler's that "the fact that Blaine did not believe that the United States had any direct interests in Korea is shown by this [quoted] statement" and, also, "there is no evidence that Blaine looked upon it [the Korean treaty] as anything more than an occasion to assert the prominent position of the United States in world affairs. The importance of Korea in Far Eastern politics in its relation to China and Japan seems not to have been considered by him.[33] It is not clear in this opinion what constituted a "direct" as opposed to a nondirect, or indirect, interest or if Korean trade was an end in itself or was perceived as a means for furthering trade with China and Japan also. But Blaine certainly made the opening of Korea's ports analagous to the opening of China's and Japan's.

Finally, Blaine's very careful wording, "it may perhaps be judicious —to put forward as the prominent purpose . . . ," certainly implies that he had other things in mind and was using the shipwreck convention as an introductory device. It is accepting the instruction too much at face value to declare wholeheartedly that this was the main reason for the treaty (a comment, incidentally, that totally ignores Shufeldt's drives). No work on Blaine does more than lift the phrase out of context and none gives it detailed consideration. None asks why Blaine should choose, very late in his term as secretary of state, to involve himself with Korea and Shufeldt. One possible answer is that interest in Korea was stimulated in 1881 by the voyage of the *Ticonderoga* and such writings as "Corea and the United States," *The Independent,* New York, November 17, 1881; "Corea the Hermit Nation," *Bulletin of the American Geographical Society* (New York 1881), no. 3; and "Corea," *Cyclopedia of Political Sci-*

ence (Chicago 1881).* More likely, however, is that Blaine, like Shufeldt, was keen to increase American trade.³⁴

Instructions thus were to be sent to Rear Admiral John Clitz to place a vessel of the Asiatic squadron at Shufeldt's disposal and to "cheerfully and cordially cooperate" with him. The commodore would be accredited to conduct the negotiations with his naval rank and as a special envoy from the United States. Blaine also insisted that while he did not feel disposed to place an absolute limit on the time for the negotiations, "the Government would not consider it compatible with a proper sense of its own dignity that you should remain in the Corean waters longer than two months unless the certainty of a successful termination of negotiations commenced in a friendly spirit and conducted with reasonable promptitude should require a moderate extension of time." He did not feel justified in prolonging indefinitely Shufeldt's time at the legation in the interests of securing the position with the Chinese Navy that he knew Shufeldt desired. The secretary presumed that such an arrangement would either have been effected already or would be abandoned when Shufeldt returned from Korea.³⁵ As Blaine penned these thoughts and instructions in November, however, he did not know that the prospects for the naval appointment for Shufeldt had rapidly receded in China; by the time that Shufeldt received the official mail on January 19 he had lost the position altogether.

---

*Of the thirty-six titles published before 1882 that Horace Underwood listed in the history section of his bibliography of works on Korea, *A Partial Bibliography of Occidental Literature on Korea from Early Times to 1930* (Seoul, 1931), 21, 23–33, 198, nineteen of the thirty-six were written in the 1870s and four more in 1880. Of the total works on Korea published before 1882 the numbers, by decades were twelve (1830s); eight (1840s); six (1850s); twenty-six (1860s); fifty-three (1870s); and fifteen (for 1880 alone).

14

The Opening of Korea, 1882

The Climax of Frustration

In July 1881, Kojong, the king of Korea, sent an envoy, Li Ying-tsung, to announce the coming to China of some Korean students. Li described to the Chinese the amount of internal opposition in Korea to the concluding of a treaty with the United States. Impressed by this opposition, the king had declined to appoint negotiators. Li Hung-chang asked Li Ying-tsung to return to Korea and request the appointment of negotiators, specifying his own concern that the treaty negotiations take place. Despite Li Hung-chang's promptings, the Korean monarch still delayed and, consequently, the Chinese viceroy was forced to respond to Shufeldt's repeated requests by referring to the Korean envoy for whom he was waiting. Eventually, the king reacted to Li Ying-tsung's urgings, resolving the debate in Korean court circles with a protreaty decision, and an envoy, Kim Yun-sik, was appointed in December 1881, as head of a cultural and trading mission containing over seventy members. Kim was to devote 80 to 90 percent of his official time to the treaty negotiations and was kept well informed by Li Hung-chang, even though Shufeldt seldom saw him and never negotiated directly with him. Despite strong opposition existing in Korea to a United States treaty, in March 1882 Kim reported that the Korean monarch had decisively requested Li Hung-chang to negotiate for him.[1]

Following his unofficial notification that Blaine's instructions would be sent by the next mail, Shufeldt felt much happier. Should the position of commissioner be given to him, he would not appear to be hanging on to Li's coattails. He had even more reason to celebrate on December 15 when Lo-fông-loh called to reveal that Kim Yun-sik had reached Tientsin and that "Corea was now willing to make a treaty with the U.S." Shufeldt sent word to Li that he did not yet know whether his government wished to negotiate with Korea. Should it be so disposed, however, he thought it possible that he or the minister at Tientsin might receive the commission. Moreover, Shufeldt told Lo-fông-loh that he doubted if anything would be undertaken before the coming spring.²

Not surprisingly, the arrival of the Korean envoy started rumors circulating in Tientsin. Shufeldt heard that the Koreans had appealed to the Chinese for assistance against "the aggressions and cruel treatment of its peoples by the Japanese officials and subjects at Foosan [sic] and Gensan." Kim Yun-sik had brought a letter from the king that included a reference to the many groups in Korea, led by the Taewon'gun, that opposed the negotiations for a treaty. The agent stated that "the only way is for the Emperor to issue an open Decree, to be given to the next tribute mission in the spring, commanding [sic] Korea to send negotiators to take up the treaty with America. In that case my King, relying upon Imperial influence, can manage the affair." Shufeldt also heard rumors that several boxes of rifles and ammunition had been sent from Tientsin, via Chefoo, to Seoul. He vouched for the Japanese "shameful treatment" from his own limited experiences and observed "this [Chinese] Government is becoming very sensitive on the Corean question." Grimly and accurately he prophesied to Holcombe, "I have regarded a war between China and Japan, on the Loochoo, Formosan and Corean complications, among the strong possibilities of the near future." The possibility did not deter him from pushing vigorously to involve American interests in the center of complications, however. Holcombe disagreed on the possibility of war, describing China as "too old, fat, and sluggish to make war upon anyone except when driven to it at the point of the bayonet, and then she will either only defend herself, or *pay* her aggressors to let her alone." Holcombe was ready to ascribe Li's fear of the Russian threat as the reason for his cooperation on the treaty and revealed that Li had already sent to Korea a scheme for a treaty with the United States.³

On January 7, 1882, in response to a dispatch from Holcombe of December 19, Chester Arthur's new secretary of state, Frederick T. Frelinghuysen, sent a telegram to the chargé merely stating, "Congratulate Shufeldt on prospect of successful negotiation." Holcombe passed on the message, adding his own sincere and personal congratulations to Frelinghuysen's. He correctly interpreted the cable to mean that negotiations were to be attempted by the new administration and that Shufeldt was to be the United States commissioner. Like his predecessor, Frelinghuysen was prepared for Shufeldt to negotiate the Korean treaty but, unlike Blaine, he was more flexible in the discretionary powers given.⁴

In a letter to Shufeldt, Frelinghuysen noted that the length of time required for communication in so isolated a country necessarily left the commodore to his own discretion in carrying out the department's instructions of November 14. He then outlined for Shufeldt his own ideas of what might constitute the necessary provisions of the treaty: "It does not appear from Mr. Holcombe's telegram whether the Corean government has expressed willingness to negotiate both of the treaties contemplated, or, if only one of them, which one. A Shipwreck convention is, naturally, of the first necessity, and should you accomplish no more than this, your mission will still have yielded admirable results." But Frelinghuysen would not have been content merely with a shipwreck convention if more were obtainable. He pointed out:

> With regard to a Commercial treaty, your own good judgment will doubtless have counselled the primary importance of not seeking to gain too many or too great advantages in a negotiation which, in the nature of things, is merely a first step in the direction of opening a hitherto closely sealed country to our trade. The provisions of such a treaty should be so simple and few as not to excite any distrust on the part of a government and people whose jealous dread of foreign association and influence has been conspicuously manifested hitherto. That *a moderate degree of friendly and mutually profitable intercourse at first will bring about its natural and necessary enlargement in time* can not reasonably be doubted. Bearing this in mind, and regarding any concession, however small, as an absolute gain, you may *safeguard future interests by a judiciously worded clause giving to the United States whatever commercial privileges may be hereafter granted by the Coreans to other countries by treaty.*

For Frelinghuysen the treaty was designed to safeguard and enlarge American trading opportunities in the future. The basis from which this enlargement would take place was equality of commercial opportunity in the present.[5]

Frelinghuysen was cautious in his endorsement of Shufeldt's mission, possibly for another reason. During the first week of January 1882, at the time that he drafted and then forwarded these instructions, the new secretary of state, with the assistance of the first assistant secretary of state, J. C. Bancroft Davis, was conducting a searching reanalysis of his predecessor's foreign policy, particularly in Latin America. As Blaine's Latin American policies fell under review, Blaine's appointees on other tasks in various areas of the world were offered no more than the necessary minimum encouragements to continue. This would account for the terse telegram and, later, a long silence when Shufeldt cabled for instructions in April and May just prior to going to Korea.[6]

On January 19, Blaine's instructions of November 14 and Shufeldt's credentials as envoy to Korea finally arrived. Admiral Clitz was also ordered to place the USS *Swatara* at his disposal. Reading the instructions cursorily and quickly, in order to catch the return mail, Shufeldt noted there was no provision for an interpreter or authority to employ one. Furthermore, he considered that the time allowed—two months, "in a country where time is of no account" and where communication and travel were slow and difficult—seemed to be too limited. He also suggested that the mouth of the Seoul River within thirty miles of Seoul would probably prove more convenient than Fusan for conducting the negotiations.[7]

At some time between January 1 and 15, Shufeldt wrote what he termed an "open letter" to his friend Aaron A. Sargent, the former senator from California (see Appendix 1 for text of letter). Expected by some Republicans to become Chester Arthur's secretary of the interior, Sargent was a powerful figure in the Republican party. The letter to him went first to Shufeldt's cousin in San Francisco, Albert Dibblee, who received it in mid-March. Dibblee, who allowed several of his friends to read the letter, as Shufeldt had authorized, knew that the *San Francisco Bulletin* would have been anxious to publish the letter, had he offered it, but later told Shufeldt that he could not permit such publication. As Dibblee heard that Sargent was due to arrive in San Francisco for a short visit, before going to Germany as United States minister, he called on the former senator on March 15, missed him in the hotel, and left the letter with a covering note. Sargent read Shufeldt's letter, recognized its importance in giving the commodore's candid views on China, and gave it to the *Bulletin* for publication, where it appeared on March 20, 1882.[8]

Shufeldt was bitter when he wrote the Sargent letter. He opened with a general statement of his own sympathies for the "downtrodden people of the earth" and the "victim of oppression."[9] He claimed that all his life he had suffered from "a sort of sentimentalism" for the underdog and had previously charged foreigners in the East with "prejudice of race, with arrogance of power, with ignorance of customs, with contempt of religious faith—never crediting them with forbearance, charity or sympathy for an inferior people." He had maintained that "the merchant seemed to force his wares and the missionary his creed, upon a passive and long-suffering community." As he had done previously, Shufeldt was careful to distinguish between the way a people should be treated and his initial belief that some peoples were "inferior." This separation of the assumption of inferiority from the method of dealing with other people allowed Shufeldt to condemn the Chinese while claiming a basic sympathy with them. He had performed a similar feat when studying South African natives, Cuban rebels, and other races on his travels. Thus, he observed, "there is an underlying truth in these [humane] sentiments, but as a practical idea the view is inapplicable to the relations, both commercial and political, which connect Asia with Europe or America." This underlying assumption became the key to the letter. After it was made, Shufeldt deliberated on several topics: Chinese attitudes toward foreigners; the roles of England and the United States in China; Li Hung-chang; the internal organization of the Chinese empire's armed forces; the role of foreign officials in China; and the part China was likely to play in international relations.

The commodore was blunt in his description of Chinese attitudes toward foreigners. Drawing on the experience of his six months residence in Tientsin and "an intimacy rather exceptional with the ruling element," he asserted that deceit and untruthfulness pervaded all intercourse with foreigners and an "ineradicable hatred" existed. Any appeal across such a barrier was useless. The only approach appreciated "is that of *force.*" Consequently, he argued, "if justice is done to these people, it must be for the sake of itself, not expecting appreciation. If justice is exacted, it must be unrelentingly. All sympathy will be construed as weakness, all pity as fear. [Above all things necessary, is tenacity of national dignity.] The least condescension fosters conceit and provokes insolence."[10] Shufeldt was convinced that "acting with such decision always when right, and even sometimes when wrong, is the only means by which foreigners can live in China with security to life and property." For the commodore it became "only a question between this and the *right* to live here at all."

Shufeldt defined the United States role in China differently from English dominance of the country. His own country was "standing, or endeavoring to stand, upon a higher plane than that of mere physical force," and was pursuing a policy in China of "moral suasion, which neither convinces nor converts the Chinaman to the doctrines of a common brotherhood of men." Such high, moral ground and appeals to the motives that ordinarily governed nations, he presumed, when unaccompanied by the use of force, were met by delay, equivalent to victory for the Chinese. Yet he prophesied:

> the United States has interests in China destined in the future to be greater than those of any other nation—possessing as we do the Pacific Ocean as a common highway—geographically with reference to the continents, politically with reference to Europe, and commercially with reference to each other. These interests should be reciprocal, but China does not care to realize this fact—does not desire any identity of interests. She would today, if she could exclude every article of foreign manufacture from her shores. She is slowly learning the Western arts, in order that by means of them she may some time not only exclude foreign goods, but the foreigner himself from the country. "China for the Chinese," is more than ever the motto of every Mandarin in the Empire. Our policy, therefore, should be positive, and governed to the extent of moral law, by American interests alone, and followed up by

the argument which they understand—the argument of force, pressure not persuasion.

It was when Shufeldt characterized Li Hung-chang and the empress of China, Tsu Hsi, that his acrimony reached a peak. The long delays to which he had been exposed, the frustrations over the naval appointment, and the uncertainty about his own position as United States commissioner, all combined to rouse his anger. Violating all diplomatic protocol with one sentence, Shufeldt declared that Li Hung-chang was "the absolute and despotic ruler of 400,000,000 of people," yet such was the system of government that "he lives upon the mere breath of the Empress, an ignorant, capricious and immoral woman."[11] This opinion of the empress, publicly expressed, was to be used by Shufeldt's opponents and the Democratic press in the United States to embarrass him, the Arthur administration, and the Korean treaty ratification measure. In addition, it fueled the flames of the Chinese exclusion bills that emanated from California congressmen in the 1880s. Of all the contents of the letter to Sargent, that phrase created the most embarrassment for Shufeldt in China and the United States.

The sentiments that Shufeldt condensed into his final remarks were designed to appeal to Sargent. The Chinese had no aggressive military or naval strength. United States policy in China and toward the Chinese in America should be *"purely selfish. . .* , by no means governed by the fallacious idea of inter-national friendship, or even the broader ground of a common brother-hood." American needs for labor should determine legislation; the supply should be limited by the demand, with the government repudiating unrestricted immigration. Nor would Shufeldt confine this policy to California alone. "Already," he warned, "undue proportions of Chinamen are flooding the Sandwich Islands [Hawaii]." This island group, both from its commercial and strategic position, was "a mere outlying county of that State [California], yielding the productions necessary to the Pacific Slope, & of vital importance in the military & naval strength of the whole country." Shufeldt left one last impression that showed his awareness of the contemporary beliefs in historical causation. The superabundant people of China would "under their imperative necessity emigrate to other lands, in constant, & irresistible currents, yet they will go toward the West, into India, rather than toward the East into America." This seemed to Shufeldt to be "the great law of movement to the human tide—from East to West." Despite his awareness of this key historical theme, Shufeldt urged upon Sargent that the "eddies & countercurrents, may be sufficiently strong to need watching" and guarding against by dikes of legislation; that would be the work of Congress.

This letter to Sargent was to shatter the composure of the Republican party in the summer of 1882. From it Shufeldt was to suffer more than from any other act in his life, and he lived to regret its publication even though he considered that its contents accurately stated the condition of Chinese affairs. Chester Holcombe later wrote a long dispatch to the State Department criticizing Shufeldt's letter as "one half of it composed of truths which had better not have been made public by an officer of our Government, while the other half is made up of erroneous impressions." But these repercussions were six months away. Ironically, shortly after he wrote the letter to Sargent, Shufeldt noted the warning in Blaine's instructions of November 14 against the danger of permitting his zeal to outrun his discretion in the effort to be the first into Korea. He even drew Frelinghuysen's attention to this warning, carefully adding that the dignity of the government would be paramount to his own advantage. Overall, the performance was similar to the excessive zeal that drew Seward's wrath over the Mexican adventure in 1862. Shufeldt's enthusiasm for Korea, like his concern for Tehuantepec, propelled him into a situation in which he gave offense to the State Department and received an admonition from it.[12]

Negotiating the Korean Treaty

Following his long indictment of China, Shufeldt informed the State Department of the difficulties facing him.[13] His experience in the East had taught him that nothing gave a Western nation greater ascendency than "a *successful* manifestation of its power." A failure, such as the American expedition of 1871 to Korea, was never forgotten. This was one of the great obstacles confronting his mission. Yet another was that success depended not so much on American efforts as on "the critical condition of the relations existing between China and Japan." Shufeldt was aware of the international complications. In his eyes a treaty made by the United States through China's influence "would tend to check the encroachments of Japan, against which China though possessing the will, lacks the nerve to protest."

Shufeldt also brought Frelinghuysen up to date on the events in China that had triggered his writing the Sargent letter. He reminded him of Holcombe's dispatch, which had indicated that the Korean king was willing to negotiate a treaty, and he warned:

> I speak of the Viceroy in all these matters because he is virtually, in all foreign affairs, the ruler of China.
>
> I quite recognize the fact that there is no "urgency" in a treaty with Corea. It is a poor country and its commerce is of small promise, both at present and in the future, but it lies in the ocean highway of Nations and *must*

be opened sooner or later: it is only a question whether our Government will take the initiative, as it did in Japan, or leave to European Powers the prestige which such action would confer upon them. Our Ships have almost disappeared from the surface of the sea—Our Navy is fast becoming a tradition, but if our diplomacy can by its *moral* force gain a point here upon the Pacific I shall take great satisfaction in my share of the work.

He also warned Frelinghuysen that Li Hung-chang was toying with a similar project with the British. Shufeldt imagined that the viceroy preferred the Americans to the British because he hoped to see a clause inserted forbidding trade in opium. He also knew that the United States would leave out the religious toleration clause upon which either France or Italy would insist.

Shufeldt soon notified Admiral Clitz that he had received the credentials as American negotiator. He hinted that if Clitz could meet him in the flagship at Chefoo on May 1, together with any other ships of the Asiatic squadron that the admiral could offer, the naval presence would give to the mission "that might and dignity which the Coreans would appreciate." If Clitz went in person, Shufeldt promised that the cooperation "will be perfectly cordial and for the public good." However, he had no intention of sharing the limelight with Clitz should the negotiations be started. To Lo-fông-loh he made it known that his instructions confined the negotiations to himself alone and required that they be carried out in Korea. Shufeldt wanted Lo to ask Cheow Fuh, the Hai Kwan taotai and negotiator in Tientsin for Li when the latter was absent from the city, what were the best means of passing the news of the arrival of his credentials to the viceroy. He informed Lo that speedy action would be desirable. Cheow Fuh forwarded Shufeldt's dispatches to Li with a message that the commodore intended to leave Chefoo in a warship for Korea about May 1.[14]

On February 2, Li replied to Shufeldt's request for an interview at Pao-ting-fu or Tientsin. The viceroy confirmed his verbal message, sent through Lo-fông-loh, that the Korean government was contemplating sending a confidential envoy to Li. He notified the commodore that "Corea as you are well aware has been from time immemorial a dependent country on the Chinese Empire, its Government will consequently act under the instruction of China." The desire to rectify the mistake in the Japanese treaty of 1876 showed that China's diplomats had learned much of Western legal forms. As far as the Korean treaty was concerned, the lesson had been learned by Ma Chien-chung, an expectant taotai of the honorary title of the second rank, who had studied political science in France. He was to attend every session of the negotiations with Li. Both were eager to have Korean dependence on China inserted in treaties with Western powers. Li, however, promised to render Shufeldt's mission successful but wanted secrecy kept at all accounts. Once known, he warned, many obstacles would be thrown in the way by "the parties who are jealous of your Government's initiating the foreign intercourse with Corea." He asked Shufeldt to come to Pao-ting-fu if he saw fit, travelling incognito in the interior.[15]

Suspecting Li's machinations, Shufeldt declined to do this. He had made arrangements to travel from Tientsin to Peking on Wednesday, February 8, in order to consult Holcombe, who had been warning him to be careful. Cheow Fuh tried desperately to prevent his going, but without success. From Peking, Shufeldt notified Li that under the condition of secrecy that he thought proper to oberve on Korean affairs, a visit to Pao-ting-fu would be inadvisable as the journey could not be made without attracting public attention. But he offered to join the viceroy at Tientsin in March if Li considered it necessary. He assured Li that he fully realized the importance of the caution necessary in initiating the proceedings. Somewhat ironically, in view of the Sargent letter en route to California, Shufeldt replied, "the trust placed in me by my own government, added to the confidence implied on the part of China, through Your Excellency, will make me very careful of the obligations connected with this duty. Your Excellency need therefore feel no apprehension of any disclosures from me." He later explained to Frelinghuysen that he did not desire at this point to give the negotiations "the character of a personal intrigue between the Viceroy & myself & I went to Peking for the purpose of ascertaining whether H. Ex. the Viceroy was acting in this matter with the sanction of the Chinese Govt. & thus place the affair on its proper basis as a friendly act on the part of this Govt. toward our own."[16] He had sacrificed an opportunity, however, for the Korean envoy was with Li at Pao-ting-fu.

Chester Holcombe had initiated this second approach to the Chinese government. On Wednesday, February 1, he had gone to the Tsungli Yamen and sounded the ministers on the Korean matter. He then wrote to Shufeldt:

> they responded more readily and freely than I had anticipated and told me some things which surprised and pleased me and which explains Li's course in the Corean matter.
>
> All matter concerning Corea have in past years been attended to by the Board of Rites here—the oldest, highest, and most intensely anti-progressive of the Six Boards.
>
> The Yamen told me that last spring, through Prince Kung's influence Corean questions were transferred from the Board of Rites to the Foreign Office; that the Emperor of China himself wrote a letter to the King of Corea, urging him to establish treaty relations with Foreign Powers, *and first*

with the United States; that Li was simply ordered to forward that letter; that the King of Corea had replied that he was willing, and even anxious to negotiate with the U.S. They added that the King and a large proportion of the people of Corea understand the situation and are ready for foreign intercourse, but that there is there, as in China an anti-foreign party.[17]

Holcombe believed this information relieved the situation for Shufeldt. It raised the question of how far Li had been assuming more credit than belonged to him.

Both Shufeldt and Holcombe were granted interviews with the Tsungli Yamen. They found the officials quite as willing for a treaty as (and Shufeldt believed more sincere than) the viceroy himself. Shufeldt also discovered that Li had the authority of the Chinese government for the negotiations. As Li was due to return to Tientsin shortly, Shufeldt invited Holcombe to be present at the interview. He wanted the chargé's expertise in the Chinese language. Furthermore, he notified the State Department that he had no personal desire to remain a moment longer than was necessary on duty "either to make it a success, or to ascertain its failure." Neither did he consider it advisable to go to Korea without the assistance of the Chinese government.

Shufeldt remained in Peking working out a preliminary draft of the treaty with Holcombe based on various United States treaties and conventions with Japan that he had brought with him while waiting for Li to return from Pao-ting-fu. Later he was to discover that his visit to the Tsungli Yamen had considerably disturbed the viceroy. The commodore believed the visit had the effect of impressing Li with the fact that Shufeldt could no longer be deceived by the pretense that his action was personal to him or was evidence of a friendly feeling for the United States. It emancipated Shufeldt from the ensnarements of the naval appointment and playing the game by Li's rules, at the expense of informing Li that he had not trusted him and missing a chance to see Kim Yun-sik at Pao-ting-fu.[18]

After Frelinghuysen's instructions arrived, Shufeldt commented that the secretary was "consequently more sanguine of a favorable result than may be justified by events." On March 9 he saw Cheow Fuh. From him he learned that Li desired to have at least four provisions inserted in the treaty: the dependence of Korea on China; prohibition of religious and missionary books; the right of Korea to establish her own tariff and to tax foreign imports both at the ports and in the interior; and the right of Korean officials to arrest Korean criminals in the houses of foreign merchants. Li had ordered Ma Chien-chung and Chêng Tsao-ju to draw up a tentative treaty "with all precautions for preserving Korean interests against foreign encroachment." Shufeldt considered that the dependence of Korea on China would be demanded because the viceroy wished to obtain the moral support of the United States "for a proposition which China has not the courage authoritatively to assert to the world." In the commodore's eyes, however, Li was defying the Japanese in particular with the help of the United States. To Shufeldt such a proposition was "inadmissible" and "not even justified by the facts." He took the legalistic view that the Japanese treaty had rendered Korea independent of China. If Li insisted on the dependency clause, he was prepared to sacrifice a possible Korean treaty by refusing the necessary acknowledgment. The other clauses presented less of a problem. Shufeldt believed they could be omitted or shaped satisfactorily to accord with other United States treaties, particularly as his instructions indicated the "possibility" of confining himself to the protection of shipwrecked seamen and property if he so desired.[19]

At 10:00 A.M. on Saturday, March 25, Shufeldt met Li Hung-chang for the first formal negotiations on Korea. Li authorized a formal statement, which Shufeldt forwarded to Washington:

> The King of Corea & his Prime Minister, are in favor of opening the country to foreigners, & are not only willing but anxious to treat with the United States; but there is a faction at court & among the people intensely hostile to the movement. A Corean envoy had recently visited H. Ex. at Pao-ting-fu, & it was then determined to ask the Corean King to send an Ambassador to China, for the purpose of making a treaty with the United States under the supervision of H. E. the Viceroy and to return to Corea when I go to that country for its ratification.[20]

Shufeldt formally submitted his first draft as early as March 22.[21] This draft noted "the perfect, permanent and universal peace" between the United States and Chosen (as Korea was referred to through the entire negotiation) and American desire to appoint a diplomatic representative at Seoul and consular representatives at ports open to foreign trade. The king of Chosen would have the right to appoint a diplomatic representative at Washington and consuls at ports in the United States. Shufeldt wanted official intercourse to be carried on in "terms of equality and courtesy." The draft then stipulated that all rules and precedents "calculated to obstruct friendly intercourse shall be totally abrogated." In their stead rules both liberal and fit to secure a firm and perpetual peace were to be established. United States citizens would be permitted to frequent the ports and cities of Chosen and reside there with their families while trading. They would be forbidden to carry on a clandestine trade with ports not open; American vessels violating this proviso would be subject to confiscation by the Chosen government. Similarly, the United States authorities were to take measures to prevent their flag from being abused by the subjects of other nations as a cover for the violation of Chosen's laws. American citizens peacefully attending to their affairs in Chosen would be placed on a common footing of amity and goodwill, under the protection of local authorities who would defend them from all insult. United States consuls could ask for military protection against mobs attacking American property. Chosen's citizens guilty of mob violence were to be punished by Chosen authorities; American citizens guilty of similar acts were to be punished by the American consul under American laws. In cases involving both nationalities, trial under the laws of the defendant would be granted with open access to authorized officials of the plaintiff's nationality. Such officials would have the right to cross-examine witnesses and protest the proceedings in detail if they wished. The law administered would be that of the officer trying the case.

Shufeldt's shipwreck and trading provisions would have allowed American ships to enter any port under stress of weather, want of fuel or provisions in order to obtain supplies, or to make repairs, in closed ports, with the expenses to be defrayed by the ships' masters. The nearest Chosen authority would be informed and would be required to send assistance to the crew, provide necessities, and take measures necessary for the salvage of the ship and the preservation of the cargo. For trading purposes, Shufeldt desired that no higher rates of tonnage dues or duties on imports and exports should be imposed in the open ports on United States vessels, produce, manufactures, or exports to the United States than were imposed or levied on vessels or cargoes of any other nation or on those of the subjects of Chosen. In return, the United States government would promise the same. The king of Chosen should agree to a maximum 10 percent *ad valorem* import and export tariff to be paid only once, with no further dues on merchandise *in transitu*. Opium was not to be imported into the ports of Chosen or the United States by citizens of the other nation. Appropriate legislation in both countries would enforce an absolute prohibition on the opium trade, and the most-favored-nation clauses in other treaties applying to opium would not be claimed by citizens of either power. The right for American marine surveyors to survey the Chosen coasts was included. Shufeldt also wanted to prescribe trade regulations for the benefits of the merchants of the respective countries but decided these could be added later. Finally, the draft expressed the desire that if the king of Chosen granted to any nation or the merchants and citizens of any nation "any right, privilege or favor connected either with navigation, commerce, political or other intercourse, which is not conferred by the Treaty, such right, privilege, and favor, shall at once freely secure to the benefit of the U.S., its public officers, merchants and citizens." This would have gathered in anything that Shufeldt might have overlooked; it applied only to Chosen and not to the United States. Shufeldt considered his draft was liberal in terms and "eminently just towards Corea—which country is yet unaccustomed to foreign intercourse—& one by which it might shape its future policy with reference to all foreign nations." Shufeldt had with him United States–Japanese treaties of March 1854, June 17, 1857, July 29, 1858, October 22, 1864, January 28, 1864, July 25, 1878, and May 17, 1880, as guidelines in negotiating with China and Korea.[22]

Li Hung-chang's first draft contained the provision that

> Korea is a vassal state of China, but has always enjoyed autonomy in both its internal and external affairs. After the conclusion of the treaty, the King of Korea and the President of the United States shall treat each other on an equal footing and the peoples of the two nations shall permanently maintain their peaceful relations. In case of any injustice or insult from other nations, mutual assistance or mediations shall be offered so as to assure each other's security.

In this draft, prepared by Ma Chien-chung and Chêng Tsao-ju and accepted by the Korean court, inland trade was to be reserved for the Koreans; opium importation was prohibited; foreigners could rent land; extraterritoriality was to be granted "temporarily"; Koreans in the service of foreigners could be arrested by Korean officials; no merchant consuls were to be allowed; missionary work was excluded; import duties were 10 percent on necessities, 30 percent on luxuries; export duties were 3 percent; and the treaty was to end in five years. T. C. Lin believed this draft was "of peculiar interest, because it reveals the motives of the government of China in encouraging the treaty and also shows the attitude of the Chinese with reference to their own treaties with foreign Powers."[23] The other clauses covered material in the four basic points specified by Cheow Fuh, the Hai Kwan taotai, on March 9. Li was thus hoping that the United States would stand as a bulwark against Japanese encroachments upon Korea.

Li arranged with Shufeldt for the commodore to meet Cheow Fuh on April 1 to present objections to each other's drafts. Shufeldt informed his secretary of state that both China and Korea were anxiously looking for protection "against the growing aggression of Japan on the peninsula."[24] Li had told him in strictest confidence that the king of Korea would welcome an American man-of-war in the river near Seoul. The viceroy also advised Shufeldt to go as near as possible to Seoul for the signing of the treaty. As he was waiting for the arrival of a Korean ambassador at Tientsin, Li told Shufeldt that if he did not arrive within thirty days, Li would either send a Chinese envoy with the commodore to Korea or give him a letter "to insure a friendly reception by the Corean Govt." Li confidentially stated that he intended to send a Chinese gunboat to accompany the American.

In reply, Shufeldt brusquely informed Li that the United States had been waiting for more than a year for the action of the Chinese authorities over Korea, that the proposition to intercede had come from Li, that the United States had accepted it in the friendliest spirit, and that he hoped there would be no delays. If there were to be no prospects of success by May 1, Shufeldt intended to advise the State Department to abandon the project. The viceroy answered that he had promised his assistance and intended "to fulfill it to the extent of his power." Shufeldt's embittered feelings filtered through to Frelinghuysen:

> if my confidence in the promises of the Viceroy has been somewhat shattered, it is from a forced conviction of their uncertainty—but my visit to Peking—which he so much deprecated—has had the effect of impressing him with the fact, that I can no longer be deceived by the pretence that his action is personal to me, or even the evidence of a friendly feeling for the United States.
>
> He is governed in fact by the orders of the Imperial government, & both the govt. & H. Ex. are moved by a policy which halts between their interests & their fears, but which points to foreign treaties on the part of Corea to save that country from absorption by Russia or Japan, to the great damage of the prestige of China.

Shufeldt was well aware of the Chinese motives in negotiating a treaty and as the prospect heightened began to feel a sense of responsibility for the work and to appreciate Holcombe's assistance.

On Wednesday, March 29, Li returned the official visit to Holcombe and Shufeldt, sending along Admiral Ting Ju-ch'ang to say he had been selected to accompany the Americans to Korea with two of his vessels. Shufeldt felt some concern over this, for both Chinese vessels had a speed of over sixteen knots and were armed with 35-ton breech-loading rifle guns, thus "presenting a marked contrast with the *Swatara,* which ship, altho' one of the best of her class in the navy, lacks all those elements of a modern man-of-war."[25] Shufeldt's hopes of a Perry-type entrance into Korea would disappear if the Chinese Navy was to provide the awe-inspiring force off the coast of Korea.

On April 1 Shufeldt met Cheow Fuh and Lo-fông-loh. He submitted a second draft combining the first Chinese and American drafts of March 25 in such a form that he believed would meet Li's approval. In return, he received a draft from Li that revealed the viceroy was standing firm on the question of Korean dependency. The first article stating this, and Shufeldt's assent to it, was made the *sine qua non* of any further discussions. Li feared that its omission, if conceded to the American, would be claimed as a precedent by other powers: "there would be a time when the Powers would forget that Korea is our vassal state, which situation would necessarily breed future troubles." The Chinese language was to be used by Chosen in making the treaty. The articles on the exchange of diplomatic representatives and consuls, shipwreck relief, Chosen's citizens trading in the United States, American residency in Chosen's open ports, opium prohibition, and the jurisprudence cover for citizens of both countries remained similar to Shufeldt's first draft. The percentage levies on exports and imports were changed to the Chinese first draft figures. Other features dealing with importing into the interior, employment of natives, arrests in houses of citizens of the other country, assistance to students, and the five-year limit on the treaty were retained from the Chinese first draft.[26]

To Shufeldt the "dependency" clause was the major point of difference over the treaty. With some difficulty he explained his objections in a letter written April 4 to the viceroy:

> I do not deny the right of a semi-dependent state to make independent treaties—on the contrary if—(as the article referred to asserts)—the Kingdom of Corea is a dependent state, in possession of sovereign powers as to its foreign & domestic relations, then I respectfully submit that the United States has the right to treat with it irrespective of the suzerainty of China. It is eminently proper that the King of Corea should take the advice, & be governed by the consent of his suzerain the Emperor of China, & the United States has no cause whatever of complaint—but the privilege remains unimpaired for the two countries to negotiate upon terms of perfect equality, & without reference to, or acknowledgement of any other power than that contained in themselves.
>
> Any reference therefore to China in this treaty would not be pertinent to it, & might be the cause of complications which the United States always desires to avoid in its foreign relations. Moreover the article in question more or less directly connects China & the United States, in such a way as to make these two great powers, the joint protectors of Corea. However willing I might be personally to see Corea enter the family of nations under such powerful escort, your Ex. will understand, that I am only authorized to make a treaty of amity & commerce, & not to enter into any political alliance.
>
> Under these circumstances I submit to Your Ex. that you should not ask me to insert in this treaty, an extraneous article which might be far-reaching in its effects, but which has no bearing upon the object, & which at the same time has no precedent.[27]

Shufeldt's objection thus rested on his inability to comprehend the Confucian framework of the Chinese empire and his unwillingness to see the

United States and China as coprotectors of the Korean peninsula after the signing of the treaty.

Chester Holcombe suggested that if Li still insisted on including a reference to China's connection with Korea, he might consider a sentence in the treaty such as "Chosen, in accordance with the advice of the Emperor of China being desirous to establish permanent relations. . . ." On April 5 he had been to the Tsungli Yamen and had found the ministers thoroughly posted on everything that had transpired at Tientsin in the negotiations. He told them that the clause about the suzerainty of China must be omitted or else there could be no treaty. The ministers thought the Americans would object to it. Holcombe notified Shufeldt that "they manifested no disposition to insist upon it." He gathered they were very much in earnest about the treaty, and he believed it would go through. He also offered to go to Tientsin to work over the Chinese and English texts for the final draft whenever Shufeldt was ready. By April 8 Holcombe was buoyant enough to proclaim that he had a plan to solve the problem over the first article and that "the treaty *will* go through." Holcombe and the Tsungli Yamen officials had agreed on a version for Article I that read, "Chosen being a dependent nation of the Chinese Empire, has nevertheless heretofore exercised her own sovereignty in all matters of internal administration and foreign relations. After the conclusion of this treaty, the Korean King promised to fulfill all obligations of this treaty in accordance with the law of nations; the President of the United States promises to recognize Korea as a dependent nation and will never interfere henceforth."[28]

On April 5 Shufeldt met Li, Cheow Fuh, Ma Chien-chung, and Lo-fông-loh. With the exception of some small emendations that they could consider later, Li's party approved of much of Shufeldt's second version. But the viceroy considered that the insertion of the dependency clause was indispensable; without it he would send neither messenger nor gunboat to accompany Shufeldt to Korea. Li explained that his own government's instructions made that imperative. Shufeldt then read out his letter of April 4 as an argument as to why the first article was inadmissible on the part of the United States in any treaty with Korea and gave the letter to Li. After "considerable discussion" with the other Chinese delegates, Li requested four days for further consideration and a final interview. Nevertheless, he intimated that the article would be sent to Korea to be inserted then, for, he insisted, it had been written at the desire of the king of Korea. Shufeldt replied that in that event he could not take the journey to Korea under the auspices of China because the article was entirely inadmissible.

A discussion next took place on the propriety of the Korean government's addressing a communication to the United States government after the signature of the treaty stating that such a treaty had been made by and with the consent of the Chinese government. Shufeldt would only commit himself so far as to promise to see that such a letter would be passed on. He insisted again that in a treaty with the United States and Korea the Chinese government had nothing to do "except so far as its friendly offices were concerned." Yet he was discussing the treaty with the viceroy of Chihli (and upbraiding him for delaying action), writing it in Tientsin in the Chinese language, and arranging it through the agency of China's diplomats for a Korean official he had never formally met and had seldom seen! He was stubbornly using the Chinese in a treaty that would help Korea throw off dependency on China, at least in Western legal terms, while accusing the Chinese of using him to secure recognition of Korean dependency.[29]

At this point in the interview Li informed the commodore that a friend in America had telegraphed to him that in a published letter Shufeldt had advocated that "force was the only argument to use in Corea." He asked him if he had written such a letter to the government. Shufeldt told him he had not. Strictly speaking, he could deny this because the letter was to Aaron Sargent. Li then asked a question about the application of force with regard to Eastern nations being a suitable policy generally. This was hitting too near the mark for Shufeldt, who retorted that he did not propose to hold himself responsible to the viceroy for any correspondence, whether official or personal. Obviously embarrassed under Li's probings, Shufeldt took the initiative. Later recalling the incident, he recounted:

> I then said to H. E. that since he had broached a subject outside of the matter under discussion, I wished him to understand that I appreciated the studied indignity with which I had been treated by him for four months—That I had on two or three occasions sought an interview & it had been denied me—That his manner had been more or less reflected by the mandarins surrounding him until the foreign residents in Tientsin had come to consider me an adventurer seeking office in China—although he himself well knew that I had come here by his own invitation & with the approval of my own Govt.—H. E. could not suppose that I would submit to such treatment without intimating it to my own Govt., or resenting it in any other manner than I might think proper—I had never, to my knowledge, given H. Ex. any reason for this palpable disregard both of my age, & my position, & yet it was so marked, that my own Minister had on two occasions advised me to leave Tientsin rather than submit to it. (I had remained, however, quietly bearing it, in order that I might see whether an American officer could be compelled to leave China under a condition of ignomiy, when his conduct had been irreproachable). I then said to H. Ex. that I did not wish any further discus-

sion to this subject & that I respectfully desired him to understand that our intercourse here after must be of an official character.[30]

The outburst, which was an indication of Shufeldt's own shock at Li's revelation, worked. Taken aback by the force of Shufeldt's comment, the startled viceroy hurriedly changed the subject. He quickly asked Shufeldt if he might recommend one of his interpreters, Pethick, in case Shufeldt went to Korea. Still ruffled, the commodore informed Li he was waiting for his own interpreter who would be responsible to his own government for his work, adding that he preferred Holcombe, if he could be spared from Peking, to any other person that his government might select. At this point the interview ended with the prospects of a final meeting in four more days. In a postscript added later, Shufeldt recalled, "the impression *may* have been conveyed to H. Ex. that I denied positively having written so to my Govt. in reference to the use of force towards Eastern nations generally but if so it was owing to the exciting nature of the accusations & its passage through an interpreter." Shufeldt also jotted down a rough draft of a letter that he probably did not send to Li, asserting that he was "suffering under a sense of personal and official annoyance such as I have never before been submitted to." But it was obvious that Li had news of the Sargent letter, even if he did not possess a copy of it.[31]

On April 10 the meeting took place. Shufeldt claimed that the Chinese had waived the first article, subject to a proposition by Li that Shufeldt would make a request to the Chinese government in writing "that owing to the fact that Corea was in a certain sense a dependent of China," he had asked "the intervention of the Chinese authorities to the accomplishment of the purpose in view." On reflection, Shufeldt saw no objection in making the request but deferred action until the treaty could be perfected and approved by the viceroy. He also agreed to transmit to the president of the United States a letter from the king of Korea in which the latter stated that the treaty had been made with the consent of the Chinese government.

The modifications in the third draft referred to the commercial articles; duties were to be paid once at the port of import or export with no further dues, fees, or taxes of any sort to be levied on the goods in the interior. Tonnage dues were to be levied on American vessels entering ports. The revenue would be applied exclusively to the proper and necessary surveying of the coast and to the construction of lighthouses, beacons, and buoys. Li also desired to substitute in the Korean treaty the favored-nation clause recently introduced in the new Brazilian and German treaties with China in place of the clause used in the treaty with the United States and China.

Shufeldt had reservations about the letter from the king of Korea. Carefully, he delineated the Chinese mood for Frelinghuysen:

> The Chinese authorities both here & at Peking are manifesting an earnest pose to have this treaty accomplished, & I have every reason to believe that there is at this moment in Tientsin, a Corean official of rank, who is being consulted at every step, & when the discussion is closed will be sent to Corea in a Chinese man-of-war, in order that the Government of that Country may be prepared to conduct the negotiation to a favorable issue.
>
> The main point which the Viceroy & the authorities at Peking seem to have in view, is the connection of China to Corea in this treaty, realizing the fact, that by such connection the encroachments of other nations upon Corea may be checked. With this idea in view, you will observe in the memorandum inclosed & marked B; that the Viceroy has submitted a proposition that when the Treaty is concluded, the King of Corea shall write to the President of the United States, by & with the consent of the Emperor of China. I simply promised on my own part, that if such a letter were written, I would see it sent to its proper destination, & thought I could promise a reply thereto.

Shufeldt was correct about the Korean official, Kim Yun-sik, being consulted, although he never met him in conference or for consultation over the treaty. At this point Shufeldt could not resist apprising Frelinghuysen of the personal affronts to his dignity which, in some measure, he considered, had been "reflected upon my own Government." He gave a long account of his "ill-treatment" at Li's hands, finishing with a testament to his frustration: "I have but little faith in the friendship of China for any nation, & believe that friendship to be measured by the pressure brought to bear upon it; & I desire to repeat my conviction that if a treaty is made with Corea, it will be owing to circumstances surrounding that country which are as threatening to China as to Corea itself; and not from any particular friendship for the United States."[32]

In the final draft of the treaty, the proposed Chinese first article was entirely omitted, for Shufeldt defined it as "outside of the object of the Treaty" and beyond his authority. He intended to ask Li, "as an act of friendship on the part of the Government of China towards that of the United States," to send the treaty to Korea, which was one way to escape the obvious fact that the treaty had been fully negotiated in Tientsin under strict Chinese control. However, the Tsungli Yamen officials had asked Chester Holcombe whether it was possible, "in some way less positive," that "the suzerainty of China over Corea might not be mentioned in the Treaty." Holcombe did not see the objections that had occurred to Shufeldt. The Tsungli Yamen had revealed to Li this seeming difference of opinion between the two Americans. Out of defer-ence to the wishes of the Tsungli Yamen and the viceroy, Shufeldt telegraphed to the State Department on April 12: "May I insert in treaty with Corea an article admitting dependence of Corea upon China. China conceding sovereign powers to Corea. They desire it. I have objected." A week later he sent another cable informing Frelinghuysen that the treaty was arranged except for the point about the first clause. The State Department remained silent, possibly because of the review of Blaine's policy but also possibly due to embarrassment over the publication of the Sargent letter.[33]

The Chinese did not wait long for Shufeldt to receive an answer. On April 23 Li revealed that the Chinese emperor had approved his memorial nominating Ma Chien-chung as Chinese intermediary "for facilitating the final arrangement of the forthcoming treaty." Ma was one of Li's closest advisers on Korea. Shufeldt approved of his appointment and noted the selection of such an officer would be regarded by the government of the United States as evidence on the part of the Chinese government of its desire "to perfect a treaty of lasting friendship between the Government and people of Corea and the country which I have the honor . . . to represent." The treaty was completed just as the viceroy's mother died, which meant his retirement from office for a period of mourning. Holcombe was assured by the Tsungli Yamen officials that Li's temporary absence would not delay the treaty.[34]

Shufeldt made arrangements to go to Korea via Shanghai and Chefoo. As late as April 28 it was not finally decided whether Fusan or the "Salee" River near Seoul would be the point for which the *Swatara* would make. He had also resolved to wait at Chefoo for a few days in case departmental instructions should come prohibiting his movement to Korea. Holcombe telegraphed on the thirtieth: "Nothing received. Better cable State hurry, business will certainly succeed." Shufeldt knew the difficulties with Japan were pushing the Chinese toward completion. He noted that "if the [treaty] herewith performed, can be made, independent of political considerations, then I see no objection under favorable circumstances of making the effort." He added for his superiors at the State Department, "it is safe to predict, that at no distant day, it [Korea] will become the battlefield of these two nations [China and Japan]."[35]

On May 4 Shufeldt arrived at Chefoo to meet the *Swatara*. On the fifth he met with Ma Chien-chung and Admiral Ting to finalize the arrangements for leaving for Korea. Ma was to sail in the Chinese flagship on May 7 and next day Shufeldt was to follow in the *Swatara* to a predetermined anchorage. From Ma Shufeldt learned that the fourth draft of the treaty had been forwarded to the Korean government "without any condition of a political character being imposed upon it by

His Excellency." He notified the State Department that he would proceed to Korea in the absence of further instructions from Washington. He also confessed he was "somewhat surprized at the evident desire of the Chinese Government to act upon this treaty without imposing any conditions whatever." Under the circumstances, he felt he should carry out his original instructions and head for Korea. As he left Holcombe, Shufeldt gratefully acknowledged the chargé's past help by telling him, "if the treaty is perfected and ratified it will be due very much to the interest you have taken in the matter."[36]

The formal ceremonies to mark the signing of the Korean treaty proved to be something of an anticlimax to the negotiations in Tientsin. Yet the timing of Shufeldt's sailing was important. The *Swatara* got underway from Chefoo in heavy fog between 6:30 and 7:00 A.M. on Monday, May 8, and Shufeldt telegraphed once more to Frelinghuysen, "Have gone to Corea." On the ninth the *North China Daily News* of Shanghai printed a copy of Shufeldt's letter to Sargent. Li could have used this as a weapon to stop the treaty had he desired. The newspapers were also full of rumors of an attempt by Robert Hart to organize a Korean customs service; this was denied by the Tsungli Yamen and by Li's Tientsin yamen. Holcombe revealed that the Tsungli Yamen was anxious for Shufeldt to conclude the treaty, for it had already been approached formally by representatives of France, Germany, Russia, England, and Japan about treaties. On May 12 Holcombe warned that its ministers were "determined to keep the others back until we get through but fear their ability to close if we delay much longer. They have urged me twice this week to telegraph again. *This I have of course declined to do.*" Yet Holcombe wanted Shufeldt to telegraph to the State Department to see if it had received his cables, and he urged the commodore to specify "time important." On the fifteenth Holcombe mentioned that the German minister, Herr Von Brandt, had revealed the news that the Shufeldt mission to Korea "had reached B[erlin] from Washington *officially,* that the U.S. was negotiating with Corea." The chargé could not understand why the State Department had not replied to Shufeldt's telegrams of April 12 and 19, and he even imagined that it might be because Secretary Frelinghuysen was seeking advice from other governments to see whether they would join in recognizing the suzerainty of China over Korea.[37]

Shufeldt in the *Swatara* found at the mouth of the Salee River one Japanese and three Chinese vessels swinging at anchor on May 9. On May 14 two Korean commissioners, Shin-Chen, the president of the Royal Cabinet, who had negotiated the Korean-Japanese treaty, and Kim Hong-Jip, a member of the cabinet and ambassador to Japan, together with a secretary, So Sang-u, and Gin Hung Dze, a chamberlain representing the Korean government, called to see Ma on the Chinese flagship and then to see Shufeldt on board the *Swatara*. They remained an hour, "were very friendly in their professions and urged a return of their visit to the town of Yin Chuin." Presents of eggs, rice, and fowl were exchanged for bread, cigars, and money from the *Swatara*. Shufeldt waited six days before returning the visit. He went to the town accompanied by his officers—Philip H. Cooper, Lieutenant Commander Perry, and Lieutenant Staunton. Once there he formally presented his documents crediting him as an envoy and also passed on the letter from President Arthur to the king of Korea. He claimed it would be delivered and answered "in terms of equality as existing between two sovereign rulers of friendly nations." A joint meeting was arranged on shore, in view of the ship's company, for the signing ceremony on May 20, but the tent where the signing was to take place was not ready, and the ceremony was fixed for the twenty second.[38]

When Shufeldt met with the Korean commissioners on the twentieth, he issued a flambuoyant "imperial decree":

Great America. Imperial Decree of Commodore Shufeldt U.S.N. Special Envoy with full power.

I enclose a copy in Chinese of a letter to me from the President of the United States authorizing me to make a treaty of friendship and commerce and will also send a letter from the President of the United States to His Majesty the King of Chosen, after the treaty is signed.

By this time Shufeldt's confidence was evident. He had been afraid of a last minute hitch in the proceedings but by the twentieth he had notified Holcombe that he did not foresee any difficulty, "as both the government and people of Corea have been perfectly friendly." To his daughter he gleefully noted, "the Corean treaty may be regarded as a *sure* thing— & that—I am sure you will consider a compensation not only for my fatigue but for the worry that it has given to both of us."[39]

At 9:30 A.M. on May 22, Shufeldt went on shore with a full complement of ship's officers and marines toward the town of "Sai mots fo" (Chemulp'o). There a ceremonial tent stood ready for the signing of the treaty. Together with Shin-Chen and Kim Hong-jip were Ma Chienchung, Admiral Ting, and Captain Clayson of the Imperial Chinese Navy. After some preliminary conversation, six copies of the treaty were signed (see Appendix 2 for the full text of the treaty). At the Koreans' suggestion the treaty included a clause prohibiting the exportation of rice and breadstuffs of every description from the open port of Yin Chuen. The *Swatara* fired a twenty-one gun salute, expending sixty-six rounds in courtesy salutes to Admiral Ting and the Korean commissioners. At the banquet to celebrate the signing, Shufeldt gave the credit of the treaty to Li and Ma, much to the chagrin of Hanabusa Yosimoto, the Japanese minister who arrived at Chemulp'o and toasted Shufeldt on his quick success! Shufeldt and his party then returned to the *Swatara*. On May 23 Hanabusa visited Shufeldt. After delaying sailing in order to wait for a letter from the king of Korea to the president, Shufeldt ordered the *Swatara* to move slowly down the Salee River and out to sea. Shufeldt's third journey to Korea, unlike the visits in the *Wachusett* and the *Ticonderoga,* had finally produced a treaty for him.[40]

The Importance of the Korean Treaty

Shufeldt was gratified by the treaty. Years later he wrote, "I am very glad for the sake of our country that we were the pioneers in accomplishing the feat of bringing the last of the exclusive countries within the pale of Western Civilization. It was as easy a thing to do, as for Columbus to stand his egg upon its end." Immediately after Shufeldt had performed the trick, other powers did likewise. Germany and Britain quickly negotiated treaties with Korea, in November 1883, demanding modifications in the rate of duties pending the exchange of the treaties. Italy completed a treaty on January 26, 1884, Russia followed suit on June 3, 1884, France on June 25, 1886, and Austria in June 1892.[41]

Shufeldt's treaty went to the Senate on July 29 and to the Foreign Relations Committee on August 9, 1882. It was delayed for six months until Senator William Windom of Minnesota reported favorably on it for the committee. On January 9, 1883, it was submitted to the Senate with five resolutions. Three of them dealt with advice and consent and the interpretation of certain clauses. The fourth resolved that the Senate

> in advising and consenting to the treaty mentioned in the foregoing resolutions does not admit or acquiesce in any right or constitutional power in the President to authorize or employ any person to negotiate treaties or carry on diplomatic negotiations with any foreign power unless such person shall have been appointed for such purpose or clothed with such power by and with the advice and consent of the Senate, except in the case of a Secretary of State or a diplomatic officer appointed by the President to fill a vacancy occurring during a recess of the Senate, and it makes the declaration in order that the means employed in the negotiations of said treaty be not drawn into a precedent.

This was the first time in almost a hundred years that the Senate had succeeded in entering a formal protest with the president against the use of executive agents. It was probably directed as much against Shufeldt, as a particular agent responsible for the Sargent letter, as against executive agents in general. It created no commotion because it was not publicized in the press. The president and secretary of state both ignored it. Henry M. Wriston, the most prominent analyst of the relationship between executive agents and foreign policy, who closely examined this aspect of the Korean treaty as it related to the use of an executive agent, condemned the resolution and was severely critical of it as naive. Yet it did represent an attempt to limit the rights of the president to appoint agents beyond the control of the Senate in the diplomatic field. The treaty itself passed the Senate and ratifications were exchanged on May 19, 1883.[42]

The importance of the Shufeldt treaty lay in two areas: its impact on the international relations of the Far East and its revelations about American commercial policy in the Pacific. It contributed toward disturbing the balance of power in the struggle between China and Japan. Both of those nations regarded Korea's status in a different light. United States commercial policy sided with Japanese denials of Korea's tributary status.

Li Hung-chang believed the treaty could help China maintain the status quo in the East by checking Japanese aggression and helping China retain her domination of Korea. Li wrote to the king of Korea that "the United States, situated at the other end of the Pacific, has never entertained any territorial ambition. By our concluding a treaty of peace and amity with her, not only will Japan's aggression be checked but also the other nations demanding trade will have a model treaty to base theirs upon." Li was pinning his hopes on the letters sent to the United States with the treaty. He declared that "since separate notes stating Korea's vassalage to China have thus been preserved in the archives of the respective Powers, in case of future attack on Korea by any of these Powers or in case of Korea's disloyalty to us, we can hold either of them responsible." The viceroy was mistaken in this belief. It is useful to compare his view with the assessments of later Korean scholars. Andrew C. Nahm, a leading writer on Korean history during this period, has commented that Li's aim was "to destroy the Japanese contention that Korea was sovereign and independent as expressed in the treaty of 1876 by inducing the U.S. to recognize China's suzerainty in Korea: secondly in the case of his failure in achieving this, he would apply a strategy of 'setting one barbarian against the other' by allowing the U.S. to sign a treaty with Korea and then weaken Japan. Li's schemes proved to be abortive in both cases." Yet this result occurred partly because of the rapid rise of Japanese military power, in relation to Chinese, between 1881 and 1894. C. I. Eugene Kim and Han-Kyo Kim, in *Korea and the Politics of Imperialism 1876-1910,* do not blame Li when they note, "the Li-Shufeldt compromise appears to have been a unilateral capitulation on Li's part . . . Thus, China's internal weakness, particularly in the military sphere, and not Li's handling of the Korean-American treaty of 1882, is responsible for the end of China's influence in Korea."[43]

The king of Korea sent two letters to Shufeldt for delivery to the president of the United States. The first was a reply to Garfield's letter that Shufeldt carried with him to Korea. The second was the letter Shufeldt agreed to accept instead of having Korean dependency written into the treaty. Chester Holcombe translated it, and Shufeldt had another translation done in Shanghai. Shufeldt's translation read:

> The King of Ta Chou Hsien Kwo (Corea) makes a communication to the President of the United States.
>
> The Chou Hsien Country (Corea) is a dependency of China, but the management of her governmental affairs, home and foreign has always been vested in the Sovereign.
>
> Now, as the Governments of the United States and Corea are about to enter into treaty relations, the intercourse between the two nations shall be carried on in every respect on terms of equality and courtesy, and the King of Corea clearly asserts that all of the articles of the treaty shall be acknowledged and carried into effect according to the laws of independent states [according to international law (as binding upon) independent states].
>
> In the matter of Corea being a dependency of China any question that may arise between them in consequence of such dependency the United States shall in no way interfere. The King has accordingly deputed commissioners for the purpose of negotiating the treaty and now as in duty bound addresses this communication for the information of the President of the United States. A necessary communication dated the 491st year of the founding of Ta Chou Hsien Kwo (Corea) and the 28th day of the 3rd moon of the 8th year of the Reign of Kwang Hsü.[44]

This letter is dated differently from the accompanying letter of greeting, being dated May 15, 1882, before the treaty was signed, a point of considerable importance to the Chinese in the dependency argument and something Shufeldt did not discover until he returned to Shanghai. Both this interpretation, and the one that Holcombe sent to Frelinghuysen, used the words "sovereign," "independent," and "international Law," words that imply complete equality between states and independent nations. These terms seemingly contradict the subsequent statement of the dependency of the Korean king.

American diplomatic reaction to the letter in the early 1880s was ambiguous. John Russell Young, American minister to China in 1882, wrote to Frelinghuysen from Philadelphia, before he set out for China, "If Corea is an independent kingdom then we can treat with its sovereign without regard to China. If Corea is a province of the Chinese empire then we should treat directly with the Peking foreign office. If the question is in doubt, as is most certainly the case, then we should consider the wisdom of the United States endeavoring to settle it by the indirect method of a commercial treaty." If one takes Young's point a stage further, it is obvious that an American commercial treaty was inextricably interwoven with the fabric of a Far Eastern political problem. Frelinghuysen, however, argued that Korea was independent in a Western political sense. He wrote to Young in August, "In view of all the circumstances, I cannot but regard the administrative independence of Korea as a pre-established fact, abundantly recognized by the events of the past few years, and not created by or recognized by the conclusion of our treaty . . . we regarded Korea as *de facto* independent, and . . . our acceptance of the friendly aid found in China was in no sense a recognition of China's suzerain power." Thus, when he sent the treaty to the Senate Foreign Relations Committee, Frelinghuysen declared, "the treaty . . . does not create Corean independence any more than like engagements concluded or now in process of negotiation between Corea and the western powers." Young, however, was prepared to equivocate more, for he was aware of the importance of a commercial treaty. As far as American good offices could be given, he declared, "they should be used to protect Corea either in the 'independence' which China will recognize, or in the tributary position which the Peking government is indisposed to surrender."[45]

While official American policy thus indirectly supported the Japanese and the proindependence party in Korea, the letter sent by the king of Korea conveyed the sense of Chinese suzerainty over Korea. To the educated Korean and Chinese of 1882, the curious Chinese phrases for "President," the "Korean King," and "international law," in the letter would all have revealed a superior-inferior relationship between China and Korea. The dating of the letter with the Chinese year-period indicated that the sender considered himself subordinate to the Chinese ruler whose year-period was being used. Everything about the letter indicated that while Americans were thinking in terms of Korean sovereignty and independence, the Koreans and the Chinese were thinking in terms of Korean dependence on China—a filial relationship that was beyond Shufeldt's (and American) ability to comprehend.

Much of the tension that characterized American policy toward Korea between 1882 and 1895 arose from the indecision over conflicting assumptions about the relationship of Korea to China. The treaty certainly helped to produce a change in the status quo in the East; the opposite result, in the long run, to that intended by Li Hung-chang. But it is difficult to disagree with the assessment, for example, of C. I. Eugene Kim and Han-Kyo Kim that the major change in Chinese relations with Korea after 1882, resulting in the end of China's influence in Korea in 1895, was due to internal weakness, particularly in the military sphere, and not to Li's or Shufeldt's handling of the negotiations. Power in upholding the changes or in meeting rising Japanese military power seeking to undermine the situation was equally as important as the form, content, and involved negotiating procedures of the treaty.[46]

American commercial policy to some extent aided Japanese contentions, despite initial Japanese reactions to the treaty. The Japanese government apparently feared a declaration of dependency would strengthen China's claim to the Ryukyu Islands. The treaty was thus one of a number of events from 1867 that culminated in the Sino-Japanese War of 1894–1895. It was not, however, naive diplomacy. It served as the standard for Korea's later treaties with other nations. The British objected to the prohibition of trade in opium, the agreement to abolish extraterritorial rights once the Korean penal code had been reformed, and the exclusion of Americans from the coasting trade. The Chinese regarded the treaty as a diplomatic victory, yet Korea was thrust into the forefront of increasing great-power rivalry in the Far East as a result. The country was left to lurch through a series of coups, *émeutes,* and military uprisings that characterized her internal struggles over the next three years until the Chinese stepped in with military force. Thereafter, the unhappy court and country became the center of an imperial struggle between China and Japan in which Shufeldt, and through him, as its accredited agent, the American government had engaged, partly because of the lure of dominating Pacific commerce and partly out of a desire to safeguard the trade routes to China and Japan.[47]

Korea and China attempted to remedy the situation by clarifying the relationship in treaty form. For example, the regulations for maritime and overland trade between Chinese and Korean subjects, published in September 1882, stated:

> All that pertains to the relations of Korea as a boundary state of China has been long ago regulated by fixed rules, and no change is required in this respect. But as new foreign countries entertain trade with Korea by water, it becomes necessary to remove at once the prohibition of sea trade hitherto enforced between China and Korea. . . . The new regulations for the maritime and overland trade now decided upon are understood to apply to the relations between China and Korea only, the former country granting to the latter certain advantages as a tributary kingdom, and treaty nations are not to participate therein. It is in this sense that the following Articles have been agreed upon.

The regulations then specified the trading rights of citizens of both countries, and were signed by Li Hung-chang, Cheow Fuh, and Ma

Chien-chung for China and Chao Ning-Hsia, Chin Hung-chi, and Yu Yun Chung for Korea.[48] Such efforts, however, gained little respite for pro-Chinese Koreans or for Chinese statesmen struggling to maintain the nature of the dependent status.

Although the assumption of moral superiority often permeates works on United States diplomatic history when dealing with American motives, especially when contrasted to the motives of other powers toward Far Eastern nations, there is little evidence, outside of constant repetition, to sustain the belief. In the specific instance of the Shufeldt treaty, no author has considered it from the overall *intent* of the American negotiator. The treaty has usually been judged in the context of Li's China policy, Korean independence, Japanese ambitions, or the genuflections historians have made toward American diplomacy after the Civil War. Some authors have preferred to stress the "good offices" clause of the Korean treaty in much the same way that they earlier stressed only the "shipwreck convention" aspect of Blaine's instructions. Yet there is no reason why "moral" clauses or "mere shipwreck conventions" should be highlighted to the exclusion of more significant aspects of the treaty, unless the basic assumption of the writer so doing is to project an image of the United States as a nation somewhat above the tactics and strategies of competing European powers. It is highly difficult to sustain a claim that American obligations under the treaty were, from a legal point of view, limited to the tender of good offices, and impossible when such a treaty is placed in the context of Evarts', Thompson's, Blaine's, and Frelinghuysen's instructions or Shufeldt's cruise in the *Ticonderoga*.[49]

Equally as important, criticism of Shufeldt has been made from a base of similar assumptions. Thus it has been claimed that the treaty "did not conform to the instructions from Secretary Frelinghuysen . . . for the protection of shipwrecked sailors"—a criticism that totally ignores the first and third paragraphs of Article III of the treaty and the fact that the secretary of state clearly stated that the treaty was to be the means to develop future American interests in Asia. A similar tactic has been to distinguish Shufeldt's desire to open Korea from the American government's "relative indifference" toward the project. Even Frederick Foo Chien declared that the United States policy in the Far East "was essentially passive: friendly intercourse with all nations, entangling alliance with none." This is a classical non sequitur, for what other nation sought an "alliance" with Korea, or China for that matter, and which other nations were not "entangled" by treaties of commerce? While one can agree with Chien that Shufeldt sought to leave his "mark on the pages of history," it was with the active concurrence of Evarts, Thompson, Blaine, Frelinghuysen, Angell, and Holcombe.[50]

Overall, however, the failure of historians to place the treaty with Korea in the context of the specific aims and intentions of Shufeldt's world cruise and his views on the developing empire of the seas is a strange omission. In the light of Shufeldt's instructions from Evarts, Thompson, and Blaine, the Korean treaty was clearly another wedge designed to open the Asian door for American trade. Nothing appears in Shufeldt's previous expressions on Korea and commercial supremacy, in the various sets of instructions he acted under, or in the role of the United States in the Far East from 1866 to 1882, to justify expressions of faith about good offices being the primary reason for the treaty. Shufeldt aimed for commercial supremacy in the Pacific. Put simply, the United States employed similar tactics based on similar interests to those used by other powers operating in the muddy shoals of foreign power politics and commercial opportunity in the Far East.

15
The Legacy of an Expansionist

The Personal Consequences of the Korean Treaty

As Shufeldt left Korea to return to Shanghai, he informed his daughter that the treaty had been signed and the Sargent letter published in America and China, "So *every*thing has happened that can." He also wrote to the secretary of the navy for permission to remain abroad in command of the Asiatic squadron in order to ratify the Korean treaty. Moving on to Yokohama and Nagasaki, however, he began to be concerned over his future. On May 28 he telegraphed to the Navy Department for the command of the squadron. Then on June 8 he wrote to Frelinghuysen: "The [State] Department must have been made aware of the reasons for the action of China by my despatch of January 23rd (No. 1) in time to recall my commission if it so desired. My telegram also of April 12th indicating that I was ready to go to Corea, could have been answered in the interval between that time and May 1st the day fixed for my departure, in time to countermand the movement if anything had occurred to render such action advisable."[1]

Aaron A. Sargent had written to Shufeldt in April, the letter reaching him on July 5, that he had grave doubts about publishing the open letter but had considered it the commodore's wish. He warned Shufeldt of Frelinghuysen's reaction in referring to it as "an extraordinary letter, brutal in its frankness." Frelinghuysen said he understood that Shufeldt's commission from the State Department to negotiate the treaty had put the commodore out of the navy; Sargent had objected to that interpretation and supported Shufeldt. The secretary of state had replied hastily "that he did not intend to speak of or do anything about it," a sentiment that must have alleviated only slightly Shufeldt's uneasiness about the official silence. Sargent mentioned the incident to put Shufeldt on his guard. As the new secretary of the navy, William E. Chandler of New Hampshire, was Sargent's personal friend, he intended to write asking that Shufeldt relieve Rear Admiral Clitz on the Asiatic station during the summer. "It won't do you any harm," Sargent explained to the commodore, "if it does no good." The impact of this letter on Shufeldt was devastating. Molly wrote that her father was worrying considerably over Sargent's warning "just received." She invoked the parallel with Perry's opening of Japan: "he had a large squadron & twenty thousand dollars worth of presents for distribution. Father went over with one *small* U.S. vessel, two *Chinese* gunboats, a *Chinese* admiral & a mandarin of high rank all sent by Li Hung-chang . . . the conduct of our Government is most extraordinary."[2]

In October, Shufeldt indicated the problems that Sargent's release of his January letter from China had created for him. On August 17 Sargent had written from the American legation at Berlin that he was disturbed over a telegram from Japan, printed in the *San Francisco Call* of July 23, which stated: "Commodore Shufeldt is now in Yokohama with the new Corean treaty. He is expected to declare emphatically that his notorious letter to Mr. Sargent was not intended for publication, and that Sargent violated confidence in printing it." Sargent was unwilling to believe that Shufeldt had made such a statement but felt it due to himself to inquire if the commodore, whom he regarded as "the soul of honor & frankness, who would suffer any consequences of a mistake, if one were made . . . rather than escape them as [at?] the expense of the honor of a friend," had, in fact, authorized the report. The letter reached Shufeldt on October 14, and he prepared at least two drafts of a reply, toning down the bitterness that occasionally crept into the first one.* His response brought the personal side of the controversy to rest, as well as revealing how deeply Shufeldt had been blistered:

> I have never said publicly or privately that you had violated my confidence in publishing my letter. . . . It was marked an "open letter" & [if being so marked means the right to publish it in the newspapers—then] you had the right so to use it—Nevertheless it was not intended for that purpose. It was sent to you as an intimate personal friend familiar with my object & interests & as a public man [possibly] (in all probability) a Cabinet officer [certainly in harmony with the Administration] (as you yourself informed me) & as an expression of my own views on a most important topic & at a critical time. . . . It was forwarded to you to be used entirely at your discretion & you wrote that you had published it after some hesitation.
>
> I have suffered for it, more than for any other act of my life—I have not seen in any public print any allusion to you in the matter—while I have been subjected to indiscriminate abuse. If there has been any such allusion I am in no way responsible for it—I have been summarily recalled from China & my

---

*The two drafts vary slightly; brackets indicate the first and parentheses the second.

Corean work to a great extent nullified—I have submitted to this without any effort to avoid the consequences or escape them "at the expense of the honor of a friend."[3]

In addition to that personal assessment of the cost of the Sargent letter, Shufeldt anticipated there would be a departmental price to pay. While he was waiting at Yokohama for an answer to his application for the command of the squadron, Assistant Secretary of the Navy John G. Walker informed him on June 2 that his orders would depend on a satisfactory explanation of his January letter to Sargent. Shufeldt considered that any explanation, however satisfactory, would tend "to impair the influence pertaining to that command [of the squadron]." Next came a letter from George Robeson, then the second-ranking member of the House Naval Committee, which had promised support and help to Shufeldt. However, Robeson added in a postscript that if the commodore failed to receive the command, "it will be on account of some letter which you wrote to Sargent attacking the Chinese Government and which the Chinese representatives here object to . . . as coming from an officer attached to the American Legation in China." Despite the promise of help and support, when Robeson spoke to the secretary about Shufeldt's employment, the news in the postscript had been the result. Realizing from these two communications that the Sargent letter had lost him the squadron he had longed to command, Shufeldt telegraphed to the department on July 8 withdrawing his application, and then he prepared to leave for Nagasaki. Unknown to him at the time, he had already been detached from his duties under instructions from the State Department at the legation. On July 10 he received a cable ordering him home immediately. He set out with Molly in mid-July bound for San Francisco.[4]

Returning to California on July 29, Shufeldt requested two months leave of absence. Physically exhausted and mentally weary from the long negotiations in China, he entered Mare Island Naval Hospital under the care of Dr. George Peck. While a controversy over his recall developed in the Navy Department and the press, he slid into acute depression and began to look upon his accomplishments as so much wasted effort. He read in the *New York Times* that his recall was "due to his open letter to ex-Senator Sargent," which was "supposed to have been written to affect legislation on the Chinese bill" then before Congress. The newspaper's editor called the letter "an admirable paper" when regarded from the point of view of "an impartial Philistine," but at the same time "a frightening piece of impudence and indiscretion, coming as it did from an officer of the United States Government temporarily charged with semi-diplomatic duties in a foreign land." Two days later the *Times* mentioned that Secretary Chandler had rejected the point that because Shufeldt's position was a diplomatic one, he had forfeited his naval rank. The *Washington Post* printed an interview with former secretary of the navy Richard W. Thompson, who referred very favorably to Shufeldt as a man of "great sagacity." Thompson argued that if the Sargent letter was confidential and sent to a friend who violated Shufeldt's confidence, then he was not guilty of any naval offense, "and his friend is more censurable then he." Shufeldt, however, lost perspective and began to think that newspaper accounts necessarily reflected what naval personnel thought of him. He saw no future for himself in the navy.[5]

There were some crumbs of comfort. Rear Admiral Clitz sent congratulations on the signing of the treaty. Shufeldt's loyal friend, Norman Farquhar, complimented him on the successful termination of the Korean negotiations and told him "the making of the treaty will place you in History beside Perry, and when your detractors will have long been forgotten your name will still shine brighter than ever." But even Farquhar considered Sargent's publication of the letter was "most inopportune" and declared himself certain that Shufeldt had not intended all of it as an open letter. Robert H. Wyman caught Shufeldt's mood much better. He likened the navy to a school of porpoises, "if one is wounded the others pounce upon him—all esprit de corps is gone—& 'tis everyone for himself." Wyman also informed Shufeldt that he was suspicious of Sargent's use of the letter; the publication was for Sargent's own ends. Wyman confided, "I never viewed S. in the light that you did." Perhaps best of all were the congratulations that Chester Holcombe sent to Shufeldt on accomplishing "a splendid piece of work." Holcombe did not know if the treaty had been changed in Korea or signed "just as we finished it at Tientsin." But he had seen the impact of the news of the treaty on the foreign staffs in China and revealed that Thomas Wade, Butzon, and the Prussian Von Brandt "are racing to see which can get to Corea first, and the Frenchman is jumping up and down & swearing." Additional support for the commodore came from the navy's medical director, Francis M. Gunnell, who had worked to obtain the Asiatic squadron for Shufeldt, gave him "a hearty welcome home," praised the Korean work, and hoped to see him soon in Washington.[6]

Shufeldt began to write long justifications and explanations of his conduct to Secretary of the Navy Chandler. He asserted that the Sargent letter had been given an exaggerated importance as far as it bore on the relations of the United States and China. Quoting from a letter received from Owen N. Denny at the Shanghai consulate, Shufeldt declared that Li Hung-chang had not been greatly offended by the letter: he asked after him kindly, desired to know when he was coming to China again, and had increased respect for Shufeldt for confirming what he himself had to say about Chinese power. But he felt driven to explain his use of the words "open letter." Shufeldt had assumed that Sargent would be in the cabinet, in harmony with the administration, and would read the letter to the president and fellow members of the cabinet. He had not expected the letter to be given to the press. He deeply regretted the reference to the empress, more because she was a woman than because she was an empress. Until the Chinese court was thrown open to the outside world, he expected such references would circulate. None of these personal remarks had affected the Korean negotiations, though Shufeldt did not inform the secretary that they might have done so if Li Hung-chang had desired to use them. Finally, Shufeldt considered the treaty was "of infinitely more importance to China than to the United States, for it has given to that country, without a war, a political preponderance in the East which it has long sought for with reference to Japan."[7]

On the subject of the command of the Asiatic squadron, Shufeldt's explanations were tinged with sorrow. He had applied in order to insure that American interest would be best served. Because the Navy Department had publicly indicated that it would require explanations, he had been forced to withdraw his request. To Chandler, Shufeldt declared, "you can readily understand how humiliating the acceptance of such a position would be to me & how prejudicial to the national dignity it would appear to others." Shufeldt had given up his desire to command the Asiatic squadron rather than explain in public what his motives had been.[8]

Over the summer of 1882, Shufeldt heard heartening news of Chandler's friendly attitude toward him from Gunnell and William H. Trescott of South Carolina, a former United States commissioner in China who met Shufeldt in Tientsin in August 1880 while revising immigration and commercial treaties for the United States. Gunnell explained that it was the State Department's sending of the *New York Times* copy of the Sargent letter to the Navy Department, with a request for an explanation, that had prevented the commodore from receiving the Asiatic squadron, which both Sargent and Gunnell thought they had secured for him. Shufeldt, however, remained depressed and low-spirited and talked of giving up the navy. After he had been given two months leave of absence, Molly urged him to relax at the Pacific Club in San Francisco. "Take care of yourself & get well & strong," she wrote to him, "so that we may enjoy the vacation before going back to the old battle ground." Shufeldt's son, Robert, had spoken with President Arthur's secretary, Phillips, who said the treaty results were "entirely satisfactory to him [the president]." Robert also sent news that the editor of the *Post* had referred to his father as the "Stupid Diplomat," scarcely an antidote for his father. Molly's mother castigated Robert as "a very bad man."⁹

On the credit side, William Elliot Griffis, the author of *The Hermit Nation,* wrote requesting particulars of Shufeldt's life. In addition, Putnam's wanted the publishing rights to any book Shufeldt might write on "Negotiations with and experiences in Corea." Griffis caught Shufeldt's mood over the summer of 1882 when he later wrote, "he died some years later feeling the sting of what he felt was the slight or ingratitude of his superiors, because a friend had betrayed his confidence." In "The Opening of Korea," Griffis added, "personally, I wonder whether his peaceful achievement does not rank with Perry's and, whether his name does not, in Korea at least, deserve a noble memorial."¹⁰

Shufeldt felt isolated in California. He feared Secretary Chandler would bypass him. But Gunnell cleared up one doubt in Shufeldt's mind, concerning the lack of acknowledgment from the State Department of his letters from Japan. "You announced you were coming," he told the commodore, "and therefore no official acknowledgment of your letter was sent." The Navy Department had no control over him until the State Department released him from the service; thus Shufeldt had been left in the dark about his future in the service. Gunnell warned him of the importance of coming to Washington. The newspaper stories derived from the navy men who disliked him and were jealous of his influence. "You cannot delight these men," Gunnell confided, "than by staying away—and if you would make them wild with joy, just talk about going on the Retired List."¹¹

Neither Gunnell nor Frelinghuysen knew the torment in Shufeldt's mind. He considered his life had been devoted to the betterment and promotion of the navy. Its seeming neglect of him now was largely imagined but, nevertheless, real to Shufeldt. Unless the department issued orders for him to go to Washington, it could wait forever for him to come voluntarily. He felt he had been badly treated for the Sargent letter. To Chandler he declared, "I regret very much that the Corean treaty, so unique in its character, & so well calculated to enhance the prestige of the United States in the East should have been surrounded by these embarrassments, but I desire to say, that my letter to Mr. Sargent was purely of a personal character, while the treaty with Corea was entirely national, and the one should not in any way or manner conflict with the other." But, there was no vote of thanks from a grateful Congress, no award of expenses to publish his manuscript of the cruise of the *Ticonderoga,* such as Perry had been granted following the opening of Japan, no plaudits from the press. President Arthur was to ignore Korea in his messages to Congress in 1882. Instead of praise, Shufeldt was subjected to party wrangling and bickering. To his sister Ellen, he confessed his loneliness. "Such a vagabond upon the face of the earth," he moaned, "such a waif and stray among men—that I do not write even to those who continue to love me in spite of myself." This was the quintessence of self-pity. He described himself at the sulphur springs where he relaxed as "a moody rheumatic old man—feeling that life has done its worst & its best for me—that I have come to the end of my tether—none the better for life with its vanities & vexations—where shall I turn next?" At sixty, he did not intend it to be Washington, "to dip again into the cesspool of politics," or anywhere with any work to do. Instead, Shufeldt claimed, he was "searching for *rest*," for he was due to retire in a year's time and "go out as the old horse to grass—then all I have done & all I have said fades away into oblivion or into history which always lies."[12]

As these thoughts were being written, the secretary of the navy was asking for Shufeldt. The latter telegraphed hopefully to the assistant secretary of the navy, John G. Walker, asking, "when my leave expires can I wait orders or have leave extended?" Walker replied, "Will do what you wish in the matter." Chandler dispatched a telegram inquiring about the condition of Shufeldt's health. He answered, "health restored, I am ready for orders if required." A second cable asked if his health would permit him to serve on duty. Finally, the department ordered him to proceed to Washington to take up his new position as president of the Second Naval Advisory Board organized under the provisions of the act of August 5, 1882. Shufeldt not only still had a future in the navy, but he was to be in charge of the board that eventually recommended and supervised the building of the White Squadron, the navy's first steel warships.[13]

President of the Naval Advisory Board

American interests in the East, as Shufeldt was well aware from his observations during the world cruise and his time in China, lay at the mercy of powerful European and developing Japanese squadrons. Growing support for a stronger navy from such senators as John T. Morgan of Alabama and John F. Miller of California and from a powerful New England group of congressmen led by Benjamin Harris of Massachusetts, together with James Gordon Bennett's *New York Herald* and the American delegation to the Berlin Conference on the Congo, headed by John A. Kasson, meant that new appropriations began to flow to the navy as it emerged from the lethargy of the early 1870s. Secretary of the Navy William H. Hunt, appointed by Garfield on March 5, 1881, held office for only a year until appointed minister to Russia on

April 5, 1882. Brought into the cabinet initially as a southern-born Republican—he was a prominent member of the New Orleans bar and a judge of the United States Court of Claims—in order to give some semblance of executive representation for the southern reconstructed states, Hunt proved an able administrator and diligent strategist for a growing navy. In July 1881, he appointed a board of fifteen naval officers headed by Rear Admiral John Rodgers to draw up plans for the navy. Its members first met on July 11 and deliberated until November 7. The Rodgers' board then recommended the acquisition of eighteen new steel cruisers of first- and second-rates, twenty fourth-rate wooden cruisers, five steel rams, five torpedo gunboats, ten cruising torpedo boats, and ten harbor torpedo boats. This proved too much for Congress, especially the House Naval Affairs Committee under Benjamin Harris of Massachusetts, to accept, and the Rodgers' board was disbanded. Inasmuch as the wooden ships were more for the relief of shipbuilders in the east rather than for the benefit of the navy, Congress decided to reject the board's report. In place of the first board a second was established by an act of August 5, 1882, to supervise the designs for a more restricted naval program. Shufeldt was ordered by Secretary Chandler, who had succeeded Hunt, to convene this statutory board at the Navy Department as soon as possible.[14]

The naval members of the board were quickly selected by the secretary: Chief Engineer Alexander Henderson, Commander John A. Howell, Lieutenant Edward W. Very, and Naval Constructor Frank L. Fernald. Shortly after arriving in Washington, Shufeldt was ordered to select the civilian members. He collected many opinions on the fitness of various rivals, but concluded that they were all likely to be "more or less influenced by their interests—or their prejudices." As he knew none of the candidates personally, he was at some loss to know who to select, finally advising Chandler to make the choice himself. Eventually, Miers Coryell, a mechanical and marine engineer, and Henry Steers, a ship architect and president of John Roach's Eleventh Ward Bank, were chosen. Assistant Naval Constructor Francis T. Bowles became secretary and Passed Assistant Engineer C. R. Roether with Assistant Engineer H. P. Norton were selected as draftsmen to serve the board. As John Roach, who had been a heavy contributor to Republican campaign funds, and Superintendent Faron of Roach's shipyard had urged Coryell's selection, it was later claimed by the *Washington Post* that the choice had given Roach "the refusal" of four out of seven on the board. Shufeldt later refuted the charge.[15]

Over the winter of 1882–1883, the Advisory Board met to discuss the new and repaired vessels that would be suitable for a new navy. Hemmed in by careful congressional authorizations laid down by the act of August 5, 1882, the second board could not be as sweeping in recommending large numbers of vessels as the Rodgers' board had been. Initially, Congress limited the number of vessels to be mentioned in the draft bill to two. One was to be a cruiser of not less than 5,000 tons nor more than 6,000 tons displacement and the other of not less than 4,300 tons nor more than 4,700 tons displacement, both to be built of domestic steel. The Naval Advisory Board eventually recommended "a comparatively modest program of five vessels" constructed of steel. One was to be a cruiser of about 4,500 tons displacement, three were to be of nearly 3,000 tons displacement each, and one a dispatch boat of 1,500 tons displacement. On March 3, 1883, Congress enacted the proposals of Shufeldt's board appropriating the money for four steel vessels, the first of that kind in the United States Navy, but removing one of the smaller cruisers from the bill before final passage. By May 2, 1883, proposals for the construction of the vessels had been invited for July 2, and contracts for the heavy cruiser *Chicago,* the light cruisers *Atlanta* and *Boston,* and the dispatch boat *Dolphin* were awarded to John Roach of New York City, who had been lowest bidder on all four vessels.[16]

In addition to supervising contractual work for the new steel vessels and completing work on ironclads, the Advisory Board also reported on October 25, 1883, its view on new work that should be undertaken in the coming year. Shufeldt recommended the construction of seven more unarmored steel vessels, three like the cruisers *Chicago* or *Boston,* two similar to the dispatch boat *Dolphin* but constructed on a different plan, and two small gunboats of about 750 tons displacement for both seagoing and shallow water navigation. The members of the board deemed it necessary to record their "emphatic disapproval" of the suggestions that "the Navy should acquire a number of extremely high-speed commerce-destroying vessels of great endurance, designed in these respects with special reference to gaining superiority over the large and swift transatlantic mail steamers." The reasons offered were the excessive cost of such vessels, the absorption of such a large proportion of the personnel of the navy as might leave other areas deficient, and the ease with which enemy mail steamers might resort to neutral flags upon a declaration of war. Nevertheless, the board members remained wedded to a concept of commerce destruction as the legitimate objective of the navy in case of war. The last paragraph of the October 25 report declared:

> The vulnerable commerce of the enemy, and the one which, if struck, will cause the greatest disaster, is the great bulk of the slow or moderate speed steamers; vessels with which ships of the *Dolphin* class are thoroughly compe-

tent to deal under any or all circumstances. Such being assuredly the case, it seems conclusive that since for the cost of one of these immense vessels eight of the *Dolphin* class could easily be built and kept at sea, no plausible reason exists for the introduction of the type into the service. The cost of building and fitting out one of these very large vessels would be at least as great as that of all seven of the ships we have recommended.[17]

On May 2, 1883, Chandler ordered Shufeldt to appear before Surgeon Francis Gunnell for an examination to determine his physical qualities for performing all duties at sea. Shufeldt was also ordered to report to Vice Admiral Stephen C. Rowan for duty as superintendent of the Naval Observatory for service until February 21, 1884. On May 10 Acting Secretary of the Navy Edward Nichols forwarded a formal commission of Shufeldt's appointment to the rank of rear admiral, dating from May 7, 1883, and for him to take rank next after Rear Admiral Charles H. Baldwin. Shufeldt's old China colleague, James B. Angell, then president of the University of Michigan, wrote to congratulate him on the appointment, considering it a well-earned honor.[18]

As the navy's newest rear admiral was assuming his duties at the Naval Observatory, he was also completing the work on the awarding of contracts for the new cruisers. He notified Chandler that all objections to clauses in the contracts had been modified to the complete satisfaction of the Advisory Board, the Bureau of Construction and Repair, the Bureau of Steam Engineering, and shipbuilder John Roach. The plans for the vessels were to be ready by July 16 and the contracts prepared for the secretary's signature. But here Shufeldt met a stumbling block. In setting up the Advisory Board, Congress had created a body to superintend the building of the new ships, a work that previously had been superintended by the Bureau of Construction and Repair. This bureau wanted to approve and pass judgment on the board's findings; institutional jealousies between board and bureau over approval of plans and appointment of inspectors of material were to create bottlenecks during the summer of 1883.

With the work of the Advisory Board seemingly coming to a conclusion, Shufeldt told Secretary Chandler that he thought it "well done—much of it has been without guide or precedent." If more ships were to be built, then the experience gained would be advantageous and the duties of the board defined and simplified. He asked for a month's respite for the board, to be reconvened in September for work on the monitors and the designs for the new ships. He hoped that once the board had completed the design stage of the new squadron, the construction could go ahead "without any of the complications which arise from divided authority." But a dispute developed over the inspectors between board and bureau officers. As far as Shufeldt was concerned, the

Bureaus of Construction and Repair and Steam Engineering had no responsibility whatever, except such as the secretary gave them. But to the admiral, the Advisory Board was defined by law "so strict that the failure or success of the ships is made to depend entirely upon its action." This was a sweeping claim for autonomy. He counselled the secretary that he was quite sure that the board, in full session, "would be unwilling to see its function become merely 'pro forma' while its responsibilities before the country & even before the world are so grave —& I feel equally certain that you in your earnest desire to see these cruisers a success & a credit to your administration—will take care that no jealousies shall interfere with the plain practical & direct method of bringing the work to a successful & creditable conclusion."[19]

Chandler agreed that the general propositions that Shufeldt had laid down were "indisputable." The board was to inspect and supervise the construction of the vessels and could have any inspection officers it might select to report to if for duty and to act "solely under their [officer's] orders, if the Board desire this." The secretary confessed that the question of form was "of no importance to me." Shufeldt soon made the necessary arrangements with Admiral Edward T. Nichols, chief of the Bureau of Yards and Docks, and Chief Constructor Theodore D. Wilson of the Bureau of Construction and Repair. Mutually satisfactory inspectors of hulls were appointed and Shufeldt informed Chandler: "you understand I am sure, that I have no wish to add to the many embarrassments which attach to the administration of the Navy. I was only anxious to make the work of the Advisory Board so clear & satisfactory as to be beyond intelligent criticism & even so far as possible beyond partisan malice." He sent Chandler the photographs of the designs for the new ships and made arrangements to have them issued by the Naval Institute together with sketches of cross sections "for the purpose of inviting criticism & interesting the Navy." The board's president wanted the Navy Department to subscribe to enough prints "to place one [copy] upon the desk of every member of Congress at the coming session." The *New York Herald* also asked for the prints, and Shufeldt wanted the paper to have them. "We have nothing to fear," he wrote from the Naval Observatory to the department, "& may have much to learn from a close inspection & a free discussion of their designs, for although the ships may be considered as typical yet they may & undoubtedly will be improved upon in the future of the new navy." By the time Shufeldt's work on the board ended, his struggle to establish the board's autonomy had dealt a blow to the old naval bureaucracy based on the rigid division of bureaus. In the 1880s Congress referred designs for the new vessels to be laid down to the continuing Naval Advisory Boards.[20]

The new navy was launched into the turbulent maelstrom of Democratic and Republican politics as well as the more natural element for which it was designed. One hostile survey of the new vessels in the *Washington Post,* two years after congressional approval for the cruisers, speculated that "it is hardly necessary to discuss the question whether Mr. Roach got the contracts to build these vessels as a necessary consequence of the peculiar organization of the board . . . or whether the peculiar organization of the board was an indispensable preliminary to a fore ordained award of the contracts to Mr. Roach." To the paper, "the result was the same in either event." When Shufeldt's own role came under review, the paper treated him kindly. It considered that while the "decadence" of the board was "evident," Shufeldt's eventual retirement from it "bereft it of its sole remaining element of popularity." Whatever may have been the former faults of the board, the criticism continued, "the high reputation, the courtly manners and the kindly spirit of Admiral Shufeldt were always redeeming features." After Shufelt read this, he sent the article to his daughter with a message that while "it goes for the Advisory Board with apparent knowledge & a real animus," he thankfully acknowledged, "it handles me gently—& for this we should be grateful."[21]

The hostility between Democrats and Republicans over the navy was reflected in Congress. With the Democrats convincingly recapturing control of the House of Representatives in 1883, navalists concentrated on the Senate for support in the push for a new navy. Shortly before he retired, Shufeldt appeared before the Senate Committee on Naval Affairs in February 1884 to give testimony on the building of the White Squadron. The committee met to discuss a bill (S698) to authorize the construction of additional steel vessels for the navy. Although a great part of the committee's report lay in probing the technical details of copper sheathing, horizontal versus vertical beam engines, boilers, brick furnaces, coals, sail power, speed, cost, contracts, and tonnage, Shufeldt found the opportunity to make a comprehensive statement of what the United States sea power should develop into in the immediate and more distant future. He stated these views in a dialogue with Senator Matthew Calbraith Butler of South Carolina, nephew of Matthew Calbraith and Oliver Hazard Perry:

SENATOR BUTLER: There are seven vessels provided for in Senate bill 698. Is it your opinion that those seven vessels, if Congress should authorize their construction, would be enough with those now being constructed?
ADMIRAL SHUFELDT: No, sir, of course not. My own opinion in regard to our Navy is simply this: that we

should make a Navy with reference to the protection of our people and our commerce abroad, outside of Europe. That is the first thing we ought to do. I am speaking now of a cruising navy. To do that I should think we ought to have at least 60,000 or 80,000 tons afloat. In a very short time the ships we have in commission now will disappear. If I were asked the question I should say that in my opinion about $5,000,000 a year expended on the Navy, first for such ships as would protect our commerce in Asia and Africa, without any reference to any European navies, because we have no ships now that will do that, and then, afterwards I would like, perhaps in the not very distant future, to build larger ships, very much more expensive; for instance, the last armored cruiser built by England is 9,000 tons, and will cost about a million pounds sterling, just about as much as we ask for all these ships.

SENATOR BUTLER: Your idea, then, would be, after completing the ships of this character, which you think ought to reach to 60,000 or 80,000 tons, to go on and build some larger vessels?

ADMIRAL SHUFELDT: I should like to see it done. I should hope it would be done for the benefit of the country. . . . I think our double turreted monitors, when completed, in addition to the present monitors that we have, will form a very respectable coast defense, and I think we ought to look now to the construction of ships for cruising abroad among the semi-barbarous peoples, because a navy not only protects commerce, but creates it. You cannot build up a new market without having a man-of-war go ahead of your merchant ship. Then commerce would inevitably come. That is the secret of half the success of the British commerce. There is hardly a port in the world where you will not find a British gun-boat.

SENATOR BUTLER: Your idea, then, is that increasing the ships of our Navy and keeping them employed would

	increase the foreign commerce of the United States?
ADMIRAL SHUFELDT:	Unquestionably. I know that from my own experience.
THE ACTING CHAIRMAN:	Do you have so much in mind the increase of the Navy as the building of these ships we have been talking about to take the place of the old ships which are rapidly going out of use?
ADMIRAL SHUFELDT:	At the present time I have only in my mind the replacing the old ships.

Later, Senator Butler asked Shufeldt that if the United States wished to acquire a fighting navy, with larger vessels, would the Congress have to appropriate more money? Shufeldt's answer indicated that he had clearly distinguished between absolute and immediate needs and desirable future building:

ADMIRAL SHUFELDT:	A great deal of money. If we want to go into the navies of the world as one of the naval powers we shall have to spend a great deal of money. I am not thinking of that now. I referred to the English new-armored cruising ship of 9,000 tons burden, carrying a ten-inch battery *en barbette,* costing not less than $5,000,000. I do not propose such a ship as that for our Navy to-day. I should like to see it, but neither our condition nor our personnel would warrant the construction of such a ship.[22]

Shufeldt had fixed on cruisers of the size of the *Chicago* as being the maximum in size appropriate for the United States in the mid-1880s, but his "I should like to see it" meant he had in mind much larger ships for the future.

In February 1884, immediately after the testimony before the committee, Shufeldt retired from the navy. On the fourteenth he was detached from all duties. The long naval career ended on a pleasant note. Samuel R. Franklin, later to become a rear admiral himself, recalled that he was ordered to relieve Shufeldt as superintendent of the Naval Observatory. When Franklin took charge of his new duties, he found that Shufeldt and his assistant, Commander William T. Sampson, had everything "in good running order, and the duties were so distributed

The Legacy of an Expansionist 319

that the right man was always to be found in the right place, and the work so arranged that the officers were employed in such branches of the scientific duties of the Observatory as suited each one's taste." This testimony to Shufeldt's organizing ability was further complemented when Franklin revealed that he had found it necessary to make "but little change," the chief innovation being the creation of a permanent board, whose duty was to formulate a work system for each year to coordinate the work of the other observatories.[23]

Korea, the Canal, and the Navy in the Mid-Eighties

As Shufeldt's retirement drew near, old dreams resurfaced. He revived his interests in Korea and the isthmian canal. He was widely regarded as the Navy Department's leading expert on the Forbidden Kingdom. In September 1883 news came to the State Department of the arrival in San Francisco of a special embassy from the king of Korea to the United States, headed by Min Yong-Ik, nephew of the king, and Hong Yong-shik, son of the chief minister. John Davis, acting secretary of state, requested the service of a naval officer "to take charge of the Embassy." Davis suggested Shufeldt for the task, "by reason of his associations hitherto with Corean affairs." The admiral was willing to serve and the Navy Department was agreeable. But because of a misunderstanding, Davis received the impression that Shufeldt's duties as a member of the Naval Advisory Board "were so onerous as to make it inconvenient for him to aid us as was desired." Consequently, two junior officers, Lieutenant Theodorus B. Mason and Ensign George C. Foulk, were detailed to meet the Korean embassy. Later Commodore Earl English told Shufeldt that the State Department had been informed of his willingness to act. Shufeldt was displeased by the oversight, and it took a personal letter from Chandler to soothe his ruffled pride.[24]

Shufeldt kept in close touch with Korean affairs after this. He promised the members of the Korean embassy that at some future time he would visit Korea. Drawing plans for such a visit, he wrote to the United States legation in Seoul to see if he would be received. Percival Lowell, who had been the foreign secretary of the Korean legation when in Washington, informed him in January 1884 that the king of Korea had offered Shufeldt "a position in the government." The exact office had not been decided, wrote Lowell, who could only say, "it will be high and that in the present state of the land just opening to the West, it will only depend upon you to make it as important as you please." Shufeldt was informed that he was "as highly thought of as you could possibly desire" in Korea. Lowell believed that he would be cordially welcomed. Similar sentiments were expressed by Soh Kwang Pom, secretary of the

Korean embassy. George Foulk, who was due to accompany the Koreans on their return home, informed Shufeldt that "He [Soh] sets great store by the hope that you may come to Korea next spring. . . . He says that what you may have to say will have very great weight, and along with other things [he] would like to tell you exactly how things stand *when* you reach Korea." Shufeldt, however, found that his professional duties in the United States compelled him to defer his visit until after his retirement. When Foulk arrived in Korea, the king urged him to advise Shufeldt to come out. Lucius Foote, United States minister to Korea, sent a telegram at the king's request, inviting the admiral to visit the country. Shufeldt found this telegram waiting for him in San Francisco when he visited there at the end of July 1884. Another invitation followed in September.[25]

At this time the struggle between pro-Japanese "progressives," Min conservatives, and pro-Chinese Korean factions was reaching a climax. Both Foulk and Foote leaned toward the progressives and urged Shufeldt to come as a military adviser to aid the progressive cause. The progressives eventually staged an anti-Min coup d'etat in December 1884, in which over three hundred people lost their lives and Korea lost six of its leading Min family conservative statesmen. The chief conspirators against the Mins were Park Yong-hyo, Soh Kwang Pom, Kim Ok Kyun, and fourteen military students trained in Japan. Chinese troops entered the palace to eject a detachment of the Japanese legation guard in a dispute over who should defend the king.[26]

The first rumblings of this storm occurred in September. Lucius Foote had telegrammed to the United States fleet in Nagasaki harbor of an attempt at revolution. The USS *Trenton* sailed for Chemulp'o and reached port on September 17. On board one of Shufeldt's friends, F. P. Gilmore, notified Shufeldt that he had expected his arrival. Had the admiral come out, Gilmore wrote, he would have seen some stirring sights and "perhaps have influenced them in a manner to prevent the occurrences of the 4th [of December]." But by the end of the summer, "after waiting several months for some written communication from the Corean Government," stating what would be required of him, Shufeldt abandoned the idea of going to Korea. He needed expense money, he was still settling into retired life, and he later confessed that he had intended "to spend the remainder of his life as leisurely as possible." George Foulk later speculated that Shufeldt's absence proved to be an embarrassment to the Korean government, for it left it without foreign advisors and deprived the progressives of leadership. If Foulk's delineation of the effect of Shufeldt's nonarrival is correct, and Foulk was certainly pro-progressive, then the progressives may have been pushed toward the December coup in the face of the conservative and pro-Chinese pressure out of fear of losing their position in the government, especially having lost the foreign and military advisers that they expected. Hilary Conroy has argued that "Admiral Shufeldt had not appeared, so the young Tokyo-trained cadets were leaderless." Shufeldt's decision not to go to Korea almost certainly damaged the progressive cause and may have accelerated the December coup.[27]

As Shufeldt turned away from Korea, he focused on the needs for an isthmian canal. While still in Washington as head of the Naval Advisory Board, he had begun a thorough investigation into the Panama canal route. In July 1884, he went to Panama to consider the merits of that route. The journey was an easy one to Colon and then by sea to San Francisco. Had his choice been limited to canals through Panama or Nicaragua, he would have preferred the Nicaraguan route. But by 1881 an alternative transportation system of transcontinental railroads was in operation. He reported unfavorably on the Panama route, declaring the work would be unfinished. In reality, however, Shufeldt now opposed the cutting of any canal across the isthmus at this time in the country's development. The Senate had just declined to ratify the Frelinghuysen-Zavala Treaty on a canal. Carrying his ideas of 1881 on the usefulness of a canal to their logical conclusion, Shufeldt explained why his views on a canal had changed:

> As to its commercial advantages, I submit that a canal across Nicaragua or any other part of the Isthmus will operate to the very great *disadvantage* of the Commerce of this Country.
> The United States now holds, by virtue of its railroads, the right of way across this Continent, & has, or ought to have, the commercial control of the Pacific Ocean. To open a canal would simply be to throw into the hands of England & other European Powers this commerce; or, in other words, we would build a canal through an American isthmus for the benefit of foreign commerce, as the French built a canal at Suez for the benefit of English commerce. The first result of this canal would be the domination of England, or Germany or France in the Pacific & the first victims to fall into the hands of either one of these Powers would be the Sandwich Islands, which in a naval or military point of view are essential to our supremacy on our Western Coast. The construction of a Canal therefore in a Commercial point of view is merely a matter of sentiment.[28]

Shufeldt feared that England would gain by the cutting of such a canal. He confessed he was unable to understand why the people of the Pacific slopes would be in favor of a project that would "inevitably shunt San Francisco off on a side track & confine that emporium of the West to its exports alone of wheat & wine." In his opinion, California should look "for a market in the Great Orient, teeming with population, which must eventually consume everything which she can produce."

The admiral thus assumed that a canal would undercut American commercial superiority in the Pacific Basin, based on control of the transcontinental railroads and California potential. He was also concerned for strategic reasons. In time of war, he confessed, the canal would be "utterly useless for naval purposes" because United States vessels would be forced to run a continuous blockade of an enemy's fleet. Even if the country's naval forces were doubled, they would have to be employed in defending the canal in a similar fashion to the English, who required their largest fleet for the protection of the English Channel. There would be an impact on neighboring states:

> it can readily be understood that any Maritime Power could blockade either terminus of the canal & that it would be impossible to return at any time by sea any garrison placed there in any forts which we might construct for its defence. Ships containing supplies or troops would be obliged to run a continuous blockade from any of our own ports to this point. . . . We would have to dominate over the States before mentioned & preserve uninterrupted railroad communication among a turbulent people through a difficult and sparsely settled country. Are we prepared to embrace within our limits those nations, under these conditions?

Shufeldt concluded that the United States should watch the progress of the Panama canal "and at the opportune moment take such means to control it as was adopted by England to control the French canal at Suez." At this point he asserted, "I believe Panama not Nicaragua to be the *Ultima thule*—the extreme limit of American domination on the American continent."

Such reflections, however, did not disturb the leisure of retirement. Shufeldt relaxed, taking daily rides in the country around Washington and dining with colleagues. But in 1885 he began to think of leaving the United States and going to live in the Far East, preferably Japan. Expenses in Washington cut deeply into his retirement salary, the Democrats were in power (and therefore by his definition the country was being mismanaged), and the Far East promised opportunities, especially in Korea, where he hoped to make his long-delayed visit. Opportunities there might be open to him that were denied him in Washington. He began to set his affairs in order, presenting his Damascus sword and the eight ivory and gold knives that he had received from the sultan of Zanzibar to the Smithsonian Institution.[29]

Soon Shufeldt set off with his daughter. He believed that he would probably not return for several years. They arrived in San Francisco, via Panama, on the steamer *San Blas* on June 26, 1886, and the next day the admiral was interviewed by a *San Francisco Chronicle* reporter at the Baldwin House Hotel.[30] Shufeldt impressed his interviewer with his "exceedingly impressive appearance, being six feet in height, massive in figure, without being portly, and with a face whose smile seemed cheerful, but whose frown might inspire dread." The overawed reporter found that the admiral also displayed "great conversational powers," especially when on the subject of the Panama canal and the American Navy. Having just observed the work on the canal as he passed through Panama, Shufeldt had not altered his opinions of three years earlier. The canal was possible and could be completed, but the time it would take to accomplish it, together with the "immeasurable sums of money" that would be swallowed up still formed the bases of his objections to the scheme. He continued to favor Nicaragua over Panama, if the choice were between those two alone. However, he told the reporter that the only scheme that should interest Americans was the Tehuantepec canal project of Captain James Eads, a ship-railroad transporting vessels on huge flatcars across the isthmus.

From the canal the *Chronicle* reporter diverted Shufeldt's attention to the condition and prospects for the service from which he had recently retired. Following his favorite division of the navy into personnel and material, Shufeldt had no hesitation in asserting that the former could be compared "without disparagement" with that of any country in the world. The fault of the navy, he argued, lay with the material. In the event of war, he anticipated that the United States naval forces would be swept from the seas by the ironclad fleets of other nations. Sharply, he preached to the nation its dangers in tones that anticipated in part Alfred Thayer Mahan's arguments of the 1890s:

> For a country so prosperous, so large in extent and numerous in population, such a state of things should not exist. We want ships—we want ships that won't sink; ships that have speed, and ships that can carry long guns. When we have these we will have a navy. As it is now, States that are insignificant and puny beside this great Nation boast of men-of-war that surpass anything we have. . . . A navy cannot be built in a day; it is like Rome. Ships require time to build, and sailors and officers require time to train and discipline. I suppose it is only a war or the prospect of a war that can awaken a sense of the necessity of a good navy. It will not be then as it was in 1861. We had in those times a merchant marine to fall back on, and now we have not. That is the difference.

Shufeldt explored the reasons for the seeming indifference in the nation and decided that it developed out of the growth and expansion of the middle states of the Union. Formerly, the seaboard cities and towns had been the pivots of power and influence. But with the center of population, industry, commerce, and enterprise rapidly being located inland, the representatives of inland states were blocking measures for a larger navy. "Of course," he added sarcastically, "they must feel that the guns and bombs of foreign men-of-war cannot possibly reach the Mississippi River. It would not hurt their interests much if New York or San Francisco were bombed to ashes." What concerned him most was the practical defenselessness of San Francisco and the west coast, but he was hopeful that this would change. The "unrest in European politics and the uncertainty of European governments" were inducing men of forethought in the country to build up the navy and the country's defenses. As he prepared to leave the country, he stated the message clearly for those men of forethought: "this navy could be made the best in the world with American workmen and material."

Retirement in the East, 1886–1889

In June Shufeldt left San Francisco for Japan and Korea. In Yokohama, he received a dispatch from the king of Korea, relayed through former United States minister Parker, urging him to make a personal visit. Consequently, he cabled to Denny and Foulk that he was coming to Korea, and, joined by his sons Mason and George, he set out with Molly. The west coast of Korea, where they landed near the capital, was vastly different from that Shufeldt had opened in 1882. The straggling fishing village of Chemulp'o by 1886 had grown into a developing commercial port, the outlet for the capital with a flourishing foreign section. The country was now the center of an open power struggle between China, Russia, and Japan, with the British acquiescing in "the avowed intention of China to reduce Corea to the condition of a province" in return for the annexation of Burma. The United States supported the Japanese contention that Korea was fully independent of China. On the power struggle in Korea, Shufeldt concluded that "while China ought perhaps to have a preponderating influence in Corea, owing to the geographical situation of the country as well as to the traditions of the people; still, at the same time, under such influences as now exist, Corea cannot look forward, either to peace or prosperity, until her political independence is secured. . . . If they, viz China, Russia and Japan would jointly guarantee the integrity of the Kingdom, its prosperity would be assured." In the international context Shufeldt was asking too much, though he had put his finger on the one solution that might have saved Korea the invasion of 1894 and 1905. Each nation believed in the paramount position of its own interests rather than in an international agreement guaranteeing Korean integrity.[31]

Shufeldt had several audiences with the king. But the admiral found that his visits excited jealousy among the pro-Chinese faction led by the Chinese resident, Yuan Shi Kai. He discontinued them after warning the king against "adopting any so-called Western ideas," especially the borrowing of money. He pointed out the "evil results of embarrassing a new nation with a public debt at a high rate of interest." Molly believed that the king was "very anxious" for Shufeldt to enter into the Korean service, but the admiral "positively refused," and the king thereupon invited him to stay as his guest at least for the winter. Shufeldt was persuaded, agreeing to remain longer than the month he had originally intended to stay.[32]

Over the winter of 1886–1887, Shufeldt lived very quietly in Seoul among the missionaries, teachers, and physicians who formed the bulk of the American community around the American legation. He wrote out for Henry Gerard Appenzeller, an American missionary who wanted his story, an account of the opening of Korea to the Western world. In January the admiral informed the king he would be leaving shortly. He would have liked to tour the country, but in view of the mounting attacks then being made on Foulk's position in the legation, he affirmed that his self-respect would not allow him to remain. He did not know when he might receive similar treatment. Though the king attempted to persuade him to stay, Shufeldt was adamant. In mid-February he left Seoul "in a blaze of glory," according to his daughter, and set out for Japan. Shufeldt's contributions to post-treaty Korea were negligible compared with his desire to see the country opened. He could have played a more significant part in Korean internal politics if he had had the motivation to challenge Yuan Shi Kai. His inclination after retirement from the navy, however, was to seek relaxation as much as possible.[33]

Shufeldt settled down in a house overlooking Nagasaki Bay, Kyushu. He noted that "everybody [is] very quiet here—the absolute freedom from excitement is really monotonous—still we enjoy it." "Living here," he noted, "nothing occurs to ruffle the even tenor of my existence, except the occasional arrival of the American mail, where I am disturbed, more particularly, by newspaper criticism upon the condition of the American navy."

For two hours every day the admiral went riding and bathing. Alternatively, he toured the countryside, taking vacations at the sulphur springs at Takeo and visiting the daimyos' old castles. He hated going into underground places, so did not enter the porcelain caves when Molly visited them. "He is not hard to please," Molly noted for her mother's benefit, "but as to asking him to make a visit of more than two or three days, you know as well as I do that it would be quite useless—he will be uncomfortable & so would everyone else." In mid-August Shufeldt stirred himself to dictate a letter on the American Navy to Molly, intending to publish it in one of the San Francisco newspapers. She observed, "we don't get on very rapidly. He does not like to dictate more than one hour or so a day in this hot weather, & as it will of course have to be copied when done, I will not probably have it ready for a mail or two." His daughter also confessed that she wished the admiral would write down his recollections of his life. Rather wistfully, she revealed, "so many people have asked him to do so, but I can't get him to consent."[34]

Shufeldt was disturbed by the indiscriminate abuse leveled at the American Navy, especially the long political squabble about the cruisers of the White Squadron; debate over the suitability of the *Dolphin* had made it "a byword and reproach throughout the world," particularly in the East. While he considered this damaging enough, he believed the antagonism between line and staff officers was undermining the harmony and efficiency he judged vital to the navy. The admiral coupled this statement on the navy to further reflections on the collapse of the American merchant marine. He sarcastically made his point by announcing that it would be more to the purpose to import the British captain and crew, because it would be much easier to build ships than train the personnel to man them. Loss of American commerce meant the disappearance of American seamen. Should a war come, he warned, the United States would have no war reserve of seamen. Disgusted, he left for a vacation with Molly in Takeo.[35]

When Shufeldt had visited Korea over the winter of 1886–1887, he had been alert to the possibility of attracting American capital into industrial and commercial enterprises. He had observed the export of hides was very largely in the hands of the American China and Japan Trading Company. Furthermore, he would have liked the Korean government to open another port on the northern coast in P'yongan Province where there were reputed to be large coal mines. Shufeldt also wished to see the government legalize the exportation of ginseng by establishing warehouses where merchants could buy it from the government at fixed prices, effectively stopping smuggling and increasing the country's wealth. He wrote to the press that "Corea is undoubtedly rich in gold, and notwithstanding that her mines are as yet undeveloped, about $2,000,000 per annum go abroad in the shape of gold dust."[36]

Two of the firms that Shufeldt hoped to interest in Korea were the American Trading Company of New York and Yokohama and the Union Ironworks of San Francisco. He kept in close touch with James R. Morse, one of the partners in the American Trading Company, who also procured orders for the Union Ironworks. One of the problems as far as Morse was concerned was the attitude of the American government with regard to Korean business opportunities. Shufeldt had written to him that George Foulk, chargé d'affaires in Seoul, would be driven from Korea by Chinese pressure. Morse agreed that "the milk and water policy of our Government has *upset* all your good work—and all Independent action in that country has been given a 'black eye' by the unscrupulous action of Judge O. N. Denny, who has proved himself unworthy the Country he hails from." Morse had discovered from the press that the Korean government proposed to give Americans mining concessions, but he glomily confessed he was becoming discouraged about business there.[37]

Shufeldt hoped for a better response from the headquarters of the Union Ironworks of San Francisco. He hoped to introduce Morse cartridges and Powler gun carriages into Korea and place the business with Union. Union's secretary, James O'B. Gunn, collected Shufeldt's check from the Navy Department each month and held it for him, serving as a bank for the admiral's drafts. Shufeldt was acting under blanket instructions from the president of Union, George W. Prescott, to enter into negotiations with the governments or residents of Japan, China, and Korea for the manufacture for them by Union of mining machinery, steam engines, iron, steel, or wooden vessels for war or commerce, railroad rolling stock, and railroad equipment. Shufeldt was also to secure franchises for the construction and management of railroads, navigation of rivers, and "any and all other franchises and rights which he may deem it advisable to obtain." All would be inoperative until approved by the company's head officers.[38]

Shufeldt eventually sent a letter from Walter D. Townsend, one of the Americans granted mining concessions by the king of Korea, to James O'B. Gunn, that analyzed the prospects for mining in Wentang district. Shufeldt believed Townsend's concession was "one of the richest districts in the country," and he wanted California capitalists to move into Korean mine development. Twice in his letter to Gunn, and obviously referring to the terms of the Union Ironworks instructions to him, Shufeldt stressed, "this is the first enterprise which I have thought proper to enter on & recommend to you." He attempted to persuade Union to offer a $2 million loan to Korea in return for the Un-san gold mining concession. Shufeldt's enthusiasm for the project was caught by his daughter. She wrote to her mother:

> I am very anxious that Father should, while out here, make some addition to his income, & so far there has been nothing which he could conscientiously recommend to his correspondences. On his present means he would never be content to live East [coast of America], nor could I ask him to let me often come from the Pacific Coast to see you, while if he had money, he would like the life in Washington, or the travel East every summer. . . . In *strict confidence,* I may say that there is a faint prospect of something good, but it is only in embryo, & *may* come to nothing.[39]

Molly, Morse, and Shufeldt were disappointed in their hopes for "something good." The Union Ironworks rejected the opportunity to stimulate American capital to move into Korean mining in 1887. Gunn notified Morse that even if it were possible to organize an American syndicate to accept the proposed conditions, it would take a very long time to accomplish it, especially on the west coast. He acknowledged that the Shufeldt-Morse correspondence had been shown to the manager of "a very strong American combination of Capital invested in mines, both in U.S. and also in Mexico," who had turned down the prospects. Political instability in a Korea beset by Russian, Japanese, and Chinese intrigues, together with the indifferent attitude of the American government were among the reasons for the refusal. Furthermore, Gunn feared that foreign intrigue would operate to block American development. He candidly asserted that "no American syndicate will make this loan" and suggested that Morse and Shufeldt undertake the development of the mines themselves. Naturally, Union could supply them with the machinery, payment in advance. Gunn, however, did thank Shufeldt for his "kindly efforts in the East [which] have done us much good." Molly wistfully commented: "There are brilliant opportunities in Korea, but they will be availed of by other nations, whose commercial enterprises are supported by their governments—Our people fear to venture & no wonder, but it is a great pity." Shufeldt missed the chance to invest in one of the richest gold mines in Asia. Townsend and the American Trading Company, however, did supply mining equipment, munitions, furniture, and railroad stock to Korea and invested in railroads and mines as well as gaining a timber-cutting concession from the Korean government. American businessmen established the first steam-driven rice cleaning plant in Korea, undertook the construction of railroads, introduced streetcars and electric light to Seoul, and began gold mining.[40]

Shufeldt settled well into the stereotyped life of the foreign community in Japan. He went to the Church of England services nearly every Sunday with Molly. The cost of living in Nagasaki was low enough for him to live comfortably on his retirement salary. Molly noted that he "could not afford to live as he liked anywhere else." However, she was keen to return to the United States, hoping something might develop to increase their income. The one disturbing factor in Shufeldt's life was still his relationship with his sons. The admiral regarded Robert as conceited and, at times, insane. Agreeing with this assessment, his daughter declared that Shufeldt had little pleasure from his sons, though George was reputed to be doing well as marshal at Shanghai. But when Mason was serving with the Asiatic squadron they did not hear from him. Later, when he did come to visit, he contracted a return bout of Madagascar fever. He remained for three months being nursed by Molly. She had no sympathy for him at all, considered him "beyond hope" in his attitudes, and blamed the Naval Academy for inspiring much of his weakness. Equally contemptuously, she thought Robert had a blood vessel on the brain that rendered him insane. To her the whole tragedy was that they had needed a strong hand over them when they were younger and their father had been away at sea too much of the time to provide it. But once grown up they were so bad, she believed, that she declared Shufeldt was "dragged down by his sons." She was prepared to tolerate George but affirmed, "as for the other two they are simply beyond hope. Father says so very plainly." Molly applied her ultimate criterion to the sons by declaring that a woman would be safe marrying George but she could not say the same thing for his two brothers. The admiral himself doted on his daughter. In November 1887, he gave her a $1,000 certificate of deposit for herself.[41]

During "the warmest weather known in Nagasaki for eighteen years" in July 1888, Shufeldt took Molly on a twenty-day cruise to Vladivostok, returning in the same steamer. Unfortunately, he picked a difficult time. The weather on the voyage was bad, and on the return journey they sailed in rain and fog. The voyage, however, refreshed him and set him thinking about his old cruises. It was probably at this time also that Shufeldt decided to return to the United States. Molly had been restless in Nagasaki for some time, but could not find it within herself to ask Shufeldt to leave his peaceful life. "I wait for some motion of his own," she confided to her mother, but at the end of the Vladivostok journey she revealed, "Father thinks we will reach home about the middle or last of March, but there is no certainty." She thought he would sell his Washington house to buy elsewhere: "he hates to live where he can so easily be reached by those sons of his." But the election of 1888 helped to change his mind. With a Republican victory expected, the country would return once more to the values of Republican party control. Deciding to return, and as he prepared to sail, he was cheered by the news of the elections results. His cousin, Albert Dibblee, informed him that "Your friends will again hold the reins—and especially Mr. Blaine will again be a power in the land." Dibblee noted for Shufeldt's sake, "This change must make Washington a more congenial home for you and perhaps may induce you to return." Shufeldt agreed and embarked on a leisurely return home. He sailed with Molly for Shimonoseki, Hong Kong, Singapore, Colombo, and the Mediterranean. He arrived in New York at the beginning of April 1889.[42]

Ebb Tide

Shufeldt wished to leave the party battles of the 1870s and 1880s behind him when he returned to Washington. For seven years he had achieved this aim despite the temptations to return to active politics. In June the new secretary of state, once again James G. Blaine, offered him the post of the United States minister to China. Shufeldt asked for time to ponder the offer. The west coast press, jealous of the interest of California in the Chinese immigration question, was enthusiastic about Shufeldt. Albert Dibblee, living in San Francisco, expected something "of a howl" in the city because a "coast man" had not been selected, but he found "nothing of the sort has appeared." The *San Francisco Evening Bulletin* wished Shufeldt, as a man "of breadth and penetration," to become "the right man in the right place" and accept the post. Dibblee considered that the government did a wise thing "to select a representative free from the Sand Lot influences upon the China question that so infest this coast." He judged that any California man would have had to pander to the violent and unreasoning prejudice that prevailed in the state. Shufeldt, however, eventually declined the offer, as it would have involved the sacrifice of his pay as a retired admiral.[43]

To fill his time, Shufeldt visited Admiral Chandler and talked with him about the strategy of Rear Admiral John G. Walker's Squadron of Evolution, designed to test the qualities of the ships of the White Squadron and the new gunboat *Yorktown* and work out tactics for the new squadron. During the summer of 1890 the press magnified the struggle for power in the navy between Admirals Walker and Bancroft Gherardi. Shufeldt took a keen interest, for he did not agree that a squadron of evolution was needed, arguing that it was "simply a repetition of history [like the 1871 European squadron] & only a pretext for having a good time in the classic waters of the Mediterranean." The retired admiral picked up his pen for the last time on naval matters:

> a Squadron of Evolution, consisting simply of steel cruisers is outside of the domain of American Naval Policy. The Navy of the United States won its highest glory in the War of 1812 on the Ocean in simple combats with the enemy, & it may be added that the only legitimate naval combat in the Rebellion was that between the *Kearsage* & the *Alabama* and was also a single combat. In point of fact these cruisers are but the rovers of the sea; destined in any war which is likely to happen to us, to cruise upon the ocean for the destruction of commerce; to alarm an enemy's coast & to destroy the confidence of the owners in the protection afforded by the flag which floats over their ships. For this purpose men will be found who like Paul Jones dared to venture even upon the English coast; or Porter, who cleared out the Pacific Ocean, or even like Semmes in the *Alabama* who caused the American Flag to disappear from all the broad seas.

Shufeldt had finally revealed his unwillingness to accept the principles of fleet supremacy that Alfred Thayer Mahan was just then beginning

The Legacy of an Expansionist 331

to popularize. In dismissing even the notion of a squadron of evolution, Shufeldt seemingly approved of cruiser warfare against commerce. He also attacked the policy of the Naval Academy in having a graduate write a thesis on subjects "more or less remote from his professional duties." He desired recruits to go to sea for training and indicated what his policy would be for the navy:

> when an officer who has scarcely been upon the water for twenty odd years[*] is appointed to command a Squadron for the instruction of his juniors in the doctrine of evolution . . . it seems to me that these ships should be sent to the ports of the world where we desire to create favorable impressions both commercial and political. We have indeed no interest whatever in European politics; we keep no armies & navies in battle array, our naval forces must necessarily consist of defensive vessels upon our own coasts. It is there alone & in the contiguous waters that we hoist the Flag of *nolime tangere.* . . . More good has come to the Country . . . by the cruises of single ships to the remote ports of the world . . . than to the presence of American Squadrons, which, wherever they may have been sent, have been, & always will be insignificant when compared with those of the other Naval Powers of the world.[44]

Within the context of the debate over naval policy that was developing in the United States, Shufeldt thus turned away from large squadrons and instead accepted the argument of coast defense and overseas vessels for political and commercial "impressions" within strict limits. He had assumed that the American Navy would always be inferior to European fleets. Though, like Mahan, he stressed the usefulness of the navy in a commercial context, Shufeldt differed in evaluating strategy for that navy. Acting with the spirit of the navalist, Mahan combined a desire for a large battleship navy with a cry for commercial outlets; Shufeldt assigned the commercial task to independent cruises, such as he had undertaken in the *Ticonderoga,* and turned down the call for an overweening navy.

In 1890 Shufeldt became seriously ill. Horace Allen, who was just then emerging as a powerful figure in Korean affairs as United States secretary of legation, wrote to him from Korea advising him to give up smoking "on the sly." Just as he was recovering from his illness, the news was broken to him of the death of Mason, in Madagascar, while employed by the organizers or the Chicago World Columbian Exposition to secure pygmies for display. Shufeldt engaged in a long wrangle with the exposition's managers, who wanted refunded the money they

---

*Walker had retired after the Civil War to be vice-president of a railroad. He later served as chief of the Bureau of Navigation from 1881–1887.

had loaned to Mason, and with Consul George F. Hollis at Cape Town, who wanted payment for funeral expenses. "It strikes me as very cold blooded that he should be left stranded in Africa," Shufeldt complained bitterly to Walker Fearn, head of the exposition's foreign affairs section. He rejected Hollis' draft. The consul responded by refusing to send Mason's effects until the matter was settled. Eventually Shufeldt paid for the burial expenses and the consul's debts.[45]

In October 1892 Shufeldt became ill again and only recovered after a vacation in Virginia. For five years after 1890 he was in generally poor health, largely as a result of influenza. This was complicated further in October 1894, when on a visit to Hamilton, Virginia, his team of horses bolted and threw him from the carriage. His left side was badly bruised and his face required stitching in two places. The admiral was confined to bed and could not move without assistance. It did not deter him from later driving the same team, but he had suffered a severe shock and, as a result, he prepared a last will. On November 14, 1894, he drafted the testament. Its terms were highly beneficial to Molly, for she was to receive regular payments from a trust administered by the National Safe Deposit Savings and Trust Company as long as she lived. After her death the payments were to go to Sarah Abercrombie Shufeldt, Robert's daughter, until she reached the age of twenty-one years, when the estate was to be conveyed to her in fee simple. Should Sarah die before Molly, or before reaching the age of twenty-one in the event that Molly died before her, the estate was to go in fee simple to "the person or persons answering the description of her *heirs* at law." Shufeldt's manuscripts were left to Molly, who was to retain those she deemed valuable and to destroy the balance. The residue and remainder of Shufeldt's personal property not specifically bequeathed to anyone was to go to Molly. Shufeldt's son Robert, who had become both a leading ornithologist and a racial bigot on the Negro question, was to receive nothing. George A. Shufeldt was allowed only his mother's portrait and any one article of Shufeldt's personal effects as a memento. If Molly were to sell Shufeldt's personal property passed to her by the terms of the will, then she was to give George $500 of the proceeds. Shufeldt regretted he could not make the amount larger. He related the will in his daughter's favor "in consideration of her devotion to my comfort and health for the past twenty five years." Moreover, he desired the most economical funeral and left clear instructions to be buried "wherever I die and to have nothing to mark my grave but the plainest headstone. I do not want any naval ceremonies of any kind at my funeral."[46]

In the summer of 1895 Shufeldt again visited the mountains of Virginia for a vacation. When he returned to Washington in September he fell ill. When his condition worsened, Francis Gunnell diagnosed an

The Legacy of an Expansionist

attack of bronchitis. Pneumonia developed and Shufeldt's condition became critical. Gunnell knew that the admiral would be unable to last another winter and prepared Molly for the inevitable. She was with her father when he died quietly at 10:30 A.M. on November 7. Despite the request in his will for no naval ceremonies, Shufeldt was buried in Arlington, the casket being borne by eight naval apprentices from the Washington navy yard, a tribute that Shufeldt would have appreciated. On a large granite monument bearing his name and age is carved the message, "Until the day dawns."[47]

Conclusion

Robert Wilson Shufeldt's career illuminates a transitional phase of American expansion, the period from 1850 to 1885. His thoughts and endeavors to extend American influence into many areas of the world during those years show him to be one of the foremost naval and commercial expansionists of the nineteenth century. Within the context of such expansion the only nineteenth-century naval officers to compare with him were David Porter, Charles Wilkes, Matthew Calbraith Perry, and Alfred Thayer Mahan. Of the four, Porter first realized the opportunities of the Pacific when he cruised in its waters in the USS *Essex* during the War of 1812, destroyed the British whaling fleet, and pressed President Madison vigorously to dispatch a government naval and military expedition to the northwest coast of America and Japan in 1815. Wilkes led the United States Exploring Expedition that sailed for southern seas, discovered Antarctica, and surveyed the Hawaiian Islands and the northwest coast from 1838 to 1842. Perry, who has long received recognition from diplomatic historians for the opening of Japan, was also an annexationist who wanted to control most of the northern Pacific islands such as the Bonins, Coffins, Hawaiian Islands, Ryukyus, and Taiwan, together with Siam, Cambodia, Cochin China, parts of Borneo and Sumatra and many islands of the Indonesian archipelago, as naval stations and dependencies. Mahan has received most attention as naval theorist, historian, and synthesizer of the naval debates of the 1890s. Of the four, however, only Perry rivalled Shufeldt in combining diplomacy and naval activity with the conscious promulgation of theories designed to extend American influence to many parts of the world.[1]

As a diplomat Shufeldt obviously differed from Perry. The admiral's treaty was negotiated in far more difficult surroundings, and in a more complicated international context, than was the commodore's. The opening of Korea consummated the work of Shufeldt's diplomatic mentor, William H. Seward, as well as rounding out Shufeldt's own dreams for Korea dating back to 1867. As Tyler Dennett has observed, the opening was "the most important political action undertaken by the United States in Asia until the occupation of the Philippines in 1898,"[2] and Shufeldt accomplished it through the agency of Li Hung-chang and the Chinese government in the dusty heat of a Tientsin summer, not through a display of force off the mouth of the Seoul River, as Perry had done in Japan. Moreover, there is little doubt that Shufeldt underestimated the forces at work in the Far East and misjudged any commitment that the United States might be prepared to make after the treaty to control those forces, which tore it apart by warfare in 1894 and 1905. But he was perfectly aware of what those forces were when he warned that Korea would become a battleground of any future wars between China, Japan, and Russia. Far from encouraging him to keep away, his diagnosis made him more eager to bring the United States into this arena.

The full significance of the Korean treaty should be measured directly in relation to the motives that caused Shufeldt to stick assiduously to his task in China during 1881 and 1882. He remained for a variety of reasons—his desire to make the Pacific an American sea, his beliefs in commercial expansion, the lure of fame for securing the opening of the Hermit Kingdom, his zeal for promoting United States policies and interests abroad, his concern for the safety of sailors engaged in commerce, his sense of power, his belief in an overriding mission for the United States in Asia, and, not least, his orders from three secretaries of state. To regard the treaty merely as a curious venture by an aberrant United States into the cockpit of oriental rivalries is to miss the point as well as the evidence. The opening of Korea forged a further link in a chain of thought that for thirty years stretched across the Pacific through California, Tehuantepec and the isthmus, Cuba, and the Mississippi River heartland.

For Shufeldt the treaty was the culmination of an interest in Korea that commenced with his tour of duty with the Asiatic squadron in 1866–1867. He willingly entered the arena of growing dispute over whether Korea was a Chinese dependency or not, and his treaty contributed to the notion that Korea was independent—a position that Secretary of State Frelinghuysen assumed once the treaty was ratified. United States policy, after Shufeldt, supported Japanese contentions, though for different reasons, that denied Chinese suzerainty over Korea. It also demonstrated that the United States was prepared to pursue an active commercial policy in East Asia that underpinned the later Open Door Notes and was not loathe to initiate negotiations that involved the country in the sensitive international relations of the area.

As a formal diplomatic negotiator in Korea, Liberia, Muscat, Madagascar, and Zanzibar, Shufeldt showed tenacity, even doggedness, but his frustrations, which surfaced most clearly in the Sargent letter and his later relations with Li Hung-chang, sometimes marred his effectiveness. This applied equally to his exchange with Seward over Mexico in 1862, with the British and Liberians over the boundary question in 1879, and with the Chinese over Korea in 1882. Yet Shufeldt also displayed, when negotiating, a willingness to support local traders against central governments, as in Madagascar in 1879, or central governments against local traders, as in Liberia earlier in the year, if the results benefited United States trade relations with the areas concerned. In all of his negotiations this latter goal was paramount, although in some his emotional fervor tended to reduce his effectiveness.

Shufeldt's Korean work attested to his fascination with the Pacific as an objective for American endeavor. Following his post-Civil War assumptions that the Pacific was the ocean bride of America and that Japan and China were the bridesmaids, his conclusion to "determine while yet in our power, that no commercial power or hostile flag can float with impunity over the long swell of the Pacific sea" was highly revealing. He related that drive to the East and West coming together and reaching the point "where search for Empire ceases & human power attains its climax." He expected California energy to be the means for bringing China into "the family of nations." Such a result anticipated his call in 1871 for a canal to join the Atlantic and Pacific oceans. Assuming that the commercial decline apparent in 1871 meant that the country had been driven off the Atlantic, the canal became a necessity because "the Pacific Ocean *is* & *must* be essentially American." Late in 1880, en route to Honolulu at the end of the *Ticonderoga*'s cruise, in a call that was echoed exactly by Secretary of the Navy Thompson's *Annual Report,* Shufeldt pointed to the acquisition of Alaska and the Aleutians and the treaties with Japan, the Hawaiian Islands, and Samoa to enlarge the commercial domain. Shufeldt also informed Thompson, writing from Japan in 1880, that America was the pioneer of the Pacific—"a position which she must not only recognize but claim"—and in 1884 he declared that the United States ought to have, by virtue of the new transcontinental railroads, the commercial control of the Pacific Ocean.

Commerce and the Pacific were the keys to the future for Shufeldt. From his pre-Civil War involvement with the Collins Line and the Louisiana–Tehuantepec Company to the signing of the Korean treaty he constantly urged the United States government to extend its commercial interests into the Caribbean, Latin America, Africa, the Pacific, and the Far East. Such commercial promptings were given a Pacific slant as well as an urgency after the Civil War because he deemed that

Conclusion

England, France, and Prussia had proved to have too much weight on the Atlantic. Thus Shufeldt described the Pacific, Alaska, and the Aleutians as the arms that America stretched forth to embrace the nations and commerce of the East. During the depression of 1877, when he considered, and published, *The Relation of the Navy to the Commerce of the United States,* Shufeldt regarded commercial expansion as the only solution to the question of deporting producers or having starving millions on hand, a clear illustration of his expectation that foreign demand would compensate for the satiation of the domestic market. Shufeldt also appreciated that force, or the presence of men-of-war, was often the means to ensure that new markets could be opened.

By the time of the centennial he was prepared to recognize Africa as the great undeveloped market remaining in a world of seemingly overstocked markets. The cruise of the *Ticonderoga* on both coasts of that continent, billed as the American Naval and Commercial Expedition to Africa, together with his wish to establish Edward Wilmot Blyden as a roving consul for the United States in the interior, the consular scheme for West Africa from the palm oil rivers to Cape Town, and the negotiation of new (together with the renegotiation of old) treaties in Madagascar, Johanna, and Zanzibar, all attest to Shufeldt's tenacity in seeking to deliver "the great commercial prize of the world" to the United States.

Shufeldt constantly reminded his government of the advantages of commerce from the more than fifty ports of call on his 36,000-mile world cruise. From Borneo he told Thompson that he wished to create a prestige in the East for the benefit of American commerce. From the Philippines he called for government protection of commerce in 1880— a message he first sent to the government from St. Helena in 1879. As early as 1867 he wanted to survey the Yangtze River, move the American shipping and trading frontier 400 miles farther up that river, and survey the Japanese Islands, the Yellow Sea, and the coast of Korea. In the 1880s he considered United States and Chinese interests greater than those of other nations, felt it was commerce that was insisting on the opening of Korea, and informed the government from Persia that the cruise of the *Ticonderoga* would be useless unless it convinced the government of the vital importance of a reorganization and extension of the United States consular system. Perhaps his clearest expression was the blunt message from Bombay, when he characterized the United States as "a nation which in the process of time must become the center of commercial power."

Commercial outlets were absolutely vital. Following the trough of the depression of 1874–1877, Shufeldt defined the problem of overproduction quite simply as "a question of starving millions." He wanted such production to increase the opportunities for commercial shipping that would require "commercial outlets" in Africa, through Liberia and the Congo, and in Asia through Korea. Moreover, he made himself active in leading expeditions into the commercial highways he identified. He had wanted to lead forces into Tehuantepec, even during the disadvantageous years of the Civil War. In 1867 he took the *Wachusett* up the Yangtze River to return Colton Salter to his consular post and, at the same time, he pointed out the great trading possibilities of the river for American commerce. His world cruise concentrated on prodding the State and Navy departments to initiate action in Africa, especially in Sierra Leone, Liberia, St. Paul de Loanda, the St. Paul River and the Niger Valley, the Congo, Madagascar, Johanna, Zanzibar, the Persian Gulf, and, finally, through the "barred gates" of Korea. Only rarely did Shufeldt extend his analysis to embrace a concept of colonial possessions, except in the case of Liberia, which he termed a "quasi-colony" of the United States; Tehuantepec, which he wanted to control and occupy militarily during the Civil War; Port Hamilton, off the southern coast of Korea, which he wanted as a bargaining pawn; or when he mentioned to Molly that he would like to "annex" the whole Orient. Although he reflected at length on the British empire, he usually did not extend his analysis to dwell on the possibility that political and military solutions for new colonies may have arisen from the British desire to preserve commercial interests from the serious challenges of new and vigorous nations.

Before and during the Civil War, Shufeldt focused additional expansionist desires outside of Tehuantepec, on the Spanish island of Cuba. He anticipated its attainment by the American Union, and although he recognized it was a problem leading to internal factional strife for the country as early as 1855, he explored the ramifications for the island for Truman Smith during the Civil War even when he feared "Africanization" and the "barbarism of another San Domingo." After the Civil War he agonized over whether bringing Cuba into the Union would create racial problems and conflicts in society, and he shied away from annexation at first on the grounds of an "extension of the area of disaffection in our own country." At one point, in May 1869, because of the racial implications, he decided that Cuba should work out "her own salvation." Yet he also believed that Grant deliberately "killed Cuba" by not intervening, and on another occasion he openly advocated annexation and imperialism. Until the 1880s he wanted Cuba, despite the racial problems he considered to be caused by slaves, Chinese, and degraded young Cubans, as a Caribbean anchor point to guard the approaches to any isthmian canal.

In such a context, the call for the opening of a canal fell logically into place. Shufeldt linked his Asian surveys with his wish to see a canal across a Central American isthmus. With the "supremacy of the Atlantic Ocean" gone from America and the Pacific still awaiting the "American flag," a ship canal would offer Americans the desired commercial opportunities in the Pacific. For years, therefore, culminating with his 1870 survey of Tehuantepec, Shufeldt pressed upon the government the necessity of an American canal under American control, so that China and Japan could be reached and thereby acquire "a new civilization & adopt a new creed." Shufeldt was fascinated by the possibilities of controlling the Isthmus of Tehuantepec for such an American transit route. During the first year of the Civil War he tempted Seward with the claim that Tehuantepec presented "the best natural highway between the Atlantic and Pacific Oceans and the shortest for us between our Eastern & Western possessions by over 1000 miles of sea travel." He feared Confederate seizure of the isthmus and went to Mexico City in 1862 partly to forestall such an eventuality. The proposed treaty that he showed to Mexican foreign minister Doblado would have placed American black colonists on the isthmus. He argued that the acquisition of Tehuantepec would circumscribe the limits of the Confederacy and prevent it spreading to the shores of the Pacific. Shortly thereafter he was ready to take possession and proposed to infuse an "American Element by the military occupation of the isthmus." He discussed indirect control with Frederick W. Seward and also mulled over the possibilities of making the Tehuantepec canal "bear the same relation to the trade of the United States that the Erie Canal does to the State of New York." He considered it was militarily defensible as well as being the shortest route between the east and west coasts. His own survey in 1870–1871 was designed to discover if such a route was practicable, and he felt triumphant when his engineer, Estevan Fuertes, found the water for a feeder at the right elevation. He wanted the government to select the route that, while satisfying interoceanic demands, would, at the same time, conduce the most to the development of United States overseas and domestic trade. Yet he judged the canal more advantageous, initially, to American, rather than world, commerce and believed that such a canal would be an extension of the Mississippi River to the Pacific Ocean and convert the Gulf of Mexico into an American lake. Paramount in his mind was the assumption that it was the only route the United States government could control and that it would render the United States and its territorial possessions "circumnavigable." As such it was the device that would enable the government and commerce "to go hand in hand to further development, until are reached and taught the remotest corners of the East and the rudest barbarians of the Pacific Isles." The canal was thus important for the access it would give the United States to the Pacific "field of our commercial triumphs."

In 1876 Shufeldt thus demanded that the United States be involved in building an isthmian canal as a link in a chain from the Mississippi across the Pacific. He showed that he placed American ability to defend and control the canal, together with its commercial proximity to the gulf, above all considerations and advocated throwing troops into Mexico, if necessary, to defend any canal built at Tehuantepec. These were the two reasons—distance and strategic considerations—why he rejected Panama and Nicaragua in favor of Tehuantepec, when he became involved in the debate of the 1880s on the desirability of a canal. In addition, he displayed an ability to think through the problem of how such a canal would involve American security and the future disposition of both Cuba and the Hawaiian Islands.

After the building of the transcontinental railroads, Shufeldt feared that the monopoly created for carrying bulk materials across the continent by virtue of those railroads might then be undermined by a canal. He recognized railroads as landed commercial highways and preached that message when he witnessed the impact of the developing South African railroad network. Though he did not dwell at great length on railroads, to Shufeldt they produced trade just as did shipping. In the 1880s he feared English dominance of an isthmian canal after the lesso of the Suez Canal takeover bid. The call for an isthmian canal in the 1880s, which corresponded almost exactly with Shufeldt's sentiments of the 1870s, drowned out the railroad-oriented opposition. Americans decided they could build a canal, defend it with the navy they were building at the same time, and control the commercial artery to the west coast and East Asia. In both cases of this support for a canal in the 1870s and his opposition to Panama and his qualified support for Nicaragua in the 1880s, Shufeldt was consistent in attempting to preserve United States control of the internal commercial carrying trade. Railroads or canals were, in the last resort, just alternative methods to preserve that control, which called for different approaches and policies in the Caribbean and on the continent to realize the desirable end result of preserving American hegemony in that trade.

The instruments to help the United States regain commercial vitality overseas would be large, fast steamships and government subsidies. Such steam vessels would be fitted for commerce destruction in time of war and merged with a navy of coast defense vessels such as the monitors. Early in his career, when Shufeldt identified himself with the younger naval officers who were engaged in promoting steam and screw propulsion for national warships, he was more attuned to the possibilities of steam for the navy. He personified the application of the early Industrial Revolution in the United States to the navy—coal energy converted into speed through steam rather than size and bulk. He respected the strength of the monitors in the Civil War, even when he was cramped in the smaller ones such as the USS *Kaatskill,* but he preferred the wider scope of the *Proteus* until he found her outsteamed by large blockade-runners. He envied the British their large, fast steamers for India, capable of carrying two thousand troops each voyage, five times a year. When dealing with successive secretaries of the navy and with Congress in the 1870s and the 1880s, he pleaded for the building or completion of monitors such as the *Puritan* and *Monadnock* but only if steamers such as the *Trenton* were added. Yet, in all of his correspondence and conversations with Secretaries of the Navy Thompson and Chandler, in his work on the second Naval Advisory Board in 1882-1883, and during the conversations in the Senate with Senator Butler in 1884, he demonstrated a sharp ability to distinguish between the immediately attainable and the prospectively desirable—between the navy of the present, which he usually considered constricted by personnel problems and congressional financing, and the navy of the future, which he contemplated in terms of the 9,000-ton vessel that the British were deploying in the 1880s. The latter navy, never articulated clearly and systematically by Shufeldt, was always conceived of as large and based on the power of steam.

Shufeldt did not, as did Mahan after him, work out a historical basis of sea power or preach for large fleet concentrations. The closest he came to a historical perspective was to review the work of the United States Navy in his pamphlets *The Relation of the Navy to the Commerce of the United States* and *The United States Navy in connection with the Foundation, Growth and Prosperity of the Republic of Liberia* and when he dropped hints about "the more ponderous ships of war" or the British vessels of 9,000 tons with guns *en barbette.* His last expression on the navy tended to disapprove of the Squadron of Evolution, which, he indicated, was "outside of the domain of American Naval Policy." To the end of his days, Shufeldt considered navies were for defending one's own coast, cruising for the destruction of commerce, clearing an enemy's coast, and driving up insurance rates to destroy the confidence of foreign owners in the abilities of their own naval forces to protect them—all of which meshed with his own considerations of the primacy of commercial expansion as national policy.

Shufeldt always considered that it was more important for the personnel of a navy, rather than the ships, to be efficient. The latter could be efficient only when the former were. The condition of the navy in Reconstruction America generally disheartened him. He called it "absolutely stagnant." He recognized that the institution was pervaded by a spirit of caste and conservatism, "prematurely old," requiring not only a reorganization but a regeneration as well. He was disturbed about the criticism within the navy itself, sufficiently to write from retirement in

Japan to the San Francisco press about it. His administrative career in the navy was tuned toward searching for, and increasing, efficiency, especially apparent in his support of the naval apprenticeship scheme and his efforts on behalf of the ordinary seaman. The search for efficiency was the key. The changes in punishment and in recruiting practices, the provision of cleaner receiving ships and training vessels, the alteration in the location of the ships' hospitals, and his call for "an intelligent revision of the naval code . . . to harmonize it with the spirit of the age," all foreshadowed a more humane treatment of the men. The latter were the backbone of the navy, more important than the ships. Efficiency on naval vessels, he considered, began with a genuine concern for the welfare of the crew. "Ships & guns," he wrote in 1878, "are subordinate in importance to the proper education of the men." His parting message for Richard W. Thompson, when he left the Bureau of Equipment and Recruiting, was that "the efficiency of the Navy depends in a very great degree upon the physical condition of its personnel," and on another occasion, he more bluntly asserted, "the efficiency of the Navy depends upon its officers and men and not upon its ships and guns."

Shufeldt spent considerable energy in attempting to convince the Navy Department and Congress of the importance of the navy as a pioneer of commerce. He related his concern to extend commerce by using the navy in his pamphlet on the relation of the navy to commerce, originally written as a letter to Congressman Leopold Morse in 1878, and he characterized the merchant marine and the navy as joint apostles for the greatness of the United States. He wanted government subsidies to steamship lines for carrying mails and passengers, such as that gained by the Collins Line and by the Louisiana–Tehuantepec Company in the 1850s. In the 1880s he called for a reorganization of the executive departments of the government to place all merchant marine interests and maritime matters under one marine department headed by a secretary of marine.

As a naval officer, Shufeldt was concerned with the acquisition of strategic bases, though he usually buried his suggestions in dispatches to the secretary of the navy. As early as 1868 he called for the annexation of Port Hamilton, off the southern coast of Korea; a call he reiterated in 1880. He wanted to use Liberia and Korea as entrances into West and East Africa, a suggestion with both commercial and strategic overtones. The logbooks of his voyages are filled with minutely detailed reports and descriptions of his investigations into the possibilities of establishing naval bases in desirable harbors along the coasts of China, Korea, Hawaii, and Africa. At one time, during the Civil War, he would have sanctioned the partition of Mexico, if the United States could have gained Tehuantepec by the act. His world cruise established for him the best location for coaling stations, and his treaties with kings Balambé and Lamarese in Madagascar and with the sultans of Johanna and Zanzibar were designed to make them accessible to American merchants and to provide ports of call for the navy's warships.

Shufeldt's desire to increase American influence in the world became a type of secular religion for him. In part it arose because of objections to the perceived influence of the British but mainly because of his belief that American civilization stood on higher ground than any other. He filled quires of paper on the British influence he encountered on his world cruise, and his reports on trade, commerce, the canal, and his Oriental ventures were all, in the last resort, designed to increase and serve the growth of American influence. At one point he told Molly that he clenched his teeth at the prospects for his country. After his initial visit to see Li Hung-chang, in 1880, he revealed that he wanted the United States to act because it was "a duty which we owe to these people to become the pioneers of a more enlightened policy in the East." His 1868 lecture on "Western Civilization in the East" to a Stamford audience pointed out the superiority of American versions of civilization. His reports of 1878–1880 confirmed such diagnoses. In a secular sense, he wanted the United States to protect weak countries, such as Siam, which he observed on his world cruise, from the encroachments of imperial powers and to encourage "commercial intercourse and intimate relations without interfering either with their policies or their religion." Yet his treaty with Korea did not, in the long run, live up to that objective, for American diplomats and missionaries did interfere in both areas after 1882. He declared that the United States, "while demanding protection for its citizens, should ask for nothing more than she is willing to concede." At times such thoughts took on a lyrical quality. When he arrived in the valley of Mesopotamia, his emotions and yearnings for the spread of the secular gospel of Americanism overflowed any dikes of reserve, and he proclaimed:

> in the process of time America has been born, the instrument perhaps, though the youngest of nations—to bring back to the Euphrates—the blessings of a liberal religion and a free Government. . . . In almost a moral and religious sense therefore the display of the American flag, in these sacred waters and over the cradle of civilization, is a duty we owe to mankind—as well as to ourselves.
>
> . . . The Government of the United States is the product of the ages of experiment. Its flag represents the result up to the 19th century of the Christian era. It is the sign and symbol of modern civilization—It involves a responsibility and dictates a course of action.

Shufeldt was not unique in holding such views. Like Mahan and John Tyler Morgan, John Fiske, Josiah Strong, Henry Cabot Lodge,

John Hay, John A. Kasson, and Theodore Roosevelt, he believed it was the duty of the United States to "uplift and civilize" the "barbarians" of the world. Though he was plainly unhappy about the activities of American Christian missionaries in Asia in 1867, when he regretted that "the preachers of a gospel of peace, should seem so often to need the interpretations of a Gunboat in order to make the heathen understand them," it was probably more because of their style of life than the nature of the message. He made this plain in his lecture, "Western Civilization in the East," when he condemned the personal luxury of missionaries living in China. But he did not mind using missionaries for his own ends as he used the Reverend Hunter Corbett, an American missionary in Chefoo, as interpreter on his first voyage to Korea in 1867. Though on one occasion he objected to the "unceasing chatter in the preaching of Christianity" and condemned the pre-Civil War attitude of the southern slaveholder that "he christianize the Negro," Shufeldt was not averse to using the power of religious proselytism for American purposes. When he lectured on Liberia in 1877, he emphasized to the American Colonization Society that Christianity was the religion of the future in Africa, "essential not only to her salvation, but to her temporal welfare," especially as a bulwark against Islam. In that lecture, he recommended Liberia as "the initial point for American effort in the Christianization of Africa." Later, when the message was sent from Africa, to the secretary of the navy, Shufeldt edited out the Christianization and substituted, "Liberia is the objective point for American trade."

Closely linked to Shufeldt's conception of civilization were his views on race, the burdens of the Anglo-Saxon, the role of the Negro in American life, and other races in foreign lands. When he was in command of the USS *Conemaugh* off Winyah Bay, South Carolina, during the Civil War, at the time that the old gray-haired slave escaped to his vessel, he claimed in his diary, "I protest that I have no prejudice of color—I have enjoyed the intellectual society of many great and good negroes—in Liberia—& St. Domingo—and yet with that detestable weakness which makes man cower to man—I have shrunk from contact with colored men in America." Shufeldt later admitted that he was "no advocate of miscegenation." Despite his youthful attentions to his Brazilian first love of 1841, the older man considered a mixture of races would be "an unmixed evil." During the Civil War, he wanted the Negro treated "as if he were human," and in Brazil in 1865, he pondered, along with James Watson Webb, the question of whether the Negro was capable of "self government and progressive civilization." In his lecture to the American Colonization Society in 1875, he urged colonization and inveighed against "the arbitrary dictum of a senseless race prejudice."

Given the ambiguities in these reflections, it is important to clarify Shufeldt's views on race and equality.

At the time of the Civil War, when he reflected sympathetically on the individual black from the South Carolina swamps, Shufeldt was particularly close to conservative Republicans such as Truman Smith, the former Whig, and to the Republican colonizationists. When he was consul general in Havana during 1861, he wrote to Charles Sumner and claimed to be intimate all of his life with the Negro, in Africa and "in the mildest form of slavery in our own society." He then suggested to the Massachusetts senator that the Isthmus of Tehuantepec should be the site of Lincoln's suggested purchase of territory for the colonization experiment. Colonization was the key to Shufeldt's view of the American black. It solved the problem of what to do with the black "contraband"—Benjamin Butler's word to cover the confusion in the debate over the characterization of slaves as "property" or "human." Colonization would also enable the United States to extend its influence into the Caribbean or Mexico through such expelled or transferred residents. To Frederick Seward, Shufeldt described the time was not far distant "when the future home of the *emancipated* negro must be found—in the genial climates of the more southern latitudes," and he suggested Tehuantepec for black colonization, especially in view of "the higher interest" of "Americanizing that point as a transit to our Pacific shores." Shufeldt constantly emphasized colonization. He even overstepped his instructions from Seward when he proposed black colonization in the eight points offered to Manuel Doblado in 1862. The isthmus, he claimed, afforded "admirable advantages for the colonization of our contraband negroes." This would bring the "happiest results to the black man, whether looked upon in either the light of economy or philanthrophy." Later, in the 1870s, Shufeldt claimed he had gone to Mexico with the authority of the president "to ascertain from that Government the practicability of settling our Southern negroes on the isthmus of Tehuantepec" by forcing them to emigrate. As an exponent of colonization for former slaves, Shufeldt was close to the conservative Republicans who suggested it.

In *Free Soil, Free Labor, Free Men,* Eric Foner has pointed out the irony that Negroes were considered "capable of becoming the agents of American empire in the Caribbean while they were being viewed at the same time as an undesirable population at home." Republicans, Foner explained, attempted to justify such ambiguities and contradictions by "appealing to the widely accepted belief that the white and black races were suited to different climates." The basis for such schemes, including the Republican one, was the assumption that "the United States was, or should be, a Nation of white men." In addition, Foner pointed to the opportunities these schemes afforded for outflanking the British in the Caribbean, blocking southern plans to expand the slave system southward, and removing the fear that "emancipation would lead to equality and intermixing of the races."[3]

What is remarkable about Shufeldt's paralleling such notions is that he clung to colonization long after it had become a political dead letter, rejected by both blacks and administration politicians. "The Continent of Africa presents itself to you as the natural home of the black men," he lectured to the American Colonization Society in 1876; "the yellow race flourishes in Asia, the white race developes its full vigor in Europe . . . each race has its allotted portion of that part of the earth's surface." A crisis was upon the blacks of the South, he conjectured, who were "no longer considered as a portion of the People of America." Yet he also considered that emigration would plant "the seed of a vigorous race upon the soil and within the latitude for which he was destined from the beginning, and to lay the foundation of a civilization, which, *if not equal* at first to that of the boasted Anglo-Saxon, will at least be bound by his own will and powers, and not by the arbitrary dictum of a senseless race prejudice." With this last comment, leveled directly at southerners in the last days of Reconstruction, Shufeldt rejected overt race prejudice for a concept of race based on geographical separateness to allotted spheres—thus southern blacks were to be removed to Mexico during the Civil War and Africa after that option was thwarted. The colonists would influence "the surrounding mass of barbarism," and he claimed that Liberia would be an "island in an ocean of barbarism." American blacks would thus be the cutting edge of his Christian propagandism into Africa.

When Shufeldt moved away from the United States black population, he dropped even such muffled qualifications of his ideas on race. The Cuban slave was outside the pale: "no construction of the laws of humanity" could place him "within the limits of citizenship—He is an absolute barbarian—totally unfit for the duties and responsibilities of civilization." The Cuban Creole in 1869 was condemned as "degraded by . . . moral and political servitude—contaminated in blood by miscegenation—it will take centuries to raise him to the dignity of real manhood." When faced with the prospect of Cuban slaves in an American Union, he was more explicit: "What will we do with 600,000 Negroes—as savage as on their native coast—or the 200,000 Chinese—the lowest dregs of Canton—Will the rule of universal suffrage work here?" he asked rhetorically. His answer, given his presuppositions, was self-evident. To Shufeldt, universal suffrage with an "unmixed condition of races & colors, is simply impossible," and he recommended imperialism before such a solution.

Outside the hemisphere he was more explicit. In South Africa, immediately following the Civil War, he deplored Christian civilization (British version) for trampling on "unoffending barbarism." Yet he viewed the native South Africans as "barbarians" and "ignorant people." Blacks in Africa were "rude people." On the world cruise he viewed Liberians as "these poor, helpless people," and while he was prepared to use educated Africans, such as Edward Wilmot Blyden, to extend American commercial opportunities, in general he considered Africans had to be taught to aspire to "a higher plane of civilization." Blacks in Africa would be better off under the rule of the white man, however despotic, he opined, than under their own chiefs, whom he dismissed as unfeeling savages. He told Leopold Morse that traders dealt with "barbarous tribes—with men who appreciate only the argument of physical force." The Mussarango tribe was an example. Shufeldt considered them to be "incorrigible rascals and robbers." The conquest of Africa, therefore, he considered to be a benevolent act. The natives of the lower Congo, who had been in contact with whites for four hundred years, had "only had ingrafted upon their innate barbarism the lowest vices of civilization." He did not perceive that a desire to preserve local customs could be viewed as successful resistance to acculturation or that "barbarism" might be well grounded in an indigenous culture. Hence he condemned Dutch efforts in Africa because he considered they led to the degeneration and degradation of natives "by nature already debased." Muscat, with its racial mixes, he described as "semi-barbarous and barbarous." Later in the cruise he wrote to Molly about Chinese immigration to the United States, "Sargent was not all wrong on the Chinese question" because "we don't want *another* race of inferior people in our Country."

Like Theodore Roosevelt, Shufeldt had his own set of priorities in judging races in an order of superiority and inferiority. Yet he tempered such divisions with a streak of humanity. He revealed this most clearly in the Sargent letter of January 1882, when he claimed to suffer "a sort of sentimentalism for underdogs" and charged foreigners in Asia "with prejudice of race, with arrogance of power, with ignorance of customs, with contempt of religious faith—never crediting them with forbearance, charity or sympathy for an inferior people." This is the key to Shufeldt's belief that he was not prejudiced and others were. While he considered that it was self-evident that certain races were inferior and should be relegated to their allotted spheres, the way that one dealt with such inferiors was the indicator of prejudice. He viewed the plight of native peoples under colonial rule, whether South African natives or Cubans, with a great deal of sympathy. Such sympathetic considerations on his part meant that people who treated an "inferior" person cruelly or harshly were prejudiced. The method of dealing with such peoples, rather than the assumption of their being inferior, was the distinguishing badge of prejudice in Shufeldt's mind. When his efforts to deal with others were translated from the personal level to the national level, it led him to preach a gospel of overseas race colonization using "civilization" to justify extending a Christian-American system in such places as Liberia or Tehuantepec, and American commerce in other areas of the world. Given such sentiments, Shufeldt closely resembled the model of Foner's Republicans.

When one turns to his personality, there is little doubt that Shufeldt was intensely ambitious, especially when seeking fame by serving his country, as he eagerly demonstrated by involving himself with Charles Wilkes' plan to remove Mason and Slidell from the *Trent* in 1861. During the Civil War he notified Seward that he was willing to lay down his life for the principle that America must be ruled by Americans. Even discounting the rhetoric, he was prepared to go to Mexico to instill Americanism and foster republican sentiment, to which end he would sacrifice his life or create his fame, for in the war "the field is already occupied—the harvest of fame has been gathered." In volunteering his services to the government to save Mexico he declared: "I will either succeed or die in the effort to vindicate the cause of republican freedom upon this Continent." He thought of himself as a military advisor to Juárez, coming to his aid from abroad. Later, he suggested seeing Juárez and offering a force of three to five thousand men to hold the Isthmus of Tehuantepec and advance American interests in that country. At the end of the war, en route to the Orient, he penned a long poem on his forty-third birthday that reflected on the stages of his life and pointed out that "Saddest of all, is Ambition's wreck . . . Lost, Lost! for ever and ever more." In 1880 at the end of his world cruise, he showed several times flashes of his desire to startle official Washington by news of his appointment as "Grand Admiral of the Chinese Navy." He indicated repeatedly that he would like to command the Asiatic squadron, especially at the anticipated culmination of the Korean treaty negotiations. To Molly he wrote, "If I only had the squadron for a few months." If he had, it is possible that he could have matched Perry's performance.

Two related personality traits stand out in Shufeldt's character. His ambitions, when frustrated, led him to despondency. He was angered in the Civil War when he thought that even Spanish officials could bully him in Havana because of the disadvantageous position of the United States. He sweated over British, Spanish, and French moves into Mexico in 1861–1862. The contretemps between the Spanish and French forces elated him, in turn, because it relieved the burden. He wanted the United States to institute actions in Mexico to prop up republican government at a time of deep difficulties in the Civil War and advocated the military occupation of the Isthmus of Tehuantepec for that purpose. He resented the intervention of what he termed the modern-day Holy Alliance. The United States, he argued, should be "co-heirs in the country" and Tehuantepec remain Mexican "until *We* want it." Seward's refusal to adopt his suggestions and his subsequent recall threw him into a deep fit of melancholy.

Secondly, Shufeldt was often lonely and able to confide in only a chosen few, such as Truman Smith and Molly, or, officially, in George M. Robeson, Richard W. Thompson, William H. Seward, and William E. Chandler. He also seemed to have the knack of alienating people. Setting out for China on good terms with Henry Haywood Bell, and with high hopes of working closely with him in the Asiatic squadron, he ended his tour of duty by declaring he would rather go home on a raft than join Bell in the *Hartford* again. He was restless under the command of superior authority, as he revealed in 1862 with Seward in Mexico and under the command of Rear Admiral Dahlgren in the blockading squadron off the South Atlantic coast. His antagonism toward his own sons is probably the best example of his alienating people once close to him. Robert, Mason, and George were all eventually disliked by their father, and his correspondence and will testified to that dislike. In this he may well have been influenced in his later years by Molly, whose dislike for Shufeldt's sons (and they for her) was apparent in her own comments to her mother in letters sent from Japan. Shufeldt's pride was partly responsible for the break, and his absences at sea may have accentuated the drift away from them. His pride spilled over at times into official correspondence. Shufeldt certainly resented Captain General Dulce's posture toward him in Cuba, and his wounded *amour propre* came out in his dealing with Seward over Mexico, with Daniel Ammen over the fate of the Tehuantepec route as judged by the Inter-Oceanic Canal Commission in 1876, and with Li Hung-chang in Tientsin in January 1882. The latter three events all testify to the fact that the Admiral had a temper that, at times, could easily be ruffled, thereby creating difficulties for him.

Shufeldt's emotions were often close to the surface, more particularly when he was on board ship. His emotions, particularly in the 1850s and during the Civil War, were manifested in his interests in spiritualism, his pity for heroic-romantic figures like the Cuban rebel Estrampez, or Kate, the object of his reminiscences about the 1850s, the "dark beauty" from his boyhood romance in Rio, the old "contraband" from the South Carolina swamps, the ordinary Jack-Tars of the navy, and the native peoples of South Africa and India, whom he regarded as exploited. He combined such romantic attachments, at times, with a fine degree of sarcasm and hostility equally as well as pity when focusing on the work of American missionaries in Asia or on the activities of imperial powers such as the Dutch in the Congo or the British in India. Mixed with his hostility toward the latter were feelings of envy and admiration when he came to view their imperial holdings in the world.

Shufeldt communicated more easily with women. He delighted in the women of Brazil, a trait he shared with Alfred Thayer Mahan. He found solace with Kate when in his "highly spiritualized condition" searching for "the eternal harmony of the spheres" in the 1850s. He recalled flirting with several women at the ball on board the HMS *Narcissus* in Rio harbor in 1865. He corresponded privately at length with Fannie V. Mangum. There is little in his papers that indicates a strong bond with his wife, Sarah, though his correspondence was edited, presumably by Molly, before presentation to the Navy Department. Sections of many personal letters are excised. A number of sad letters from Sarah to him in 1869 and 1870 have survived that reveal her own loneliness when running the farm he had purchased in Connecticut after the Civil War. He did take her to Tehuantepec while he surveyed it. Other than that the only clue to his thoughts on his wife are in the sad reflections he penned on leaving behind members of his family as he sailed on the *Hartford* for East Asia in 1865 and his depression when he left the returning isthmian surveying party in 1871 at Savannah to return home overland, following Sarah's death.

At times of loneliness such as the *Hartford* voyage in 1865–1866, Shufeldt wrote poems and songs for the crew. His own writings contain numerous literary samplings from Pascal, Louis XII of France, Dr. Johnson, John de Witt Tator to William III of England, "Old Martin" in Scott's *Monastery,* the Bible, Cicero, Voltaire, "Mademoiselle de Camargo" from *Men and Women of the XIX Century* by Argene Houssaye, Coleridge, Emerson, Seneca, Bacon, Harriet W. Beecher, Emile Souvestre, Shakespere's *Henry VIII,* Napoleon's *Ideas,* Dryden, Catullus to Lesbia, and others, but it is impossible to ascertain whether he jotted the snippets from magazines or read the originals. The only book that his correspondence shows he read directly was *Jane Eyre,* yet, his son, Robert, recalled reading extensively from his father's library on board the USS *Proteus,* so the evidence indicates that Shufeldt read widely. He was more prone to respond to situations with emotion and elation rather than with quotations.

Shufeldt was loath to become involved actively in political campaigns though he reflected at times on presidential elections and the state of parties. He confessed during the Civil War to approaching politics with "extreme caution." Events in 1868 depressed him considerably, leading him to lose his faith in the capacity of his countrymen for self-government. He preferred strong men at the helm, "who can ride the storm—who can defy the elements—who can *create* destiny—*control* fate." He thought that General Benjamin Butler fit this description near the close of the 1864 election, and he preferred Grant as a "man on horseback" during Reconstruction. One clue as to why lies in his view of history as but the life of the individual "who vindicated our immortality—whose voice is the voice of God."

Naval power obviously appealed to Shufeldt. In 1867, when the squadron consisting of the *Hartford, Wyoming, Ashuelot, Monocacy, Aristook, Madrilla,* and *Wachusett* lay in Hong Kong harbor, he wished to "have a dash . . . at some foe worthy of our steel." At that point he thought a war would be a blessing for the nationality of Americans, to help overcome post-Civil War bitterness. He may have had this in his mind when urging Bell to make a display of force on the Korean coast or to seize Port Hamilton. In 1869, at the time of the Cuban rebellion, he longed for the "silent eloquence" of the *Miantonomoh,* although he accepted David Dixon Porter's complaint that "the Navy was all gone." In 1880, he also wished to use force in Korea at different points on the coast, at unexpected moments, to "so intimidate the authorities as to bring them to terms," or to take possession of Port Hamilton, as he had advocated in 1868. In the Sargent letter of 1882, he insisted that the only argument the Chinese appreciated was force.

The recognition that Shufeldt expected for the Korean treaty never came. Partly as a result of the Sargent letter, partly because he was a James G. Blaine appointee serving the Chester Arthur administration, which was just beginning to wrestle with the problem of Korean dependency, and partly because Frederick T. Frelinghuysen, as the evidence reveals, would have preferred John Russell Young to negotiate the Korean treaty, Shufeldt was passed over for any rewards. Moreover, during the two major periods of diplomatic activity in which he was engaged, Shufeldt suffered on both occasions for letting his zeal outrun his rationality. Despite his active help for Wilkes in the *Trent* affair, he was later reprimanded by Seward for the conversations with Minister Doblado in 1862. Twenty years later, he was ignored by Frelinghuysen and Chester Arthur because of the embarrassments of the Sargent letter. Feeling rejected by his party leaders, alienated from his sons, loved only by his adopted daughter, and loving only her in return, Shufeldt led a lonely life of regret and travel in exile until his return to the United States in 1890 for what he deemed little reward. He might have accepted the position as minister to China, offered to him in 1889 by Blaine, but wisely declined on account of his wishes for the quieter life that his continuing pension would enable him to enjoy.

The admiral was an emotional, but not necessarily a complicated, person, who suffered periods of depression and elation for schemes and hopes for himself and his country. There is little doubt that he believed in some overriding sense of power that he deified in terms of the sea. He gave a rare insight into his thinking when he confessed to his diary on September 2, 1865, "I love the sea because it brings into play that part of my being nearest akin to *Power.*" He gloried in storms and the consciousness of strength, "not to defy but to control the elements." He put this into practice personally when he proved his competence in crippled vessels, in the barque *Marion* in 1846; the wrecked Collins Line steamer *Atlantic* as she limped into Cork in 1851; and in the *Quaker City* as she lay helpless in an October gale in 1859. Sometimes his sense of power was Napoleonic, based on the notion of power over "barbarians" and "rude peoples" of the world. In addition, he displayed a willingness to use that power, and would have done so, especially against the Spanish, French, and Koreans, if not restrained by Seward and Thompson.

Shufeldt was also tenacious. He fought hard for his visions and dreams about Tehuantepec, Cuba, the China survey, and the African treaties when they began to fade away. His character development between 1865 and 1880 reveals how his dreams of territorial expansion, displayed most militantly toward Cuba and Mexico during the Civil War, began to wane only as opportunities for commercial expansion in the Orient and Africa waxed. The period from 1866 to 1871 was crucial, for he was introduced to the pull of East Asia at a time when his ambitions still lay in Mexico. Gradually, his attitudes toward the latter were modified and Shufeldt concentrated on extending influence in the Pacific and Indian oceans.

At the time his ambitions changed direction, however, Shufeldt also buckled down to the routine of administering one of the Navy Department's bureaus at a critical time. In that period his greatest achievements were in overhauling the naval apprenticeship scheme, improving recruitment facilities, reducing punishment, and, later, supervising the building of the White Squadron. The admiral was effective as a reformer when working for change in the condition of the personnel of the navy. He was scarcely the conservatively oriented navalist that has been the model for numerous generalizations about officers of the United States Navy of the 1870s. Overall, his vision of the usefulness of the navy, for commercial expansion in all areas of the world and as an outlet for discontented boys in society, was a quasi-philosophical statement of the needs of American society that antedated Mahan's by fifteen years.

Despite the administration's neglect of his diplomatic role in the opening of Korea in the 1880s, Shufeldt's career provides an important case study of nineteenth-century expansion. As a person, a writer of poetry, a romantic, and, at times, a mystic, Shufeldt was interesting. His views on race afford another example of conservative Republican attitudes in the post-Civil War period. As a naval officer his work, which culminated with superintending the designs for the White Squadron, was of significance in keeping the navy before the public eye in the 1870s and 1880s. From the perspective of an analyst and advocate of commercial expansion he was highly important. As a diplomat he completed in one area of East Asia the gospels he had preached for many areas of the world. He was one of the earliest of the post-Civil War strategists to evolve and apply concepts of commercial penetration into Africa and Asia. His efforts postdated the visionary schemes of William H. Seward and predated the imperial school of the 1890s. Shufeldt thus exemplifies the important continuing threads between the commercial drives of the pre-Civil War period and the successful applications of national power to those drives in the 1880s and the 1890s.

Appendix 1:
The Sargent Letter

The United States and China

A letter to Hon. A. A. Sargent   Tientsin, China, Jany. 1882

Dear Sir—

You know me well enough to understand that the current of my sympathies for the human race has always been in favor of the "down trodden" people of the Earth.

The African or the Asiatic, whether at home, or as a slave or emigrant upon foreign shores has always seemed to me—more or less the victim of oppression & I have fired my indignation upon the Oppressor with a force never equal to my zeal & with a sincerity never greater than my convictions. I have indeed early analysed the causes but always warmed up over its effects. In other words I have all my life suffered under a sort of sentimentalism, an unquestioning sympathy for the "under dog."

With reference to the Eastern Nations, I have charged foreigners dwelling among them, with prejudice of race, with arrogance of power, with ignorance of custom, with contempt of religious faith—never crediting them with forbearance, charity or sympathy for an inferior people. To me the merchant seemed to force his wares & the missionary his creed upon a passive & long suffering community. There is an underlying truth in these sentiments, but as a practical idea inapplicable to the relations both commercial & political, which connect Asia with Europe or America.

Six months residence in this city, the political centre of the Chinese Government and an intimacy rather exceptional with the ruling Element has convinced me that deceit & untruthfulness pervade all intercourse with foreigners—that an ineradicable hatred exists & that any appeal across the barrier, either of sympathy, or gratitude is utterly idle. The only appeal or argument is that of *force*. If justice is done to these people it must be for the sake of itself—not expecting appreciation—if justice is exacted it must be unrelentingly. All sympathy will be construed as weakness, all pity as fear.* The least condescencion fosters conceit & provokes insolence.

It is quite true however that Europe permits or encourages Western Civilization in China to the extent of subordination. It fosters the pretext of strength, sells guns & ships knowing that it is not in the genius of the Chinese to handle them, that in time of war they simply become easy prizes to the first European enemy. But commercially England alone controls China. Eighty-six per cent of the foreign trade is English. The Imperial Customs which collects all duties upon foreign imports are managed by an English Inspector Genl. Under him is a Corps of foreign officials which controls the Customs Houses, commands the Gun boats & revenue cruisers & maintains the light house systems. In fact almost everything which filters into China from the outside world goes through this strange excrescence upon its body politic.

Diplomatically also, England rules China—recognizing the hard logic of facts, she has imposed a wholesome dread of her power by always following the word with the blow. The murder of Margary for instance, on the westernmost confines of the country, among an insubordinate people, was avenged on demand. Sir Thomas Wade, H.B.M.'s Minister said, "Do this, or I will haul down my flag": no squirming could evade the issue, no lies deceive. He insisted upon the trial of the murderers in the presence of a British officer, & it was done. I do not go into the equity of this case, or the real responsibility of the Peking Govt. but I am convinced, that acting with such decision, is the only means by which foreigners can live in China with security to life & property. It is only a question between this, & the *right* to live here at all. But the United States standing, or endeavoring to stand, upon a higher plain than that of mere physical force, pursues in China a policy of moral suasion, which neither convinces, nor converts the Chinaman to the doctrines of a common brotherhood of men or nations; for, high as the Heaven is above the earth so high is his conceit; & deep as the waters of the sea, is the measure of his contempt for the "outside barbarian."

Any high moral ground in the field of diplomacy any appeal to the motives which ordinarily govern nations—indeed any argument unaccompanied by the outward, visible sign of force, is used only for the purpose of delay, which in the end is equivalent to victory. Yet the U. States has interests in China destined in the future to be greater than those of any other nation; possessing as we do the Pacific Ocean as a common highway. Geographically, with reference to the continents;

*Here the sentence "Above all things necessary, is tenacity of national dignity" was added to the text in the newspaper account that appeared in the *San Francisco Evening Bulletin,* Monday, March 20, 1882, presumably by either Sargent or the editor of the newspaper. One possibility is that Molly, or whoever transcribed the letter, omitted that sentence when making the copy. This copy is the manuscript in the Robert Wilson Shufeldt Papers, box 4, Korean Letterbook, pp. 31-40.

politically, with reference to Europe; and commercially, with reference to each other, these interests should be reciprocal; but China does not care to realize this fact, does not desire any identity of interest. She would today, if she could, exclude every article of foreign commerce or manufacture from her shores. She is slowly learning the western arts, in order that by means of them, she may sometime not only exclude foreign goods, but the *foreigner himself* from the country. "China for the Chinese" is more than ever the motto of every mandarin in the Empire. Our policy therefore should be positive & governed to the extent of moral law by American interests alone, & urged by the arguments which they understand, the argument of force—pressure, not persuasion.

Li Hung-Chang, Senior Guardian of the Emperor; Grand Secretary; Commander-in-Chief of Eighteen provinces; Commissioner of Coast Defences; etc, etc, sits in his vice-regal chair at Tientsin, the gate of the capital of China; regulates the ingress & egress of foreign diplomats to the Court, & defines the foreign, & dictates the domestic policy of the country. Li Hung-Chang is therefore the absolute & despotic ruler of 400,000,000 of people. Yet, such are the anomalies of his Govt., he lives upon the mere breath of the Empress, an ignorant capricious, & immoral woman. A word from her, & his power would vanish like the morning mist, & his courtiers would shrink from him as a man with the plague.

He is fifty-nine years of age; six feet two inches in height, has a clear, cold, cruel eye, & an imperious manner. He is a thorough Oriental, & an intense Chinaman. These imply contempt for western nations, & hatred for all foreigners. Li Hung-Chang is the Bismarck of the East; he keeps together an incongruous Empire & an effête dynasty by the repressive force of an indomitable will. He suppresses rebellions by decapitation, & quiets the turbulent with the bamboo—yet he is great— not because he is so much in advance of his countrymen, but because he is not so far behind as they are in an appreciation of the arts political & physical which govern the modern world. He at least recognizes the value of these forces; he buys ships of war; constructs forts, experiments in torpedoes; & drills troops with modern arms. He has learned that despite the protestations of civilization, the sword yet remains the arbiter of nations, & that China to be respected must be feared. But he does not know that standing in the way of his military & naval aspirations is the fact, that in China there is no military & naval spirit.

Antedating all other nations in their traditions, standing as it were upon this rock of ages, China has taught her people to believe that there is something derogatory to honor in the character of a soldier; that the road to true glory lies through the fields of literature, & to emolument by the paths of commerce. Throughout the centuries, generations have been imbued with these ideas, until by the very doctrine of the "survival of the fittest" all martial spirit has died out of the race. The Chinese will suffer & endure, will if cornered fight; will rise against local oppression, but under these circumstances their wars become murders, or retaliations shocking from their cruelty. There is absolutely no chivalry which makes the soldier an agent of civilization no "esprit du corps" which creates heroes & national leaders. The only idea of discipline is the fear of corporeal punishment. The bamboo is the dread alike of the general & the private. The civil button of the mandarin takes precedence over military rank, & defines relative subordination. Under such a system there can be no *organization,* none of that spirit which distinguishes an army from an armed mob.

Li Hung-Chang, as the Viceroy of the Imperial province, guards & garrisons with his own provincial army, the capital city of Peking. He has a partially trained force of about 35,000 men, armed with breech-loaders & a complement of field pieces. He has also in store 200,000 or 300,000 stand of arms, & several hundred pieces of artillery. His forts on the seaboard of the Gulf of Pechihli, are of modern construction, & are armed with heavy modern ordnance. But although his troops have been more or less drilled & organized by foreign officers, they are at all times liable to be dispersed for labor upon the public works, thus continually destroying what their instructors are endeavoring to create in them, namely the élan, & spirit of a military corps.

Over these men, the Viceroy appoints the generals, & perhaps the colonels, but the subordinate-officers are simply hired by the month & degraded or bambooed at the caprice of their superiors. The men are obedient, apt, & only insubordinate when not paid. They are pure volunteers & paid like coolie laborers by the month. There is no military code of justice, & no such thing as a court-martial.

But this small force forms no type of the immense mass of men, which has been & can be collected into a so-called army, nor is it even a nucleus for a well-drilled force. The first, & almost insurmountable obstacle, in addition to what has been stated, is the absence of any consolidated national feeling, or love of country as a whole. The political divisions of the Empire have cut through every stratum of society, have established customs, & created languages or dialects, making each of the nineteen provinces not only a distinct, but a hostile nationality. Besides, each of these provinces is governed by a Viceroy, almost independent of Peking, & only bound to it, & to each other by the mythical tie of a common Emperor, who rules as the "Son of Heaven."

It is impossible to convince these antagonistic people, that they can have any common cause, or move them by any common motive. For these reasons it will be seen how difficult it would be to create a National Army.

As it is with the Army, so with the Navy. There are four distinct naval fleets; each independent of the other; & although nominally under the control of two "Commissioners of Coast Defence"—of whom Li Hung-Chang is one, & the vice-roy of Nanking the other; yet there is no combination nor unity. A few years ago, the Foochow arsenal & fleet, under the able administration of M. Giquel, a French officer, gave promise of forming at least the nucleus of an Imperial force—but after twenty years of labor, that gentleman has gone away, & both the arsenal & fleet are lapsing into decay.

Under the pressure of a war iminent [sic] with Russia, Viceroy Li, undertook to form a squadron for the protection of the approaches to Peking; & within a year or two, he has collected a force of almost twelve small ships, six of them are gun boats of unique type, being remarkable for carrying the heaviest gun—35 tons—on the smallest displacement of any vessel afloat—two others of similar type but longer, & with very high speed, carry two guns each of 35 tons. These were all built by Sir Wm. Armstrong. The other vessels of the squadron are composite built at Foochow, & armed with light guns of French pattern: besides these, there are being built in Germany, two iron-clads of the "Sachsen" class of the German Navy. Every modern appliance in the art of naval warfare has been placed on these new ships. Guns with large calibre & high velocity, moved by hydraulic power—machine guns—electric lights; torpedoes & torpedo-boats—engines with twin screws—steel rams—etc. etc. etc.—indeed the materiel of this squadron is complete. Yet it is evident that in order to be really effective, it needs an intelligent personnel, & a thorough organization. It represents indeed a large amount of money expended, & has deluded the Chinese govt. & to some extent the world, into the belief that China is really in possession of a Navy. But the vices & weaknesses of the Chinese system of administration, pervade & permeate it. The absence of naval rank, & consequently of esprit du corps'; of maritime experience; & knowledge of the outside world among the officers—incongruous crews from different provinces, wanting in that pluck & dash which a national feeling & a national flag alone can create,—deep seated & ineradicable financial corruption—all these combine to neutralize the qualities of the ships & render them useless as a fighting force.

To increase the inherent defects of this organization, & under the semblance of strength, in reality to add to its weakness, are the intrigues & jealousies of foreign officers both in, & about the service. The Inspector-General of the Customs, an Englishman—in addition to his great power in that office, would like to administer the Navy. The ships were built in England under his contracts. Since their arrival in China, the Commissioner of Customs at Tientsin—a German—has managed to secure their control. Three Englishmen—quasi-officers of the Royal Navy, but now belonging to the Imperial Customs Service afloat, are on board of the ships as "advisers" to the Chinese admiral & captains. Two ex-officers of the French Navy, employed at high salaries for some purpose never yet specified, make up three nationalities, each jealous of the other, & all despising the Chinese, while aspiring to control its naval service.

With such discordant parts, it will be easily seen—how difficult it is to create a harmonious whole; while the Viceroy, astute in all things but the wisdom of the outside world, is more or less a victim to the flatteries or the arts of these ambitious men, who persuade him that he has a Navy. But the Ministers of the Western Powers, who watch every movement of the Chinese toward the acquisition of military or naval strength, & who are determined that they shall go "thus far & no further"; know that, sold at large profits by their constituents, & officered by their countrymen; it is only a toy to amuse his Ex—the Viceroy in time of peace, & a prize to be captured in time of war.

When we consider the enormous power of the 400,000,000 of people, if turned in any intelligent direction—unrestrained by any moral obligation—unhindered by any physical obstacle—over-running countries —exterminating races—I am forced to agree with these experienced diplomats, that Chinese progress in the art of war, is a thing to be checked rather than accelerated by Western Nations. But, notwithstanding the heavy hand which the representatives of Europe lays upon China whenever it attempts to move, contrasted with the scarcely perceptible pressure of American influence, China is really more in sympathy with Europe than with America. Russia, with a long co-terminous border, exerts great power over its foreign policy, rendered easy by the assimilation of race, & forcible by the dread of aggression. But it is to our form of government that China is most antagonistic. The mandarins are beginning to understand, that if by the force of our example, liberal principles should be introduced into the Empire, there would be an end to the "heaven-born" dynasty, as well as to the taxation & tyranny upon which they now fatten & flourish. This fact has been illustrated lately by the treatment of the Chinese students peremptorily brought back from the United States before their educational course was completed. Where ever these youths have been distributed in the public service they seem to have been regarded as the embodiment of Americanism, & the determination has been shown to repress it even by the cruelest means. They have fallen upon evil times; yet thoroughly embued as they are with the spirit of free institutions, it is not likely that even the bamboo will entirely drive out of them the knowledge of better things. But today they are the victims of Oriental hatred to popular institutions, & the innocent cause of dislike on the part of the Mandarins for everything American.

The visit of Genl. Grant to China, was dramatic, rather than real in its effects. Li Hung-Chang was pleased to meet a man whom he could consider his peer both as a soldier & a statesman & at the same time, one who, like himself had risen to greatness by virtue of his own genius. The prominent visitors coming to China from Europe, have usually been mere scions of royalty, immature boys, or wandering princes, but Genl. Grant had been the ruler of a great people, & more than that the Viceroy expected that he would be again. It was this, indeed, which gave the General's visit its impressiveness. The Russian bear was growling on the border of China, & the English lion inspired by the imperial policy of Beaconsfield, was crouching for a spring upon anything or any where that threatened English trade or supremacy, while the friendship of the United States, personified in Genl. Grant, was easily secured by the out-stretched hand, and more in friendship than diplomacy by the astute Viceroy. But it would be a mistake to think that the visit had any permanent effect upon the foreign policy of China. The good it really did, was to draw the attention of the U. States to that country with its immense possibilities for American commerce. During our war, China had almost been forgotten, & our trade almost annihilated. Gl. Grant's visit revived these memories: indeed around the world his visit had this significance. It reminded both the East & the West, that America still lived. Gl. Grant represented a character which abroad, many of his countrymen are ashamed to confess—a *Republican* by conviction, & an American at all times, whether in camps or courts.

As an adjunct to the Navy & Army, China has four Arsenals—at Foochow, Shanghai, Tientsin, & Nanking. At the first three, are docks, & plants for building & repairing small ships of war, & engines; & distributed among them are factories for making powder, metallic cartridges —torpedoes—steam launches etc. etc. etc. At Shanghai, heavy ordnance is fabricated for the Navy, & at Nanking, fieldpieces for the Army. All of these establishments have been, or are, more or less under foreign supervision; but it is at Tientsin alone, that at present, under the rigorous determination of Li Hung-Chang to arm China, there are any signs of vitality. The others are in a state of gradual decadence.

With such warlike means & methods, & under the conditions I have enumerated, China is growing into fictitious strength, & keeping imaginary pace with Western improvements. Concomitant with these, there is an increasing & undying feeling of hostility to foreigners of all & every nationality.

Under these circumstances, portrayed without prejudice, but without sentiment; I am of the earnest conviction, that the policy of the U. States in China, & towards the Chinese in America, should be with us, as it is with them, *purely selfish.* Coming as it ought to, under the common law of right, & justice, but by no means governed by the fallacious idea of inter-national friendship, or even the broader ground of a common brother-hood.

We should legislate—to the extent of our own needs for labor. We should regulate & limit the supply by the demand, & with reference to these people, repudiate the doctrine of unrestricted immigration. Nor should our policy in this matter be confined to California. Already undue proportions of Chinamen are flooding the Sandwich Islands. This group, both from its commercial & strategic position, is a mere outlying county of that state, yielding the productions necessary to the Pacific slope; & of vital importance in the military & naval strength of the whole country. Any evil inflicted upon these islands, will eventually affect ourselves.

The points I have endeavored to make in this letter are:

1st That China has no *real* aggresive military or naval strength.
2nd That there is, & can be, no affinity between the people of the U. States & China.
3rd That the Govt. of the U. States, as the Govts. of Europe, should *insist* upon its rights in China, conceding no more than is granted, & trusting no more than it is trusted.
4th That although the two countries are so situated as to invite, there can never be any intimate political or commercial relations between them, except upon the basis of such as the United States may demand.

Farther, I desire to express the opinion, that although the superabundant people of China will, under their imperative necessity emigrate to other lands, in constant, & irresistible currents, yet they will go towards the West, into India, rather than towards the East into America. This seems to be the great law of movement to the human tide—from East to West. Nevertheless, the eddies & countercurrents, may be sufficiently strong to need watching, & providing against. It will be for Congress to judge of the limit of legislation necessary to effect this purpose.

In my next letter, I will endeavor to elucidate the three questions which have vexed, & still vex the "Tsung-li-Yamen" at Peking, & in which we are more or less interested.

I address these letters to you, because I remember, that you were the earnest opponent of unlimited Chinese immigration into the United States, both as a Senator, & a citizen of your state, although at the time I did not fully concur with you.

         I am very truly—
         Your friend
         (signed) R. W. Shufeldt

Appendix 2:
Treaty of Amity and Commerce between the United States of America and Korea, May 22, 1882

The United States of America and the Kingdom of Chosen, being sincerely desirous of establishing permanent relations of amity and friendship between their respective peoples, have to this end appointed, that is to say: the President of the United States, R. W. SHUFELDT, Commodore, U. S. Navy, as his Commissioner Plenipotentiary; and His Majesty the King of Chosen, SHIN CHEN, President of the Royal Cabinet, CHIN HONG-CHI, Member of the Royal Cabinet, as his Commissioners Plenipotentiary: who, having reciprocally examined their respective full powers, which have been found to be in due form, have agreed upon the several following Articles:

ARTICLE I. There shall be perpetual peace and friendship between the President of the United States and the King of Chosen and the citizens and subjects of their respective Governments.

If other Powers deal unjustly or oppressively with either Government, the other will exert their good offices, on being informed of the case, to bring about an amicable arrangement, thus showing their friendly feelings.

ARTICLE II. After the conclusion of this treaty of amity and commerce, the high contracting Powers may each appoint Diplomatic Representatives to reside at the Court of the other, and may each appoint Consular Representatives at the ports of the other which are open to foreign commerce, at their own convenience.

These officials shall have relations with the corresponding local authorities of equal rank upon a basis of mutual equality.

The Diplomatic and Consular Representatives of the two Governments shall receive mutually all the privileges rights and immunities, without discrimination, which are accorded to the same classes of Representatives from the most favored nation.

Consuls shall exercise their functions only on receipt of an exequatur from the Government to which they are accredited. Consular authorities shall be bona fide officials. No merchants shall be permitted to exercise the duties of the office, nor shall consular officers be allowed to engage in trade. At ports to which no Consular Representatives have been appointed, the Consuls of other Powers may be invited to act, provided that no merchant shall be allowed to assume consular functions, or the provisions of this treaty may, in such case, be enforced by the local authorities.

If Consular Representatives of the United States in Chosen conduct their business in an improper manner, their exequaturs may be revoked, subject to the approval, previously obtained of the Diplomatic Representative of the United States.

ARTICLE III. Whenever United States vessels, either because of stress of weather or by want of fuel or provisions, cannot reach the nearest open port in Chosen, they may enter any port or harbor either to take refuge therein or to get supplies of wood, coal, and other necessaries, or to make repairs; the expenses incurred thereby being defrayed by the ship's master. In such event, the officers and people of the locality shall display their sympathy by rendering full assistance, and their liberality by furnishing the necessities required.

If a vessel of the United States carries on a clandestine trade at a port not open to foreign commerce, such vessel with her cargo shall be seized and confiscated.

If a United States vessel be wrecked on the coast of Chosen, the local authorities on being informed of the occurrence, shall immediately render assistance to the crew, provide for their present necessities, and take the measures necessary for the salvage of the ship and the preservation of her cargo. They shall also bring the matter to the knowledge of the nearest consular representative of the United States in order that steps may be taken to send the crew home and to save the ship and cargo. The necessary expenses shall be defrayed either by the ship's master or by the United States.

ARTICLE IV. All citizens of the United States of America in Chosen, peaceably attending to their own affairs, shall receive and enjoy for themselves and everything appertaining to them the protection of the local authorities of the Government of Chosen, who shall defend them from all insult and injury of any sort. If their dwellings or property be threatened or attacked by mobs, incendiaries, or other violent or lawless persons, the local officers, on requisition of the Consul, shall immediately dispatch a military force to disperse the rioters, apprehend the guilty individuals, and punish them with the utmost rigor of the law.

Subjects of Chosen, guilty of any criminal act towards citizens of the United States, shall be punished by the authorities of Chosen according to the laws of Chosen; and citizens of the United States, either on shore or in any merchant vessel, who may insult, trouble, or wound the persons, or injure the property of the people of Chosen, shall be arrested and punished only by the Consul or other public functionary of the United States thereto authorized, according to the laws of the United States.

When controversies arise in the Kingdom of Chosen, between citizens of the United States and the subjects of His Majesty which need to be examined and decided by the public officers of the two nations, it is agreed between the Governments of the United States and Chosen that such cases shall be tried by the proper official of the nationality of the defendent, according to the laws of that nation. The properly authorized official of the plaintiff's nationality shall be freely permitted to attend the trial, and shall be treated with the courtesy due to his position. He shall be granted all proper facilities for watching the proceedings in the interests of justice. If he so desires, he shall have the right to present, to examine, and to cross examine witnesses. If he is dissatisfied with the proceedings, he shall be permitted to protest against them in detail.

It is, however, mutually agreed and understood between the High Contracting Powers, that whenever the King of Chosen shall have so far modified and reformed the statutes and judicial procedure of His Kingdom that, in the judgment of the United States, they conform to the laws and course of justice in the United States, the right of ex-territorial jurisdiction over United States citizens in Chosen shall be abandoned, and thereafter United States citizens, when within the limits of the Kingdom of Chosen, shall be subject to the jurisdiction of the native authorities.

ARTICLE V. Merchants and merchant vessels of Chosen visiting the United States for purposes of traffic shall pay duties and tonnage dues and all fees according to the Customs Regulations of the United States, but no higher or other rates of duties and tonnage dues shall be exacted of them than are levied upon citizens of the United States or upon citizens or subjects of the most favored nation.

Merchants and merchant vessels of the United States visiting Chosen for purposes of traffic shall pay duties upon all merchandise imported and exported. The authority to levy duties is of right vested in the Government of Chosen. The tariff of duties upon exports and imports, together with the customs regulations for the prevention of smuggling and other irregularities, will be fixed by the authorities of Chosen and communicated to the proper officials of the United States, to be by the latter notified to their citizens and duly observed.

It is, however, agreed in the first instance as a general measure, that the tariff upon such imports as are articles of daily use shall not exceed an *ad valorem* duty of ten *per centum;* that the tariff upon such imports as are luxuries, as, for instance, foreign wines, foreign tobacco, clocks and watches, shall not exceed an *ad valorem* duty of thirty *per centum;* and that native produce exported shall pay a duty not to exceed five *per centum ad valorem.* And it is further agreed that the duty upon foreign imports shall be paid once for all at the port of entry, and that no other dues, duties, fees, taxes, or charges of any sort shall be levied upon such imports either in the interior of Chosen or at the ports.

United States merchant vessels entering the ports of Chosen shall pay tonnage dues at the rate of five mace per ton, payable once in three months on each vessel, according to the Chinese calendar.

ARTICLE VI. Subjects of Chosen who may visit the United States shall be permitted to reside and to rent premises, purchase land, or to construct residences or warehouses, in all parts of the country. They shall be freely permitted to pursue their various callings and avocations and to traffic in all merchandise, raw and manufactured, that is not declared contraband by law.

Citizens of the United States who may resort to the ports of Chosen which are open to foreign commerce shall be permitted to reside at such open ports within the limits of the concessions, and to lease buildings or land or to construct residences or warehouses therein. They shall be freely permitted to pursue their various callings and avocations within the limits of the ports, and to traffic in all merchandise, raw and manufactured, that is not declared contraband by law.

No coercion or intimidation in the acquisition of land or buildings shall be permitted, and the land rent as fixed by the authorities of Chosen shall be paid. And it is expressly agreed that land so acquired in the open ports of Chosen still remains an integral part of the Kingdom, and that all rights of jurisdiction over persons and property within such areas remain vested in the authorities of Chosen, except in so far as such rights have been expressly relinquished by this treaty.

American citizens are not permitted either to transport foreign imports to the interior for sale or to proceed thither to purchase native produce from one open port to another open port. Violations of this rule will subject such merchandise to confiscation, and the merchant offending will be handed over to the Consular authorities to be dealt with.

ARTICLE VII. The Governments of the United States and Chosen mutually agree and undertake that subjects of Chosen shall not be permitted to import opium into any of the ports of the United States, and citizens of the United States shall not be permitted to import opium into any of the open ports of Chosen, to transport it from one open port to another open port, or to traffic in it in Chosen. This absolute prohibition, which extends to vessels owned by the citizens or subjects of either Power, to foreign vessels employed by them, and to vessels owned by the citizens or subjects of either Power and employed by other persons for the transportation of opium, shall be enforced by appropriate legislation on the part of the United States and of Chosen, and offenders against it shall be severely punished.

ARTICLE VIII. Whenever the Government of Chosen shall have reason to apprehend a scarcity of food within the limits of the kingdom, His Majesty may, by decree, temporarily prohibit the export of all breadstuffs, and such decree shall be binding on all citizens of the United States in Chosen, upon due notice having been given them by the authorities of Chosen through the proper officers of the United States [; but it is to be understood that the exportation of rice and breadstuffs of every description is prohibited from the open port of Yin-Chuen.]

Chosen having of old prohibited the exportation of red ginseng, if citizens of the United States clandestinely purchase it for export, it shall be confiscated, and the offenders punished.

ARTICLE IX. The purchase of cannon, small arms, swords, gunpowder, shot, and all munitions of war is permitted only to officials of the Government of Chosen, and they may be imported by citizens of the United States only under a written permit from the authorities of Chosen. If these articles are clandestinely imported, they shall be confiscated, and the offending party shall be punished.

ARTICLE X. The officers and people of either nation residing in the other shall have the right to employ natives for all kinds of lawful work.

Should, however, subjects of Chosen, guilty of violation of the laws of the kingdom, or against whom any action has been brought, conceal themselves in the residences or warehouses of United States' citizens or on board United States' merchant vessels, the Consular authorities of the United States, on being notified of the fact by the local authorities, will either permit the latter to despatch constables to make the arrests, or the persons will be arrested by the Consular authorities and handed over to the local constables.

Officials or citizens of the United States shall not harbor such persons.

ARTICLE XI. Students of either nationality who may proceed to the country of the other, in order to study the language, literature, laws, or arts, shall be given all possible protection and assistance, in evidence of cordial goodwill.

ARTICLE XII. This being the first treaty negotiated by Chosen, and hence being general and incomplete in its provisions shall in the first instance be put into operation in all things stipulated herein. As to stipulations not contained herein, after an interval of five years, when the officers and people of the two Powers shall have become more familiar with each other's language, a further negotiation of commercial provisions and regulations in detail, in conformity with international law and without unequal discriminations on either part shall be had.

ARTICLE XIII. This Treaty and future official correspondence between the two contracting governments shall be made, on the part of Chosen, in the Chinese language.

The United States shall either use the Chinese language, or if English be used, it shall be accompanied with a Chinese version, in order to avoid misunderstanding.

ARTICLE XIV. The High Contracting Powers hereby agree that, should at any time the King of Chosen grant to any nation, or to the merchants or citizens of any nation, any right, privilege, or favor, connected either with navigation, commerce, political or other intercourse, which is not conferred by this Treaty, such right, privilege, and favor shall freely inure to the benefit of the United States, its public officers, merchants, and citizens; provided always, that whenever such right, privilege, or favor is accompanied by any condition or equivalent concession granted by the other nation interested, the United States, its officers and people, shall only be entitled to the benefit of such right, privilege or favor upon complying with the conditions or concessions connected therewith.

In faith whereof, the respective Commissioners Plenipotentiary have signed and sealed the foregoing at Yin-Chuen in English and Chinese, being three originals of each text, of even tenor and date, the ratifications of which shall be exchanged at Yin-Chuen within one year from the date of its execution, and immediately thereafter this Treaty shall be in all its provisions publicly proclaimed and made known by both Governments in their respective countries, in order that it may be obeyed by their citizens and subjects respectively.

    Chosen, May the 22nd, A.D. 1882.
        (Signed) R. W. Shufeldt, Commodore, U.S.N. Envoy of the U.S. to Chosen.
        (Signed) Shin Chen   (In Chinese)
        (Signed) Chin Hong-Chi   (In Chinese)

The manuscript of the original treaty with Korea is in the Robert Wilson Shufeldt Papers, box 24, Folio (Treaties, Korea). The section enclosed in brackets in ARTICLE VIII was added in Korea.

Note on Sources

The most important collection of Robert Wilson Shufeldt's papers is in the Manuscripts Division of the Library of Congress. They were deposited there by the Naval Historical Foundation, which received them from Mary Abercrombie (Miller) Shufeldt. In October 1968, the Manuscripts Division prepared a final Register for Shufeldt's papers after recataloging them in thirty-seven boxes. The Register, obtainable from the Manuscripts Division, has a short "scope and content" note; a "description of series" dividing the papers into subgroups; and a "container list," which is a short guide to the individual box holdings. The papers are thus organized into series and each series has a number of containers in it. Box numbers and content headings are as follows:

Container Number	*Contents*
1	Diaries, Notebooks, Logbooks, and Journals, 1865–1880
2	Diaries, Notebooks, Logbooks, and Journals, 1865–1880
3	Letterbooks, Letterpress Books, and Letter Index Books, 1864–1880
4	Letterbooks, Letterpress Books, and Letter Index Books, 1864–1880
5	Official Correspondence, 1839–1862
6	Official Correspondence, 1863–1865
7	Official Correspondence, 1866
8	Official Correspondence, 1867
9	Official Correspondence, 1868–1872
10	Official Correspondence, 1873–1889
11	General Correspondence, 1838–1861
12	General Correspondence, 1862–1867
13	General Correspondence, 1868–1870
14	General Correspondence, 1870–1871
15	General Correspondence, 1872–1875

16	General Correspondence, 1876–1884
17	General Correspondence, 1887–1900 and undated
18	Subject File, Cuba, 1861–1863 and undated, correspondence, May 1861–January 1862
19	Subject File, Cuba, 1861–1863 and undated, correspondence, February 1862–April 1863 and undated
20	Subject File, Tehuantepec, Correspondence and Survey Expedition, 1861–1873
21	Subject File, Bills, receipts, miscellany, newspaper clippings, and printed matter
22	Subject File, World Cruise of the *Ticonderoga,* West Africa to Japan
23	Subject File, World Cruise of the *Ticonderoga,* Liberia
24	Subject File, World Cruise of the *Ticonderoga,* China and Korea
25	Subject File, General correspondence, maps, Oriental documents, and miscellany
26	Subject File, Unpublished manuscript, chapters 1–14
27	Subject File, Unpublished manuscript, chapters 15–19, and collected materials, Liberia to India
28	Subject File, Collected materials, Singapore to Korea
29	Subject File, Miscellany
30	Newspaper Clippings, 1859–1899 and undated; China; Gheradi-Walker controversy; Japan; interoceanic canal; and Korea
31	Newspaper Clippings, Liberia, miscellany, St. Helena, Sierra Leone, U.S. Navy, SS *Quaker City,* USS *Ticonderoga*
32	Printed Matter, 1849–1910 and undated, 1849–1910
33	USS *Miantonomoh,* 1869–1870
34	Miscellany, 1836–1893 and undated, account book, 1876–1877, and calling cards and invitations, 1870–1882; fragments, poetry, inventories, registers, blueprints
35	Bills, receipts, and inventories, 1862–1893; copies of treaties between the United States and foreign countries; certificates, awards and passports, 1853–1861; poems, songs, and essays written on board USS *Proteus* and USS *Hartford,* 1864–1868
36	Mason A. Shufeldt File, 1883–1893 and undated, general correspondence and Madagascar expedition
37	Mason A. Shufeldt File, Printed matter, reports and writings, Columbian World Exposition, and miscellany

Other letters and collections used in the research, grouped according to manuscript locations, are the Nelson Brewster Papers, Truman Smith letters, 1842–1883, and Gideon Welles letters, Connecticut Historical Society; Estevan A. Fuertes letters, Henry Sage Papers, and broadsides and pamphlets on Tehuantepec, Regional History Collection, Cornell University; John A. Quitman letters, William W. Rockhill Papers, and Charles Sumner Papers, Houghton Library, Harvard University; Gideon Welles letters, Henry E. Huntington Library, San

Marino, California; Richard W. Thompson letters, Indiana University Library; Willam E. Chandler Papers and Manuscripts, John A. Dahlgren Papers, Louis M. Goldsborough Papers, Stephen B. Luce Papers, Willie P. Mangum Papers, Edward L. Plumb Papers, David D. Porter Papers, George C. Remey Papers, William H. Seward Papers, and Charles Wilkes Papers, Manuscripts Division, Library of Congress; James B. Angell Papers, Michigan Historical Collections, University of Michigan; Robert W. Shufeldt letters, New York Public Library; William H. Seward Collection, Rush-Rhees Library, University of Rochester; Pierce Butler Papers, Special Collections Division, Tulane University Library; Roger S. Baldwin Papers, William C. Redfield Papers, Sterling Memorial Library; and Truman Smith letters, Beinecke Rare Book Room and Manuscript Library, Yale University. Most significant for the study were the Angell, Chandler, Luce, Mangum, Porter, Seward, and Wilkes papers. The Shufeldt manuscript collection dovetails neatly with correspondence in these collections. A number of Shufeldt's letters and questions on the navy and Korea can be found in them and their replies in his correspondence.

The following State Department Archives, National Archives, Record Group 59 were used extensively. References are followed by an RG microcopy number and roll number: Diplomatic Instructions of the Department of State, 1801–1906, to Ministers in *China*, vol. 3 (Jan. 1, 1879–Feb. 28, 1885), M-77 r. 40; *Great Britain*, vol. 25 (Aug. 3, 1877–Sept. 30, 1880), M-77, r. 84; *Japan*, vols. 2–3 (July 2, 1872–Nov. 21, 1890), M-77, rs. 105–106; *Liberia*, vol. 2 (Oct. 6, 1875–July 19, 1906), M-77, r. 110; and *Mexico*, vols. 17–18 (May 6, 1854–Apr. 26, 1873), M-77, rs. 113–114. Diplomatic Instructions of the Department of State, 1801–1906, to Consuls, vols. 31 (1862) and 98 (1881). Diplomatic Dispatches from United States Ministers to *China*, vols. 23–24 (Jan. 6, 1866–Sept. 26, 1868), M-92, rs. 24–25, and vols. 57–61 (Mar. 3, 1881–Oct. 17, 1882), M-92, rs. 58–62; *Japan*, vols. 41–46 (Nov. 6, 1879–May 23, 1882), M-133, rs. 41–46; *Korea*, vols. 1–2 (Mar. 13, 1883–Oct. 15, 1885), M-134, rs. 1–2; *Liberia*, vols. 7–8 (Nov. 18, 1877–May 5, 1882), M-170, rs. 7–8; and *Mexico*, vols. 28–29 (Dec. 21, 1859–May 1, 1863), M-97, rs. 29–30.

In addition, the following consular dispatches and notes to legations were used: Dispatches from United States Consuls to the Department of State from Consuls in *Bombay*, vol. 3 (Jan. 13, 1870–May 5, 1881), T-168, r. 3; *Cape Town*, vol. 11 (June 20, 1872–June 14, 1880), T-191, r. 11; *Chefoo*, vol. 1 (Mar. 10, 1863–Oct. 10, 1869), M-102, r. 1; *Chinkiang*, vol. 1 (Sept. 16, 1864–Dec. 31, 1869), M-103, r. 1; *Foochow*, vol. 3 (Jan. 2, 1864–Dec. 31, 1869), M-105, r. 3; *Gabon*, vol. 1 (Apr. 2, 1856–Feb. 24, 1888), T-466, r. 1; *Havana*, vols. 41–45 (Jan. 3, 1861–

Dec. 31, 1862, and supplementary volumes for 1861 and from 1854–1862), T–20, rs. 41–45; *Hong Kong,* vols. 5–6 (Nov. 20, 1855–Dec. 31, 1869), M–108, rs. 5–6; *Manila,* vol. 7 (July 4, 1879–June 16, 1882), T–43, r. 6; *Mexico City,* vols. 11–12 (Jan. 15, 1861–Dec. 10, 1869), M–296, r. 6; *Minatitlan,* vols. 1–2 (June 2, 1853–July 5, 1881), T–221, rs. 1–2; *Monrovia,* vol. 3 (Apr. 15, 1875–Aug. 11, 1882), M–169, r. 3; *Nagasaki,* vol. 3 (Mar. 29, 1877–Jan. 23, 1883), M–131, r. 3; *Shanghai,* vols. 8, 33 (Feb. 22, 1866–Dec. 27, 1867, and Jan. 3, 1882–Feb. 19, 1883), M–112, rs. 8, 33; *Singapore,* vol. 13 (May 2, 1879–July 1, 1880), T–128, r. 13; *St. Helena,* vol. 16 (Mar. 23, 1875–Oct. 12, 1880), T–426, r. 16; *Tamatave,* vol. 2 (Jan. 5, 1870–May 20, 1886), T–60, r. 2; *Tehuantepec,* vol. 1 (June 22, 1850–Dec. 17, 1867), M–305, r. 1; *Zanzibar,* vol. 6 (Feb. 2, 1870–Oct. 25, 1882), T–100, r. 6. Notes to Foreign Legations in the United States from the Department of State: *Great Britain,* vols. 17, 18 (July 28, 1875–Mar. 8, 1882), M–99, rs. 46–47. Notes from Foreign Legations in the United States to the Department of State: *Great Britain,* vols. 103–104 (Feb. 9, 1878–Dec. 29, 1879), M–50, rs. T–103–104, and *Liberia,* vol. 1 (July 9, 1862–Feb. 16, 1898), T–807, r. 1. Miscellaneous Letters of the Department of State, vols. 523–582 (Oct. 18, 1878–Mar. 31, 1881), M–179, rs. 523–582. Domestic Letters of the Department of State, vols. 125–136 (Oct. 22, 1878–Dec. 31, 1881), M–40, rs. 87–97.

Navy Department archives used included Letters sent by the Secretary of the Navy to Chiefs of Navy Bureaus, vols. 5–7 (Jan. 9, 1869–Nov. 13, 1886) and Letters Received by the Secretary of the Navy from Chiefs of Navy Bureaus, vols. 71–76 (Jan. 2, 1874–Dec. 29, 1879), both RG 45. Other archival sources included British Foreign Office Papers, Public Record Office, London, F.O. 72/1013 and 1041, British Consul General in *Havana,* 1861, and Shufeldt's will, located in Registrar of Wills, United States District Court for the District of Columbia, Washington, D.C., Administration no. 6962, Nov. 11, 1895.

Abbreviations Used in Notes and Bibliographical Essay

AfNL	*Africana Newsletter*
AGSJ	*American Geographical Society Journal*
AGSNYJ	*American Geographical Society of New York Journal*
AH	*American Heritage*
AHI	*American History Illustrated*
AHR	*American Historical Review*
AJIL	*American Journal of International Law*
AN	*American Neptune*
AP	*American Perspective*
ARAHA	*Annual Report of the American Historical Association*
ARCBER	*Annual Report of the Chief of the Bureau of Equipment and Recruiting*
ARSN	*Annual Report of the Secretary of the Navy*
AW	*African World*
BAGS	*Bulletin of the American Geographical Society*
BBAAS	*Bulletin of the British Association of American Studies*
BDAC	*Biographical Directory of the American Congress*
BIHR	*Bulletin of the Institute of Historical Research*
BUPAH	*Boston University Publications in African History*
CD	Dispatches from United States Consuls
Cd'HM	*Cahiers d'Histoire Mondiale*
CI	Instructions of the Department of State to Consuls
CPS	*Cyclopedia of Political Science*
CSPSR	*Chinese Social and Political Science Review*
CWH	*Civil War History*
DAB	*Dictionary of American Biography*
DBR	*Debow's Review*
DD	Diplomatic Dispatches from United States Ministers

DI	Diplomatic Instructions of the Department of State
DLDS	Domestic Letters of the Department of State
DUM	*Dublin University Magazine*
EIHC	*Essex Institute Historical Collections*
FEER	*Far Eastern Economic Review*
FHQ	*Florida Historical Quarterly*
FO	British Foreign Office Papers
For Rel	*Papers Relating to the Foreign Relations of the United States*
GC	General Correspondence, Robert Wilson Shufeldt Papers
GR	*Geographical Review*
H	*Historian*
HAHR	*Hispanic-American Historical Review*
HJAS	*Harvard Journal of Asiatic Studies*
HUEARCPC	*Harvard University East Asian Research Center Papers on China*
JAfH	*Journal of African History*
JAH	*Journal of American History*
JAS	*Journal of Asian Studies*
JAticS	*Journal of Asiatic Studies*
JHR	*Journal of Human Relations*
JHSN	*Journal of the Historical Society of Nigeria*
JMissH	*Journal of Mississippi History*
JNH	*Journal of Negro History*
JSH	*Journal of Southern History*
JSS	*Journal of Social Sciences*
KA	*Korean Affairs*
KC	*Korean Culture*
KJ	*Korea Journal*
KLBK	Korean Letterbook, formal letters to the Secretary of the Navy and the Secretary of State, from July 1, 1881 to Aug. 3, 1882
KM	*Korea Magazine*
KQ	*Koreana Quarterly*
KR	*Korea Review*
KRep	*Korean Repository*
KS	*Korean Survey*
LH	*Louisiana History*
LHQ	*Louisiana Historical Quarterly*
LPCOC	Letterpress copies of official correspondence prepared during global cruise of the USS *Ticonderoga*
LRBC	Letters Received by Secretaries of the Navy from Chiefs of Navy Bureaus

Abbreviations

MA	*Military Affairs*
M-Am	*Mid-America*
MAQR	*Michigan Alumnus Quarterly Review*
MASALP	*Michigan Academy of Science, Arts and Letters, Papers*
MDLC	Manuscripts Division, Library of Congress
ML	*Medical Life* (New York)
MLDS	Miscellaneous Letters of the Department of State
MN	*Monumenta Nipponica*
MVHR	*Mississippi Valley Historical Review*
NA	National Archives
NAR	*North American Review*
NJHSP	*New Jersey Historical Society Proceedings*
NSEQ	*Nankai Social and Economic Quarterly*
NYGBR	*New York Genealogical and Biographical Record*
OC	Official Correspondence, Robert Wilson Shufeldt Papers
OR	*Official Records of the War of the Rebellion*
ORUCN	*Official Records of the Union and Confederate Navies in the War of the Rebellion*
P	*Phylon*
PHR	*Pacific Historical Review*
PRO	Public Record Office, London
PSQ	*Political Science Quarterly*
RGSJ	*Royal Geographical Society Journal*
RWS	Robert Wilson Shufeldt Papers
SA	*Studies on Asia*
SL	*Studies on the Left*
SLBC	Letters sent by Secretaries of the Navy to Chiefs of Navy Bureaus
SM	*Sunday Magazine* (New York, Nineteenth Century)
TKBRAS	*Transactions of the Korean Branch of the Royal Asiatic Society*
TNR	*Tanganyika Notes and Records*
TRHS	*Transactions of the Royal Historical Society*
USNIP	*United States Naval Institute Proceedings*
YBDCHS	*Year Book of the Dutchess County Historical Society*

Notes

CHAPTER I

1. Shufeldt's description is taken from a passport, no. 2636, issued Aug. 29, 1861: "Age 36 [*sic*], Height 6 feet 1½ inches, Forehead high and broad, Eyes blue, Nose prominent, Mouth medium, Chin round, Hair dark brown, Complexion dark, Face full." Robert Wilson Shufeldt Papers [hereafter RWS], Manuscripts Division, Library of Congress [hereafter cited as MDLC], box 35, Miscellany, 1836–1893, and undated folio (certificates, awards, and passports, 1853–1861). The items of news are in Shufeldt [hereafter S.] to Gentlemen (newspaper owners), Apr. 4, 1855, RWS 11, General Correspondence [hereafter GC], 1838–1900, and undated (1843–1857).

2. Fox to S., Dec. 6, 1873, RWS 15, GC, 1838–1900, and undated (Dec. 1873).

3. G. A. Shufeldt to S., Feb. 18, 1841, RWS 11 (1838–1847).

4. H. H. Shufeldt to S., Mar. 16, 1870, RWS 13, GC, and undated (Mar. 1870).

5. Hiram Paulding [name removed] to G. A. Shufeldt and to S., Aug. 5 and Oct. 31, 1839, RWS 5, Official Correspondence [hereafter OC], 1839–1862 (1839).

6. S., diary entry, Oct. 28, 1865, vol. USS *Hartford,* "On a Cruise to the China Seas," Aug.–Dec. 1865, RWS 1, Diaries, Notebooks, Logbooks, and Journals, 1865–1880.

7. G. A. Shufeldt to S., Feb. 18, 1841, RWS 11 (1838–1847).

8. Goldsborough to Elizabeth W. Goldsborough, Feb. 21, 1842, Louis M. Goldsborough Papers 5 (Apr. 29, 1841–Feb. 1847), 719–720, MDLC. For background to the cruise, see C. G. Ridgely to S., Aug. 11, 1841, RWS 5 (1841–1842).

9. On the years between 1842 and 1844, see Abel P. Upshur to S., June 16, Aug. 8 and 16, Dec. 3, 1842 and May 3, 1843; Charles H. Winder to S., Aug. 4, 1842; David Henshaw to S., Sept. 26, Oct. 18, and Nov. 24, 1843; D. Connor to S. and J. S. Bohrer, July 9 and Aug. 29, 1844; T. A. Gillis to S., Sept. 19, 1844, in RWS 5 (1841–1842) and (1843–1844).

10. G. A. W. Stoker to S., Aug. 12, 1841; Belt to S., Mar. 17 and 21, 1842; Goldsborough to "whom it may concern," June 22, 1842; J. M. Pearson to S., Dec. 9, 1842; D. F. Johnston to S., Apr. 27 and June 22, 1843, all in *ibid.*

11. Morgan to S., Apr. 30, 1845; Surgeon B. F. Bache to [Morgan], May 29, 1845; G. C. Read to S., June 2, 1845; George Bancroft to S., June 5 and 20, 1845 (for the naval school); Davis to S., Aug. 7, 1845 and Feb. 12 and 18, 1846; J. Hull to S., Feb. 21, 1846; A. D. Bache to S., Feb. 25, 1846 (for the Coast Survey); Bancroft to S., Feb. 23 and Apr. 9, 1846 (West African squadron), all in RWS 5 (1845) and (1846-1848).

12. Read to S., Sept. 1, 1846, *ibid.*; S. to E. and G. W. Blunt, Sept. 15, 1848, and to Redfield, Oct. 25, 1848, in William C. Redfield MSS, Yale University Library; *London Nautical Magazine* (1849): 39; Redfield to S., Oct. 6, 1848, RWS 5 (1846-1848).

13. H. B. Shufelt, *Our Folks: A History of the Shufelt Family* (Claverack, New York, 1929), 50; on Reverend James Abercrombie, see R. W. Shufeldt, Jr., "Life History of an American Naturalist," *ML* 31, no. 2 (Feb. 1924): 69, n. 1; Barlow's passes in RWS 5 (1846-1848); Davis to S., Nov. 11, 1848, RWS 11 (1848-1857).

14. Davis to S., Nov. 11, 1848, RWS 11 (1848-1857); J. Y. Mason to S., Sept. 16, 1848, Feb. 27 and Mar. 16, 1849; A. O. Dayton to S., Jan. 23, 1849; A. D. Bache to S., Mar. 24, 1849; W. B. Preston to S., June 16, 1849, in RWS 5 (1846-1848) and (1849).

15. Preston to J. West and S., June 18, Aug. 9, and Oct. 25, 1849, and Apr. 13, 1850; C. S. Boggs to W. H. Davage, Mar. 11, 1850 and to S., Mar. 12, 1850, RWS 5 (1849) and (1850-1851); Dayton to S., Feb. 12, 1850, RWS 11 (1848-1857).

16. Report of J. West, Jan. 22, 1851; Statement of Lieutenant Shufeldt, *New York Evening Post,* Feb. 17, 1851; also in *New York Daily Tribune,* Feb. 17, 1851; *London Times,* Feb. 5, 1851, quoting *Cork Reporter,* Jan. 25, 1851.

17. Boyd to S., Jan. 24, 1851, and West to S., Jan. 27, 1851, RWS 5 (1850-1851); *New York Evening Post,* Feb. 17, 1851; passenger resolutions in *New York Daily Tribune,* Feb. 17, 1851; *London Times,* Feb. 5, 1851; *Albany Argus,* Feb. 18, 1851; *New Orleans Daily Picayune,* Feb. 20 and 26, 1851. Letters of thanks, James Brown to S., and two unidentified letters to S., March 8, 10, and April 2, 1851, RWS 5 (1850-1851).

18. R. W. Shufeldt, Jr., "Life History of an American Naturalist," 68.

19. For assignment to the *Georgia,* see S. to Sir [J. Brown?], Apr. 12, 1851; W. A. Graham to S., Apr. 11, 1851; M. C. Perry to S., Apr. 15, 19, and May 8, 1851; Graham to Perry, May 5, 1851; for detachment from the *Georgia,* see Graham to Perry, Sept. 11, 1851; for the furloughs, see Graham to S., Feb. 28, 1852; John P. Kennedy to W. R. King and to S., Aug. 30, 1852, and Mar. 12, 1853; Dobbin to S., Mar. 23 and Sept. 5, 1853, all in RWS 5 (1850-1851) and (1852-1853). For promotions, see Robert Wilson Shufeldt file, National Archives [hereafter NA].

20. G. M. Parker to S., Nov. 10, 1858, RWS 11 (Nov. 1858); Shufeldt file, NA. The birthdates of Shufeldt's sons are in H. B. Shufelt, *Our Folks,* 52.

21. Essay on "Spiritualism," RWS 35, Diary, 1864-1868; the "Original

poems, songs, essays, and other writings [Shufeldt composed] aboard the USS *Proteus* and the USS *Hartford,* 1864-1868," are also in this diary [hereafter Diary, 1864-1868].

CHAPTER 2

1. S. to Seward, Nov. 16, 1861, RWS 20, official and other papers on Tehuantepec-Nicaragua Survey Expedition, 1870-1871 (1861-Sept. 1870); also in Dispatches from United States Consuls in Havana [hereafter CD, Havana], vol. 41 (Jan. 3-Dec. 31, 1861), dated Nov. 21, 1861; "Through Mexico to the Pacific—In Search of a Canal Route" [undated but post-1870], 26, RWS 21, official and other papers on Tehuantepec-Nicaragua Survey Expedition (written reports). See the bibliography for secondary materials used.

2. *New Orleans Daily Picayune,* Apr. 21, Sept. 18, 29, and 30, 1857; S. to Quitman, Feb. 15, 1857, Quitman Papers, Houghton Library, Harvard University, box bMS Am (196), also for the next two paragraphs.

3. *New Orleans Daily Picayune,* Aug. 2, Sept. 29 and 30, and Nov. 19, 1857.

4. C. Gardner, comp., *New Orleans Directory for the Year 1858,* 186; *Directory for the Year 1859,* 177 and 372; P. A. Hargous to S., Oct. 8, 1858, RWS 11 (Jan.-Oct. 1858); *New Orleans Daily Picayune,* Sept. 18 and 29 and Oct. 10, 1857.

5. Company operations can be followed in N. S. Stevens to S., Jan. 7, 1858; L. Hermann to S., Feb. 4, 1858; C. Walsh to S., Oct. 28, 1858; Y. M. Zangroniz to S., Nov. 2, 1858; S. H. Ackerman and W. Boardman to S., Nov. 5, 1858; Ackerman to S., Nov. 5, 1858, and Jan. 3, 1859; L. Heyliger to S., Nov. 11, 1858; E. J. Strong to S., Nov. 12, 1858; T. Dibblee to S., Nov. 6, Dec. 2 and 18, 1858; H. M. Humphrey to S., Nov. 25, 1858; Hargous to S., Nov. 20, 1858, and Jan. 9, 1859; J. M. Murphy to [?] Perry, Jan. 28, 1859, all in RWS 11 (Jan.-Oct. 1858), (Nov. 1858), (Dec. 1858), and (Jan. 1859). See also the Record of Treasury fees received at Minatitlan ending the quarter to Dec. 31, 1858, CD, Minatitlan, vol. 1 (June 2, 1853-Dec. 1, 1869). The room location and the French lessons are recalled in R. W. Shufeldt, Jr., "Life History of an American Naturalist," *ML* 31, no. 2 (Feb. 1924): 68; on Shufeldt's "flattering paragraphs," see R. D. Hatch to S., Jan. 18, 1859, RWS 11 (Jan. 1859).

6. Hatch to S., Jan. 31, 1859; see also H. S. Stevens to S., Feb. 16, 1859, both in RWS 11 (Jan. 1859) and (Feb. 1859).

7. R. S. Bunker to S., Apr. 24, 1859, RWS 11 (Jan.-Oct. 1859); *New Orleans Daily True Delta,* May 27, 1859; Hargous to S., Apr. 18 and 25, 1862; RWS 20 (1861-Sept. 1870); Petition of Truman Smith "at the instance of Peter A. Hargous, Esq. merchant of the City of New York," to William H. Seward, Jan. 27, 1862, in RWS 20 (1861-Sept. 1870).

8. The incident is covered fully in S. to Messrs. Hargous & Co., Oct. 7, 1859, in the *New York Times,* Oct. 13, 1859. See "Accident to the Steamship *Quaker City,*" *New York Times,* Oct. 10, 1859; "The Disaster to the *Quaker City,*" *Norfolk Herald,* Oct. 11, 1859; "The Accident to the *Quaker City,*" *New York Herald,* Oct. 11, 1859; "The *Quaker City* Disaster" and "A New York Steamship in Peril," *New York Express,* Oct. 11, 1859; "The Fate of the *Quaker City,*" *New York Times,* Oct. 12, 1859; "Fate of the *Quaker City,*" *New York Daily Tribune,* Oct. 13,

1859; "The Disaster to the *Quaker City,*" *New York Herald,* Oct. 13, 1859; "Captain Shufeldt's Statement," *New York Daily Tribune,* Oct. 14, 1859. The Hargous interview is in the *New York Express,* Oct. 11, 1859; the recollections about Shufeldt are in S. P. G. to the editor of the *Herald,* Oct. 12, 1859.

9. "Arrival of the Rescued Passengers," and "Narrative of a Lady Passenger," given in "The Fate of the *Quaker City,*" in the *New York Daily Tribune,* Oct. 13, 1859; A. B. Neilson, president of the New York Board of Underwriters, to Howell Cobb, Oct. 10 and 11, 1859, *New York Herald,* Oct. 11, 1859; on the Havana run, see S. to J. D. Bulloch, June 13, 1860, RWS 11 (1860). Shufeldt was now living in New York City at the LaFarge Hotel on Broadway, from where his son, Robert, attended a public school on Bleeker Street.

10. S., "Are We Prepared for War?" *New York Herald,* May 29, 1858, copy in RWS 31, newspaper clippings (naval policies 1850s-1880s).

11. For the location and the details of the house in Stamford, see R. W. Shufeldt, Jr., "Life History of an American Naturalist," nos. 2 and 4 (Feb. and Apr. 1924): 69-70 and 140-141.

12. There is no biography of Smith. For information on him see, F. C. Drake, ed., "Secret History of the Slave Trade to Cuba Written by an American Naval Officer, 1861," *JNH* 55 (1970): 218-219. For possible contacts between Smith and Shufeldt, see W. Boardman to S., Nov. 5 and 19, 1858, and J. B. Ferris to S., Nov. 5, 1858; Smith to S., June 19, 1861, RWS 11 (Nov. 1858) and (Jan.-Oct. 1861), and Smith to G. Welles, June 18, 1861, Gideon Welles Papers, Connecticut Historical Society.

13. For the treaty of April 7, 1862, see *Papers Relating to the Foreign Relations of the United States, 1862* [hereafter *For Rel*] (Washington, D.C., 1862), 64-65, 158-159, 164-165, 181, 185, 289, and 473; A. Taylor Milne, "The Lyons-Seward Treaty of 1862," *AHR* 38 (1932-1933): 511-525. Shufeldt's account of the Cuban slave trade is in S. to Smith, Jan. 6, 1861, "The Secret History of the Slave Trade," RWS 11 (Jan.-Oct. 1861). This document, summarized here, is given in full in Drake, "Secret History of the Slave Trade to Cuba," 218-235.

14. The British Consul General in Havana, Joseph T. Crawford, estimated the profitability of the slave trade in the late 1850s as follows: cost $150,000; proceeds, $540,000 (450 slaves at $1,200 each); profit $389,850. See W. S. Howard, *American Slavers and the Federal Law* (Berkeley, 1963), Appendix C, 236-237, who estimated the trade cost at $159,000; proceeds at $250,000 (500 slaves at $500 each); and profit at $90,500. Shufeldt's estimate of cost is much lower than Crawford's or Howard's because it omits provisions, food, etc., but his proceeds and profits are halfway between their estimates.

15. Howard estimated the number from 1857-1859 at 6,000 each year and in 1859-1860, 11,000 per year, *ibid.,* Appendix K, 256. Hubert S. Aimes, in *A History of Slavery in Cuba 1511 to 1868* (New York, 1907), Appendix II, 269, put the number at 9,000 for 1856-1859 (2,500 per year), and 3,000 for 1860, 2,000 for 1861, and 600 for 1862.

16. S. to Seward, draft, Nov. 16, 1861, RWS 20 (1861-Sept. 1870) and a final version, Nov. 21, 1861, in CD, Havana 41.

17. "Through Mexico to the Pacific—In Search of a Canal Route," RWS 21 (written reports).

CHAPTER 3

1. Breese to the Secretary of the Navy, Apr. 25, 1861, in Richard Rush et al., eds., *Official Records of the Union and Confederate Navies in the War of the Rebellion* [hereafter *ORUCN*] (Washington, D.C., 1894-1914), ser. 1, vol. 4:332; Report of Flag Officer Stringham, July 23, 1861, *ibid.,* 6:30; Smith to S., June 19, 1861, RWS 11 (Nov. 1861) and (Jan.-Oct. 1861); "Memorandum on Foreign Appointments," ca. Apr. 1861, in R. P. Basler, ed., *The Collected Works of Abraham Lincoln* (New Brunswick, 1953), 4:310; S. to Seward, Apr. 7, 22, and July 4, 1861, in CD, Havana 41; W. H. Aspinwall to Welles, Apr. 29, 1861, *ORUCN,* ser. 1, 4:349. An expanded version of the first two sections of this chapter has appeared in F. C. Drake, "The Cuban Background of the *Trent* Affair," *CWH* 19 (1973): 29-49, and the author is grateful to the editor of *CWH* for permission to reprint.

2. S. to Robert Jr. in R. W. Shufeldt, Jr., "Life History of an American Naturalist," *ML* 31, no. 2 (Feb. 1924): 70.

3. On the descriptions of the house, schooling, family anecdotes, and neighbors, see *ibid.,* 70-72, 74-76.

4. Information on Crawford from *London Times,* Aug. 24 and 25, 1864. Crawford to Russell, no. 15, Apr. 6, 1861, and to Milne, Apr. 17, 1861, British Foreign Office Papers [hereafter FO], 72/1013 British Consul General in Havana, 1861, Spain, Consuls at Havana, Trinidad de Cuba; Crawford, Smith (Jan.-Dec. 1861), Public Record Office, London [hereafter PRO].

5. S. to Seward, nos. 26 and 29, May 9 and 14, 1861, CD, Havana 41; Don Blas Garcia de Quesada to S., May 7 and 10, 1861, nos. 1 and 2, with no. 29, of May 14.

6. Crawford to S., May 11 and 12, 1861; S. to Crawford, May 11, 1861; Garcia de Quesada to S., May 11, 1861; S. to Garcia de Quesada, May 11, 1861, enclosures nos. 2, 4-7, with S. to Seward, no. 29, May 14, 1861, CD, Havana 41; Crawford to S., May 10, 1861, in RWS 18, subject file, Official and Other Papers on Cuban Matters (May 1861), clearly gives Shufeldt information on the *Webb*'s purchase, which he may not have received when he informed Seward that he had received no notification of the transfer.

7. S. to Serrano, May 13, 1861, no. 10 enclosure, with S. to Seward, no. 29, May 14, 1861, which listed all the irregularities that Shufeldt found in the *Webb* case; Serrano to S., May [?], 1861, enclosure with no. 1, S. to Seward, no. 31, May 16, 1861, CD, Havana 41.

8. Quarterly returns of American vessels in CD, Havana 44 (Supplements, Oct. 24, 1858 to Dec. 29, 1862); similar reports in F. Chase to S., May 28, 1861, RWS 18 (May 1861); S. to Seward, nos. 38 and 39, June 18, 1861, CD, Havana 41; latter also in *ORUCN,* ser. 1, 16:564-565; Welles to Mervine, July 29, 1861, *ibid.,* 564.

9. Virginia Mason, ed., *The Public Life and Diplomatic Correspondence of James M. Mason* (New York, 1906), 199-203, 209-214; Mason's reports to Robert M. T. Hunter, Oct. 9 and 18, 1861, *ORUCN,* ser. 1, 1:150-151; Wilkes' movements in Wilkes to Welles, Nov. 15 and 16, 1861, *ibid.,* 129-130 and 144, and also in R. N. Scott et al., eds., *Official Records of the War of the Rebellion* [hereafter *OR*] (Washington, D.C., 1880-1901), ser. 2, 2:1080-1081.

10. S. to Seward, no. 73, Oct. 24, 1861, CD, Havana 42 (Supplement, Aug. 20–Oct. 25, 1861), marked "rec'd Nov. 1, 1861"; Seward to Welles, Oct. 15, 1861, William H. Seward Papers, box 1, MDLC.

11. S. to Seward, no. 74, Oct. 25, 1861, CD, Havana 42, and no. 76, Nov. 4, 1861, *ibid.*, 41; Crawford's denial is in Crawford to Lord Lyons, Dec. 2, 1861, FO 72/1013, PRO. The visit is mentioned in Mason, *James M. Mason*, 214, and Louis M. Sears, *John Slidell* (Durham, N. C., 1925), 181.

12. S. to Seward, no. 76, Nov. 4, 1861, CD, Havana 41; see also R. W. Shufeldt, Jr., "Life History of an American Naturalist," 72.

13. S. to Seward, nos. 76 and 79, Nov. 4 and 9, 1861, CD, Havana 41.

14. S. to Seward, no. 79, Nov. 9, 1861, *ibid.*

15. For examples of such claims, see T. L. Harris, *The Trent Affair* (Indianapolis, 1896), 100, and J. S. Long, "Glory-Hunting Off Havana: Wilkes and the *Trent* Affair," *CWH* 9 (1963): 138–139 and n. 11.

16. S. to Wilkes, Dec. 20, 1861, Charles D. Wilkes Papers, Family Papers Special Correspondence [hereafter Wilkes Papers], box 8, "*Trent* Affair" (Letters, Dec. 1861), MDLC; S. to Seward, no. 79, Nov. 9, 1861, CD, Havana 41.

17. Mason, *James M. Mason,* 215; Sears, *John Slidell,* 181.

18. S. to Seward, nos. 76 and 79, Nov. 4 and 9, 1861, CD, Havana 41; Wilkes to Welles, Nov. 15, 1861, *ORUCN,* ser. 1, 1:129, and *OR,* ser. 2, 2:1080.

19. Horner to Wilkes, Dec. 22, 1861; S. to Wilkes, Dec. 20, 1861, Wilkes Papers, box 8; Wilkes to Welles, Nov. 15, 1861, *ORUCN,* ser. 1, 1:129, and *OR,* ser. 2, 2:1080.

20. Long, "Glory-Hunting Off Havana," 139–141; Abbot to S., Nov. 21, 1861; P. S. Shelton, T. Smith, and O. Coles to S., Nov. 25 and 30, 1861; Wilkes to S., Dec. 5, 1861, in RWS 11 (Nov. 1861) and (Dec. 1861).

21. S. to Wilkes, Dec. 20, 1861, Wilkes Papers, box 8.

22. Crawford to Lord Lyons, Nov. 23, 1861, and Crawford to Russell, no. 51, Nov. 23, 1861, FO 72/1013.

23. Crawford to Lord Lyons, Dec. 2, 1861; Crawford to Russell, no. 54, Dec. 3, 1861, *ibid.*

24. S. to Seward, nos. 91 and 109, Nov. 27 and Dec. 24, 1861, CD, Havana 41; Russell's reprimand to Crawford, no. 3, Feb. 17, 1862, FO 72/1041.

25. S. to Seward, no. 91, Nov. 27, 1861, CD, Havana 41; S. to Wilkes, Dec. 20, 1861, Wilkes Papers, box 8.

26. S. to Seward, no. 91, Nov. 27, 1861, CD, Havana 41.

27. S. to Seward, nos. 76, 91, and 109, Nov. 4, 27, and Dec. 24, 1861, CD, Havana 41; Helm on the *Blockade and the Rights of Neutrals* to Don Francisco Serrano, Dec. 5, 1861; S. to Serrano, Dec. 12, 1861, RWS 18 (Dec. 1861); Helm to William M. Browne, Acting Secretary of State (Richmond), Dec. 21, 1861, *ORUCN,* ser. 2, 3:310; S. to F. W. Seward, Oct. 8, 1861, *OR,* ser. 2, 2:93.

28. R. W. Shufeldt, Jr., "Life History of an American Naturalist," 72.

29. S. to Seward, no. 91, Nov. 27, 1861, CD, Havana 41.

30. "Through Mexico to the Pacific—In Search of a Canal Route," 27, RWS 21 (written reports).

31. S. to Seward, no. 87, Nov. 21, 1861, CD, Havana 41, with a draft dated Nov. 16, 1861, in RWS 20 (1861–Sept. 1870).

32. Seward to Corwin, no. 15, Aug. 24, 1861, marked "not sent," and no. 17, Sept. 2, 1861, which was sent, in Diplomatic Instructions of the Department of State, Mexico [hereafter DI, Mexico], vol. 17 (May 6, 1854–Nov. 20, 1867), 360–366 and 368–371; Corwin to Seward, nos. 3–5, 7, July 29, Aug. 28, Sept. 7, and Oct. 29, 1861, in Dispatches from United States Ministers to Mexico [hereafter DD, Mexico], vol. 28 (Dec. 21, 1859–Feb. 5, 1862).

33. S. to Seward, nos. 75, 81, 89, and 96, Oct. 25, Nov. 15 and 22, and Dec. 5, 1861, CD, Havana 42, 41; see also Carl H. Bock, *Prelude to Tragedy: The Negotiation and Breakdown of the Tripartite Convention of London, Oct. 31, 1861* (Philadelphia, 1966), 263, 274–275, and James M. Callahan, *Evolution of Seward's Mexican Policy*, (Morgantown, W. Va., 1909), 28.

34. S. to Seward, no. 96, Dec. 5, 1861, CD, Havana 41.

35. S. to F. W. Seward, Dec. 10, 1861, William Henry Seward Collection, Rush-Rhees Library, University of Rochester [cited as Seward Collection and with permission].

36. S. to Seward, no. 100, Dec. 9, 1861, CD, Havana 41; S. to F. W. Seward, Dec. 10, 1861, Seward Collection.

37. S. to Seward, nos. 114 and 117, Dec. 28 and 31, 1861, CD, Havana 41.

38. S. to Seward, no. 4, Jan. 14, 1862, CD, Havana 45 (Jan. 12–Dec. 31, 1862); S. to F. W. Seward, Jan. 16, 1862, *ibid.*, and also in *OR*, ser. 3, 1: 871–872.

39. S. to Sumner, Jan. 17, 1862, Charles Sumner Collection, Houghton Library, Harvard University, vol. 56, no. 15. Rough draft in RWS 18 (Jan. 1862).

40. S. to Seward, nos. 4, 6, and 8, Jan. 14, 17, and 24, 1862, CD, Havana 45. Shufeldt's estimate coincided exactly with that of the British commander, Commodore Hugh Dunlop, who reported 500 Spanish troops ill by January 15, 1862, mentioned in Bock, *Prelude to Tragedy*, 296, n. 24, and 297, n. 40, citing Dunlop to Admiralty, no. 3, Jan. 15, 1862, FO 50/370, PRO.

41. For the proclamation of the allies, see Callahan, *Evolution of Seward's Mexican Policy*, 29–30. For other pressures on Seward, see Smith to S., Jan 17, 26, and Feb. 3, 1862; Hargous to S., Feb. 4, 1862, RWS 12, GC, 1862–1867 (Jan. 1862) and (Feb. 1862).

42. Bock, *Prelude to Tragedy*, 292; H. H. Bancroft, *History of Mexico* (San Francisco, 1888), 6, 39, n. 28; S. to Seward, no. 13, Feb. 6, 1862, CD, Havana 45.

43. S. to Seward, no. 13, Feb. 6, 1862, CD, Havana 45. By this time General Prim had ordered 600 sick troops back to Havana, and the number rose to 1,000 by the end of February, for which see Bock, *Prelude to Tragedy*, 316 and 327.

44. S. to Seward, no. 20 [unnumbered but between 19 and 21], Feb. 14, 1862, CD, Havana 45.

45. S. to Seward, no. 13, Feb. 6, 1862, *ibid.*

CHAPTER 4

1. S. to Seward, Feb. 24, 1862, and Seward to S., Mar. 1862, preliminary draft of private note, Seward Collection.

2. For Plumb's treaties, see Seward to Plumb, Apr. 11, 1862, DI, Mexico 17, and Plumb Papers, MDLC, especially vol. 5, Plumb to Corwin, Jan. 29, 1862,

Plumb to Seward, Mar. 19, 1862, and vol. 6, Plumb to Seward, Mar. 31, 1862; for Shufeldt's recommendation, see S. to F. W. Seward, Jan. 16, 1862, Seward Collection; for Shufeldt's delight at Scott's appointment, see S. to F. W. Seward, no. 20, Feb. 14, 1862, CD, Havana 45; Plumb to S., Jan. 29 and Feb. 4, 1862, RWS 12 (Jan. 1862) and (Feb. 1862).

3. Plumb to S., Feb. 19, 1862, RWS 12 (Feb. 1862).

4. Plumb to S., Feb. 28, 1862, *ibid.*

5. S. to Seward, private letter, Feb. 24, 1862, Seward Collection and no. 28, Feb. 28, 1862, CD, Havana 45; and Seward's response in "Seward's Diary or Notes on the War, Mar. 10, 1862," in George E. Baker, ed., *The Works of William H. Seward* (Boston, 1883), 5:49.

6. S. to Seward, no. 28, Feb. 28, 1862, and Dunnell to S., Mar. 3, 1862, CD, Havana 45.

7. S. to Seward, no. 31, Mar. 7, 1862; Dunnell to S., Mar. 3, 1862; CD, Havana 45; cf. Dunnell's sober reporting in Dunnell to S., Mar. 22, 1862, *ibid.*, with Plumb's optimistic letters from Washington, Plumb to S., Mar. 11, 1862, RWS 12 (Mar. 1862); and RWS 19, subject file, Official and Other Papers on Cuban Matters (Mexico, 1862).

8. Seward quotation from James M. Callahan, *Evolution of Seward's Mexican Policy* (Morgantown, W. Va., 1909), 31-33; S. to Seward, Mar. 12, 1862, CD, Havana 45. Shufeldt remained suspicious of Prim until April, for which see S. to Seward, no. 43, Apr. 1, 1862, *ibid.*

9. S. to F. W. Seward, private letter, Mar. 20, 1862, CD, Havana 45.

10. S. to F. W. Seward, private letter, Apr. 1, 1862, *ibid.*

11. S. to Seward, no. 37, Mar. 22, 1862, *ibid.*

12. Quoted in James M. Callahan, *American Foreign Policy in Mexican Relations* (New York, 1932), 288, and *Evolution of Seward's Mexican Policy,* 33; J. F. Rippy, *The United States and Mexico* (New York, 1926), 259; Seward to S., two letters, Mar. 31, 1862, in Instructions of the Department of State to Consuls [hereafter CI], Havana, vol. 31:332-334, copies in RWS 19 (Mexico, 1862).

13. S. to Seward, nos. 48, 50, 51, Apr. 10, 16, and 17, 1862, CD, Havana 45. On Orizaba, see H. H. Bancroft, *History of Mexico* (San Francisco, 1888), 6:42; C. H. Bock, *Prelude to Tragedy: The Negotiation and Breakdown of the Tripartite Convention of London, Oct. 31, 1861* (Philadelphia, 1966), 555-570, Appendix T, "Protocol of the Final Conference of the Allied Commissioners, Orizaba, April 9, 1862," and for the final breach, see 417-418 and 425-429.

14. S. to Seward, private letter, Apr. 17, 1862, CD, Havana 45.

15. S. to Seward, two letters, May 1, 1862, with a manifesto of the French residents of Mexico against the French occupation, *ibid.* For background on the French movement, see Callahan, *Evolution of Seward's Mexican Policy,* 30-31; Bancroft, *History of Mexico,* 6:46; and Bock, *Prelude to Tragedy,* 425 and 429.

16. S. to Seward, May 1 and no. 2, May 3, 1862, long quotation from the latter, CD, Havana 45; on Plumb's arrival, see Plumb to Seward, May 4, 1862, DD, Mexico 29 (Feb. 18, 1862-May 1, 1863).

17. S. to Seward, no. 2, May 3, 1862, CD, Havana 45.

18. S. to Seward, nos. 2 and 3, May 3 and 8, with a short letter also dated May 8, 1862, CD, Havana 45; Plumb to Seward, May 8, 1862, DD, Mexico 29.

19. S. to Seward, May 8 and June 5, 1862, CD, Havana 45; Corwin to Seward, no. 24, May 20, 1862, DD, Mexico 29.

20. S. to Doblado, May 16, 1862, with S. to Seward, June 5, 1862, CD, Havana 45.

21. Doblado to S., May 19, 1862, *ibid.*

22. Corwin to S., June 27, 1862, RWS 12 (June-July, 1862) and July 11, 1862, RWS 19 (May-Sept. 1862); Corwin to Seward, no. 24, and private letter [received June 14 between nos. 28 and 29], May 20 and 22, 1862, DD, Mexico 29.

23. Seward to S., May 23, 1862, CI, Havana 31, 408-409.

24. S. to Seward, June 5, 1862, CD, Havana 45.

25. S. to Seward, private letter, June 5, 1862, *ibid.*

26. Seward to S., June 24, 1862, CI, Havana 31, 437-438, copy in RWS 19 (May-Sept. 1862).

27. S. to Seward, no. 68, July 4, 1862, CD, Havana 45.

28. S. to Seward, no. 68, July 4, 1862, *ibid.*; S. to F. W. Seward, July 5, 1862, Seward Collection.

29. Quotation from Frederic Bancroft, *The Life of William H. Seward* (Gloucester, Mass., 1967), 2:430, esp. 419-442.

30. Seward to S., July 15, 1862, CI, Havana 31, 466-468, a copy in RWS 19 (May-Sept. 1862).

31. Memorandum of Slidell's interview with the emperor, July 16, 1862, in Slidell to Benjamin, July 25, 1862, *ORUCN*, ser. 2, 3:486-487.

32. S. to Seward, private letter, Oct. 9, 1862, RWS 19 (Oct.-Dec. 1862); S. to F. W. Seward, Nov. 25, 1862, Seward Collection; "Through Mexico to the Pacific—In Search of a Canal Route," 29-30, in RWS 21 (written reports).

33. S. to Seward, nos. 84, 85, 96, 97, and 100, Aug. 15 and 30, Oct. 9 and 13, 1862, Nov. 20, 1861, CD, Havana 41; S. to B. des Essard, Oct. 4, 1862; and to F. W. Seward, nos. 103 and 108, Oct. 24 and Nov. 14, 1862, CD, Havana 45, with copy of S. to Seward, Oct. 13, 1862, in RWS 19 (Oct.-Dec. 1862). For the quotation, see S. to Seward, Jan. 24, 1863, Seward Collection; it also appeared in S. to Rear Admiral David G. Farragut, Dec. 1, 1862, *ORUCN*, ser. 1, 19:386-387.

34. On Dulce, see S. to Seward, no. 116, Dec. 11, 1862, CD, Havana 45; for Shufeldt's feelings, see S. to Seward, private letter, Jan. 24, 1863, Seward Collection.

35. For Spanish partiality over the *Florida*, see S. to Seward, no. 8, Jan. 24, 1863 [mistakenly dated 1862 and thus filed in CD, Havana 44 (Oct. 24, 1858-Dec. 29, 1862)], copy in *ORUCN*, ser. 1, 2:49-51, dated 1863, accompanying S. to Seward, Jan 21, 1863, *ibid.*, 47-49. See also Helm to Benjamin, Jan. 26, 1863, *ibid.*, ser. 2, 3:670, and ser. 1, 2:641; Farragut to S., Jan. 26, Feb. 3, 6, and 26, 1863, in RWS 6, OC, 1863-1865 (Jan.-Apr. 1863), also in *ORUCN*, ser. 1, 19:582, 597, and 604; S. to Farragut, Jan. 29, 1863, *ibid.*, ser. 1, 2:64-65, and ser. 1, 19:598; S. to Seward, private letter, Jan. 24, 1863, Seward Collection.

36. Shufeldt's plans to rejoin the navy are revealed in Smith to S., May 30 and Nov. 21, 1861, Jan. 3, 7, and 17, Mar. 4, 14, and 18, and Dec. 16, 1862, RWS 18 (May 1861), RWS 11 (Nov. 1861), RWS 12 (Jan. 1862) and (Mar.

1862), and RWS 19 (Oct.-Dec. 1862), respectively; Fox to Seward, Mar. 14, 1863, RWS 18 (Aug.-Oct. 1861).

37. Seward to S., Apr. 15, 1863; Welles to S., Apr. 17, 1863; and F. W. Seward to S., Apr. 21, 1863, RWS 6 (Jan.-Apr. 1863) and RWS 19 (Feb.-Apr. 1863).

CHAPTER 5

1. Welles to S., May 8, 1863, and S. to DuPont, June 1, 1863, RWS 6 (May-June 1863); for the *Conemaugh,* see *ORUCN,* ser. 1, 14:229-230.

2. Abstract log of USS *Conemaugh,* June 8, 1863; *ORUCN,* ser. 1, 14:245; S. to DuPont, June 8, 1863, RWS 6 (May-June 1863); DuPont to S., June 12, 1863, *ORUCN,* ser. 1, 14:244.

3. Essay on "Contraband," in RWS 35, Diary, 1864-1868.

4. Dahlgren to S., June 12, 1863; DuPont to S., June 12 and July 5, 1863; S. to DuPont, June 16 and 26, 1863; S. C. Rowan to S., July 8, 1863, and W. C. Reynolds to S., July 17 to 26, 1863, in RWS 6 (May-June 1863) and (July 1863), with Rowan's July 8 letter in *ORUCN,* ser. 1, 14:315-316; Dahlgren to S., July 12, 1863, John A. Dahlgren Papers, General Correspondence, box 8, Letterbook, June 27-July 29, 1863, 31, MDLC; S. to Dahlgren, July 27, 1863, *ibid.,* box 5, Sept. 1861-July 1863, folder (July 21-31, 1863).

5. Dahlgren to S., Sept. 2 and 12, 1863, RWS 6 (Sept. 1863), also in *ORUCN,* ser. 1, 14:580, and Dahlgren Papers, General Correspondence, box 8, Letterbook, Aug. 28-Oct. 10, 1863, 68 and 272; S. to Welles, Sept. 5, 1863, and S. to Dahlgren, Sept. 5, 1863, RWS 6 (Sept. 1863); Dahlgren to Welles, Oct. 30, 1863, *ORUCN,* ser. 1, 15:92.

6. Welles to S., Sept. 17, 1863, Welles Collection, Henry E. Huntington Library, San Marino, California. This letter is a reply to a second Shufeldt letter of Sept. 5 (which has not survived), discussing the effectiveness of the Charleston blockade.

7. Howard K. Beale, ed., *Diary of Gideon Welles: Secretary of the Navy under Lincoln and Johnson* (New York, 1960), 1:434, entry for Sept. 15, 1863.

8. *Ibid.,* 466-467, entry for Sat., Oct. 3, 1863.

9. Welles to S., Sept. 17, 1863, Welles Collection.

10. Welles to S., Oct. 6, 1863, RWS 6 (Oct.-Dec. 1863); vessel's description in R. W. Shufeldt, Jr., "Life History of an American Naturalist," *ML* 31, no. 4 (Apr. 1924): 142-144; Becky [Mrs. R. Watson] to S., Jan. 31, 1864; M. A. Shufeldt to S., Feb. 9, 1864; R. H. Wyman to S., Feb. 9 and 27, 1864, RWS 12 (Jan.-Feb. 1864); R. H. Wyman to S., Mar. 14, 1864, RWS 6 (Jan.-Mar. 1864); H. B. Shufelt, in *Our Folks: A History of the Shufelt Family* (Claverack, New York), 50, mentions the death of Shufeldt's baby.

11. Wyman to S., Mar. 4, 1864, RWS 12 (Mar.-Dec. 1864); Wyman to S., Mar. 14, 1864; Welles to S., Mar. 28, 30, Apr. 5, 1864; Bailey to S., Apr. [?], Apr. 30, 1864, RWS 6 (Jan.-Mar. 1864) and (Apr. 1864); "Report of Commander Shufeldt, commanding USS *Proteus,* of the cruise of that vessel from New York to Key West," Florida, Apr. 27, 1864, *ORUCN,* ser. 1, 3:6; the Letterbook [hereafter LBK] of the USS *Proteus,* 1864-1865, RWS 3, gives a list of blockade-runners at Nassau, Apr. 21, 1864. Several of these letters are in *ORUCN,* ser. 1, 3:6 and 20; *ibid.,* ser. 1, 17:679, 690-691.

12. T. Bailey to S., May 28, 1864, RWS 6 (May–Aug. 1864); *ORUCN,* ser. 1, 17:709; S. to Welles, June 9, 1864, LBK, USS *Proteus,* 1864–1865, nos. 2 and 5, RWS 3; also in *ORUCN,* ser. 1, 17:715–716; on prize money, see H. H. Shufeldt to S., July 13, 1866, RWS 12 (1866), which recalled that Shufeldt had given Henry $550 in prize money to invest for him and that by 1866 it had grown to $1,125.

13. On *Jupiter,* see "Report of Commander Shufeldt, June 27, 1864," in S. to Welles and to the Secretary of the District, Boston; "Report of Commander Shufeldt, USS *Proteus,* regarding the cruise of that vessel," July 23, 1864, LBK, USS *Proteus,* 1864–1865, nos. 8, 9, 15, RWS box 3; these reports also in *ORUCN,* ser. 1, 17:725, 727–728.

14. "Report of Commander Shufeldt . . . regarding the capture of the British schooner *Ann Louisa* . . . Sept. 6, 1864," LBK, USS *Proteus,* 1864–1865, no. 21, RWS box 3; also in *ORUCN,* ser. 1, 17:753; R. W. Shufeldt, Jr., "Life History of an American Naturalist," 148, recalled the chase of the *Francis;* S. to Greene, Sept. 12, 1864, LBK, USS *Proteus,* 1864–1865, RWS box 3.

15. Cruising order in C. K. Stribling to S., Nov. 1864, RWS 6 (Sept.–Dec. 1864); T. Smith to S., Nov. 30, 1864; the Butler quotation is in "August, 1864," from essay "At Sea," RWS 35, Diary, 1864–1868; R. W. Shufeldt, Jr. "Life History of an American Naturalist," nos. 5 and 8 (May and Aug. 1924), 198, 202 (quotation), 203, 309, 316–320, and 324.

16. F. Shufeldt to S., Nov. 8, 1864; G. Shufeldt to S., Dec. 29, 1864; L. E. Hargous to S., Jan. 2, 1865, RWS 12 (Mar.–Dec. 1864) and (1865); "Oh Woman," "At Sea," "Contraband," and "Spiritualism" RWS 35, Diary, 1864–1868.

17. "Quarante Trois!" RWS 35, Diary, 1864–1868, written aboard the USS *Proteus,* Feb. 20, 1865.

18. G. A. Shufeldt to S., Dec. 29, 1864, RWS 12 (Mar.–Dec. 1864).

19. Stribling to S., Jan. 17, 20, 26, Feb. 4 and 15, 1865; R. Winder to S., Jan. 19, 1865, RWS 6 (Jan. 1865) and (Feb.–Mar. 1865); "Report of Commander Shufeldt, Feb. 27, 1865," *ORUCN,* ser. 1, 17:822, and LBK, USS *Proteus,* 1864–1865, RWS 3; a picture of the *Ruby's* remains is in Francis T. Miller, ed., *The Photographic History of the Civil War* (New York, 1911), vol. 6, *The Navies,* 107.

20. S. to Stribling, Mar. 9, 1865, LBK, USS *Proteus,* 1864–1865, RWS 3; Stribling repeated Shufeldt's words exactly in his report to G. Welles, Mar. 14, 1865, *ORUCN,* ser. 1, 17:814; "Report of operations by Major General (Acting) John Newton, Mar. 19, 1865," *OR,* ser. 1, 49, pt. 1:58.

21. Stribling to S., Mar. 2, 1865, RWS 6 (Feb.–Mar. 1865); S. to Stribling, Mar. 7, 1865, LBK, USS *Proteus,* 1864–1865, RWS 3; "Report of operations by Major General (Acting) John Newton, Mar. 19, 1865," *OR,* ser. 1, 49, pt. 1:58.

22. This conclusion is obvious from reading Newton's report, *OR,* ser. 1, 49, pt. 1:58–59, and the "Report of Major Edmund Weeks to the Assistant Adjutant General, Mar. 9, 1865," *ibid.,* 69–70.

23. S. to Stribling, Mar. 7, 1865, LBK, USS *Proteus,* 1864–1865, RWS 3.

24. S. to Stribling, Mar. 9, 1865, *ibid.*

25. "Report of operations by Brigadier General J. Newton . . . Mar. 19,

1865," *OR,* ser. 1, 49, pt. 1:58-61; "Preliminary report of operations by Brigadier General J. Newton . . . Mar. 15, 1865 "; Brigadier General J. Newton to Assistant Adjutant General C. T. Christenson, Apr. 6, 17, and 19, 1865; "Report of Major General Sam Jones, CSA to General J. E. Johnston, Mar. 20, 1865" in *OR,* ser. 1, 49, pt. 1:57, 60-62, 64-65, 66-67 and pt. 2:1134-1136, respectively.

26. S. to Stribling, Mar. 7 and 9, 1865, LBK, USS *Proteus,* 1864-1865, RWS 3; "Report of Lieutenant Commander Gibson, Mar. 21, 1865," *ORUCN,* ser. 1, 17:818-819.

27. Newton's charges are in "Reports of operations by Brigadier J. Newton . . . Mar. 15, 19, 1865"; Newton to C. T. Christenson, Apr. 6 and 19, 1865, *OR,* ser. 1, 19, pt. 1:57, 58-62, 64-65, 66-67; Stribling to Welles, Mar. 3, 1865, and "Detailed report of Acting Rear Admiral C. K. Stribling, U.S. Navy, regarding the expedition, Mar. 14, 1865," *ORUCN,* ser. 1, 17:812-814; Stribling to S., Mar. 14, 1865, RWS 6 (Feb.-Mar. 1865); S. to Stribling, Mar. 7, 1865, LBK, USS *Proteus,* 1864-1865, RWS 3; Newton to S., Mar. 8, 1865, *ibid.,* and also in RWS 6 (Feb.-Mar. 1865).

28. W. K. Beard, Special Order, no. 49, Mar. 9, 1865, *OR,* ser. 1, 49, pt. 1:62; S. to Stribling, Mar. 7, 1865, LBK, USS *Proteus,* 1864-1865, RWS 3; "Detailed report of Acting Rear Admiral Stribling, Mar. 14, 1865," *ORUCN,* ser. 1, 17:814.

29. Stribling to S., Mar. 20, Apr. 17 and 24, 1865, RWS 6 (Feb.-Mar. 1865) and (Apr.-May 1865); S. to Stribling, Apr. 12, 1865, and S. to Welles, Apr. 29, 1865, LBK, USS *Proteus,* 1864-1865, RWS 3.

CHAPTER 6

1. S. to Bell, May 23, 1865, RWS 6 (Apr.-May 1865); Bell to S., May 25, [1865], RWS 17, General Miscellany (GC, undated).

2. P. Drayton to S., June 13, 1865; E. B. Latch to R. Townsend, July 7, 1865; C. H. Bell to Bell or S., Aug. 4, 1865; W. B. Whiting to S., Aug. 7, 1865, RWS 6 (June-July 1865) and (Aug.-Dec. 1865); Bell to S., June 16, 1865, RWS 17 (undated).

3. Diary entries for Aug. 27, Sept. 2 and 24, and Oct. 28, 1865, vol. USS *Hartford,* "On a Cruise to the China Seas," Aug.-Dec. 1865, RWS 1, Diaries, Notebooks, Logbooks, and Journals, 1865-1880. The poem "A Dream" follows (pp. 12-13) the essay on "Spiritualism," and the quotation about the sea comes from the three-page essay, "Brazil," written in Rio de Janeiro.

4. On the anti-British sentiment, see diary entries of Oct. 28 and Nov. 28, 1865, USS *Hartford,* "On a Cruise to the China Seas," Aug.-Dec. 1865, RWS 1; "Brazil," RWS 35, Diary, 1864-1868.

5. "Cape Town, Cape Colony, South Africa," RWS 35, Diary, 1864-1868.

6. *Ibid.*

7. Allen to Seward, Feb. 10 and Apr. 9, 1866, CD, Hong Kong 5 (Nov. 20, 1855-Aug. 10, 1866); G. Sanford to Seward, Jan. 11, 1866, CD, Chefoo 1 (Mar. 10, 1863-Oct. 10, 1869).

8. For the ports visited, see the letters in RWS 7, OC, 1866 (Jan.-Feb. 1866) to (Sept. 1866); on Shufeldt's appointment, see Bell to S., Sept. 5, 1866, and

General Orders nos. 12 and 16, Sept. 1 and 11, 1866, *ibid.* (Sept. 1866) and (Nov. 1866); Mrs. Brewer to S., and Jonathan Smith to S., Aug. 21 and 18, 1866, RWS 12 (1866). On Townsend, see Bell to Townsend, Apr. 2 and 17, June 20, and July 7, 1866, RWS 7 (Mar.-Apr. 1866), (June 1866), and (July 1866). Townsend's death is reported in G. F. Seward to Seward, Aug. 18, 1866, CD, Shanghai 8 (Feb. 22, 1866-Dec. 23, 1867); J. L. Kiernan to Seward, Aug. 20, 1866, CD, Chinkiang 1 (Sept. 16, 1864-Dec. 31, 1869). Also see Louis H. Bolander *DAB*, s.v. "Robert Townsend."

9. Allen to Seward, Sept. 29 and Nov. 27, 1866, CD, Hong Kong 6 (Sept. 29, 1866-Dec. 31, 1869); Bell to S., Sept. 9, 10, and 11, 1866, RWS 7 (Sept. 1866); S. to Bell, no. 24, Nov. 1, 1866, RWS 3, LBK, USS *Wachusett*, Sept. 1866-Jan. 1869; Allen to S., Oct. 2, 1866, RWS 7 (Oct. 1866).

10. S. to Bell, no. 11, Oct. 3, 1866; Allen to S., Oct. 3, 1866, RWS 3, LBK, USS *Wachusett*, 1866-1869.

11. Bell to S., Oct. 15 and 17, and Nov. 1, 1866, RWS 7 (Oct. 1866) and RWS 12 (1866).

12. S. to Bell, nos. 19 and 25, Oct. 30 and Nov. 1, 1866, RWS 3, LBK, USS *Wachusett*, 1866-1868.

13. Jones to S., Nov. 21, 1866, with enclosures nos. 1 and 2, translations of communications from the Acting Taotai of Chang Chow to the Taotai of Amoy, Nov. 25, [1865] 1866, and a letter of Jones to the Acting Taotai of Amoy, Nov. 27, 1866, in RWS 7 (Nov. 1866); S. to Bell, nos. 27 and 29, Nov. 22 and 30, 1866, RWS 3, LBK, USS *Wachusett*, 1866-1868.

14. S. to Bell, no. 29, Nov. 30, 1866, RWS 3, LBK, USS *Wachusett*, 1866-1868; M. J[?]. Knowlton to S., Sept. 3, 1869 [1867?], RWS 13 (1868-Jan. 1870); on Shufeldt's analysis of Christianity in China, see page 115.

15. Jones to S., Nov. 27, 1866, RWS 7 (Nov. 1866) and Jan. 10, 1867, RWS 12 (Jan.-Feb. 1867); on the refit, see S. to Bell, nos. 32 and 33, Dec. 17 and 24, 1866, RWS 3, LBK, USS *Wachusett*, 1866-1868.

16. Bell to S., Dec. 27, 1866, RWS 7 (Dec. 1866).

17. For background information on Korea, see the bibliographical essay for chap. 6.

18. Sanford to Seward, Dec. 31, 1866, CD, Chefoo 1; *For Rel, 1867,* pt. 1, 415, 427-428.

19. The Tsungli Yamen was set up to handle relations with nontributary barbarian states, i.e., Western powers. A more complete translation of the term is "The Office for the General Management of Affairs Concerning the Various Countries." Burlingame to Seward, no. 124, Dec. 15, 1866, DD, China 23 (Jan. 6-Dec. 18, 1866). Additional dispatches on the case from Sanford, Apr. 1, 17, Nov. 20, 23, and Dec. 3, 1867, and Aug. 27, 1869, are in CD, Chefoo 1.

20. Bell to Welles, no. 63, Dec. 14, 1866, in "Letters received by the Secretary of the Navy from Commanding Officers of Squadrons, 1841-1866," General Records of the Department of the Navy, NA, RG 60, series M-89, reel 252.

21. Bell to S., Dec. 24, 27, and 31, 1866, RWS 7 (Dec. 1866).

22. S. to Bell, no. 37, Jan. 8, 1867, RWS 3, LBK, USS *Wachusett*, 1866-1868.

23. "Memorandum of an interview between Commander R. W. Shufeldt of

the USS *Wachusett* and Father Rydell and another missionary of the Roman Catholic Church, Shanghai, Jan. 8, 1867," RWS 3, LBK, USS *Wachusett, 1866-1868*, with a copy and an abstract of the conversation sent to Bell, RWS 8, OC, 1867 (Jan. 1867).

24. S. to Bell, nos. 41 and 42, Jan. 19, 1867, RWS 3, LBK, USS *Wachusett, 1866-1868*; Bell to S., Jan. 18, 1867, RWS 12 (Jan.-Feb. 1867).

25. S. to Bell, nos. 41 and 42, Jan. 19, 1867, RWS 3, LBK, USS *Wachusett, 1866-1868*.

26. *Ibid.*, no. 41; and H. G. Appenzeller, "The Opening of Korea: Admiral Shufeldt's Account of It," *KRep* 1 (1892): 57-62, n. 1. On Corbett, see F. M. Beck, "Interpreting for Captain Shufelt [*sic*]," *KM* 1 (1917): 239-240. Corbett claimed in his account, erroneously, that the *Wachusett* went up the Yalu River.

27. S. to Bell, following no. 43 memorandum, Jan. 25, 1867, and Jan. 30, 1867, RWS 3, LBK, USS *Wachusett, 1866-1868*.

28. S. to His Majesty, the King of Korea, translation from the Chinese document, no. 44, Jan. 24, 1867; S. to His Excellency, the Presiding Officer of the district of Chang Yuen Heen [Chang-yon], Jan. 25, 1867, *ibid.*

29. S. to Bell, Jan. 25, 1867, RWS 3, LBK, USS *Wachusett, 1866-1869*; S. to Bell, private letter, [Jan.-Feb. 1867], RWS 12 (June-Dec. 1867). A reply that came to Shufeldt from Pak Kyusu, "Governor of Pyeng yang province," and a statement by Pak Sŏng hui, "Governor of Hwanghae province," which probably did not reach him before he sailed, are given in E. M. Cable, "United States-Korean Relations, 1866-1871," *TKBRAS* 28 (1938): 48-52.

30. "Memorandum of an interview between Commander Shufeldt of the USS *Wachusett* and a Corean official from the district city of Hae Chow Poo on the Tai Tong [*sic*] River, Jan. 29, 1867," with no. 46, RWS 3, LBK, USS *Wachusett, 1866-1868*.

31. S. to Bell, no. 47, Jan. 30, 1867, RWS 3, LBK, USS *Wachusett, 1866-1868*.

32. Appenzeller, "The Opening of Korea: Admiral Shufeldt's Account of It," 59; Beck, "Interpreting for Captain Shufelt," 240; S. to Bell, nos. 47 and 50, Jan. 30 and Feb. 3, 1867, RWS 3, LBK, USS *Wachusett, 1866-1868*; Bell to S., Feb. 9 and 14, 1867, RWS 8 (Feb. 1867) and (July 1867) records the Admiral's appreciation for Shufeldt's work in Korea.

33. Febiger to S., enclosing a letter from the King of Korea to S., May 19, 1868, RWS 28, World Cruise of the USS *Ticonderoga, 1879-1883*, and undated, collected material for the manuscript (China and Japan); "Despatch from Corean authorities to USS *Wachusetts* [*sic*] regarding the *Genl. Sherman* case," *China Overland Trade Report*, Hong Kong, July 18, 1868, RWS 9, OC, 1868-1872 (1868-Apr. 1869).

34. Appenzeller, "The Opening of Korea: Admiral Shufeldt's Account of It," 59-60; C. O. Paullin, "The Opening of Korea by Commodore Shufeldt," *PSQ* 25 (1910): 472. The Korean records about the *Sherman* affair are translated in E. M. Cable, "United States-Korean Relations, 1866-1871," *TKBRAS* 28 (1938): 11-32. The visit of the *Shenandoah* in 1868 is confused with the visit of the *Wachusett* in 1867 in Cable's chapter on Yi dynasty annals, chap. 23, 54-62; S. to Bell, no. 47, Jan. 30, 1867, RWS 3, LBK, USS *Wachusett, 1866-1868*.

35. S. to Bell, nos. 51 and 52, Feb. 3 and 5, 1867, *ibid.,* gives Shufeldt's report on the islands. For the occupancy of the islands and Port Hamilton, see [unsigned note in Shufeldt's handwriting] to [no name, but Bell, for the dispatch mentioned Bell's "private note of Jan'y 18," which is the only one of that date in the Shufeldt Papers], Jan.-Feb. 1867, RWS 12 (June-Dec. 1867). The note is similar to S. to Bell, Jan. 25 and 30, 1867, RWS 3, LBK, USS *Wachusett,* 1866-1868.

36. Salter to S., Feb. 20, 1867; Mangum to S., Feb. 20, 1867, RWS 8 (Feb. 1867).

37. S. to Bell, no. 61, Feb. 25, 1867, RWS 3, LBK, USS *Wachusett,* 1866-1868.

38. Bell to S., Feb. 23, and two letters of Mar. 4, 1867; Salter to S., Feb. 20, 1867; Mangum to S., Feb. 20, 1867; O. B. Bradford to S., Feb. 21, 1867, in RWS 8 (Feb. 1867) and (Mar. 1867); S. to Bell, nos. 61, 63, and 65, Feb. 25, Mar. 7 and 17, 1867; "Dispatches from the Acting Taotai at Kiu Kiang . . . to Shu [*sic*], Commander of the Naval Troops of the Great Country of America," nos. 64 and 68, Mar. 20, 1867, in RWS 3, LBK, USS *Wachusett,* 1866-1868; Salter to S., Mar. 13, 1867, and S. Dabey to S., Mar. 13, 1867, RWS 12 (Mar. 1867). See Kemp Tolley, *Yangtze Patrol: The U. S. Navy in China* (Annapolis, 1971), 15, 18, and E. M. Tate, "Admiral Bell and the New Asiatic Squadron 1865-1868," *AN* 23 (1972): 130.

39. S. to Bell, no. 71, (second letter), Apr. 1, 1867; S. to G. Tyson (first letter), Mar. 30, 1867, RWS 3, LBK, USS *Wachusett,* 1866-1868; J. MacGowan to S., Mar. 14, 1867, RWS 12 (Mar. 1867); Bell to S., Mar. 27, 1867, RWS 8 (Mar. 1867).

40. Salter to S., Apr. 9, 1867, RWS 8 (Apr. 1867); S. to Bell, nos. 81 and 82, Apr. 18, 1867, RWS 3, LBK, USS *Wachusett,* 1866-1868. On the *Wachusett*'s defects, see letters in RWS 7 (Jan.-Feb. 1866), (July 1866), and (Dec. 1866); RWS 8 (Apr. 1867), (May 1867), and (July 1867).

41. Salter to S., Mar. 13, 1867, RWS 12 (Mar. 1867); proposed survey in S. to Jenkins, 1867, misfiled in RWS 24, World Cruise, USS *Ticonderoga,* 1879-1883, and undated (China and Korea Correspondence, 1882).

42. See Kwang-Ching Liu, *Anglo-American Steam Ship Rivalry in China 1862-1874* (Cambridge, Mass., 1962), 69-70, 71, table 17; S. to Jenkins, 1867, RWS 24 (China and Korea Correspondence, 1882).

43. S. to Jenkins, 1867, RWS 24 (China and Korea Correspondence, 1882); Bell to S., June 6 and 27, 1867, RWS 8 (June 1867).

44. Bell to S., June 6 and 27, 1867; A. Lawton to Latch, June 7, 1867, RWS 8 (June 1867); S. to My Friend [F. V. Mangum], Sept. 3, 1867, Willie P. Mangum Papers, Family Papers, vol. 11 (1862-1868) [hereafter Mangum Papers], MDLC.

45. S. to F. V. Mangum, Sept. 3, Oct. 6, 1867, and Mar. 8, 1868; S. to My Friend [W. P. Mangum], Sept. 6, 1867, and Feb. 15, 1868; Burlingame to Mangum, Sept. 10, 1867, Mangum Papers 11.

46. Bell to S., Sept. 12 and 17, 1867; I. Stone to S., Oct. 2, 1867; J. M. Gideon to S., Dec. 14, 1867; T. Fitman to S., Dec. 14, 1867, in RWS 8 (Sept. 1867), (Oct. 1867), and (Dec. 1867); S. to Welles, nos. 115 and 122, Dec. 14,

1867 and Jan. 29, 1868; S. to Wise, Jenkins, and Lenthall, nos. 116, 117, and 121, USS *Wachusett,* Jan. 1, 9, and 27, 1868, RWS 3, LBK, USS *Wachusett,* 1866-1868; Jenkins to S., Feb. 1, 1868, RWS 9 (1868-Apr. 1869).

CHAPTER 7

1. S. to Mangum, Feb. 15, 1868, and to F. V. Mangum, Mar. 8, 1868, Mangum Papers 11; R. W. Shufeldt, Jr., "Life History of an American Naturalist," *ML* 31, no. 8 (Aug. 1924): 325.

2. S., *Western Civilization in the East* (Stamford, 1868). Thirty-four pages of manuscript for this talk are in RWS 5, Diary, 1864-1868. The quotation on pages 115-116 is from the conclusion. Shufeldt mentioned the lectures on China and "Outward Bound" to F. V. Mangum, Mar. 8, 1868, Mangum Papers 11. See also Lois Bayles, "The Story of Waveny," *New Canaan Historical Society Annual* 6, no. 3 (1969): 15, and Charlotte C. Fairley, "A History of New Canaan 1801-1901," *Readings in New Canaan History* (New Canaan Historical Society, 1949), 157-290, 228.

3. S. to F. V. Mangum, Mar. 8, June 1, and Nov. 1, 1868, Mangum Papers 11; Jenkins to S., Oct. 30, 1868, RWS 9 (1868-Apr. 1869); Smith to Seward, May 26, 1868; Jones to Morgan, May 25, 1868, RWS 13 (1868).

4. Jenkins to S., Oct. 30, 1868, RWS 9 (1868-Apr. 1869); S. to F. V. Mangum, Nov. 1, 1868, Mangum Papers 11.

5. Jenkins to S., Nov. 13, 1868, RWS 9 (1868-Apr. 1869); "The Creole in Cuba," *Philadelphia Press,* Dec. 2, 1868, not signed but with several identifying passages from other Shufeldt manuscripts on the subject; copy in RWS 31, Newspaper Clippings, 1859-1899, and undated (Miscellany).

6. Jenkins to S., Jan. 21, 1869; Godon to S., Jan. 22, 1869; J. Alden to S., Apr. 22, 1869, RWS 9 (1868-Apr. 1869); S. to Porter, Mar. 12, 1869, RWS 35, at front of box; second copy of page 1 in RWS 19 (General Miscellany) and box 25, GC, Maps, Oriental Documents, and Miscellany (Miscellany).

7. Smith to Sumner and to Fish, Apr. 21, 1869, S 13 (Jan.-Sept. 1869); S. to Porter, Mar. 12, 1869, RWS 35, front of box; W. Dibblee to Fish, Apr. 21, 1869, RWS 13 (Jan.-Sept. 1869); J. Alden to S., Apr. 22, 1869, RWS 9 (1868-Apr. 1869).

8. "The Annexation of Cuba," "The Independence of Cuba," and "The Future of Cuba," RWS 19 (General Miscellany). The latter can be pieced together from halves of two separate copies overlapping by one page in RWS 25 (Miscellany Oriental Documents).

9. This quotation from "The Independence of Cuba" was written after the appointment of Motley as minister to Great Britain, April 12, 1869, and before April 25. The manuscript "The Annexation of Cuba" was clothed in a context of past filibustering schemes in the 1850s.

10. In "The Future of Cuba" Shufeldt claimed that "the superior activity & energy always implied & often manifested by the Yankee is a constant reproach to the poco á poco Cuban & a source of concealed contempt on the one hand & concealed dislike on the other."

11. On the Cuban junta in New York, see A. Nevins, *Hamilton Fish: The Inner History of the Grant Administration* (New York, 1937), 179-187; *Quaker City,* 338-

341; the Cuban revolt, 177-200, 243-248, 294-303, 335-363, 615-637, and 667-694. Shufeldt's observations in the following three paragraphs are from S. to My Dear Sir [Porter?], mid-May and June 14, 1869 [former dated from contents], RWS 35, unfiled at front of box, and RWS 13 (Jan.-Sept. 1869).

12. S. to [Porter?], mid-May 1869, RWS 35, unfiled at front of box; Adams to S., Oct. 24, 1869, RWS 13 (Oct. 1869); S. to W. P. Mangum, May 9, 1869, Mangum Papers 12 (1869-1906 and undated).

13. S. to Porter, undated [but Mar. 29, 1869, dated by Porter's reply of Apr. 2, 1869, mentioning the Mar. 29 letter]. For the survey proposed to Jenkins, see pages 111-112 and 391, n. 41. Porter to S., Apr. 2, 1869, two letters, RWS 9 (1868-Apr. 1869).

14. S. to Mangum, May 9 and Dec. 12, 1869, and to F. V. Mangum, July 15, 1869, Mangum Papers 12 (1869-1906 and undated).

15. Porter to S., May 23, 1870, RWS 13 (May 1-15, 1870) and (May 17-30, 1870); Alden to S., May 17, 1870; on the captaincy, see Robeson to S., Nov. 6 and 26, 1869; M. Smith to S., Dec. 18, 1869; Godon to S., Dec. 31, 1869; Robeson to S., Jan. 4 and Feb. 1, 1870, all in RWS 9 (May-Oct. 1870), (Nov. 1869), (June-Oct. 1869), (Dec. 1869), (Jan. 1870), and (Feb. 1870); S. to the Mangums, Dec. 12, 1869, Mangum Papers 12; a number of letters from Sarah Shufeldt, commencing Feb. 3 and continuing to May 28, 1870, in RWS 13 (Feb. 1870), (Mar. 1870), (Apr. 1870), (May 1-15, 1870), and (May 17-30, 1870); R. W. Shufeldt, Jr., "Life History of an American Naturalist," 139-140.

16. Quotation in S., rough draft of a proposal to go before Congress, with a condensed version in RWS 21 (written reports).

17. United States Congress Joint Resolution for a survey for a ship canal across the Isthmus of Tehuantepec, 41st Cong. 2nd Sess. S. R. 161, Mar. 18, 1870, copy in RWS 13 (Mar. 1870). See also Peter Karsten, *The Naval Aristocracy: The Golden Age of Annapolis and the Emergence of Modern American Navalism* (New York, 1972), 151-152, n. 28, 161.

18. Broadside of the Tehuantepec Railway Company, Aug. 1873, overcrossed July 30, 1875, signed by Simon Stevens, president, Tehuantepec Railway Company, Cornell University Regional History Collection, no. 2072; Jackson Crowell, "The United States and a Central American Canal, 1869-1877," *HAHR* 49 (1969): 27-52, esp. 28-32, for Grant's interests; Karsten, *The Naval Aristocracy,* 151, note.

19. W. A. Buckingham to S., May 21, 1870; Porter to S., May 23, 1870, in RWS 13 (May 17-31, 1870); *Annual Reports of the Secretary of the Navy, 1870* [hereafter *ARSN,* followed by year] (Washington, D.C., 1870-1873), 9-10; *ARSN, 1871,* 8-10; *ARSN, 1872,* 9-13; and *ARSN, 1873,* 9, respectively.

20. T. S. Negus to S., May 31, 1870, RWS 13 (May 17-31, 1870) on the problems of American commerce. Further letters of July 22 and Aug. 5, 1870, RWS 14, GC, July 1870-Dec. 1871 (July 17-30, 1870) and (Aug. 1870), cover the decline in American commerce.

21. Murphy to S., June 2, 7, 14, 20, 23, July 1, 2, 19, and 22, Aug. 5, 1870, RWS 13 (May 17-31, 1870), (June 2-19, 1870) and (June 20-30, 1870) and RWS 14 GC, July 1870-Dec. 1871 (July 1-15, 1870), (July 17-30, 1870), and

(Aug. 1870), respectively; John McLeod Murphy, "The Isthmus of Tehuantepec," *AGSNYJ* 1 (1859): 162-177; a short sketch of Murphy is in C. E. Brasseur de Bourbourg, *Voyage sur L'Isthme de Tehuantepec dans L'État de Chiapas et la République de Guatémala Execute dans les Années 1859 et 1860* (Paris, 1861), 11-12, and 201.

22. Starkweather to S., June 25, 1870; W. C. Wise to S., May 30, 1870; Buckingham to S., June 28, 1870, in RWS 13 (May 17-31, 1870) and (June 20-30, 1870); Porter to S., June 25, 1870, RWS 20 (1861-Sept. 1870); Smith to S., July 7, 1870, RWS 14 (July 1-15, 1870).

23. On the Darien expedition, see *ARSN, 1870,* 9; Crowell, "The United States and a Central American Canal, 1869-1877," 28 and n. 6. The visit to Sumner is recalled in "Through Mexico to the Pacific—In Search of a Canal Route," RWS 21 (written reports). Sumner's resolution was an amendment to H. R. 2165, referred to the Committee on Appropriations, July 4, 1870, 41st Cong. 2nd Sess., and a copy is in RWS 14 (July 4-15, 1870); *New York Tribune,* July 13, 1870; and unidentified clipping, July 12, 1870, in RWS 14 (July 17-30, 1870).

24. Broadside of the Tehuantepec Railway Company, Aug. 1873, Cornell Regional History Collection, no. 2072. For the Nicaraguan lobby, see Crowell, "The United States and a Central American Canal, 1869-1877," 29-30; Ziegler to S., July 1, 6, and 17, 1870, RWS 20 (1861-Sept. 1870) and RWS 14 (July 1-15, 1870) and (July 17-30, 1870).

25. Ziegler to S., July 6, 17, and Aug. 4, 1870, RWS 14 (July 1-15, 1870), (July 17-30, 1870), and (Aug. 1870); Fish to T. H. Nelson, Oct. 22, 1870, DI, Mexico 18; C. N. Riotte, United States Minister to Nicaragua, to Fish, Sept. 7, 1870, with enclosures of Riotte to the *New York Gazette,* July 26, 1870, RWS 20 (1861-Sept. 1870). For Riotte's pressure on Fish, see Crowell, "The United States and a Central American Canal, 1869-1877," 29, nn. 12-14.

26. "Through Mexico to the Pacific—In Search of a Canal Route," 32, RWS 21 (written reports); Smith to S., July 7, 1870; W. Temple to S., July 28, 1870; Porter to S., Aug. 24, 1870, RWS 14 (July 1-15, 1870), (July 17-30, 1870), and (Aug. 1870).

27. Porter to S., Aug. 30, 1870; Porter to Grant, Aug. 31, 1870, RWS 14 (Aug. 1870).

28. On Grant's desires for a Central American canal, see Crowell, "The United States and a Central American Canal, 1869-1877," 27-28; "Through Mexico to the Pacific—In Search of a Canal Route," 33, RWS 21 (written reports); Alden to S., Sept. 3 and 9, 1870, RWS 9 (May-Oct. 1870) and RWS 20 (1861-Sept. 1870); two-page manuscript on an isthmian transit route and another draft in RWS 21 (written reports); Buckingham to S., June 28, 1870, RWS 13 (June 20-30, 1870); Calvin G. Child to S., July 6, 1870, RWS 14 (July 1-15, 1870).

29. On Stevens, see Simon Stevens, *The new route of Commerce by the Isthmus of Tehuantepec and the Tehuantepec railway; its location, features and advantages under the La Sère grant of 1869* (New York, 1869); Stevens to S., Sept. 10 and 12, 1870; S. to Abert, Sept. 11 and telegram of Sept. 12; Murphy to S., Sept. 24 and Oct. 3, 1870, RWS 20 (1861-Sept. 1870), (Sept. 13-Oct. 22, 1870), and RWS 14

(Sept. 1-21, 1870) and (Sept. 22-30, 1870); Shufeldt's copy of Abert's work is in RWS 21 (printed matters, reports). For Fuertes' references, see A. W. Craven to S., June 10, 1870, and Murphy to S., June 18, 1870, RWS 13 (June 2-19, 1870); Fuertes to S., Sept. 17 and 26, 1870; V. G. Wheeler to S., Sept. 18, 1870; M. F. Merritt to S., Sept. 19, 1870; A. T. Mahan to W. P. Moran, Sept. 8, 1870, RWS 14 (Sept. 1-21, 1870).

30. S. to Robeson, Sept. 26, 1870, RWS 20 (1861-Sept. 1870), and a rough copy in RWS 14 (Sept. 22-30, 1870). The rough draft in RWS 21 (written reports) offering reasons for a surveying expedition links the ideas about Tehuantepec in particular to the more sweeping ideas of capturing the commerce of the Pacific.

31. Robeson to S., Oct. 4 and 6, 1870, RWS 20 (Sept. 22-Oct. 13, 1870); J. B. Ferris to S., Oct. 5, 1870; Mary A. Miller to S., Sept. 23, 1870, thanking Shufeldt for taking her to Tehuantepec, RWS 14 (Oct. 1870) and (Sept. 22-30, 1870).

CHAPTER 8

1. S. to Robeson, Oct. 24, Nov. 1, 13, and 18, 1870; S. to Nelson, telegram and letter, Nov. 17, 1870, in RWS 3, Letterbook, USS *Kansas,* Oct.-Nov. 1870 and USS *Mayflower,* Nov. 1870-Mar. 1871 [hereafter Tehuantepec LBK I], 1-2, 46-50; Nelson to S., Oct. 19 and Nov. 28, 1870, RWS 20 (Oct. 14-Nov. 15, 1870) and (Nov. 16-Dec. 12, 1870); Fish to Nelson, no. 127, Dec. 10, 1870, DI, Mexico 18; RWS 2, "Journal of the Tehuantepec and Nicaragua Surveying Expedition including the United States Steamers *Kansas* and *Mayflower* under the command of Captain R. W. Shufeldt, USN, 1870" [hereafter Abstract Journal: Tehuantepec], entries for Nov. 11 to 21, 1870.

2. Memorandum, instruction to Lieutenant Commander N. Farquhar, Dec. 3, 1870, RWS 3, Tehuantepec LBK I, 24-27, copy in RWS 21 (written reports); S. to Farquhar, Nov. 24, 1870; instructions to Spear, Nov. 8, 1870, RWS 3, Tehuantepec LBK I, 51-52 (Farquhar) and 21-24 (Spear); copy in RWS 20 (Oct. 14-15, 1870).

3. RWS 2, Abstract Journal: Tehuantepec, entries for Nov. 28 to Dec. 19, 1870; "Remarks arranged as a Journal," Thomas Skeel to S., Dec. 23, 1870, RWS 20 (Dec. 23-31, 1870); S. to J. N. Wolf, Dec. 12, 1870; S. to Robeson, Dec. 12, 1870; S. to Albine Juninez, Dec. 17, 1870, RWS 3, Tehuantepec LBK I, 52-55.

4. S. to Robeson, Jan. 2 and 3, 1870; S. to F. Garcia, Dec. 22, 1870; S. to "the commanding officer of any man-of-war that may visit Ventosa under instructions . . . ," Dec. 26, 1870, RWS 3, Tehuantepec LBK I, 56-61; RWS 2, Abstract Journal: Tehuantepec, entries for Dec. 18-27, 1870; N. Farquhar to S., Dec. 12 and 20, 1870; J. A. Winslow to A. Hopkins, Dec., 1870, RWS 20 (Nov. 16-Dec. 12, 1870) and (Dec. 13-22, 1870).

5. Stevens to Robeson, Nov. 29, 1870; Robeson to S., Dec. 1, 1870, RWS 20 (Nov. 16-Dec. 12, 1870).

6. On Stevens' concerns and being "a good deal excited" that Shufeldt's report might not be "as favorable as they wish it to be," see Negus to S., Nov. 8 and Dec. 18, 1870, RWS 14 (Nov. 1870) and (Dec. 1870); Porter to S., Nov.

10, 1870; Nelson to S., Dec. 25, 1870, RWS 20 (Oct. 14-Nov. 15, 1870) and (Dec. 21-31, 1870); Broadside of the Tehuantepec Railway Company, Aug. 1873, Cornell University Regional History Collection, no. 2072; "The Tehuantepec Canal Concession . . ."; Benito Juárez to Blas Balcarel, Dec. 20, 1870, RWS 21 (printed matters, reports); S. to M. Z. Chazaro, Jan. 10, 1871, RWS 3, Tehuantepec LBK I, 64.

7. RWS 2, Abstract Journal: Tehuantepec, entries for Feb. 5-17, 1871; Farquhar to S., Feb. 3 and 11, 1871, RWS 20 (Feb. 1871); Mary [Molly] A. Miller to S., Jan. 28, 1871, RWS 15 (misfiled in Jan.-Apr. 1872); Sarah's illness is mentioned in Molly to S., Feb. 8, 1871, RWS 14 (Jan.-June 1871).

8. S. to Fuertes, Feb. 13, 1871, RWS 3, Tehuantepec LBK I, 67; Fuertes to S., Jan. 16 and Feb. 6, 10, and 17, 1871, in RWS 14 (Jan.-June 1871), RWS 13 (misfiled in Feb. 1870), and RWS 20 (Feb. 1871).

9. Fuertes to S., Feb. 17 and 21, 1871; Remey to S., Feb. 21, 1871; and Bartlett to S., Feb. 24, 1871, all in RWS 20 (Feb. 1871).

10. S. to Robeson, Feb. 20, 1871, RWS 3, Tehuantepec LBK I, 68-69; Bartlett to S., Feb. 24, 1871, RWS 20 (Feb. 1871).

11. Remey to S., Mar. 4, 1871; Fuertes to S., Mar. 6 and 9, 1871, in RWS 20 (Mar. 1871) and (Apr. 1871), with a memorandum from Shufeldt attached to page 3; S. to Robeson, Mar. 16, 1871, in RWS 3, Tehuantepec LBK I, 77-79.

12. Fuertes to S., Apr. 4, 1871, RWS 20 (Apr. 1871); S. to Robeson, Apr. 18, 1871, RWS 3, Letterbook USS *Mayflower,* Mar.-Aug. 1871 [hereafter Tehuantepec LBK II], 29.

13. Four-page essay at the front of *ibid.* 2-6. On the role of the naval officer, see Peter Karsten, *The Naval Aristocracy: The Golden Age of Annapolis and the Emergence of Modern American Navalism* (New York, 1972), 150-178.

14. Hopkins to S., Apr. 15, 1871; Fuertes to S., Apr. 27, 1871, RWS 20 (Apr. 1871).

15. Events of May 1871 are recorded in RWS 2, Abstract Journal: Tehuantepec, entries for May 1, 5, 10, 12, 15, and 16, 1871; Shufeldt mentioned being ill to Surgeon Spear, July 24, 1871; also see S. to Robeson, May 1 and 6, 1871; S. to Robeson and K. Jasper, May 15 and 16, 1871, Tehuantepec LBK II, 75, 47, 65, 67, and 69, respectively; Robert and Mason to S., Oct. 28 and Nov. 15, 1871, RWS 14 (July-Oct. 1871) and (Nov.-Dec. 1871). Formal notifications that Shufeldt adopted Molly are in S. to F. V. Mangum, May 9, 1872, Mangum Papers 12; Smith to Mary M. Shufeldt, Feb. 28, 1877, RWS 16, GC, 1876-1884 (1877); and in Shufeldt's will, Administration no. 6962, filed Nov. 11, 1895, Registrar of Wills, U.S. District Court for the District of Columbia, Washington, D.C., 1. Robert Jr.'s recollection is in "Life History of an American Naturalist," *ML* 31, no. 4 (Apr. 1924): 139-140.

16. "Report of Captain R. W. Shufeldt, USN, to Hon. George M. Robeson, Aug. 11, 1871," in *Report of Explorations and Surveys to ascertain the Practicability of a Ship Canal between the Atlantic and Pacific Oceans by way of the Isthmus of Tehuantepec* [hereafter *Tehuantepec Report*] (Washington, D.C., 1872), 1, filed as *Sen. Ex. Doc.,* no. 6, 42nd Cong. 2nd Sess., and the manuscript of which is in RWS 2 in front of the Abstract Journal: Tehuantepec. Jackson Crowell, in "The United States and a Central American Canal, 1869-1877," *HAHR* 49

(1969): 28, noted that the canal would be impracticable as an interoceanic route because of the length and number of locks.

17. Concluding remarks of the *Tehuantepec Report,* 20. The long quotation about the Gulf of Mexico being an American lake was first used in a letter from S. to Truman Smith, Mar. 23, 1871, RWS 14 (Jan.-June 1871), with a copy in RWS 3, Tehuantepec LBK II, 9-15. The letter, with minor changes, became the concluding remarks of *Tehuantepec Report,* 20.

18. Crowell, "The United States and a Central American Canal, 1869-1877," 33-35, 36-37; William B. Hesseltine, *Ulysses S. Grant: Politician* (New York, 1957), 204-205; see also Karsten, *The Naval Aristocracy,* 153, 181-182, n. 31.

19. "Through Mexico to the Pacific—In Search of a Canal Route," 35, 51-52, RWS 21 (written reports).

20. *Tehuantepec Report,* 20-21; S. to Robeson, Aug. 11 and 16, 1871, RWS 3 Tehuantepec LBK II, 77-79.

21. Alden to S., Aug. 7, 1871, and D. Ammen to S., Oct. 18 and 23, 1871, in Letters to Captain Robert W. Shufeldt, 1871-1873, New York Public Library [hereafter Shufeldt MSS, NYPL], with a copy in RWS 14 (July-Oct. 1871); Porter to S., Oct. 24 and 30, 1871, *ibid.;* S. to F. V. Mangum, May 9, 1872, Mangum Papers 12.

22. Ziegler to S., Feb. 28, 1872, RWS 15 (Jan.-Apr. 1872); S. to F. V. Mangum, May 9, 1872, Mangum Papers 12; 1890 quotation from "Flag Officer Walker: His Squadron of Evolution," RWS 35 (Naval Personnel and Rank Information).

23. I. O. U. to Rebecca Watson, Aug. 1, 1871, RWS 14 (July-Oct. 1871); S. to Molly, Sept. 20, 1872, RWS 17 (Family Correspondence, undated); Alden to S., Sept. 24 and 28, and Oct. 20, 1872, Shufeldt MSS, NYPL.

24. Alden to S., Dec. 23, 1872, and Jan. 17, 1873, Shufeldt MSS, NYPL; B. F. Stevens to S., Feb. 13, 26, and 27, 1873; S. to Sprague, Feb. 6, 1873; Governor General of the Cape Verde Islands to S., Mar. 13, 1873, RWS 15 (Jan.-Nov. 1873) and RWS 10, OC, 1873-1889 (1873); Ammen to S., June 24, 1873, *ibid.;* "Movement of the Fleets—European Fleet," *ARSN, 1873,* 24-25.

25. On correspondence with Shufeldt over the *Virginius,* see Farquhar to S., Dec. 5, 1873; L. M. Monroe to S., Nov. 29, 1873; Fox to S., Dec. 6, 1873, in RWS 15 (Dec. 1873) and (Jan.-Nov. 1873).

26. Telegram of Feb. 5, 1874, RWS 15 (Feb. 1874); Ammen to S., Jan. 29, 1874, RWS 21 (written reports); Daniel Ammen, *The Old Navy and the New* (Philadelphia, 1891), 463 and 474; Crowell, "The United States and a Central American Canal, 1869-1877," 31-52.

27. Fuertes to S., Feb. 7, 1874, RWS 21 (written reports).

28. S. to the Isthmian Canal Commission, Feb. 11, and to D. Ammen, Feb. 13, 1874, RWS 35 (front of volume) and RWS 21 (written reports); R. W. Shufeldt, Jr., to S., Feb. 10, 1874, and G. A. Shufeldt to S., Feb. 14, 1874, RWS 15 (Feb. 1874).

29. Ammen to S., Feb. 12, 1874, and S. to the I.C.C., Feb. 11, 1874, RWS 21 (written reports) and RWS 35 (front of volume).

30. S., *New York Herald,* Feb. 13, 1874; S. to Ammen, Feb. 13, 1874, and

with estimates, in RWS 21 (written reports); Farquhar to S., Feb. 14, 1874; Humphreys to S., Feb. 16, 1874, RWS 15 (Feb. 1874); for background, see Crowell, "The United States and a Central American Canal, 1869-1877," 29-30.

31. Fuertes to S., Mar. 7, 1874, RWS 15 (Mar. 1874); Ammen, *The Old Navy and the New,* 474-475, 478-483, 490-498, and 523; N. Farquhar to S., May 4, 1874, RWS 15 (May 1874). See also *ARSN, 1874,* 15-16, and Crowell, "The United States and a Central American Canal, 1869-1877," 31-32 and 37-38.

32. S. to the editor of the *Nautical Gazette* [undated, but written on New York navy yard paper, 1874], RWS 9 (front of box).

Chapter 9

1. Woodford to S., Feb. 21, 1874; Smith to S., Mar. 7, 18, and 29, 1874; Buckingham, Ferry, Hawley, Starkweather, and Kellogg to Robeson, Mar. 8, 1874; Buckingham to S., Mar. 20, 1874; Mullany to S., Apr. 9 and July 5, 1874; Farquhar to S., Jan. 30, Feb. 14, and May 4, 1874; Parker to S., July 7, 1874; R. W. Shufeldt, Jr., to S., Apr. 29, 1874; W. Matthews to S., July 16, 1874, in RWS 15 (Jan. 1874), (Feb. 1874), (Mar. 1874), (Apr. 1874), (May 1874), and (June-July 1874); Hanscom to S., July 20, 1874, RWS 10 (1874-1875).

2. Sage to Robeson, July 17, 1874; Hatch to S., July 17, Aug. 6 and 12, 1874; S. to Hatch, July 18, 31, and Aug. 24, 1874; S. to Ammen, July 18, 1874; Parker to S., July 22, 1874; Wyman to S., July 21, 1874; A. Bryson to S., July 24, 1874; J. W. Philips to S., Aug. 13, 1874; C. C. Carpenter to S., Aug. 21, 1874, in RWS 15 (June-July 1874), (Aug. 1874); Robeson to S., July 30 and Aug. 5, 1874; Hanscom to S., July 30, 1874; S. to Robeson, Aug. 7, 1874, RWS 10 (1874).

3. Mullany to S., July 5, 1874; F. Augustus Miller to S., Nov. 9, 1872; C. R. P. Rodgers to S., Sept. 6 and Nov. 26, 1872, and May 21, 1874; H. Bartlett to S., Dec. 7, 1872; M. A. Shufeldt to S., Mar. 15, 1872; quotations from Mullany to S., Apr. 22 and July 5, 1874; Farquhar to S., May 4, 1874, RWS 15 (Sept.-Oct. 1872), (Nov.-Dec. 1872), (Jan.-Apr. 1872), (Apr. 1874), (May 1874), and (June-July 1874).

4. Mullany to S., July 5, 1874, RWS 15 (June-July 1874).

5. Parker to S., July 22, 1874, *ibid.*

6. Rowan to S., Sept. 1, 1874; W. Reynolds to S., Aug. 8 and 19, 1874; "Historical Sketch of the Navy Yard, New York," vols. 1-3, RWS 10 (1874).

7. The bureaus, employees, and expenditures are listed in various letters of bureau chiefs to a new secretary of the navy, Richard W. Thompson, Jan. 16 (6 letters) and 19 (1 letter), 1878, in Letters Received by the Secretary of the Navy from Chiefs of Navy Bureaus [hereafter LRBC], vol. 75 (Jan. 4-Dec. 30, 1878), letters 5, 6, 8, 10, 11, 13, and 40. For Shufeldt's work, see S. to Molly, Jan. 23, 1875, RWS 15 (1875); Robeson to S., Feb. 13, 1875, in Letters sent by the Secretary of the Navy to Chiefs of Navy Bureaus, 1852-1886 [hereafter SLBC], vol. 5 (Jan. 9, 1869-June 30, 1880): 402; S. Diaries for 1875-1878, RWS 2, Diaries, 1875, 1876, 1877, 1878.

8. S. to Robeson, Feb. 10 and Mar. 11, 1875, LRBC 72 (Jan. 4-Dec. 31,

1875): 30 and 57; S. to Molly, May 11, 12, and 14, 1875, RWS 15 (1875); Robeson to S., July 13, Oct. 26, Nov. 18, 1875, and Jan. 10, 1876, SLBC 5:409, 417, 418, and 420; other travel duties for the bureau came on Dec. 6, 1876, Jan. 27, Aug. 16, 1877, and July 3, 1878, *ibid.*, 439, 444, 467, and 498. His commission as commodore came September 21, 1876, with Howell to S., Sept. 29, 1876, RWS 10 (1876).

9. *New Orleans Republican,* Nov. 16, 1876; S. to Molly, Nov. 15 and 18, 1876, RWS 17 (Family Correspondence, undated); Robeson to S., Nov. 13, 1876, SLBC 5:438-439.

10. S. to Molly, Nov. 20, 1876, RWS 17 (Family Correspondence, undated); Robeson to S., Dec. 6, 1876, SLBC 5:438-439.

11. Porter to Grant, Aug. 18, 1876, and Grant to Robeson, Aug. 18, 1876; Robeson to Grant, Aug [?], 1876, RWS 10 (1876). See also C. O. Paullin, *DAB,* s.v. "David Dixon Porter," and Porter's "Chronicles," pp. 1114, 1116-1117, 1120, 1123-1125, and 1137, in David Dixon Porter Papers, vol. 9, Writings A-C, MDLC. On Shufeldt's service with Porter, see above, p. 11, n. 19, and R. S. West, Jr., *The Second Admiral: A Life of David Dixon Porter, 1813-1891* (New York, 1937), 54-56. The congressional investigation of Robeson's administration is in *House Misc. Doc.,* no. 170, 44th Cong. 1st Sess.; *House Reports,* nos. 788 and 789, 44th Cong. 1st Sess.; Charles R. Erdman, Jr., *DAB,* s.v., "George Maxwell Robeson."

12. S. to Robeson, Oct. 23, 1876, *Annual Report of the Chief of the Bureau of Equipment and Recruiting to the Secretary of the Navy for the Year Ending June 30, 1876* [hereafter *ARCBER, 1876* and likewise by year], included with *ARSN, 1876,* 104-105; *ARCBER, 1877,* 4, and *ARCBER, 1878,* 59-60; S. to Robeson, Apr. 29, 1875; LRBC 72:98; Bradley A. Fiske, *From Midshipman to Rear Admiral* (New York, 1919), 44-45, with details of Fiske's apparatus, p. 40.

13. *ARCBER, 1875,* 85; S. to I. Bell, Apr. 29, 1872, Stephen B. Luce Papers, box 7 (1872), MDLC, quoted also, in part, in Albert Gleaves, *Life and Letters of Rear Admiral Stephen B. Luce* (New York, 1925), 134; S. to Luce, Apr. 15, 28, and May 5, 1875, Luce Papers, box 7 (1875).

14. *ARCBER, 1875, 1876, 1877,* and *1878,* pp. 85, 108-109, 6-8, and 61-63, respectively. William Kimmel, representative from Maryland, in "Enlistments in the Navy," a *Report from the House Committee on Naval Affairs to accompany H. R. 2240,* no. 452, 45th Cong. 2nd Sess., showed strong support for Shufeldt's scheme. Shufeldt's main correspondence with Luce, indicating cooperation, is dated Apr. 23, May 24, June 25, July 31, and Dec. 12, 1875, Feb. 26, Mar. 3, Sept. 24, Oct. 1, 5, 6, 9, 11, 12, and Nov. 3, 1877, and Luce to S., Sept. 27, Oct. 11, 22, and 24, 1877, in Luce Papers, box 7 (1875) and (1877). See also S. to B. F. Mauiere, Dec. 1878, in RWS 35 (Naval Personnel and Rank Information).

15. *ARCBER, 1875, 1876, 1877,* and *1878,* pp. 85-86, 105-107, 5, and 56, respectively; S. to Robeson, Nov. 6, 1875, LRBC 72:181-182.

16. *ARCBER, 1876, 1877,* and *1878,* pp. 105-107, 5, and 56, respectively; S. to Robeson, Nov. 6, 1875, LRBC 72:181-182; cf. the deck plans of the USS *Richmond, Swatara,* and *Miantonomoh,* enclosed with *ARCBER, 1877.*

17. *ARCBER, 1877* and *1878,* pp. 6 and 61, respectively.

18. *ARCBER, 1876,* 106 and 108; for an individual case, Paymaster's Teaman, Charles G. Gray, see S. to Robeson, Aug. 9, 1875, LRBC 72:137.

19. Statistics from *ARCBER, 1876, 1877,* and *1878,* pp. 108, 5, and 61, respectively; Fragment on "Naval Affairs," ca. 1876-1877, RWS 17 (Fragments); S. to Thompson, Oct. 30, 1878, LRBC 75:268.

20. *ARCBER, 1878,* 63. The *Newark Daily Journal,* Jan. 20, 1877, "The Coming Navy," with favorable comment on Shufeldt's *ARCBER, 1876;* clipping in RWS 31 (Naval Policies, 1850s-1880s). *ARSN, 1878, 1879,* and *1880,* pp. 30-32, 19-20, and 23-24.

21. Thompson to S., Ammen, Jeffers, and Shock, Jan. 14, 1878, SLBC 5:479.

22. Harold Sprout and Margaret Sprout, *The Rise of American Naval Power, 1776-1918* (Princeton, 1939), 181; cf. with W. R. Herrick, *The American Naval Revolution* (Baton Rouge, 1966), 17-21, esp. 20-21. *ARSN, 1877, 1878, 1879,* and *1880,* clearly show Thompson's increasing emphasis on the need for commercial expansion.

23. S. to Thompson, Jan. 16, 1878, LRBC 75:14 (for next seven, unnumbered pages).

24. The board's reply to Thompson, Feb. 19, 1879, *ibid.,* 86 and 87.

25. S., *The Relation of the Navy to the Commerce of the United States: A Letter Written by Request to Hon. Leopold Morse, M. C., Member of the Naval Committee, House of Representatives* (Washington, D.C., 1878); copy in Navy Department Library. The copy in RWS 32 (Commerce, U.S. Navy, 1878) is missing pp. 5-9.

26. The italics are Shufeldt's.

27. Quoted in Walter LaFeber, *The New Empire: An Interpretation of American Expansion: 1860-1898* (Ithaca, 1963), 40-41. On Evarts' recognition of the urgent need for commercial expansion, see his speech to the New England Society, Dec. 22, 1878, in Sherman Evarts, ed., *Arguments and Speeches of William Maxwell Evarts* (New York, 1919), 391-397.

28. S. to Luce, May 5, 1875, Luce Papers, box 7 (1875).

29. *The Statistical History of the United States from Colonial Times to the Present* (Stamford, 1965), 538, series U1-14, "Value of Exports and Imports: 1790-1857," gives $1,151,000,000 for 1877, with an excess of $167,000,000 in exports over imports. Compare similar arguments in Robert Seager II, "Ten Years before Mahan: The Unofficial Case for the New Navy, 1880-1890," *MVHR* 40 (1953): 493.

30. Seager, "Ten Years before Mahan," 498-500. Compare Secretary Thompson's comments on the importance of the navy for commerce in *ARSN, 1877, 1878, 1879,* and *1880,* pp. 8-10 and 11, 11-16, 26, and 34-35, respectively, with Shufeldt's ideas. Shufeldt was most probably Thompson's source of information for the commercial passages of the secretary's reports. See also "The State of the Navy," *New York Daily Tribune,* Nov. 28, 1879.

31. S. to Molly, Aug. 28, 1877, RWS 16 (1877); *ARSN, 1875* and *1876,* pp. 14 and 15-16, respectively; E. B. Glick, *Straddling the Isthmus of Tehuantepec* (Gainesville, Fla., 1959), 7-27.

32. Coppinger to S., Nov. 16, 1875, and Jan. 7 and 21, 1876; Orcutt to S., Jan. 29, 1876, in RWS 16 (Jan. 1876) and RWS 23, World Cruise of the USS

Ticonderoga 1878-1879 (Liberian Correspondence, 1875-1879); S., "Exodus of a Race," RWS 23 (Printed Matter), with MS copy, *ibid.* (Miscellany); *Appeal of the Executive Committee of the American Colonization Society* (Washington, D.C., 1876), RWS 16 (1876).

33. S., "Exodus of a Race," RWS 23; cf. with Richard Hofstadter, *Social Darwinism in American Thought* (Boston, 1962), 172, 176, and generally, 172-184 and 191-194.

34. S., *The United States Navy in Connection with the Foundation, Growth and Prosperity of the Republic of Liberia: An Address Delivered before the American Colonization Society* (Washington, D.C., 1877), 10, 16, 17, 18, and 25.

35. For appointments, see *Minutes of the 62nd Annual Report of the American Colonization Society, Jan. 21 and 22, 1879* (Washington, D.C., 1879); copy in RWS 23 (Printed Matter). G. Washington Warren, *The Duty of Strengthening Liberia. Jan. 20, 1880* (Washington, D.C., 1880), 4.

36. S. to Thompson, Nov. 1, 1878, LRBC 75:274; S. to Luce, Oct. 24, 1878, Luce Papers, box 7 (1878); Thompson to S., Nov. 19, 1878, RWS 10 (1877-1880).

CHAPTER 10

1. Gilbert Haven, "America in Africa," *NAR* 125 (July 1877): 147-158, quotation p. 158. See the bibliographical essay for further details.

2. Thompson to S., Oct. 29, 1878, Lettercopy book of Richard Wigginton Thompson, 190-194, Thompson MSS, Indiana University Library; Evarts to Thompson, Oct. 23 and Nov. 9, 1878, Domestic Letters of the Department of State [hereafter DLDS], vol. 125 (Oct. 22-Dec. 31, 1878): 23, 206-212; Thompson to Evarts, Oct. 24 and 29, 1878, Miscellaneous Letters of the Department of State [hereafter MLDS], (Oct. 18-31, 1878); instructions also summarized in "The Cruise of the *Ticonderoga*" and "A Commodore's Cruise," *St. Helena Guardian,* July 3, 1879, clipping in RWS 2, Journal of Frederick Augustus Miller [hereafter Miller's Journal], USS *Ticonderoga,* vol. 3 (Dec. 1879-May 1880): 2.

3. Evarts to Thompson, Oct. 23, Nov. 9 and 12, 1878, DLDS 125:23 and 206-212, copy in RWS 23 (Liberian Boundary Dispute, Nov. 1878-Jan. 1879); Thompson to Evarts, Oct. 24 and 29, 1878, MLDS (Oct. 18-31, 1878); Milton Plesur, "Across the Wide Pacific," *PHR* 28 (1959): 78-79; *Monrovia Observer,* Nov. 14, 1878. For Sargent's resolution, see *U.S. Congressional Record,* 45th Cong. 2nd Sess., 7, pt. 3:2324 and 2600-2601.

4. Evarts to Thompson, Oct. 23, Nov. 9 and 12, 1878, DLDS 125:23 and 206-212; Thompson to S., Oct. 29, 1878, Lettercopy book of Thompson, 190-194 (for all Thompson's quotations); for the instructions on the Liberian Boundary Dispute, see Smyth to Evarts, nos. 13 and 8, Oct. 17, 1878, and Jan. 7, 1879, DD, Liberia 7 (Nov. 18, 1877-Dec. 29, 1879), copy in RWS 23 (Liberian Boundary Dispute, Nov. 1878-Jan. 1879); Evarts to Smyth, nos. 13 and 21, Nov. 12, 1878, and Feb. 20, 1879, DI, Liberia 2 (Oct. 6, 1875-July 18, 1906): 60 and 68-69; *Monrovia Observer,* Nov. 14, 1878, RWS 31 (Liberia, Oct.-Nov. 1878); Evarts to Sir Edward Thornton, Nov. 12, 1878, Notes to Foreign Legations in the United States from the Department of State, Great Britain,

vol. 17 (July 28, 1875–Feb. 26, 1879): 632; Thornton to Evarts, Nov. 13, 1878, Notes from the British Legation in the United States to the Department of State, vol. 103 (Feb. 9, 1878–Nov. 12, 1878); copy in RWS 23 (Liberian Boundary Dispute, Nov. 1878–Jan. 1879); Thompson to Evarts, Nov. 15, 1878, MLDS (Nov. 15–30, 1878); Evarts to Thompson, Dec. 2, 1878, DLDS 125:437–438, copy in RWS 23 (Liberian Boundary Dispute, Nov. 1878–Jan. 1879).

5. The description of the vessel is from George L. Allen, *The Pilgrimage of the* Ticonderoga (San Francisco, 1880). Allen was chief petty officer on board; see pp. 81–85.

6. S. to Molly, Nov. 23, 25, 26, and Dec. 7, 1878, RWS 17 (Family Correspondence, undated) and RWS 16 (1878).

7. S. to Molly, Christmas, 1878, and Jan. 8, 1879, RWS 16 (1878) and (Jan. 1879); S. to Thompson, Dec. 26, 1878, and no. 3, Jan. 15, 1879, RWS 4, USS *Ticonderoga* Letter Press Book, Dec. 24, 1878–Nov. 8, 1880: Letters to the Secretary of the Navy from S. [hereafter *Ticonderoga* LSN], 2 and 13–16; S. to William LeRoy, Dec. 26, 1878, RWS 4 (Letterpress copies of official correspondence prepared during global cruise, Dec. 26, 1878–Mar. 5, 1880) [cited hereafter as LPCOC, with dates and page nos.]; guides to letters in RWS 3 (general index to letters sent and received, Dec. 24, 1878–Nov. 1880). The unpublished manuscript of the *Ticonderoga*'s cruise is in the Shufeldt Papers, RWS 26 (World Cruise of the USS *Ticonderoga:* West Coast of Africa), RWS 27 (World Cruise of the USS *Ticonderoga:* East Coast of Africa), and RWS 28 (World Cruise of the USS *Ticonderoga:* Penang to Japan). There is a bound, two-volume copy in the Navy Department Archives, Record Group 45, Naval Records Collections of the Office of Naval Records and Library, Appendix A, Entry 25, Letters from Officers Commanding Expeditions, Jan. 1818–Dec. 1885, series entry item 11. Shufeldt's letters to the secretary of the navy are also in RG 45, entry 464, Subject File, box 351, OC, Cruises and Voyages (Special), 1878–1884.

8. RWS 2, Miller's Journal 1 (Dec. 1878–Aug. 1879): 3–4; Allen, *The Pilgrimage of the* Ticonderoga, 1; S. to Brown, Dec. 29, 1878, RWS 4 (LPCOC, Dec. 26, 1878–Mar. 5, 1879).

9. S. to Thompson, no. 2, Jan. 7, 1879, RWS 4, *Ticonderoga* LSN, 4–10; S. to Molly, Jan. 5 and 8, 1879, RWS 16 (Jan. 1879).

10. S. to Thompson, no. 3, Jan. 15, 1879, RWS 4, *Ticonderoga* LSN, 13–16; S. to Molly, Jan. 19, 1879, RWS 16 (Jan. 1879).

11. Evarts to Thompson, Dec. 4, 1878, DLDS 125:458; Thompson to S., Dec. 5, 1878, RWS 22, World Cruise of USS *Ticonderoga*, 1879–1883, and undated (West Africa reports: Sierra Leone–St. Helena); S. to Thompson, nos. 4 and 6, Jan. 15 and 20, 1879, RWS 4, *Ticonderoga* LSN, 17 and 21–25; S. to Molly, Jan. 19 and 26, 1879, RWS 16 (Jan. 1879); *Freetown Watchman and West African Record,* Jan. 31, 1879; *West African Reporter,* Feb. 5 and 12, 1879, copies in RWS 31 (Sierra Leone, Jan.–Feb. 1879).

12. "The *Ticonderoga*'s Mission" and "The American Naval and Commercial Expedition to Africa," *West African Reporter,* Jan. 29, 1879, with a half-column taken from the *New York Times,* RWS 31 (Sierra Leone, Jan.–Feb. 1879).

See also "The Voyage of the *Ticonderoga:* The Effort to Extend Our Foreign Trade," by "Mack," *New York Daily Graphic,* Feb. 28, 1879, RWS 2, Miller's Journal 3:2-3.

13. Morris to S., Dec. 10, 1878; Blyden to Morris, Apr. 4 and Nov. 6, 1877; Morris to Blyden, Oct. 1, 1877; Blyden to S., Apr. 18, 1879, all in RWS 23 (Liberian Boundary Dispute Correspondence, Mar.-Dec. 1879) and another, of Apr. 18, 1879, in RWS 27, Cruise MSS, pt. 2, "On the Liberian Boundary Question of 1879": Correspondence, Second Session.

14. S. to Thompson, no. 8, Jan. 29, 1879, RWS 4, *Ticonderoga* LSN, 27-29, and RWS 26, Cruise MSS, pt. 2, chap. 1, "Sierra Leone"; S. to Blyden, Jan. 29, 1879, and S. to F. J. Drake, Feb. 26, 1879, RWS 4 (LPCOC, Dec. 26, 1878-Mar. 5, 1880), 19-22 and 34-37.

15. S. to Thompson, no. 9, Commercial Dispatch no. 1, Jan. 30, 1879, RWS 4, Commercial Dispatch Letterbook [hereafter ComDis]; S. to Blyden, Jan. 29, 1879, RWS 4 (LPCOC, Dec. 26, 1878-Mar. 5, 1880), 19-22, and RWS 26, Cruise MSS, pt. 2, chap. 1, "Sierra Leone." See also "The Trip of the *Ticonderoga:* The Liberian Boundary Dispute to be Arbitrated by an American Commodore," *New York Daily Graphic,* Apr. 16, 1879; RWS 2, Miller's Journal 3:3.

16. S. to Thompson, nos. 5, 10, and 12, Jan. 15 and 31, and Feb. 16, 1879, RWS 4, *Ticonderoga* LSN, 17, 21-25, and 34-36; for a longer, more detailed outline, see RWS 26, Cruise MSS, pt. 2, chap. 2, "The Mixed Commission." King to S. and to Governor Rowe, Jan. 21 to Feb. 13, 1879, RWS 26, Cruise MSS, pt. 2, chap. "Part First of the Appendix North West Boundary Commission . . . correspondence . . . of the Mixed Commission,"; RWS 4 (LPCOC, Dec. 26, 1878-Mar. 5, 1880), 8, 11, 13, 15-16, 25, and 29; S. to Molly, Jan. 19 and 26, 1879, RWS 16 (Jan. 1879); *Freetown Watchman and West African Record,* Jan. 31, 1879; *West African Reporter,* Feb. 5 and 12, 1879, copies in RWS 31 (Sierra Leone, Jan.-Feb. 1879).

17. Hopkins to S., Jan. 29, 1879; King to S., Jan. 29, 1879, RWS 23 (Liberian Boundary Dispute Correspondence, Nov. 1878-Jan. 1879); S. to Molly, Feb. 10 and undated [but before Feb. 11], 1879, RWS 16 (Feb. 1879). Apologies for the delay were sent to Evarts and acknowledged in his letter to Thornton, Apr. 12, 1879, Notes to Foreign Legations in the United States from the Department of State, vol. 18 (Great Britain, Mar. 3, 1879-Mar. 18, 1882): 36; copy in RWS 31 (Sierra Leone, Jan.-Feb. 1879); *African Times,* Feb. 1, 1879, 15.

18. "Synopsis of the Proceedings of the Mixed Commission held under the provisions of the draft proposals for the settlement of the Liberian Boundary Question" [hereafter "Synopsis"], *Monrovia Observer,* Feb. 27, 1879, and *West African Reporter,* Mar. 19, 1879; copies in RWS 31 (Liberia) and (Sierra Leone, Mar. 1879). Copy sent by Smyth to Evarts with no. 14, Mar. 5, 1879, DD, Liberia 7; RWS 26, Cruise MSS, pt. 2, chap. 2, "The Mixed Commission"; Streeton to S., Feb. 12, 1879, RWS 23 (Liberian Boundary Dispute, Feb. 1879).

19. S. to Thompson, no. 12, Feb. 16, 1879, RWS 4, *Ticonderoga* LSN, 34-42; S. to G. W. Gibson, Feb. 27, 1879, RWS 4 (LPCOC, Dec. 26, 1878-Mar.

5, 1880), 41-44; S. to Molly, Feb. 14, 1879, RWS 16 (Feb. 1879); RWS 26, Cruise MSS, pt. 2, chap. 2, "The Mixed Commission."

20. "Synopsis," *Monrovia Observer,* Feb. 27, 1879; Smyth to Evarts, no. 14, Mar. 5, 1879, DD, Liberia 7; Gibson to S., Mar. 1, 1879, RWS 27, Cruise MSS, pt. 2, "On the Liberian Boundary Question of 1879"; résumé in S. to Thompson, no. 12, Feb. 16, 1879, RWS 4, *Ticonderoga* LSN, 37-38; RWS 26, Cruise MSS, pt. 2, chap. 2, "The Mixed Commission"; Gibson to S., rec'd Mar. 5, 1879, RWS 23 (Liberian Boundary Dispute, Mar.-Dec. 1879); S. to Streeton and Hopkins, Feb. 14, 1879, RWS 4 (LPCOC, Dec. 26, 1878-Mar. 5, 1880), 30-31.

21. S. to Thompson, no. 12, Feb. 16, 1879, RWS 4, *Ticonderoga* LSN, 39-40, italics Shufeldt's; RWS 26, Cruise MSS, pt. 2, chap. 2, "The Mixed Commission"; 29th Report of the American Colonization Society (1846) with W. Coppinger to S., Nov. 30, 1878, RWS 23 (Liberian Boundary Dispute Correspondence, Mar.-Dec. 1879).

22. S. to Molly, Feb. 23, 1879, RWS 16 (Feb. 1879).

23. RWS 2, Miller's Journal 1:15; Smyth to Evarts, nos. 13 and 15, Feb. 22 and Mar. 6, 1879, DD, Liberia 7; Gibson to Smyth, Feb. 18, 1879; Smyth to S., Feb. 24 and 25, 1879; S. to Smyth, Feb. 26, 1879 in RWS 23 (Liberian Boundary Dispute, Feb. correspondence, 1879), and all four enclosed with Smyth to Evarts, Mar. 6, 1879, RWS 4 (LPCOC, Dec. 26, 1878-Mar. 5, 1880), 39-40; Evarts' reply to Smyth, July 12, 1879, DI, Liberia 2:79.

24. Smyth to S., Mar. 2, 1879, RWS 23 (Liberian Boundary Dispute Correspondence, Mar.-Dec. 1879); S. to Molly, Mar. 7, 1879, RWS 16 (Mar. 1879); Smyth to Evarts, no. 16, Mar. 7, 1879, DD, Liberia 7; *Monrovia Observer,* Mar. 13, 1879, RWS 31 (Liberia, Mar.-Apr. 1879).

25. Gibson to J. T. Gibson, Mar. 3, 1879, RWS 22 (West Africa reports, Angola-Capetown); RWS 26, Cruise MSS, pt. 2, chap. 4, "Cruise to Tabou and the Return."

26. S. to Julio, Mar. 8, 1879, and to King Nimleh, Mar. 10, 1879, RWS 4 (LPCOC, Dec. 26, 1878-Mar. 5, 1880), 52-55; Smyth to Evarts, no. 31, June 12, 1879, DD, Liberia 7, including a "Manifesto of the G'Debo Chiefs, Apr. 5, 1879." *Monrovia Observer,* June 12, 1879, copy in RWS 2, Miller's Journal, 3:5; Gemut Vahson to S., Mar. 24, 1879, RWS 22 (West Africa reports, Sierra Leone-St. Helena); "Memorandum of a meeting of the Superintendent of Maryland County, Liberia, and certain chiefs of the G'Debo tribe of natives, on board the Flag Ship *Ticonderoga* at Cape Palmas roads, Mar. 14, 1879," RWS 23 (Reports).

27. S. to Thompson, no. 17, Mar. 19, 1879, RWS 4, *Ticonderoga* LSN, 52-56; RWS 26, Cruise MSS, pt. 2, chap. 4, "Cruise to Tabou and the Return."

28. S. to President A. W. Gardner, Feb. 24, 1879, RWS 4 (LPCOC, Dec. 26, 1878-Mar. 5, 1880), 32-33; Gibson to S., Feb. 25, 1879, RWS 23 (Liberian Correspondence, 1875-1879); Drake to S., Mar. 17, 1879, RWS 23 (Reports), which has the same illustrations as Shufeldt's own report on Liberia, RWS 26, Cruise MSS, pt. 2, chap. 3, "Liberia." See also "Africa Stretches out her hands, The Civilization, Christianization and Material Development of Africa," *New York Daily Graphic,* Aug. 20. 1879, copy in RWS 2, Miller's Jour-

nal 3:11-12; Drake to S., Apr. 28, 1879, S. to W. D. Whiting, May 19, 1879, enclosing Drake's reports, Whiting to S., July 28, 1879, all in RWS 23 (Reports), (Liberian Correspondence, 1875-1879), and (Liberian Boundary Dispute Correspondence, Mar.-Dec. 1879).

29. S. to Thompson, no. 11, Feb. 11, 1879, RWS 4, *Ticonderoga* LSN, 32-33. Part of the quotation about Liberia being the "objective point for American trade" also appears in S. to G. W. Gibson, Mar. 2, 1879, RWS 4 (LPCOC, Dec. 26, 1879-Mar. 5, 1880), 47; RWS 26, Cruise MSS, pt. 2, chap. 3, "Liberia."

30. S. to Thompson, no. 16, Mar. 19, 1879, RWS 4, *Ticonderoga* LSN, 47-50; Van Volkenburgh and Leavitt to Thompson, June 3, 1880, RWS 22 (West Africa reports, Congo Cotton); RWS 26, Cruise MSS, pt. 2, chap. 3, "Liberia."

31. S. to Molly, Mar. 20, 1879, RWS 16 (Mar. 1879).

32. Hopkins to S., Apr. 1, 1879, RWS 23 (Liberian Boundary Dispute Correspondence, Mar.-Dec. 1879); S. to Molly, Mar. 20 and 30, and Apr. 5, 1879, RWS 16 (Mar. 1879) and (Apr. 1879).

33. Gibson to S., Mar. 19, 1879; S. to the Commissioners of the North West Boundary Commission, Apr. 6, 8, and 9, 1879; Laborde to S., Apr. 5, 1879; the Commissioners to S., Apr. 7, 1879, in RWS 27, Cruise MSS, pt. 2, "On the Liberian Boundary Question of 1879"; Davis to S., Apr. 7, 1879; Streeton to S., Apr. 8, 1879, RWS 23 (Liberian Boundary Dispute Correspondence, Mar.-Dec. 1879) and RWS 4 (LPCOC, Dec. 26, 1878-Mar. 5, 1880), 72, 74, and 76; *Monrovia Observer,* Apr. 24, 1879; S. to Molly, Apr. 11, 1879, RWS 16 (Apr. 1879).

34. S. to Thompson, nos. 20 and 24, Apr. 11 and 25, 1879, RWS 4, *Ticonderoga* LSN, 59-60 and 68-73; another copy of latter in RWS 27, Cruise MSS, pt. 2, "On the Liberian Boundary Question of 1879," and RWS 26, Cruise MSS, pt. 2, chap. 5 "On the Spot and the end of the Mixed Commission." Shufeldt heard again from Edward Blyden on the dangers of British trader, John Myers Harris, being left in control of Solyman—"a very demoralizing influence upon the Native" would be sustained, supposedly by the British government. Harris's "undisputed pre-eminence" would then "stimulate confusion and wars and even slavery in that country in the interest of his trade." Blyden to S., Apr. 18, 1879, RWS 23 (Liberian Boundary Dispute Correspondence, Mar.-Dec. 1879). See also G. Moore and L. H. Williams to S., Apr. 21, 1879, and A. B. King to S., Apr. 22, 1879, RWS 27, Cruise MSS, pt. 2 "On the Liberian Boundary Question of 1879" and "Liberia: The Present Condition of the Republic, America's Foster Child," *New York Herald,* May 7, 1879, RWS 2, Miller's Journal 3:5-6.

35. *Monrovia Observer,* Apr. 24, 1879, RWS 31 (Liberia, Mar.-Apr. 1879); S. to Molly, Apr. 26, 1879, RWS 16 (Apr. 1879); S. to Thompson, no. 24, Apr. 25, 1879, RWS 4, *Ticonderoga* LSN, 68-73; "Liberia's Future—The Fate that awaits a Colony established by the people of this country," *New York Herald,* July 7, 1879; "Liberian Boundary Question Failure of the Commission and its Consequences," by "Mack," *New York Daily Graphic,* Aug. 15, 1879; "Liberia: The Present Condition of the Republic, America's Foster Child," *New York Herald,*

May 7, 1879, RWS 2, Miller's Journal 3:5-6, and 10. "England's Policy in Africa," *West African Reporter,* Apr. 2, 1879; "The Boundary Commission," *ibid.,* Apr. 16, 1879; "The North West Boundary Commission," *Monrovia Observer,* July 3, 1879; RWS 27, Cruise MSS, pt. 2, "On the Liberian Boundary Question of 1879," and RWS 26, Cruise MSS, pt. 2, chap. 5, "On the Spot and the end of the Mixed Commission."

36. Mannix to King, Apr. 23 and 24, 1879; Laborde to S., Apr. 24, 1879; King to Mannix, Apr. 24, 1879; Mannix to Laborde, Apr. 24, 1879, in RWS 23 (Liberian Boundary Dispute Correspondence, Mar.-Dec. 1879); Gibson to S., Apr. 28, 1879, RWS 27, Cruise MSS, pt. 2, "On the Liberian Boundary Question of 1879"; S. to Molly, Apr. 26 and May 2, 1879, RWS 16 (Apr. 1879 and May 1879); on the "disintegrating influences" quotation, see RWS 26, Cruise MSS, pt. 2, chap. 2, "The Mixed Commission."

37. Evarts to W. J. Hoppin, no. 446, Apr. 21, 1880, DI, Great Britain 25 (Aug. 3, 1877-Sept. 30, 1880): 627; Evarts to E. F. Noyes, Apr. 21, 1880, quoted in G. A. Pennanen, "The Foreign Policy of William Maxwell Evarts," (Ph.D. diss. University of Wisconsin, 1969), 222; Smyth to F. W. Seward, Apr. 28, 1879, CD, Monrovia 3 (Apr. 15, 1875-Aug. 11, 1882); Gibson to Evarts, May 15, 1879, Notes from the Liberian Legation in the United States to the Department of State, vol. 1 (July 9, 1862-Feb. 16, 1898); Smyth to Evarts, no. 26, May 12, 1879, DD, Liberia 7; S. to Thompson, no. 26, Apr. 28, 1879, RWS 4, *Ticonderoga* LSN, 76-77, also in RWS 27, Cruise MSS, pt. 2, "On the Liberian Boundary Question of 1879." See also Hunter to Noyes, July 17, 1879, *For Rel, 1879,* 341; "Documents Relating to the United States and Liberia," *AJIL* 4 (1910), Documents, 188-229, esp. 221-222, which includes Evarts to Smyth, Feb. 2, 1880.

38. S. to Thompson, no. 29, May 6, 1879, RWS 4, *Ticonderoga* LSN, 80-81, RWS 27, Cruise MSS, pt. 2, "On the Liberian Boundary Question of 1879," S. to Molly, May 14, 1879, RWS 16 (May 1879); see also Smyth to F. W. Seward and to Hunter, Aug. 4 and 21, 1879, CD, Monrovia 3; Evarts to Smyth, nos. 29 and 43, June 17, 1879, and Feb. 2, 1880, DI, Liberia 22, where Evarts wanted evidence that the Boundary Question Commission had ended and took cognizance of the great importance and potential of Liberian trade and the interior of Africa for the United States; *62nd Annual Report of the American Colonization Society* (Washington, D.C., 1879), 14-16, which used Shufeldt's cruise to request steamship connections and a stimulated competition with European powers for "The Open Gate" to Africa. Further information is in "The Cruise of the *Ticonderoga:* Indifference to Liberian Interests a National Folly," and the editorial, "Progress in Liberia," *New York Daily Graphic,* June 17, 1879; "Liberia Present and Future, the Negro Republic Not a Failure," by "Mack," *ibid.,* July 12, 1879; RWS 2, Miller's Journal 3:7-8, 9-10.

39. Evarts to Thompson, Feb. 3, 1879, Thompson to S., Feb. 25, 1879, RWS 22 (West Africa reports, Congo Cotton) and RWS 27, Cruise MSS, pt. 2, "On the Liberian Boundary Question of 1879."

40. S. to Thompson, no. 31, May 14, 1879, RWS 4, *Ticonderoga* LSN, 82; RWS 26, Cruise MSS, pt. 2, chap. 6, "Fernando Po"; S. to Thompson, no. 30, Commercial Dispatch no. 4, May 14, 1879, RWS 4, ComDis, 15-19; on the oil rivers, see G. I. Jones, *The Trading States of the Oil Rivers* (London, 1963),

88-101; "Liberian Boundary Question, Failure of the Commission and its Consequences: The Cruise of the *Ticonderoga*—Missionaries and Great Rivers," by "Mack," *New York Daily Graphic,* Aug. 15, 1879; RWS 2, Miller's Journal 3:10.

41. S. to Molly, May 14, 1879, RWS 16 (May 1879).

42. On the Gabon mission station, see S. to Molly, May 19, 1879, *ibid.;* S. to Thompson, nos. 32 and 33, May 19 and 21, 1879, RWS 4, *Ticonderoga* LSN, 85, 86-90. See also "Commodore Shufeldt in Africa: Work of the Presbyterian Missions—The 'Opening of Africa' A Delusion," *New York Times,* Aug. 15, 1879. For the Congo River area, see RWS 26, Cruise MSS, pt. 2, chap. 8, "An American Man of War up the Congo"; S. to Thompson, nos. 34 and 37, June 3 and 20, 1879, RWS 4, *Ticonderoga* LSN, 92, 100-101, the latter containing extracts of Drake's interview; S. to Thompson, Commercial Dispatch no. 5, June 19, 1879, RWS 4, ComDis, 24; "Commodore Shufeldt in Africa," *New York Times,* Aug. 15, 1879; RWS 26, Cruise MSS, pt. 2, chap. 7, "The Great Gaboon," and chap. 8, "An American Man of War up the Congo"; RWS 2, Miller's Journal 1:47-48.

43. S. to Thompson, no. 34, June 3, 1879, RWS 4, *Ticonderoga* LSN, 92-99, and no. 35, Commercial Dispatch no. 5, June 19, 1879, RWS 4, ComDis, 20-24; RWS 26, Cruise MSS, pt. 2, chap. 8, "An American Man of War up the Congo"; "Commodore Shufeldt in Africa," *New York Times,* Aug. 15, 1879; *African Times,* Dec. 1, 1879, 141-142.

44. S. to Thompson, no. 34, June 3, 1879, RWS 4, *Ticonderoga* LSN, 97; and no. 35, Commercial Dispatch no. 5, June 19, 1879, RWS 4, ComDis, 20-24; RWS 26, Cruise MSS, pt. 2, chap. 8, "An American Man of War up the Congo."

45. S. to Thompson, nos. 35 and 36, Commercial Dispatches nos. 5 and 6, June 19 and 20, 1879, RWS 4, ComDis, 20-23, 25-28; RWS 26, Cruise MSS, pt. 2, chap. 8, "An American Man of War up the Congo." On Silva Porto, see James Duffy, *Portuguese Africa* (Cambridge, Mass., 1959), 176-177, 192-194, or *Portugal in Africa* (Cambridge, Mass., 1962), 104-106.

46. S. to Thompson, no. 45, Aug. 2, 1879, RWS 4, *Ticonderoga* LSN, 123-130.

47. S. to Molly, Aug. 10, 1879, RWS 16 (Aug. 1879).

48. Several official announcements were sent from the State and Navy departments, for example, Evarts to Thompson, Feb. 3, 1879; Thompson to S., Feb. 25, 1879; Hunter (State Department) to Thompson, Sept. 1, 1879; and Jeffers to S., Sept. 8, 1879, in RWS 22 (West Africa reports, Congo Cotton) and (West Africa reports, Sierra Leone-St. Helena). The Evarts' quotations are in Evarts to Thompson, Sept. 22, 1879, RWS 22 (West Africa reports). "[I]n relation to the commercial interests of the West Coast of Africa," Evarts noted in a second letter of the same day, "The information is important and valuable, and will be considered in connection with the Consular system for that locality."

CHAPTER II

1. *ARSN, 1879,* 4.

2. S. to Thompson, Sept. 10, 1879, RWS 4, *Ticonderoga* LSN, 137-143;

RWS 26, Cruise MSS, pt. 2, chap. 11, "Cape Town"; report printed in "South African Colonies: A Report upon Their Condition and Prospects," *New York Times,* Nov. 28, 1879; editorial, *ibid.*

3. S. to Thompson, Sept. 10, 1879, RWS 4, *Ticonderoga* LSN, 145–148, 152–153; also in RWS 26, Cruise MSS, pt. 2, chap. 11, "Cape Town"; "Letter from the *Ticonderoga:* Table Bay and Cape Town—Cosmopolitan Character of Cape Colony," by "Mack," *New York Daily Graphic,* Oct. 1879, clipping in RWS 2, Miller's Journal 3:15.

4. RWS 27, Cruise MSS, pt. 3 "The East Coast of Africa," chaps. 15, "Madagascar and East Africa," and 16, "Malagasy, East Africa"; S. to Thompson, no. 50, Sept. 20, 1879, and to Commodore Earl English, unnumbered, Sept. 21, 1879, RWS 4, *Ticonderoga* LSN, 155–160, 164–167; RWS 22 (East Africa reports, Madagascar); "Letter from the *Ticonderoga:* Madagascar —The Present Natives—Foreign Traders and Pirates," by "Mack," *New York Daily Graphic,* Nov. 23, 1879, in RWS 2, Miller's Journal 3.

5. S. to Thompson, nos. 50 and 54, Sept. 20 and Oct. 14, 1879, and to Commodore Earl English, unnumbered, Sept. 21, 1879, RWS 4, *Ticonderoga* LSN, 160–163, 182–183, and 164–167, respectively.

6. W. W. Robinson to W. Hunter, July 21, Aug. 24 and 26, Oct. 21, 1879, and Jan. 12, 1880, CD, Tamatave 2 (Jan. 5, 1870–May 20, 1880). See also dispatches nos. 69, 74, and 81 of Aug. 31, 1880, Jan. 15 and June 9, 1881, *ibid.,* vol. 3 (July 2, 1880–June 14, 1883), for the threat of the French protectorate.

7. S. to Thompson, no. 57, Oct. 29, 1879, RWS 4, *Ticonderoga* LSN, 202–206; RWS 27, Cruise MSS, pt. 3, chap. 16, "Malagasy, East Africa."

8. C. Payson to Robinson, no. 59, Jan. 21, 1881, CI, vol. 98 (Nov. 18, 1880–Mar. 3, 1881): 363–367.

9. Johanna (Anjouan), Mayotte, Mohilla (Mohéli), and Great Comoro are the four islands in the group. S. to Thompson, no. 51, Oct. 5, 1879, RWS 4, *Ticonderoga* LSN, 174–177; RWS 27, Cruise MSS, pt. 3, chap. 17, "Johanna"; S. to Molly, Oct. 12, 1879, RWS 16 (Oct. 1879).

10. S. to Thompson, no. 53, Oct. 9, 1879, RWS 4, *Ticonderoga* LSN, 178–181; S. to W. H. Hathorne, Oct. 14, 1879, and S. to Sultan Abdallah, Oct. 7, 1879, RWS 4 (LPCOC, Dec. 26, 1878–Mar. 5, 1880), 124–127; Abdallah to S., Oct. 5, 1879, and Hathorne to S., Oct. 14, 1879, RWS 22 (East Africa reports, Cotton Johanna); see RWS 2, Miller's Journal 2 (Aug. 1879–Dec. 1879): 20, on Wilson.

11. "Treaty between the Government of the United States of America and His Highness, Sultan Abdallah, King of Johanna," with S. to Thompson, Oct. 5, 1879, RWS 4, *Ticonderoga* LSN, 168–173; copies in RWS 22 (East Africa reports, Cotton Johanna) and in RWS 27, Cruise MSS, pt. 3, chap. 17, "Johanna." See W. Stull Holt, *Treaties Defeated by the Senate* (Baltimore, 1933), 131–132.

12. Sultan Abdallah to Rutherford B. Hayes, Oct. 5, 1879, with S. to Thompson, no. 51, Oct. 5, 1879, RWS 4, *Ticonderoga* LSN, 178–179; copies in RWS 22 (East Africa reports, Cotton Johanna); RWS 27, Cruise MSS, pt. 3, chap. 17, "Johanna," RWS 2, Miller's Journal 2:21.

13. S. to Molly, Oct. 12 and 15, 1879, RWS 16 (Oct. 1879); Hathorne to the

Department of State, Oct. 17, 1879, CD, Zanzibar 6 (Feb. 2, 1870-Oct. 25, 1882).

14. S. to Thompson, no. 55, Oct. 25, 1879, RWS 4, *Ticonderoga* LSN, 184-187; RWS 27, Cruise MSS, pt. 3, chap. 18, "Zanzibar and the Zanzibaris."

15. S. to Thompson, no. 55, Oct. 25, 1879, RWS 4, *Ticonderoga* LSN, 184-187 (including Hathorne quotation) and 190-192; S. to Molly, Oct. 15, 1879, RWS 16 (Oct. 1879).

16. S. to Thompson, no. 56, Oct. 28, 1879, RWS 4, *Ticonderoga* LSN, 193-197; RWS 27, Cruise MSS, pt. 3, chap. 19, "The East African Slave Trade"; J. Kirk to the British Foreign Office, Oct. 15 and Nov. 23, 1879, Q-22, Zanzibar Archives, quoted in Norman Bennett, "Americans in Zanzibar: 1865-1915," *EIHC* 98 (1962): n. 77. On this dispatch, see Evarts to Thompson, Feb. 10, 1880, RWS 22 (East Africa reports, Zanzibar).

17. S. to Thompson, nos. 55 and 56, Oct. 25 and 28, 1879, RWS 4, *Ticonderoga* LSN, 190-192, 198-201; RWS 27, Cruise MSS, pt. 3, chaps. 18 and 19, "Zanzibar and the Zanzibaris" and "The East African Slave Trade."

18. Information and quotations in S. to Thompson, no. 56, Oct. 28, 1879, RWS 4, *Ticonderoga* LSN, 201; RWS 27, Cruise MSS, pt. 3, chap. 18, "Zanzibar"; shipping figures in R. Coupland, *The Exploitation of East Africa, 1859-1890: The Slave Trade and the Scramble* (London, 1939), 319-323, 322, and see the comment by John Kirk, British representative in Zanzibar in the 1860s and 1870s: "It is impossible to obtain accurate and reliable statistics of the trade of Zanzibar, everyone being interested in representing the imports and exports as less than they actually are," in Coupland, p. 77, also quoted in N. Bennett, "Americans in Zanzibar: 1865-1915," 49, n. 2. For further information on the increase in British trade, see John M. Gray, "Zanzibar and the Coastal Belt, 1840-1884," in Roland Oliver and Gervase Mathew, eds., *History of East Africa* (Oxford, 1963), 1:236-237 and 242-243.

19. LeDoulx à Ministère des Affaires Étranges, Oct. 16, 1880, Polit., Zanzibar, t. 5, quoted in N. Bennett, "Americans in Zanzibar: 1865-1915," n. 79.

20. S. to Thompson, no. 59, Nov. 5, 1879, RWS 4, *Ticonderoga* LSN, 209-210; S. to Molly, Nov. 5, 1879, RWS 16 (Nov. 1879).

21. S. to Thompson, no. 61, Nov. 12, 1879, RWS 4, *Ticonderoga* LSN, 213-216; S. to Molly, Nov. 5, 1879, RWS 16 (Nov. 1879); S. to [?], Nov. 14, 1879, RWS 22 (East Africa reports, Zanzibar); *New York Daily Graphic,* Jan. 7, 1880, RWS 31 *(Ticonderoga).*

22. S. to Thompson, no. 64, Nov. 24, 1879, RWS 4, *Ticonderoga* LSN, 219-223. For the impact of the *Ticonderoga*'s cruise on an American resident of Muscat, see N. A. Bachelder to the editor of the *Salem Register,* Nov. 29, 1879, RWS 2, Miller's Journal 3, frontispiece. See also Coupland, *The Exploitation of East Africa,* 375-376.

23. S. to Molly, Nov. 20, 1879, RWS 16 (Nov. 1879); S. to Thompson, no. 64, Nov. 24, 1879, RWS 4, *Ticonderoga* LSN, 219-225.

24. S. to Thompson, no. 64, Nov. 24, 1879, RWS 4, *Ticonderoga* LSN, 223-225.

25. S. to Thompson, *ibid.,* 226-227; S. to Molly, Nov. 20 and Dec. 4, 1879, RWS 16 (Nov. 1879) and (Dec. 1879).

26. S. to Molly, Dec. 4 and 12, 1879, RWS 16 (Dec. 1879).

27. S. to Thompson, no. 66, "Bussorah, Asiatic Turkey," Dec. 6, 1879, RWS 4, *Ticonderoga* LSN 229-230; S. to Molly, Dec. 4 and 12, 1879, RWS 16 (Dec. 1879).

28. Evarts to Thompson, Feb. 10 and 17, 1880, RWS 22 (East Africa reports, Zanzibar) and (Cotton Johanna); Thompson's letter to the Board of Trade in New York is in a clipping pasted to the flyleaf of RWS 2, Miller's Journal 3, frontispiece; Wilson and Bradbury to Thompson, May 25, 1880; Aub and Hackenburg to Thompson, May 13, 1880; Brainerd and Armstrong to Thompson, May 13, 1880; Van Volkenburgh and Leavitt to Thompson, June 3, 1880; W. L. Strong and Co. to Thompson, June 4, 1880; T. O. Hague to Thompson, June 7, 1880; and Edward Atkinson to Thompson, Mar. 24, 1880, all dealing with cotton, are in RWS 22 (East Africa reports, Zanzibar) and (Cotton Johanna), (Middle East, Asia, Pacific reports), and (West Africa reports, Congo Cotton).

29. S. to Thompson, no. 67, Dec. 18, 1879, RWS 4, *Ticonderoga* LSN, 234-255, and 238-230 for quotation; Abraham Yeselson, *United States-Persian Diplomatic Relations 1883-1921* (New Brunswick, 1956), 3; RWS 2, Miller's Journal 2:43.

30. S. to Thompson, no. 67, Dec. 18, 1879, RWS 4, *Ticonderoga* LSN, 240-247; A. and T. J. Malcolm to S., Dec. 21, 1879, RWS 22 (Middle East, Asia, Pacific reports).

31. S. to Molly, Christmas, 1879, RWS 16 (Dec. 1879).

32. S. to Molly, Jan. 2 and 9, 1880, RWS 16 (Jan.-Feb. 1880); S. to Thompson, no. 1, Jan. 2, 1880, RWS 27, Cruise MSS, pt. 3, chap. 20, "Bombay"; RWS 2, Miller's Journal 3 includes the clippings "Arrival of the *Ticonderoga*," *Bombay Times,* Jan. 3, 1880; "Busy Bombay," by "Mack," *New York Daily Graphic,* Apr. 8, 1880; and "What England has inflicted upon India," *Bombay Gazette,* Dec. 27, 1879.

33. S. to Thompson, no. 2, Jan. 20, 1880, "British Rule in Asia and Africa," RWS 4, *Ticonderoga* LSN, 258-259, 262, 266-270; RWS 27, Cruise MSS, pt. 3, chap. 20, "Bombay"; Evarts to Thompson, Mar. 2, 1880, RWS 22 (Middle East, Asia, Pacific reports); S. to Molly, Jan. 22, 1880, RWS 16 (Jan.-Feb. 1880).

34. S. to Thompson, no. 4, Feb. 4, 1880, RWS 4, *Ticonderoga* LSN, 277-279; RWS 28, Cruise MSS, pt. 3, chap. 22, "Penang, Singapore and Straits Settlements."

35. S. to D. B. Sickels, Feb. 22, 1880, RWS 28, Cruise MSS, pt. 3, chap. 22, "Penang, Singapore and Straits Settlements"; D. B. Sickels to S., Feb. 12, 1880, RWS 22 (Middle East, Asia, Pacific reports); S. to Molly, Feb. 6, 1880, RWS 16 (Jan.-Feb. 1880); "Letter from the *Ticonderoga:* Point de Galle—Penang—Singapore—Bruni [*sic*]—Manila—Hong Kong—Nagasaki," by "Mack," *New York Daily Graphic,* June 11, 1880.

36. S. to Molly, Feb. 6, 16, and 22, 1880, RWS 16 (Jan.-Feb. 1880); also discussed in S. to Thompson, no. 6, Feb. 18, 1880; B. J. Cromwell to S., Feb. 3, 1880; three letters of F. A. Miller, Feb. 3 and 4, 1880; S. to F. A. Miller, Feb. 4, 1880, RWS 4, *Ticonderoga* LSN, 282-298; RWS 28, Cruise MSS, pt. 3,

chap. 22, "Penang, Singapore and Straits Settlements." The quotation on "annexation" is in a private letter to Molly, not to Thompson.

37. S. to Thompson, no. 7, Feb. 21, 1880, RWS 4, *Ticonderoga* LSN 303-304; S. to W. H. Read, Feb. 21, 1880, RWS 4 (LPCOC, Dec. 26, 1878-Mar. 5, 1880), 171-176; A. G. Strider to J. Hay, Mar. 20, 1880, CD, Singapore 13 (May 2, 1878-July 1, 1880); Strider to S., no. 78, Apr. 14, 1880, RWS 22 (Middle East, Asia, Pacific reports).

38. S. to Thompson, no. 9, Mar. 4, 1880; Mannix to S., Mar. 2, 1880, RWS 4, *Ticonderoga* LSN, 309-322; S. to the Sultan of Borneo [Brunei], Mar. 1, 1880, RWS 4 (LPCOC, Dec. 26, 1878-Mar. 5, 1880), 171-176; entry for Feb. 1, 1880, RWS 2, Miller's Journal 3:31-32.

39. S. to Thompson, no. 9, Mar. 4, 1880, RWS 4, *Ticonderoga* LSN, 309-322.

40. S. to Molly, Mar. 15, 1880, RWS 16 (Mar.-May 1880).

41. S. to Thompson, "American Policy in the Asiatic Archipelago and Siam," no. 14, Apr. 28, 1880, RWS 4, *Ticonderoga* LSN, 331-333, 336-339, 339-341; RWS 28, Cruise MSS, pt. 3, "Manila"; Edward A. Youngs to J. Hay, July 10, 1880; CD, Manila 7 (July 4, 1879-June 16, 1882).

42. S. to Thompson, no. 14, Apr. 28, 1880, RWS 4, *Ticonderoga* LSN, 336-339, 339-341; for background, see "Letter from the *Ticonderoga,*" *New York Daily Graphic,* June 11, 1880.

43. S. to Thompson, no. 14, Apr. 28, 1880, RWS 4, *Ticonderoga* LSN, 343; RWS 28, Cruise MSS, pt. 3, "Manila."

44. S. to Thompson, nos. 12 and 13, Hong Kong, Mar. 30 and Apr. 26, 1880, RWS 4, *Ticonderoga* LSN, 325-327; S. to Molly, Apr. 28, 1880, RWS 16 (Mar.-May 1880).

CHAPTER 12

1. *For Rel, 1870,* 333-339; E. M. Cable, "United States-Korean Relations, 1866-1871," *TKBRAS* 28 (1938): 1-230, esp. 63-66; Paul H. Clyde, "Attitudes and Policies of George F. Seward, American Minister at Peking, 1876-1880, Some Phases of the Co-operative Policy," *PHR* 2 (1933): 388; Yong-Ho Ch'oe, "Sino-Korean Relations, 1866-1876: A Study of Korea's Tributary Relationship to China," *JAS* 9 (1966): 148-149; Francis C. Jones, "Foreign Diplomacy in Korea, 1866-1894" (Ph.D. diss., Harvard, 1935), chap. 2, "George F. Seward and the American Expedition, 1868-1871"; Hyman Kublin, "The Attitude of China during the Liu-ch'iu Controversy, 1871-1881," *PHR* 18 (1949): 213-231; Tingfu F. Tsiang, "Sino-Japanese Diplomatic Relations, 1870-1894," *CSPSR* 17 (1933): 4-53; Mary C. Wright, "The Adaptability of Ch'ing Diplomacy: The Case of Korea," *JAS* 17 (1958): 363-381, esp. 373-374 and 380-381; Albert P. Ludwig, "Li Hung-Chang and Chinese Foreign Policy, 1870-1885" (Ph.D. diss., University of California, Berkeley, 1936), chaps. 5-8 and 10.

2. John K. Fairbank, "A Preliminary Framework," in J. K. Fairbank, ed., *The Chinese World Order: Traditional China's Foreign Relations* (Cambridge, Mass., 1968), 2-3; see also the fine essays by Mark Mancall, "The Ch'ing Tribute System: An Interpretive Essay," 63-89, and Lien-sheng Yang, "Historical Notes

on the Chinese World Order," 20–33, together with J. K. Fairbank and Ssu-yü Teng, "On the Ch'ing Tributary System," 107–215, in *Ch'ing Administration: Three Studies* (Cambridge, Mass., 1960).

3. T'ung Chi Lin, "Li Hung-chang: His Korea Policies, 1870–1885," *CSPSR* 19 (1935): 202–233, esp. 203–204; Tsiang, "Sino-Japanese Diplomatic Relations, 1870–1894," 1–106, esp. 53–54.

4. Lin, "Li Hung-chang: His Korea Policies," 213–214. Lin was answering "legal-minded Occidentals," especially Tyler Dennett, *Americans in Eastern Asia: A Critical Study of United States Policy in the Far East in the Nineteenth Century* (New York, 1922), 436 and 450–451. See also Ch'oe, "Sino-Korean Relations, 1866–1876," 151–153, and for a rationalization of the Yamen's dilemma, see Wright, "The Adaptability of Ch'ing Diplomacy," 373.

5. Lin, "Li Hung-chang: His Korea Policies," 206, 210, and 214–220; Ch'oe, "Sino-Korean Relations, 1866–1876," 151–181, has a good discussion of the background of the 1876 treaty, esp. 165–169 and 173–179. See also Frederick F. Chien, *The Opening of Korea: A Study of Chinese Diplomacy, 1876–1885* (N. p., 1967), 18–48; Hosea B. Morse, *The International Relations of the Chinese Empire* (London, 1918), 3:9; Hilary Conroy, *The Japanese Seizure of Korea, 1868–1910: A Study of Realism and Idealism in International Relations* (Philadelphia, 1960), 17–77; and Ludwig, "Li Hung Chang and Chinese Foreign Policy, 1870–1885," 339–358.

6. On the power of the Taewon'gun, see Soo B. Choi, "Political dynamics in hermit Korea: the rise of royal power in the decade of the Tae Wun Kun, 1864–1873" (Ph.D. diss., University of Maryland, 1963), chaps. 3 and 4, in some ways the best account available, which, however, has the drawback of interpreting the regent's actions without a corresponding analysis of his thoughts about those actions; see esp. 42–84, 85–114, and 129–215. For a discussion of the domestic reforms, see Carl F. Bartz, Jr., "The Korean Seclusion Policy, 1860–1876" (Ph.D. diss., University of California, Berkeley, 1953), 67–69; Wright, "The Adaptability of Ch'ing Diplomacy," 368, tends to downplay this "little program of domestic reform" as "neither an attempt to meet, nor even a recognition of, new problems." On internal events within Korea during and after the rule of the Taewon'gun, see Ch'oe, "Sino-Korean Relations, 1866–1876," 173–181; Woonsang Choi, "The Korean-Japanese Relations, 1870–1910," *KA* 1 (1962): 162–188, 300–318, and 2 (1963): 51–60; Andrew C. Nahm, "Reaction and Response to the Opening of Korea, 1876–1884," *SA* 6 (1965): 61–64, and "Korea's Response to International Rivalries: Korean Domestic Policies, 1876–84," *MASALP* 50 (1964): 445–465.

7. Nahm, "Reaction and Response to the Opening of Korea, 1876–1884," 61–66; W. Choi, "The Korean-Japanese Relations, 1870–1910," 172–174; Kwang Hi Ro, "Power Politics in Korea and its Impact on Korean Foreign and Domestic Affairs, 1882–1907" (Ph.D. diss., University of Oklahoma, 1966), 5–8; Andrew C. Nahm, "Kim Ok-Kyun and the Korean Progressive Movement, 1882–1884" (Ph.D. diss., Stanford, 1961), 20–27, 30–31, 39–40.

8. S. to Bingham, Feb. 14, 1880; Bingham to S., Mar. 12, 1880, RWS 28, Cruise MSS, pt. 3, chap. 22, "Penang, Singapore and Straits Settlements," and chap. on "Korea"; RWS 4 (LPCOC, Dec. 26, 1878-Mar. 5, 1880), 158–

160; telegram of Feb. 14, 1880, RWS 25 (General Correspondence); Bingham to Evarts, no. 1090, Mar. 20, 1880; Bingham to Inouye Kaoru, Mar. 12, 1880, DD, Japan 41 (Nov. 6, 1879-Mar. 24, 1880); Evarts to Bingham, nos. 495 and 504, Apr. 1 and 28, 1880, DI, Japan 2 (July 2, 1872-Aug. 30, 1880), 570-572, 579.

9. Inouye Kaoru to Bingham, Apr. 7, 1880; Inouye Kaoru to Kondo Masuki, Apr. 20, 1880, RWS 28, Cruise MSS, pt. 3, "Korea"; Evarts to Bingham, nos. 504 and 516, Apr. 23 and June 25, 1880, DI, Japan 2:579 and 587.

10. Bingham to S., Apr. 20, 1880, RWS 24 (Korea, Mar.-June 1880).

11. S. to Molly, Apr. 28, 1880, RWS 16 (Mar.-May 1880); Mangum to Hay, telegram received Apr. 26, 1880, with reply in CD, Nagasaki 3 (Mar. 29, 1877-Jan. 23, 1883); RWS 2, Miller's Journal 3:61-65, Apr. 15, 18, and 20, 1880; S. to Thompson, Apr. 26 and telegram of Apr. 27, 1880, RWS 4, *Ticonderoga* LSN, 326-329; copy in RWS 28, Cruise MSS, pt. 3, "Korea"; Thompson to S., Apr. 26, 1880, RWS 24 (Korea, Mar.-June 1880).

12. S. to Molly, Apr. 28 and May 3, 1880, RWS 16 (Mar.-May 1880) and RWS 17 (Family Correspondence, undated) [latter in box for 1882].

13. S. to the King of Korea, May 4, 1880, enclosed with S. to Thompson, no. 15, May 29, RWS 4, *Ticonderoga* LSN, 345-350; copies in RWS 24 (Korea, Mar.-June 1880) and RWS 28, Cruise MSS, pt. 3, "Korea"; RWS 2, Miller's Journal 3:66, 68-69.

14. M. Kondo to S., May 5 and 6, 1880, RWS 24 (Korea, Mar.-June 1880); copies in RWS 4, *Ticonderoga* LSN, 351; S. to M. Kondo, May 6, 1880, RWS 24 (Korea, Mar.-June 1880); see unidentified newspaper clipping in RWS 2, Miller's Journal 3:71, entry for May 6, 1880; *Japan Gazette,* May 27, 1880, RWS 30 (Japan); *North China Herald,* June 8, 1880: "Letter from Fusan, Corea," translated from the Japanese newspaper *Osaka Shimpo* and taken from the *Japan Daily Herald,* May 28, 1880, in RWS 28, Cruise MSS, pt. 3, "Korea."

15. S. to Molly, May 13, 1880, RWS 16 (Mar.-May 1880), where Shufeldt also was cheered "by the handsome acknowledgements of the State Dept. Everything seems to meet the cordial approbation of the Secy. of State"; RWS 2, Miller's Journal 3:70-71, entries for May 5-6, 1880.

16. The second interview took place in Inouye's home. J. A. Bingham to Inouye Kaoru, May 21, 1880, RWS 28, Cruise MSS, pt. 3, "Korea"; Bingham to S., May 17 and 18, 1880, RWS 24 (China Correspondence, 1880-1881), and other copies *ibid.* (Korea, Mar.-June 1880) and May 24, 1880, RWS 28, Cruise MSS, pt. 3, "Korea"; RWS 2, Miller's Journal 3:77-78, May 20, 1880.

17. S. to Molly, May 22, 1880, RWS 16 (Mar.-May 1880).

18. S. to Bingham, May 26, 1880; Bingham to S., May 27 and 29, 1880 (quotations from the 29th); Inouye Kaoru to His Excellency the Minister of Ceremony of the Corean Government, May 29, 1880; Bingham to Inouye Kaoru, May 21, 1880, RWS 28, Cruise MSS, pt. 3, "Korea," and, in part, in RWS 24 (Korea, Mar.-June 1880); Bingham to Evarts, no. 1126, May 31, 1880, DD, Japan 42 (Apr. 9, 1880-July 26, 1880); RWS 2, Miller's Journal 3:80, May 24, 1880; "The Cruise of the *Ticonderoga,*" *Japan Gazette,* May 27, 1880, 232-235; "Arrival of Shufeldt with Consul Kondo in Korea," and

"Arrival of *Ticonderoga,*" *ibid.;* copies in RWS 28, Cruise MSS, pt. 3, "Korea," and RWS 30 (Japan); Evarts to Bingham, no. 523, Aug. 5, 1880, DI, Japan 2:592–593. For an account that is incorrect, see Dennett, *Americans in Eastern Asia,* 457.

19. S. to Thompson, no. 15, May 29, 1880, RWS 4, *Ticonderoga* LSN, 348–350; also, with a few alterations, in RWS 28, Cruise MSS, 3, "Korea."

20. S. to Molly, May 30, 1880, RWS 16 (Mar.–May 1880); S. to Thompson, no number, confidential, May 31, 1880, RWS 4, *Ticonderoga* LSN, 352–355. Shufeldt sent clippings from the *Japan Gazette,* May 27, 1880, to show the state of public opinion in Japan on the Korean question. Other clippings on the international situation over Korea were *North China Daily News,* Aug. 13, 1880; *Japan Daily Herald,* May 29, 1880; *Mainichi Shinbun, Shanghai Courier,* and *Japan Daily Mail,* in RWS 2, Miller's Journal 3:86; S. to Molly, June 11, 1880, RWS 16 (June–Oct. 1880).

21. S. to Molly, Apr. 28, June 11, July 1 and 22, 1880, RWS 16 (Mar.–May 1880) and (June–Oct. 1880); S. to Thompson, nos. 16, no number, and 17, June 30, July 1, and Aug. 2, 1880, RWS 4, *Ticonderoga* LSN, 356–358; copy in RWS 22 (Japan Correspondence); Thompson to S., telegram no. 8, June 30, 1880, RWS 24 (Korea, Mar.–June 1880). The *North China Herald* of June 8, 1880, suggested that the British government should place men-of-war under Shufeldt's command for the opening of Korea, a novel, if unlikely, possibility.

22. S. to Molly, July 1, 1880, RWS 16 (June–Oct. 1880); S. "Corea's Troubles," *San Francisco Chronicle,* Oct. 30, 1887, MSS in RWS 17 (June–Aug. 1887).

23. Bingham to S., no. 927, July 12, 1880, RWS 24 (Korea Correspondence, 1880–1881), enclosing Kondo Masuki to Inouye Kaoru, June 10, 1880, *ibid.* (Korea, Mar.–June 1880), also in RWS 28, Cruise MSS, pt. 3, "Korea"; Inouye Kaoru to Bingham, June 25, 1880, quoted in Payson J. Treat, *Diplomatic Relations between the United States and Japan, 1853–1895* (Stanford, 1932), 2:139; S. to Molly, July 22, 1880, RWS 16 (June–Oct. 1880).

24. Li Hung-chang to "Sheffield [*sic*]," July 23, 1880; Ü Tsing to S., Aug. 9, 1880; S. to Ü Tsing, Aug. 9, 1880; and S. to Li Hung-chang, Aug. 8, 1880; RWS 24 (China Correspondence, 1880–1881); RWS 2, Miller's Journal 3:103, Aug. 8, 1880.

25. S. to Thompson, nos. 18 and 19, Aug. 10 and 13, 1880, RWS 4, *Ticonderoga* LSN, 364–366 and 371–372; also discussed in S. to Molly, Aug. 13, 1880, RWS 16 (June–Oct. 1880).

26. S. to Molly, Aug. 13, 1880, RWS 16 (June–Oct. 1880).

27. In-jisho to Inouye Kaoru, Kanoye-Fatsu, enclosed with Bingham to S., Aug. 6, 1880, and covered by Wooyeno Kagenori to Bingham, Aug. 4, 1880, RWS 24 (Korea Correspondence, 1880–1881).

28. For different interpretations, see Dennett, *Americans in Eastern Asia,* who was misled by Charles O. Paullin, "The Opening of Korea by Commodore Shufeldt," *PSQ* 25 (1910): 480, which blurred together Shufeldt's thoughts of August and October. Others who have been misled include M. Fredrick Nelson, *Korea and the Old Orders in Eastern Asia* (Baton Rouge, 1946), 139–140; Lin,

"Li Hung-chang: His Korea Policies," 220; Tsiang, "Sino-Japanese Diplomatic Relations, 1870-1894," 64, and Alice F. Tyler, *The Foreign Policy of James G. Blaine* (Hamden, Conn., 1965), 264-265. More accurate, on this specific point only, is Treat, *Diplomatic Relations between the United States and Japan*, 2:123-124, and W. Choi, "The Korean-Japanese Relations, 1870-1910, Part I," 162-163, 165, n. 10, and 166.

29. S. to Thompson, no. 20, Aug. 17, 1880, RWS 4, *Ticonderoga* LSN, 375-376; Hag-w'on Sunoo, "A Study of the U. S.-Korean treaty of 1882," *KR* 2 (1949): 25-44.

30. Bingham to S., Sept. 7, 1880, RWS 24 (Korea Correspondence, 1880-1881); J. Hay to Bingham, no. 543, Nov. 11, 1880, DI, Japan 3 (Sept. 6, 1880-Nov. 21, 1890): 11, gives the State Department reply. See clippings on "Corea," *North China Daily News*, Aug. 13, 1880, "The Opening of Corea," "The Isolation of Corea," and "Corea," all in RWS 2, Miller's Journal 3:86.

31. S. to Thompson, no. 21, Aug. 30, 1880, RWS 4, *Ticonderoga* LSN, 377-381; also briefly outlined in S. to Molly, Sept. 9, 1880, RWS 16 (June-Oct. 1880). Shufeldt informed Thompson in no. 23, Oct. 13, 1880, RWS 4, *Ticonderoga* LSN, 385-386 and 401-402, that "His Excellency Li Hung-Chang, . . . informed me that it was through the influence of the government of China the treaty was effected between Corea and Japan and one of the parties who visited Corea on a private Expedition states that he was informed by Corean Officials that no treaty would be made with foreign Countries without the consent of China." See also RWS 2, Miller's Journal 3:110, entry for Aug. 26, 1880. For the number of Russian warships off the north China coast, see Sunoo, "A Study of the U. S.-Korean Treaty of 1882," 27, n. 17.

32. S. to Thompson, no. 24, Oct. 13, 1880, RWS 4, *Ticonderoga* LSN, 387-388; telegram, Sept. 10, 1880, *ibid.*, 384; compare the long quotation with Secretary Thompson's *ARSN, 1880,* 28. See also Charles Roll, *Colonel Dick Thompson The Persistent Whig* (Indianapolis, 1948), 241, and "Commodore Shufeldt on China," *North China Herald,* May 20, 1881, which published Shufeldt's dispatch.

33. The quarantine is recalled in H. G. Appenzeller, "The Opening of Korea: Admiral Shufeldt's Account of It," *KRep* 1 (1892): 60, which has no anti-Japanese expressions.

34. S. to Bingham, Sept. 19, 1880, RWS 4 (LPCOC, Dec 26, 1878-Mar. 5, 1880), 224.

35. S. to Thompson, no. 24, Oct. 13, 1880, RWS 4, *Ticonderoga* LSN, 391-400; used in Milton Plesur, "Across the Wide Pacific," *PHR* 28 (1959): 79, and compare with President Chester Arthur, who succeeded James A. Garfield when the latter was assassinated and claimed the United States was "the chief Pacific power." James D. Richardson, *A Compilation of the Messages and Papers of the Presidents, 1789-1897* (Washington, D.C., 1900), 8:43.

36. S. to Thompson, no. 24, Oct. 13, 1880, RWS 4, *Ticonderoga* LSN, 391-400.

37. S. to Thompson, nos. 25-26, Oct. 21 and Nov. 8, 1880, RWS 4, *Ticonderoga* LSN, 403-404, 405-406, and 409.

38. "The Cruise of the *Ticonderoga,*" *ARSN, 1880,* 27-28.

CHAPTER 13

1. S. to Molly, Oct. 24, 1880, RWS 16 (June-Oct. 1880).

2. Sargent to Molly, Sept. 20, 1880; S. to Molly, Apr. 11, 1880, *ibid.* and (Apr. 1879).

3. "A Bureau of Commerce, Commodore Shufeldt suggests Regulations for our Merchant Marine," *New York Times,* Dec. 28, 1880.

4. Rough eight-page draft, "The Need of a Navy: an appeal rather than an argument," RWS 35 (Miscellany), written in late 1880 or early 1881 as Shufeldt commenced "recently in making a voyage . . . around the world." Compare "Our Foreign Relations and the Need of a Navy," *New York Herald,* Dec. 12, 1881.

5. "Commodore Shufeldt's Views: an impartial comparison of the Inter-Oceanic Routes," *Washington Post,* Feb. 7, 1881, RWS 30 (Inter-Oceanic Canal, 1881-Mar. 1884); "An American Lake," also used in "The Need of a Navy: an appeal rather than an argument," RWS 35 (Miscellany).

6. Tseng Laisun to S., Sept. 21, 1880, RWS 24 (China Correspondence, 1880-1881), an extract (corrected by Shufeldt) given in S. to Chester Holcombe, Jan. 1882, RWS 4, Korean Letterbook, being all of the formal letters to the Secretary of the Navy and the Secretary of State from July 1, 1881 to Aug. 3, 1882 [cited hereafter as KLBK], 26-27.

7. C. L. Fisher to S., Mar. 3, 1881, RWS 24 (Korea Correspondence, 1880-1881), with the latter part after "The Viceroy says . . ." quoted in S. to Chester Holcombe, Jan. 1881, KLBK, 27, where Shufeldt mentioned declining to organize the Chinese Navy in August, 1880.

8. H. G. Appenzeller, "The Opening of Korea: Admiral Shufeldt's Account of It," *KRep* 1 (1892): 61; Hunt to S., Mar. 18, 1881, at back of RWS 4, KLBK; copy in RWS 24 (China Correspondence, 1880-1881); Rand to S., June 15, 1881; Ward to S., Mar. 15, 1881, RWS 16 (Jan.-June 1881); *North China Herald,* May 13, 1881; "The Treaties with China and Our Policy in Asia," and "Commodore Shufeldt and the Chinese Navy," *New York Herald,* Jan. 15 and Mar. 26, 1881; "Notes from Washington," *New York Times,* Mar. 26, 1881, stressed commercial negotiations and denied that Shufeldt had been sent to reorganize the Chinese Navy.

9. Blaine to S., May 9, 1881, RWS 24 (China Correspondence, 1880-1881); Blaine to Angell, no. 94, May 9, 1881, DI, China 3 (Jan. 1879-Feb. 1885).

10. Molly to mother, June 22 and July 4, 1881, RWS 16 (Jan.-June 1881) and RWS 17 (Fragments); J. B. Angell to S., June 30, 1881, and S. to Angell, July 2 and 4, 1881, James B. Angell Papers [hereafter Angell MSS], vol. 7, University of Michigan Historical Collections, copy in RWS 24 (China Correspondence, 1880-1881). Frederick F. Chien, *The Opening of Korea: A Study of Chinese Diplomacy, 1876-1885* (N.p., 1967), 261-262, n. 50, is in error in assuming that Angell knew of Shufeldt's coming, and Shufeldt mentioned the last-minute placing of the instructions in the dispatch box.

11. Description of Li in S. to Sargent, Jan. 1882, RWS 4, KLBK, 32-34; Angell's description in Esson M. Gale, "President James Burrill Angell's Diary as United States Treaty Commissioner and Minister to China, 1880-1881,"

MAQR 49 (1942-1943): 195-208; Molly's description of Li is in Molly to mother, July 4, 1881, RWS 17 (Fragments); S. to Angell, July 2, 1881, Angell MSS 7; S. to Blaine, July 1, 1881, RWS 4, KLBK, 1, also in DD, China 57 (Mar. 3-Aug. 30, 1881). The treaty between Russia and China was the Treaty of St. Petersburg, February 12-14, 1881, text in H. F. McNair, *Modern Chinese History: Selected Readings* (Shanghai, 1927), 475-477, and Hosea B. Morse, *The International Relations of the Chinese Empire* (London, 1918), 2:337-339. For the Korean visitor to Li, see Chien, *The Opening of Korea,* 78.

12. S. to Blaine, July 1, 1881, RWS 4, KLBK, 1-2; S. to Angell, July 4, 1881, Angell MSS 7, revealed that Li seemed annoyed. In September Shufeldt learned that Bingham had approached the Chinese, see Angell to S., Sept. 14, 1881, RWS 16 (July-Sept. 1881), mentioning a Bingham letter of June 30, 1881; see also Chien, *The Opening of Korea,* 78-79.

13. S. to Blaine, July 1, 1881, KLBK, 3-4; S. to Angell, July 2 and Sept. 15, 1881, Angell MSS 7; P. J. Treat, *Diplomatic Relations between the United States and Japan,* 1853-1895 (Stanford, 1932), 2:140-141; see T. C. Lin, "Li Hung-chang: His Korea Policies, 1870-1885," *CSPSR* 19 (1935-1936): 221-223.

14. S. to Angell, July 2 and 3, 1881, Angell MSS 7; Molly to mother, July 4, 1881, RWS 17 (Fragments); Gale, "Angell's Diary," 206.

15. S. to Hunt, July 7, 1881, and receipt for dispatch box, Angell to S., July 7, 1881, RWS 24 (China Correspondence, 1880-1881); endorsement of Hunt's orders, Mar. 18, 1881, loose sheet at back of RWS 4, KLBK; S. to Molly, July 7 and 9, 1881, RWS 16 (July-Sept. 1881).

16. S. to Molly, "Sunday" and "Tuesday" [July 10 and 12, 1881 from internal evidence], RWS 16 (Oct.-Dec. 1881) and RWS 17 (Family Correspondence, undated); S. to Angell, July 15, 1881, Angell MSS 7.

17. S. to Angell, July 15, 1881, RWS 4, KLBK, 4-6.

18. S. to Angell, July 15 and 18, 1881, *ibid.,* and Angell MSS 7.

19. S. to Angell, July 18, 1881, Angell MSS 7; Angell to S., July 19, 1881, RWS 24 (Korea Correspondence, 1880-1881); Angell to Blaine, no. 187, July 16, 1881, DD, China 57.

20. On the power struggle in New York, see T. Negus to S., July 28, 1881, RWS 16 (July-Sept. 1881); S. to Angell, July 30, 1881, Angell MSS 7.

21. S. to Angell, July 30 and Aug. 4, 1881, Angell MSS 7.

22. S. to Angell, July 15 and 30, Aug. 4 and 11, 1881, *ibid.*

23. Angell to S., Aug. 1, 12, and 17, 1881, RWS 16 (July-Sept. 1881); S. to Angell, Aug. 18, 1881, Angell MSS 7.

24. S to Angell, Aug. 18 and 21, 1881, Angell MSS 7; Molly to mother, Aug. 26, 1881, RWS 16 (July-Sept. 1881); "The Chinese Navy—Proposition submitted by request to H. E. The Viceroy," RWS 24 (China), with five more pages on the navy dated 8.12.81 in *ibid.* (China Correspondence, 1880-1881).

25. Angell to S., Aug. 21 and 22, 1881, and S. to Angell, Aug. 21 and 24, 1881, Angell MSS 7 and RWS 16 (July-Sept. 1881). The rival attempts of different nations to control the Chinese Navy are outlined in E. V. G. Kiernan, *British Diplomacy in China: 1880-1885* (Cambridge, Mass., 1939), 215-218.

26. B. R. S[tevens] to S. and O. N. Denny to S., both Sept. 21, 1881, RWS 24 (China Correspondence, 1880-1881). Stevens telegraphed "Garfield is

dead. What are we to look for now." S. to Angell, Sept. 23 and Oct. 1, 1881, Angell MSS 7; Angell to S., Sept. 25 and Oct. 8, 1881, RWS 16 (July-Sept. 1881) and (Oct.-Dec. 1881); Angell to S., Oct. 14, 1881, misfiled in RWS 17 (Sept.-Dec. 1887). On Holcombe, see Kenneth S. Latourette, *DAB*, s.v. "Chester Holcombe."

27. Molly to mother, Oct. 4, 22, and Nov. 6, 1881, RWS 16 (Oct.-Dec. 1881), together with pp. 13-16 of another dated only 1881 on "the Corean business"; S. to Holcombe, Nov. 27, 1881, RWS 4, KLBK, 6-7; Holcombe to S., Nov. 9 and 26, 1881, RWS 24 (China Correspondence, 1880-1881).

28. S. to Lo-fông-loh, Nov. 27, 1881, copied in S. to Holcombe, Nov. 27, 1881, RWS 4, KLBK, 7-8; "candle" quote in S. to Holcombe, Dec. 4, 1881, *ibid.,* 9-10.

29. Holcombe to S., Nov. 30, 1881, RWS 24 (Korea Correspondence, 1880-1881).

30. S. to Holcombe, Dec. 4, 1881, RWS 4, KLBK, 10-11.

31. *Ibid.*

32. Blaine to S., Nov. 14, 1881, and Chester Arthur's letter, both on loose sheets at the back of KLBK; a copy of Blaine's letters is in DI, China 3.

33. Blaine to S., Nov. 14, 1881, RWS 4, KLBK; Alice F. Tyler, *The Foreign Policy of James G. Blaine* (Hamden, Conn., 1965), 266 and 269. Others who stress casual interest are Tyler Dennett, *Americans in Eastern Asia: A Critical Study of United States Policy in the Far East in the Nineteenth Century* (New York, 1922), 461; C. O. Paullin, "The Opening of Korea by Commodore Shufeldt," *PSQ* 25 (1910): 487; Robert T. Pollard, "American Relations with Korea, 1882-1895," *CSPSR* 16 (1932-1933): 425, n. 1; and Richard C. Winchester, "James G. Blaine and the Ideology of American Expansion" (Ph.D. diss., University of Rochester, 1966), 61. Yet, see Blaine's clever analysis, within a context of Latin American trade potential, of peace as a prerequisite for a large increase in commerce and exports in James G. Blaine, "The Foreign Policy of the Garfield Administration," in *Political Discussions: Legislative, Diplomatic and Popular 1856-1886* (Norwich, Conn., 1887), 411-419.

34. Blaine to S., Nov. 14, 1881, RWS 4, KLBK, at back of volume; Blaine to Holcombe, no. 134, Nov. 14, 1881, *ibid.;* and DI, China 3.

35. Nichols to Clitz, Nov. 12, 1881, copy in RWS 24 (Oriental Documents); Blaine to S., Nov. 14, RWS 4, KLBK.

CHAPTER 14

1. On Kim Yun-sik, see C. I. E. Kim and H.-K. Kim, *Korea and the Politics of Imperialism 1876-1910* (Berkeley, 1967), 20-21, 24, and n. 19; F. F. Chien, *The Opening of Korea: A Study of Chinese Diplomacy, 1876-1885* (N.p., 1967), 80-81; T. F. Tsiang, "Sino-Japanese Diplomatic Relations, 1870-1894," *CSPSR* 17 (1933): 66-67, and T. C. Lin, "Li Hung-chang: His Korea Policies, 1870-1885," *CSPSR* 19 (1935): 223. Russell Smith, "Robert Shufeldt and the Opening of Korea" (M.A. thesis, University of Virginia, 1953) speculated that there was no Korean envoy, but the works of the above authors reveal that there was, and his importance. See also H. G. Appenzeller, "The Opening of Korea: Admiral Shufeldt's Account of It," *KRep* 1 (1892): 61, "The negotiations were tedious, from the fact, that although the Korean Commissioners were in Tien-

tsin, I rarely saw them, and the affair was conducted through the subordinates of the Viceroy, whose object seemed to be, to make an American Treaty for the benefit of China."

2. S. to Holcombe, Dec. 16, 1881, RWS 4, KLBK, 11, 13-14. Holcombe passed on the news to Blaine, Dec. 19, DD, China 58 (Sept. 1, 1881-Feb. 21, 1882). See also Holcombe to S., Jan. 3, 1882, RWS 24 (Korea).

3. S. to Holcombe, Dec. 21, 1881, RWS 4, KLBK, 19; the illustration of the nature of Korean dependency is given in Tsiang, "Sino-Japanese Diplomatic Relations, 1870-1894," 67; C. Holcombe to S., Dec. 27, 1881, RWS 24 (Korea Correspondence, 1880-1881).

4. Holcombe to Frelinghuysen, no. 30, Dec. 19, 1881, DD, China 58; Frelinghuysen to Holcombe, Jan. 7, 1882, with Holcombe to S., Jan. 13, 1882, RWS 4, KLBK, 11; Holcombe to S., Jan. 14 and 17, 1882, RWS 24 (Korea Correspondence, Jan.-Apr. 1882).

5. Frelinghuysen to S., Jan. 6, 1882, instructions on loose sheet, back of RWS 4, KLBK. My italics. Shufeldt had to ask Holcombe who Freylinghuysen was; see S. to Holcombe, Jan. 24, 1882, RWS 24 (Korea Correspondence, Jan.-Apr. 1882).

6. R. H. Bastert, "Diplomatic Reversal: Frelinghuysen's Opposition to Blaine's Pan-American Policy in 1882," *MVHR* 42 (1956): 653-671, esp. 659-660, n. 14, and 661-662.

7. S. to Holcombe, Jan. 16, 1882, and S. to Assistant Secretary of State, R. Hitt, Jan. 20, 1882, KLBK, 12, 15-16; Clitz to S., Dec. 13, 1881, and Holcombe to S., Jan. 19, 24, and 31, RWS 24 (Korea Correspondence, 1880-1881) and (Korea Correspondence, Jan.-Apr. 1882).

8. P. O. Ray, *DAB*, s. v. "Aaron A. Sargent"; Dibblee to S., Mar. 15, 1882, and Negus to S., Mar. 23, 1882, RWS 16 (Jan.-Apr. 1882); S. to Sargent, Jan. 1882, RWS 4, KLBK, 31-40, a copy with some insertions is in *San Francisco Evening Bulletin,* Mar. 20, 1882, and *New York Times,* Mar. 30, 1882; copies with Holcombe to Frelinghuysen, no. 108, DD, China 59 (Feb. 23-May 13, 1882); *North China Daily News,* May 9, 1882; RWS 30 (China, 1870-Mar. 1882). The letter is reprinted in Paul H. Clyde, *United States Policy Toward China: Diplomatic and Public Documents, 1839-1939* (Durham, N. C., 1940), 159-165, and summarized in Tyler Dennett, *Americans in Eastern Asia: A Critical Study of United States Policy in the Far East in the Nineteenth Century* (New York, 1922), 462-464.

9. S. to Sargent, Jan. 1882, RWS 4, KLBK, 30-41. Quotations are from the MS letter, not the newspaper.

10. Words in brackets are not in the MS but were apparently added to the newspaper account, presumably by Sargent or the editor.

11. Shufeldt's description of Li, given on p. 262, follows this sentence.

12. S. to Frelinghuysen, no. 1, Jan. 23, 1882, RWS 4, KLBK, 22-25; DD, China 58; Holcombe to Frelinghuysen, no. 108, May 23, *ibid.,* 60 (May 15-July 30, 1882). For the press comments, see "Policy of China—Shufeldt's Observations," and "Strangely Eventful Life," in *San Francisco Evening Bulletin,* Mar. 20, 1882, with the editorial, *ibid.,* Mar. 21, 1882; "China for the Chinese: Results of Commodore Shufeldt's Observations," and "A Valuable Witness," *New York Times,* Mar. 30, 1882.

13. S. to Frelinghuysen, no. 1, Jan. 23, 1882, RWS 4, KLBK, 22-25; DD,

China 58; S. to Holcombe, Jan. [no date but the 25th, dated by Holcombe to S., Jan. 31, 1882, RWS 24 (Korea Correspondence, Jan.-Apr. 1882)], RWS 4, KLBK, 26-29.

14. S. to Clitz, Jan. 20, 1882; S. to Lo-fông-loh, Jan. 20, 1882, and S. to Li Hung-chang, Jan. 23, 1882, RWS 4, KLBK, 16-18, 20-21; Clitz to S., Feb. 27, 1882, RWS 24 (China Correspondence, 1882).

15. Li Hung-chang to S., Feb. 2, 1882, RWS 24 (Korea Correspondence, Jan.-Apr. 1882), enclosed with S. to Frelinghuysen, no. 2, Mar. 11, 1882, DD, China 59; Tsiang, "Sino-Japanese Diplomatic Relations, 1870-1895," 68; M. F. Nelson, *Korea and the Old Orders in Eastern Asia* (Baton Rouge, 1946), 143. On Ma Chien-chung, see S-y. Teng and J. K. Fairbank, *China's Response to the West: A Documentary Survey, 1839-1923* (Cambridge, Mass., 1965), 95-97, document 25.

16. Holcombe to S., Jan. 23 and Feb. 4, 1882; Cheow Fuh to S., Feb. 6, 1882, RWS 24 (Korea Correspondence, Jan.-Apr. 1882); S. to Li Hung-chang, Feb. 8, 1882; S. to Frelinghuysen, no. 2, Mar. 11, 1882; and S. to Cheow Fuh, Feb. 8, 1882, RWS 4, KLBK, 42-44, 46; Molly to mother, Feb. 12, 1882, RWS 16 (Jan.-Apr. 1882).

17. Holcombe to S., Feb. 4, 1882, RWS 24 (Korea Correspondence, Jan.-Apr. 1882); Holcombe to Frelinghuysen, no. 60, Feb. 4, 1882, DD, China 58.

18. S. to Frelinghuysen, nos. 2 and 4, Mar. 11 and 30, 1882, RWS 4, KLBK, 46-47, 51-52; former in DD, China 59; M. C. Wright, "The Adaptability of Ch'ing Diplomacy: The Case of Korea," *JAS* 17 (1958): 363.

19. S. to Frelinghuysen, no. 2, Mar. 11, 1882, RWS 4, KLBK; Lin, "Li Hung-chang: His Korea Policies," 223. Shufeldt's views on China's courage and Li's reasons for the treaty are disputed in Chien, *The Opening of Korea,* 263-264, n. 67.

20. Given in S. to Frelinghuysen, no. 4, Mar. 30, 1882, RWS 4, KLBK, 51; DD, China 59. The envoy was Kim Yun-sik, who was not present at the Li-Shufeldt meeting.

21. First American draft, RWS 24 (Treaties, Korea).

22. S. to Li Hung-chang, Apr. 4, 1882, RWS 4, KLBK; Treaties in RWS 35 (Japan, Treaties) and (Printed copies of Foreign Treaties of the United States, 1876-1880).

23. Lin, "Li Hung-chang: His Korea Policies," 223-224; Chien, *The Opening of Korea,* 83; Kim and Kim, *Korea and the Politics of Imperialism,* 22, n. 14. Other drafts had been prepared by Yi To-jin, a Japanese-educated Korean, and by Huang Tsŭn-hsien, Counselor of the Chinese Legation in Tokyo.

24. Lo-fông-loh to S., Mar. 23, 1882, RWS 24 (China Correspondence, 1882); S. to Frelinghuysen, no. 4, Mar. 30, 1882, RWS 4,KLBK, 51-53.

25. S. to Frelinghuysen, no. 4, Mar. 30, 1882, RWS 4, KLBK, 52-53. On March 27 Shufeldt again wrote to Admiral Clitz asking about the possibility of other ships, but received the same answer as before, *ibid.,* 48-49.

26. Chinese draft no. 2, RWS 24 (Korean Treaties); S. to Li Hung-chang, Apr. 4, 1882, RWS 4, KLBK, 54-55, recapping the Chinese draft; Lin, "Li Hung-chang: His Korea Policies," 224; and see Hag-W'on Sunoo, "A Study of the U. S.-Korean Treaty of 1882," *KR* 2 (1949): 32, n. 41, for another view.

27. S. to Li Hung-chang, Apr. 4, 1882, RWS 4, KLBK, 54-55. It is obvious

that this debate was somewhat similar to the Li-Mori debate preceeding the Japanese-Korean Treaty of 1876; for an example, see Yong-ho Ch'oe, "Sino-Korean Relations, 1866-1876: A Study of Korea's Tributary Relationship to China," *JAS* 9 (1966): 169.

28. Holcombe to S., Apr. 5, 6, and 18, 1882, RWS 24 (Korea Correspondence, Jan.-Apr. 1882); Chien, *Opening of Korea,* 85.

29. Memorandum, Apr. 6, 1882, RWS 4, KLBK, 56; S. to Li Hung-chang, Apr. 4, 1882, RWS 4, KLBK, 54-55; Nelson, *Korea and the Old Orders in Eastern Asia,* 144; C. O. Paullin, *Diplomatic Negotiations of American Naval Officers 1778-1883* (Baltimore, 1912), 322, and "The Opening of Korea by Commodore Shufeldt," *PSQ* 25 (1910): 492; Dennett, *Americans in Eastern Asia,* 459, evades this point.

30. Memorandum, Apr. 6, 1882, RWS 4, KLBK, 56-57.

31. Memorandum, Apr. 6, 1882, RWS 4, KLBK, 56-57; RWS 24 (Korean Treaty items, 1881-1882) for the rough draft of the letter. Lawrence H. Battistini is incorrect in arguing that "its [the letter's] contents were not known in the Far East until after Shufeldt had concluded his treaty," for which see "The Korean Problem in the Nineteenth Century," *MN* 8 (1952): 52, n. 15.

32. Treaty draft no. 3, RWS 24 (Treaties, Korea); Lin, "Li Hung-chang: His Korea Policies," 224-225; S. to Frelinghuysen, no. 5, Apr. 10, 1882, RWS 4, KLBK, 58-59; DD, China 59.

33. S. to Frelinghuysen, no. 5, Apr. 10, 1882, RWS 4, KLBK, 58-59; S. to Frelinghuysen, telegraph cables, Apr. 12 and 19, 1882, RWS 4, KLBK, 60, and no. 7, Apr. 28, 1882, 62-63.

34. Li Hung-chang to S., Apr. 23, 1882, RWS 24 (China Correspondence, 1882) and RWS 16 (Apr. 1882). Ma Chien-chung is called Ma Kiet chung in Shufeldt's letters; S. to Li Hung-chang, May 6, 1882, RWS 4, KLBK, 64-66; Holcombe to S., Apr. 26 and May 5, 1882, RWS 24 (Korea Correspondence, Jan.-Apr. 1882) and RWS 16 (May 1882).

35. S. to Frelinghuysen, no. 7, Apr. 28, 1882; Holcombe to S., May 5, 1882, RWS 16 (May 1882).

36. S. to Li Hung-chang, May 6, 1882, and to Holcombe, May 6, 1882, RWS 4, KLBK, 63-67; log of the *Swatara,* May 8, 1882, *ibid.,* 68; Holcombe to S., May 5, 1882, RWS 16 (May 1882).

37. Log of *Swatara,* May 8, 1882, S. to Denny, May 7, 1882, RWS 4, KLBK, 68, 67; Molly to mother, May 11, 1882, RWS 16 (May 1882); *North China Daily News,* May 9, 1882; Holcombe to S., May 12 and 15, 1882, RWS 24 (Korean Correspondence, May-Dec. 1882).

38. S. to Frelinghuysen, no. 8, June 8, 1882, RWS 4, KLBK, 84; DD, China 60; J. A. Bingham to S., Apr. 26, 1882, and S. to Bingham, "Salee River," May 12, 1882, RWS 4, KLBK, 68-69; S. to the Full Power Board of Civil Office of Chosen, May 20, 1882, log of the *Swatara,* May 9-14, 1882, memorandum of May 20 and 22, 1882; S. to Holcombe, May 20, 1882, RWS 4, KLBK, 68-74, 80-84.

39. S. to the Full Power Board of Civil Office of Chosen, May 20, 1882, log of the *Swatara,* and memorandum of May 20 and 22, 1882, RWS 4, KLBK, 73-74, 80-84; Commissioner Shin to S., May 21, 1882; Ma Chien-chung to S., May 19, 1882, RWS 24 (Korea Correspondence, May-Dec. 1882); S. to

Holcombe, May 20, 1882, RWS 4, KLBK, 72; S. to Molly, May 20, 1882, RWS 16 (May 1882).

40. Log of the *Swatara,* May 22, 1882; S. to Frelinghuysen, no. 8, June 8, 1882, RWS 4, KLBK, 74-75, 84; copy of latter in DD, China 60; Yosimoto Hanabusa to S., May 17, 1882, and S. to Frelinghuysen, undated [but Aug. 23, 1882, from internal evidence], RWS 24 (Korea Correspondence, May-Dec. 1882), (Korea Correspondence, 1883, and undated), and (Korea Treaty items). The full text of the treaty is printed in *United States Statutes at Large* (Washington, D.C., 1850-1943), 23:720-725, and William T. Malloy, *Treaties Conventions . . . between the United States and other Powers, 1776-1909* (Washington, D.C., 1909), 1:334-339; Tsiang, "Sino-Japanese Diplomatic Relations, 1870-1894," 69; Chien, *The Opening of Korea,* 87; *North China Herald,* June 2, 1882, 593.

41. Appenzeller, "The Opening of Korea: Admiral Shufeldt's Account of It," 62; Lin, "Li Hung-chang: His Korea Policies," 226; E. V. G. Kiernan, *British Diplomacy in China, 1880-1885* (Cambridge, Mass., 1939), 73-85, 101-102; Andrew C. Nahm, "Korea's Response to International Rivalries: Korean Domestic Politics, 1876-84," *MASALP* 50 (1964): 446, n. 3.

42. Henry M. Wriston, *Executive Agents in American Foreign Affairs* (Baltimore, 1929), 275-277, has a long analysis. Other views are in Frelinghuysen to J. R. Young, no. 30, Aug. 30, 1882, DI, China 3; Sunoo, "A Study of the U.S.-Korean Treaty of 1882," 39-41; and Senate *Executive Journal* 23:584-585. Ratifications exchanged in L. Foote to Frelinghuysen, May 24, 1883, *For Rel, 1883,* 241.

43. Lin, "Li Hung-chang: His Korea Policies," 225-226; cf. with Nahm, "Korea's Response to International Rivalries," 449; Kim and Kim, *Korea and the Politics of Imperialism,* 18-19, 27-28.

44. Appended with S. to Frelinghuysen, no. 7 [2nd], May 29, 1882, addenda no. 2, in RWS 4, KLBK, 76-80; the second letter is dated after the signing of the treaty, May 22, 1882. For the section in brackets, see F. D. Cheshire to S., June 8, 1882, RWS 24 (Korea Correspondence, May-Dec. 1882). Holcombe to Frelinghuysen, no. 133, June 26, 1882, offers a different translation of the letters. This letter has been subjected to rigorous scholastic analysis; it is given in *For Rel, 1888,* pt. 2:255-256, W. W. Rockhill, *China's Intercourse with Korea from the XVth Century to 1895* (London, 1905), 2, n. 2, and Nelson, *Korea and the Old Orders in Eastern Asia,* 145-149, which also analyzes the Chinese version.

45. Young to Frelinghuysen, May 1, 1882, DD, China 59; also in P. J. Treat, *Diplomatic Relations between the United States and Japan, 1853-1895* (Stanford, 1932), 2:160; cf. with Bingham to Frelinghuysen, no. 1527, July 12, 1882, DD, Japan 47; Frelinghuysen to Young, no. 30, Aug. 4, 1882, DI, China 3. For Young, see Dennett, "Documents, American Choices in the Far East in 1882," *AHR* 30 (1924): 84-86, and 87-98 for Young's dispatch of October 2, 1882, which discussed the relationship of Korea to China and Japan; Acting Secretary of State John W. Davis to Young, no. 81, Jan. 22, 1883, DI, China 3; Li Hung-chang attempted to discuss the position, reported in Young to Frelinghuysen, Aug. 8, 1883, DD, China 65; Department of State, Report Book, 1882, 653; see also Kim and Kim, *Korea and the Politics of Imperialism,* 26-27; and

George M. McCune and John A. Harrison, eds., *Korean-American Relations: Documents Pertaining to the Far Eastern Diplomacy of the United States,* vol. 1, *The Initial Period, 1883–1886* (Berkeley, 1951), 25.

46. Nelson, *Korea and the Old Orders in Eastern Asia,* 145–149, has the best analysis; for the reference to the work of C. I. Eugene Kim and Han-Kyo Kim, see *Korea and the Politics of Imperialism,* 26–27.

47. For other interpretations, see Dennett, *Americans in Eastern Asia,* 450–451, 460–461; R. T. Pollard, "Americans Relations with Korea, 1882–1895," *CSPSR* 16 (1932–1933): 470, n. 18; P. J. Treat, "China and Korea, 1885–1895," *PSQ* 49 (1934): 515, 532, n. 51, and 542–543; Rockhill, *China's Intercourse with Korea,* 1; Noble, "The United States and Sino-Korean Relations, 1885–1887," *PHR* 2 (1933): 297–298, 304; and Chien, *The Opening of Korea,* 87–89, 90–92, 267–268, and nn. 108, 109–114. Post-1882 contacts are explored in Harold F. Cook, "Kim Ok-Kyun and the Background of the 1884 Émeute" (Ph.D. diss., Harvard, 1969), 2 vols.; Martina Deuchler, "The Opening of Korea, 1875–1884" (Ph.D. diss., Harvard, 1967), chap. 6; H.-K. Kim, "The Demise of the Kingdom of Korea: 1882–1910" (Ph.D. diss., University of Chicago, 1962), chap. 2 "Political Disturbances after the 'Opening,' " and the chapter of the same title in Kim and Kim, *Korea and the Politics of Imperialism,* 33–58; F. C. Jones, "Foreign Diplomacy in Korea, 1866–1894" (Ph.D. diss., Harvard, 1935), chap. 9; A. C. Nahm, "Kim Ok-Kyun and the Korean Progressive Movement, 1882–1884" (Ph.D. diss., Stanford, 1961); Gregory Henderson, *Korea: The Politics of the Vortex* (Cambridge, Mass., 1968), 57–71; Ch'oe, "Sino-Korean Relations, 1866–1876," 182–183; and Fred H. Harrington, *God, Mammon and the Japanese: Dr. Horace N. Allen and Korean-American Relations, 1884–1905* (Madison, 1944).

48. Carnegie Endowment for International Peace, Division of International Law, no. 43, *Korea Treaties and Agreements* (Washington, D.C., 1921), 1–6, esp. 1. For a different translation, see Lin, "Li Hung-chang: His Korea Policies," 227–228.

49. For example, see Dennett, *Americans in Eastern Asia,* 461–462; Pollard, "American Relations with Korea," 425, 428, n. 1, and 470; Sunoo, "A Study of the U.S.-Korean Treaty of 1882," 35.

50. For example, see Paullin, "The Opening of Korea by Commodore Shufeldt," 498; Dennett, *Americans in Eastern Asia,* 461–462; Dennett, "Early American Policy in Korea, 1883–1887," *PSQ* 38 (1923): 84; P. M. Brown, "Frederick Theodore Frelinghuysen," in Samuel F. Bemis, ed., *The American Secretaries of State and Their Diplomacy* (New York, 1958), 8:37; Sunoo, "A Study of the U.S.-Korean Treaty of 1882," 35; Chien, *The Opening of Korea,* 260, n. 128.

CHAPTER 15

1. S. to Molly, May 27, 1882, RWS 16 (May 1882); S. to Frelinghuysen, nos. 7 and 8, May 29 and June 8, 1882, and to Chandler, May 29, 1882, RWS 4, KLBK, 77, 80, and 83–84; S. to Chandler, May 28, 1882, RWS 10 (1882).

2. Sargent to S., Apr. 20, 1882; Molly to Mrs. A. Dibblee, July 5, 1882, RWS 16 (Jan.–Apr. 1882) and (June–Aug. 1882); Henry M. Wriston, *Executive Agents in American Foreign Relations* (Baltimore, 1929), 164, n. 126, and 174.

3. Sargent to S., Aug. 17, 1882, RWS 16 (June–Aug. 1882); S. to Sargent, Oct. 15, 1882, RWS 24 (Sept.–Dec. 1882). The two drafts vary slightly, distinguished by parentheses and brackets.

4. Acting Secretary J. G. Walker to S., June 30, 1882, RWS 25 (Official Correspondence Departure and Return); George Robeson to S., June 4, 1882, RWS 24 (China Correspondence, 1882); S. to Chandler, July 8, 1882, RWS 4, KLBK, 85, and July 30, 1882, RWS 24 (Korean Treaty items), copy in William E. Chandler Papers [hereafter Chandler Papers], vol. 54, 1882 (June 8–Aug. 2, 1882), 111111–111112, MDLC.

5. S. to Chandler, July 30, 1882, Chandler Papers 54, 111111–111112; "Army and Navy News," "Recall of Shufeldt," "Commodore Shufeldt's Recall," and "Shufeldt's Recall," in *New York Times,* July 4 and 6, 1882; "Commodore Shufeldt Recalled," "Commodore Shufeldt's Trouble," "Shufeldt not to be Displaced," and "Corea and Shufeldt," in *Washington Post,* July 4, 5, 6, and 18, 1882; "Commodore Shufeldt Recalled" and "Corea and Commodore Shufeldt," in *New York Tribune,* July 4 and 31, 1882; "Shufeldt" and "Shufeldt —He Told the Truth, which should not be told at all Times," *Chicago Daily Tribune,* July 4 and 5, 1882. Thompson forwarded the interview report to S., Aug. 27, 1882, RWS 16 (June–Aug. 1882).

6. Clitz to S., June 13, 1882; Holcombe to S., May 26, 1882, RWS 24 (Korea Correspondence, May–Dec. 1882); Farquhar to S., Aug. 8, 1882; Wyman to S., Sept. 1, 1882; Gunnell to S., July 25, 1882, RWS 16 (June–Aug. 1882) and (Sept.–Dec. 1882).

7. S. to Chandler, two letters, July 30, 1882, Chandler Papers 54, 111111–111114; Gunnell to S., July 25, 1882; Denny to S., June 26, 1882, in RWS 16 (June–Aug. 1882), copies in RWS 24 (Korea Treaty items).

8. S. to Chandler, July 30, 1882, Chandler Papers 54, 111111–111114.

9. Gunnell to S., July 25 and Aug. 11, 1882; Trescott to S., Sept. 20, 1882; Wyman to S., Aug. 11, 1882; Molly to S., Aug. 23, 1882; John McKee to S., Aug. 27, 1882; R. W. Shufeldt, Jr., to S., Aug. 13 and Sept 3, 1882, RWS 16 (June–Aug. 1882) and (Sept.–Dec. 1882); Martha [Molly's mother] to S., Sept. 4, 1882, RWS 17 (undated). On Shufeldt's low spirits, see Walker to S., Aug. 12, 1882, and S. to Walker, Aug. 21, 1882, RWS 10 (1882).

10. Griffis to S., Aug. 14, 1882; Putnam to S., Aug. 4, 1882, RWS 16 (June–Aug. 1882); William E. Griffis, "The Opening of Korea," *KM* 1 (1917): 509.

11. Gunnell to S., Sept. 20, 1882; Whitelaw Reid and Trescott to S., Sept. 10 and 20, 1882, sent friendly greetings, RWS 16 (Sept.–Dec. 1882); Shufeldt forwarded the remaining copies of the Korean treaty in his possession to Frelinghuysen, Aug. 23, 1882 [dated from internal evidence], with certified drafts of the treaty between Li Hung-chang and himself; acknowledged in Hunter to S., Sept. 6, 1882, RWS 24 (Korea Treaty items) and (Korea Correspondence, May–Dec. 1882).

12. S. to Chandler, two letters, official and personal, July 30, 1882, Chandler Papers 54, 111111–111114; S. to Walker, Sept. 21, 1882, RWS 16 (Sept.–Dec. 1882); Walker to S., Sept. 23, 1882, RWS 10 (1882); S. to [Ellen?], Sept. 27, 1882, RWS 16 (Sept.–Dec. 1882).

13. Chandler to S., Oct. 2 and 9, 1882; S. to Chandler, Oct. 2, 1882; J. Roach to S., Oct. 3, 1882; S. to Walker, Oct. 3, 1882; Walker to S., Oct. 6, 1882; E. Nichols to S., Nov. 4, 1882, in RWS 10 (1882); Gunnell to S., Sept. 28, 1882, RWS 16 (Sept.-Dec. 1882).

14. R. Seager II, "Ten Years before Mahan: The Unofficial Case for the New Navy, 1880-1890," *MVHR* 40 (1953): 491-500; William H. Hunt's report, Nov. 28, 1881, *ARSN, 1881,* 27. On Hunt, see T. Hunt, *The Life of William H. Hunt* (Brattleboro, Vt., 1922), 216-224, 230, 232-233, and Livingston Hunt, "Founder of the New Navy," *USNIP* 31 (1905): 173-199. On the navy, see C. S. Alden and A. Westcott, *The United States Navy: A History,* (Chicago, 1943), 284-286; H. Sprout and M. Sprout, *The Rise of American Naval Power* (Princeton, 1939), 185-187; G. T. Davis, *A Navy Second to None: The Development of Modern American Naval Policy* (New York, 1940), 30-36; D. W. Mitchell, *History of the Modern American Navy from 1883 through Pearl Harbor* (New York, 1946), 10-11, 14-15; and Edward Simpson, "The United States Navy in Transition," *Harper's* 72 (June 1886): 4-26. Frank M. Bennett, *The Steam Navy of the United States* (Pittsburgh, 1896), 773-774, gives the composition and subjects for discussion of the Rodgers' Board of 1881 and on p. 776 the details of the bill authorizing the second Naval Advisory Board. Shufeldt's orders are in Chandler to S., Oct. 9, 1882, RWS 10 (1882).

15. Chandler to S., Oct. 9, 1882; Walker to S., Oct. 26 and 28, 1882; Hunter to S., Oct. 10, 1882, in RWS 10 (1882); S. to Chandler, telegrams, Nov. 2 and 7, 1882, and letter of Nov. 3, 1882, in Chandler Papers 57 (Oct. 25-Dec. 10, 1882), 111630, 111650, and 111633; copy of telegram Nov. 2, in RWS 16 (Sept.-Dec. 1882); "Secretary Whitney's Task, Some Account of the Old Original Naval Advisory Board With its Plans, Performances and Results Clearly and Closely Outlined," *Washington Post,* Sept. 13, 1885, copy in RWS 31 (Naval Policies, 1850s-1880s); Shufeldt's comment, "The American Navy," *San Francisco Sunday Chronicle,* Nov. 6, 1887, with a MS in RWS 35 (Naval Personnel and Rank Information). Members of the board are given in Bennett, *Steam Navy of the United States,* 777; see also *ARSN, 1883,* 4.

16. S. to Chandler, Nov. 3, Chandler Papers 57, 111633-111635; "Armored Vessels," Report of the Naval Advisory Board, Oct. 25, 1882, attached to *ARSN, 1883,* 74-93, esp. 74-75, "Inclosure A," 77-78, 83-84; Mitchell, *History of the Modern American Navy from 1883 through Pearl Harbor,* 11-12, 16, 19; Sprout and Sprout, *The Rise of American Naval Power,* 188; Bennett, *The Steam Navy of the United States,* 776-779, 781-782; Hunt, *The Life of William H. Hunt,* 224; *ARSN, 1883,* 4-5.

17. "Additional New Vessels Proposed," *ARSN, 1883,* 6-7, and "Additional Cruisers," *ibid.,* 85-88, quotation from p. 88.

18. E. Nichols to S., two letters, May 10, 1883; Walker to S., May 2, 1883; Chandler to S., May 2, 1883, RWS 10 (May-Aug. 1883); Angell to S., May 8, 1883, RWS 16 (Jan.-Aug. 1883); "Naval Observatory," *ARSN, 1883,* 24-25.

19. S. to Chandler, July 4, 12, 16, and 28, Aug. 4, telegram of Aug. 7, letters of Aug. 8 and 10, 1883, Chandler Papers 63 (July 9-Sept. 7, 1883), 989, 997, 1005, 1039, 1040-1042, 1061-1067, 1085-1086, 1101-1102, and 1110-1111.

20. Chandler to S., Aug. 6, 1883, RWS 16 (Jan.-Aug. 1883). The rivalry

between the board and bureau over details of ship construction was explored in the Senate Committee on Naval Affairs by Senator McPherson, *Report* no. 161, Appendix 7, "Additional Steel Vessels," 4-5, 48th Cong. 1st Sess.; S. to Chandler, Aug. 8 (quotation) and 10 (designs), 1882, Chandler Papers 63, 1101-1102 and 1110-1111.

21. "Secretary Whitney's Task, Some Account of the Old Original Naval Advisory Board . . . ," *Washington Post,* Sept. 13, 1885; S., "The American Navy," *San Francisco Sunday Chronicle,* Nov. 6, 1887, RWS 31 (Naval Policies, 1850s-1880s); S. to Molly [no date, but Sept. 13, 1885, dated from *Post* article], RWS 17 (General Correspondence, 1885); for works on the navy discussing the controversy, see the bibliographical essay.

22. Dialogue from Senate Report no. 161, Appendix 7, "Views submitted to the Committee on Naval Affairs," 12-20, quotations from pp. 21-22, 48th Cong. 1st Sess. On Butler, see Francis P. Gaines, *DAB,* s.v. "Matthew Calbraith Butler."

23. S. R. Franklin, *Memories of a Rear Admiral* (London, 1898), 293-294.

24. Foote to S., July 13, 1883, RWS 16 (Jan.-Aug. 1883); Davis to Chandler, Sept. 13 and 29, 1883; English to Davis, Sept. 13, 1883; Davis to English, Sept. 13, 1883; English to S., Sept. 14, 1883, and no date, two letters; Chandler to Davis, Sept. 28, 1883; Chandler to S., Sept. 28, 1883, in RWS 24 (Korea Correspondence, 1883, and undated).

25. P. Lowell to S., Jan. 24, 1884; G. C. Foulk to S., Feb. 26, 1884, and recollections in Oct. 4, 1886, RWS 16 (1884) and RWS 17 (General Correspondence, 1886); also recalled in S., "Corea's Troubles," *San Francisco Chronicle,* Oct. 30, 1887, copy in RWS 30 (Korea); and an MS copy of the article dated Takeo [on Kyushu], Aug. 1887, is in RWS 17 (June-Aug. 1887) (the *Chronicle* misprinted the address as Tokio, 700 miles from Takeo); Foote to S., June 30 and Sept. 25, 1884, RWS 24 (Korea Correspondence, 1883, and undated) and (China, Miscellany).

26. A number of works discuss the struggles in Korea; see the bibliographical essay, p. 448.

27. Foote to S., Sept. 25, 1884, RWS 24 (China Miscellany); Gilmore to S., Dec. 27, 1884, RWS 16 (1884); interview in *New York Times,* July 6, 1886, RWS 30 (Korea); Foote to Frelinghuysen, nos. 105 and 110, Sept. 3 and 17, 1884, DD, Korea 1 (Mar. 13, 1883-Sept. 24, 1884); Foulk to the State Department, no. 128, Dec. 4-7, 1884, with Foote to Frelinghuysen, no. 128, Dec. 17, 1884, *ibid.,* 2 (Oct. 4, 1884-Oct. 15, 1885); H. Conroy, *The Japanese Seizure of Korea, 1868-1910* (Philadelphia, 1960), 144.

28. Molly to mother, July 5, 1884 [incorrectly marked 1887], RWS 17 (Family Correspondence, undated) recalls the examination of the Panama canal route, as does "Admiral Shufeldt: the Veteran Officer on the Panama Canal and Coast Defenses," *San Franciso Chronicle,* June 28, 1886, reprinted in the *New York Times,* July 6, 1886; quotations from letter to the *Washington Post,* Feb. 3, 1885, with a rough copy in RWS 21 (Written reports) and partly reprinted in "Canal Question and Admiral Shufeldt," *The Nation* 40, no. 1024, (Feb. 12, 1885): 128. For background clippings, see *Panama Star and Herald,* Mar. 6, Apr. 17, July 24 and 31, two letters Aug. 7, 1884, in RWS 30 (Inter-Ocean Canal,

1881-Mar. 1884), (Inter-Ocean Canal, July-Aug. 1884), and (Inter-Ocean Canal); C. Douglas, editor of the *Panama Star,* to S., July 12, 1884, RWS 16 (1884).

29. S. to Molly, Sept. 13 [dated from contents mentioning *Washington Post* of Sept. 13], 1885; Secretary of the Smithsonian to S., June 2, 1886, RWS 17 (General Correspondence, 1885) and (General Correspondence, 1886).

30. "Admiral Shufeldt: the Veteran Officer on the Panama Canal and Coast Defenses," *San Francisco Chronicle,* June 28, 1886, reprinted in *New York Times,* July 6, 1886 (for all Shufeldt quotations); other background from F. Barber to S., Apr. 17, 1887, RWS 17 (Apr. 1887); "One Cruiser all right," and "Steel for Guns and Armor," with "The *Atlanta*'s Trial Trip," *New York Times,* Apr. 15 and 16, 1887.

31. Denny to S., Aug. 11, 25, and no date [but Oct. 16 and 17], 1886; Molly to mother, Sept. 16, Oct. 11 and 24, 1886; Foulk to S., Oct. 4 and no date [but Oct. 16], 1886, RWS 17 (General Correspondence, 1886) and (General Correspondence, undated); S. "Corea's Troubles," *San Francisco Chronicle,* Oct. 30, 1887, RWS 30 (Korea), with MS in RWS 16 (June-Aug. 1887).

32. Molly to mother, Oct. 24 and Nov. 7, 1886; Foulk to S., Oct. 16, 1886, RWS 17 (General Correspondence) and (General Correspondence, undated); "Corea's Troubles," *San Franciso Chronicle,* Oct. 30, 1887.

33. H. G. Appenzeller, "The Opening of Korea: Admiral Shufeldt's Account of It," *KRep* 1 (1892): 57-62; Foulk to S., Mar. 18, Apr. 9, 18, and 29, May 2, 9, and 30, June 19, and Aug. 5, 1887; Molly to mother, Feb. 18 and 27, 1887, RWS 17 (General Correspondence, Jan.-Mar. 1887), (Apr. 1887), (May 1887), and (June-Aug. 1887).

34. S. to W. W. Rockhill, Feb. 28, 1887, Papers of W. W. Rockhill, no. 46M-386 (2481), Houghton Library, Harvard; Molly to mother, Mar. 17, Apr. 26, May 3, 14, and 28, June 24, July 6 and 18, Aug. 12 and 19, 1887, RWS 17 (Jan.-Mar. 1887), (Apr. 1887), (May 1887), (June-Aug. 1887), and (Family Correspondence, undated); S., "The American Navy," *San Francisco Sunday Chronicle,* Nov. 6, 1887, RWS 31 (Naval Policies, 1850s-1880s).

35. "The American Navy," *San Francisco Sunday Chronicle,* Nov. 6, 1887, RWS 31 (Naval Policies, 1850s-1880s); Molly to mother, Sept. 25 and Oct. 11, 1887, RWS 17 (Sept.-Dec. 1887).

36. S., "Corea's Troubles," *San Francisco Chronicle,* Oct. 30, 1887, RWS 30 (Korea).

37. J. R. Morse to S., Mar. 1, Apr. 8, May 30, and Aug. 20, 1887; J. O'B. Gunn to S., Oct. 16, 1888, and Apr. 24, 1889, RWS 17 (Jan.-Mar. 1887), (Apr. 1887), (May 1887), (June-Aug. 1887), (Aug.-Dec. 1888), and (Jan.-Apr. 1889).

38. S. to J. O'B. Gunn, Sept. 10, 1887; J. O'B. Gunn to S., Nov. 9, 1887, Oct. 16, 1888, and Apr. 24 and 26, 1889; Molly to mother, Sept. 16, 1887, RWS 17 (Sept.-Dec. 1887), (Aug.-Dec. 1888), and (Jan.-Apr. 1889); George W. Prescott and J. O'B. Gunn, Proclamation of the Union Ironworks, July 8, 1886, RWS 25 (World Cruise, Miscellany, Fragments).

39. S. to Gunn, Sept. 10, 1887; Gunn to S., Nov. 9, 1887; Molly to mother, Sept. 16, 1887, RWS 17 (Sept.-Dec. 1887).

40. Gunn to Morse, Oct. 11, 1887; Morse to S., Nov. 5, 1887; Gunn to S., Nov. 9, 1887 and Apr. 26, 1889 (for his thanks); Molly to mother, Nov. 19, 1887 (for the quotation), RWS 17 (Sept.-Dec. 1887) and (Jan.-Apr. 1889). For the development in Korea by businessmen, see D. S. MacDonald, "The American Role in the Opening of Korea to the West," *TKBRAS* 35 (1959): 64; Spencer J. Palmer, "American Gold Mining in Korea's Unsan District," *PHR* 31 (1962): 379-391; "Corea's Troubled State," *New York Times,* Aug. 14, 1891, in RWS 30 (Korea); and for the Unsan project, see Fred H. Harrington, *God, Mammon and the Japanese: Dr. Horace N. Allen and Korean American Relations, 1894-1905* (Madison, 1944), 144-167.

41. Assessments in Molly to mother, Oct. 20, Nov. 13 and 19, Dec. 5 and 26, 1887; Jan. 2, 8, 15, and 29, Feb. 6, 13, and 27, Mar. 5, 18, and 23, Apr. 7 and 16, May 5, 15, and 31, June 24, Aug. 20, Sept. 1, Oct. 21 and 28, Dec. 27, 1888, and Jan. 1, 1889, RWS 17 (Sept.-Dec. 1887), (Jan.-Mar. 1888), (Apr.-July 1888), (Aug.-Dec. 1888), and (Jan.-Apr. 1889).

42. Molly to mother, July 1, 9, 22, Aug. 2, 12, and 20, Sept. 23, Oct. 7, 14, and 28, Nov. 5, 11, and 23, Dec. 5, 1888, Jan. 12 and 29, Feb. 6 and 16, and Mar. 5, 1889; Barber to S., July 21, 1888; Dibblee to S., Nov. 26, 1888; Gunn to S., Oct. 16, 1888, RWS 17 (Apr.-July 1888), (Aug.-Dec. 1888), (Jan.-Apr. 1889), and (Family Correspondence, undated).

43. Dibblee to S., June 30, 1880; Horace Allen to S., Jan. 22, Feb. 19 and 28, Oct. 3, 1890, and Aug. 10, 1891; Holcombe to S., Sept. 25, 1890, RWS 17 (June-Dec. 1889), (1890), and (1891); *San Francisco Evening Bulletin,* June 19, 1889.

44. N. C. Wood to S., May 28, 1889, RWS 10 (1887-1889); G. P. Goff to S., June 3, 1889, RWS 17 (June-Dec. 1889); S., "Flag Officer Walker: His Squadron of Evolution," RWS 35 (Naval Personnel and Rank Information). See "War at Bar Harbor," and "St. Thomas Island for Our Naval Station," *New York Herald,* Aug. 30 and Sept. 24, 1891, and the *New York Times* articles "That Naval Incident," Aug. 20, "The Acting Admiral's Pull," Aug. 29, "Bad Excuses for Walker," Sept. 1, "Justice for Gherardi," Sept. 8, "Subordination and Discipline in the Navy" and "That Pull of Walker's," Sept. 9, "Walker to Lose a Ship," Sept. 10, "Reducing Walker's Fleet" and "The Naval Transfers," Sept. 11, "The Autocrat of the Navy," Sept. 16, "May Lose the *Chicago,*" Sept. 18, "Walker Uses His Pull," Sept. 19, "Gherardi-Walker," Sept. 21, and "Admiral Walker's Future," Sept. 22, all in 1891.

45. H. Allen to S., Jan. 11, 1892; R. L. Fearn to Molly, Feb. 4, 9, and 26, 1892, and to S., May 18, 1892; S. to Fearn, May 20, 1892; S. to G. F. Hollis, May 21, 1892; Hollis to S., May 31, 1892; W. F. Wharton to S., Jan. 10, 1893; C. Silberbauer to S., Nov. 9 and 23, Dec. 6, 1892, and Jan. 11, 1893, in RWS 17 (1892) and (1893); Hollis to S., Feb. 3, 1892, RWS 36 (General Correspondence, 1884-1893); "Consul Hollis Censored," *New York Herald,* Feb. 5, 1891.

46. "Admiral Shufeldt's Injuries," *New York Times,* Oct. 4, 1894; Register of Wills, Administration no. 6962, Estate of Robert Wilson Shufeldt, U.S. District Court for the District of Columbia, filed Nov. 11, 1895.

47. Obituaries in *New York Daily Tribune,* Nov. 8, 1895; United States *Army and Navy Journal* 33 (1895-1896), Nov. 9, 1895, 169, and Nov. 16, 1895, 175;

Washington Post, Nov. 8, 1895; *Chicago Tribune,* Nov. 8, 1895. The gravestone is located at Arlington National Cemetery, Humphreys Drive, section 1, no. 222.

CONCLUSION

1. For works on Mahan, Perry, and other nineteenth-century naval expansionists, see the bibliographical essay, pp. 448-449.

2. Tyler Dennett, *Americans in Eastern Asia: A Critical Study of United States Policy in the Far East in the Nineteenth Century* (New York, 1922), 450.

3. Eric Foner, *Free Soil, Free Labor, Free Men: The Ideology of the Republican Party before the Civil War* (New York, 1970), 272-273, 269.

Bibliographical Essay

This essay indicates the manuscript and archival materials used in the biography as well as a selection of the important secondary source materials, such as unpublished dissertations, books, articles, and newspaper accounts, used.

Introduction
Apart from cyclopedia articles in *Appleton's* (New York, 1862-1875) and *Appleton's American Annual* (New York, 1876-1895), the earliest works on Shufeldt dealt with his Korean treaty, such as Henry G. Appenzeller, "The Opening of Korea: Admiral Shufeldt's Account of It," *KRep* 1 (1892): 57-62; Charles O. Paullin, "The Opening of Korea by Commodore Shufeldt," *PSQ* 25 (1910): 470-499; F. M. Beck, "Interpreting for Captain Shufeldt," *KM* 1 (1917): 239-240, and "Admiral Shufeldt's Visits to Korea," *ibid.*, 243-248; and William E. Griffis, "The Opening of Korea," *ibid.*, 506-510. An exception to this trend was A. S. Hickey, "Rear Admiral Robert Wilson Shufeldt, United States Navy, Gentleman and Diplomat," *USNIP* 69 (1943): 73-80. Recent theses and dissertations include Russell W. Smith, "The Opening of Korea by Commodore Robert W. Shufeldt" (M.A. thesis, University of Virginia, 1953); F. C. Drake, " 'The Empire of the Seas': A Biography of Robert Wilson Shufeldt, USN" (Ph.D. diss., Cornell, 1970); and William J. Brinker, "Robert W. Shufeldt and the Changing Navy" (Ph.D. diss., Indiana University, 1973). Recent interest in Shufeldt has been concentrated on his naval ideas, especially in the work of Kenneth J. Hagan, *American Gunboat Diplomacy and the Old Navy: 1877-1889* (Westport, Conn., 1973); Clayton J. Barrow, ed., *America Spreads Her Sails* (Annapolis, 1973); and Thomas J. Noer, "Commodore Robert W. Shufeldt and America's South African Strategy," *AN* 34 (1974): 81-88, which paraphrases a previously published Shufeldt dispatch (see *New York Times*, Nov. 28, 1879) on South Africa. More recently, see Michael Robinson, "Unlikely Neighbors: An Overview of Korean-American Relations, 1882-1982," *KC* 3, no. 2 (July 1982): 2-9.

Chapter 1   Background of an Expansionist
The Southern drive for Cuba before the Civil War is covered in Robert E. May, *The Southern Dream of a Caribbean Empire, 1845-1861* (Baton Rouge, 1973); Basil Rauch's *American Interest in Cuba, 1848-1855* (New York, 1948); and James M. Callahan's *Cuba and International Relations* (Baltimore, 1899). On John Quincy Adams' interest, see his letter to Hugh Nelson, Apr. 18, 1823, in Worthington C. Ford, ed., *The*

Writings of John Quincy Adams (New York, 1913-1917), vol. 7, 371-381. For López, see Robert G. Caldwell, *The López Expeditions to Cuba, 1848-1851* (Princeton, 1915). On Quitman, consult J. F. H. Claibourne, *Life and Correspondence of John A. Quitman* (New York, 1860); Charles S. Urban's "The Abortive Quitman Filibustering Expedition, 1853-1855," *JMissH* 18 (1956): 175-196, and "New Orleans and the Cuba Question During the López Expeditions of 1849-1851: A Local Study in 'Manifest Destiny'," *LHQ* 22 (1939): 1095-1167. Compare with Ray Broussard, "Governor John Anthony Quitman and the López Expeditions of 1851-1852," *JMissH* 28 (1966): 103-120.

Diplomatic relations with Spain over Cuba are covered in Amos A. Ettinger, *The Mission to Spain of Pierre Soulé, 1853-1855* (New Haven, 1932), and "The Proposed Anglo-American Treaty of 1852 to Guarantee Cuba to Spain," *TRHS*, 4th ser., 13 (1930): 149-165; Gavin Henderson, "Southern Designs on Cuba, 1854-1857, and Some European Opinions," *JSH* 5 (1939): 371-385; Holman Hamilton, *Zachary Taylor: Soldier in the White House* (Indianapolis, 1951), vol. 2:368-371; Ivor D. Spencer, *The Victor and the Spoils* (Providence, 1959), 318-338; Roy F. Nichols, *Franklin Pierce* (Philadelphia, 1931); Sidney Webster, "Mr. Marcy, the Cuban Question and the Ostend Manifesto," *PSQ* 8 (1893): 1-38; and John B. Moore, "A Great Secretary of State, William L. Marcy," *ibid.*, 30 (1915): 377-396. The best work on the *Virginius* affair of 1873 is Richard H. Bradford, *The* Virginius *Affair* (Boulder, Colorado, 1980), and on the *Black Warrior* affair of 1854, see Henry L. Janes, "The *Black Warrior* Affair," *AHR* 12 (1907): 280-298.

On Shufeldt's background, the story of the Palatine exodus is well recorded in Walter A. Knittle, *Early Eighteenth Century Palatine Emigration* (Philadelphia, 1937); Sanford H. Cobb, *The Story of the Palatines* (New York, 1897); and "Papers Relating to the Palatines," in Edward B. O'Callaghan, *The Documentary History of the State of New York* (Albany, 1849), vol. 3, chaps. 9 and 10. The Kocherthal records are in Lou D. MacWethy, *The Book of Names Especially Relating to the Early Palatines* (Baltimore, 1969), 15-57. Material on the Shufeldt family in Dutchess County can be located in Frank Hasbrouck, ed., *The History of Dutchess County* (Poughkeepsie, 1909), 45-46, 50-52, 77-81, 95, 112, and 131; James H. Smith, *A History of Dutchess County, New York* (Syracuse, 1882), 173; and Philip H. Smith, *General History of Dutchess County from 1609 to 1876* (Pawling, N.Y., 1877), 372. On Red Hook, see Frances E. Crouse, "Red Hook Local History," *YBDCHS* 5 (Oct. 1915-Oct. 1916). Family genealogy is covered in Henry B. Shufelt, *Our Folks: A History of the Shufelt Family* (Claverack, N.Y., 1929), 17-21. Family baptismal and marriage records can be quarried in the articles on baptism and marriage for the Dutch Reformed churches of Claverack, Columbia County, Rhinebeck Flats, Dutchess County, and the German Reformed Church of Rhinebeck, New St. Paul's Lutheran Church, Red Hook, New York, in *NYGBR* 76 (1945), 81-90 (1950-1959), 94 (1963), and 96 (1965), four editions each year. Information on Shufeldt's college is contained in two letters from Janet Penner, Registrar of Middlebury College, Apr. 23 and Sept. 17, 1973, to the author, and in Duane L. Robinson, *General Catalogue of Middlebury College* (Middlebury, 1950).

For the African squadron, the best work is Alan R. Booth, "The United States African Squadron 1843-1861," *BUPAH* 1 (1964): 79-117. On the steamship rivalry between Cunard and Collins, see Robert G. Albion, *DAB*, s.v. "E. K. Collins," and *The Rise of New York Port: 1815-1860* (Hamden, Conn., 1961), 45 and 327-328, with Edward Collins et al., *Memorial to the Senate and House of Representatives of the United States of America* (New York, 1851). For American commerce and the Collins Line on the Atlantic, see John G. B. Hutchins, *The American Maritime Industries and Public Policy 1789-1914: An Economic History* (Cambridge, Mass., 1941), Harvard

Economic Studies 71:353-358, and Winthrop L. Marvin, *The American Merchant Marine: Its History and Romance since 1620 to 1902* (New York, 1902), 246-251. On Porter and the *Georgia,* see Richard S. West, Jr., *The Second Admiral: A Life of David Dixon Porter, 1813-1891* (New York, 1937), 54-66; Hutchins, *American Maritime Industries,* 359-361; Albion, *Rise of New York Port,* 365-366; and Rauch, *American Interest in Cuba,* 192-194, 212-215, 227-235. Some details of Shufeldt's movements in the 1850s are in the recollections of his son, Robert, "Life History of an American Naturalist," *ML* 31, no. 2 (Feb. 1924): 68-69.

Chapter 2   An Education in Expansion

The best general introduction to isthmian matters is still Gerstle Mack, *The Land Divided* (New York, 1944), but also see Mary W. Williams, *Anglo-American Isthmian Diplomacy 1815-1915* (Washington, 1916), and W. W. Pierson, Jr., "The Political Influences of an Interoceanic Canal," *HAHR* 6 (1926): 205-231. General introductions to Tehuantepec are in Miguel Covarrubias, *Mexico South: The Isthmus of Tehuantepec* (New York, 1962), and Joanne Phillips, "American Interest in the Isthmus of Tehuantepec Prior to 1853" (M.A. thesis, University of Alabama, 1951), chaps. 2 and 4. For the Garay grant, see José de Garay, *An Account of the Isthmus of Tehuantepec in the Republic of Mexico* (London, 1846); John J. Williams, *The Isthmus of Tehuantepec* (New York, 1852); R. Dale, *Notes of an Excursion to the Isthmus of Tehuantepec in the Republic of Mexico* (London, 1851); and "Survey of the Isthmus of Tehuantepec 1842-43 under a scientific commission appointed by the projector, Don José Garay," *RGSJ* 14 (1844): 306ff. Considerable interest in Tehuantepec was expressed in *DeBow's Review,* particularly vols. 3 (June 1847): 496-502; 4 (1847): 164; 7 (1849): 1-37; 10 (1851): 94-96; 13 (July 1852): 45-52; 14 (1853): 1-24 and 407-414; 22 (Jan. 1857): 193-197 and 365; 25 (Aug. 1858): 232-233; and 26 (Mar. 1859): 340-341. See also James McLeod Murphy, "The Isthmus of Tehuantepec: its inhabitants and resources," *AGSJ* 1 (1859): 162-177, and the article "New Route from San Francisco to New Orleans," *DUM* 55 (1860): 485.

Mexican and United States government differences over Tehuantepec in the late 1840s and early 1850s can be followed in Manuel Larrainzer, *La Cuestion de Tehuantepec* (New York, 1852); *A Review of the report of the Committee on Foreign Affairs, of the Senate of the United States, relative to the Tehuantepec matters* (N. p., 1852); Milo M. Quaife, ed., *The Diary of James K. Polk During His Presidency* (Chicago, 1910), vol. 2, 472-474; *Senate Ex. Doc.* 52, 30th Cong. 1st Sess., 7, ser. 509; *Senate Ex. Doc.* 97, 32nd Cong. 1st Sess., 10, ser. 621; and *Senate Ex. Doc.* 72, 35th Cong. 1st Sess., 13, ser. 930; W. R. Manning, ed., *Diplomatic Correspondence of the United States Inter-American Affairs, 1831-1860* (Washington, 1937), vol. 9, *Mexico, 1848-1860;* Fletcher Webster, ed., *The Writings and Speeches of Daniel Webster* (Boston, 1903), vols. 18:451, 16:633, and 14:504-548; José F. Ramirez, ed., *Memorias negociaciones y documentos, para servir a la historia de las diferencias que han suscitado entre Mexico y los Estados Unidos* (Mexico, 1853), and *A Memorial setting forth the Rights and Just Reasons which the Government of the United States of Mexico has for not recognizing the validity of the privilege granted to D. José Garay* (New York, 1852).

Of the works on diplomacy relating to Tehuantepec the most adequate are Paul N. Garber, *The Gadsden Treaty* (Philadelphia, 1923): Gwilyn Arwyn Edwards, "Anglo-American Foreign Relations 1841-1861, with special reference to Trans-Isthmian Communication" (M.A. thesis, University of Wales, Aberystwyth, 1951); and J. Fred Rippy's *The United States and Mexico* (New York, 1926) and his "The Diplomacy of the United States and Mexico Regarding the Isthmus of Tehuantepec, 1848-1860," *MVHR* 6 (1920): 503-521, supplemented by James M. Callahan, "The Mexican Policy of Southern Leaders Under Buchanan's Administration," *ARAHA,* (1910): 135-151, and *American Foreign Policy in Mexican Relations* (New York, 1932).

The best study of New Orleans' commercial interests in the 1850s is Merl E. Reed's *New Orleans and the Railroads: The Struggle for Commercial Empire, 1830-1860* (Baton Rouge, 1966) and "Government Investment and Economic Growth: Louisiana's Ante Bellum Railroads," *JSH* 28 (1962): 183-201. The special interests of partners in the Louisiana-Tehuantepec Company are covered in Pierce Butler, *Judah P. Benjamin* (Philadelphia, 1906); Judah P. Benjamin, "A Card," *New Orleans Daily Picayune,* Aug. 9, 1851; and Robert D. Meade, *Judah P. Benjamin: Confederate Statesman* (New York, 1943). On La Sère, see A. L. Diket, "Slidell's Right Hand: Emile La Sère," *LH* 4 (1963): 177-205, and Edward L. Tinker, *Les Écrits de Langue Française en Louisiane à XIXe Siècle* (Paris, 1932), 273-274. On Hargous, see Peter A. Hargous, "Petition offering to the consideration of Congress the advantages of a railroad across the Isthmus of Tehuantepec, Feb. 6, 1849," *Senate Misc. Docs.* 50, 30th Cong. 2nd Sess., 1849, ser. 533; Peter A. Hargous, *Remonstrance against the report and resolutions of the Mexican Congress annulling the Tehuantepec grant* (Washington, 1852); and his letter to James G. Bennett, "The Tehuantepec Route: Another Side," *New York Herald,* Aug. 12, 1856.

In addition, consult "Address of the President and the Directors of the Tehuantepec Company to the Public, May 9, 1857," *New Orleans Daily Picayune,* May 11, 1857; J. Preston Moore, "Correspondence of Pierre Soulé: The Louisiana Tehuantepec Company," *HAHR* 32 (1952): 59-72, and his "Pierre Soulé: Southern Expansionist and Promoter," *JSH* 21 (1955): 203-223; and M. L'Abbé Brasseur de Bourbourg, *Voyage sur L'Isthme de Tehuantepec dans L'État de Chiapas et la République de Guatémala Execute dans les Années 1859 et 1860* (Paris, 1861).

The diplomatic activity relating to the slave trade to Cuba is well covered in Harrel E. Landry, "Slavery and the Slave Trade in Atlantic Diplomacy, 1850-1861," *JSH* 27 (1961): 184-207; A. T. Milne's two articles "The Slave Trade and Anglo-American relations, 1807-1862," *BIHR* 9 (1931-1932): 126-129, and "The Lyons-Seward Treaty of 1862," *AHR* 38 (1932-1933): 511-525; Daniel P. Mannix with Malcolm Cowley, *Black Cargoes: A History of the Atlantic Slave Trade, 1518-1865* (London, 1963); and Warren S. Howard, *American Slavers and the Federal Law* (Berkeley, 1963). On slavery within Cuba, see Hubert S. Aimes, *A History of Slavery in Cuba 1511 to 1868* (New York, 1907).

On Truman Smith, see Edward C. Smith, *DAB,* s.v. "Truman Smith"; "Truman Smith," *Biographical Directory of the American Congress: 1774-1961* (Washington, 1961), 1624; Franklin B. Dexter, *Biographical Sketches of the Graduates of Yale College* (New Haven, 1912), vol. 6, *Sept. 1805-Sept. 1815,* 793-794; and Frederick C. Drake, ed., "Secret History of the Slave Trade to Cuba Written by an American Naval Officer, Robert Wilson Shufeldt, 1861," *JNH* 55 (1970): 218-220. For Smith's appointment, see Roy F. Basler, ed., *The Collected Works of Abraham Lincoln* (New Brunswick, 1953), vols. 4:138 and 5:339.

Chapter 3   Consul General to Cuba, 1861-1862

For Howland and Aspinwall, see Robert G. Albion, *The Rise of New York Port: 1815-1860* (Hamden, Conn., 1961), 174-175, 201-202, 230-246, 264-265. On Buckingham, see Samuel G. Buckingham, *The Life of William A. Buckingham* (Springfield, 1894), and for Crawford's obituary and notice of death, see *London Times,* Aug. 24 and 25, 1864. Materials on the *Trent* affair are discussed in Frederick C. Drake, "The Cuban Background of the *Trent* Affair," *CWH* 19 (1973): 29-49, nn. 1-2. The best study is Gordon H. Warren, *Fountain of Discontent: The* Trent *Affair and Freedom of the Seas* (Boston, 1981). Other interpretations can be found in David P.

Crook, *The North, The South and The Powers, 1861-1865* (New York, 1974), chaps. 5-6; Brian Jenkins, *Great Britain and the War for the Union* (Montreal, 1975); and, less satisfactory, Norman B. Ferris, *The* Trent *Affair: A Diplomatic Crisis* (Knoxville, 1977).

There are no good biographies of Mason and Slidell. On Mason in Cuba, see Virginia Mason, ed., *The Public Life and Diplomatic Correspondence of James M. Mason* (New York, 1906), 199-203, 209-214. Mason's official report is in Richard Rush et al., eds., *Official Records of the Union and Confederate Navies in the War of the Rebellion* (Washington, 1894-1914), ser. 1, vol. 1, 150-151. For Slidell, see Beckles Willson, *John Slidell and the Confederates in Paris: 1862-1865* (New York, 1932).

For Wilkes, the standard biography is Daniel Henderson's *Hidden Coasts: A Biography of Admiral Charles Wilkes* (New York, 1953), which should be supplemented by consulting the *Autobiography of Rear Admiral Charles Wilkes, U.S. Navy 1798-1877* (Washington, 1978), edited by William J. Morgan, David B. Tyler, Joyce L. Leonhart, and Mary F. Loughlin. See also John S. Long, "Glory-Hunting off Havana: Wilkes and the *Trent* Affair," *CWH* 9 (1963): 133-144; William N. Jeffries, "The Civil War Career of Charles Wilkes," *JSH* 11 (1945): 324-348; and James D. Hill, "Charles Wilkes—Turbulent Scholar of the Old Navy," *USNIP* 57 (1931): 867-887. For details of incidents and living quarters, see Robert W. Shufeldt, Jr., "Life History of an American Naturalist," *ML* 31, no. 2 (Feb. 1924): 67-76.

Chapter 4   Consul General to Cuba, 1862-1863

The French intervention in Mexico has received widespread study. Lynn M. Case and Warren F. Spencer have been justly acclaimed for their *France and the American Civil War* (Philadelphia, 1969), which revises Percy F. Martin, *Maximilian in Mexico: The Story of the French Intervention 1861-1867* (London, 1914). Also worth reading is Henry Blumenthal's mature *A Re-appraisal of Franco-American Relations, 1830-1871* (Chapel Hill, 1959), and one should consult as well Halford L. Hoskins, "French Views of the Monroe Doctrine, and the Mexican Expedition," *HAHR* 4 (1921): 677-689, and Benjamin F. Gilbert, "French Warships on the Mexican West Coast," *PHR* 24 (1955): 25-38.

On Mexican responses the best coverage is in Mathias Romero, ed., *Correspondencia de la Legacion Mexicana en Washington Durante la Intervención Estranjera, 1860-1868: Collection de Documentos Para Formar La Historia de la Intervención* (Mexico, 1870-1892), 10 vols., and Hilarian F. y Soto, *México y los Estados Unidos durante la Intervención Francesa* (1901). For the immediate background of the intervention the definitive work is Carl H. Bock's long study *Prelude to Tragedy: The Negotiations and Breakdown of the Tripartite Convention of London, October 31, 1861* (Philadelphia, 1966). See also James M. Callahan, *American Foreign Policy in Mexican Relations* (New York, 1932), 282-286, and his *Evolution of Seward's Mexican Policy* (Morgantown, W. Va., 1909), 1-18, 28-34; J. Fred Rippy, *The United States and Mexico* (New York, 1926); and Herbert J. Priestly, *The Mexican Nation: A History* (New York, 1969). Corwin's treaty is in W. Stull Holt, *Treaties Defeated by the Senate: A Study of the Struggle between President and Senate over the Conduct of Foreign Affairs* (Baltimore, 1933). Compare with Howard L. Wilson, "President Buchanan's Proposed Intervention in Mexico," *AHR* 5 (1900): 687-701.

On colonization, start with Brainerd Dyer, "The Persistence of the Idea of Negro Colonization," *PHR* 12 (1943): 53-66, and Charles H. Wesley, "Lincoln's Plan for Colonizing Emancipated Negroes," *JNH* 4 (1919): 7-21.

Seward has received considerable analysis in Ernest N. Paolino, *The Foundations of the American Empire: William Henry Seward and U.S. Foreign Policy* (Ithaca, 1973), and Walter LaFeber, *The New Empire: An Interpretation of American Expansion, 1860-*

1898 (Ithaca, 1963), 1-60. The major biography is Glyndon G. Van Deusen's *William Henry Seward* (New York, 1967), but better studies of Seward as an expansionist are J. G. Whelan, "William Henry Seward, Expansionist" (Ph.D. diss., University of Rochester, 1959); William G. Sharrow's "William Henry Seward: A Study in Nineteenth Century Politics and Nationalism" (Ph.D. diss., University of Rochester, 1965) and "William Henry Seward and the Basis for American Empire, 1850-1860," *PHR* 36 (1967): 325-362. Compare with the imaginative essay by Major L. Wilson, "The Repressible Conflict: Seward's Concept of Progress and the Free-Soil Movement," *JSH* 37 (1971): 533-556. Works that place Seward in a context of pre- and postwar expansion include Charles Vevier's "American Continentalism: An Idea of Expansion, 1845-1910," *AHR* 65 (1960): 325-335, and his "The Collins Overland Line and American Continentalism," *PHR* 28 (1959): 237-253, and Julius W. Pratt's "The Ideology of American Expansion," in *Essays in Honor of William E. Dodd* (Chicago, 1935), edited by Avery Craven.

Chapter 5   The Blockade of the Southern Coast
For happenings at Fort Wagner, see Richard S. West, Jr., *Mr. Lincoln's Navy* (New York, 1957), 239-241; Bruce Catton, *Never Call Retreat* (New York, 1965), 217-226; and Madeleine V. Dahlgren, *Memoir of John A. Dahlgren* (Boston, 1882), 400-433. For information on the Charleston blockade before Shufeldt joined the squadron, see Craig L. Symons, ed., *Charleston Blockade: The Journals of John B. Marchand, U.S. Navy, 1861-1862,* U.S. Naval War College Historical Monograph Series, no. 2 (Newport, R.I., 1976). On the blockade generally, see David T. Chambers, "A Critical Analysis of the Part Played by the Blockade in the Defeat of the South in the American Civil War, 1861-1865" (M.A. thesis, University of Wales, Aberystwyth, 1966). A picture of the *Ruby* is in Francis T. Miller, ed., *The Photographic History of the Civil War* (New York, 1911-1912), vol. 6, *The Navies.* For an account of the fight at the bridge near St. Mark's, see Mark F. Boyd, "The Joint Operations of the Federal Army and Navy near St. Mark's, Florida, March 1865," *FHQ* 29 (1950): 96-124, which focuses on the army's fight but neglects the navy's efforts. Personal recollections by Shufeldt's son are in Robert W. Shufeldt, Jr., "Life History of an American Naturalist," *ML* 31, nos. 3-5, 8 (Mar.-May and Aug. 1924): 67-76, 105-115, 138-149, 193-203, and 307-326.

Chapter 6   The Asiatic Station, 1865-1867
Post-Civil War United States policy in Asia and the Pacific should be approached through the many excellent studies of foreign policy, especially Walter LaFeber's *The New Empire: An Interpretation of American Expansion, 1860-1898* (Ithaca, 1963); Akira Iriye's *Across the Pacific* (New York, 1967); Richard Van Alstyne's *The Rising American Empire* (New York, 1960) and his *American Diplomacy in Action* (Stanford, 1944); William A. Williams, *The Roots of the Modern American Empire* (New York, 1969); Marilyn B. Young's perceptive essay, "American Expansion 1870-1900: The Far East," in Barton J. Bernstein, ed., *Towards a New Left* (New York, 1968), 176-201, which is much better than Lawrence H. Battistini, *The Rise of American Influence in Asia and the Pacific* (East Lansing, 1960). Other works of distinction include Tyler Dennett's *Americans in Eastern Asia* (New York, 1922) and Milton Plesur's "Across the Wide Pacific," *PHR* 28 (1959), 73-80.

The study of post-Civil War naval activity in northern Pacific waters was pioneered by Charles O. Paullin with such works as "The American Navy in the Orient in Recent Years," *USNIP* 37 (1911): 1137-1176, the last three-quarters of which are virtually the same as his "The Opening of Korea by Commodore Shufeldt," *PSQ* 25 (1910), which is also a chapter in *Diplomatic Negotiations of American Naval*

Officers, 1778-1883 (Baltimore, 1912). More general accounts of the navy in this area are in Edwin A. Falk, *From Perry to Pearl Harbor* (Garden City, New York, 1943), 40-68; Kemp Tolley, *Yangtze Patrol: The U.S. Navy in China* (Annapolis, 1971); and E. Mowbray Tate, "Admiral Bell and the New Asiatic Squadron 1865-1868," *AN* 32 (1972): 123-135.

Early European contacts with Korea are discussed in Ralph M. Cory, "Some Notes on Father Gregorio de Cespedes, Korea's First European Visitor," *TKBRAS* 27 (1937): 1-55; Hendrick Hamel, "An Account of the Shipwreck of a Dutch Vessel on the Coast of the Isle of Quelpaert, together with the Description of the Kingdom of Corea," *ibid.*, 9 (1918): 91-148; "Captain Basil Hall's Account of His Voyage to the West Coast of Corea in 1816," *ibid.*, 11 (1920): 1-37; "The Korean Record of Captain Basil Hall's Voyage of Discovery to the West Coast of Korea," *ibid.*, 24 (1935): 15-19; Pyong-Do Yi, "The Impact of the Western World on Korea in the 19th Century," *Cd'HM* 5 (1960): 957-974; and *A Narrative of the French Expedition to Korea in 1866: The United States Expedition of HMS Ringdove in 1871* (reprinted from *North China Herald*, Shanghai, 1871). Also see the early chapters of works mentioned in the bibliographical essay for chapter 12.

Early United States interest in Korea can be followed in "Extension of American Commerce—Proposed Mission to Japan and Corea," (Washington, 1845); *House Exec. Doc.* 138, 28th Cong. 2nd Sess., 3; "Recommendation re: treaty with Korea," Congressional *Globe* 14:294; and William E. Griffis, "Corea: The Last of the Hermit Nations," *SM*, New York (May 1878). *Papers Relating to the Foreign Relations of the United States, 1867* and *1870 [For Rel]* (Washington, 1868 and 1871), 414-416 and 333-339, has some material on Korea. In dealing with Shufeldt, Yur-bok Lee, *Diplomatic Relations between the United States and Korea, 1866-1887* (New York, 1970), has serious errors. Several important documents are in E. M. Cable, *United States-Korean Relations, 1866-1871* (Seoul, 1939), 1-54, which was reprinted from *TKBRAS* 28 (1938): 1-230. The account of the four shipwrecked Americans is from Earl Swisher, "The Adventure of Four Americans in Korea and Peking in 1855," *PHR* 21 (1952): 237-242. See also Hong Yul Yoo, "The Unwritten Part of the Early Stages of Korean-American Diplomatic Relations," *KQ* 5 (1963): 68-69.

On the *General Sherman* case, see James S. Gale, "The Fate of the *General Sherman:* From an Eye Witness Account," *KR* 2 (1895): 252-254; Henry Appenzeller's "The Opening of Korea: Admiral Shufeldt's Account of It," *KRep* 1 (1892): 57-62; Cable, *United States-Korean Relations, 1866-1871*, and Moon W. Oh, "The Two Visits of Rev. R. J. Thomas to Korea," *TKBRAS* 22 (1933): 95-123.

To gauge the Korean relationship to China first consult the excellent study edited by John King Fairbank, *The Chinese World Order: Traditional China's Foreign Relations* (Cambridge, Mass., 1968), especially the essays by Mark Mancall, Lien-sheng Yang, and Hae-jong Chun. Three excellent works on Chinese diplomacy are Mary C. Wright's "The Adaptability of Ch'ing Diplomacy, The Case of Korea," *JAS* 17 (1958): 363-381; Yong-ho Ch'oe, "Sino-Korean Relations, 1866-1876: A Study of Korea's Tributary Relationship to China," *JAticS* 9 (1966): 131-185; and M. Frederick Nelson, *Korea and the Old Orders in Eastern Asia* (Baton Rouge, 1946), especially chaps. 1 and 6. For a criticism of Nelson's analogies, see Hilary Conroy, *The Japanese Seizure of Korea, 1868-1910* (Philadelphia, 1960), 108-109. Other good studies are J. K. Fairbank and Ssu-yü Teng, "On the Ch'ing Tributary System," in *Ch'ing Administration: Three Studies* (Cambridge, Mass., 1960), 107-215, reprinted from *HJAS* 6 (1941); Doo-hun Kim, "Confucian Influence on Korean Society," *KJ* 3 (1963): 17-21 and 40-41; and Key P. Yang and Gregory Henderson, "An Outline History of Korean Confucianism, Part I" and "Part II," *JAS* 18 (1958): 81-101 and 259-276. James B. Palais, "Korea on the Eve of the Kanghwa Treaty, 1873-1876"

(Ph.D. diss., Harvard, 1968), published as *Politics and Policy in Traditional Korea* (Cambridge, Mass., 1975), offers a sound overview.

The Taewon'gun usually receives harsh treatment in Western hands because of his antimissionary activities. See, for example, Clarence N. Weems, ed., *Hulbert's History of Korea* (London, 1962); Carl F. Bartz, Jr., "The Korean Exclusion Policy, 1860-1876" (Ph.D. diss., University of California, Berkeley, 1953); and Ching Young Choe, "A Decade of the Taewŏngun: Reform, Seclusion and Disaster" (Ph.D. diss., Harvard, 1960), chaps. 4-7, published as *The Rule of the Taewŏn'gun, 1864-1873: Restoration in Yi Korea,* Harvard East Asian Monographs, no. 45 (Cambridge, Mass., 1972). For a detailed and sympathetic account, see Soo Bock Choi, "Political Dynamics in Hermit Korea: The Rise of Royal Power in the Decade of the Tae wŏn kun, 1864-1873" (Ph.D. diss., University of Maryland, 1963), chaps. 3 and 4. Pyong-Do Yi, in "The Impact of the Western World on Korea in the 19th Century," assumes that the persecution was severe. The later Chinese move to remove the Regent is in Dong Jae Yim, "The Abduction of the Tae Wŏngun: 1882," *HUEARCPC* 21 (Feb. 1966): 99-130.

On the historical dispute over whether Burlingame's dispatches sparked Seward to propose to the French a joint expedition against Korea, see Tyler Dennett, "Seward's Far Eastern Policy," *AHR* 28 (1922): 45-62, and *Americans in Eastern Asia,* 418-420; Francis C. Jones, "Foreign Diplomacy in Korea, 1866-1894" (Ph.D. diss., Harvard, 1935), chap. 1; Ernest Paolino, *The Foundations of the American Empire* (Ithaca, 1973), 197-199; and Glyndon Van Deusen, *William Henry Seward* (New York, 1967), 522 and 627, n. 13. Prince Kung's reply is discussed extensively in Yong-ho Ch'oe, "Sino-Korean Relations, 1866-1876," 147-148.

The Korean-American war of 1871 can be followed in E. M. Cable, "United States-Korean Relations, 1866-1871," 63ff; Wilbert W. Dubin, "United States Diplomatic Relations with Korea, 1866-1882"; Albert Castel and Andrew C. Nahm, "Our Little War with the Heathen," *AH* 19 (1968): 18-23 and 72-75; H. A. Gosnell, "The Navy in Korea, 1871," *AN* 7 (1947): 107-114; William M. Leary, Jr., "Our Other War in Korea," *USNIP* 94 (1968): 46-53, with a response from Peter Karsten and Thomas H. Patterson, "Reply to Leary, Our Other War in Korea," *ibid.,* (1969): 112-114; Bernard C. Nalty and Truman Strobridge, "Our First Korean War," *AHI* 2 (1967): 10-19; Jack K. Bauer, "The Korea Expedition of 1871," *USNIP* 74 (1948): 197-204; Jones, "Foreign Diplomacy in Korea, 1866-1894," chap. 2; and Egbert S. Oliver, "Opening the Korean Kingdom," *KS* 5 (1956), which excuses American intentions. The same article was republished as "American Korean Relations and China," *FEER* 21 (Dec. 20, 1956), 795-798. A more recent study is Robert Swartout, Jr., "Cultural Conflict and Gunboat Diplomacy: The Development of the 1871 Korean American Incident," *JSSH* 43 (June 1976): 117-169. Documents on the war are in *Annual Report of the Secretary of the Navy, 1871* [ARSN] (Washington, 1871), *Report of the Expedition to Corea by Rear-Admiral John Rodgers, USS Colorado,* June 3, 1871, 275-313, Appendix 18; and *For Rel, 1871,* 115-125 and 141-149. On Low, see Paul H. Clyde, "Frederick F. Low and the Tientsin Massacre," *PHR* 2 (1933): 100-124.

The best account of the Nien fei rebellion along the Yangtze is in Siang-tseh Chiang, *The Nien Fee Rebellion* (Seattle, 1954), 105-107, 116-122, and there is good information in Ssu-yü Teng, *The Taiping Rebellion and the Western Powers: A Comprehensive Survey* (Oxford, 1971), 365, 397-399.

Chapter 7 The China-Cuba-Mexico Axis, 1868-1870

For the Cuban revolution of 1868, start with Allan Nevins, *Hamilton Fish: The History of the Grant Administration* (New York, 1937); James M. Callahan, *Cuba and Inter-*

national Relations (Baltimore, 1899), 364-413; and the essay by Joseph V. Fuller, "Hamilton Fish," in Samuel F. Bemis, *The American Secretaries of State and Their Diplomacy* (New York, 1958), 7:125-214. For the comparison with Brooks Adams, see Adams' own *Law of Civilization and Decay* (New York, 1916), 352. The best study of the *Alabama* claims is Adrian Cook, *The* Alabama *Claims: American Politics and Anglo-American Relations, 1865-1872* (Ithaca and London, 1975).

The decline of American commerce after the Civil War is traced effectively in John G. B. Hutchins, *The American Maritime Industries and Public Policy, 1789-1914: An Economic History* (Cambridge, Mass., 1941); Winthrop L. Marvin, *The American Merchant Marine: Its History and Romance since 1620 to 1902* (New York, 1902); George W. Dalzell, *The Flight from the Flag* (Chapel Hill, 1940); Arthur H. Clark, *The Clipper Ship Era* (Pittsburgh, 1896); Abraham Berglund, *Ocean Transportation* (New York, 1931); and the fine overview by Robert G. Albion and Jennie B. Pope, *Sea Lanes in Wartime: The American Experience, 1775-1945* (New York, 1968).

Chapter 8   The Tehuantepec Dream, 1870-1874

A number of official reports and documents reveal intensely increased interest in isthmian canals in the early 1870s. The *Annual Reports of the Secretary of the Navy* [*ARSN*] in the 1870s contain several appendices on isthmian matters; see *ARSN, 1870,* Appendix 12, 133-141; *ARSN, 1871,* Appendix 14, 178-203; *ARSN, 1873,* Appendix 12, 164-180, Appendix 13, 180-207, and Appendix 15, 260-264; and *ARSN, 1875,* Appendix 12, 206-235, and Appendix 13, 235-269. In addition, see Shufeldt's report on Tehuantepec, *Sen. Ex. Docs.* 6, 42nd Cong. 2nd Sess., and Selfridge's report on explorations and surveys by way of Darien, *House Misc. Docs.* 113, 42nd Cong. 3rd Sess., 5.

On the revival of interest in Tehuantepec during the 1870s, see Simon Stevens, *The new route of Commerce by the Isthmus of Tehuantepec and the Tehuantepec railway* (New York, 1869), and "The new route of commerce by the Isthmus of Tehuantepec," *AGSNYJ* (Ann. Rep.) 3 (1872): 300-343.

The notion of exclusive control of a canal during and following Grant's term of office can be traced in Jackson Crowell, "The United States and a Central American Canal, 1869-1877," *HAHR* 49 (1969): 27-52; Philip M. Brown, "Frederick Theodore Frelinghuysen," in Samuel F. Bemis, *American Secretaries of State and Their Diplomacy* (New York, 1958), 8:28-29, and 31 for Rutherford B. Hayes' remarks on a canal under American control; Walter LaFeber, *The New Empire: An Interpretation of American Expansion, 1860-1898* (Ithaca, 1963), 49-50; and Alice Felt Tyler, *The Foreign Policy of James G. Blaine* (Hamden, Conn., 1965), 32-34, especially 33. On the excitement in the United States over the *Virginius* affair, see Allan Nevins, *Hamilton Fish: The History of the Grant Administration* (New York, 1937), 667-694, and Richard H. Bradford, *The* Virginius *Affair* (Boulder, Colorado, 1980).

Chapter 9   The Naval Theorist, 1875-1878

The decline of the American Navy after the Civil War has been well documented in Harold Sprout and Margaret Sprout, *The Rise of American Naval Power, 1776-1918* (Princeton, 1939), 165-182; George T. Davis, *A Navy Second to None: The Development of Modern American Naval Policy* (New York, 1940), 11-23; Donald W. Mitchell, *History of the Modern American Navy from 1883 through Pearl Harbor* (New York, 1946), 3-9; Dudley W. Knox, *A History of the United States Navy* (New York, 1948), chap. 24; Carroll S. Alden and Allen Westcott, *The United States Navy, A History* (Chicago, 1943), 281-284; and Walter R. Herrick, *The American Naval Revolution* (Baton Rouge, 1966). For a dissenting approach, see Peter Karsten's composite biography of the naval elite, *The Naval Aristocracy: The Golden Age of Annapolis and the Emergence of*

Modern American Navalism (Pittsburgh, 1972). Four thoughtful essays that should be read carefully are Robert Seager II, "Ten Years before Mahan: The Unofficial Case for a New Navy, 1880-1890," *MVHR* 40 (1953): 491-512; Stanley Sandler, "A Navy in Decay: Some Strategic Technological Results of Disarmament, 1865-1869, in the U. S. Navy," *MA* 35 (1971): 138-142; and Lance C. Buhl's two essays, "Mariners and Machines: Resistance to Technological Change in the American Navy, 1865-1869," *JAH* 61, no. 3 (1974): 703-727, and "Maintaining an American Navy, 1865-1889," in Kenneth J. Hagan, ed., *In Peace and War: Interpretations of American Naval History, 1775-1978* (Westport, Conn., 1978), based on his "The Smooth Water Navy: American Naval Policy and Politics, 1865-1876," (Ph.D. diss., Harvard, 1968). In addition, see Hagan's *American Gunboat Diplomacy and the Old Navy, 1877-1889* (Westport, Conn., 1973) and Clayton J. Barrow's *America Spreads Her Sails* (Annapolis, 1973).

Works on other aspects of naval policies that should be consulted are Seward W. Livermore, "American Naval Base Policy in the Far East, 1850-1914," *PHR* 13 (1944): 113-135; Gordon Lewis, "The Rise of the American Mediterranean," *SL* 2 (1961): 42-58; and Charles O. Paullin's "A Half Century of Naval Administration," *USNIP* 39 (1913): 1217-1267.

On the naval personnel with whom Shufeldt worked, see Charles R. Erdman, Jr., *DAB*, s.v. "George Maxwell Robeson"; Livingston Hunt, "Founder of the New Navy," *USNIP* 21 (1905): 173-199; and Thomas Hunt, *The Life of William H. Hunt* (Brattleboro, Vt., 1922). The best study of Chandler is Leon Burr Richardson, *William E. Chandler, Republican* (New York, 1940), but also see F. L. Paxon, *DAB*, s.v. "William Eaton Chandler," and for Thompson and Butler, see Charles Roll, *Colonel Dick Thompson: The Persistent Whig* (Indianapolis, 1948), and Francis P. Gaines, *DAB*, s.v. "Matthew Calbraith Butler."

For the violence at election times in Louisiana, see Williams A. Dunning, *Reconstruction, Political and Economic, 1865-1877* (New York, 1962), chaps. 20 and 21; C. Vann Woodward, *Reunion and Reaction: The Compromise of 1877 and the End of Reconstruction* (New York, 1956); and Robert S. Henry, *The Story of Reconstruction* (Indianapolis, 1938), which has a good bibliography on the disputed election.

The impact of the depression of 1877 can be traced in Robert V. Bruce, *1877: Year of Violence* (Indianapolis, 1959); Walter LaFeber, *The New Empire: An Interpretation of America Expansion, 1860-1898* (Ithaca, 1963), 6-24, 34-35, and 40-41; William A. Williams, *The Roots of the Modern American Empire* (New York, 1969), chaps. 7-8; and the chapter "Depression and Dilemma," in Gary A. Pennanen, "The Foreign Policy of William Maxwell Evarts" (Ph.D. diss., University of Wisconsin, 1969). Shufeldt's letter to Leopold Morse is now printed in full in Milton Plesur, ed., *Creating an American Empire 1865-1914* (New York, 1971), 35-41.

On Luce's role in promoting manning reforms in the navy and marine, see John D. Hayes and John B. Hattendorf, eds., *The Writings of Stephen B. Luce* (Newport, R.I., 1975); Luce's own "The Manning of Our Navy and Merchantile Marine," *USNIP* 1 (1874): 17-37; and John A. S. Grenville and George B. Young, "The Admiral in Politics: Stephen B. Luce and the Foundations of the Modern American Navy," in the book they edited, *Politics and American Diplomacy: Studies in Foreign Policy, 1873-1917* (New Haven, 1966). Albert Gleaves, *Life and Letters of Rear Admiral Stephen B. Luce, U.S. Navy* (New York, 1925), is useful for the letters.

Chapter 10   The Cruise of the *Ticonderoga*: Cape Henry to Cape Town
The material on the imperial endeavors of European powers in Africa is enormous in variety and uneven in quality. To explore the background of Shufeldt's cruise, however, see W. David McIntyre, *The Imperial Frontier in the Tropics, 1865-75* (New

York, 1967); Ronald Robinson and John Gallagher, *Africa and the Victorians* (London, 1961); and the two works by Lewis H. Gann and Peter Duignan, *Burden of Empire* (New York, 1967), and *Colonialism in Africa 1870-1960* (Cambridge, 1969), vol. 1, *The History and Politics of Colonialism 1870-1914*.

With the exception of two pages in Wayne S. Cole's *An Interpretive History of American Foreign Relations* (Homewood, Ill., 1974), 150-152, there is nothing on nineteenth-century relations with Africa in any of the standard textbooks of United States diplomatic history. David M. Pletcher, *The Awkward Years: American Foreign Relations under Garfield and Arthur* (Columbia, Mo., 1962), 17:308-324, and Milton Plesur's two works, *America's Outward Thrust* (DeKalb, Ill., 1971) and *Creating an American Empire,* have drawn attention to United States interests in Africa during the 1870s and 1880s.

The opening remarks in chapter 10 and the background information through to chapter 11 are based on a careful study of the following: Daniel P. Mannix and Malcolm Cowley, *Black Cargoes: A History of the Atlantic Slave Trade, 1518-1865* (London, 1963); Clarence G. Glendenen, Robert Collins, and Peter Duignan, *Americans in Africa 1865-1900* (Stanford, 1966); Glendenen and Duignan, *Americans in Black Africa Up to 1865* (Stanford, 1964); Charles O. Paullin, *Diplomatic Negotiations of American Naval Officers, 1778-1883* (Baltimore, 1912), 43-121, 352-362; Plesur, *America's Outward Thrust,* 144-156; Tyler Dennett, *Americans in Eastern Asia* (New York, 1922), 30, 128-132; Samuel E. Morison, *The Maritime History of Massachusetts 1782-1860* (Boston, 1961), 32-34, 220-223, 324, and 367-368; Norman Bennett and George E. Brooks, eds., *New England Merchants in Africa* (Boston, 1965); George E. Brooks, *Yankee Traders, Old Coasters and African Middlemen* (Boston, 1970); Warren S. Howard, *American Slavers and the Federal Law* (Berkeley, 1963); Elizabeth Donnan, ed., *Documents Illustrative of the History of the Slave Trade to America* (New York, 1965), 3:311-404 and 4:164-172, 471-586, 630-635, and 661-671; Eric Rosenthal, *Stars and Stripes in Africa* (London, 1938); Edmund Roberts, *Embassy to the Eastern Courts of Cochin China, Siam and Muscat in the U.S. Sloop of War,* Peacock, *1832-1834* (New York, 1837); A. Toussaint, *Early American Trade with Mauritius* (Port Louis, Mauritius, 1954); Reginald Coupland, *East Africa and Its Invaders from the Earliest Times to the Death of Seyyid Said in 1856* (Oxford, 1938), chap. 12.

Some articles of varying worth include Milton Plesur, "Spotlight on the Dark Continent: American Interest in Africa in the Nineteenth Century," *AW* (June 1956): 14-15; Baljit Singh, "American-Liberian Relations in the Nineteenth Century," *JHR* 10 (1962): 405-418; E. J. Algoa, comp., "Preliminary Inventory of the Records of the United States Diplomatic and Consular Posts in West Africa, 1856-1935," *JHSN* 2, no. 1 (1960): 78-104; Edwin S. Balch, "American Explorers of Africa," *GR* 5 (1918): 274-281; Harold E. Hammond, "American Interest in the Exploration of the Dark Continent," *H* 18 (1956): 202-229; Richard K. MacMaster, "The United States Navy and African Exploration 1851-1860," *M-Am* 46 (1964): 187-203; Morris Rieger, "United States consular agencies in Africa, 1789-1939," *AfNL* 2, no. 2 (1964): 36-41; and Gilbert Haven, "Americans in Africa *NAR* 125 (1877): 147-158. See also articles by George Shepperson, especially "The United States and East Africa," *P* 13 (1952): 25-34, and "Africa and America," *BBAAS,* n.s., 3 (1961): 25-30.

For the views of Evarts and Thompson on commerce, see Charles Roll, *Colonel Dick Thompson: The Persistent Whig* (Indianapolis, 1948), 248; Gary Pennanen, "The Foreign Policy of William Maxwell Evarts" (Ph.D. diss., University of Wisconsin, 1969), 217-240, the chapter on "Shufeldt and Grant," 217-220, 101-105, and 120 n. 50. Other works on Evarts' furtherance of American commerce are Brainerd Dyer, *The Public Career of William M. Evarts* (New York, 1969), especially 234; Chester L. Barrows, *William M. Evarts* (Chapel Hill, 1941), chap. 25, 379–392, chap. 24, 375–376 for Evarts' interest in "full trade" and commerce, and above 168 n. 27 for further references to Evarts' commercialism. Alice Felt Tyler, *The Foreign Policy of James G. Blaine* (Hamden, Conn., 1965), 263, misses the commercial point over Korea. Lawrence H. Battistini, in "The Korean Problem in the Nineteenth Century," *MN* 8 (1952): 51, is incorrect in his view of Evarts' and Hayes' supposed lack of interest in Korea. See Thompson, *ARSN, 1878,* 6. Other works on Evarts of value are Sherman Evarts, *Arguments and Speeches of William Maxwell Evarts* (New York, 1919) and Frederick C. Hicks, *DAB,* s.v. "William Maxwell Evarts." For Hayes, see Kenneth E. Davidson, *The Presidency of Rutherford B. Hayes* (Westport, Conn., 1972); Hamilton J. Eckenrode, *Rutherford B. Hayes: Statesman of Reunion* (New York, 1930); and T. Harry Williams, *Hayes: The Diary of a President 1875–1881* (New York, 1964). Evarts is astutely handled in William A. Williams, *The Roots of the Modern American Empire* (New York, 1969), 210–216. See also Claude G. Bowers and Helen D. Reid, "William M. Evarts," in Samuel F. Bemis, *American Secretaries of State and Their Diplomacy* (New York, 1958), 7:217–259.

There is no biography of Sargent. For Sargent's resolution and role, see U.S. *Congressional Record,* 45th Cong. 2nd Sess. 8, pt. 3: 2324 and 2600–2601, and W. E. Griffis, "The Opening of Korea," *KM* 1 (1917): 508, and "Corea, The Last of the Hermit Nations," *SM* (May 1878).

For Blyden, see Hollis R. Lynch, *Edward Wilmot Blyden* (London, 1967), and "Edward W. Blyden: Pioneer West African Nationalist," *JAfH* 6 (1965): 373–388; with Christopher Fyfe, *Edward W. Blyden, Christianity, Islam and the Negro Race* (Edinburgh, 1967).

For a view of early Liberian boundary negotiations using official British sources, see Christopher Fyfe, *A History of Sierra Leone* (Oxford, 1962), 250, 307–308, 320–321, 362–363, 384–385, 430–432, 457, and 513. A short but useful summary is in John Hargreaves, *Prelude to the Partition of West Africa* (London, 1963), 242–243, which reveals the Royal Navy's solution by force.

American relationships with Liberia, outside of the slave resettlement and colonization programs, is covered in Raymond L. Buell, *The Native Problem in Africa* (New York, 1928), 2 vols.; John P. Mitchell, *America's Liberian Policy* (Chicago, 1955); Raymond Bixler, *The Foreign Policy of the United States in Liberia* (New York, 1957); Singh, "American-Liberian Relations in the Nineteenth Century," 405–418; J. H. Mower, "The Republic of Liberia: A Study of the Degree and Nature of American Interference," *JNH* 32 (1947): 265–306; and J. A. Padgett, "United States Ministers to Liberia, 1863–1936," *ibid.,* 22 (1937): 50–92. See also the American Colonization Society after the Civil War, in *Minutes of the Sixty-second and Sixty-third Annual Reports, Jan. 21st–22nd, 1879* (Washington, 1879) and *Jan. 20th–21st, 1880* (Washington, 1880), and *Appeal of the Executive Committee of the American Colonization Society* (Washington, 1876). Further views on the boundary question are in John Hargreaves, "African Colonization in the Nineteenth Century: Liberia and Sierra Leone," in Jeffrey Butler, ed., *BUPAH* 1 (Boston, 1964): 57–76, which implies that Liberia had a weak case. For a different assessment, see Thomas G. Addison and Byron Sunderland, *England and Liberia* (Washington, 1884), 13–15.

On the palm oil rivers of West Africa the outstanding work is C. I. Jones, *The Trading States of the Oil Rivers: A Study of Political Development in Eastern Nigeria* (London, 1963). For the Dutch in the Congo a good account is in Roger Anstey, *Britain and the Congo in the Nineteenth Century* (Oxford, 1962), 30–32. For the Portuguese, see James Duffy, *Portuguese Africa* (Cambridge, Mass., 1959), and *Portugal in Africa* (Cambridge, Mass., 1962).

Chapter 11 The Cruise of the *Ticonderoga*: South Africa to Japan

On Shufeldt's visit to Cape Town there is a paraphrase of his report in Thomas J. Noer, "Commodore Robert W. Shufeldt and America's South African Strategy," *AN* 34 (1974), which Noer claimed had not previously been published but which had already been published in the *New York Times,* Nov. 28, 1879.

The background of the Zanzibar treaty, Zanzibar's relations with the United States, and the division of Muscat and Zanzibar can be followed in Tyler Dennett, *Americans in Eastern Asia* (New York, 1922), 134; Sir John M. Gray, "Seyyid Said and the United States of America," in his *History of Zanzibar from the Middle Ages to 1856* (London, 1962), 194-223; "Zanzibar and the Coastal Belt, 1840-1884," in Roland Oliver and Gervase Mathew, eds., *History of East Africa* (Oxford, 1963), 1:212-252; and "Early Connections between the United States and East Africa," *TNR* 20 (1946): 55-86; G. S. P. Freeman-Grenville, "The Coast 1498-1840," in Oliver and Mathew, *History of East Africa,* 1:157-161; and Edmund Roberts, *Embassy to the Eastern Courts of Cochin China, Siam and Muscat in the U.S. Sloop of War, Peacock, 1832-1834* (New York, 1837). On Kilwa see G. S. P. Freeman-Grenville, *The French at Kilwa Island: An Episode in Eighteenth Century East African History* (Oxford, 1965).

United States commercial interests in Zanzibar are outlined in Norman Bennett and George E. Brooks, eds., *New England Merchants in Africa* (Boston, 1965), 189-269, 340-545, with the treaty of 1833, 549-551; Norman Bennett, "Americans in Zanzibar: 1825-1845," "Americans in Zanzibar: 1845-1865," and "Americans in Zanzibar: 1865-1915," all in *EIHC* 95 (1959): 239-262, 97 (1961): 31-56, and 98 (1962): 36-61, respectively, which have been reprinted in *TNR* 56 (1961): 93-108, 57 (1961): 121-138, and 60 (1963): 49-66.

There is good coverage of the continuing interest in Johanna and the Wilson-Sultan argument in Kenneth J. Hagan, *American Gunboat Diplomacy and the Old Navy, 1877-1889* (Westport, Conn., 1973), 89-93. Two excellent, and overlapping, presentations of Anglo-Russian rivalry over Iran in 1879-1880 are given in Firuz Kazemzadeh, *Russia and Britain in Persia, 1864-1914: A Study in Imperialism* (London, 1968), 49-72, and 148-240 and John B. Kelly, *Britain and the Persian Gulf, 1795-1880* (Oxford, 1968). See also Sir Arnold T. Wilson, *The Persian Gulf* (Oxford, 1928), 36-43, 254-273.

The United States-Borneo Treaty of June 1850 is mentioned in K. C. Tregonning, "American Activity in North Borneo, 1865-1881," *PHR* 23 (1954), 357-372, especially 359-361, 366-370, and James M. Callahan, *American Relations in the Pacific and the Far East: 1784-1900* (Baltimore, 1901), 48, 73-74. The development of diplomatic problems over Borneo is treated in Graham Irwin, *Nineteenth-Century Borneo* ('S-Gravenhage, 1955), 181-182, 195-208, and 214-215; Martin Meadows, "The Philippine Claim to North Borneo," *PSQ* 77 (1962): 321-335; Chester F. Barnes and Irving Kaplan, eds., *North Borneo, Brunei, Sarawak* (New Haven, 1956), 14-15; and John Bastin and Robin W. Winks, eds., *Malaysia: Selected Historical Readings* (London, 1966), 329, 215, 418-419.

Chapter 12 The Cruise of the *Ticonderoga*: The Mission to Open Korea

The unhappy position of Korea in the 1880s is strikingly presented in C. I. Eugene Kim and Han-Kyo Kim, *Korea and the Politics of Imperialism, 1876-1910* (Berkeley, 1967), and Gregory Henderson, *Korea: The Politics of the Vortex* (Cambridge, Mass., 1968). M. Frederick Nelson, *Korea and the Old Orders in Eastern Asia* (Baton Rouge, 1946), is a fine study, and Nam-Yearl Choi, "Asian Attitudes toward International Law: A Case Study of Korea" (Ph.D. diss., University of Pennsylvania, 1967) sheds light on Korean attitudes. There is a concise account of Korea in Lark June George Paik, *The History of Protestant Missions in Korea, 1832-1910* (Pyeng Yang, Korea, 1929; reprinted in Seoul, 1970), chap. 1, and a general survey in Tae-hung Ha, *Korea: Forty-three Centuries* (Seoul, 1958). The first popular American account was William E. Griffis, *Corea, Without and Within* (Philadelphia, 1885) followed by *Corea: The Hermit Nation* (New York, 1888), good books by an author who never visited Korea. In addition see William R. Carles, *Life in Corea* (London, 1888), an account by the British consul; Horace N. Allen, *Things Korean* (New York, 1908), by the United States secretary of legation and medico-extraordinary. Two early reports are "Corea," *CPS* (Chicago, 1881) and "Corea The Hermit Nation," *BAGS* 3 (New York, 1881).

Apart from works cited in the bibliographical essay for chapter 6 (pp. 436-438), the United States' role in opening Korea can be followed in Russell W. Smith, "The Opening of Korea by Commodore Robert W. Shufeldt" (M.A. thesis, University of Virginia, 1953); Griffis, "The Opening of Korea," *KM* 1 (1917); Harold J. Noble, "Korea and Her Relations with the United States before 1895" (Ph.D. diss., Berkeley, 1932); Philip L. Bridgham, "American Policy toward Korean Independence 1866-1910" (Ph.D. diss., Fletcher School of Law and Diplomacy, 1951); Philip L. Bridgham and William L. Neumann, "Korea and the United States: The Background," *AP* 4 (1950): 225-245; Martina Deuchler, "The Opening of Korea, 1875-1884" (Ph.D. diss., Harvard, 1967), chap. 2, published as *Confucian Gentlemen and Barbarian Envoys: The Opening of Korea, 1875-1885* (Seattle, 1977); and Donald S. MacDonald, "The American Role in the Opening of Korea to the West," *TKBRAS* 35 (1959): 51-66, which appears naive about American intentions. See also Tyler Dennett's "American Choices in the Far East in 1882," *AHR* 30 (1924): 84-108, and "American 'Good Offices' in Asia," *AJIL* 16 (1922): 1-24.

The charge of Japanese bad faith from May 1880 onward is made in Charles O. Paullin, "The Opening of Korea by Commodore Shufeldt," *PSQ* 25 (1910): 480, picked up by Dennett in *Americans in Eastern Asia* (New York, 1922), 457, and relayed in Lawrence H. Battistini, "The Korean Problem in the Nineteenth Century," *MN* 8 (1952): 51. Japanese intentions are also briefly discussed in Hilary Conroy, *The Japanese Seizure of Korea: 1868-1910* (Philadelphia, 1960), 100 nn. 28-30. Payson J. Treat's *Diplomatic Relations between the United States and Japan, 1853-1895* (Stanford, 1932), 2:123, and *Japan and the United States 1853-1921* (Boston, 1921), while both are pro-Japanese in general, are accurate about Shufeldt's views in May. For some general background reading, see Kiyoshi Kawakami, *American-Japanese Relations: An Inside View of Japan's Politics and Purposes* (New York, 1912).

Chapter 13   The Opening of Korea, 1881

On Sargent, see P. O. Ray, *DAB*, s.v. "Aaron Augustus Sargent." For other materials on the canal question, see "An Imperative Duty," "The Panama Canal and the Navy'" and "The Isthmian Canal and the Monroe Doctrine," *New York Herald*, Dec. 5, 9, and 17, 1881. The best study of Blaine's foreign policy is in Richard C. Winchester, "James G. Blaine and the Ideology of American Expansionism" (Ph.D. diss., University of Rochester, 1966), especially chaps. 3 and 7. Compare with Alice Felt Tyler, *The Foreign Policy of James G. Blaine* (Hamden, Conn., 1965), 32-45. On later canal diplomacy, see Philip M. Brown, "Frederick Theodore Frelinghuysen," in Samuel F. Bemis, *American Secretaries of State and Their Diplomacy* (New York, 1958), 8:27-31. On Hunt, see Thomas Hunt, *Life of William H. Hunt* (Brattleboro, Vt., 1922), 216; Melvin J. White, *DAB*, s.v. "William Henry Hunt"; *New York Herald*, Mar. 3, 1881; *Washington Post*, Feb. 28 and Apr. 9, 1881.

Li Hung-chang has received considerable attention as the dominant figure in the last years of the Ch'ing dynasty. See particularly A. P. Ludwig, "Li Hung Chang and Chinese Foreign Policy, 1870-1885" (Ph.D. diss., University of California, Berkeley, 1936), chaps. 1 and 2; Paul E. Quimby, "A Study of the Foreign Policies of Li Hung-chang" (Ph.D. diss., University of Southern California, 1940), chaps. 1 and 2; the fine account by Stanley Spector, *Li Hung-chang and the Huai Army; A Study in Nineteenth Century Chinese Regionalism* (Seattle, 1964); T'ung Chi Lin, "Li Hung-chang: His Korea Policies, 1870-1885," *CSPSR* 19 (1935): 202-233, answering "legal-minded Occidentals" such as Tyler Dennett; and Kwang C. Liu, "Confucian as Patriot and Pragmatist: Li Hung-chang's Formative Years, 1823-1866," *HJAS* 30 (1970): 5-45, a sympathetic study. John O. P. Bland, *Li Hung-chang* (London, 1917), is still useful.

James Burrill Angell is something of a forgotten figure in Asian relations, but see his *The Reminiscences of James Burrill Angell* (New York, 1912), 128-168, and his article "The Diplomatic Relations Between the United States and China," *JSS* 17 (1883): 24-36; Esson M. Gale, "President James Burrill Angell's Diary as United States Treaty Commissioner and Minister to China, 1880-1881," *MAQR* 49 (1942-1943): 195-206; and Paul H. Clyde, *United States Policy Toward China: Diplomatic and Public Documents, 1839-1939* (Durham, N.C., 1940), 152-156, for the treaties that he negotiated.

For Garfield, the standard works are Robert G. Caldwell, *James A. Garfield: Party Chieftain* (New York, 1931); Theodore C. Smith, *The Life and Letters of James Abram Garfield* (New Haven, 1925), 2 vols.; and the two campaign biographies by John C. Ridpath, *The Life and Work of James A. Garfield* (Cincinnati, 1881), and William M. Thayer, *From Log-Cabin to the White House: Life of James A. Garfield* (Boston, 1881). For the struggle between Garfield and Conkling, see David M. Jordan, *Roscoe Conkling: Voice in the Senate* (Ithaca, 1971), 380-409, and Caldwell, *James A. Garfield*, 342-348.

Chaper 14   The Opening of Korea, 1882
The Korean visitor, Kim Yun-sik, is mentioned in C. I. Eugene Kim and Han-Kyo Kim, *Korea and the Politics of Imperialism 1876-1910* (Berkeley, 1967), 20-21, 24, and n. 19; Frederick F. Chien, *The Opening of Korea: A Study of Chinese Diplomacy, 1876-1885* (N.p., 1967), 80-81; the article by Tingfu F. Tsiang, "Sino-Japanese Diplomatic Relations, 1870-1894," *CSPSR* 17 (1933): 66-67; and T'ung Chi Lin, "Li Hung-chang: His Korea Policies, 1870-1885," *CSPSR* 19 (1935): 23. Russell W. Smith, in "Robert W. Shufeldt and the Opening of Korea" (M.A. thesis, University of Virginia, 1953), speculated, incorrectly, that no envoy came from Korea.

For American perceptions of Korea in 1882, see Shannon McCune, "The American Perception of Korea in 1882: A Bibliographical Sketch," *KC* 3, no. 2 (July 1982): 10-20. For Holcombe, see Kenneth S. Latourette, *DAB*, s.v. "Chester Holcombe." For Frelinghuysen, see F. J. Hageman, "The Life, Character and Services of Frederick T. Frelinghuysen," *NJHSP* 2nd ser., 9 (1887): 47-75; *New York Times*, Dec. 13, 1881; Russell H. Bastert, "Diplomatic Reversal: Frelinghuysen's Opposition to Blaine's Pan-American Policy in 1882," *MVHR* 42 (1956): 653-671; and "Blaine to the President," *New York Herald*, Feb. 3, 1882. The best biography of Chester Arthur is Thomas C. Reeves, *Gentleman Boss* (New York, 1975), and also solid is George F. Howe, *Chester A. Arthur: A Quarter Century of Machine Politics* (New York, 1934).

The anti-Chinese movement in California is covered in Elmer C. Meyer, *The Anti-Chinese Movement in California* (Urbana, Ill., 1939).

Background information on Shufeldt's treaty can be traced in Francis C. Jones, "Foreign Diplomacy in Korea, 1866-1894" (Ph.D. diss., Harvard, 1935), chap. 7;

Chien, *The Opening of Korea: A Study of Chinese Diplomacy,* 79 and chap. 3: Hag-w'on Sunoo, "A Study of the U.S.-Korean Treaty of 1882," *KR* 2 (1949): 25-44. The treaty is printed in Henry Chung, ed., *Korean Treaties* (New York, 1919).

For John Russell Young's interpretation of the treaty, October 2, 1882, and the relation of Korea to China, see Tyler Dennett, "American Choices in the Far East in 1882," *AHR* 30 (1924): 84-98. Acting Secretary of State John W. Davis' reaffirmation of the American view is in a letter to Young, DI, China 3, no. 81. Li Hungchang's discussion with Young of the Chinese position is reported in Young to Frelinghuysen, Aug. 8, 1883, DD, China 65; Department of State, Report Book, 1882, 653. See also Kim and Kim, *Korea and the Politics of Imperialism,* 26-27; George M. McCune and John A. Harrison, eds., *Korean-American Relations* (Berkeley, 1951), vol. 1, *The Initial Period, 1883-1886,* 25. Other works on the tensions in American policy are Dennett, *Americans in Eastern Asia* (New York, 1922), 461-462; Dennett, "Early American Policy in Korea, 1882-1887," *PSQ* 38 (1923): 82-103; Harold J. Noble, "The United States and Sino-Korean Relations, 1885-1887," *PHR* 2 (1933): 292-304; *DAB,* s.v. "George Clayton Foulk"; and Payson J. Treat, *Diplomatic Relations between the United States and Japan, 1853-1895* (Stanford, 1932), 2:160-166, and his article "China and Korea, 1885-1895," *PSQ* 49 (1934): 506-543. The articles by Tsiang, "Sino-Japanese Diplomatic Relations, 1870-1894," 1-106; Lin, "Li Hung-chang: His Korea Policies, 1870-1885," 202-233; Robert T. Pollard, "American Relations with Korea, 1882-1895," *CSPSR* 16 (1932-1933): 425-471; and James S. Gale, "The Influence of China upon Korea," *TKBRAS* 1 (1900): 1-24; and the book by Paul H. Clyde, *United States Policy Toward China; Diplomatic and Public Documents, 1839-1939* (Durham, N.C., 1940), generally accept a Chinese suzerainty over Korea, which Treat rejects. For an account which calls the Treaty of Kanghwa the "critical turn," see Yong-ho Ch'oe, "Sino-Korean Relations, 1866-1876: A Study of Korea's Tributary Relationship to China," *JAticS* 9 (1966): 182-183.

Useful introductions to the subject of Chinese foreign relations and the structure of Asiatic rivalries are Mingchien Bau, *The Foreign Relations of China* (London, 1922); Harold Vinacke, *A History of the Far East in Modern Times* (London, 1960); and the older but still valuable work by Hosea B. Morse, *The International Relations of the Chinese Empire* (London, 1918), 3 vols. On the Tsungli Yamen, the Chinese "Foreign Office," see Masatake Banno, *China and the West 1858-1861* (Cambridge, Mass., 1965); Tingfu F. Tsiang, "The Origins of the Tsungli Yamen," *CSPSR* 15 (1931-1932): 92-97, and S. M. Mêng, *The Tsungli Yamen: Its Organization and Functions* (Cambridge, Mass., 1962).

Adding considerably to the picture of Chinese reactions to other nations at the end of the nineteenth century are Michael Loewe, *Imperial China: The Historical Background to the Modern Age* (London, 1946); Ernest R. Hughes, *The Invasion of China by the Western World* (London, 1937); and Ssu-yü Teng and John K. Fairbank, *China's Response to the West: A Documentary History, 1839-1923* (Cambridge, Mass., 1965). On the T'ung Chih restoration, see the superb study by Mary C. Wright, *The Last Stand of Chinese Conservatism* (Stanford, 1957). E. Victor G. Kiernan, *British Diplomacy in China 1880-1885* (Cambridge, Mass., 1939), has useful background on British activities covering the period of Shufeldt's visit.

United States relations with China should be followed in Fairbank, *The United States and China* (Cambridge, Mass., 1962), and the work in which he joined Edwin O. Reischauer and Albert Craig, *History of East Asian Civilization* (London, 1965), vol. 2, *East Asia: The Modern Transformation;* A. Whitney Griswold, *The Far Eastern Policy of the United States* (New Haven, 1938); and three works by Paul H. Clyde, *The Far East* (New York, 1952); *United States Policy Toward China;* and "Attitudes and

Policies of George F. Seward, American Minister at Peking, 1876–1880: Some Phases of the Co-operative Policy," *PHR* (1937): 387–404. The fine studies by Kwang-Ching Liu, *Anglo-American Steamship Rivalry in China: 1862–1874* (Cambridge, Mass., 1962), and *Americans and Chinese: A Historical Essay and a Bibliography* (Cambridge, Mass., 1963), were highly useful for placing Shufeldt's visions about the Yangtze in 1867 in context.

Sino-Japanese relations from midcentury to 1895 can be followed in the works cited by Tsiang and Treat, with the latter's "The Cause of the Sino-Japanese War, 1894," *PHR* 8 (1939): 149–157; Yoshisaburo Kuno, *Japanese Expansion on the Asiatic Continent* (Berkeley, 1940); Trumbull White, *The War in the East: Japan, China and Corea* (Philadelphia, 1895); together with the article by Hyman Kublin, "The Attitude of China during the Liu Ch'iu Controversy," *PHR* 18 (1949): 213–232, and Ok Y. Kim, "The American Role in Korean-Japanese Relations" (Ph.D. diss., Bryn Mawr College, 1937).

Chapter 15   The Legacy of an Expansionist

On the navy in 1882 and the Naval Advisory Board, see the works cited in the bibliographical essay for chapter 9: Seager, "Ten Years before Mahan," 491–500; Alden and Westcott, *The United States Navy,* 284–286; H. Sprout and M. Sprout, *The Rise of American Naval Power,* 185–187; Davis, *A Navy Second to None,* 30–40; Mitchell, *History of the Modern American Navy,* 10–11, 14–15; T. Hunt, *The Life of William H. Hunt,* 216–224, 230–233; L. Hunt, "Founder of the New Navy," 173–199; Hunt's annual report, *ARSN, 1881,* 27; F. L. Paxon, *DAB,* s.v. "William Eaton Chandler"; and Livermore, "American Naval Base Policy in the Far East," 114–115. See also Frank M. Bennett, *The Steam Navy of the United States* (Pittsburgh, 1896), 773–779; *Sen. Report* 161, 48th Cong. 1st Sess., "Report to accompany Bill S. 698 to authorize the construction of additional steel vessels for the Navy"; and the report of the Naval Advisory Board, "New Steam Cruisers for the United States Navy," *ARSN, 1883,* Appendix 2. On Roach, see Leonard A. Swann, Jr., *John Roach, Maritime Entrepreneur: The Years as Naval Contractor, 1862–1886* (Annapolis, 1965), and Dean C. Allard, Jr., "The Influence of the United States Navy upon the American Steel Industry, 1880–1900" (M.A. thesis, Georgetown University, 1959).

Post-treaty, Korean–United States contacts are explored in Harold J. Noble's articles, "The Korean Mission to the United States in 1883," *TKBRAS* 18 (1929): 1–27, "The United States and Sino-Korean Relations, 1885–1887," *PHR* 2 (1933), and *DAB,* s.v. "George Clayton Foulk." On Foulk, who went to Korea as United States minister to implement the Shufeldt treaty, see George M. McCune and John A. Harrison, eds., *Korean-American Relations* (Berkeley, 1951), vol. 1, *The Initial Period, 1883–1886,* and the second volume by Spencer J. Palmer, ed., *The Period of Growing Influence, 1887–1895* (Berkeley, 1963). For differing speculations as to why Shufeldt may have left Korea, see Robert T. Pollard, "American Relations with Korea 1882–1895," *CSPSR* 16 (1932–1933): 435–436, n. 30; T'ung Chi Lin, "Li Hung-chang: His Korea Policies, 1870–1885," *CSPSR* 19 (1935): 228–230; Noble, "The United States and Sino-Korean Relations," 292–304, and his "Political Activities of American Missionaries in Korea before 1905," *NSEQ* 9 (1936); Ting-fu F. Tsiang, "Sino-Japanese Diplomatic Relations, 1870–1894," *CSPSR* 17 (1933): 104.

Reactions within and without Korea to the opening of the country are well surveyed in the works of K. Hwang, *A Study in Transition in Intra-Asian Relations* (Cambridge, 1978); Andrew Nahm, "Kim Ok-Kyun and the Korean Progressive Movement, 1882–1884" (Ph.D. diss., Stanford University, 1961); Nahm's "Korea's Response to International Rivalries: Korean Domestic Politics, 1876–84,"

MASALP 50 (1965): 445-465; and his similar "Reaction and Response to the Opening of Korea, 1876-1884," *SA* 6 (1965): 61-80, all generally anti-Min, anti-Confucianist, and pro-Kim family. See also Kwang Hi Ro, "Power Politics in Korea and its Impact on Korean Foreign and Domestic Affairs, 1882-1907" (Ph.D. diss., University of Oklahoma, 1966); Harold F. Cook, "Kim Ok-Kyun and the Background of the 1884 Émeute" (Ph.D. diss., Harvard, 1969), 2 vols., now published as *Korea's 1884 Incident: Its Background and Kim Ok-kyun's Elusive Dream* (Seoul, 1972). Other studies include Martina Deuchler, "The Opening of Korea, 1875-1884" (Ph.D. diss., Harvard, 1967), chap. 6, published as *Confucian Gentlemen and Barbarian Envoys: The Opening of Korea, 1875-1885* (Seattle, 1977); Han-Kyo Kim, "The Demise of the Kingdom of Korea: 1882-1910" (Ph.D. diss., University of Chicago, 1962), chap. 2; C. I. Eugene Kim and Han-Kyo Kim, *Korea and the Politics of Imperialism, 1876-1910* (Berkeley, 1967), 33-58; and Francis C. Jones, "Foreign Diplomacy in Korea, 1866-1894" (Ph.D. diss., Harvard, 1935), chap. 9.

For the attempts to weaken the queen's influence, see William R. Carles, *Life in Corea* (London, 1888), chap. 18, whose information was based on eye-witness accounts; William E. Griffis, *Corea: The Hermit Nation* (New York, 1888), 464-469; McCune and Harrison, *Korean-American Relations*, 1:96-114; Hosea B. Morse, *The International Relations of the Chinese Empire* (London, 1918), 3:11; M. Frederick Nelson, *Korea and the Old Orders in Eastern Asia* (Baton Rouge, 1946), 183-184: Pollard, "American Relations with Korea," 430, 435-436, 439; Frederick F. Chien, *The Opening of Korea: A Study of Chinese Diplomacy, 1876-1885* (N.p., 1967), 147-168; Hilary Conroy, *The Japanese Seizure of Korea: 1868-1910* (Philadelphia, 1960), 139-159; Tsiang, "Sino-Japanese Diplomatic Relations," 80-84; Lin, "Li Hung-chang: His Korea Policies, 1870-1885," 229; Tyler Dennett, *Americans in Eastern Asia* (New York, 1922) 478-479; and Payson J. Treat, "China and Korea, 1885-1894," *PSQ* 49 (1934): 513-516, which blames Li Hung-chang and the Chinese. See also F. H. Morsel, "Event leading to the Émeute of 1884," *KRep* 4 (1897): 95-98, 135-140, 212-219. Two new, good studies are Key-Huik Kim, *The Last Phase of the East Asian World Order: Korea, Japan and the Chinese Empire* (Berkeley, 1980) and Robert Swartout, Jr., *Mandarins, Gunboats, and Power Politics: Owen Nickerson Denny and the International Rivalries in Korea* (Honolulu, 1980).

On Korea's relations with Japan, see Woonsang Choi, "The Korean-Japanese Relations, 1870-1910," pt. 1-2, *KA* 1 (1962): 162-188, 300-318, and pt. 3, *KA* 2 (1963): 51-60, who believed the Mins were "extreme radicals"; Lawrence H. Battistini, "The Korean Problem in the Nineteenth Century," *MN* 8 (1952): 47-66; and Chon Dong, "Japanese Annexation of Korea: A Study of Korean-Japanese Relations to 1910" (Ph.D. diss., University of Colorado, 1955). Finally, see Jongsuk Chay, "The United States and the Closing Door in Korea: American-Korean Relations, 1894-1905" (Ph.D. diss., University of Michigan, 1965) and Dong H. Choi, "The United States Policy toward the Japanese Protectorate and Annexation of Korea, 1904-1910" (Ph.D. diss., Fletcher School of Law and Diplomacy, 1965).

On later American activity, see Spencer J. Palmer, "American Gold Mining in Korea's Unsan District," *PHR* 31 (1962): 379-391, and Fred H. Harrington, *God, Mammon and the Japanese* (Madison, 1944).

Conclusion

For the context of navalists and naval expansionists, see Allen B. Cole, ed., "Captain David Porter's Proposed Expedition to the Pacific and Japan, 1815," *PHR* 9 (1940): 61-65; W. Patrick Strauss, "Captain David Porter: Pioneer Pacific Strategist," *USNIP* 93 (1967): 158-160; and David F. Long, *Nothing Too Daring* (Annapolis, 1970). On Perry, see Samuel E. Morison, *"Old Bruin": Commodore Matthew C.*

Perry, 1794-1858 (London, 1968); E. M. Barrow, *The Great Commodore* (Indianapolis, 1935); and for astute reflections, see William L. Neumann, "Religion, Morality and Freedom: The Ideological Background of the Perry Expedition," *PHR* 23 (1954): 247-258; Earl Swisher, "Commodore Perry's Imperialism in Relation to America's Present Day Position in the Pacific," *ibid.*, 16 (1947): 30-40; and Tyler Dennett, "Perry's Proposals for Far Eastern Policy," in *Americans in Eastern Asia* (New York, 1922), 270-278. Mahan has attracted considerable writing, the best of which is now Robert Seager II, *Alfred Thayer Mahan The Man and His Letters* (Annapolis, 1976). See, in addition, Robert Seager and Doris D. Maguire, eds., *Letters and Papers of Alfred Thayer Mahan* (Annapolis, 1976), 3 vols. Still useful are W. D. Puleston, *Mahan: The Life and Works of Captain Alfred Thayer Mahan* (New Haven, 1939); William E. Livesey, *Mahan on Sea Power* (Norman, Oklahoma, 1947); and Allan Westcott, *Mahan on Naval Warfare* (Boston, 1948). In addition, see Peter Karsten, "Mahan Reconsidered," in *The Naval Aristocracy: The Golden Age of Annapolis and the Emergence of Modern American Navalism* (Pittsburgh, 1972), 326-352 and Walter LaFeber, *The New Empire: An Interpretation of American Expansion, 1860-1898* (Ithaca, 1963), 85-95, and his article "A Note on the 'Mercantilistic Imperialism' of Alfred Thayer Mahan," *MVHR* 48 (1962): 674-685.

Index

NAME INDEX

Abdallah, Sultan (Johanna), 214–215, 253
Abercrombie, Sarah Hutchins: daughter of Reverend James Abercrombie, 8, 8n; *see* Shufeldt, Sarah H.
Abert, Sylvanus Thayer, 132
Adams, John Quincy, 2, 3
Adee, Alvey A., 199
Alden, Rear Admiral James, 132, 146
Allen, Horace: U.S. secretary of legation in Seoul, 331
Allen, Isaac J.: U.S. consul in Hong Kong, 92, 94
Almonte, General Juan Nepomucene, 54, 58; Almonte government, 59
Ammen, Rear Admiral Daniel: heads Inter-Oceanic Canal Commission, 148, 150, 151; chairs naval committee (1870s), 171; mentioned, 349
Angell, James B.: U.S. minister in China, 262; describes Li Hung-chang, 262; discusses Li, 265; meets Shufeldt, 262, 264; urges State Department to appoint negotiator for Korea, 266; warns Shufeldt in Tientsin, 267, 268; changes mind on Li's intentions, 268; leaves China, 268; congratulates Shufeldt on promotion, 314; mentioned, 303
Appenzeller, Henry Gerard, 325
Arthur, Chester: succeeds to presidency, 268; ignores Shufeldt's Korean treaty, 308; mentioned, xii, 207, 281, 297, 351

Bailey, Rear Admiral Theodorus, 78
Balambé: king of the Malagasy tribe, 211, 253, 343
Balestier, Captain Joseph, 228
Barghash, Sultan (Zanzibar, after 1870), 216
Bartlett, Lieutenant Commander John R., 136, 139
Bell, Rear Admiral Henry Haywood: commands Asiatic squadron, 88; instructions to cooperate with British, 92, 94; approves convoy of *Parsee*, 95; orders Shufeldt to investigate disappearance of *General Sherman*, 97, 100; approves Shufeldt's excursion up Yangtze, 109; punitive expedition to Formosa, 112; mentioned, 108, 349, 351
Belt, Commander William J.: USS *Marion*, (1841), praises Shufeldt, 7–8
Benjamin, Senator Judah P., 14; leader of Louisiana-Tehuantepec Company, 16; Confederate secretary of state, 68; mentioned, 25, 26, 43
Bennett, James Gordon: provides African slogan for *New York Herald*, 182; supports growing navy, 311; mentioned, 148, 177
Biddle, Commodore James: visits Japan, 247
Bigelow, John: U.S. consul in Paris (1864), 67
Bingham, John A.: U.S. minister to Japan, arranges Shufeldt visit, 238–239, 241, 242; consoles Shufeldt, 248; annoys Li Hung-chang, 263
Blaine, James G.: secretary of state, commercial policy in Far East, 261, 274, 418, n33; intervenes to secure position for Shufeldt, 261; wants information on military and naval organization of China, 261; instructs Shufeldt on Korea treaty, 272–275; instructions of November 1881, 278, 282; offers Shufeldt position as U.S. minister to China, 330; mentioned, xii, 259, 266, 303, 351
Blyden, Edward W.: Liberian minister plenipotentiary to Court of St. James, 184; Shufeldt wishes to use as roving consul, 184–185; mentioned, 255, 337, 347
Breese, Samuel L.: New York navy yard (1861), 28
Buckingham, Governor William, 29, 153; U.S. senator, 118, 126, 128
Buel, R. H., 132; finds water of Corte, 139
Burlingame, Anson: U.S. minister to China (1867), 98
Butler, General Benjamin F.: supports bill to

relieve American shipping, 128; supports Shufeldt's survey, 131; defines "contraband" status of slaves, 345; mentioned, 80, 351
Butler, Senator Matthew Calbraith: discusses navy with Shufeldt, 316–318, 341

Céspedes, Don Manuel de: lawyer and Cuban revolutionary, 117, 121
Cespedes, Father Gregario de: first recorded Western visitor to Korea, 97
Chandler, William E.: secretary of the navy, orders Shufeldt to Naval Advisory Board, 305–306, 308, 309, 310, 311; orders medical for Shufeldt, 314, 315; soothes Shufeldt's ruffled pride, 319; mentioned, 341, 349
Chêng Tsao-ju: ordered to prepare first draft for treaty (March 1881), 265, 288
Cheow Fuh: meets Shufeldt, 283; attempts to dissuade Shufeldt from visiting Tsungli Yamen, 284; negotiates treaty, 285; signs commercial treaty, 302; mentioned, 288, 289, 291
Chien, Frederick Foo, 303
Clitz, Admiral John B.: U.S. Asiatic squadron, 246; meets Shufeldt, 274, 278, 283, 306; sends congratulations, 308
Collins, Edward Knight, 9
Conkling, Roscoe: leader of New York Stalwarts, 266; presses for commission to discuss trans-African railroad, 255
Conroy, Hilary, 321
Coppinger, William: secretary of American Colonization Society, 171, 191
Corbett, Reverend Hunter: assists Shufeldt, 103, 106, 344
Corwin, Thomas: U.S. minister to Mexico (1862), 44; negotiates loan treaties with Mexico, 52, 53, 59; meets Shufeldt, 61, 62; exchanges ratifications, 62; praises Shufeldt, 62
Crawford, Joseph T.: British consul general in Havana, 30; concerned over British trade, 30; books passage for Mason and Slidell, 34; introduces Mason and Slidell to captain general of Cuba, 35; justifies conduct, 35; belligerent, 39; refuses to authorize U.S. mail bags to be carried, 40; reprimanded, 40; estimate of slave trade in Cuba, 380, n14
Cromwell, Commander Bartlett J.: captain USS *Ticonderoga*, 180–181, 182, 244; trouble with Shufeldt's nephew, 228

Dahlgren, Rear Admiral John, 75, 76, 349
Davis, Lieutenant Charles Stacey: commands Shufeldt on Coast Survey (1845–1846), 8, 9; congratulates Shufeldt on marriage, 9
Davis, John: reviews Blaine's policies, 278; acting secretary of state, 319
Dayton, William Lewis: U.S. minister to France, 57

de Garay, José: leader of Louisiana–Tehuantepec Company, 16
de la Concha, José: Spanish captain general of Cuba (1864), 2
de Lorencez, General: leader of French troops in Mexico, 58
de Nargas y Muchucas, Brigadier General Carlos: second military officer of Puerto Rico, 46
Dennett, Tyler, 241, 250; on Japanese intentions, 238; on Shufeldt treaty, 335
Denny, Owen Nickerson, 308, 324, 327
de Saligny, Alphonse Dubois: French minister to Mexico, 44, 50, 55
des Essard, Bernard: French consul general in Havana, 69–70
Diaz, Manuel: Mexican consul in Havana, 45
Dibblee, Albert, receives Sargent letter, 279; mentioned, 329, 330
Doblado, Manuel: Mexican foreign minister, 54; responds to Shufeldt's colonization scheme, 60, 62; assessed by Seward, 68; mentioned, 59, 219, 339, 345, 352
Drake, Lieutenant Franklin J.: leads surveys, 185, 193–194; negotiates with Mussarango tribe, 201; mentioned, 254
Dulce, Domingo: captain general of Cuba, 70, 349
Dunlop, Commodore Hugh: Royal Navy, detains General Miramón, 50
Dunnell, Mark Hill: U.S. consul at Veracruz, 54
DuPont, Samuel F., 73, 75

Eads, Captain James: ship-railroad scheme, 323
Estrampez: Cuban nationalist, executed, 1; Shufeldt's views on, 3, 13, 26, 349
Evarts, William M.: secretary of state, 163; views as commercial expansionist, 168, 400, n27, 406, n38; desires commercial treaty with Korea, 179; instructs Shufeldt, 177–180; joint policy with Secretary Thompson, 177, 206, 222; on intervention in Liberia, 192; instructions re: Zanzibar, 215; re: Borneo, 228; approves Bingham's actions in Japan, 238; thanks Japanese minister, 242–243; leaves office, 257; mentioned, 175, 199, 200, 208, 231, 253, 303

Fairbank, John K.: defines Korea's relationship to China, 234
Farquhar, Norman: on Tehuantepec survey, 136, 138, 151; supports Shufeldt for bureau position, 153–154; on navy, 155; compliments Shufeldt on treaty, 308; mentioned, 150
Farragut, Admiral David G.: captures New Orleans, 62, 88; Shufeldt proposes to occupy Matamoras, 54; mentioned, 35n
Febiger, Commander John: visits Korea, 106–107

Name Index

Fenton, Senator Rueben E.: resolution for ship canal, 126
Fernandez, Manuel: Mexican commissioner, 139
Ferris, Senator Orris S., 118
Fish, Hamilton: secretary of state, 118, 233; on international arrangements for isthmian canal, 144; offers help to Tehuantepec Railway Company, 130
Fisher, Charles L.: U.S. consul at Tientsin, informs Shufeldt of Li's interest, 260-261
Foner, Eric, 345
Foote, Lucius: U.S. minister to Korea, 320
Foulk, George C.: U.S. chargé d'affaires in Korea; detailed to meet Korean embassy, 319, 320; in Korea, 324, 325, 326
Fox, Gustavus Vasa, 71
Franklin, Samuel R., 318
Frelinghuysen, Frederick T.: secretary of state, 207, 271; reviews Blaine's policy, 278; telegraphs to Holcombe, 277; ideas on a Korean treaty, 277-278; Shufeldt informs, 282, 305; silent on treaty, 294; argues for Korean independence, 300-301; mentioned, 283, 289, 293, 294, 296, 303, 310, 335, 351
Fuertes, Estevan A.: Tehuantepec survey chief engineer, 132, 136; finds water for canal, 139-140; reports canal practicable, 141; estimates for a canal, 149; aids Shufeldt, 151; mentioned, 339

Garfield, James A.: attempt on life of, influences Shufeldt's plans, 264, 268; mentioned, 257, 258, 259, 266, 299
Gasset, Major General Don Manuel: leader of Spanish expedition to Mexico, 46; resigns, 50
Gibson, Garretson W.: Liberian secretary of state, 190-191
Gibson, James T.: superintendent of Cape Palmas, 192
Gibson, Lieutenant Commander William, 82
Godon, Rear Admiral Sylvanus W., 117
Goldsborough, Captain Louis M., 7
Gore-Jones: Bristish Admiral in India, 225
Grant, Ulysses S.: on Cuba, 124-125; on exclusive control of an isthmian canal, 126, 144; appoints Shufeldt to lead survey of isthmus, 131; visits India, 225; visits China, 230-231, App. 1; mentioned, 81, 117, 148, 157, 351
Griffis, William E., 310
Grimes, Senator James W., 71
Gunn, James O'B.: Union Ironworks, 327; on slow movement of American capital, 328
Gunnell, Francis, 308, 309; urges Shufeldt to come to Washington, 310; diagnoses Shufeldt's last illness, 332-333; mentioned, 314
Gutièrrez de Rubalcava, Admiral Don Joaquin: leads initial Spanish expedition to Mexico, 45, 50

Hag-w'on Sunoo: on U.S.-Korean treaty, 247-248
Hale, Senator John Parker, 71
Hargous, Peter A.: backer of Louisiana-Tehuantepec Company, 17; praises Shufeldt, 17, 18; financial losses, 17, 25
Harris, Benjamin, 311, 312
Harris, John Myers, 197, 405, n34
Hart, Robert, in charge of Chinese customs, 264, 296
Hatch, R. D.: SS *Quaker City*, 17; invites Shufeldt to join Pacific Mail Ship Company, 154
Hathorne, W. H.: U.S. consul, Zanzibar, 214, 215
Haven, Bishop Gilbert: on African commerce, 177
Hayes, Rutherford B., 158, 163, 253
Helm, Charles J.: former U.S. consul, Havana, 21; Confederate agent in Havana, 23, 41
Hilton, Joseph H.: Liberian commissioner, 186, 188, 189
Hogarth, George: *General Sherman*, 100, 105
Holcombe, Chester: U.S. chargé d'affaires at Tientsin, 269; advises Shufeldt to leave Tientsin, 269; changes advice, 271; on Korean treaty matter, 271; on possibility of China-Japan war, 277; criticizes Shufeldt for Sargent letter, 282; initiates second approach to Tsungli Yamen, 284-285; on Tsungli Yamen and treaty, 296; on dependency clause, 290-291; translates Korean monarch's letter to Garfield, 300; congratulates Shufeldt, 308; mentioned, 277, 289, 294, 295, 303
Hollis, George: U.S. consul, Cape Town, 332
Hong Yong-shik: son of chief minister of Korea, 237, 319
Hopkins, Alfred A.: assigned to survey Pacific coast of Mexico, 138; reports, 141
Hopkins, David: British consul for Bights of Benin and Biafra, Niger River, and Fernando Po; on Liberian Boundary Commission, 186, 189
Horner, James H.: U.S. consul at Sagua la Grande, 37; misunderstands Shufeldt's instructions over *Trent* departure, 37-38; defends conduct, 38
Humphreys, Brigadier General Andrew A., 151
Hunt, William H.: secretary of the navy (1881), 261; appoints (First) Naval Advisory Board, 311-312

In-jisho: Korean minister of ceremony, rejects Shufeldt's letter of approach, 247
Inouye Kaoru: Japanese minister of foreign affairs, 238; interviews Shufeldt on Korea, 241; advises Korea to negotiate treaty with U.S., 242; sends letter to Korea, 242; holds off foreign inquiries re: Korea, 245; thanked by Shufeldt, 251; mentioned, 235, 247, 272

Jeffers, William N., 164, 166
Jones, William Patterson: U.S. consul at Amoy, requests Shufeldt's help, 95; mentioned, 116
Juárez, Benito: president of Mexico, 42, 47, 50, 58, 68, 348; approves terms of transit grant (1868), 126
Julio: trader in area disputed by Liberia, 191, 192–193
Jurien de la Gravière, Rear Admiral Jean: leads French expedition to Mexico, 47; instructions differ from Saligny's, 55

Kasson, John A.: supervises electoral count in New Orleans (1876), 157; leads U.S. delegation to Berlin conference, 311; mentioned, 344
Kate, 12; mentioned, 349, 350
Kim, C. I. Eugene and Kim, Han-Kyo, on China's loss of power, 299, 301
Kim Hong-jip: member of Korean cabinet and ambassador to Japan, 296, 297
Kim Ok-Kyun, 237, 320
Kim P'yong-muk, 236, 237
Kim Yun-sik: Korean negotiator for a treaty with the U.S., 276; at Pao-ting-fu, 284; mentioned, 277, 294
Kirk, John: British consul in Zanzibar, 214, 217; on Shufeldt, 217
Kojong (Ch'ol jong): king of Korea, 97, 236, 276; interviews Shufeldt, 324
Kondo Masuki: Japanese consul in Fusan (Pusan), forwards Shufeldt's letter, 247; thanked for services, 251; mentioned, 238, 239, 240, 245, 246, 247
Kung, Prince: head of Tsungli Yamen, 98, 249, 264, 265

Lamarese: king of the Sakalava tribe, 211, 253, 343
La Sère, Emile: Louisiana–Tehuantepec Company, 16; forms new isthmian canal company, 126
Lee, William D.: Louisiana–Tehuantepec Company, 16
Le Ke Yung: interview with Shufeldt (1867), 105–106
Li Hung-chang: Viceroy of Chihli (Hopei), alarmed at Japanese-Korean treaty (1876), 236; writes to Shufeldt, 245–246; interviews Shufeldt, 248–249; fears war with Russia, 248; influences Shufeldt's views on Japan (1880), 251; praises Shufeldt, 260; described by Shufeldt, 262, 280–281, App. 1; keeps Shufeldt close by, 262, 265; neglects to mention naval appointment, 257, 264; discusses importance of a Korean treaty with Shufeldt, 263; proposes Shufeldt should go to Korea, 265; requests a Korean envoy, 276; wishes to see Shufeldt at Pao-ting-fu, 283; negotiates with Shufeldt, 284–285, 288; will send Chinese warships to Korea, 288; stands firm on dependency clause, 290, 291; on Sargent letter, 292, 308–309; temporary absence, 295; role in treaty negotiations praised by Shufeldt, 297; policy hopes for Korea treaty, 299, 301, 303; signs commercial treaty with Korea, 302; mentioned, 245, 260, 272, 276, 283, 284, 289, 294, 296, 306, 309, 335, 336, 343, 349
Lin, T. C., 28, 234
Lincoln, Abraham, 24, 48, 61, 64, 69; on Shufeldt's proposed convention with Mexico, 67 68
Li Ying-tsung: Korean envoy to China, 276
Llorencez, Colonel (Spanish), 49
Lo-fông-loh: Li Hung-chang's naval secretary, reveals Korean negotiator has arrived, 276; mentioned, 270, 277, 283, 289, 291
López, Narcisco, invades Cuba, 2, 2n
Low, Frederick F.: U.S. minister to China, 179, 233, 234
Lowell, Percival: secretary to Korean legation in Washington, 319
Luce, Stephen: on apprenticeship scheme, 159–160; Shufeldt discusses loss of sailing ships, 168; Shufeldt informs him of need to continue training system, 175; mentioned, xii, 153, 154
Lyons, Lord: British minister in Washington, 21, 39

Ma Chien-chung: ordered to prepare drafts for treaty (March 1881), 265; main Chinese intermediary for Korean treaty, 283, 295; given treaty credit by Shufeldt, 297; signs commercial treaty with Korea, 302; mentioned, 285, 288, 291, 296, 297
McCaslin, Captain: of *Surprise,* 98, 101
McConnell, James B.: captain of *W. H. Webb,* 31
McLane, Robert M.: U.S. minister to Mexico (1859), 42
Mahan, Alfred Thayer: declines appointment to isthmian surveying expedition, 132; mentioned, xi, xii, 171, 323, 330, 331, 334, 343, 350, 352
Mangum, Fannie V.: befriends Shufeldt in China, 112; Shufeldt writes to, 114; mentioned, 350
Mangum, Willie P.: U.S. consul, Shanghai, befriends Shufeldt in China, 112; praises Rear Admiral Bell, 113; Shufeldt writes to, 114; Shufeldt analyzes state of the country for, 123–124; mentioned, 122, 239
Mannix, Daniel P.: commands marines on USS *Ticonderoga,* 182, 229; Chinese torpedo school, 260, 267
Marcy, William L.: secretary of state (1853), 2n
Marigny, Antoine J.: Louisiana–Tehuantepec Company, 16
Mason, James M.: Confederate commissioner to the Court of St. James, 33; leaves Charleston, 33, 34; recollects stay in Havana, 37; captured by Charles Wilkes, 32–33, 41–42; mentioned, 35, 36, 348

Name Index

Maximilian of Austria, 54, 58
Miller, Lieutenant Frederick A. (nephew): keeps daily journal of *Ticonderoga* cruise, 181; leaves vessel at Singapore, 228; mentioned, 228, 244, 254
Miller, Mary (niece), 134; *see* Shufeldt, Molly (Mary Miller)
Milne, Rear Admiral Sir Alexander: commander-in-chief, British naval forces, North American and West Indies station, 30
Min Yong-Ik: nephew of Korean king, 319
Miramón, General Miguel: leader of Conservatives, 49; Jecker debt, 50; detained by British, 50
Mori Akinori, 235
Morse, Congressman Leopold: House Committee on Naval Affairs, 167, 169, 175, 342, 347
Morgan, Senator John T.: interest in Congo, 207; support for a growing navy, 311, 343
Mullany, James Madison R.: Philadelphia navy yard, 154-155; on conditions in navy, 155; complaints about naval conditions heeded, 160
Murphy, James McLeod: Shufeldt turns to for help with survey of isthmus, 128-129; rejects Williams as isthmian surveyor, 132

Nahm, Andrew C.: on Li's aim for the Korean treaty, 299
Napoleon III, 28, 51, 69; comments on Corwin's treaty, 68
Nelson, Thomas H.: U.S. minister to Mexico City; authorized to help Tehuantepec Railway Company, 130, 135
Newton, Brigadier General John: expedition to St. Mark's, Florida, 82-87
Nichols, Admiral Edward T., 314, 315
Nichols, William H.: retired U.S. consul at Aden, 179
Nimleh, King: chief of the Grebos, 193

Oppert, Ernest, 101
Orcutt, John: American Colonization Society, 172

Pak Won-Kuei: impressed by U.S. trade advantages, 262-263
Pak Yong-hyo, 237, 320
Pao Ch'ao, General: fighting Nien fei banditti, 109
Parker, Rear Admiral Foxhall: supports Shufeldt for bureau, 154, 155-156
Parm, Dr. John A.: U.S. acting consul, Freetown, 183
Patterson, Rear Admiral Thomas H.: declines to turn over command of Asiatic squadron to Shufeldt, 244
Paulding, Rear Admiral Hiram, 71
Paullin, Charles O.: re: Japanese intentions, 238, 241, 250
Payson, Charles: State Department, 212-213
Peirce, Benjamin: superintendent of the U.S. Coast Survey on the Inter-Oceanic Canal Commission, 148
Perry, Commodore Matthew Calbraith: compared with Shufeldt, 308; mentioned, xi, xii, xiii, 306, 310, 334, 335, 348
Perry, Lieutenant Commander, 296-297
Phillips: Chester Arthur's secretary comments on Shufeldt, 309
Plumb, Edward Lee: attaché, U.S. Legation, Mexico, 52, 53; visits Havana, Cuba, 52; travels to Mexico City with Shufeldt, 59-60; brings treaties to Mexico, 62
Porter, Admiral David Dixon: as lieutenant on SS *Georgia,* 11; Shufeldt asks for help to secure position of consul general in Havana, 118; Shufeldt petitions to for vessels for China, mourns passing of navy, 123; supports Shufeldt's isthmian survey, 126, 129, 131, 146; supports Shufeldt for bureau, 154; view of navy in 1870s, 154; dispute with Secretary of the Navy Robeson, 158; fails to influence legislation for recruits, 163; mentioned, xii, 117, 128, 158, 351
Preston, W. B.: owner of *General Sherman,* 96, 100
Preston, William Ballou: secretary of the navy (1849), 9
Prim, General Don Juan, Marqués de los Castillejos: assumes overall command of Spanish expedition, 47; arrives in Cuba, 50; urges Mexico to adopt monarchy, 55; reembarks Spanish troops, 55; mentioned, 54, 55, 59
Puizon, Admiral: Spanish Pacific squadron, 66

Quitman, General John A., 2, 56; governor of Mississippi, 15, 25, 26

Ranavalona II (Queen of Madagascar), 212
Rand, Stephen: paymaster USS *Canonicus,* 157-158
Ransom, Captain George: USS *Colorado,* 153, 171
Read, Commodore George: West African squadron (1846), 8, 173
Remey, George C.: isthmian survey party, 132; reports Fuertes has traced feeder, 140; mentioned, 136
Reynolds, William: Shufeldt's predecessor at Bureau of Equipment and Recruiting, 155
Ridgely, Commodore Charles G.: New York, 6; commands USS *Santiago de Cuba,* 40
Roach, John: suspected of influencing (Second) Naval Advisory Board, 312; receives contracts for White Squadron, 313; mentioned, 314, 316
Roberts, Edmund: treaty with Muscat (1833), 176, 215
Roberts, Marshall O.: New York shipowner, 11; heads a rival isthmian company, 131
Robertson, William H.: U.S. consul in Havana (1855), 4

Robeson, George: secretary of the navy (1869–1877), 11; informed of Shufeldt's views on isthmian canal, 132; orders Shufeldt to proceed on survey of Tehuantepec, 134; mentions Stevens party on isthmus, 138; content with navy, 163; on the Sargent letter, 307; mentioned, 140, 158, 162, 163, 349

Robinson, W. W.: U.S. consul at Tamatave, 212–213

Rodgers, Rear Admiral John: attempts to open Korea by force (1871), 233; appointed to (First) Naval Advisory Board, 312; mentioned, 154, 234

Roosevelt, Theodore, 124, 344, 347

Rose, Admiral Pierre Gustav: leader of French expedition to Korea, 98

Rost, Pierre A.: Confederate envoy to Europe, 30

Russell, Lord John: British foreign secretary, 30; reprimands Crawford, 40

Rydell, Father Felix: escapes from Korea, 98; meets Shufeldt, 101; briefs Shufeldt on fate of *General Sherman,* 102

Salisbury, Marquis of: British foreign secretary, 188

Salter, Colton: U.S. consul at Hankow, 109, 110, 338; discusses Yangtze trade with Shufeldt, 111

Sanford, E. T.: U.S. consul at Chefoo, 98

Sanford, Henry Shelton: interest in Congo, 200, 202, 207

Sargent, Senator Aaron A.: Senate Committee on Naval Affairs, calls for treaty with Korea through Japan, 178–179; leads anti-Chinese movement in California, 257; introduces resolution to open Korea, 258; receives Shufeldt's "open letter," 279, App. 1; writes explanation of his conduct to Shufeldt, 305–306; Shufeldt cites on use of force, 351; mentioned, 292, 336, 347, 351

Scott, Winfield S., 52; anaconda plan for crushing South, 81

Selfridge, Commander Thomas O.: surveys Darien, 128, 150, 152

Serrano, Don Francisco: captain general of Cuba, 30, 32, 34, 35, 36; discontented with Prim, 50, 54; recalled, 70

Seward, Frederick W.: Shufeldt reports to, 46; praises Shufeldt, 71–72; Shufeldt warns on Helm, 41; on Spain and Mexico, 47, 48, 56, 66, 69; mentioned, 339, 345

Seward, William Henry: secretary of state, informed of Shufeldt's suspicions re: Louisiana–Tehuantepec Company, 15; Lyons–Seward treaty, 21; influences Shufeldt, 24–25; recommends Shufeldt to Lincoln, 29; desires capture of Mason and Slidell, 34; authorizes Corwin to negotiate treaty with Mexico, 44; declines invitation to cooperate with allies in Mexico, 45; responds to Shufeldt's urgings re: Mexican agent, 57; debate with Shufeldt over Mexico, 55–67; rejects Shufeldt's scheme for Mexico, 64, 67; Shufeldt proposes convention to, 65–66; praises Shufeldt's fidelity, 68; orders Shufeldt's return from Mexico, 62; communicates information on Mexico to Bigelow, 67; institutes new policy of exclusive control of isthmian canal, 144; mentioned, xi, xii, 29, 32, 35, 36, 37, 43, 47, 48, 50, 51, 52, 53, 54, 59, 67, 69, 71, 92, 334, 336, 348, 349, 352, 353

Seyyid Majid, Sultan (Zanzibar), 216

Seyyid Said, Sultan (Muscat and Zanzibar), 215–216

Seyyid Thuwain, Sultan (Muscat), 216

Seyyid Turki, Sultan (Muscat), 220

Sheridan, General Philip: in command of troops in New Orleans, 1876, 157

Shewfelts of Dutchess County, 5

Shin Chen: President of Korean Royal Council, signs Korean treaty, 296–297, App. 2

Shock, William: on committee to reexamine the navy, 164, 225

Shufeldt, Charles (fourth son), 77

Shufeldt, George Adam (father): children of, 5; lawyer, 5, 6; Van Buren Democrat, 6; disturbed by absence of news from son, 6

Shufeldt, George Adam (third son): born, 11; attends school in Havana, 29; accompanies father on European cruise, 147; writes briefly, 244; accompanies father to Korea, 324; assessed by Molly, 328, 329; terms of will affect, 332; mentioned, 77, 349

Shufeldt, Mary Howey [née Wilson] (mother), 5

Shufeldt, Mason Abercrombie (second son): born, 11; attends school in Stamford, 20; in Havana, 29; charges father with neglect in death of mother, 142; attends Naval Academy 147; believes Naval Academy teaching program outdated, 155; neglects to write, 244; accompanies father to Korea, 324; assessed by Molly, 328–329; dies in Madagascar, 331–332; mentioned, 77, 349

Shufeldt, Molly [Mary Miller] (niece): adopted as daughter by Shufeldt, 134, 142; accompanies Shufeldt to Europe, 147; receives letters on world cruise, 191, 200, 239, 244; engaged as Shufeldt's secretary, 261; impressed by Shanghai, describes Li Hung-chang, 262; judges Shufeldt's relations with Li Hung-chang to be good, 268; worried over parallel with Perry, 306; urges Shufeldt to rest, 309; accompanies Shufeldt to Korea, 324; reflections on Korean monarch, 325; comments on Shufeldt, 325–326; judges prospects in Korea, 327; judges Shufeldt's sons, 328–329; receives gift from Shufeldt, 329; chief beneficiary in Shufeldt's will, 332; with Shufeldt, at death, 333; mentioned, 156, 158, 225, 227–228, 232, 305, 338, 349, 350, 351

Name Index

Shufeldt, Robert Wilson (1822-1895): [subjects arranged under AFRICA, BACKGROUND AND CHARACTER, CHINA, COMMERCE, CUBA, EMPIRE, ENGLAND, KOREA, LECTURES, LIBERIA, MERCHANT SHIPS, MEXICAN INVASION, NAVAL POSITONS, NAVY, U.S., PROMOTIONS, PACIFIC, POLITICS, RACE, SLAVES AND SLAVERY, SOUTHERN EMPIRE, TEHUANTEPEC, *TICONDEROGA, TRENT* AFFAIR, U.S. DESTINY]. AFRICA: on Islam in, 173, 344; views on British in, 174; visits Sierra Leone, 185; Liberia, 191-193, 195-196; on Africa as the great commercial prize of the world, 185, 194, 201, 202, 204, 206, 207, 218, 220; on civilization in, 202-204; on Portuguese in, 202; on Dutch in, 204; visits Congo, 204; calls for consular service for, 204-206; railroads in South Africa, 209; Cape Town, 206-208; reports from Cape Town, 208-210; draws parallel between United States and South African history, 210; treaties with chiefs of the Malagasy and Sakalava tribes, 211; visits Madagascar, 211-213, Zanzibar, 218-219, Aden, 220-221, Muscat, 220; *see also* Liberia. BACKGROUND AND CHARACTER: descriptions of, 1, n1, 322-333; born (Feb. 21, 1822), 5; education, 5-6; remembered as young man, 6; rejects father's advice to become lawyer, 6; eulogized by passengers, 18; reputation for diplomacy, 28; character traits, ambitious, 15, 81, 195, 348, dreamer, 6, emotions, 89, excess of zeal, 282, headstrong, 58, impatient, 6, lone wolf, 6, romantic, 6, 90, views on individual, 79, God, sea, and heaven, 89, man, 89, manners, 29, mysticism and spiritualism, 12-13, 90, on power, 51, 89-90, 173; writes poetry, 6, 81, 89; writes diary, 80-81, 88-89, 89, 350; health (1845), 8, yellow fever, 42, recalls bad health (1871), 146, feeling old, 227-228, ill after treaty negotiated, 307, ill (1892), 332, (1895), 332; home in Stamford, 77; Shufeldt on Shufeldt, 124, 157, 195, App. 2; relations with women, 6-7, 12, 90, 157; meets Kate, 12, 157; relations with sons, 328-329; retirement in Japan, 322-323, 325-329; death, 333; mentioned, xi-xiv, 275. CHINA: (1866-1867), anticipates Orient, 91; on commerce of, 94-95; piracy in, 94; opium in, 94, 115; coolie trade of, 95, 115; missionaries in, 95-96, 115; Nien fei, 110; scheme to open Yangtze, 108, 110-112, 116, 123; visits Hankow, 109; Ningpo, 108; returns from, 113; views on United States power in Asia, 125; views on China's lack of power, 167; (1880-1882) hopes for naval post from Li Hung-chang, 245-246, 257, 267; admires Li, 249; influenced by Li's views of Japan, 251; views on Far Eastern nations, 252; delivers treaties, 264; received by Li Hung-chang, 262; invited by Li to visit Taku and Port Arthur, 267; prepares paper on Chinese Navy, 267-268; forecasts war between China and Japan, 267; judges China sensitive on the Korean question, 277; advocates use of force in, 280-281; on Chinese, 270, App. 2; defines United States role in China, 280-281; disillusioned with Li, 288, 289, 292; negotiates Korean treaty through agency of Li, 295; writes letter to Sargent on, 279-282, App. 1; describes Chinese empress as "immoral," 281; explains letters to Sargent, 282, 309; suffers from Sargent letter, 282; denies having written to government about use of force, 293; regrets reference to Chinese empress, 309; on power struggle in the Far East, 324; declines post as U.S. minister to China, 330, 351. COMMERCE: Shufeldt desires to stimulate American commerce, 128, 167, 168, 170, 326; heads drive for commercial expansion in Africa and Asia, 175, 185; desires government intervention to aid, 167-168; steamship lines for, 174, 182; relationship of to the navy, 167, 169; defines United States as commercial rival of Europe, 184-185; as a commercial expansionist, xi, 16, 26, 45, 145, 254-255, 258, 336; Suez Canal, influence of, 143; *see also* Pacific. CUBA: consul general in Havana (1861-1863), photograph, ii; visits Cuba, 1; execution of Estrampez, 3-4; seeks position as consul at Trinidad de Cuba, 15, 16; appointed Havana, 29; deals with *Webb* case, 31-32; relations with Joseph T. Crawford, 31-32; as prime mover in *Trent* affair, 34; desired blockade vessels off Havana, 32, 46; Shufeldt's views on Cuba, 2, 3-4, 13, 15, 16, 119, 121-122, 392, nn9-10; wrestles with *Jules et Marie* case, 40; feels humiliated with position, 69, 70; resigns, 71; praised by F. W. Seward, 71-72; toys with applying again (1868), 116; offered position, 116-117; declines, 117-118; opposes annexation of, 119; proposes annexation of, 122; wishes to use force on, 120, 122; scorns Cuban efforts, 120-122; on Grant's stance on, 124; see also *Trent* affair. EMPIRE: American, xi-xii, 169, 219, 253-256, 258; Shufeldt on, 24-25, 145, 226-227, 228, 255: Brazilian, 90; British, 217, 218, 221, 222-226, 229, 231, 255; Chinese, 233; Dutch, 255; French, 255; Portuguese, 255. ENGLAND: anti-English, 19, 40, 70, 90, 115, 321; compliments English, 50; on Suez, 152; on greed for territory, 198; on the Royal Navy (1858), 19, 23, (1879-1880), 224, 226; on consular and naval practice of, 205; British Empire, 224-226. KOREA: (1867-1868); maps, 99, 104; investigates disappearance of *General Sherman,* 97, 101, 103-108; views on

China's control over Korea, 102; sends letter to king of Korea, 103-104; interviews Korean officials, 106; desires to annex Port Hamilton, 108; desire to use force in, 107-108; claims desire to open Korea conceived in 1867, 107: (1880-1882): Shufeldt determined to open Korea, 178, 239; Japanese help with, 243; waits at Nagasaki, 246; reasons for treaty with, 248, 249-251, 251-252, 415, n31; prepares statement on, 240, 243, 272; considers force against, 243-244, 282; American interests in Korea, 249-251; changes views on in October, 250-251; treaty: Blaine's instructions, 261, 272-275; Korean factions in, 263; claims indifference over, 266-267; anticipates success, 264, 276; seeks authorization to negotiate treaty, 261, 265-266; turns to Holcombe for advice, 269, 270-271; negotiations with Li Hung-chang in Tientsin for, 263, 264-265, 266, 269, 286; on Li, 282, 284; visits Tsungli Yamen, 285; embarrassed by Li, 292; terms of, 286-287, App. 2; the dependency question in, 271, 286, 290-291, 293, 294-295; preliminary drafts, (first) 285, 286, 287; (second), 289-290; (third), 291-292; (final) 293-295; visits Korea, 238, 295, 297; issues "Imperial Decree," 297; agrees to transmit letter from king of Korea to president, 293, 294; Korea as a future battleground, 295; justifies conduct over treaty, 296, 305, 308, 310; opening of, Shufeldt on treaty, 297, 298, 309; leaves Korea, 305; Sargent letter revealed, 306; impact of Sargent letter, 306; ordered home, 307; invited to Korea, 1884, 319-320, 321; visits, 1886-1887, 325; assesses mining prospects in, 327-328; misses opportunity to invest in, 328. LECTURES: on "Western Civilization in the East," 115; "Exodus of a Race," 172; "The United States Navy in connection with the Foundation, Growth and Prosperity of the Republic of Liberia," 173-174. LIBERIA: on Liberia, 171, 173, 190, 191, 195, 198, 200; seeks to use Blyden as a roving consul, 184; arbitrator for Liberian Boundary Commission, 185-191, 195-198; map of, 187; desires to be advocate for Liberians, 186; "On the Spot" investigation of boundary, 189; prophesies Liberia will be absorbed by Sierra Leone, 190; on Liberian commercial possibilities, 190, 194, 197, 199, 206; visits Tabou district, 191-195; refuses to attend commission, 196; exasperated with commission, 195; criticizes Liberia's color line, 198-199; could weep for Liberia, 200. MERCHANT SHIPS: joins SS *Atlantic,* 9; superintends building of *Black Warrior* and *Cahawba,* 11; *Quaker City,* 16-18, 26, 28, 352; views on lost commerce, 125. MEXICAN INVASION (1861-1862): Shufeldt fears Spain in Mexico, 42, 45, 46, 47, 49, 50-51, 53-54; observes troops disembarking, 45, 47; believes collision between United States and Spain certain, 46; not originally worried by French, 44; believes Saligny in sympathy with Confederacy, 44; suggests occupation of Matamoras, 48; on Quadruple Alliance, 49, 58; delighted over English seizure of Miramón, 50; advises Seward over Mexican affairs, 43, 45, 63-64, 66; desires alliance of American republics, 51; suggests confidential agent to, 55-56; volunteers for service in Mexico, 47, 48, 56, 57; accuses French, 57; proposes to see Juárez, 59, 60; journey to Mexico City, 58-62; meets Doblado, 61; proposes eight-point convention with Mexico re: colonization, 61, 65, 69; debate with Seward over Mexican dilemmas, 55-57, 64-65; admonished by Seward and Lincoln, 67, 69. NAVAL POSITIONS: Home Squadron (1839), 6; Brazil squadron, 7; USS *Potomac* (1840), 6; USS *Marion,* 7; Pensacola (1844), 7; Naval School, Philadelphia (1845), 7; USS *United States,* West African squadron, 8; USS *Marion* (1846-1848), 8; Coast Survey, serves on revenue cutter *Morris,* 9, furloughed (1852-1854), 11, resigns (June 1854), 11; recalls first naval career, 15; rejoins navy (1863), 71; prize money in Civil War, 78; relations with Gideon Welles, 75-76; blockade in Civil War, 73-87; commands *Fort Jackson,* 71, 73; South Atlantic squadron, 73; commands USS *Conemaugh,* 73; commands USS *Proteus,* 77; roving commission under Admiral Theodorus Bailey, 78, 87; leads expedition against St. Mark's, 86; maps of, 84, 85; praised by Stribling, 86; New York naval yard, 87; appointed to flag captaincy, Asiatic squadron, 88; map of Asiatic Station, 93; commands USS *Wachusett,* 92; coordinates movements of Asiatic squadron, 112; relationship with Rear Admiral Bell, 113; offered position as inspector of ordnance, Portsmouth, 125; New York Naval Rendezvous, 117, 118, 125; Portsmouth navy yard, 125, 132; commands USS *Congress,* 147; USS *Plymouth,* 147; European squadron (1871-1873), 147-148; executive officer, New York navy yard, 148; secretary of Board of Examiners, Naval Academy, 156; writes history of New York naval yard, 156; serves on Courts of Inquiry, 156; Chief of Bureau of Equipment and Recruiting, 153, 156-157, 157-158, 158-159, 160-163; resigns from, 175, 342; acting secretary of the navy, 174; commodore of the American commercial and naval expedition to Africa and Asia, 175, 177, 182-183; would like to command Asiatic squadron, 242, 244, 245; naval attaché in Tientsin, 261; chairman of the Naval Advisory Board (Second), 311-318; superintendent, Naval Observatory, 314-315,

318–319; retires, 318–319. NAVY, U.S.: views on steam vessels, 19; recruiting for, 153, 159, 163; desires items of American manufacture, 159; apprentices in, 159, 160, 169; modifies punishments in, 160–161; desires revision of naval code, 162; on desire for efficiency and reform in the navy, 159, 160, 161, 162, 167, 169; defensive needs of a navy, 165, 165–167; using the navy to survey unexplored coasts, 179; on usefulness of wooden warships, 160, 231; on commerce destroyers, 313–314; dialogue on the navy with Senator Butler, 316–318; believes U.S. Navy could be best in world, 323–324; on the line staff controversy, 326; assesses Squadron of Evolution, 330–331, 341; reflections on the role of the navy, 18–20, 22, 157, 164, 168, 258, 325–326, 341–342; writings on navy of 1877–1878 assessed, 171. PROMOTIONS: warranted as passed midshipman, 8; Coast Survey, 9; master (1853), 11; lieutenant (1853), 11; commander, 71; commissioned as captain (1869), 125; commodore (1875), 157; appointed rear admiral (1883), 314; hopes for appointment in Chinese Navy, 245–246, 261, 267, 269; loses hope for Chinese naval position, 270, 274, 416, n7; supervises Naval Advisory Board's design of the White Squadron, 312–315; construction recommendations, 313; attacked by *Washington Post*, 316; argues for board predominancy, 315. PACIFIC: on the Pacific Ocean, 145; the importance of a canal for, 144–146, 340; the United States in the Pacific, 252, 280, 282, 304. POLITICS: on Seward, 24; on Lincoln, 79; on Benjamin Butler, 79–80, 131; on imperialism, 124; on Grant, 116, 131; on Reconstruction America, 114, 124; on Louisiana election (1876), 158; on social unrest, 167; United States, 228. RACE: on barbarians, 13, 27, 144, 172, 173, 174, 220–221, 258, 339, 344–346, 347; on blacks, 90; on civilization and, 90–91, 115, 279, 346; on Irish, 124; American blacks in Africa, 174; African blacks in Africa, 209; on race conflict, 210; on Chinese, 258, App. 1; on prejudice, 279. SLAVES AND SLAVERY: experiences with the West African squadron, 8; briefs Truman Smith on slave trade in Cuba, 20–24; informs Charles Sumner of position on slavery and race, 48; "contraband," 48, 74–75; proposes settlement for blacks in Tehuantepec, 48–49, 59, 65; plight of Negro, 74; compassion for slaves, 75; denounces slavery, 91; vice-president of American Colonization Society (1878), 174. SOUTHERN EMPIRE: associates with New Orleans expansionists, 14; extols Quitman, 15; resides New Orleans, 16–17; views failure of Louisiana–Tehuantepec Company, 24–25; discerns southern threat, 25, 26; fears Confederate designs on Mexico, 43. TEHUANTEPEC: recalls hiring by Louisiana–Tehuantepec Company, 14–15, desires to control Tehuantepec, 18, 43, 45; proposes to colonize Tehuantepec, 59–60, 65; relates to Asian commerce, 125; desires survey, 125–126; gains support, 131; surveys isthmus, 135–136, 138; discusses with Grant, 131; maps of, 127, 137; notifies Robeson of discoveries, 132–134, 140; bottles optimism on water for canal, 140; reports on condition of Oaxaca, 141; completes report on, 142–143; wants national government to construct canal, accepts notion of exclusive control of canal, 144; estimate of costs, 143–144; link to East, 144–146, 340; views on a canal, 132–135, 139, 143, 145–146, 150, 152, 259; appears before Inter-Oceanic Canal Commission, 148–152; writes *Washington Post,* and *New York Herald* on canal, 150, 259; wishes to defend with troops, 260; explores canal issue, 321, 322; links with railroads, 321–322; Panama canal, 323. *TICONDEROGA:* instructions for world cruise, 177–180; reports begun, 181; Sierra Leone informed of objectives, 187–198; visits Liberia, 191–193, 195–196, 200; visits Cape Town, 207–210; urges use of American silver at Madagascar, 212; negotiates treaties with Malagasy and Sakalavas, 211–212; repudiates authority of Hova government, 211–212; visits Johanna, 214; signs treaty with Sultan, 214; Zanzibar key to East African trade, 216; map of cruise, endsheets; opinion on United States–Zanzibar treaty of 1833, 216; fears for Zanzibar, 217; visits Muscat, 220; visits Persia, 221, 222, 223; views on Mesopotamia, 223–224; urges legation in Persia, 223; urges appearance of U.S. men-of-war, 220; visits India, 225; visits Borneo, 229; Philippines, 230; Japan, 232, 239, 242–248; Fusan, 240–241; Tientsin, 248–249; Honolulu, 250–251; San Francisco, 252. *TRENT* AFFAIR: consults authorities on international law with Wilkes, 35, 36; presents Wilkes to Don Francisco Serrano, 35; justifies Wilkes' actions, 36; reveals time of departure, 37; informs Horner at Sagua la Grande, 38; praises Wilkes for capture, 39; view of Joseph T. Crawford on, 40–41; fears British retaliation over, 40; on Mason and Slidell, 36, 42. U.S. DESTINY, 24–25, 123, 342; on American republics, 50, 55; on benefits of flag, 224, 256, 258–259; on potential power, 226–227; desires to spread influence, 343; on force, 351

Shufeldt, Robert Wilson, Jr. (first son): born (1850), 10; nearly lost at sea, 11; attends schools, Stamford, 20, Havana, 29, 30; recalls visits of Wilkes and Farragut, 35n; recalls assassination attempt on father, 41; goes to sea in USS *Proteus,* 78; almost loses life, 80; charges father with neglect in death of mother, 142; attends Cornell, 147; neglects to write, 244; sends news of reaction to Korean treaty, 309-310; on Molly, 142; assessed by Molly, 329; omitted from father's will, 332; mentioned, 77, 349

Shufeldt, Sarah Abercrombie (granddaughter): beneficiary in Shufeldt's will, 332

Shufeldt, Sarah H. [née Abercrombie] (wife): marries Shufeldt, 8-9; almost loses son overboard, 11; entertains Joseph T. Crawford's wife, 36-37; ill, 77, 114, 125, 139; accompanies Shufeldt to isthmus, 134; dies of apparent heart attack, 142; mentioned, 114, 350

Shufeldt family, 4-5

Shufelt, Henry Ball: author of *Our Folks: A History of the Shufelt Family,* 8

Shufelts of Livingston Manor, 5

Sickels, David B.: U.S. consul at Bangkok, 227

Slidell, Senator John: southern expansionist, 14; Confederate commissioner to Napoleon III, 33; discusses Shufeldt's Mexican mission, 68-69; mentioned, 25, 26, 34, 35, 36, 43, 44, 69; see also *Trent* affair

Smith, James S.: Liberian commissioner, 186; agrees to investigations of North West Boundary, 189

Smith, Senator Truman: influences Shufeldt, 20-21; aids election of Zachary Taylor, 20; discusses slave trade with Shufeldt, 20, 21; appointed judge, 21; aids Shufeldt's career, 71, 118, 129, 153; views on Tehuantepec similar to Shufeldt's, 144; mentioned, 24, 28-29, 52, 80, 116, 131, 338, 345, 349

Smyth, John H.: U.S. minister to Liberia, 180; recommends Shufeldt to intervene in Liberia, 192

Soh Kwang Pom: secretary of the Korean embassy to U.S., 237, 319-320

Soulé, Pierre: U.S. minister to Madrid, 2n, 4; opponent of Louisiana-Tehuantepec Company, 16

Spear, John C.: surgeon on Tehuantepec expedition, 132, 136; attends Sarah Shufeldt, 139

Stanley, Henry Morton: African explorer and commercial opportunist, 148, 177, 207

Starkweather, Congressman Henry Howard, 129

Staunton, Lieutenant: visits Korea with Shufeldt, 296-297

Stevens, Simon: president of Tehuantepec Railway Company, 130; offers help to Shufeldt, 132; informs Robeson of attempt to build isthmian railway, 138

Streeton, William Worrell: acting chief justice, Sierra Leone, 186; British Sierra Leone commissioner, 188-189, 196

Stribling, Rear Admiral Cornelius K.: Philadelphia navy yard (1863), 73; authorizes St. Mark's expedition for Shufeldt, 81, 82, 86

Strider, A. G.: U.S. consul in Singapore, 178, 229

Sumner, Senator Charles, 48; chairman Senate Foreign Relations Committee, 53, 118; view of allied naval expedition to Mexico, 53; political opportunism of, 122n; supports Shufeldt's isthmian scheme, 129; eulogized by Shufeldt, 131; mentioned, 52, 56, 345

Taewon'gun: regent of Korea, 236-237, 277

Thompson, John: American businessman in Cuba, 1, 2

Thompson, Richard Wigginton, secretary of the navy; poses questions on future of the navy, 164; sorry to lose Shufeldt as bureau head, 175; instructions jointly with Evarts for world cruise, 175, 177-180; informs eastern seaboard firms of commercial opportunities in Africa, 220; informed of Li Hung-chang's offer on Korea, 246; keeps tight rein on Shufeldt, 244; informs Congress of cruise, 254; reports echo Shufeldt's writings, 249, 336; leaves office, 257; praises Shufeldt, 308; mentioned, 162, 166, 175, 199, 208, 225, 230, 231, 239, 252, 303, 337, 341, 342, 349, 352

Thompson, William J.: paymaster, drafts commercial reports on cruise, 202, 254

Tilden, Samuel: unsuccessful presidential candidate (1876), 158

Tisdel, Willard: agent in Congo, 207

Ting Ju-chang, Admiral, 289, 295, 297

Toevelts of Dutchess County, 5

Torrey, Joseph W.: U.S. vice-consul at Bangkok, 178; American Trading Company, 228

Townsend, Walter D.: granted mining concession in Korea, 327, 328

Trescott, William H.: former U.S. commissioner in China, 309; working for Shufeldt, 309

Tsiang, Tingfu: on relationship of China to Korea, 234-235

Tsu Hsi: Chinese empress, 268-269; described by Shufeldt, 281

Tyler, Alice Felt: on Blaine's Korean policy, 274

Tyson, George: Shanghai Steam Navigation Company, 109-110

Tzu An: death of disrupts Shufeldt's plans for treaty, 268

Underwood, Horace, 274n

Upshur, Abel P.: statement on U.S. interest in Liberia, 191, 199

Ü Tsing: Chinese consul in Nagasaki, 239, 240; translates Shufeldt's letter to king of Korea, 244; delivers Li's letters and flatters Shufeldt, 245, 246

Van Volkenburgh and Leavitt: New York traders in Africa, 194, 222

Von Brandt: German minister to China, 296, 308

Vreeland, Charles E.: prepares survey reports in Liberia, 185, 193, 254

Wade, Sir Thomas: British minister in Peking, 264, 308, App. 1
Walker, John G.: desires explanation of Sargent letter, 307; Squadron of Evolution, 311, 311n, 330
Waters, Richard P.: establishes U.S. consulate in Zanzibar, 217
Watkins, Lieutenant Mayo C.: desired survey of St. Paul River, 194
Watson, Rebecca, recalls loan from Shufeldt, 147
Webb, James Watson, U.S. minister to Brazil, 90; discusses black empire with Shufeldt, 90, 344
Welles, Gideon: secretary of the navy, 28; commends Shufeldt's suggestions, 32; opinion of Shufeldt, 75, 76–77; Bell requests reinforcements for Asiatic squadron, 98
West, Captain James, of SS *Atlantic*, 9, 10
Wilkes, Captain Charles: USS *San Jacinto*, 33; claims re: *Trent*, 33; waits at Sagua for Shufeldt's information, 33–34; three "disappointments," 34; lionized in North, 38–39; explorer, 334; mentioned, 37, 348, 351
Williams, Colonel John J.: engineer for Tehuantepec Railway Company, 130, 132, 138
Williams, James I.: representative of American commercial houses in East Africa, 220; consular applicant, Aden, 219
Wilson, Dr. Benjamin F., 214
Wilson, Commander Steven Bayard, U.S. Navy (Shufeldt's uncle), 6, 7

Windom, Senator William: reports on Korean treaty in senate, 298
Wolf, John N.: U.S. vice-consul at Tehuantepec, 136
Wool, General John: organizes Union Defense Committee, 28
Wooyeno Kagenori: Japanese vice-minister for foreign affairs, 238
Worrell, John Wallace: counsel to Liberian commissioners, 186; new commissioner, 196
Wriston, Henry M., 298
Wyman, Robert H.: suspicious of Sargent, 308; urges Shufeldt to hold on to naval position, 154

Yaku-Gaku-Liu-Ko-Shaku: Korean officer at Fusan, 240
Yancey, William L.: Confederate envoy to Europe, 30
Yi Man-son, 236
Yosimoto Hanabusa: Japanese minister to Korea, 247, 297
Young, John Russell: U.S. minister to China, 300; view of Korea as independent, 301; mentioned, 230, 351; gauges relationship of Korea to China, 300
Youngs, Edward A.: U.S. vice-consul at Manila, 230
Yuan shi kai, 324, 325
Yu Yun Chung: signs commercial treaty, 302

Zachary, J. W.: suspected Confederate agent, Havana, 40
Ziegler, John Q. A.: chief engineer of USS *Miantonomoh* used as agent by Shufeldt, 130

Subject Index

Accolades: for Shufeldt from Angell, James B., 314; Belt, William J., 7–8; Chandler, William E., 319; Clitz, Admiral John B., 308; Corwin, Thomas B., 62; Farquhar, Norman, 308; Frelinghuysen, Frederick T., 277; Griffis, William E., 310; Holcombe, Chester, 308; Liberian Government, 198; Li Hung-chang, 246, 260; Seward, Frederick W., 71–72; Seward, William H., 68; Thompson, Richard Wigginton, 175, 308; Welles, Gideon, 32, 75
Aden, 209, 219, 220, 255
Africa: views of nineteenth-century Americans on, 176; mentioned, 148, 254, 338, 342, 346, 347. *See* Shufeldt, Robert Wilson: Africa
Africanization, of Cuba, 2, 24, 27, 338. *See* Shufeldt, Robert Wilson: Cuba
Alabama claims, 122, 122n
Alaska, 249, 337
Aleutian islands, 336, 337
American China and Japan Trading Company, 326
American Colonization Society: flourishes after Civil War, 171–174; interest in Africa, 344, 346

American flag, 224, 256, 258–259, 343
Ammen Committee: on needs of the navy, 164–168
Amoy, 92, 95, 96
Annexation: in Africa, 196; of Cuba, 2–3, 119, 122; "Annexation of Cuba, The," Shufeldt's manuscript, 118, 119–120; on "Orient," 228; mentioned, 338, 342
Antananarivo: capital of Madagascar, 211–212
Asiatic squadron, (1865–1868), 88, 93, 91–96, 108–109, 112–113; (1881–1882), 274, 283; Shufeldt's views on (1868), 112; Shufeldt's desire to command (1879–1880), 225, 239, 245; Shufeldt loses command of, 246, 308, 309, 328. *See also* Squadrons, and Shufeldt, Robert Wilson: Naval Positions; Asiatic squadron
Aub and Hackenburg: machine silk manufacturers, 222

Barbarians: Shufeldt's views on, 173, 174, 220–221, 339, 344, 346, 347, 352. *See* Shufeldt, Robert Wilson: Race
Basra, 221, 222
Battery Wagner attack, 75

Berlin Conference on the Congo: United States interest in, 207; international conference, 311
Blacks: Shufeldt's views on recaptured Negroes, 23; views on, 50, 119, 124, 172, 344-346. *See* Shufeldt, Robert Wilson: Race; Slaves and Slavery
Black Warrior affair, 2n
Blanche affair, 69-70
Blockade, Charleston, 73
Board of Rites, Chinese, 235, 284
Bombay, 225, 227, 337
Borneo (Brunei): Shufeldt to visit, 178; visits, 228, 229, 255; mentioned, 334, 337
Brainerd and Armstrong, silk manufacturers, 222
Brazil, 6, 344
Brazil squadron: Shufeldt serves in, 6-7
British: in Indian Ocean, 217-228; in Asia, 229, 231-232, 233; Shufeldt analyzes "Paramountcy," 255-256. *See* Shufeldt, Robert Wilson: England
British government: requests American arbitrator for Liberian Boundary Question, 180
Buchanan administration: loan policy toward Mexico, 42
Bureau of Commerce: advocated by Shufeldt, 258
Bureau of Construction and Repair, 314, 315
Bureau of Equipment and Recruiting, 153, 154 (described), 156-163, 174, 342. *See* Shufeldt, Robert Wilson: Naval Positions
Bureau of Steam Engineering, 314, 315
Bureau of Yards and Docks, 315
Burma, 178, 227, 233

Canal: at Tehuantepec, 35; possible dimensions of, 142; judged impracticable, 396-397, n16; canal, transisthmian, 259, 336, 338-339. *See* Shufeldt, Robert Wilson: Tehuantepec and Tehuantepec, Isthmus of
Canton, 92, 269
Cape Palmas, Liberia, 193, 205; threat of war at, 171
Cape Town, 200, 208-210, 254; as last link with West, 90-91
Cat Island Battery, South Island, Winyah Bay, 73
Chang Chow, 95, 96
Chefoo, 92, 96, 100, 102, 277, 283, 295, 296
Chemulp'o, 320, 324
China: to acquire a new civilization, 145; analyzed by Shufeldt, App. 1; customs of, App. 1; defines commercial relations with Korea, 302; four arsenals of, App. 1; relationship to Korea, 234; Shufeldt on, 281; as source of "true liberty," 125; war with Russia feared, App. 1; weaknesses of, 301; mentioned, 92, 107, 282, 324, 327, 328, 336, 338, 339, 342, 347.
China Overland Trade Report: offers rules of visit to Korea, 107
Chinese: army, App. 1; Board of Rites, 235, 284; coolie trade, 115; content of Korean treaty, 292; empire, 233; empress, xiii, 281, App. 1; exclusion bills, 281; immigration, subject of virulent American political campaign (1882), 257, App. 1; language in Korean treaty, 296; Navy, 245, 260, App. 1; naval vessels go to Korea, 289; opium trade, 115; Shufeldt's views on, 119, 124, App. 1; students in United States, App. 1; views of Western language, 301; views of foreigners, App. 1; view of Treaty of Kanghwa, 236
Chivela, 135, 136, 138, 139
Chosen: Korean name adopted by United States, for treaty, 272
Choson (Inch'on), port, 101, 102
Christianity: in Africa, 173, 174, 344; in China, 96, 115, 344
Chusan Islands, off Chekiang Province, 96, 112
Civilization: 90-91; in Africa, 202; and barbarism, 183; Shufeldt's views on, 115. *See* Shufeldt, Robert Wilson: Race
Coachapa River, 128, 138
Coatzacoalcos River, Mexico, 14, 16, 133
Collins Steamship Company, 9-10, 336, 342
Colonization schemes, 48-49, 56, 65; outlined by Shufeldt, 61; Republicans on, 345-346, 348
Commerce: American need to aggrandize, 169; Chinese in Yangtze, 111, 337-338; emphasized, 278. *See* Shufeldt, Robert Wilson: Commerce
Commerce destroyers, 168
Commercial expansion, xi, xii; New Orleans, 14; and American destiny, 340; policy of in East, 301-302. *See* Shufeldt, Robert Wilson: Commerce
Comoro Islands, 213, 215, 255
Confucian culture, 234-235
Congo, 200, 205, 255, 338, 347
Congress, Mexican: passes canal concession (1870), 135
Congress, United States: appropriates funds for canal survey, 129, 131; cuts number of seamen in navy, 160; debates new navy (1882), 315-318; discusses naval priorities in 1870s, 163; Shufeldt warns of naval dangers, 161
Consular system for Africa: Shufeldt urges, 202, 204-207
Continentalism: provides new frontier on the Pacific, 145; who controls, 27
Contrabands: status of escaped slaves, 74. *See* Shufeldt, Robert Wilson: Race; Slaves and Slavery
Coolie trade, 95, 115
Corea: *see* Korea
Cuba: diplomatic significance of, 2, 3-4; future with United States, 1, 24; mentioned with canal, 133; problems discussed, 120; revolution in (1868), 117, 351; Shufeldt analyzes for press, 118-122; slave trade, 20-24, 27. *See* Shufeldt, Robert Wilson: Cuba
Cuban Creoles, 117-118, 346

Subject Index 463

Cuban junta, 117, 120–121
Cuban slave trade, 23, 119, 120, 346; Shufeldt's views on, 20–24. *See also* Shufeldt, Robert Wilson: Cuba
Cunard Steamship Company, 9

Darien (Panama): proposed canal site, 126, 128, 129, 150, 152
Debate on National Policy: Seward and Shufeldt, 63–69
Dependency clause: key to Korean treaty, 288, 290; letter to President Arthur as substitute for, 291
Desertions in navy (1876–1878), 162
Diplomatic reactions: to United States–Korean treaty, 300–302
Dutch, possession of Congo, 201–202, 255, 347, 350
Dutchess County, New York: agricultural decline in (1830s), 6; censuses of, 5; population explosion in (1750s), 5

El Dorado affair, 1, 2, 3, 13
Émeute, Korean (1882), 237; (1884), 320
Empire: American, 219, 256; Shufeldt on, 24–25, 145, 226–227, 228, 255; Brazilian, Shufeldt on, 90; British, Shufeldt on the nature of, 217, 218, 221, 224, 229, 231, 255; in Persian Gulf, 222–223; in India, 225–226; Shufeldt compares with Roman, 225–226; British, naval strength of, 221; Chinese, 233; Dutch, Shufeldt attacks, 255; French, Shufeldt fears, 255; Portuguese, Shufeldt sneers at, 255
Empire of the Seas, xi–xii, 169, 253–256, 258
England, 209, 296, 321, 337. *See* Shufeldt, Robert Wilson: England
European squadron, 146–148; social effects of, recalled (1890), 146–147
"Exodus of a Race," lecture scheduled, 172

Fernando Po (Bioko): Spanish colony, 194, 200–201, 205, 255; Shufeldt assesses as key to palm oil trade, 201
Folly Island: home of Battery Wagner, 75
France: government sends expeditions, to Mexico, 47; to Korea, 97; naval officers in employ of Li Hung-chang, 268, App. 1; mentioned, 233, 296, 337, 348, 352
Freetown, Sierra Leone, 182
Fusan (Pusan), Korean port: center for Japanese-Korean trade, 247; Shufeldt visits, 240–241; mentioned, 238, 239, 242, 272, 295
"Future of Cuba, The," Shufeldt manuscript, 118, 119–120

Gabon, 200, 205, 255
Gallinas chiefs: treaties with Liberia cause confusion, 185–186, 195
General Sherman affair: Rear Admiral Bell hears fate of, 98; crew murdered, 100; schooner described, 96; Shufeldt investigates the disappearance of, 101–105, 107; mentioned, 234, 237, 240

Grenville, Lord: instructions (1870) re: Sugury district dictate terms of Liberian Boundary Question, 189
"Grounds for Capture," Wilkes' justification for seizing the *Trent,* 36
Gulf of Mexico, 53; as American lake, 143, 259, 397, n17

Hall, Sir James islands, off Korean west coast, 103
Havana, 1, 2, 4, 11, 16, 17, 23, 24, 28–72, 116, 118, 121, 122, 142. *See* Shufeldt, Robert Wilson: Cuba
Hawaiian Islands, 334, 336, 340, 342; Honolulu, 336; *see* Sandwich Islands
Hermit Kingdom: *see* Korea
Hong Kong, 92, 94, 112, 113, 232, 329; smuggling market, 94
Hova government, Madagascar, 212, 213
Howland and Aspinwall, New York shipping company, 28
Hunan soldiers: seize American missionary chapel, 95; Shufeldt investigates case of, 95–96

I'chang, 110, 111, 112
Île Boisée (Kanghwa Island), French land expedition at, 97
Imperial Board of Directors (Korean), address Shufeldt, 107
Imperialism: British, Shufeldt analyzes craze for, 210, 255; Shufeldt asserts to be panacea for ills of United States, 114
Imperialist, The, 124
Imperial School of the 1890s, 353. *See* Shufeldt, Robert Wilson: Empire
"Independence of Cuba," Shufeldt manuscript, 118, 119–120
India, 219, 220, 226, 255. *See also* Bombay
Inter-Oceanic Canal Commission (1872–1876): established (1872), 148; accepts Nicaraguan route, 151, 171, 349

Japan: aids Shufeldt, 239–241; annexes Liu Ch'iu Islands, 236; defeat of China (1894), 237; early relations with Korea, 247; government reactions to United States–Korean treaty, 301–302; Hideyoshi invasion of Korea (1592–1598), 247; Japanese-Korean treaty, 235–236, 237, 239; Shufeldt wants to survey, 123, 337; to acquire a new civilization, 145; visits, 232, 233; Shufeldt suspects, 249–251; Shufeldt resides in, 325–329; mentioned, 282, 296, 301, 324, 325, 327, 328, 336, 339
Jecker debt: complicates French-Mexican relations, 50
Johanna (Anjouan), Comoro Islands, 213–214, 337, 338; town of, 213
Juárez government, Mexico, 54, 56
Jules et Marie case, 40, 69

Kanghwa Island, 97, 101
King of Korea: Shufeldt's letter to, 106–107; offers position to Shufeldt, 319–320; entertains Shufeldt as his guest, 324–325

Kiukiang, 109, 110, 111
Korea: attitudes toward foreigners, 97-98; early contacts with, 97; special embassy to U.S., 319; family division in, 236-237; government sends confidential envoy, 283; Hideyoshi invasions of (1592-1598), 247; ignorance of, in Western governments, 97; international power struggle over, 302; Japan's challenge to China's control of, 236; Japanese treaty (1876) with, known to Evarts, 179; king of, memorializes China's Board of Rites, 235; maps of, 99, 104; messengers executed (1868), 106; opening of, as part of Shufeldt's life work, xii, 4, 276-304; political factions opposed to opening, 263, 276; relationship to China, 97, 98, 102, 234-238, 243, 300; Shufeldt to visit, 178; Shufeldt, hopes to open like an oyster, 230; finds gates closed, 241; treaty with United States, 301, 302; mentioned, xii, 100, 232, 236, 242, 255, 260, 276, 319-320, 324-325, 327, 335-336, 338, 342, 343, 351, 352. *See* Shufeldt, Robert Wilson: Korea

Labuan Island (Borneo), 229
Laws, abolishing grog and floggings, in United States Navy, 161
Letters, sent by king of Korea: to Shufeldt, 107; to Shufeldt for Garfield (1882), 299
Liberia: established (1821), 176; as area for colonization of American blacks, 171; commercial importance of, defined by Shufeldt, 190; object of resettlement, 23; prosperity of the republic, 173; treaty relations with the United States, 177-178; mentioned, 177, 180, 194, 199, 200, 254, 255, 335, 336, 338, 342, 344, 348. *See* Shufeldt, Robert Wilson: Liberia
Liberian Boundary Commission: commissioners, 183; established (1879), 185-191, 195-198; first session, 185-191; Grenville instructions, 188-189; second session, 195-198; Shufeldt as arbitrator, 180, 188, 189, 195, 198
Liu Ch'iu (Ryukyu) Islands, 232, 233, 302, 334
Louisiana: disputed election in (1876), 157-158
Louisiana-Tehuantepec Company: crashes, 17-18; employs Shufeldt, 14-15; obtains new charter, 16; Shufeldt's doubts about, 24; reflections on failure, 145; mentioned, 27, 43, 44, 65, 128, 336, 342
Low-Rodgers expedition: invades Korea (1871), 108, 179; mentioned, 234, 235, 240, 243, 252, 253
Lubra: looted by pirates, 94, 95, 115

Macao, 92, 95
Madagascar: Shufeldt to visit, 178; visits, 211-213; mentioned, 254, 255, 335-336, 337, 338
Malcolm, A. and T. J., American merchant house in Persia, 223

Manila, 230, 232
Merchant marine: as joint apostle with navy, 170
Mesopotamia, 221, 223, 343
Mexico: allied expedition against, 43, 45-46, 48, 49-50; Garden of Eden to Shufeldt, 51; government suspends payment on foreign debt, 42-43; government promulgates grant for Louisiana-Tehuantepec Company, 16; railroads in, 259; sovereignty in jeopardy, 61; mentioned, 25, 336, 339, 340, 342, 345, 348, 352. *See also* Tehuantepec and Shufeldt, Robert Wilson: Tehuantepec
Min family and faction, 237, 320
Minatitlan, 14, 139, 141
Missionaries, Shufeldt's views on, 96, 173, 344
Mississippi River, 143, 339-340
Monitors, 121, 165, 166
Monroe Doctrine, 4, 47
Monrovia, 191, 255
Muscat: divided from Zanzibar, 216; 1833 treaty revision desired, 178; Shufeldt to visit, 177; trade relations with United States, 176, 220; mentioned, 220, 254, 255, 335, 347

Nagasaki, 92, 232, 239, 305, 307, 328
Nan Hoo Islands, off southern coast of Korea, 100, 108
National Safe Deposit Savings and Trust Company, 332
Natural Bridge, Florida: engagement at, 83
Naval Advisory Board (First), 312
Naval Advisory Board (Second): discusses new vessels, 312-313; members of, 312; reports, 313-314; superintends building of White Squadron (1882), xiii, 312-315, 341
Naval apprenticeship scheme, 159-160, 163, 352
Naval debate (1883), 316-318
Naval Observatory: Shufeldt at, 314, 315
Navy, United States: bureaus listed, 156; as joint apostle with merchant marine, 170; need for reform in, 155; personnel in, 159; relationship to Liberia, 173; shortage of vessels in, 131; stagnating, 154. *See* Shufeldt, Robert Wilson: Naval
Negro slavery: *see* Shufeldt, Robert Wilson: Race; Slaves and Slavery
New Canaan: Shufeldt acquires large farm in, 114, 117
New Orleans, expansionist sentiment in (1850s), 1-2; Shufeldt acquires residence in (1854), 11; Shufeldt commands naval forces in, 157-158
New York and Alabama Steamship Company, 1, 11
New York Evening Post: on Shufeldt's experiences with SS *Atlantic*, 10; editorial policy against government interference with merchant shipping, 10
New York Herald: promotes African trade,

Subject Index 465

182, 200; on Shufeldt, 18; publishes letter by Shufeldt, 18–20; mentioned, 148, 315
New York Times: on Shufeldt's letter to Sargent, 307, 308, 309
Nicaragua: canal issue, 321; included in Shufeldt's (1871) survey, 146; government lobby, 151; mentioned, 340
Nien fei: Chinese banditti, 109, 110
Niger Valley, 184, 255, 338
North China Daily News: prints Sargent letter, 296

Orizaba, Convention of: leads to withdrawal of British and Spanish from Mexico, 58
Ostend Manifesto: statement of intent to seize Cuba, 2

Pacific Ocean: Rear Admiral Bell considers United States masters of, 100; center for United States commercial activity, 249; Shufeldt's views on America's role in, 115–116, 125–126, 128, 152, 252, 253, 321–322, 336; Shufeldt links canal to, 133; mentioned, 337, 339, 352
Pacific squadron, 11
Palm oil rivers of West Africa, 200–201; map of, 203
Panama: proposed canal site, *see* Darien; Shufeldt visits, 321–322, 323–324
Pao-ting-fu, 283, 284, 286
Persia: Shufeldt anticipates as battleground between England and Russia, 223; United States Legation established in (1883), 223; mentioned, 253, 337
Persian Gulf, 221–222, 224, 254, 255, 338
Philadelphia Press: Shufeldt's articles on Cuba in, 117–118
Philippines, 230, 255, 337
"Ping Yang" (Taedong) River, Korean west coast: confused by Shufeldt, 100, 103
Pirates, Chinese: 92, 94
Port Hamilton: anchorage on largest of Nan Hoo Islands, 98, 100, 106, 107; Shufeldt desires to annex, 100, 255; mentioned, 244, 255, 338, 342, 351
Power: Shufeldt's views on, 352
Prejudice, 345–348. *See* Shufeldt, Robert Wilson: Race
Punishments in navy: diminish (1876–1878), 162
P'yongan Province, 101, 103, 326

Race prejudice: in California, 258; Shufeldt's views on, 119, 124, 209–210; discussed, 344–348
Railroads, South African, 209, 340
Receiving ships, 156n, 159, 161
Reformers: in navy (1870s), 155
Relation of the Navy to the Commerce of the United States, The, published, 167; quoted in *West African Reporter,* 183; mentioned, 337, 341
Rio de Janeiro, 6, 350
Role of the navy, 163
Royal Navy: helps annex disputed land from Liberians, 198; strength of in Persian Gulf, 19, 23, 221, 224, 226, 341
Russia: pressure on Korea, 97; war with China threatening, App. 1; mentioned, 221, 224, 233, 263, 271, 296, 324, 328
Ryukyu Islands: *see* Liu Ch'iu Islands

St. Mark's, Florida: expedition against, led by Shufeldt, 82–87; encounters difficulties in, 82–83, 86–87; map of army action at, 85; map of naval action at, 84; plans for attack on, 82, last port of Confederacy open, 81–82; results of attack on, 86–87
St. Paul River, 193, 338
Sakalava tribe, 211, 212, 213
Samoa, 249, 336
San Domingo: Grant and, 144, 338, 344
Sandwich Islands, 249, 321
San Francisco, 252, 321, 322
San Francisco Bulletin: publishes Shufeldt's "open letter," 279, 330
San Francisco Chronicle: interviews Shufeldt, 322–323
Sargent letter, 279–280, 281–282; text, App. 1
Secretaries of the Navy: *See* Chandler, William E.; Dobbin, James C.; Hunt, William H.; Preston, William B.; Robeson, George M.; Thompson, Richard W.; Welles, Gideon
Secretaries of State: *See* Blaine, James G.; Evarts, William M.; Fish, Hamilton; Frelinghuysen, Frederick T.; Marcy, William L.; Seward, William H.
Senate Committee on Naval Affairs, 71
Senate, United States: nominates General Winfield Scott as minister to Mexico, 52; ratifies postal convention with Mexico, 53
Seoul: capital of Korea, 97, 101, 236, 277
Shanghai, 92, 100, 111, 117, 261, 262, 269, 295, 308
Shanghai Steam Navigation Company: owns Yangtze River steamers, 109, 110–111
Shipping companies: Collins Steamship Company, 9–10, 336, 342; Cunard Steamship Company, 9; Howland and Aspinwall, 28; Louisiana–Tehuantepec Company, 14, 16, 17–18, 24, 27, 43, 44, 65, 128, 145, 336, 342; New York and Alabama Steamship Company, 1, 11; Pacific Mail Ship Company, 154; Shanghai Steam Navigation Company, 109, 110–111; United States Steamship Company, 11
Ships: SAILING, *Ann Louisa,* schooner, 79; *Estelle,* brig, destroyed by CSS *Florida,* 70; *General Sherman,* 96, 98, 100–102, 105, 107, 108, 234; *Grapeshot,* 120; *Guiding Star,* schooner, 79; *Lubra,* 94, 95, 115; *Surprise,* schooner, 98, 101, 103; *Kingfisher,* schooner, 18
Ships: STEAMSHIPS, *Atlantic,* Collins Line, 9, 10, 352; *Arctic,* Collins Line, 9; *Avon,* English, bound for Veracruz, 49; *Baltic,* Collins Line, 9; *Bienville,* 29; *Black*

Warrior, 2, 2n, Shufeldt superintends building of, 11; *Blanche*, 69-70; *Cahawba*, Shufeldt superintends building of, 11; *City of Peking*, and *City of Tokio*, Pacific Mail Ship Company, 154; *El Dorado*, 1-3, 13; *Emperor*, 101; *Francis*, vessel lost by USS *Proteus*, 79; *Georgia*, 11; *Henry Burden*, for Cuban junta, 120; *Hornet*, Shufeldt declines offer of command by Cuban junta, 121; *Jules et Marie*, 40, 69; *Jupiter*, 78; *Karnak*, 28; *Let Her Be*, lost by USS *Proteus*, 78; *Pacific*, 9; *Parsee*, 94, 115; *Perritt*, Cuban junta, 120; *Quaker City*, switched to New Orleans-Coatzacoalcos run, operated by Shufeldt, 16, 17, 18, 26, 28, 352, gunrunning, 121; *Ruby*, 81; *San Blas*, 322; *Santa Martha*, 79; *Spark*, 95, 115; *State of Georgia*, tows *Quaker City*, 18; *Suchil*, 16; *Theodora*, carries Mason and Slidell to Nassau, 33-34; *Trent*, Royal Mail steamer intercepted by USS *San Jacinto*, 33-35, 37-38, 39, 40-42, 71; *Union*, 80; *Virginius*, 4, 4n, 148; *W. H. Webb*, 31, 32, 41

Ships: WAR VESSELS, CONFEDERATE, CSS *Alabama*, 122n, 168; CSS *Florida*, 70-71, 78; CSS *Spray*, 83; Foreign BRITISH; *Malabar*, 227; HMS *Narcissus*, Shufeldt attends ball on, 90, 350; HMS *Pelonis*, 100; FRENCH; HIMS *Prinoquet*, 100; SPANISH; *Concepcion*, 45; *Sealtad*, 45; UNITED STATES, USS *Adams*, 165;USS *Ajax*, 166; USS *Alaska*, 165; USS *Aristook*, 351; USS *Ashuelot*, 95, 123, 351; USS *Atlanta*, 313; USS *Bainbridge*, 8; USS *Bermuda*, Shufeldt takes passage in, 73; USS *Boston*, 313; USS *Britannia*, 82, 83; USS *Brooklyn*, 88; USS *Canonicus*, 157; USS *Colorado*, 153; USS *Columbus*, compared with USS *Ticonderoga*, 247-248, 251; USS *Chicago*, 313, 318; USS *Conemaugh*, 73, 73n, 74, 75, 344; USS *Congress*, Shufeldt switches command to, in Europe, 147; USS *Dolphin*, 313, 314, 326; USS *Enterprize*, 7; USS *Essex*, 334; USS *Fort Henry*, 82, 83, 86; USS *Fort Jackson*, 71, 73; USS *Hartford*, flagship of Asiatic squadron, 88, 90, 91, 92, 95, 112, 113, 349, 350, 351; USS *Hendrick Hudson*, 82; USS *Hibiscus*, 82, 83; USS *Honduras*, 82, 83; USS *Isonomia*, 82; USS *Iuka*, 82; USS *Kaatskill*, Shufeldt ordered to (1863), 75, 341; USS *Kansas*, assigned to isthmian survey, 132, 136, 142; USS *Madrilla*, 351; USS *Mahaska*, 82, 83; USS *Magnolia*, 82; USS *Marion*, Brazil squadron, 7, 8, 165, 180, 352; USS *Massachusetts*, 11; USS *Matthew Vassar*, 82; USS *Mayflower*, assigned to isthmian survey, 132, 136, 142; USS *Miantonomoh*, 118, 120, 122, 125, 130, 351; USS *Minnesota*, 159; USS *Monadnock*, 341; USS *Monocacy*, joins Asiatic squadron, 95, 112, 123, 351; USS *Montgomery*, 69; USS *Morris*, 9; USS *Ohio*, 8; USS *O. H. Lee*, 82; USS *Plymouth*, Shufeldt switched to command, 147, returns home in, 173, mentioned, 189; USS *Potomac*, Atlantic squadron, 6, 8; USS *Powhatan*, 33, 37; USS *Proteus*, described, 77, Shufeldt transferred to, 77, cruise off Cardenas, 78, boards vessels, 78, 79, 80, 81, mentioned, 82, 87, 88, 341; USS *Puritan*, 341; USS *Richmond*, 161; USS *Sabine*, 159; USS *San Jacinto*, vessel commanded by Captain Charles Wilkes, 33, 36, 37, 38, 40; USS *Santiago de Cuba*, 39; USS *Shenandoah*, joins Asiatic squadron, 95, 106-107, 112; USS *Spirea*, 82, 83; USS *Stars and Stripes*, 82, 83; USS *Supply*, 159; USS *Susquehanna*, 217; USS *Swatara*, 161, 278, 289, 295, 296, 297; USS *Ticonderoga*, xi, described, 180; USS *Tioga*, 78; USS *Two Sisters*, 82; USS *Trenton*, 165, 168, 320, 341; USS *Union*, 80; USS *United States*, 6, West African squadron, 8; USS *Wabash*, Shufeldt appointed to (1870), 146; USS *Wachusett*, used against pirates, 91, 92, escorts *Parsee*, 94-95, cruises Macao, Hong Kong, 95-96, visits Amoy and Chang Chow, 95-96, Chefoo and Shanghai, 100, 101, off coast of Korea, 103, 105, 106, 108, visits Hankow, 109, 110, 112, 113, crack in main shaft, 111, leaves Asiatic squadron, 112, mentioned, 100, 101, 115, 298, 338, 351; USS *Washington*, 8; USS *Weehawken*, 75; USS *Worcester*, flagship at Key West, 155; USS *Wyoming*, 92, 112, 351; USS *Yorktown*, 330

Siam, 230-231, 232, 334
Sierra Leone, 180, 205, 254, 338
Singapore, 231, 329
Slaves: British action in regard to, 217-218; Cuban, 346; slave trade company (Havana), 21; slave trade, expenses of, 22; profits from, 22; numbers in, 379, n7; incident with old slave, Winyah Bay, 74; crew's reaction to slave, 74; owned by Jurie Toevelt and Jurie Adam Toevelt, 5; Shufeldt's experience with (1846), 8; *see* Shufeldt, Robert Wilson: Slaves and Slavery
Smithsonian Institution, 136, 322
Social Darwinism: Shufeldt on, 172, 346
Soledad Convention, 53, 54
South Africa, 176, 340. *See* Cape Town
Spain, 121, 122, 348, 352
Spanish colonies in the East, 228, 230
Spanish naval expedition to Mexico, 45-46, 49, 50
Spanish policy in Cuba, 22
Spiritualism: Shufeldt's views on, 12
Squadrons: Asiatic, (1865-1868), 88, 93, 91-97, 108-109, 112-113, 123; (1879) Shufeldt desires to command, 225, 239-240, 245-246; to allocate vessel for Korea, 274-275, 283; Shufeldt loses chance for, 308, 309; Mason serves with, 328; power of, 350-351; Brazil, 6-7; European, 146-148; of Evolution, 330, 341; Home, 6; Pacific, 11; South Atlantic, 73, 73n, 344; West African, 8-9, 176; White, the, xiii, 311, 316, 341

Stamford: Shufeldt home in, 1851, 11; purchases home and land in, 20, 343
Steam power, 340–341
Steamship lines: need to subsidize, 170, 340; *see* Ships, steamships
Suez Canal, 126, 143, 152, 259, 321, 340; impact on British East African trade, 219

Tabou, 192, 205; district visited by Shufeldt, 191–193
TaeDong Man (bay), west coast of Korea, 103
Taedong River, 98, 101, 103
Taewon'gun: regent of Korea, 97, 237
Taiping Rebellion, 110
"Tai Tong" (Taedong) River, 97
Takeo, 325, 326
Tehuantepec, Isthmus of, 339; advantages to the United States, 133; canal discussed, 145–146; 43, 139, 174, 259, 338, 340, 342, 348, 350; House of Representatives resolution on, 126; map of, 127, 137; object of pre-Civil War southern expansionist hopes, 14; proposed canal site, 126, 127; relation to Asia, 125; rejected as viable route by Inter-Oceanic Canal Commission (1876), 135; Shufeldt proposes to open to black colonists, 48, 56, 59; proposes survey of, 125–134; survey by Shufeldt, 135–141; fades into Shufeldt's background, 171; as a transit route, map of, 127; transit rights as proposed guarantee of United States loan, 42; mentioned, 345, 349. *See* Shufeldt, Robert Wilson: Tehuantepec; Mexico
Tehuantepec Railway Company (1850s), 128; formed by La Sère, incorporated in Vermont (1870s), 126; commences work on isthmian railroad, 130, 132, 138; fails to gain canal concession, 129–130
Ticonderoga, USS, cruise of: history of cruise, 177, 181; covered in press, 182; Sierra Leone, 182–183, 189; Monrovia, 191, 192, 193, 195, 196, 200; Fernando Po, and Congo, 201, 204; Cape Town, 206, 208, 210; Tullear Bay, Madagascar, and Johanna, 211, 212, 213, 214, 215; Zanzibar, 218, 219; Aden, 220, 221; Persia, 221, 223; India, 225, 227; Singapore, Borneo, and the Spanish colonies in the East, 228, 229, 230, 232; Nagasaki, 233, 238, 242, 244, 247; Fusan, 240; Tientsin, 248, 249, 251; San Francisco, 252, 260; cruise results, 253–256, 258, 263, 274, 298, mentioned, 177, 257, 303, 310, 331, 337. *See also* Shufeldt, Robert Wilson: *Ticonderoga*
Tientsin, 96, 269, 277, 292, 296
Trading companies: Afrikaansche Handelsverenniging Company (Dutch), 201–202; African Trade Society, 207; American China and Japan Trading Company, 326; American Trading Company, 178, 228, 326; American Trading Company of New York and Yokohama, 326; Bateman and Allen: Boston and Portland African Traders, 182; Bertram, John and Company: Salem traders in Aden and Zanzibar, 213, 215, 219; Dent, Overbeck and Company, Borneo, 228, 229, 253; Emmerton and Company, 217; Hauge, T. D. and Company, 222; Hines, Arnold and Company, New York and Zanzibar, 217, 219; Hondlette and Company, Mauritius, 214; Jardine, Matheson and Company, 101; Meadows and Company, 96, 100; O'swald and Company (German), Zanzibar, 217; Ropes, Emmerton and Company, Salem, Zanzibar, 217; Ropes, George and Company, Boston and Zanzibar, 217; Russell and Company, China, 111; Yates and Porterfield, New York and Freetown, 185
Treaties: Adams-Onís, 2; Austrian-Korean, 298; Brazilian-Chinese, 293; Chinese-Korean, 288; Clayton-Bulwer, 144; Frelinghuysen-Zavala, 321; French-Korean, 298; German-Chinese, 293; German-Korean, 298; Great Britain-Korean, 298; Italian-Korean, 298; of Kanghwa (Japanese-Korean, 1876), 235–236, 237; of Livadia (China-Russia), 233; McLane-Ocampo, 42; Russian-Korean, 298; United States–Borneo (1850), 228–229; United States–China, immigration and commercial, 261; United States–Japanese, basis for United States–Korean treaty, 273; United States–Johanna (1879), dies in Senate, 215; United States–Korean (May 1882), xi, 272, 283, first draft, 285, 288, objections to drafts presented, 288, second draft, 290–291, third draft, 293, modifications of third draft, 293, final draft, 294–295, commercial provisions of, 287, formal signing 296, 297, importance of, 299, 300–302, 335–336, not primarily for "good offices," 303, from Shufeldt's intent, 303; text of, App. 2; United States–Liberian (1862), discussed, 177–178, 192; United States–Madagascar commercial (of 1867), 211, 213; United States–Muscat and Zanzibar (1833), 178, 215; of Washington (1871), 122n; Webster-Ashburton (1842), 8; treaty making, 211–216
Trent affair, diplomatic crisis over, 33–34, 36, 37; strengthens Shufeldt's relations with Cuban authorities, 41; mentioned, 71, 348, 351
Tsungli Yamen, 98, 245, 264, 265, 271, 284, 291, 294, 296, 389, n19; flexible on dependency claims, 291, 295
Tullear Bay, Madagascar, 211, 212

Union Ironworks, San Francisco, 326, 327
United States: consul at Cape Town, 176; consulates in Africa, 176; Exploring Expedition, 334; financial climate in disturbed, 328; policy in China, App. 1; policy in the Pacific, 304; railroads, 321; relations with China, 233; Senate, 53, discusses United States–Korean treaty, 298–299; offers to assume payment of interest on Mexican

foreign debt, 53; troops looked to by Mexicans, 60; mentioned, 324, 349
United States Navy in connection with the Foundation, Growth and Prosperity of the Republic of Liberia, The, 341

Ventosa, 14, 138
Veracruz, 46, 47; allies occupy, 49, 50, 54; U.S. consulates in, 52, 54; British and Spanish withdrawal, 57–58; Shufeldt in, 58, 59; Shufeldt dispatches from, 63; mentioned, 52, 62

Washington Post, The: attacks Naval Advisory Board, 312; hostile to designs of White Squadron, 316; Shufeldt writes to on canal, 259; on Shufeldt's letter to Sargent, 308; mentioned, 310
Webb case, 31, 32, 41
West African Reporter, The: promotes commercial aspects of Shufeldt's cruise, 183
West African squadron, 8–9; in African waters, 176

"Western Civilization in the East," 115, 343–344
Whampoa, 92, 96
White Squadron, the, xiii, 311, 352
Wilson and Bradbury, merchants, 222
Winyah Bay, Shufeldt's first Civil War action, 73–74

yangban, opposed to opening of Korea, 236, 263
Yangtze: Shufeldt desires to survey, 108–112, 122–123; mentioned, 337
Yucatan: mentioned with canal, 133; governor of refuses troops to oppose French, 63
Yokohama, 92, 232, 305

Zanzibar, 253; Shufeldt's views on as key to East African trade, 219; Shufeldt to visit, 178; trade statistics of, 217, 218; treaty revision desired, 178; mentioned, 254, 255, 336, 337, 338; mentioned, 209, 215–216, 217

About the Author

Frederick C. Drake was born at Barrow-in-Furness, Cumbria, England and was educated at the University of Manchester, where he received his B.A. (1959) and M.A. (1961) degrees, and at Cornell University, where he was awarded the Ph.D. in history in 1970. He has taught at University College, London; the University of the West Indies; University College of Wales, Aberystwyth; and is at present associate professor of history at Brock University in St. Catharines, Ontario, Canada. He has published in *American Quarterly, Civil War History, Journal of Negro History,* and *Lincoln Herald,* and has contributed articles on diplomatic and naval history to the *Encyclopedia of Southern History.*

Production Notes

This book was designed by Roger Eggers. Composition and paging were done on the Quadex Composing System and typesetting on the Compugraphic 8400 by the design and production staff of University of Hawaii Press.

The text and display typeface is Baskerville.

Offset presswork and binding were done by Vail-Ballou Press, Inc. Text paper is Glatfelter Hi-Brite Offset Vellum, basis 55.

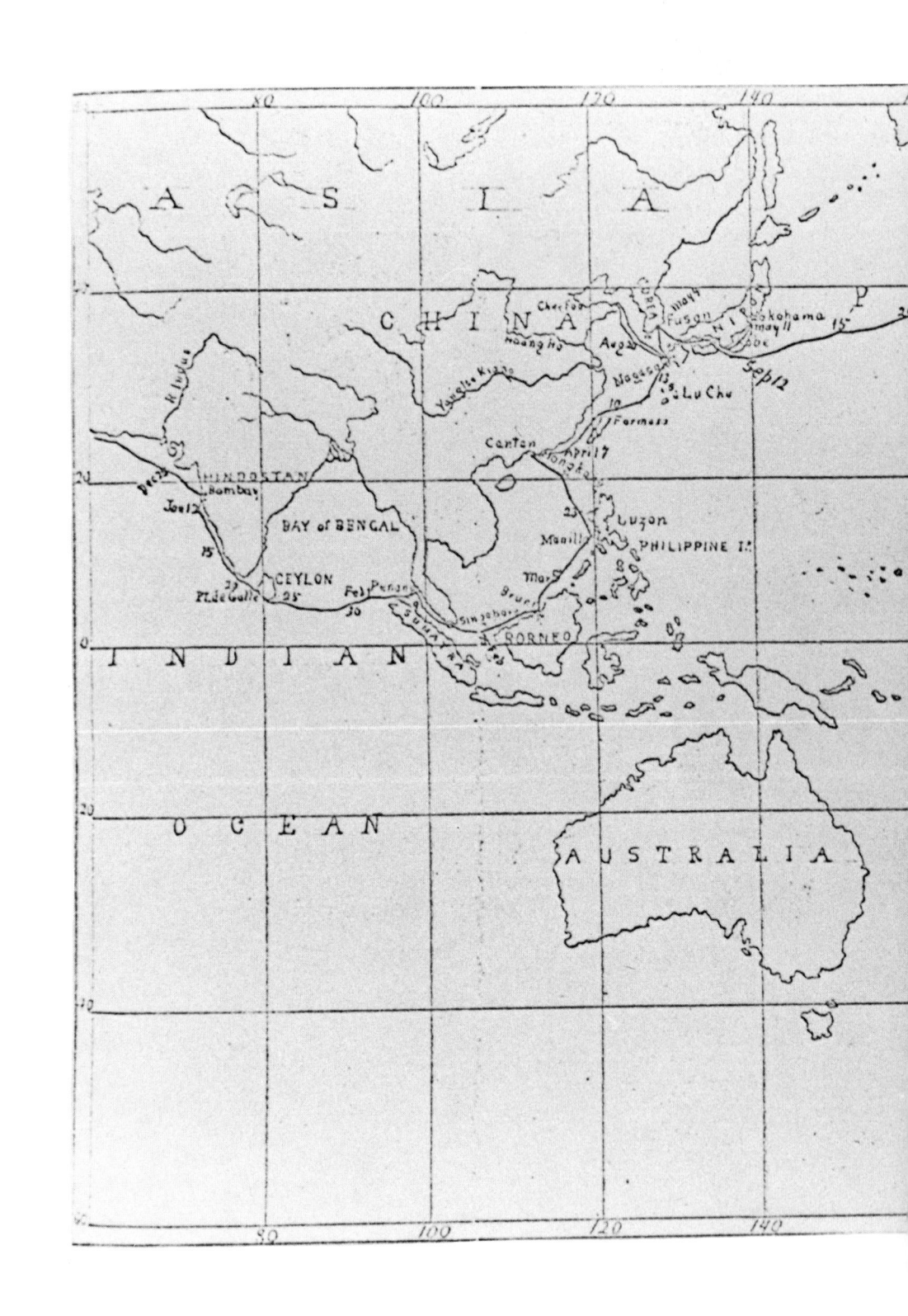